(Continued on back endsheets)

DICTIONARY OF LITERARY BIOGRAPHY

DOCUMENTARY SERIES

AN ILLUSTRATED CHRONICLE

VOLUME TWELVE

Depicting The Lives And Work of
Authors—Including Photographs,
Manuscript Facsimiles, Letters,
Notebooks, Interviews, And
Contemporary Assessments

DICTIONARY OF LITERARY BIOGRAPHY

DOCUMENTARY SERIES

AN ILLUSTRATED CHRONICLE

VOL.  TWELVE

SOUTHERN WOMEN WRITERS:
FLANNERY O'CONNOR
KATHERINE ANNE PORTER
EUDORA WELTY

EDITED BY
MARY ANN WIMSATT AND KAREN L. ROOD

A BRUCCOLI CLARK LAYMAN BOOK
GALE RESEARCH INC.
DETROIT, WASHINGTON, D.C., LONDON

PERMISSIONS

PERMISSIONS

CONTENTS

For

Louis D. Rubin, Jr., and Lewis P. Simpson

PREFACE

DLB: *Documentary Series* is a reference source with a twofold purpose: 1) it makes significant literary documents accessible to students and scholars, as well as nonacademic readers; and 2) it supplements the *Dictionary of Literary Biography* (1978–). The *Documentary Series* has been conceived to provide access to a range of material that many students never have the opportunity to see. By itself it is a portable archive. Used with *DLB*, it expands the biographical and critical coverage of the essays by presenting key documents on which the essays are based. *DLB* places authors' lives and works in the perspective of literary history; the *Documentary Series* chronicles literary history in the making.

Each volume in the *Documentary Series* concentrates on major figures of a particular literary period, movement, or genre. *DS 12* covers the careers of Katherine Anne Porter, Eudora Welty, and Flannery O'Connor, three prominent authors associated with the literary movement known as the Southern Renascence. *Renascence,* of course, means "rebirth." When applied to the South, the term describes the remarkable flowering of writing that occurred in that region between the years 1920 and 1950. By 1920 the South had suffered for more than half a century from the grave wounds inflicted by the Civil War; yet despite continuing economic hardship it had begun to experience an intellectual rebirth. As Allen Tate wrote in "The New Provincialism" (1945), "With the war of 1914–1918, the South reentered the world — but gave a backward glance as it slipped over the border: that backward glance gave us the Southern renascence, a literature conscious of the past in the present." The result was what a British scholar has called "the literature of memory." Tate and his wife, Caroline Gordon, were among the authors whose careers began or flourished during the Renascence, as were William Faulkner, Robert Penn Warren, Thomas Wolfe, John Crowe Ransom, Katherine Anne Porter, Eudora Welty, and Flannery O'Connor.

During the Renascence, the South's conception of itself — which had originated during the colonial era and had first emerged clearly in the antebellum period — crystallized. Central to self-image, as expressed through the writing of Renascence authors, is the belief that the region has a distinctive, cohesive culture characterized by an attachment to the land and an agrarian economic system, a strong sense of place, an equally strong awareness of time and the past, and a clearly demarcated class and caste system that results in a firm sense of community.

In one way or another, the South figures importantly in the writing of Katherine Anne Porter, Welty, and O'Connor. Yet, not surprisingly, it assumes a different cast in the work of each because of individual circumstances of birth, turn of mind, and upbringing. Porter, the oldest of the three authors, was born in Texas, a state whose many-stranded Southern, Southwestern, and Hispanic heritage gives it a colorful history markedly different from that of other southern states. The most restless and peripatetic of the three women, Porter spent considerable time in Mexico, where she became involved in revolutionary politics — a fact reflected in "Flowering Judas," the title story of her first collection of tales (1930). Her association with Mexico is also reflected in such notable works as "María Concepción," likewise collected in her first book, and *Hacienda* (1934).

Porter also lived and traveled extensively in Europe, as is apparent in works such as "The Leaning Tower," the title story in her 1944 volume of short fiction, and in her long novel, *Ship of Fools* (1962). Yet what many readers consider Porter's most memorable body of work is solidly grounded in Southern regional and social patterns, including agrarian-based principles and persistent, if oppressive, family ties. This work includes the stories Porter grouped together as "The Old Order" in *The Collected Stories* (1965) and the short novels "Old Mortality," "Noon Wine," and "Pale Horse, Pale Rider" — published together in 1939. Much of this fiction centers on Porter's semi-autobiographical character Miranda Gay and her difficult progress from childhood to young maturity. Porter's interest in the South and her determination to treat it in fiction was strengthened by her long friendship with Allen Tate and Caroline Gordon, much of whose writing carries forward the Agrarian principles articulated in *I'll Take My Stand* (1930).

Porter and Eudora Welty first met in summer 1938, when, through the agency of mutual friends, Welty visited Porter in Baton Rouge, Louisiana. As Porter remarked later, the two "spent a pleasant evening together talking in the cool old house with all the windows open." After this visit the women became congenial professional associates. In summer 1941 Welty joined Porter for a short time at the Yaddo writers' and artists' colony near Saratoga Springs, New York. Porter had tried to help Welty find a publisher for her first collection of tales, *A Curtain of Green* (1941); she assisted the young author further by writing the introduction to the volume after Doubleday, Doran agreed to publish it. Welty and Porter exchanged warm letters, and in 1965 Welty wrote a perceptive appreciation of Porter's fictional method, "Katherine Anne Porter: The Eye of the Story." She also warmly reviewed Porter's *The Never-Ending Wrong* (1977) and wrote a long memoir, "My Introduction to Katherine Anne Porter"(1990), in which she acknowledges Porter's contribution toward launching her literary career.

Welty was born in Jackson, Mississippi, and except for her college years, brief periods in New York, and occasional travel in the United States and abroad, she has spent her life in Jackson. Mississippi and its people figure centrally in both her writing and her photographs. She and Faulkner are the most famous authors the state has produced; her reputation at home is reflected by the fact that Governor William Waller proclaimed 2 May 1973 "Eudora Welty Day." (A few days later Welty's novel *The Optimist's Daughter* won the Pulitzer Prize for fiction.) To honor its native daughter, the city of Jackson organized a week of festivities (1–6 May) which brought together Welty's literary friends — such as her agent Diarmuid Russell; editor Lambert Davis; and writers Reynolds Price, Kenneth Millar (Ross Macdonald), and the Brainard Cheneys — as well as personal friends from Jackson and elsewhere. Describing the occasion for *The New York Times*, Nona Balakian observed Welty in the midst of so many friends and remarked, "Writers in America are not supposed to be famous and happy at the same time. . . . Yet here was a writer perfectly attuned to her milieu, the lilt in her voice and simplicity of her manner giving her away as no words could. No gloss. No front. Only a sharp, intense responsiveness, a feeling of comradeship." In an equally perceptive, much earlier statement, Porter had noted in her introduction to *A Curtain of Green* that Welty was fortunate in possessing "an ancient system of ethics, an unanswerable, indispensable moral law, on which she is grounded firmly."

For all this emphasis on Welty's belonging, more than one reader — including the prominent Southern historian C. Vann Woodward — has identified an outsider's perspective in Welty's fiction, derived from the fact that neither of her parents was born or raised in the South. At the same time Welty's long residence in Mississippi and her devoted attachment to place — articulated in her well-known essay "Place in Fiction" (1955) — give her an insider's status as well. This dual perspective permeates a body of writing in which the South, though an essential and even inevitable setting for the action, is neither criticized nor polemically defended.

An outsider's perspective of another kind may be detected in the writing of Flannery O'Connor, a young writer befriended early in her short career by Gordon, Tate, Porter, and other Renascence authors. Although her father's and mother's families had lived in the South for several generations, O'Connor's Roman Catholicism gave her minority status in a predominantly Protestant South. Devoted to her religion and possessing an intense, deeply individual moral and theological vision, O'Connor was concerned throughout the fiction of her maturity to make plain the manifold operations of divine grace upon the lives of her characters, who for the most part are southern Protestants living out their violence-ridden existence against the relatively bleak backgrounds of the rural and small-town South. Because of its powerful religious content, O'Connor's fiction has generated a mixed and complicated response. In one of her most frequently delivered lectures, "The Catholic Novelist in the Protestant South," she explains the relationship of her theology to her view of the South.

Among the most perceptive reviews of O'Connor's writing are those by such friends and fellow Roman Catholics as Caroline Gordon and Brainard Cheney, as well as several Roman Catholic clerics. Yet her fiction was also widely admired by non-Catholics, including novelist John Hawkes, who shared O'Connor's vision of a violent modern world even as he disagreed with her understanding of the devil.

O'Connor's relationship with the talented writer Caroline Gordon deserves special mention. Gordon read the penultimate draft of O'Connor's first novel, *Wise Blood* (1952), offering long lists of suggestions, which O'Connor valued. From that time forward O'Connor showed Gordon drafts of all her fiction, appreciating her detailed responses even when she occasionally disagreed with some of Gordon's comments.

By Christmas 1950, while still at work on her first novel, O'Connor had begun to exhibit the symptoms of lupus, a debilitating disease that would kill her as it had her father. With rare and graceful courage, she nevertheless embarked on a remarkably active literary career. After her death in 1964 at age thirty-nine, Southern novelist Guy Davenport remarked, "Miss O'Connor knew the difference between art and religion, and never confused the two. . . . Only by being a writer of hair-raising insight could she deliver such a wallop to our moral complacency."

— *Mary Ann Wimsatt and Karen L. Rood*

ACKNOWLEDGMENTS

This book was produced by Bruccoli Clark Layman, Inc.

Production coordinator is James W. Hipp. Photography editor is Bruce Andrew Bowlin. Photographic copy work was performed by Joseph M. Bruccoli. Layout and graphics supervisor is Penney L. Haughton. Copyediting supervisors are Bill Adams and Denise W. Edwards. Typesetting supervisor is Kathleen M. Flanagan. Julie E. Frick is editorial associate. Systems manager is George F. Dodge. The production staff includes Phyllis A. Avant, Ann M. Cheschi, Melody W. Clegg, Patricia Coate, Brigitte B. de Guzman, Joyce Fowler, Laurel M. Gladden, Mendy Claire Gladden, Stephanie C. Hatchell, Leslie Haynsworth, Rebecca Mayo, Kathy Lawler Merlette, Jeff Miller, Pamela D. Norton, Delores I. Plastow, Patricia F. Salisbury, William L. Thomas, Jr., and Robert Trogden.

Walter W. Ross and Robert S. McConnell did library research. They were assisted by the following librarians at the Thomas Cooper Library of the University of South Carolina: Linda Holderfield and the interlibrary-loan staff; reference-department head Virginia Weathers; reference librarians Marilee Birchfield, Stefanie Buck, Cathy Eckman, Rebecca Feind, Jill Holman, Karen Joseph, Jean Rhyne, Kwamine Washington, and Connie Widney; circulation-department head Caroline ("Tucky") Taylor; and acquisitions-searching supervisor David Haggard. Virginia Hodges and Kreg Abshire, graduate research assistants at the University of South Carolina, helped with library research and proofreading.

The editors would like to thank the following individuals for their invaluable assistance and advice: Beth Alvarez, Curator of Literary Manuscripts, University of Maryland at College Park Libraries; Nancy Davis Bray, Curator of Special Collections, Ina Dillard Russell Library, Georgia College; Forrest W. Gayley, Head of Special Collections, and H. T. Holmes, Director of Archives and Library Division, Mississippi Department of Archives and History; William Erwin, Manuscripts Division, William R. Perkins Library, Duke University; Professor Ashley Brown, University of South Carolina; Professor Sarah Gordon, Georgia College; Professor Emerita Louise Y. Gossett, Salem College; Professor Emeritus Thomas Gossett, Wake Forest University; Professor Suzanne Marrs, Millsaps College; and Professor Peggy Whitman Prenshaw, Louisiana State University.

DICTIONARY OF LITERARY BIOGRAPHY

DOCUMENTARY SERIES

AN ILLUSTRATED CHRONICLE

VOLUME TWELVE

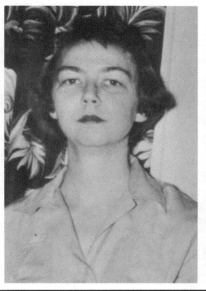

FLANNERY O'CONNOR

(25 March 1925 – 3 August 1964)

See the Flannery O'Connor entry in DLB 2: American Novelists Since World War II.

BOOKS:

Wise Blood (New York: Harcourt, Brace, 1952; London: Spearman, 1955);

A Good Man Is Hard to Find and Other Stories (New York: Harcourt, Brace, 1955); republished as *The Artificial Nigger and Other Tales* (London: Spearman, 1957);

The Violent Bear It Away (New York: Farrar, Straus & Cudahy, 1960; London: Longmans, Green, 1960);

Everything That Rises Must Converge (New York: Farrar, Straus & Giroux, 1965; London: Faber & Faber, 1966);

Mystery and Manners: Occasional Prose, edited by Sally and Robert Fitzgerald (New York: Farrar, Straus & Giroux, 1969; London: Faber & Faber, 1972);

The Complete Stories (New York: Farrar, Straus & Giroux, 1971);

The Presence of Grace and Other Book Reviews, compiled by Leo J. Zuber, edited by Carter W. Martin (Athens: University of Georgia Press, 1983).

BIBLIOGRAPHIES:

Robert E. Golden and Mary C. Sullivan, *Flannery O'Connor and Caroline Gordon: A Reference Guide* (Boston: G. K. Hall, 1977);

David Farmer, *Flannery O'Connor: A Descriptive Bibliography* (New York & London: Garland, 1981);

Stephen G. Driggers and Robert J. Dunn, with Sarah Gordon, *The Manuscripts of Flannery O'Connor at Georgia College* (Athens & London: University of Georgia Press, 1989).

LETTERS:

The Habit of Being, edited by Sally Fitzgerald (New York: Farrar Straus Giroux, 1979);

The Correspondence of Flannery O'Connor and the Brainard Cheneys, edited by C. Ralph Stephens (Jackson & London: University Press of Mississippi, 1986).

INTERVIEWS:

Conversations with Flannery O'Connor, edited by Rosemary M. Magee (Jackson & London: University Press of Mississippi, 1987).

LOCATION OF ARCHIVES:

The Flannery O'Connor Collection is at the Ina Dillard Russell Library at Georgia College, Milledgeville, Georgia.

Mary Flannery O'Connor, photographed at age two with her mother (left) and at three (right), was born on 25 March 1925 to a prominent Roman Catholic family in Savannah, Georgia. She lived there for the first twelve years of her life, attending St. Vincent's School and, briefly, Sacred Heart High School.

O'Connor's parents, Regina Cline O'Connor and Edward Francis O'Connor. O'Connor's father served in the army as a lieutenant and returned to Savannah to work in real estate and participate in local politics. When he became seriously ill with lupus in 1938, the family moved to Regina O'Connor's hometown, Milledgeville, Georgia, where he died on 1 February 1941, less than two months before his only child's sixteenth birthday.

Flannery O'Connor at seven, on the occasion of her First Communion, and at twelve, the age at which she started writing in a small notebook with a warning on the first page: "I know some folks that don't mind thier own bisnis."

When the O'Connors went to live in Milledgeville, they moved into Regina O'Connor's family home (above), bought by her father, Peter Cline, in 1886. Before the state capital was relocated from Milledgeville to Atlanta in 1868, the house, which was built in 1820, was the governor's mansion.

Tuesday, December 16, 1941.   THE PEABODY PALLADIUM

MARY FLANNERY O'CONNOR

Peabodite Reveals Strange Hobby

"Mary Flannery, what's your hobby?"

"Collecting rejection slips."

"What?"

"Publisher's rejection slips!"

And so the secret slipped out! Mary Flannery O'Connor is an author—of three whole books—illustrations and everything! But nothing can be put beyond Mary Flannery.—Nothing is impossible.

She began writing at the delicate age of six and just kept right on writing until "Mistaken Identity," "Elmo," and "Gertrude" were produced.

These, incidentally, are the same three books mentioned above. Each one of them is about a goose. They are of a novelty type—too old for young children and too young for older people.

As for Mary Flannery's ambition, she wants to keep right on writing, particularly satires.

One doesn't mention her without saying something about her pets. Herman is her remarkable gander who hatched out a brood of eight goslings. Mary Flannery brought him to school last summer and painted its portrait in art class. Hailie Selassie, her pet rooster, also served as a model.

Winston, a black crow, was added to her menageries when a neighbor shot the feathered rascal stealing pecans. Adolph, another rooster who roomed with Hailie, is now dead. His name was changed when neighbors began wondering about the "Here Adolph's!!" issued from Mary Flannery's back yard. Always there is an interesting collection of pets on the premises.

This Peabodite not only collects pets in the flesh, but also has a hundred and fifty replicas of them in china and glass.

And Mary Flannery is a musician. She plays a clarinet, accordian, and bull fiddle, "because," she says, referring to the latter, "I am the only one who can hold it up."

The cartoons in the Palladium by the art editor—Mary Flannery again—show the orginality and a keen sense of humor characteristic of the cartoonist. Cartoons, in fact, are right down her alley.

The note book which she has painted with oils and covered with cellophane is the envy of all Peabody. Recently, a collection of original lapel pins designed and executed by Mary Flannery were placed on sale at a local store.

A most unassuming person is Mary Flannery O'Connor, and clearly is one of Peabody's most outstanding personalities.

In Milledgeville O'Connor attended Peabody High School, run by the education department of Georgia State College for Women (now Georgia College). This article published in the Peabody student newspaper during O'Connor's senior year reveals that she had already started her lifelong hobby of raising barnyard fowl and had used one of them as a model for three children's stories.

"Music Appreciation Hath Charms" and "These two express the universal feeling of heart-brokenness over school closing," two of the block-print cartoons O'Connor contributed to The Peabody Palladium

"Hrump—not enough price to build a nest!"

"Isn't it fortunate that Genevieve has completely escaped that boy-crazy stage?"

After O'Connor enrolled at Georgia State College for Women in Milledgeville in autumn 1942, she began contributing her cartoons to the college newpaper, The Colonnade, *which had published nearly sixty of them by the time she graduated with an A.B. in social science in June 1945. These cartoons appeared in* The Colonnade *during her senior year (left: 19 April 1945; right: 2 May 1945).*

The 1944–1945 staff of the college literary quarterly, The Corinthian, *which O'Connor (seated at center) edited during her last year at Georgia State College for Women. During her three years at the school O'Connor contributed nonfiction, fiction, and verse to the magazine.*

The passing chapel speaker theses days is wont to refer with euphu-
istice enthusiasm to the part we students will play in the pest war
world. It is doubtful, however, if even seen from the poopdeck position
of a speakers platform , we would inspire such optimism from anyone not
bound by the obligations of tact or politeness to the heads of our particular institution. As far as we are concerned, the speaker who with
arms outstretched defines us as the alert guardians of the future is
hitting the nail squarely on the gold fish bowl, and the gold fish, byt
this time, is sitting on the sofa consulting his insurance dealer.

Apparantly, in the eyes of the usual speaker, youth carries with
it all the qualities of interest, activeness, and that dauntless courage
which will lead us into a sun of our own manufacture. Obviously, he s
should stick around awhile and see our duplicate copies of Uncle Bohah
and Aunt Euphegia or the wavering new products of uncertaintty. What
each is going to do to the future izzzzi will not be one thousandth
of what the future is going to do to each.

All this is a sharp reversal of the youth-going-to-the-dogs theory
expounded since the Pleistocene age by adults who were not necessarily
convinced of it by personal experience; as a matter of fact they are s
still expounding it with an enthusiasm equal to our friends who are
convinced, even less by personal experience, that we are headed toward
certain glory, but in a college, we seldom hear from the former group.
Izxxxxfxxdixgxthxzxhxxd That would not be giming us our moneys worth.
Perhaps equal parts of the predictions of both groups might reasonably
turn out to match our own particular color. At least we are certain,
those of us who are not yet afraid to be certain, that we are neither
color unmixed.

Let him who is expecting our alert little minds to grasp and grapple with the interminable problems of postwar security view those little
minds in action; in other words, let him expose his opinion to the

First page of a working draft for "Education's Only Hope," a humorous essay O'Connor published in the Spring 1945 issue of The Corinthian *(The Flannery O'Connor Collection, Ina Dillard Russell Library, Georgia College)*

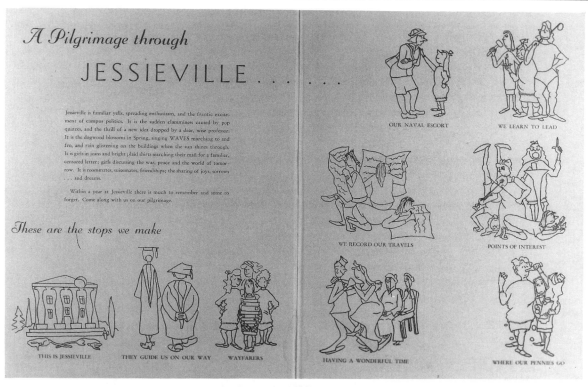

As features editor for The 1945 Spectrum, *her college yearbook, O'Connor planned its thematic organization and drew the cartoons that appear on the contents pages (top) and individually on each section title page. She also drew the endsheets (bottom). "Jessieville" is a nickname for Georgia State College for Women.*

15.

out of his eyes. He shuffled to the chair by the window. The geranium wasn't there but he saw where it was. Down in the alley a cracked flower pot was scattered over a spray of dirt, and the head of a pink geranium stuck out of a green paper bow. There was a man sitting in the window where the geranium should have been. Old Dudley raised himself up on the window ledge.

"Why don't you pick up your geranium?" he said.

The man recrossed his arms. "Why don't you, wise guy?"

"I'm gona," Old Dudley murmured.

*   *   *   *

"Flopped like a jelly fish," Mr. Sagelli was telling the little group outside number 10 sixth floor. "Right in front of my eyes. Must have been off his nut."

"He did seem a little queer," a negro in a business suit said. "You know, I talked to him just this morning."

"So what about you?" Mr. Sagelli snorted. "I seen him when he done it."

Minor matters of detail — you don't hunt quail with a rifle — and nobody gets ten out of one covey.

After graduating from Georgia State College for Women, O'Connor attended the Writers' Workshop at the University of Iowa, where she studied fiction writing with workshop director Paul Engle, who probably wrote the note on this last page of a late draft for "The Geranium" (The Flannery O'Connor Collection, Ina Dillard Russell Library, Georgia College). The first of six stories that O'Connor submitted as her M.F.A. thesis in 1947, "The Geranium" was published in the Summer 1946 issue of Accent. *During the last year of her life O'Connor extensively reworked the story and retitled it "Judgement Day."*

LETTER:
Flannery O'Connor to Sally and Robert Fitzgerald, mid September 1951; in *The Habit of Being*, edited by Sally Fitzgerald (New York: Farrar Straus Giroux, 1979), pp. 27–28.

After earning an M.F.A. at Iowa in 1947, O'Connor stayed on for another academic year, working on her first novel, Wise Blood *(1952). In September 1948 she went to Yaddo, an artists' colony near Saratoga Springs, New York, where the other writers-in-residence included poet Robert Lowell and novelist Elizabeth Hardwick, Lowell's future wife. In February 1949 Lowell introduced O'Connor to her future publisher, Robert Giroux, then editor in chief at Harcourt, Brace. The following month, after the three writers had left Yaddo, Lowell and Hardwick took O'Connor to meet poet-translator Robert Fitzgerald and his wife, Sally Fitzgerald, future editor of O'Connor's letters, at their New York City apartment. After a few weeks in New York O'Connor spent the rest of the spring in Milledgeville but returned to New York for the summer. In September she moved to Ridgefield, Connecticut, where she rented the room and bath above the garage of a house the Fitzgeralds had recently bought there.*

By December 1950 O'Connor had completed Wise Blood, *which she sent to Giroux the following March, and she had begun to experience the first symptoms of lupus, the disease that eventually killed her. On the train trip home for Christmas 1950, O'Connor became seriously ill. She was hospitalized on arrival and nearly died. A doctor at Emory University Hospital in Atlanta diagnosed her illness and was able to stabilize her condition with ACTH, a cortisone derivative, releasing her in March 1951.*

By the time she wrote this letter to the Fitzgeralds, O'Connor had revised Wise Blood *according to suggestions made by Giroux and novelist Caroline Gordon, who had been sent the manuscript by her friends and fellow Roman Catholics the Fitzgeralds. In her previous letter to the Fitzgeralds, O'Connor, who did not have Gordon's address, had asked if Gordon would read the revised version because, "All the changes are efforts after what she sugested...."* (One of Gordon's suggestions had been that O'Connor should make the narrator's voice clearly distinct from the voice of the characters.) *Gordon did read the manuscript again, and she*

O'Connor (right) and Peggy George, business manager of The Corinthian, *in a photograph published in* The 1945 Spectrum

remained a valued literary adviser for the rest of O'Connor's career. The House of Fiction *(1950), an anthology edited with commentary by Gordon and her husband, poet Allen Tate, became a sort of textbook of literary technique for O'Connor. O'Connor's comparison of J. D. Salinger's* The Catcher in the Rye *(1951) to the fiction of Ring Lardner is high praise. Lardner was one of her favorite writers.*

I certainly enjoyed *Catcher in the Rye*. Read it up the same day it came. Regina said I was going to RUIN MY EYES reading all that in one afternoon. I reckon that man owes a lot to Ring Lardner. Anyway he is very good. Regina said would she like to read it and I said, well it was very fine. She said yes but would *she* like to read it, so I said she would have to try it and see. She hasn't tried it yet. She likes books with Frank Buck and a lot of wild animals.

Thank you for sending the ms. to Caroline. She sent it back to me with some nine pages of comments and she certainly increased my education thereby. So I am doing some more things to it and then I mean to send it off for the LAST time...

You ought to hear all the hollering down here about the Separation of Church & State.

O'Connor during her college years

After her release from the hospital, O'Connor was too weak to climb the stairs at the house in Milledgeville, so she and her mother moved to Andalusia, a farm five miles away that her mother had inherited from a brother and had been running while living in town. In this letter O'Connor, who regularly regaled the Fitzgeralds with stories about her mother and various southern "characters," reported an episode that made its way into "The Displaced Person," a story first published in the Autumn 1954 issue of Sewanee Review *and collected in* A Good Man Is Hard to Find and Other Stories *(1954).*

A very noisy Christmas to you all and assorted blessings for the new year. My mamma is getting ready for what she hopes will be one of her blessings: a refugee family to arrive here Christmas night. She has to fix up and furnish a house for them, don't know how many there will be or what nationality or occupation or nothing. She and Mrs. P., the dairyman's wife, have been making curtains for the windows out of flowered chicken-feed sacks. Regina was complaining that the green sacks wouldn't look so good in the same room where the pink ones were and Mrs. P. (who has no teeth on one side of her mouth) says in a very superior voice, "Do you think they'll know what colors even is?" Usually the families that have been got around here for dairy work have turned out to be . . . shoemakers and have headed for Chicago just as soon as they could save the money. For which they can't be blamed. However, we are waiting to see how this comes out.

What I forgot to say the last time I wrote was don't send me any two weeks rent that you may think you owe me. If the Lord is with me this next year I aim to visit you, at which time I will be glad to eat it out. I am only a little stiff in the heels so far this winter and am taking a new kind of ACTH, put up in glue, and I am on a pretty low maintenance dose. I only hope I can keep it that way.

My momma sends hers for the season.

They are having conventions all over the place and making resolutions and having the time of their lives. You'd think the Pope was about to annex the Sovereign State of Georgia.

What ever happened to Jacques Maritain? Is he still at Princeton or did Frank the Spell man [Cardinal Francis Spellman] get him a job in some Catholic institution?

Regina is glad you liked the cake and will send you the recipe when she finds it. I think she just throws stuff in. She likes em dry and Sister [Miss Mary Cline] likes em wet. That was Sister's recipe.

I am glad you have come to favor chickens. You won't favor them so much when you have to clean up their apartment but the eggs are certainly worth it. I have got me five geese. We also have turkeys. They all have the sorehead and the cure for that is liquid black shoe polish — so we have about fifteen turkeys running around in blackface. They look like domesticated vultures.

LETTER:
Flannery O'Connor to Sally and Robert Fitzgerald, Christmas 1951; in *The Habit of Being*, p. 30.

INTERVIEW:

"May 15 Is Publication Date of Novel by Flannery O'Connor, Milledgeville," *Milledgeville* [Ga.] *Union-Recorder*, 24 April 1952, p. 1; in *Conversations with Flannery O'Connor*, edited by Rosemary M. Magee (Jackson &

London: University Press of Mississippi, 1987), pp. 3–4.

The announcement that O'Connor would soon be a published novelist was greeted with enthusiasm by her hometown newspaper. The gorilla episode mentioned in this interview and in O'Connor's 3 May 1952 letter to Robert Lowell occurs in "Enoch and the Gorilla," first published in New World Writing *(April 1952) and revised as chapter 11 of* Wise Blood. *O'Connor's anecdote about having owned a chicken that could walk backward was one of her favorites, and she repeated it in various later interviews.*

Harcourt, Brace and Company, one of the country's leading publishing houses, has announced May 15 as the publication date for *Wise Blood,* a novel by Flannery O'Connor of Milledgeville.

Although advance copies of the book are not yet available, a prepublication review of it by the New York critic, Caroline Gordon, says in part: "I was more impressed by *Wise Blood* than any novel I have read in a long time. Her picture of the modern world is literally terrifying. Kafka is almost the only one of our contemporaries who has achieved such effects."

Editorial comment by the publishers describes the book as an "extraordinary novel, which introduces an important new talent, relating the story of Hazel Motes, who comes from Eastrod, Tennessee, and has discovered a new religion which he preaches from the hood of his rat-colored Essex. . . . Haze, a primitive figure, represents the most primitive issue of our time or any time — religion. In his fight for truth as he sees it, he clashes with two other evangelists. . . ."

Wise Blood, say the publishers, "has great humor, and horror, and compassion, and its satire is reminiscent of the Evelyn Waugh of *The Loved One.*"

Although a native of Savannah, the 26-year-old author of the new book is a member of the Cline family of Milledgeville and in 1938 returned here with her mother, Mrs. Edward O'Connor, and she completed high school at Peabody and her college studies at Georgia State College for Women. From GSCW she went to the State University of Iowa and studied writing under Paul Engle, receiving a Master of Fine Arts in Literature in 1947. She had a fellowship in English at Iowa for two years.

She began her novel in 1947, living for seven months of that year [i.e., 1947–1948] at Yaddo, Saratoga Springs, N.Y., which is an estate left by the Trask family for writers, painters and musicians who are doing creative work. Later she lived in the country with friends in Connecticut.

Back in Milledgeville for the past year, Miss O'Connor is living for the present with her mother at "Andalusia," a rambling, storybook farm owned by the Cline family.

"I write every day for at least two hours," says the young author, "and I spend the rest of my time largely in the society of ducks." Raising ducks is her hobby and she owns, also, geese, pheasants, quails and one frizzly chicken. A frizzly chicken, she explained, is a chicken that looks more like a wet fur coat than anything else.

Miss O'Connor's interest in feathered friends dates back to the time she was about 11 years old and she owned a chicken that got in *Pathé News* by the simple (but exceedingly singular) procedure of walking backwards. A *Pathé* cameraman traveled across several states to film the hen that went places in reverse with as much ease as most birds stroll forward. "Since that big event," remarked the chicken's proud owner as she looked back on the excitement of that bygone day, "my life has been an anti-climax."

She gives credit to an advertisement in the *Union-Recorder* for an idea that led to one of the chapters in her book. A local theater offered free passes to fans who would shake hands with a gorilla appearing here "in person" on the day of the particular film's showing. This chapter happens to be one of the several printed as separate stories in various literary magazines prior to publication of her novel.

Flannery O'Connor's first story was published in *Accent* in 1946. Since then she has had stories or chapters of her novel in such publications as *Sewanee Review, Partisan Review, Mademoiselle, Tomorrow,* and *New World Writing.* She writes only fiction and is interested in the novel only as art.

Her book is dedicated to her mother.

LETTER:
Flannery O'Connor to Robert Lowell, 2 May 1952; in *The Habit of Being,* pp. 35–36.

In responding to Robert Lowell's praise for "Enoch and the Gorilla," O'Connor mentioned two hobbies, painting and raising barnyard fowl. Some of her paintings are still hanging on the walls at Andalusia.

Flannery O'Connor
Workshop

SYNOPSIS: (after first four chapters)

After getting off the bus, Haze meets Asa Moats and his wife, Sabbath, on the street. Asa is a missionary for David's Aspirants, a local evangelical religious group. Haze talks to them and becomes interested in what they have to say. Sabbath is a big gaunt woman. She has seen God. For just a second once He flashed in her eyes and took away her breath. She has even seen Mr. Cruise, the founder of the David's Aspirants. (He writes pamphlets which Asa and the other missionaries distribute.) The Moats make a deep impression on Haze; he gives Sabbath the peeler he was sold on the street and talks to them for a long while. They walk home with him and say they will come to see him. The thought of God begins to worry him after this, but a more immediate problem is that of conquering the city--which is to be done by becoming like Bill Hill. He meets Lea, his sister's second floor friend, and is attracted to her. Bill Hill has a cocktail party during which the Moats come to see Haze who is ashamed, in this setting, to own such friends and pretends he has never seen them before. The next day his conscience is in so raw a condition that he finally goes out to hunt them. Lea joins him on the way and when he sees them on the street corner, he does not stop. After this he plans to forget the Moats but he continues to be haunted by the ugly face of Sabbath and to be worried by thoughts of God. He remembers the agonized hard-shell religion of his mother and some of her pronouncements on eternal damnation.

On the one hand he is drawn toward Lea, Bill Hill, and the city and on the other toward the Moats and the wonderful Mr. Cruise they talk about. His sister rents the other half of his room to a stu-

Opening page from a synopsis of O'Connor's first novel, Wise Blood, *submitted with completed chapters in O'Connor's application for the 1947 Rinehart-Iowa Fiction Award, which she won (The Flannery O'Connor Collection, Ina Dillard Russell Library, Georgia College)*

I was powerful glad to hear from you and I am pleased that you liked the gorilla. I hope you'll like the whole thing. I asked Bob Giroux to send you one.

I've been in Georgia with the buzzards for the last year and a half on acct. of arthritis but I am going to Conn. in June to see the Fitzgeralds. They have about a million children, all with terrific names and all beautiful. I'm living with my mother in the country. She raises cows and I raise ducks and pheasants. The pheasant cock has horns and looks like some of those devilish people and dogs in Rousseau's paintings. I have been taking painting myself, painting mostly chickens and guineas and pheasants. My mother thinks they're great stuff. She prefers me painting to me writing. She hasn't learned to love Mrs. Watts. Harcourt sent my book to Evelyn Waugh and his comment was: "If this is really the unaided work of a young lady, it is a remarkable product." My mother was vastly insulted. She put the emphasis on *if* and *lady*. Does he suppose you're not a lady? she says. WHO is he?

I'm all with Elizabeth on the sightseeing and will take mine sitting down or not at all. I like food with mine instead of politics, though.

If you ever see Omar [Pound] give him my regards. I met a doctor recently who had been at St. Elizabeth's and knew Mr. and Mrs. [Ezra] Pound, and liked them very much. He said a lot of people came out to see Pound and one who came insistently had sprouted a beard and a French collar.

The best to you both.

BOOK REVIEW:
William Goyen, "Unending Vengeance," review of *Wise Blood, New York Times Book Review,* 18 May 1952, p. 4.

By 23 May 1952 O'Connor could report to a friend that Wise Blood *had gotten good reviews in* Newsweek, The New York Times, *and* The New York Herald Tribune. *The anonymous* Newsweek *reviewer called O'Connor "perhaps the most naturally gifted of the young generation of novelists" (19 May 1952), while in* The New York Herald Tribune Book Review, *Sylvia Stallings praised the novel as "at once delicate and grotesque" (18 May 1952). The enthusiastic* New York Times *review was written by Texas native William Goyen, who had achieved critical success with his first novel,* House of Breath *(1952). His perceptive reading of* Wise Blood *anticipates later critical commentary on O'Connor.*

Written by a Southerner from Georgia, this first novel, whose language is Tennessee-Georgia dialect expertly wrought into a clipped, elliptic and blunt style, introduces its author as a writer of power. There is in Flannery O'Connor a fierceness of literary gesture, an angriness of observation, a facility for catching, as an animal eye in a wilderness, cunningly and at one sharp glance, the shape and detail and animal intention of enemy and foe. The world of "Wise Blood" is one of clashing in a wilderness.

When Hazel Motes, from Eastrod, Tenn., is released from the Army at the age of 22, he comes to a Southern city near his birthplace. He falls under the spell of Asa Hawks, a "blind" street preacher who shambles through the city with his degenerate daughter, Lily Sabbath Hawks, age 15. The encounter with Hawks turns Hazel Motes back into his childhood traumatic experience with his grandfather who was a preacher traveling about the South in an old Ford. The story of this novel, darting through rapid, brute, bare episodes told with power and keenness, develops the disintegration and final destruction of Hazel who physically and psychologically becomes Hawks and parrot-preaches (in vain) to the city crowds from the hood of his second-hand Essex.

In a series of grim picaresque incidents Hazel struggles to outfox and outpreach Hawks. He announces a new religion called "The Church Without Christ."

In Taulkinham, U. S. A., the city of Fiendish Evangelists, one is brought into a world not so much of accursed or victimized human beings as into the company of an ill-tempered and driven collection of one-dimensional creatures of sheer meanness and orneriness, scheming landladies, cursing waitresses, haunted-house people, prostitutes, fake blind men who take on, as they increase in number, the nature and small size of downright skullduggery and alum-mouthed contrariness. One is never convinced of any genuine evil in these people, only of a sourness; they seem not to belong to the human race at all, they are what the geneticist calls a race of "sports."

The stark dramatic power of the scenes is percussive and stabbing, but Miss O'Connor seems to tell her story through clenched teeth in a kind of Tomboy, Mean-Moll glee, and a few times she writes herself into episodes that have to contrive themselves to deliver her out of them, and then she is compelled to go on too far beyond or in the direction of sensationalism.

When he got out of the army, he bought the glare-blue suit and the black wool hat and, looking the same way he had looked when he left Eastrod, he went back to it. He knew all the time that it would not be there. He didn't know it in words but he knew it, and when the plank fell out of the ceiling onto his head, he was prepared with a numbness that would keep him from feeling anything. But it fell deeper than he thought. When it fell, he saw everything, for an instant, outside and in, falling. He saw his despair lit up like a whole village exploding. Everything he had believed was gone as well as everything he had known. He saw it for only a second and then his mind closed over it and he didn't know why he had felt the shock he had been prepared for. He got up in the middle of the night and tied the chifforobe to the floor and left the note in each of the drawers. That was left, and so was his sister, Ruby. He transferred all of Eastrod to her. The peculiar edge of her character was dim to him. She was seven years older than he was.

The taxi driver who took him where she lived had a long bluish neck and a leather cap. The tip of a cigar stuck from around the corner of his face. Haze leaned forward talking to him over the back of the seat. "I ain't seen her for three years," he said. "I cant think what she looks like."

"Well that's tough," the driver said. He put his head out the window and spit just before a car passed him, and then he swerved the taxi down a side street as if he wanted to drive it along the fronts of the houses. All of a sudden he lurched it to a stop in front of an potato-looking house, about six stories high. It had brown blinds on some of the windows and there was a porch all the way across the front. There was a swing on the porch and a woman swinging in it, going fast with her legs stuck out in front. The taxi driver turned around and looked at Haze. He was looking out the window at the woman. "That's her yonder in that swing," he said. He didn't make any move to get out the taxi.

"If you don't know what she looks like how you know that's her?" the driver said.

Opening pages from chapter 2 of an early, incomplete draft for Wise Blood (The Flannery O'Connor Collection, Ina Dillard Russell Library, Georgia College)

2

She had grown dim to him. She was seven years older than he, and in Eastrod they had not been close or not close. When he went away, she wrote him a few letters and at Christmas she sent him a ready packed box. Now, although he didn't know it, everything depended on ~~his sister~~ his Ruby. He didn't know this himself in words because he had ~~very~~ few words to think with, but he knew it in his hands and feet and inthe muscles of his face and in his blood. There was something sewed into his blood to be a reminder for what he had forgotten and what he couldn't know. ~~He could not say what he thought, but he could do it. He was always ahead of what he knew.~~

The taxi driver who took him to his sister's had a long bluish ~~from~~ neck and a leather cap. The tip of a cigar stuck from around the corner of his face. Haze leaned forward talking to him over the back of the seat. "I ain't seen her in three years," he said. "I cant think what she looks like."

"Well that's tough," the driver said. He put his head out the window and spit just before a car passed him, and then he swerved the taxi down a side street as if he wanted to drive it along the fronts of the houses. All of a sudden he lurched it to a stop in front of an old potato looking house, about six stories high. It had brown blinds on some of the windows and there ~~was a porch all the way across the front. There was a swing on the porch and~~ ~~was~~ a woman swinging in it, going fast with her legs stuck out in front. The taxi ~~xxx~~ driver turned around and looked at Haze. Haze was looking out the window. ~~His face was going from one expression to another~~ "That's her yonder in that swing," he said. He didn't make any move to get out the taxi.

"If you don't know what she looks like how you know that's her?" the driver said.

"I remember now."

"What you waitin on?" the driver asked. "A buck thirty-five. You ain't gonna sit here all day squinting at her.

She turned her head and looked at the taxi, but Haze was getting his money out the pouch to pay the driver. "I remember ~~all about her~~," he said, giving him the money. "If I had seen her in ~~a thousand people~~ I would have known her right away."

The photograph of O'Connor that appears on the dust jacket of Wise Blood. *She disliked this picture, in which her face is swollen as a side effect of taking ACTH, commenting to Sally and Robert Fitzgerald, "I . . . looked as if I had just bitten my grandmother and that this was one of my few pleasures. . . ."*

Miss O'Connor's style is tight to choking and as direct and uncompounded as the order to a firing squad to shoot a man against a wall. It perfectly communicates this devilish intent of the inhabitants of Taulkinham to be mean, or cadge or afflict each other. One cannot take this book lightly or lightly turn away from it, because it is inflicted upon one in the same way its people take their lives: like an indefensible blow delivered in the dark. Perhaps this sense of being physically struck and wounded is only the beginning of an arousal of one's questioning of the credibility of such a world of horror.

In such a world, all living things have vanished and what remains exists in a redemptionless clashing of unending vengeance, alienated from any source of understanding, the absence of which does not even define a world of darkness, not even that — for there has been no light to take away.

BOOK REVIEW:
Oliver LaFarge, "Manic Gloom," review of *Wise Blood, Saturday Review,* 35 (24 May 1952): 22.

The reviews for Wise Blood *were not all positive. The most negative response came from Oliver LaFarge, best known for his fiction and nonfiction about the Southwest, who was not alone in misunderstanding the novel.*

The trick of achieving satire and humor through turning values inside out and describing the most outrageous behavior and ideas with complete calmness is not as easy as one would think. Grotesques, to hold interest, must be extra convincing, and there is danger that outrageousness will turn into mere sordidness. Also, a continuous succession of bizarre actions can become as dull as any other form of repetition.

Edgar Mittelholzer pulled the trick off remarkably well in "Shadows Move Among Them." He has there accepted behavior that ordinarily one would violently reject; yet he, with his fine sense of humor, occasionally failed.

Miss O'Connor has taken up this device with a vengeance. Her story is built around a fanatic who believes that there is no Christ, no redemption, and no soul, and who goes about preaching this doctrine with complete dedication. There are possibilities in the idea, but they are not realized, for one reason, because the individual is so repulsive that one cannot become interested in him.

This individual, "Haze," is surrounded by a supporting cast that ranges from imbecility to viciousness. The result is inevitably a gloomy tale. The author tries to lighten it with humor, but unfortunately her idea of humor is almost exclusively variations on the pratfall. If a character carries an umbrella, the umbrella collapses; if he walks in the aisle of a train, he falls over someone.

Neither satire nor humor is achieved. Perhaps it was only the blurb-writer's idea that it was intended. Perhaps Miss Flannery's aim was a savage and bitter study of the nethermost depths of a small town, with special reference to the viciousness of itinerant preachers. Savage she certainly manages to be.

Two incidents involving policemen indicate the nature of the whole book. In one, a policeman learns that Haze has no driver's license, so he whimsically pushes Haze's jalopy over a cliff. Later, when Haze is blind, deathly ill, and, as far as I can make out, completely insane, he disappears in a storm and an alarm is sent out for him. Two policemen find him in a ditch, barely alive, so one of them clubs him over the head, killing him. At least this policeman does the reader the service of terminating a story which has long since become sheer monotony.

BOOK REVIEW:

Brainard Cheney, Review of Wise Blood, *Shenandoah*, 3 (August 1952): 55–60; in *The Correspondence of Flannery O'Connor and the Brainard Cheneys,* edited by C. Ralph Stephens (Jackson & London: University Press of Mississippi, 1986), pp. 195–199.

After reading this review — which may be seen as an answer to LaFarge and other critics who failed to distinguish O'Connor's point of view from her protagonist's — O'Connor wrote to Cheney to thank him for "reading my book and writing about it so carefully and with so much understanding" (8 February 1953). O'Connor later met Brainard Cheney and his wife, Frances Neel Chaney, Nashville friends of Caroline Gordon and Allen Tate, when they visited Andalusia on 6 June 1953. They remained friends for the rest of her life.

Complaint about our Patent Electric Blanket has been common enough. In varied note it has make [*sic*] up the bulk of our literature and art for half a century, to be sure — not to mention the more oblique use of it in political oratory.

The day when the outcry arose over who could or should come under the blanket, or how far it could or should be stretched, now dims in memory (except for Politics' ghostly official ritual). And for a long time now complaint has been directed at the blanket itself.

Political short-circuits having produced two devastating general electrocutions in the past forty years and brought about a chronic state of localized slaughter, no one even among its manufacturers regards the old blanket with complacence any more. Inspecting it and proposing fumigation, renovation, etc., are the preoccupations of our age. In this country, where the blanket was warmest and most of the people slept next to it, in the raw, there was paradoxically in the distant South a ravelling edge.

The edge of man's social covering has always interested the artist, and the existence of these loose antique strands in the South has not gone without notice. It has received literary treatment

a novel by **Flannery O'Connor**

WISE BLOOD

Dust jacket for O'Connor's first novel. In an author's note for the 1962 edition she wrote, "It is a comic novel about a Christian malgré lui *[despite himself], and as such, very serious; for all comic novels that are any good must be about matters of life and death."*

over more than two decades. The significance of our unravelling even has been suspected.

No more dramatic representation of it, however, has come to my attention than that made in *Wise Blood* by Miss Flannery O'Connor. And let me add, no wiser blood had brooded and beat over the meaning of the grim rupture in our social fabric than that of this twenty-six year old Georgia girl in this, her first novel.

Two earlier novels dealing substantially with the same material — Erskine Caldwell's *Tobacco Road* and William Faulkner's *As I Lay Dying* — can, I believe, be drawn upon to illuminate and give us perspective for Miss O'Connor's dramatic revelation. These three stories present the same sort of people in the same passage of history, although a quarter of a century separates the Lesters and the Bundrens from Hazel Motes. To be sure a little more has transpired historically for "Haze," than had for Jeeter or Anse. There has been a po-

O'Connor (seated) at an autograph party held at Georgia State College for Women a few days after the publication of Wise Blood

litical revolution in this country and another world war. But this is of no great importance in their predicament.

The significant difference comes in the creator's definition of this predicament.

Caldwell — no artist and only a dull pornographer and entitled to mention in this company only because of the accident of his comment on the material in question and public reaction to it — saw only the physical poverty and hunger of his Lesters in *Tobacco Road*. In the Marxist *morality* which he reflected, this was mortal sin, and, with the anger of the sentimental and confused, he heaped every conceivable indignity that could be heaped on the human animal, upon them.

Perhaps the only reason why he did not do them deeper degradation was because he knew of no other dimension in which to degrade them. His references to religion were purely nominal. He had too little imagination to use his woman preacher, Bessie, for anything more than a labelled effigy on which to smear sexual imbecilities. He granted Jeeter and Ada Lester a tragic

death only because death for him was merely phenomenal — and literary.

In *As I Lay Dying*, Faulkner knows that death is not merely phenomenal and he remembers that there is a more persistent hunger than physical hunger. The Bundrens are not absorbed in their precarious economy. At the story's opening, however, Addie, the religious one, is dying and their drama concerns itself with the ritual burial of her remains. Their religious rite gives them significance while it engages them, yet they do not seek salvation and when it is ended they slip back into naturalistic anonymity. Faulkner, one of the great visionaries of our time, showed religious perspective here, but he had not then been granted the grace of vision.

To be sure time has passed, events have transpired and we all understand more about the limitations of materialism than we did twenty years ago. This is true even for artists and their Lesters, Bundrens and Moteses, too. *Tobacco Road* received serious critical as well as popular acceptance and praise, while Faulkner was being rebuked for *As I Lay Dying* by those who slept warmly, in the raw, next to The Blanket. But to make my point, the suspicion I wish to give voice to here is that Lesters, Bundrens and Moteses alike, were gnawed by the same secret hunger.

It has remained for Miss O'Connor, twenty years after their earlier appearance, to see what these people's destitution signifies and to fully appreciate their motivation.

Wise Blood is not about belly hunger, nor religious nostalgia, but about the persistent craving of the soul. It is not about a man whose religious allegiance is name for a shiftlessness and fatalism that make him degenerate in poverty and bestial before hunger, nor about a family of rustics who sink in naturalistic anonymity when the religious elevation of their burial rite is over. It is about man's inescapable need of his fearful, if blind, search for salvation. Miss O'Connor has not been confused by the symptoms.

And she centers her story frankly and directly on the religious activity and experience of her simple and squalid folk. Didactically stated her story seems over-simple: Hazel Motes, an hysterical fringe preacher, tries to found a church "Without Christ" and, progressively preaching nihilism, negates his way back to the cross.

The point is, however, that there is nothing didactic about her statement of it. Her statement is completely dramatic and dramatically profound.

I would agree, however, that Miss O'Connor could not have done what she has done twenty years ago. We have here essentially the same people and the same essential motivation, but the Lesters and Bundrens could not have been made to force the issue of the Church Without Christ. The technique Miss O'Connor employs had not ripened then and, if it had been so employed perhaps could not have been generally understood.

In contrast to Caldwell's reportorial naturalism and Faulkner's poetic expressionism, she uses, under the face of naturalism a theologically weighted symbolism.

When the story opens, Hazel Motes, from Eastrod, Tennessee, and just released from the Army after four years' service, is on his way to preach "the church without Jesus Christ Crucified." He doesn't believe in Jesus and he doesn't believe in sin, he confides to passengers on the train taking him to Taulkinham, the city.

His first act to disprove his belief in sin on his arrival is to share the bed of Mrs. Leora Watts, said to be the "friendliest bed in town." His mission complicates his life with that of a phony, blind, street-corner beggar-preacher and his young daughter, whom Haze plans to seduce to prove to the blind preacher that he is serious in his repudiation of Christianity.

Haze is impressed with the preacher's story that he blinded himself with quick lime to justify his belief that Christ had redeemed him. Still Haze suspects its validity. In the course of events he succeeds in finding out what the reader already knows, that the preacher had funked his demonstration with the quick lime and not put it in his eyes, and is not blind. Moreover, the preacher's fifteen-year old nymphomaniac daughter turns the tables on Haze in his plans to seduce her and forces him to take her into his bed.

To the theater crowds, he preaches nightly from the hood of his rat-colored, high-back automobile, which he bought for $40.00 — preaches at the outset that "Jesus Christ is just a nigger trick," and he talks about a "new Jesus." Later he contends that he cannot commit blasphemy, because there is nothing to blaspheme.

His talk about a new jesus attracts a street mountebank who wants to join him, capitalize on his *idea* and make money out of it. When Haze refuses, the mountebank, Onnie Jay Holy, finds a double for Haze and tries to carry on without him.

Haze, who feels that he is trying to bring Truth to the world — the truth that there is no truth — will have no counterfeit of himself preaching a new jesus to take people's money. When warning does not stop his deceitful imitator, he runs him down with his car and kills him.

In his treasured automobile, he plans to drive to another city to found his church, leaving behind his crime, the people who did not appreciate his message of truth, and the preacher's feckless daughter who has proved too much for him. On the journey, he is overtaken by a traffic cop, who, when he finds Haze has no driver's license, has him drive his jalopy up on the next hill-top, to see the "puttiest view you ever did see." Here the cop pushes Haze's car over the embankment to its destruction, with the words, "Them that don't have a car, don't need a license."

For a long time Haze stares at the desolate view "that extended from his eyes to the blank gray sky that went on, depth after depth, into space." When the now solicitous patrolman offers to give Haze a lift, he says he wasn't going anywhere.

Up to this point the surface action has simulated naturalistic motivation, but evidently Miss O'Connor felt that, to a world which does not yet accept the idea of the devil, she had better emphasize his allegorical appearance. It is the first apparent clue to Haze's reemboidment [sic] of the Christ myth, this ironic *temptation* from the mountain-top.

He returns to blind himself with quick lime and spends his remaining days in mortifying the flesh. The anti-Christ messiah's lone disciple is his hard-bitten landlady, a shrew who had always felt cheated. And her curiosity to know what that "crazy fool," sitting on her porch, staring off into space with his sight-less eyes *sees,* finally gets her. "Why had he destroyed his eyes and saved himself unless he had some plan, unless he saw something that he couldn't get without being blind to everything else?" And his other silent penance — rocks and broken glass in his shoes, barbed wire around his chest — when she nosily discovers it, fascinates her by its very illogic: she suspects that she is being cheated somehow, because of something he sees that she can't see. She pursues him, finally falls in love with him, and with mixed motives tries to force him to marry her.

He will not "treat" with her, flees her house into a storm, dies of exposure and a policeman's billy. His death only fixes his fascination for her.

Miss O'Connor employs symbolic motivation, allusion, parallel, irony and understatement, among other things, to suggest her indirect and deeper meanings. The surface story as a whole makes its allegorical point. These are all known devices, but she employs them with fine skill and tact and dramatic insight.

There is the obvious suggestion in *Wise Blood* that that terrible heretical misconception of religious freedom which regards every man as potentially his own priest, has come to the end of its row. But the dramatic impact for me lay in my share of the landlady's chill (and fascination) over the undescribed vision that filled Haze Motes' sightless eyes — Haze Motes, who had never got far enough under the Patent Electric Blanket to be lulled to sleep in its security.

BOOK REVIEW:
Review of *Wise Blood, Times Literary Supplement,* 2 September 1955, p. 505.

The British edition of Wise Blood, *published in June 1955, was not widely reviewed, but a respectful and perceptive notice appeared in the* Times Literary Supplement.

Miss Flannery O'Connor is one of those writers from the American South whose gifts, intense, erratic and strange, demand more than a customary effort of understanding from the English reader. Nevertheless, the gifts are notable: and in *Wise Blood,* her first novel, Miss O'Connor adds to the passion with which she searches for moral absolutes a subtle, ironic humour.

The story she tells is that of a fiercely militant atheist named Hazel Motes who preaches, from the nose of his rat-coloured old forty-dollar car, the doctrine of the Church Without Christ:

> I preach there are all kinds of truth, your truth and somebody else's, but behind all of them, there's only one truth and that is that there's no truth. No truth behind all truths is what I and this church preach!

Hazel is subjected to many deceits and temptations during the course of his pilgrimage towards truth. The blind preacher whom he follows proves not to be blind at all; he had determined to blind himself with lime, but flinched at the last moment from such an ultimate act of faith. The preacher's daughter pursues Hazel with threats, or promises, of partnership in deliberate sexual degradation. The one convert made by the Church Without Christ is a shyster who simply uses it as a vehicle for profitable rhetoric. Hazel's integrity is proof against them all. The time comes when he should

blind himself to express his faith in nothingness, and he does not falter. Yet even this act does not prove to have any final meaning, and the end of Hazel's story has a terrible, fantastic consistency. Miss O'Connor may become an important writer. She is certainly a serious one.

LETTER:
Flannery O'Connor to Robie Macauley, 18 May 1955; in *The Habit of Being,* pp. 80–82.

O'Connor was awarded Kenyon Review Fellowships for 1953 and 1954 and reported to the Fitzgeralds that, as a result, "My kinfolks think I am a commercial writer." By December 1954 she was walking with a cane. Either the ACTH she was taking or her disease itself was causing her upper leg and hip bones to deteriorate, and a year later she was using crutches. At the same time she began taking a new cortisone drug with fewer side effects than ACTH. Even before these changes, which improved her mobility, she was able to travel on a limited basis. This letter mentions a writers' conference in Greensboro, North Carolina, that she attended in March 1955 and an upcoming television appearance in New York, in which she was interviewed in connection with a dramatization of the beginning of "The Life You Save May Be Your Own," one of the ten stories in her second book, A Good Man Is Hard to Find and Other Stories, *published on 12 May 1955. This letter to novelist Robie Macauley, who had been at the Iowa Writers' Workshop with O'Connor, is a response to his praise for the book. The Ashley mentioned in this letter is Ashley Brown, whose memoir of O'Connor is included in this volume.*

I certainly am glad you like the stories because now I feel it's not bad that I like them so much. The truth is I like them better than anybody and I read them over and over and laugh and laugh, then get embarrassed when I remember I was the one wrote them. Unlike *Wise Blood,* they were all relatively painless to me; but now I have to quit enjoying life and get on with the second novel. The first chapter of it is going to be published in the fall in the *New World Writing* thing and is to be called "You Can't Be Any Poorer Than Dead" — which is the way I feel every time I get to work on it.

Nobody has given me any gold even in a medal, but you are right about the television. I am going to New York on the 30th to be, if you

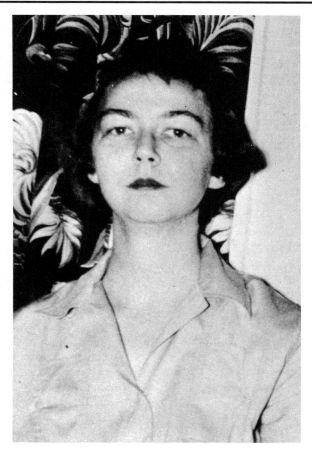

O'Connor in 1953

please, interviewed by Mr. Harvey Breit (on the 31st) on a program he is starting up over NBC-TV [*Gallery-Proof*]. They are also going to dramatize the opening scene from "The Life You Save" etc. Do you reckon this is going to corrupt me? I already feel like a combination of Msgr. Sheen and Gorgeous George [a wrestler]. Everybody who has read *Wise Blood* thinks I'm a hillbilly nihilist, whereas I would like to create the impression over the television that I'm a hillbilly Thomist, but I will probably not be able to think of anything to say to Mr. Harvey Breit but "Huh?" and "Ah dunno." When I come back I'll probably have to spend three months day and night in the chicken pen to counteract these evil influences.

Although I am a prominent Georgia Author I have never went to Washington but I have went over it and shall this time at an altitude of 14,000 feet compliments Eastern Airlines.

Greensboro was moderately ghastly, the more so than it would have been if you and Anne had come down. The panel was the worst as I never can think of anything to say about a story and the conferences were high comedy. I had one with a bearded intellectual delinquent from Kenyon who wouldn't be convinced he hadn't written a story, and the rest with girls writing about life in the dormitory.

A couple of weeks ago Ashley came down of a Sunday afternoon with [a friend] and they took in the architecture and had supper with me. Ashley was telling me that you are an admirer of Dr. Frank Crane [a newspaper columnist], my favorite Protestant theologian (salvation by the compliment club). I was glad to hear this because I think the doctor ought to be more widely appreciated. He is really a combination minister and masseur, don't you think? He appears in the Atlanta *Constitution* on the same page as the funnies. I like to hear him tell Alma A. that she can keep her husband by losing 75 pounds and just the other day he told a girl who was terrified of toads how not to let this ruin her life — know the truth & the truth shall make you free. However, his best column was where he told about getting the letter from the convict who had joined the compliment club. I hope you saw that one.

Please thank Mr. W. P. Southard for liking my stories. I am always glad to know I have a reader of quality because I have so many who aren't. I get some letters from people I might have created myself . . . [like] one from a young man in California who was starting a magazine to be called *Hearse* — "a vehicle to convey stories and poems to the great cemetery of the American intellect." Then I got a message from two theological students at Alexandria who said they had read *Wise Blood* and that I was their pin-up girl — the grimmest distinction to date. I got a real ugly letter from a Boston lady about that story called "A Temple of the Holy Ghost." She said she was a Catholic and so she couldn't understand how anybody could even HAVE such thoughts. I wrote her a letter that could have been signed by the bishop and now she is my fast friend and recently wrote me that her husband had run for attorney general but hadn't been elected. I wish somebody real intelligent would write me sometime but I seem to attract the lunatic fringe mainly.

I will be real glad when this television thing is over with. I keep having a mental picture of my glacial glare being sent out over the nation onto millions of children who are waiting impatiently for *The Batman* to come on.

Best to you and Anne and write me again before my next book comes out because that may be in 1984.

LETTER:
Flannery O'Connor to Sally and Robert Fitzgerald, 10 June 1955; in *The Habit of Being*, pp. 85–86.

Although O'Connor's interview on Harvey Breit's television show (included in Conversations with Flannery O'Connor, *pp. 5–10) is described as "mildly ghastly" in the letter to the Fitzgeralds, she was able to say more than "Huh" and "Ah dunno," as she had predicted to Macauley. (It is true, however, that Breit's questions tended to be longer than O'Connor's answers.) Most of this letter is a report about public and private responses to* A Good Man Is Hard to Find, *which went through four printings of a total of sixty-five hundred copies by 18 June 1956. This letter also alludes to Robert Giroux's move from Harcourt, Brace to Farrar, Straus and explains a legal and ethical way in which O'Connor could leave Harcourt, Brace if she became unhappy with her treatment there.*

Gladjer got the book. You are right about "A Stroke of Good Fortune." It don't appeal to me either and I really didn't want it there but Giroux thought it ought to be. It is, in its way, Catholic, being about the rejection of life at the source, but too much of a farce to bear the weight . . .

I have just got back from a week in New York at the expense of Harcourt, Brace, being, if you please, on a television program with Harvey Breit. They dramatized "The Life You Save" up to the point where the old woman says she'll give $17.50 if Mr. Shiftlet will marry the idiot daughter. Harvey Breit narrated the story and they had three live actors and then he interviewed me. It was all mildly ghastly as you may well imagine. I had interviews with this one and that one, ate with this one and that one . . . and generally managed to conduct myself as if this were all very well but I had business at home. This book is getting much more attention than *Wise Blood* and may even sell a few copies.

The atmosphere at Harcourt, Brace, at least in regard to meself, has changed to one of eager enthusiasm. I had tea with Giroux and he told me all about it. He looks better than when I saw him in the fall. He advised me to have a clause in my contract saying that my editor had to be a certain Miss Carver whom I like or the contract would be void so this has been done. If she leaves I can escape the textbook people if they prove to be too much. I liked Denver Lindley fine and am satisfied at Harcourt, Brace as long as he and Miss Carver are there.

I spent the weekend in Conn. with Caroline [Gordon Tate] and Sue Jenkins [friend of Mrs. Tate]. They had a party at which the chief guests were dear old Malcolm Cowley and dear old Van Wyke [Wyck] Brooks. Dear old Van Wyke insisted that I read a story at which horror-stricken looks appeared on the faces of both Caroline and Sue. "Read the shortest one!" they both screamed. I read "A Good Man Is Hard to Find" and Mr. Brooks later remarked to Miss Jenkins that it was a shame someone with so much talent should look upon life as a horror story. Malcolm was very polite and asked me if I had a wooden leg.

Congratulations on the Shelley Memorial Award which certainly sounds elegant. I am going to apply for a Guggenheim, hoping that now that my need is not so great they may see fit to reward me . . .

I have never read *The Golden Bowl* but I guess that condition will have to be corrected.

BOOK REVIEW:
Caroline Gordon, "With a Glitter of Evil," review of *A Good Man Is Hard to Find and Other Stories*, New York Times Book Review, 12 June 1955, p. 5.

Caroline Gordon had declined to review Wise Blood *because she had provided a dust-jacket blurb (in which she compared O'Connor to Franz Kafka). Having seen the stories in* A Good Man Is Hard to Find *at various stages of their composition, Gordon reviewed O'Connor's book with perception as well as enthusiasm, making cogent observations about her skillful handling of symbolism, incidents, and "the cadences of everyday speech."*

This first collection of short stories by Flannery O'Connor exhibits what Henry James, in "a partial portrait" of Guy de Maupassant, called "the artful brevity of a master." James added that Maupassant was "a 'case,' an embarrassment, a lion in the path." The contemporary reviewer, called upon to evaluate the achievement of the young American writer, may well feel that a lioness has strayed across *his* path. Miss O'Connor's works, like Maupassant's, are characterized by precision, density and an almost alarming circumscription. There are few landscapes in her stories. Her characters seem to move in the hard, white glare of a searchlight — or perhaps it is more as if the author viewed her subjects through the knothole in a fence or wall.

James complained that Maupassant's work lacked a dimension, because he "took no account of the moral nature of man. . . . The very compact mansion in which he dwells presents on that side a perfectly dead wall." This charge cannot be laid at Miss O'Connor's door. The difference lies in the eye that is applied to the crack in the wall of her "very compact mansion." Miss O'Connor, for all her apparent preoccupation with the visible scene, is also fiercely concerned with moral, even theological, problems. In these stories the rural South is, for the first time, viewed by a writer whose orthodoxy matches her talent. The results are revolutionary.

Miss O'Connor has an unerring eye in the selection of detail and the most exquisite ear I know of for the cadences of everyday speech. The longer, statelier sentence which has come down to us from the great masters of English prose and which, in the hands of a writer like Joyce, throws into such dramatic relief his mastery of the ver-

nacular, is not as yet in her repertory. She is, like Maupassant, very much of her time; and her stories, like his, have a certain glitter, as it were, of evil, which pervades them and astonishingly contributes to their lifelikeness.

In "A Good Man Is Hard to Find" an American family, father, mother, three children and grandmother, set off on a vacation motor trip, their aim being to cover as much ground as possible in the time allotted for the vacation. "Let's go through Georgia fast, so we won't have to look at it much" is the way 8-year-old John Wesley puts it. Before they are through they have all six confronted eternity — through the agency of a gunman escaped from a penitentiary who employs the interval, during which his two henchmen are off in the wood murdering the father and mother and three children, in discussing the problem of death and resurrection with the grandmother.

In "The Displaced Person" Mrs. Shortley, the wife of a dairyman, reads the Apocalypse and communes with her soul so long and earnestly that she has visions. Mrs. McIntyre, the owner of the dairy farm, being more sophisticated than Mrs. Shortley, does not have as easy access to spiritual comforts and, when hard pressed, turns to the memory of her late husband, "the Judge." She sometimes sits and meditates in his study, which she has kept unchanged since his death as a sort of memorial to him.

Mrs. McIntyre married the Judge because she thought he was rich — and wise. His estate proved to consist of "fifty acres and the house." His wisdom is still embodied in pithy vulgarization of proverbs: "One fellow's misery is the other fellow's gain." "The devil you know is better than the devil you don't."

Miss O'Connor is as realistic and down to earth a writer as one can find. Yet many people profess to find her work hard to understand. This may be because she uses symbolism in a way in which it has not been used by any of her young contemporaries. Mrs. Hopewell in "Good Country People" is thrifty, kind-hearted and optimistic, abounding in aphorisms such as "A smile never hurt anyone," "It takes all kinds to make a world." She cannot understand why her daughter Joy is not happy. Joy, who had her leg blown off in a shotgun explosion when she was 8 years old, has a doctor's degree in philosophy, a bad complexion and poor eyesight and at 28 is so joyless that she has changed her name to "Hulga" because she thinks that is an ugly name. It is not

2

the grandmother

~~Of course she~~ was the first one ready to load up the next morning at six

o'clock. She had Baby Brother's bucking bronco ~~that~~ and ~~basketing~~ what she

called her "~~Pile~~" and Pitty Sing, the cat, ~~all three~~ packed in the car before

Boatwrite had a chance to ~~get anything at her in~~ *get the* ~~come out of the door with the~~

rest of the luggage.out of the hall. They got off at seven-thirty, Boatwrite

and ~~Baby~~ the children's mother in the front and Granny, John Wesley, Baby Brother,

Little Sister Mayy Ann, Pitty Sing, and the bucking bronco in the back.

"Why the hell did you bring that goddam rocking horse?" Boatwrite asked

because as soon as ~~the car began to move,~~ *they were out of the city & on the smooth highway,* Baby Brother began to squall to get

on the bucking bronco. "He can't get on that thing in this car and that's final,"

his father who was a stern man said.

"Can we open the lunch now?" Little Sister ~~Maryxxxx~~ asked. "It'll shut

Baby Brother up. Mamma, can we open up the lunch?"

"No," their grandmother said. *It's only eight-thirty.*

Their mother was ~~still~~ reading SCREEN MOTHERS AND THEIR CHILDREN. "Yeah,

sure," she said.without looking up. She was all dressed up today. She had on

a purple silk dress and a hat and ~~xxxxxxxxx~~ *her red* a choker of pink beads and a new

pocket book, and high heel pumps.

"Let's go through Georgia quick so we won't have to look at it much," John

Wesley said. "~~I seen enough of it myself.~~"

"You should see Tennessee," his grandmother said. "Now there is a *beautiful* state."

"Like hell," John Wesley said. "That's just a hillbilly dumping ground."

"Ha *ha*," his mother said, and nudged Boatwrite. "Didjer hear that?" *she was*

from Arkansas. They ate their lunch and got along fine ~~after that~~ for a while until Pitty

Sing who had been asleep jumped into the front of the car and caused Boatwrite

to swerve to the right into a ditch. Pitty Sing was a large grey-striped cat

with a yellow hind leg and a ~~x~~ *big* soiled white face. Granny thought that she

was the only person in the world that he really loved but he had never ~~really~~ *the truth was*

looked ~~anyfarxupxxxxhxxxfxxx any~~ farther *up* than her middle and he didn't even

like other cats. He jumped snarling into the front seat and Boatwrite's shoulders

Second and third pages from an early draft for "A Good Man Is Hard to Find," the title story in O'Connor's second book
(The Flannery O'Connor Collection, Ina Russell Dillard Library, Georgia College)

3

snapped above his head and in one second ~~theyzxx~~ the car was nose-down in ~~the~~

a red embankment.

"count the children, count the children!" Granny screamed for her first

thoughts were always for others. The children were all there but Pitty Sing ~~had~~

                                                    slowly
jumped out the window and was down in the embankment, digging a ~~x~~ small hole.

in the ~~xxxxhx~~ clay.

Boatwrite was cursing so softly that the children might have thought *him*
        only
he ~~xx~~ ~~was~~ humming a popular tune.

hard to find in the two women figures of the "Old" and "New" South.

Perhaps a profounder symbolism underlies "The Displaced Person." The Judge, a "dirty, snuff-dipping courthouse figure," may also — for the orthodox — symbolize the "Old" South, his study, "a dark, closet-like space as dark and quiet as a chapel," the scanty provision which the "Old" South was able to make for the spiritual needs of her children.

LETTER:
Flannery O'Connor to "A," 20 July 1955; in *The Habit of Being*, p. 90.

In summer 1955 O'Connor received a letter from a young woman with whom she was to carry on a nine-year correspondence; they met only infrequently. Because this woman chose to remain anonymous, she is called "A" throughout The Habit of Being. *In her letters to "A," an aspiring fiction writer, O'Connor made some of her most clearly articulated statements about her religious and literary views. In this first letter to "A," O'Connor defended the so-called brutality of the stories in* A Good Man Is Hard to Find. *The "moronic" review in* The New Yorker *is a brief, anonymous note asserting, "There is brutality in these stories, but since the brutes are as mindless as their victims, all we have, in the end, is a series of tales about creatures who collide and drown, or survive to float passively in the isolated sea of the author's compassion, which accepts them without reflecting anything" (18 June 1955).*

I am very pleased to have your letter. Perhaps it is even more startling to me to find someone who recognizes my work for what I try to make it than it is for you to find a God-conscious writer near at hand. The distance is 87 miles but I feel the spiritual distance is shorter.

I write the way I do because (not though) I am a Catholic. This is a fact and nothing covers it like the bald statement. However, I am a Catholic peculiarly possessed of the modern consciousness, that thing Jung describes as unhistorical, solitary, and guilty. To possess this *within* the Church is to bear a burden, the necessary burden for the conscious Catholic. It's to feel the contemporary situation at the ultimate level. I think that the Church is the only thing that is going to make the terrible world we are coming to endurable; the only thing that makes the Church endurable is that it is somehow the body of Christ and that on this we

are fed. It seems to be a fact that you have to suffer as much from the Church as for it but if you believe in the divinity of Christ, you have to cherish the world at the same time that you struggle to endure it. This may explain the lack of bitterness in the stories.

The notice in the *New Yorker* was not only moronic, it was unsigned. It was a case in which it is easy to see that the moral sense has been bred out of certain sections of the population, like the wings have been bred off certain chickens to produce more white meat on them. This is a generation of wingless chickens, which I suppose is what Nietzsche meant when he said God was dead.

I am mighty tired of reading reviews that call *A Good Man* brutal and sarcastic. The stories are hard but they are hard because there is nothing harder or less sentimental than Christian realism. I believe that there are many rough beasts now slouching toward Bethlehem to be born and that I have reported the progress of a few of them, and when I see these stories described as horror stories I am always amused because the reviewer always has hold of the wrong horror.

You were very kind to write to me and the measure of my appreciation must be to ask you to write me again. I would like to know who this is who understands my stories.

LETTER:
Flannery O'Connor to "A," 28 August 1955; in *The Habit of Being*, pp. 97–99.

In this letter O'Connor defends her adherence to Roman Catholic dogma in light of the suggestion that her views might be considered "fascist." She also provides a list of writers who influenced her religious and literary ideas.

I wish St. Thomas were handy to consult about the fascist business. Of course this word doesn't really exist uncapitalized, so in making it that way you have the advantage of using a word with a private meaning and a public odor; which you must not do. But if it does mean a doubt of the efficacy of love and if this is to be observed in my fiction, then it has to be explained or partly explained by what happens to conviction (I believe love to be efficacious in the loooong run) when it is translated into fiction designed for a public with a predisposition to believe the opposite. This along with the limitations of the writer could account for the negative appearance. But find another word than fascist, for me and St. Thomas too. And totalitarian won't do either. Both St. Thomas and St. John of the Cross, dissimilar as they were, were entirely united by the same belief. The more I read St. Thomas the more flexible he appears to me. Incidentally, St. John would have been able to sit down with the prostitute and said, "Daughter, let us consider this," but St. Thomas doubtless knew his own nature and knew that he had to get rid of her with a poker or she would overcome him. I am not only for St. Thomas here but am in accord with his use of the poker. I call this being tolerantly realistic, not being a fascist.

Another reason for the negative appearance: if you live today you breathe in nihilism. In or out of the Church, it's the gas you breathe. If I hadn't had the Church to fight it with or to tell me the necessity of fighting it, I would be the stinkingest logical positivist you ever saw right now. With such a current to write against, the result almost has to be negative. It does well just to be.

Then another thing, what one has as a born Catholic is something given and accepted before it is experienced. I am only slowly coming to experience things that I have all along accepted. I suppose the fullest writing comes from what has been accepted and experienced both and that I have just not got that far yet all the time. Conviction without experience makes for harshness.

The magazine that had the piece on Simone Weil is called *The Third Hour* and is put out spasmodically (when she can get the money) by a Russian lady named Helene Iswolsky who teaches at Fordham. I used to go with her nephew so I heard considerable about it and ordered some back issues. The old lady is a Catholic of the Eastern Rite persuasion and sort of a one-man Catholic ecumenical movement. The enclosed of Edith Stein came out of there too. I've never read anything E. Stein wrote. None of it that I know of has been translated. There is a new biography by Hilda Graef but I have not seen it. My interest in both of them comes only from what they have done, which overshadows anything they may have written. But I would very much like you to lend me the books of Simone Weil's when you get through with them . . .

Mrs. Tate is Caroline Gordon Tate, the wife of Allen Tate. She writes fiction as good as anybody, though I have not read much of it myself. They, with John Crowe Ransom and R. P. Warren, were prominent in the '20s in that group at Vanderbilt that called itself the Fugitives. The Fugitives are now here there and yonder. Anyway Mrs. Tate has taught me a lot about writing.

Which brings me to the embarrassing subject of what I have not read and been influenced by. I hope nobody ever asks me in public. If so I intend to look dark and mutter, "Henry James Henry James" — which will be the veriest lie, but no matter. I have not been influenced by the best people. The only good things I read when I was a child were the Greek and Roman myths which I got out of a set of child's encyclopedia called *The Book of Knowledge*. The rest of what I read was Slop with a capital S. The Slop period was followed by the Edgar Allan Poe period which lasted for years and consisted chiefly in a volume called *The Humerous* [sic] *Tales of E. A. Poe*. These were mighty humerous — one about a young man who was too vain to wear his glasses and consequently married his grandmother by accident; another about a fine figure of a man who in his room removed wooden arms, wooden legs, hair piece, artificial teeth, voice box, etc. etc.; another about the inmates of a lunatic asylum who take over the establishment and run it to suit themselves. This is an influence I would rather not think about. I went to a progressive high school where one did not read if one did not wish to; I did not wish to (except the *Humerous Tales* etc.). In college I read works of social-science, so-called. The only thing that kept me from being a social-scientist was the grace of God and the fact that I couldn't remember the stuff but a few days after reading it.

I didn't really start to read until I went to Graduate School and then I began to read and write at the same time. When I went to Iowa I had never heard of Faulkner, Kafka, Joyce, much less read them. Then I began to read everything at once, so much so that I didn't have time I suppose to be influenced by any one writer. I read all the Catholic novelists, Mauriac, Bernanos, Bloy, Greene, Waugh; I read all the nuts like Djuna Barnes and Dorothy Richardson and Va. Woolf (unfair to the dear lady of course); I read the best Southern writers like Faulkner and the Tates, K. A. Porter, Eudora Welty and Peter Taylor; read the Russians, not Tolstoy so much but Dostoevsky, Turgenev, Chekhov and Gogol. I became a great admirer of Conrad and have read almost all his fiction. I have totally skipped such people as Dreiser, Anderson (except for a few stories) and Thomas Wolfe. I have learned something from Hawthorne, Flaubert, Balzac and something from Kafka, though I have never been able to finish one of his novels. I've read almost all of

Henry James — from a sense of High Duty and because when I read James I feel something is happening to me, in slow motion but happening nevertheless. I admire Dr. Johnson's *Lives of the Poets*. But always the largest thing that looms up is *The Humerous Tales of Edgar Allan Poe*. I am sure he wrote them all while drunk too.

I have more to say about the figure of Christ as merely human but this has gone on long enough and I will save it. Have you read Romano Guardini? . . . In my opinion there is nothing like [his book, *The Lord*] anywhere, certainly not in this country. I can lend it to you if you would like to see it.

LETTER:
Flannery O'Connor to "A," 16 December 1955; in *The Habit of Being*, pp. 123–126.

This wide-ranging letter to "A" begins with comments on other fiction writers — Henry James, Nelson Algren, Shirley Ann Grau, Louis-Ferdinand Céline, and Françoise Sagan — and goes on to a discussion of O'Connor's fiction and experiences at literary gatherings.

The subject of the moral basis of fiction is one of the most complicated and I don't doubt that I contradict myself on it, for I have no foolproof aesthetic theory. However, I think we are talking about different things or mean different things here by moral basis. I continue to think that art doesn't require rectitude of the appetite but this is not to say that it does not have (fiction anyway) a moral basis. I identify this with James' *felt life* and not with any particular moral system and I believe that the fiction writer's moral sense must coincide with his dramatic sense. I don't like Nelson Algren because his moral sense sticks out, is not one with his dramatic sense. With the Grau stories, I can't discover that life is felt at a moral depth at all. As I remember Céline, I felt that he did feel life at a moral depth — or rather that his work made me feel life at a moral depth; what he feels I can't care about. Focus is a bad word anyway.

When I said that the devil was a better writer than Mlle. Saigon [Sagan], I meant to indicate that the devil's moral sense coincides at all points with his dramatic sense.

As I understand it, the Church teaches that our resurrected bodies will be intact as to personality, that is, intact with all the contradictions beautiful to you, except the contradiction of sin; sin is the contradiction, the interference, of a greater good by a lesser good. I look for all variety in that unity but not for a choice: for when all you see will be God, all you will want will be God.

About it's being cowardly to accept only the nun's embrace: remember that when the nun hugged the child, the crucifix on her belt was mashed into the side of the child's face, so that one accepted embrace was marked with the ultimate all-inclusive symbol of love, and that when the child saw the sun again, it was a red ball, like an elevated Host drenched in blood and it left a line like a red clay road in the sky. Now here the martyrdom that she had thought about in a childish way (which turned into a happy sleeping with the lions) is shown in the final way that it has to be for us all — an acceptance of the Crucifixtion, Christ's and our own. As near as I get to saying what purity is in this story ["A Temple of the Holy Ghost"] is saying that it is an acceptance of what God wills for us, an acceptance of our individual circumstances. Now to accept renunciation, when those are your circumstances, is not cowardly but of course I am reading you short here too. I understand that you don't mean that renunciation is cowardly. What you do mean, I don't in so many words know. Understand though, that, like the child, I believe the Host is actually the body and blood of Christ, not a symbol. If the story grows for you it is because of the mystery of the Eucharist in it.

I was once, five or six years ago, taken by some friends to have dinner with Mary McCarthy and her husband, Mr. Broadwater. (She just wrote that book, *A Charmed Life*.) She departed the Church at the age of 15 and is a Big Intellectual. We went at eight and at one, I hadn't opened my mouth once, there being nothing for me in such company to say. The people who took me were Robert Lowell and his now wife, Elizabeth Hardwick. Having me there was like having a dog present who had been trained to say a few words but overcome with inadequacy had forgotten them. Well, toward morning the conversation turned on the Eucharist, which I, being the Catholic, was obviously supposed to defend. Mrs. Broadwater said when she was a child and received the Host, she thought of it as the Holy Ghost, He being the "most portable" person of the Trinity; now she thought of it as a symbol and implied that it was a pretty good one. I then said, in a very shaky voice, "Well, if it's a symbol, to hell with it." That was all the defense I was capable of but I realize now that this is all I will ever be able to say about it, outside of a story, except that it is the center of existence for me; all the rest of life is expendable.

Why didn't the lady say I identified myself with St. Thomas? I was recommending to these innocents self-knowledge as the way to overcome regionalism — to know oneself is to know one's region, it is also to know the world, and it is also, paradoxically, a form of exile from that world, to know oneself is above all to know what one lacks, etc. etc. etc. I then went on to say that St. Catherine of Siena had called self-knowledge a "cell," and that she, an unlettered woman, had remained in it literally for three years and had emerged to change the politics of Italy. The first product of self-knowledge was humility, I said, and added that this was not a virtue conspicuous in the Southern character. Well, betwixt us two, I do not identify myself with St. Catherine. What's furthermore, I never quoted St. Augustine. Anyway, I'm real pleased to have impressed with my attire. Nothing shocks like conventionality and this will remind me when attending the fire sales where I buy my clothes not to get anything the Duchesser Windsor wouldn't eat with the Duke in.

Tuesday I attended another one of these things [a literary gathering]. There are always one or two that I would like to see again although I never can remember the names or am not given them. I reported on the characteristics of the short story and afterwards they asked questions, such as, "What do you think of the frame-within-a-frame short story?" They know all the "frames." Most of them live in a world God never made. There is one of them who attends all these things who reminds you of Stone Mountain on the move. She's a large grey mass, near-sighted, pious, and talks about "messages" all the time. I haven't got her name yet but she is going to pursue me in dreams I feel.

If the fact that I am a "celebrity" makes you feel silly, what dear girl do you think it makes me feel? It's a comic distinction shared with Roy Rogers's horse and Miss Watermelon of 1955. In a great many ways it makes things difficult, for the only friends you can have are old friends or new ones who are willing to ignore it. I am very thankful that you are willing to ignore it.

LETTER:
Flannery O'Connor to "A," 24 August 1956 [excerpt]; in *The Habit of Being*, pp. 170–171.

The personal reading of "Good Country People" offered in this letter to "A" reveals O'Connor's sympathy for and understanding of even her most grotesque characters. Her compassion was rooted in self-knowledge.

. . . About GCP ["Good Country People"] let me say that you are not reading the story itself. Where do you get the idea that Hulga's need to worship "comes to flower" in GCP? Or that she had never had any faith at any time? or never loved anybody before? None of these things are said in the story. She is full of contempt for the Bible salesman until she finds he is full of contempt for her. Nothing "comes to flower" here except her realization in the end that she ain't so smart. It's not said that she has never had any faith but it is implied that her fine education has got rid of it for her, that purity has been overridden by pride of intellect through her fine education. Further it's not said that she's never loved anybody, only that she's never been kissed by anybody — a very different thing. And of course I have thrown you off myself by informing you that Hulga is like me. So is Nelson, so is Haze, so is Enoch, but you cannot read a story from what you get out of a letter. Nor I repeat, can you, in spite of anything Sister Sewell may say, read the author by the story. You may but you shouldn't — See T. S. Eliot.

That my stories scream to you that I have never consented to be in love with anybody is merely to prove that they are screaming an historical inaccuracy. I have God help me consented to this frequently. Now that Hulga is repugnant to you only makes her more believable. I had a letter from a man who said Allen Tate was wrong about the story that Hulga was not a "maimed soul," she was just like us all. He ended the letter by saying he was in love with Hulga and he hoped some day she would learn to love him. Quaint. But I stick neither with you nor with that gent here but with Mr. Allen Tate. A maimed soul is a maimed soul.

I have also led you astray by talking of technique as if it were something that could be separated from the rest of the story. Technique can't operate at all, of course, except on believable material. But there was less conscious technical control in GCP than in any story I've ever written. Technique works best when it is unconscious, and it was unconscious there.[. . .]

MEMOIR:
Ashley Brown, "Flannery O'Connor: A Literary Memoir," in *Realist of Distances: Flannery*

O'Connor Revisited, edited by Karl-Heinz Westarp and Jan Nordby Gretlund (Aarhus, Denmark: Aarhus University Press, 1987), pp. 18–29.

As he explains in this memoir, Ashley Brown, now a professor at the University of South Carolina, began reading O'Connor's fiction in the late 1940s and met her in July 1953 at the home of his old friends the Brainard Cheneys near Nashville, Tennessee. His memoir provides a valuable description of O'Connor's literary connections and influences.

My friendship with Flannery O'Connor began in the American way, through correspondence, in 1952. The early correspondence, long since lost, had to do with *Wise Blood,* the novel with which she made a small reputation in the spring of that year. It was reviewed in *Time* and *Newsweek* and the New York *Times* — no mean feat for a first novel. I, like some others, had read and remembered three disconnected episodes published back in the late 1940s in the *Sewanee Review* and the *Partisan Review,* and in those days I tended to set my literary standards by the writers who were admitted to their pages. Now the novel was out, and the fragments took their place within a design. *Wise Blood,* I thought and still think, is somewhat episodic, and when I talked to Flannery about it the following year she altogether agreed. The very format of the first edition, with its spacing between the chapters, suggests this. But what made me buy the book immediately was a statement on the jacket by Caroline Gordon, a writer for whom I had the utmost respect. She said there, "I was more impressed by *Wise Blood* than any novel I have read for a long time. Her picture of the modern world is literally terrifying. Kafka is almost the only one of our contemporaries who has achieved such effects." Caroline Gordon had already assisted Faulkner in his comeback with an important review of the *Portable Faulkner* in the New York *Times* in 1946, and she was doing as much as anyone to revive Ford Madox Ford during the early 1950s. Now she was recommending another genius. And to put this young writer beside Kafka, who was a special literary hero of that period! How percipient she was. In retrospect the comparison seems just; the scale of Flannery O'Connor's work is much the same as Kafka's; their thematic concerns are indeed similar.

In 1952 I was living in Virginia as an instructor at Washington and Lee University, where I had helped to found and edit a small literary quarterly called *Shenandoah.* It was great fun thinking up projects for writers we admired, some of them not at all famous at that time. I decided that we must run a longish review of *Wise Blood,* something more substantial than the notices in *Time* and *Newsweek.* So I turned to the Tennessee novelist Brainard Cheney, who I knew was a close friend of Caroline Gordon and Allen Tate. He responded with a splendid review that we published in our Autumn 1952 issue, immediately following Faulkner's little review of *The Old Man and the Sea.* The five pages of Mr. Cheney's piece are too long to summarize here, but I like especially the way in which he brings together *Wise Blood,* Erskine Caldwell's *Tobacco Road,* and Faulkner's *As I Lay Dying,* three novels which "present the same sort of people in the same passage of history." Caldwell he dismisses as "no artist and only a dull pornographer" who refuses to allow his characters a religious dimension in which to fulfill their wretched existence. Faulkner, on the other hand, "knows that death is not merely phenomenal and he remembers that there is a more persistent hunger than physical hunger. The Bundrens are not absorbed in their precarious economy. . . . Faulkner, one of the great visionaries of our time, showed religious perspective here, but he had not then been granted the grace of vision." *Wise Blood,* says Mr. Cheney, "is about man's inescapable need of his fearful, if blind, search for salvation. Miss O'Connor has not been confused by the symptoms." Then he makes this interesting observation:

> I would agree, however, that Miss O'Connor could not have done what she has done twenty years ago. We have here essentially the same people and the same essential motivation, but the Lesters and the Bundrens could not have been made to force the issue of the Church Without Christ. The technique Miss O'Connor employs had not ripened then, and if it had been so employed perhaps could not have been generally understood. In contrast to Caldwell's reportorial naturalism and Faulkner's poetic expressionism, she uses, under the face of naturalism, a theologically weighted symbolism.

This, I submit, was the best review that *Wise Blood* had at its first appearance. Rather curiously, neither the *Sewanee Review* nor the *Partisan Review,* which had originally published those episodes, bothered to review the completed novel at any time.

Flannery was very pleased with Brainard Cheney's piece. Before long she was writing to him, and her first letter, which dates from February, 1953, marks the beginning of another friendship. As for *Shenandoah,* we were quite poor and always apologized to our contributors for not paying them anything, but I went ahead and asked Flannery if she had a story we could use. No, she had nothing new that wasn't already spoken for, but she wanted to retrieve an old story and have it reprinted. That is how we happened to publish "A Stroke of Good Fortune," which had originally appeared in a magazine called *Tomorrow* in 1949. It came out in our issue for Spring 1953. It was in fact the earliest written of the stories that were eventually collected in *A Good Man Is Hard to Find,* but by 1954 Flannery had second thoughts about using it in a collection at all; it was "too much of a farce," she wrote to the Fitzgeralds. It is clearly not one of her best things, but I have found that university students rather enjoy it as an example of literary craft. They love the way in which the author deploys the various ages of mankind through a limited cast of characters within a highly restricted setting and time scheme. And they like the raucous treatment of the Fountain of Youth theme. It may be the work of a superior creative writing student, but one is always glad to have it in the *Complete Stories.*

I finally met Flannery in July of that year, 1953. The Brainard Cheneys had stopped by Andalusia Farm that spring during one of their trips to south Georgia and invited her to a house party at their place in Tennessee. I had known them since my student days at Vanderbilt and was of course delighted to be included. The Cheneys, I gathered, had recently become Roman Catholics through the influence of Caroline Gordon and had a special interest in Flannery at this moment. She had in person that same wonderful combination of caustic wit and friendly assurance that she had conveyed in her letters. The Cheneys had mentioned something about a disability that imposed certain restrictions on her, but at this time she wasn't on crutches and she never referred to her illness. I was indeed very ignorant of lupus then; I had simply never heard of it. A photograph made on this occasion depicts Flannery sitting on the steps of an abandoned smokehouse at the Cheneys' place; the steps are rotting away, the vines are gradually taking over. She is quite ladylike in a dark blue dress with white trim and the only earrings that I ever saw her wear; perhaps they were suggested by her mother. She looks relaxed

O'Connor during her July 1953 visit to the Brainard Cheneys

though she is unsmiling. There is nothing to arouse her sense of humor, not even the slight incongruity of the setting. I prefer this photograph to one that appeared in *Harper's Bazaar* two years later. This time she is sitting on the front steps of Andalusia — I can tell by the pattern of the bricks — dressed in a work shirt, as though she had just stepped out from her typewriter. But the camera shot is done in a kind of soft focus; she is looking away with a strangely evasive glance; the effect, though "glamorous" as they used to say, isn't at all natural. The photograph is almost belied by Flannery's accompanying comment: "A lady in Macon told me she read me under the dryer. I was gratified."

The Cheneys' house in those days was called Cold Chimneys; later, after central heating was installed, it became Idler's Retreat. A large brick house in the Greek Revival manner, not quite antebellum, it stands outside Smyrna, a little town perhaps twenty miles from Nashville. The Cheneys gradually moved themselves out there from the city after the Second World War, but they were very busy people and could not at first find the endless time that it takes to keep up such a place. Brainard or "Lon" Cheney, as he has been known to hundreds of people for decades, has been a journalist often involved with politics during a long career; now and then he has managed to buy the time to write his four novels and his literary and theological essays. Frances or Fannie is an eminent librarian, at one time president of the American Library Association. The Cheneys attended Vanderbilt during Fugitive days, and their friendships with the Nashville literati go back more than half a century. Cold Chimneys has always been a center of hospitality, for the young and unknown as well as the famous. Here, in the 1950s, one might meet Allen Tate and Caroline Gordon, or "Red" Warren, or on one occasion Katherine Anne Porter. A frequent guest was Andrew Lytle who had known Flannery longer than any of us, because he had been one of her teachers at Iowa. Young writers from Nashville were always bringing out their first novels or books of poems, and they soon took their place at the Cheneys' table.

Cleanth Brooks and others have suggested that there are some similarities between the literary renaissance in Ireland and that in the Southern United States. In retrospect it seems to me that Cold Chimneys was something like Coole Park in County Galway, Lady Gregory's house, where for thirty years William Butler Yeats and his friends gathered. Nothing at Coole Park remains except the ruins of the foundations, the tree on which the visiting writers carved their names, and of course the famous swans. Yeats celebrated the house and what it stood for in a memorable poem which will outlast everything else. Nobody, I believe, has celebrated Cold Chimneys except a former student of mine, a brilliant youth named Tom Carter from Virginia; he spent one year of his short life as a graduate student at Vanderbilt. Upon leaving Tennessee for Virginia in 1956, never to return, he wrote something entitled "Stray Stanzas from an Occasional Poem for Some Friends." I quote one of his eight quatrains, this about our host and hostess:

Convivial Lon, Odysseus wise,
loves God and politics and plays.
Sweet Fannie graced to civilize
articulates Smyrna soirées. ["Coole Park"]

Since I have retrieved the poem, I can't resist quoting another quatrain, because Flannery wrote an amusing prose account of the same occasion in a letter dated 20 October 1955; the subject is Russell Kirk, the philosopher of conservatism who was also a house guest at Cold Chimneys:

The procrastinator Kirk, hambone in hand,
speaks joyfully of his barren land;

then having been most amply dined,
expounds the simple, conservative mind.

In July 1953, when she first visited Cold Chimneys, Flannery had just published three stories: "A Good Man Is Hard to Find," "The Life You Save May Be Your Own," and "The River." "A Stroke of Good Fortune" had been reprinted in *Shenandoah* and "A Late Encounter with the Enemy" was about to come out in *Harper's Bazaar*. During the next two years she would bring out five more stories. All of these were collected in *A Good Man Is Hard to Find* in 1955. This seems to me her great creative moment; after that, as we know, she wrote another ten stories, perhaps one a year, and in 1959 she managed to finish a short novel, *The Violent Bear It Away*, on which she had been working for seven years. In 1953, when these stories were being published so quickly, they weren't always easy to take account of. I remember very well Flannery's first reading of "A Good Man Is Hard To Find" in the great library at Cold Chimneys. A few people came out from Nashville to meet her, but hardly anyone had read this new story. She started out in her Georgia drawl that was so perfect for rendering those awful selfish children, John Wesley and June Star, and their grandmother; it was comedy in a Southern tradition that goes back to Longstreet's *Georgia Scenes*, written, as Allen Tate once said, "by an accomplished gentleman for other accomplished gentlemen" (*Essays of Four Decades*, 1968, p. 591). Flannery's modern Georgia scene is much funnier than Longstreet's; the social details are more sharply observed, her ear for the vernacular is better. We all succumbed to laughter by the time we reached Red Sammy's barbecue place along the highway. The author had us in her hands. Then, at a certain point after Pitty Sing the cat sprang onto Bailey's shoulder, thus causing the accident, something sinister came into the narrative. Our reactions began to be crossed, and by the time that the grandmother found herself alone with The Misfit we were stunned into silence. It was a masterful performance. Flannery was not a trained reader. Once she got out into public she felt she should try other stories, but nothing ever seemed to work as well as this one, which eventually she called her "reading story." I grew to know her version of it well, as one knows a favorite musical composition that never fails to delight no matter how often one hears it. Incidentally, I think that the note of the sinister comes with a very short sentence at the end of the paragraph describing The Misfit's two companions: "Neither spoke." The little world of the story is an oral culture; everybody talks at one level or another; to withhold comment is to be inhuman.

In July, 1953, I was just about to visit Ireland for the first time. This would be the first stage in a kind of *Wanderjahr,* and I was already looking forward to my descent on Coole Park and Joyce's Martello tower and Bowen's Court. It was to be a literary pilgrimage all the way. I was astonished when Flannery brought me up short by saying, "Whatever do you want to go *there* for?" She had in fact a rather developed prejudice against Ireland which I, not Irish at all, could never understand. She was right to make fun of the sham Irishness that takes in so many people, and her caustic remark about Baloney Castle is worthy of Joyce himself. All the same, I thought this was a curious attitude on her part. She gave me the address of one of her favorite writers, J. F. Powers, who was then living in County Wicklow. Powers of course is Irish-American. His first book of stories, *Prince of Darkness,* had been published in 1947 to considerable acclaim, and I was impressed by the esteem in which he was held by other short-story writers of my acquaintance, Flannery and Peter Taylor and Robie Macauley. In 1953 he was writing some of the stories that he would collect in a volume called *The Presence of Grace* (1956), and later he extended his career with a fine novel, *Morte D'Urban* (1962), and another collection of stories, *Look How the Fish Live* (1975). He isn't a very fashionable writer now; I haven't seen one of his stories in an anthology for at least a decade. He really deserves a better reputation than many others. This is all apart from the fact that he was the first Catholic writer of the highest quality in the United States. His fictional world of priests and parish houses in the Midwest might seem to promise no more than Flannery's; his tone is light even when his issues are serious; but his work is a remarkable achievement. I suspect that he was a kind of model for Flannery when she was still trying herself out as a writer at the State University of Iowa, and her first story, "The Geranium," was published in *Accent,* the little magazine at the University of Illinois that was chiefly responsible for sponsoring Powers' work. It is no accident that she listed him first among American Catholic writers in a letter written to Father John McCown in March, 1964.

Another Catholic writer of a quite different sort whom we argued about in the 1950s was François Mauriac. After he won the Nobel Prize in 1952 many of his earlier books were translated and published, usually by Farrar, Straus and Cudahy, who were to be Flannery's publishers. Some of our friends had misgivings about his Jansenist tendencies, especially Caroline Gordon. Indeed her strictures about him were in an essay called "Some Readings and Misreadings," which came out in the *Sewanee Review,* Summer 1953; it was lying at hand in the library at Cold Chimneys during Flannery's first visit. This issue was rather prominently displayed, because it also contained Flannery's story "The River" as well as essays by Warren and Lytle. Caroline's general argument against the most eminent living Catholic novelist (as he was then) is that he denies the natural order, unlike Yeats and Faulkner, whose "patient, passionate portrayal of natural objects" is at least "Christian in hope":

> Mauriac's loftiest edifices, lacking such a solid foundation, seem always on the verge of toppling. The lurid flames that light up his scenes make them appear less rather than more substantial. He has said that he regrets that he does not find human nature more admirable but that he must portray it as he sees it. One wonders if he would not be a better novelist if he found it *natural?*

This is a long and very subtle essay which Flannery, like the rest of us, pondered at the time. I am sure that it influenced her thinking about the art of fiction. Her admiration for Mauriac, however, continued to the end. She owned at least fifteen of his books and I used to think that her work resembled his in certain respects. But she seems to have had some misgivings about him, and in January, 1956, she said, in a letter to Father John Mc-Cown:

> The Catholic fiction writer has very little high-powered "Catholic" fiction to influence him except that written by these three, Bloy, Bernanos, and Mauriac, and Greene. But at some point reading them reaches the place of diminishing returns and you get more benefit reading someone like Hemingway, where there is apparently a hunger for a Catholic completeness in life, or Joyce who can't get rid of it no matter what he does. It may be a matter of recognizing the Holy Ghost in fiction by the way He chooses to conceal himself.

In her essay on "Some Readings and Misreadings" Caroline Gordon has some things to say

O'Connor in 1957

about Evelyn Waugh. She has distinct reservations about his earlier novels, simply because he "does not explore the consciousness of any one of his characters . . ." But then she takes up *Brideshead Revisited* and finds that he has a new subject, "which arouses not moral indignation but awe, a rendering of the mystery of human existence." She finally attributes to this novel a "love of the natural order" which she doesn't find in Mauriac, Bernanos, or Graham Greene. Flannery had enjoyed Waugh's earlier novels, especially *A Handful of Dust* and *Vile Bodies*, but she had no particular enthusiasm for *Brideshead Revisited*. Waugh in his turn read *Wise Blood*, and on the jacket of the first British edition, published in 1955, he stated: "If this is really the unaided work of a young lady, it is a remarkable product." The jacket, by the way, is dominated by a ghastly picture of Hazel Motes, presumably in the act of prayer, his eyes lifted up, his mouth open, the figure posed against a pink background. I bought the book in London many years ago just for the jacket. On the back, beneath the same photograph of Flannery that appears on the first American edition, is the information that she "is at present completing her second novel, *Whom the Plague Beckons,* to be published by us in the autumn." Well, as we know, the novel took another four years to finish and eventually it had another title. Back to Evelyn Waugh. I was very fond of his mil-

itary trilogy, *The Sword of Honour,* which had started appearing in 1952, and I sent Flannery a paperback of the first two parts in 1961. But it was the third part, called *Unconditional Surrender* in the British edition, that aroused her full enthusiasm. I had the idea that Waugh had modelled his trilogy on the first three parts of Ford Madox Ford's *Parade's End,* which is a tetralogy. Waugh, I think, got this notion by way of Graham Greene, who had been a great friend of Ford. But Flannery, it turned out, simply couldn't read *Parade's End.* I see now that it was a question of fictional method. Waugh, even in his trilogy, had a style of great economy and precision, not unlike Flannery's, whereas Ford is expansive with his endless time-shifts. Flannery certainly heard about Ford at Cold Chimneys, because his name was held in great regard in that house. He had never set foot there during his visits to Tennessee in the 1930s, but Fannie Cheney had been acquainted with him and was about the only person around who had a coherent account of the famous banquet given for John Crowe Ransom's departure in 1937, at which occasion Ford was the master of ceremonies. He was a real literary hero in that part of Tennessee.

My former student, Tom Carter, didn't meet Flannery till July, 1955, at Cold Chimneys, but they had frequently corresponded and seemed to understand each other immediately. Tom had been the editor of *Shenandoah* at Washington and Lee, and this post led to all kinds of literary relationships. Unlike most of his contemporaries, he never travelled much, and I suppose he was content to know people at a distance. Among his correspondents were Ezra Pound and Wyndham Lewis. He met Pound just once, in St. Elizabeth's Hospital in Washington when I happened to be along. After that I believe they wrote each other every day. Pound was always looking for disciples. Wyndham Lewis was a very remote figure then, living out his last years at Notting Hill Gate in London where few people saw him. This famous survivor of the 1914 Vortex was almost blind; he could no longer paint or draw, but he had an extraordinary burst of literary creativity near the end. "Milton had his daughters," he used to say. "but I have my dictaphone." Tom Carter edited a special issue of *Shenandoah* in honor of Lewis in 1953; several writers contributed, including T. S. Eliot, Marshall McLuhan, and Lewis himself, who wrote a story especially for this issue. In September, 1953, I called on him twice, the first time bearing an advance copy of Tom's magazine. Tom communicated his interest in Lewis to a number of friends, especially Flannery, and I suppose she read at least ten of his books, from the early Vorticist novel *Tarr* to a late one called *Self Condemned.* I think there are some real affinities between his work and hers; she refers to him quite a few times in her letters. But as she said in a letter to "A" in November, 1956, "I'm more interested in the way Lewis writes than what he has to say." Tom also sent Flannery a copy of Marshall McLuhan's early book, *The Mechanical Bride,* an outrageous but funny satire on modern advertising. McLuhan wasn't famous at that time, around 1954, but he, a Canadian Catholic, had for some years been interested in the South, and one of his essays, "The Southern Quality" (1947), made a great impression on Flannery. She was fascinated to learn that he was the original for one of the characters in *Self Condemned.*

I used to be very amused when I listened to Flannery and Tom; they were likely to say anything. They decided one day that most books, especially novels, were too long and that 250 pages should be the limit. This was what they called The Test. I think Flannery was at least half serious about this. Perhaps she was rationalizing her own tendencies, because she seemed almost inevitably a short-story writer. In her lecture on "The Grotesque in Southern Literature," she says:

> Instead of reflecting a balance from the world around him, the novelist now has to achieve one from a felt balance inside himself. . . . The direction of many of us will be towards concentration and the distortion that is necessary to get our vision across; it will be toward poetry rather than the traditional novel. The problem for such a novelist will be to know how far he can distort without destroying. . . .

The "concentration" that she speaks of was deliberate and almost precluded novels as they are generally written. Flannery, after all, had been brought up on the short story; it was an American tradition that went back to Poe and Hawthorne, her first masters. In February, 1956, she wrote to the Cheneys, "I have just got through writing a story about a lady who gets gored by a bull. I get so sick of my novel that I have to have a diversion." Nearly all of the modern American fiction that she liked best came in the short form: the early stories of Peter Taylor and J. F. Powers, Bernard Malamud's *The Magic Barrel,* some of Caroline's stories in *The Forest of the South,* some of Katherine Anne Porter's. What of Faulkner? Flannery had read some of the great early novels

when they were reissued in the 1940s, but she took no interest in the work of his long decline — *Requiem for a Nun, The Town, A Fable,* and the others. The story of Faulkner's that she always described as "the work of a master" was "Spotted Horses."

One novel that we all read in the 1950s was Caroline Gordon's *The Malefactors.* From the day it came out in 1956 it was a kind of *cause célèbre* for us. Everybody knew that she had based some of her characters on Dorothy Day (to whom the novel was originally dedicated), Hart Crane, and others, living or dead; the general assumption was that Caroline was using Allen Tate as the central figure, a poet whom she calls Tom Claiborne. It seemed to Flannery, as to me, a remarkable portrayal of the dilemma of a modern poet whose creativity has dwindled away and who is eventually brought to the edge of a religious conversion. I think that Caroline did not simply use Allen for her model; her poet is much more like Allen's friend John Peale Bishop. We thought the novel was a splendid technical achievement, a tribute to Henry James, whom Caroline adored. Allen Tate, by the way, always liked the novel, and towards the end of his life he included it in a short list of neglected books of the 20th Century. What Flannery objected to was not Caroline's human figures but a prize bull who figures in the first part of the novel. The scene is a kind of harvest festival given on the estate owned by the poet's rich wife, and her bull is a major symbol of the action at this point. Nearby is an exhibit sponsored by a society for breeding cattle through artificial insemination. Caroline here introduces an old Dunkard farmer who heartily disapproves of this practice, and clearly the author has him as her spokesman. This is the situation that caused Flannery to remark in a letter to "A" in May, 1956: "I agree with you about the bulls. Nothing wrong with artificial insemination as long as it's animals and bringing those Hookers or Shakers or whatever they were and their disapproval to bear just confused the moral point, if any. But I suspect that she just wasn't able to resist doing that inseminator, as she had him down." Flannery felt that the bull episode threw the novel off balance.

This wasn't quite the end of the story. In October, 1959, I drove Caroline to Andalusia for her first visit. Andalusia was a real farm which Regina O'Connor operated with the practical instincts that she had developed there; she was never sentimental about it. Anyway, I didn't know this at the time but it seems that the matter of artificial insemination was discussed by Regina and Caroline, who considered the practice a crime against the natural order. Now that Caroline has departed from this life, I can't resist quoting part of a letter that Flannery wrote to me upon my return to South Carolina:

> My own nerves were jangled when it was over — the job of trying to keep the two ladies' personalities from meeting head-on. While you were opening gates, there was a little altercation about artificial breeding. All those cows sitting there, I guess it was inevitable. I am afraid Caroline forthwith consigned us to hell. She does not seem to make the necessary distinction between man and animal . . . She was at her best doctoring my prose.

Although I don't think that the issue ever came up between them, Flannery and Caroline would certainly have disagreed about another novelist who was becoming famous. In the summer of 1956 Donald Davie, the English poet-critic then living in Dublin, sent me a copy of the original edition of Nabokov's *Lolita*, I can't remember why. Nabokov, I gathered, had been unable to get his novel published in the United States, and so he turned to the Olympia Press in Paris. The Olympia Press published writers like Henry Miller, but most of their product was hardly more than pornography. So *Lolita* arrived unexpectedly one day, two little paperback volumes bound in a horrid shade of green. I was dissertation-writing at the time and stoutly refused to be tempted by this diversion from abroad. It went first to a friend in Nashville, who happened to be the mother of a young daughter; she returned it indignantly the next day. Then off it went to Flannery, and a week or so later she returned it with a note stating flatly that *Lolita* was the funniest novel she had ever read. She was one of the first people in the United States to have seen a copy. Actually Nabokov had been a favorite writer of hers for some time. I don't think she had yet read his first novel in English, *The Real Life of Sebastian Knight*, but she certainly admired his second, *Bend Sinister*, a satire on totalitarianism. She mentions it in a letter to John Hawkes in July 1959. *Bend Sinister* was published in 1947; Allen Tate, who was then associated with a publishing house in New York, had something to do with this, and Caroline was very disapproving; she could never accept any of Nabokov's books. Flannery's favorite among his works may have been his little book on Gogol, simply because of her great admiration for *Dead Souls*, which she

read at Iowa. Our friend Robie Macauley, then a young writer of the most cosmopolitan sort who was a great partisan of Gogol, insisted that *Dead Souls* was a necessary part of one's literary equipment. In Flannery's case his enthusiasm took hold.

Flannery O'Connor's stories take their place in the great American tradition of short fiction, and one can already see her as the heir to Hawthorne, Poe, Stephen Crane, and a dozen others. Indeed, twenty years after her death, she is the last American writer to have attained this kind of classic status. Although she certainly belongs to the mode of American romance, as it has been described by Richard Chase and other critics, I am inclined to place her, in matters of style, closer to a tradition of modern British fiction, as represented by the early Wyndham Lewis, Anthony Powell, Evelyn Waugh, and Muriel Spark. These are the writers who have resisted the descent into introspection represented by Joyce, Virginia Woolf, and Lawrence. They are usually comic writers, unillusioned, witty, astringent at times; the surfaces of their work have a bright clarity of definition. To some Americans they seem cruel. But then we have never had such novelists, with the possible exception of Nathanael West. Flannery liked writers of this kind; she never wanted to imitate them, but they had achieved a distant kind of perfection that was an ideal for a young American woman who deplored the "general mess of imprecision of feeling" in many of her contemporaries. (The phrase is T. S. Eliot's in *East Coker*.) There is much more to be said about her as a writer; these are merely notes on part of her literary experience during the period when I first knew her.

LETTER:
Flannery O'Connor to Caroline Gordon, 10 December 1957; in *The Habit of Being*, pp. 257–258.

"The Enduring Chill," discussed in this letter to Caroline Gordon, was published in the July 1958 issue of Harper's Bazaar *and collected in* Everything That Rises Must Converge *(1965). O'Connor's comments here and in her 20 December 1957 letter to "A" suggest how much she valued the advice not only of Gordon but also of Allen Tate, Brainard Cheney, and other literary friends.*

The "pilgrimage" mentioned in the last paragraph is a trip to Europe O'Connor and her mother took in April and May 1958. They went to

Lourdes, where O'Connor bathed in the waters famous for effecting miracle cures, and to Rome, where they had an audience with the pope and visited Robert and Sally Fitzgerald, who had been living in Italy since 1953.

I'm busy with the Holy Ghost. He is going to be a waterstain — very obvious but the only thing possible. I also have a fine visitor for Asbury to liven him up slightly. I'm highly obliged for your thoughts on this ["The Enduring Chill"] and I am making the most of them. When I get this finished I'd like you to see it again because it is already much improved — but I notice my stories get longer and longer and I'm afraid this one may be too long. If I've finished with it, I'd like to send it to the Cheneys for a Christmas card and will hope that you might have time to look at it there. If not, I'll send it to you after Christmas . . .

I have lately been getting dizzy because I am taking a new medicine and have got an overdose of it. So I figure I'll do my staggering around at home. It takes some time for the dose to get regulated. Every time something new is invented I get in on the ground floor with it. There have been five improvements in the medicine in the 7 years I've had the lupus, and they are all great improvements.

A friend of mine at Wesleyan, a Dr. Gossett, wrote me that he and his wife had just come from the Modern Language Asso. convention in Knoxville or somewhere and had heard Willard Thorpe read a paper on "The Grotesque in Southern Literature." He (Thorpe) allowed as how the roots of it were in antebellum Southern writings but that the grotesque you met with in Southern writing today was something else and has serious implications which the other didn't approach. He said he had no satisfactory explanation for the change. The Gossetts decided the reason he didn't was because he doesn't know enough theology. I seem to remember that he wrote one of the better reviews of *The Malefactors*, but I may be mixed up on the name.

You are more sanguine about this pilgrimage than I am. It's not that I'd rather be a tourist; I'd rather stay at home. You are good to ask us to stop by Princeton, but knowing the difficulties of getting anywhere, I doubt we could engineer it. I envy you that energy you have. I wish you would come to see us. We have a lovely place — as evidenced by my reluctance to leave it for 17 days of Holy Culture and Pious Exhaustion. Pray that the Lord will (gently) improve my attitude so I can at least endure it . . .

LETTER:
Flannery O'Connor to "A," 28 December 1957 [excerpt]; in *The Habit of Being*, p. 261.

This excerpt from a letter that accompanied revisions to "The Enduring Chill" reveals O'Connor's thinking about the main character and his sister and how she needed to convey her ideas about them in the story.

[. . .] Enclose a new front and back, but I have not changed the last sentence as no other way seems to improve it. I was supposed to go to Nashville to see the Cheneys on the weekend of the 20th but I didn't feel like getting myself in those Christmas crowds at the airport so I didn't go. Caroline and Allen [Tate] did and were there for all of them. Allen had read the story ["The Enduring Chill"] to them . . . When I talked to Allen he said do one thing to that story for me and I said what and he said get the Holy Ghost in the first page or two. That is very good advice and it is what I have proceeded to do. Lon said that he hadn't known whether Asbury was coming or going there at the end, that the Holy Ghost came too fast. I think there is something in that too. So I have let it be known that he undeniably realizes that he's going to live with the new knowledge that he knows nothing. That really is what he is frozen in — humility. Faith can come later. I have it in mind to take Asbury further maybe in other stories. I also think Mary George is a monster who ought to have a little comedown. I have carefully not killed anybody off, you observe, so that I can have more to do with them later. Besides I don't want to be known as a killer, though death is the end of us all as the old man said heartily from his coffin . . .

LETTER:
Flannery O'Connor to "A," 4 April 1958; in *The Habit of Being*, pp. 274–275.

O'Connor's friends Thomas and Louise Gossett — at the time of this letter English professors at colleges in Macon, Georgia — brought Katherine Anne Porter and other people to Andalusia to meet O'Connor on 27 March 1958. O'Connor described the visit in several letters. (Her dating of it in this letter is off by one day.) The letter also makes the surprising revelation that she had read relatively little fiction by Caroline Gordon, her most trusted literary adviser (though she had read more than she implies here).

The first meeting of Katherine Anne Porter and Flannery O'Connor at Andalusia, the O'Connors' farm, 27 March 1958

I have been holding the fort alone since Sunday night. In the middle of the night my mother had a severe pain in her back, so bad that she went to the hospital in the middle of the night . . . She hit her back on the edge of the sink somehow Saturday when the telephone rang. She appears to be better and hopes to come home tomorrow. I don't know what this will lead to for her; pray that this will be the end of it . . . The doctor thinks she will be all right and able to go on the trip. She wants to go. Since I've never much wanted to go anyhow, I am more than willing to call it off, but we will just have to wait and see how she gets on when she gets home. This has convinced me of one thing: that I must learn to drive. Louise stays with me at night but as to getting in town I am dependent on Sister . . .

I haven't read [Caroline Gordon's] *None Shall Look Back* but I have heard Lon Cheney expound on it. He says that the antagonist in NSLB is Death — the foe we don't know but all care about. You will see I really haven't ever read Caroline, just a few things here and there. I agree that Tom and his dreams don't work — it's really abstract, too much like an equation.

About the novel of religious conversion. You can't have a stable character being converted, you are right, but I think you are wrong that heroes have to be stable. If they were stable there wouldn't be any story. It seems to me that all good stories are about conversion, about a character's changing. If it is the Church he's converted to, the Church remains stable and he has to change as you say — so why do you also say the character has to remain stable? The action of grace changes a character. Grace can't be experienced in itself. An example: when you go to Communion, you receive grace but you experience nothing; or if you do experience something, what you experience is not the grace but an emotion caused by it. Therefore in a story all you can do with grace is to show that it is changing the character. Mr. Head [in "The Artificial Nigger"] is changed by his experience even though he remains Mr. Head. He is stable but not the same man at the end of the story. Stable in the sense that he bears his same physical contours and peculiarities but they are all ordered to a new vision. Part of the difficulty of all this is that you write for an audience who doesn't know what grace is and don't recognize it when they see it. All my stories are about the action of grace on a character who is not very willing to support it, but most people think of these stories as hard, hopeless, brutal, etc.

Katherine Anne Porter read in Macon on the 27th and the next day the Gossetts brought her over to have lunch with us. She was very pleasant . . . When she asked me where we were going in Europe and I said Lourdes, a very strange expression came over her face, just a slight shock as if some sensitive spot had been touched. She said that she had always wanted to go to Lourdes, perhaps she would get there some day and make a novena that she would finish her novel [*Ship of Fools*] — she's been on it 27 years. After that the conversation somehow got on the subject of death — there were two professors from North Carolina and the Gossetts and us and her — in the way that death is discussed at dinner tables, as if it were a funny subject. She said she thought it was very nice to believe that we would all meet in heaven and she rather hoped we would but she didn't really know. She wished she knew who exactly was in charge of this universe, and where she was going. She would be glad to go where she was expected if she knew. All this accompanied by much banter from the gentlemen. It was a little coy and a little wistful but there was a terrible need evident underneath it . . .

ARTICLE:
Robert McCown, S.J., "Flannery O'Connor and the Reality of Sin," *Catholic World,* 188 (January 1959): 285–291.

At a time when many reviewers, including some Roman Catholics, failed to recognize the grounding of O'Connor's writing in Catholic theology and criticized her use of the grotesque, this article by a perceptive Jesuit priest was an important and valuable corrective.

It has been over three years now since the appearance of Flannery O'Connor's *A Good Man Is Hard to Find* (Harcourt, 1955). This collection of extraordinary short stories won immediate and enthusiastic praise, and placed its author, then still in her twenties, in the first ranks of contemporary fiction writers.

Those who first reviewed the volume, however, seemed to limit their comments either to points of style, or to her power of realism, or to her skill as a satirist, with only few and inconclusive comments about the positive contents of the stories. *Time,* for example, eagerly praised what it termed her "sardonic brutality," her style "as balefully direct as a death sentence," without, however, venturing to consider whether or not what she had to say was worth the saying.

Among Catholic periodicals, *Commonweal* (July 22, 1955) carried an appreciative review by James Greene who expressed warm admiration for "her detached style [which] manages to preserve the complexity of the lives she takes up" . . . "a superb story-teller" . . . "a musician's ear for the progress and qualities of sound"; but, on the whole, he seemed to shy away from any definite evaluation of the spiritual content of her stories or characters. Since then, Miss O'Connor has not been mentioned as often as one would like in the columns of Catholic critics. Last year, however, her name did appear again in *Commonweal* (March 7, 1958), but only to have her writing related by William Esty to what he called a "a cult of the Gratuitous Grotesque" — a surprisingly short-sighted charge from such a source, and very unfair in my estimation. It does, nonetheless, sum up the ordinary negative reactions to her writing, and has thus occasioned the following reflections.

Flannery O'Connor's phenomenal power of giving life to her characters is due to a complete mastery of her art which renders with rapid precision their psychological makeup. What Mr. Esty mistakes for the gratuitous grotesque is, much of the time, none other than this realism in picturing living, breathing, sweating humanity. As to the physical deformities, only three or four of the two dozen or so major characters of *A Good Man Is Hard to Find* should come under this category, not a large proportion when compared to the writings of such authors as Dostoevski, or Bernanos, or, for that matter, to reality itself. Far from being outside the legitimate domain of art, physical afflictions have their special place, particularly when they point to privations of the mind, ignorance and prejudice, or, even deeper, to the need of redemption of souls out of joint with themselves and reality. Flannery O'Connor, a Catholic by conviction as well as by birth, writes from a deep Christian concern for the spiritual. Her stories, the characters that live in them, the excellencies of her style, are not ends in themselves but rigorously subordinated means of showing us reality, the quality of goodness and the subtle malice of sin, either of which have power to determine our destiny.

One of the first things which strike us in these stories is the peculiar rigor with which the author limits her canvas to things of her own direct and intimate knowledge — people with whom she has grown up, against the countryside of her own native Georgia. In many of the stories the setting is the same: a small dairy farm owned by a widow struggling to make ends meet, with her children, the tenant family, the Negro help, visited by an occasional faith healer, Bible salesman, or hobo. Yet, within these self-imposed limits, she has created characters of extraordinary depth, originality, and color; with all the strength of mind, prejudices, fears — fears of shame, of poverty, of the foreigner — which go to make a Southerner.

Miss O'Connor is admittedly influenced by the writers of the Catholic revival of France and England, notably Bloy, Mauriac, and Greene. Like them she is deeply concerned with the palpable reality of sin, of the blight it can bring to human existence, and of its mysterious communication from one generation to another. Her stories often show that God-fearing, humble parents, no matter how ignorant and shiftless, will generally produce psychologically and morally sound children; whereas the children of the proud and contemptuous, whatever natural gifts they may otherwise have, are likely to turn out warped in some way. This is the central idea of the excellent story, "Greenleaf," which was published in the *Kenyon Review* and which won first prize in the O. Henry Contest for best short stories of 1957. We see it also in the character of the precocious and mischievous child in "A Temple of the Holy Ghost," with her first stirrings of pride and her adolescent conflicts, who, nonetheless, has an essentially pious and healthy mind thanks to her good, intelligent mother.

Another penetrating study of children is "A Circle in the Fire." Mrs. Cope, a widow who cannot thank God enough for not having made her like other women, has a dairy farm which she manages with great efficiency, but also in constant fear of losing everything by a fire or some other mishap. In contrast to her primness, her only child is a ruthless, violent, malicious girl. One summer evening an anemic twelve-year-old boy from the development area of the city returns for a visit to the farm whose many pleasures he had known when once his father had been a tenant there. He and his two companions begin, to the patronizing annoyance of Mrs. Cope, to make themselves at home by sneaking rides on the horses, stealing milk from the barn, camping and smoking in her valuable stand of pines. In the swelling psychological conflict which follows and moves steadily toward disaster there is such perfection of balance and restraint in the narrative that the reader finds it hard to take sides either with the self-righteous woman as she strives to maintain her dignity and the semblance of benevolence in the face of this encroachment, or with the delinquent boys whose insolence soon grows to lawlessness. Implicitly the root causes of social strife are laid bare as the envy and violence of the *have-nots* contend with the pharisaical pride and avarice of the *haves*. We find here a fully developed tragedy of character and circumstance, written with an astonishing command of details, in barely seventeen pages.

"The River" is the best example of Flannery O'Connor's remarkable talent for creating children characters, and of molding them, as it were, from the inside out, exploring with tenderness, but without a trace of sentimentality, the mysterious processes of their thought and motivation. In this story Bevel, a five-year-old child of pagan and pleasure-loving parents, is disposed of for a day of party-making by being left in the keeping of Mrs. Connin, a good Christian woman, who takes him out to her farm. After reading to him from *The Life of Jesus Christ for Readers Under Twelve*, she leads him and her own children off to the river to hear a youthful faith healer, knee-deep in the muddy stream preach to a mixed crowd of whole and afflicted, believers and scoffers: "Listen, you people! There ain't but one river and that's the River of Life, made out of Jesus' Blood. That's the river you have to lay your pain in . . . it's the River full of pain itself, pain itself, moving toward the Kingdom of Christ. . . ."

After the preaching, the woman has the healer baptize the child by immersion, and then takes him home, wet and tired. But the words of the preacher have taken root in his heart, for waking up the next morning to the tedium of the existence of an unwanted child, he makes a decision. Stealing a car-token from his sleeping mother's purse, he makes off alone to the river again. This time he will not fool with preachers, but will baptize himself, and keep on going until he finds really and truly the Kingdom of Christ in the river. The story achieves an effect of exquisite sadness, but then of exaltation, as the reader realizes that the forces working in the child's pilgrim soul were none other than divine grace.

The extraordinary quality of Miss O'Connor's humor and the ease with which she puts it into a compressed yet lucid prose come from a thorough knowledge of the people of whom she writes, of the bits of wisdom, truths and half-truths — and downright prejudices — which make up their mental equipment. "The Artificial Nigger" will one day be considered a classic of American humor. Mr. Head, a little old man of an almost incredible combination of innocence, ignorance, and prejudice, decides to take his grandson, Nelson, for his first trip to the sinful city "to get his fill once and for all."

Throughout the day a sort of duel of worldly knowledge between grandfather and grandson continues as they lose their lunch, get lost themselves, and spend long hours looking for the train station. Tired and hungry, and in a moment of confusion, they are separated. Mr. Head finds Nelson just as in his panic he upsets a woman shopper, who calls wildly for a policeman, and maintains that Mr. Head must pay the doctor's bill for her injured ankle. Terror-stricken, he denies his own flesh and blood, and pays for it by agonizing for a long while under the child's burning scorn. Finally, by an incident of delightful

O'Connor showing some of her pet fowl to Katherine Anne Porter, Hugh Holman, a professor of English at the University of North Carolina, and Arlin Turner, an English professor at Duke University, during their 27 March 1958 visit to Andalusia. In a letter to a friend O'Connor described Porter as "Very pleasant and agreeable, crazy about my peacocks; plowed all over the yard in her spike-heeled shoes to see my various kinds of chickens."

comedy and pathos they are reconciled, and return home, both much the wiser. The old man learns humility through his chastisement, the boy in his turn learns forgiveness.

Miss O'Connor's genius for catching the psychological attitude of her characters in brief, penetrating descriptions and bits of dialogue is seen in "The Life You Save May Be Your Own," a sort of tragedy in miniature. An old woman living in the country alone with her mute-idiot daughter is visited one day by an one-armed hobo, Mr. Shiftlet. To pay for his food and a place to sleep in the shed, he does odd jobs about the house, mends the roof, builds a pig-pen, and even resurrects her old automobile. The woman is ravenous for a son-in-law, and talks him into marrying her idiot daughter, offering to pay for the license and a two-day honeymoon in the car. Mr. Shiftlet accepts, but after driving a hundred or so miles, abandons the girl, asleep at the counter of a roadside cafe, and continues on in the car with some remorse.

We are left to imagine for ourselves the fear and suffering awaiting the girl upon awakening alone and lost in a strange place, as well as the anxiety and regret of the old mother. The quality of the tragic element of this story is even higher than that of "A Circle in the Fire." The picture of helpless innocence being ground to death among the conflicting forces of pride, hatred, and prejudice, is one of the most important spiritual elements in Flannery O'Connor's writing. We see it first in the title story, "A Good Man Is Hard to Find," but it receives its most complete development in "The Displaced Person."

In "A Good Man Is Hard to Find" the blood-curdling realism describing the treatment of the helpless family by The Misfit, an escaped convict, following directly upon the light and humorous atmosphere of the first part of the story, might prove a bit too much for the unsuspecting reader. Also, since this story is placed first in the collection, and titles it, it has given rise to much of the adverse criticism of the whole volume. Of course, this fierce contrast of black against white — or very light gray — has its purposes, and there is no denying the mastery of description in the simple strokes which draw the sinister visitant. In two or three pages we see the horror of a soul blasted by the sin of despair, a soul which, we feel, had at one time had a glimpse of the light and of a way of peace, but had rejected it.

" 'I call myself The Misfit,' he said, 'because I can't make what all I done wrong fit what all I gone through in punishment. . . . Jesus was the only One that ever raised the dead . . . and He shouldn't have done it. He thown everything off balance. If He did what He said, then it's nothing for you to do but thow away everything and follow Him, and if He didn't, then it's nothing for you to do but enjoy the few minutes you got left the best way you can — by killing somebody or burning down his house or doing some other meanness to him. No pleasure but meanness,' he said, and his voice had become almost a snarl."

Although the structure of "The Displaced Person" is somewhat looser and, in a few places, its punch weaker, it is undoubtedly the *pièce de résistance* of the volume. Here are stated explicitly many of the ideas only hinted at in the other stories. The Displaced Person, Mr. Guizac, is the father of a family of Polish refugees imported as labor on a small dairy farm, who falls a victim to the dark forces of hatred, fear, and prejudice, which surround him, but of which he is fatally ignorant. One of the characters of the story is an old priest, an incurable bore in his tactless efforts to convert people, yet one whose genuine charity commands much sympathy. The dream of the old widow, merciless in her decision to fire the Displaced Person, strikes the central idea of the story: "One night she dreamed that the priest came to call and droned on and on, saying, 'Dear Lady, I know your tender heart won't suffer you to turn the porrrr man out. Think of the thousands of them, think of the ovens and the boxcars and the camps and the sick children and Christ Our Lord.'

" 'He's extra and he's upset the balance around here,' she said, 'and I'm a logical, practical woman and there are no ovens here and no camps and no Christ Our Lord and when he leaves, he'll make more money. He'll work at the mill and buy a car and don't talk to me — all they want is a car.'

" 'The ovens and the boxcars and the sick children,' droned the priest, 'and our dear Lord.'

" 'Just one too many,' she said."

Thus, in the figure of the awkward, inarticulate foreigner, Mr. Guizac, mistrusted and despised by everyone, is seen the suffering Body of Christ. The scene of his murder is perhaps the most powerfully moving of the whole book.

There are few modern writers whose wit is more unexpected and brilliant, or whose satire is more scathing than Flannery O'Connor's — a sample of her when she *really* wants to be mean is her satire on the South and its nostalgia for the days of glory long-past-but-not-forgotten, in "A Late Encounter With the Enemy" — yet her greatest strength lies in another quality which is at a premium among satirists: compassion for those whom she satirizes. The current of irony runs deep throughout her stories, but rarely does it run as deep as her compassion. It is in "Good Country People" that is found the richest blend of these two qualities. The story is of a girl with an acute but confused mind, who, as a result of a childhood accident, has a wooden leg. Out of spite for this affliction and the mediocrity of her surroundings, she changes her name from Joy to Hulga, studies to be a Ph.D. in philosophy, and becomes an embittered atheist. When a youthful itinerant Bible salesman asks her to go for a walk, she lures him into a hayloft and would seduce him. But instead of the "good country people" she had supposed him to be, her victim turns the tables on her and proves to be more a nihilist than herself. For a moment the girl experiences the burning shame of being confronted with an image of her own intellectual and moral darkness, but then is completely undone when the youth runs off with her wooden leg in his valise.

Because of her genuine horror of sentimentality, at just the point where many writers would soften, Flannery O'Connor's wit appears to become more wry and her satire more scathing, the result being a quality of humor remarkably akin to that of Chaucer in which the author tells with apparent ease and gusto side-splitting stories, which, nonetheless, contain implicitly matter for some very sobering thought.

In "Good Country People," particularly, we must look beyond the bluff and the sparkling wit to the heart of the matter, to the girl's loss of faith in God's providence resulting from her bitter affliction, to the loneliness, to the wasted talent, to the lack of understanding or sympathy in those who surround her, which have driven her so far into the wasteland of self that she can only be brought back to reality by the scourge of self-knowledge and humiliation. It was against this story in particular that Mr. Esty leveled the charge of "gratuitous grotesque." I think, to the contrary, that it contains a delicately balanced, Christian humanism — an opinion which, I believe, comes much closer to Allen Tate's judgment of the story.

In her first novel, *Wise Blood* (Harcourt, 1952), Flannery O'Connor showed an extraordinary writing ability; in *A Good Man Is Hard to Find* she proved herself a storyteller of genius. In not a few respects one might offer her to aspirant young writers as a model to be imitated: in her dedication to her art, in the clear understanding she shows of the limitations of fiction and of the fiction writer, in her many varieties of humor, in her aversion to the apologetic approach. But more than all these there is a certain quality which gives the reader of her stories the immediate impression of being confronted with something real and living, something of one piece with his own experience.

Who would not recognize the dusty clay hills of Georgia covered with granite pines, the speckled old women, the tow-headed children with silver-rimmed spectacles before pale, vacant eyes, their strange wisdom and unpredictable energy, the middle-aged widows with their invincible prejudices. Flannery O'Connor has great talent indeed, but it is, above all, her fidelity to truth which gives her stories their quality of realism; it is a fearless trust in reality itself as something eminently worth knowing, and, when known, more satisfying than all its substitutes.

LETTERS:

Ashley Brown, "An Unwritten Drama: Susan Jenkins Brown and Flannery O'Connor," *Southern Review*, 22 (Autumn 1986): 727–737.

In 1958 Caroline Gordon suggested that her friend Susan Jenkins Brown write a play based on one of O'Connor's stories. The results of this suggestion are recorded in the letters published in this article. At the time O'Connor was hard at work on her second novel, The Violent Bear It Away *(1960). None of O'Connor's letters to Susan Jenkins Brown is included in* The Habit of Being. *The remark in one of the letters about the "doleful" news regarding "the House of Tate" refers to*

O'Connor and Brainard Cheney in 1959

the impending divorce of Allen Tate and Caroline Gordon.

The letters in the following exchange were found among some papers left by the late Susan Jenkins Brown, who often appears in the literary memoirs of the 1920s. She was born in Pennsylvania and attended high school with Malcolm Cowley and Kenneth Burke; then as a young woman she moved to Greenwich Village, where she quickly made friends with other writers of her generation, including Hart Crane, Allen Tate, and Caroline Gordon. Although she became an experienced editor who gave practical advice to her friends, her only major publication during her long life was *Robber Rocks,* the book about Hart Crane which came out in 1969. (A section of the book was first published in the *Southern Review* in Autumn 1968 under the title of "Hart Crane: The End of Harvest.") The letters here concern her brief friendship with Flannery O'Connor.

Sue Jenkins, as she usually called herself, met Flannery O'Connor only once, early in June 1955. On this occasion Caroline Gordon brought Flannery to Tory Valley, a literary enclave on the Connecticut–New York border, where Sue had owned a farmhouse, "Robber Rocks," since the mid-twenties. (She had originally bought it with her second husband, Slater Brown.) Malcolm

Cowley and other friends have always lived in the vicinity, and during the winter of 1925–26 Hart Crane and the Tates rented a house down the road from "Robber Rocks." Flannery O'Connor's rather amusing account of her visit is recorded in a letter to Sally and Robert Fitzgerald, dated 10 June '55.

Later that year (December 19, 1955) Sue Jenkins tried to enlist Flannery's help in promoting *The Malefactors,* Caroline's novel which was soon to be published by Harcourt Brace. Denver Lindley, an editor at that house, was very enthusiastic about it. And since *A Good Man Is Hard to Find* had been published with some success by Harcourt Brace earlier that year, it seemed natural that Sue should turn to Flannery. I quote the relevant parts of her letter:

There are certain persons who should know about this book and its theme and I think you know who they are better than I do. Caroline probably (certainly) won't be able to do this sort of job and I don't see how Allen can although I shall confer with him when he arrives here around Dec. 21st. You've got a good head, I decided when I spent those several days with you in the country. Enough good sense not to go to church in Body and Fender work. Any ideas you can offer (both to me and to Lindley at Harcourt Brace) will be appreciated. It will help Caroline a lot, I think, if this book is pushed and can be made to go over. I am using hardboiled terms but then I'm just an old publishing hack and books are so many bricks to me when it comes to throwing them out to the public. How much do they weigh, and who's going to think they are the foundation of his culture?

And — most important — I don't want you ever to mention to Caroline that I made this suggestion re her book to you. I could explain but I think it isn't necessary. And may the good Lord be kind to you, my child.

Sue

Flannery O'Connor had more than the usual interest in *The Malefactors,* as many of her letters in *The Habit of Being* make clear. She was not directly involved in promoting it, as Sue Jenkins had suggested, but she wrote a short review, one of her first, for *The Bulletin,* the diocesan paper. This has recently been reprinted in *The Presence of Grace* (University of Georgia Press, 1983). Of course very few literary people saw it when it was originally published in 1956. Then in the following year Flannery wrote a review of Caroline Gordon's *How to Read a Novel.* Sue Jenkins had done much of the editorial work on this book, and in gratitude Caroline dedicated it to her. But Flannery's review was never published in *The Bulletin.* (It too is included in *The Presence of Grace.*)

About this time, at the end of 1957, Sue Jenkins decided to write a play. She had had some small experience in the theater during her youth, because her first husband, James Light, was a director with the old Provincetown Players when they were producing Eugene O'Neill's early dramas. According to her account of that period, she read the manuscripts of unsolicited plays which came into the office of the Provincetown Players by the dozen every day. But her idea about playwriting was entirely literary: she would make a play from some work of fiction that she admired. At one time she considered James's *The Awkward Age,* an obviously "dramatic" novel written mostly in dialogue, as her project. Early in 1958 she was thinking of "The Captive," Caroline Gordon's story about a pioneer woman captured by Indians. For this purpose she borrowed a copy of *The Forest of the South* from Scribner's, who had been Caroline's publisher. A few days later, however, Caroline had another suggestion. (The following letter, undated, was quite certainly written in mid-January 1958.)

Eight o'clock
Tuesday a.m.

Dear Sue:

What a zombie I am! It became plain — to me, at any rate — at half past six this morning who your author is. Flannery O'Connor. She has enough fame to get a producer's attention AND she bristles with dialogue and could turn out reams more at a moment's notice if wanted. There is a conversation in the story she sent up to Nashville to be read by the petit cercle that is MADE for the stage.

I have been running over the stories in my mind, handicapped, as usual, by the fact that I can't put my hand on the book needed, but never mind: she's in paperback. I'll get one next time I come to town and bring it to you.

I find myself coming back to the one she read in the country: A Good Man Is Hard to Find. And also the one about the little boy who was drowned in the river, while getting baptized. I believe in my soul that that's the one. The young mother in A Good Man is not a very attractive female — of course she could be made so — but the young mother in The River is today's young mother. You could get a terrific contrast there between the living room scenes, drinking, discussion etc. and the goings on of the Holy Rollers.

One would, so to speak, carry the other. That Holy Roller baby sitter is a powerful figure. Of course the grandmother in A Good Man is, too, but she doesn't seem to me — who knows nothing about it — to have as good a supporting cast.

The more I think about this the more I like the idea. The fact that your author has plenty of time on her hands and is a saint to boot ought to be enormously helpful. As you know, I will do anything I can. Allen, too.

Really, I am pretty steamed up over this!

Caroline

You know Red Warren's "Understanding the Drama"? Most practical they tell me.

A Good Man, it seems to me, has everything. In the living room scenes there could be a discussion about the way to raise children. (All the way to Morristown Sunday Peto, in the back seat, was mumbling about a teen age friend of his who had a mother who had a psychiatrist "who must be crazy." The psychiatrist had told her that maybe she ought to go to Venice for the next few months and then she might be better able to cope with children when she came back.) Anyhow, as every taxi driver in NY knows, the fact that parents let the children get away with murder in the home has a hell of a lot to do with the murders they commit in the parks. You have here a subject that is in everybody's mind — that's the way to be successful and famous. Take something everybody is already thinking about and think it through better than they can. The Holy Roller baby sitter knows what's wrong with the child but her remedy is too tough for him; he goes under while taking it. Everybody loves little children — they better! Here's innocence sacrificed between two extreme points of view. A little common sense, plus real, not fantastical religion, would have saved this child's life. . . . Yes, I know it is your play or going to be. I'll shut up, after this. But do read it.

A few comments are in order here. The new story that Flannery had sent to Nashville for the Tates and the Brainard Cheneys to read was "The Enduring Chill." Caroline's letters, usually typed, were written at great speed, as all her friends know. The reference to "Understanding the Drama" should be to *Understanding Drama* by Cleanth Brooks and Robert B. Heilman, not by Warren. In the last paragraph she is thinking of "The River," not of "A Good Man Is Hard to Find." Peto is one of Caroline's grandsons.

Sue Jenkins immediately took up Caroline's suggestion and wrote to Flannery:

January 16, 1958

Dear Flannery:

Try not to be too shocked and dismayed. For some time I have been itching to dramatize a suitable work of fiction and at last, encouraged by Caroline, I have picked on you. Will you permit it?

One reason I have picked on you is because of your dialogue. I don't want my play to be *my* play but the play of the original creator. In some of your stories, I declare to goodness, I think my role would be little more than copying down as fast as my pencil and typewriter can fly and arranging dialogue into scenes.

Caroline so far favors "A Good Man" or "The River"; she also mentioned as likely material for dramatizing a story you sent to Nashville (I suppose last Christmas) which I probably haven't read. Nor have I read *Wise Blood;* I haven't been able to get it. I have your collection of stories, *A View of the Woods* (which I don't see as suitable) and *You Can't Be Any Poorer Than Dead* in #8 New World Writing. This last would be my tentative choice. I've already worked out a scheme for one act, presumably the first. It practically dramatizes itself. One set would do it, I think, with lowered curtain and change of light to indicate passage of time (as well as the program), and the last scene done downstage before a back drop, with only the faces lit. The incidents at the lawyer's office, etc., could be brought out in dialogue at the coffin-porch scene. The opening scene would be the school teacher and social worker at the cabin, the "shot-gun" scene.

But its suitability for drama would have to be determined by the rest of it. How far along are you? May I read what you have written so far?

You'll want to know what makes me think I could do this. The point is: you would be the final judge. It would have to be collaboration — not my dramatization of your work. You'd have to supply more dialogue. (And maybe you'd prefer to do this without my intervention.) At any rate, for the last few months as I read fiction my mind has been trying to turn what I read into a play. Sometimes it's a great nuisance because the material isn't suitable and I wrench and strain at it, throwing some incidents out as not dramatic and giving it up as a bad job. So I wouldn't try to work with a piece of fiction that didn't dramatize itself in my mind. I suppose I'm suffering for sins of the past; for some years I was associated with the Provincetown Players in their days of glory — reading plays, preparing scripts, holding script at rehearsals, other odd jobs. Now I'm dreaming in plays; it's caught up with me.

I could do a few scenes of *Poorer Than Dead* and send it to you as a sample — or of something

Milledgeville
Georgia
17 January 58

Dear Sue,

Off hand it sounds like a fine idea. I don't know Thing One
about the theatre myself and I wouldn't want to write a play myself for fear it would throw me off from my proper bent. However,
if you planned the thing out, you could probably find enough dialogue
in it, with my supplying a little more, to make due. I have only done
70 pages of this novel and I am rampant to finish it but it goes so
fast and no faster. I have added a good deal to that first chapter,
notably emphasizing the school teacher's little boy who looks like
Old Tarwater. This is a feeble-minded child. When Tarwater goes
to town to the school teacher, he is of course reminded constantly
of the old man by this child (whose name is Bishop). The rest of
the action of the book is concerned with the school teacher's
attempt to "adjust" Tarwater to modern life, rid him of his religious
ideas, make him a normal American boy etc etc. Tarwater on the
other hand is torn between his real desire to be a prophet like the
old man intended and his feeling that he ain't been called; in
other words the dead old man and the school teacher are in a struggle
for his soul. And I mean for the old man to win. I tentatively
have it in mind that Tarwater will drown the little boy, Bishop, in
an attempt to free himself from the old man's image. This doesn't
upset the school teacher too much as he's rather glad to have him child
out of the way. The school teacher thinks he won, but in the
end Tarwater burns up the school teacher's house too and sets off
to prophesy. The old man has won because the old man was right.

This is very rough and as I say there are only 70 pages of
it. I'm hogwild to finish it but it just doesn't go very fast.
As you can see it's a good deal to have to make believable. I
would rather wait until I do a little more on it before I show it
to anybody.

You might find Wise Blood could be done something with. Anyway
I enclose it, and if you want to see the one I sent to Nashville,
Caroline has a copy of it. A Good Man is a available, but The River
is being considered by a young man for a movie. He contends it will
make a wonderful movie, but if he actually does anything, I intend
to keep a firm hand on him because I am afraid he will sentimentalize
it.

Elizabeth McKee is my agent. She works with Mavis McIntosh.
You could ask her about this if you want to as she has been interested
in the possiblity of a play out of something of mine. I don't know
how these things are worked out myself, but if anybody does anything
with my stuff I would like it to be somebody like you that I
know wouldn't turn the meaning upside down. I sold the story called
The Life You Save for a tv play; the result was nauseous.

You can let me know your further thoughts on the subject.
Meanwhile cheers.

Flannery

*O'Connor's response to Susan Jenkins Brown's proposal to dramatize one of O'Connor's stories (Collection of
Ashley Brown)*

else if this is too incomplete to be worked with . . . I have cordial relations with a key staff member of the producers of O'Neill's *Long Day's Journey* and *Iceman Cometh* and could get a script read by them. But so could your agent; is it still McIntosh?

Caroline tells me you're going abroad — when, I don't recall. Can you make up your mind before that? I'd like to work on this right away. And could you send me anything I should read (that I haven't got) before making a choice? I do hope this isn't too much of a bombshell.

Cordially, Sue Brown

There is of course no collection of stories called *A View of the Woods;* the collection is *A Good Man Is Hard to Find*. Since Sue Jenkins decided at this point that she wanted to dramatize a novel that was far from completed, the next move was up to Flannery. Sue was very impressed by "You Can't Be Any Poorer Than Dead," which had appeared in *New World Writing* (October 1955) and which would eventually be revised as the opening chapter of *The Violent Bear It Away*. (Robert Giroux has included the original version in *The Complete Stories*.) Flannery replied immediately to Sue Jenkins; her letter is dated 17 January, but I think that it must have been written the following day.

Dear Sue,

Off hand it sounds like a fine idea. I don't know Thing One about the theatre myself and I wouldn't want to write a play myself for fear it would throw me off from my proper bent. However, if you planned the thing out, you could probably find enough dialogue in it, with my supplying a little more, to make due. I have only done 70 pages of this novel and I am rampant to finish it but it goes so fast and no faster. I have added a good deal to that first chapter, notably emphasizing the school teacher's little boy who looks like Old Tarwater. This is a feeble-minded child. When Tarwater goes to town to the school teacher, he is of course reminded constantly of the old man by this child (whose name is Bishop). The rest of the action of the book is concerned with the school teacher's attempt to "adjust" Tarwater to modern life, rid him of his religious ideas, make him a normal American boy etc etc. Tarwater on the other hand is torn between his real desire to be a prophet like the old man intended and his feeling that he ain't been called; in other words the dead old man and the school teacher are in a struggle for his soul. And I mean for the old man to win. I tentatively have it in mind that Tarwater will drown the little boy,

Bishop, in an attempt to free himself from the old man's image. This doesn't upset the school teacher too much as he's rather glad to have his child out of the way. The school teacher thinks he's won, but in the end Tarwater burns up the school teacher's house too and sets off to prophesy. The old man has won because the old man was right.

This is very rough and as I say there are only 70 pages of it so far. I'm hogwild to finish it but it just doesn't go very fast. As you can see it's a good deal to have to make believable. I would rather wait until I do a little more on it before I show it to anybody.

You might find Wise Blood could be done something with. Anyway I am sending it in another envelope, and if you want to see the one I sent to Nashville, Caroline has a copy of it. A Good Man is available, but The River is being considered by a young man for a movie. He contends it will make a wonderful movie, but if he actually does anything, I intend to keep a firm hand on him because I am afraid he will sentimentalize it.

Elizabeth McKee is my agent. She works with Mavis McIntosh. You could ask her about this if you want to as she has been interested in the possibility of a play out of something of mine. I don't know how these things are worked out myself, but if anybody does anything with my stuff I would like it to be somebody like you that I know wouldn't turn the meaning upside down. I sold the story called The Life You Save for a tv play; the result was nauseous.

You can let me know your further thoughts on the subject. Meanwhile cheers.

Flannery

On January 23 Sue Jenkins replied to Flannery on a postcard. She couldn't see *Wise Blood* as a play; she would now read the stories with the idea that one of them could be dramatized; but she still hoped that the novel in progress would be finished so that she could work it into dramatic form with Flannery's collaboration. She left a few scattered notes based on "You Can't Be Any Poorer Than Dead" and obviously thought that the image of the old man in the coffin was powerful enough to set the drama going. As for Flannery, she had been trying to get back to her novel for years; she had started it in 1952. In March 1958, she met Katherine Anne Porter (this was the first of Miss Porter's visits to Andalusia Farm) and was appalled to hear that *Ship of Fools* was unfinished after twenty-seven years. Flannery mentioned this to several friends, including myself, and very likely the thought of Miss Porter's delays on her novel caused Flannery to finish hers as quickly as she did.

At any rate, Sue Jenkins waited a year before returning to the subject. Her next letter was undated but written probably in March 1959:

Dear Flannery:

Just a short note to ask how the novel is coming and when I can hope to receive it. I'm winding up matters in NYC, have sublet my apartment, and will go to the country on or about June 12th. I'll be there until September, going back on my job around October 1. This gives me three good months to see what I can do with dramatizing — enough to find out if it's possible, I should think.

I suppose you have been kept informed of the news of the House of Tate, most of it doleful.

My best,

Congratulations on your grant — Ford, wasn't it? I got a lot of pleasure, seeing your name in the list.

Sue

Flannery had received a Ford Foundation grant of $8,000 in February 1959, and perhaps this encouraged her to think about a play despite her misgivings. Her next letter is dated 29 March '59:

Dear Sue,

I have finished my novel and if you are still interested in seeing it, I'll send you a copy as soon as I get my final corrections settled upon and get it typed. All this will probably take me a month anyway.

I don't know whether it could be dramatized or not. The hero has a penchant for setting fires and you wouldn't want to burn up the theatre. Also he has visions; but if you want to see it, lemme know.

The name of it is THE VIOLENT BEAR IT AWAY. If anybody tries to dramatize it, I would like it to be you.

Yours,
Flannery

But it was June before Flannery was satisfied with her manuscript. The next two letters are evidently her last word on the subject of a play.

7 June 59

Dear Sue,

It looks like everything takes longer than you think. I have been doing over the middle section of the novel which I was not satisfied with. I'll try to get you a copy to Sherman sometime after the 15th of June. It may not be a final draft but enough of one for you to see if you think it can be dramatized. I have my doubts.

I haven't heard from Caroline in a couple of weeks but I hope the news is no more doleful than it was then. She did say she had started on a novel which I should think would be the best place for her mind to be set right now.

You will hear from me shortly with the ms. I'd like to hear what you think of it.

Best,
Flannery

14 June 59

Dear Sue,

This is it. I'd be much obliged if you didn't show it to anybody but yourself and if you see at once that it can't be dramatized, send it back to me. You'll be a good one if you can do anything with this.

Cheers + thanks,
Flannery

Two weeks later Sue Jenkins regretfully returned the manuscript of *The Violent Bear It Away* to Flannery. She admitted that she simply couldn't develop her drama beyond the original scene that she had read and admired in *New World Writing* in 1955.

June 30, 1959

Dear Flannery:

It's a great disappointment to have to agree with you, but I don't find myself able to make a play out of your most interesting novel. I rather imagine that somebody with more dramatic imagination than I, and more skill at dramatizing, could do so. But I've mulled it over, and the only way I seem able to figure anything visual out of it is by doing scene after scene, for the last two thirds of a play. And that's not good. I feel I could do a beautiful first act, one which would be largely your work. But the whole part of the book which has to do with the little boy and the relations between Tarwater and the schoolteacher has me completely stumped.

I regret giving up the idea of it because I think something interesting dramatically could be done with the scenes between Tarwater and his other self.

So now I revert to the idea of one of your short stories. I'm about to re-read those in the collection, and I have read the one in the Partisan Review, also one in Ms. I'll write you again if I have anything sensible to write about.

My best,
Sue

Sherman, Conn., RD
Tuesday, July 14, 1959

Dear Flannery:

I regret to say I've had an idea for a dramatic scheme
for "A Good Man" -- the regret because it's so pleasant to be lazy
in the summer and because it would entail a lot of work for somebody,
including you. I almost hope you won't like it.

Act One. Opens with arrival of the familyat Red Sammy's.
Scene shows both outside and inside of The Tower. Dialogue introduces everything that went on at home in Atlanta and in the dar --
The Misfit, grandmother's hankering after a visit to east Tennessee
and romanticizing about life on the Old Plantation. Bailey and
wife sort of doze off while grandmother tells children astory about
the house she wants them to visit, which leads into

Act Two. This would have to introduce new material,
an expansion of the grandmothers fantasy of the Old South. It's
played in front of a back drop showing a romanticized picture of
the Old Plantation. Grandmother and children are seen in kxwax front
right or left, occasionally spotlighted when the children interrupt
her sarcastically. Finally she succeeds in focusing their interest
on the secret panel, and the Old Plantation drop is raised. Children
clamor for trip back to dirt road, as in the story

Attitude toward grandmother's picture: could be ironic,
and I'm inclined to think it should be. Perhaps she could spin some
well known incident from "Gone With the Wind" which June Star spots.
The actors in the Old South scene could be limited to pantomime and
dance, with grandmother supplying the dialogue. Or else they can
act out a scene from her imaginings and pseudo-recollections.

To be decided on: Omit baby? How to handle Pity Sing.

Act Three. After the accident.

I forgot: after Bailey is finally prevailed upon to
make the detour (end of Act Two, after disappearance of the Old South
and return to The Tower scene) grandmother remembers, for the benefit
of the audience, that the secret panel house is in Tennessee.

I have it worked out in much greater detail in my mind,
but since the scheme depends on your liking the new material for
Act Two, which is an expansion of what you don't develop in the story
but merely summarize, and which would mean your supplying incidents
and dialogue, there's no point in burdening you with more detail
until you have passed on this.

My feelings won't be hurt if you don't see it at all,
or don't want to be bothered with it. Of course, if the task
were undertaken, it couldn't be finished this summer, although I
think I could get a very rough draft down, for you to work on
during the fall and winter, or whenever you could.

Suggestion: make June Star 11 or 12, and John Wesley
10 or 11. Would be easier to handle.

* July: Would the children be familiar with My best, Sue Gone With Wind?

Letter to O'Connor in which Susan Jenkins Brown outlined a dramatic version of "A Good Man Is Hard to Find"
(Collection of Ashley Brown)

Sue Jenkins made another try, and her final letter in this exchange is certainly interesting, not least because it illustrates so well the difficulty that many writers have had in moving from fiction to drama.

Thursday, July 14, 1959

Dear Flannery:

I regret to say I've had an idea for a dramatic scheme for "A Good Man" — the regret because it's so pleasant to be lazy in the summer and because it would entail a lot of work for somebody, including you. I almost hope you won't like it.

Act One. Opens with arrival of the family at Red Sammy's. Scene shows both outside and inside of The Tower. Dialogue introduces everything that went on at home in Atlanta and in the car — The Misfit, grandmother's hankering after a visit to east Tennessee and romanticizing about life on the Old Plantation. Bailey and wife sort of doze off while grandmother tells children a story about the house she wants them to visit, which leads into

Act Two. This would have to introduce new material, an expansion of the grandmother's fantasy of the Old South. It's played in front of a back drop showing a romanticized picture of the Old Plantation. Grandmother and children are seen in front right or left, occasionally spotlighted when the children interrupt her sarcastically. Finally she succeeds in focusing their interest on the secret panel, and the Old Plantation drop is raised. Children clamor for trip back to dirt road as in the story.

Attitude toward grandmother's picture: could be ironic, and I'm inclined to think it should be. Perhaps she could spin some well known incident from "Gone With the Wind" which June Star spots. The actors in the Old South scene could be limited to pantomime and dance, with grandmother supplying the dialogue. Or else they can act out a scene from her imaginings and pseudo-recollections.

To be decided on: Omit baby? How to handle Pitty Sing.

Act Three. After the accident.

I forgot: after Bailey is finally prevailed upon to make the detour (end of Act Two, after disappearance of the Old South and return to The Tower scene) grandmother remembers, for the benefit of the audience, that the secret panel house is in Tennessee.

I have it worked out in much great detail in my mind, but since the scheme depends on your liking the new material for Act Two, which is an expansion of what you don't develop in the story but merely summarize, and which would mean your supplying incidents and dialogue, there's no point in burdening you with more detail until you have passed on this.

My feelings won't be hurt if you don't see it at all, or don't want to be bothered with it. Of course, if the task were undertaken, it couldn't be finished this summer, although I think I could get a very rough draft down, for you to work on during the fall and winter, or whenever you could.

Suggestion: make June Star 11 or 12, and John Wesley 10 or 11. Would be easier to handle.

My best, Sue

This seems to close the episode. Flannery, as she firmly stated, knew nothing about the theater, but it is worth recalling that some of her southern contemporaries, including Faulkner and Warren, were trying to move into it. Carson McCullers and Eudora Welty had had a great success in New York with the plays made from *The Member of the Wedding* and *The Ponder Heart*. Several of Flannery's friends, among them Brainard Cheney and Peter Taylor, were spending much of their creative energy during the 1950s in trying to establish a regional drama based on the established literary talent of the South. So this little episode, though it came to nothing, was altogether typical of the period.

LETTER:
Flannery O'Connor to "A," 25 July 1959; in *The Habit of Being*, pp. 342–343.

O'Connor sent a complete draft of The Violent Bear It Away *to Caroline Gordon in January 1959 and worked on revisions until 17 July, when she sent copies of the final draft to her agent, the Fitzgeralds, and "A." This letter is a response to comments from "A."*

. . . Thank you for what you say about the novel. Your appreciation always adds something to my own. I will shore it up against the day when I am faced with the misunderstanding reviews. I expect this one to be pounced on and torn limb from limb. Nevertheless, I am pleased with it myself, everything in it seems to me to be inevitable in the economy of the situation.

Now about Tarwater's future. He must of course not live to realize his mission, but die to realize it. The children of God I daresay will dispatch him pretty quick. Nor am I saying that he has a great mission or that God's solution for the problems of our particular world are prophets like Tarwater. Tarwater's mission might only be to baptize a few more idiots. The prophets in the

Bible are only the great ones but there is doubtless unwritten sacred history like uncanonized saints. Someday if I get up enough courage I may write a story or a novella about Tarwater in the city. There would be no reformatory I assure you. That murder is forgotten by God and of no interest to society, and I would proceed quickly to show what the children of God do to him. I am much more interested in the nobility of unnaturalness than in the nobility of naturalness. As Robert [Fitzgerald] says, it is the business of the artist to uncover the strangeness of truth. The violent are not natural. St. Thomas's gloss on this verse is that the violent Christ is here talking about repre-sent those ascetics who strain against mere nature. St. Augustine concurs.

I will take just as much naturalness as I need to accomplish my purposes, no more, but a Freud-ian could read this novel and explain it all on the basis of Freud. Many will think that the author shares Rayber's point of view and praise the book on account of it. This book is less grotesque than *Wise Blood* and as you say less funny. But if it had been funny, the tone would have been destroyed at once. In some places I may have gone too near the edge already. As you say, one distraction, one look aside or up or down, and the jig is up.

I will not be doing any more after the book is published than at any other time. I do not attend book parties . . .

LETTER:
Flannery O'Connor to John Hawkes, 13 Septem-
    ber 1959; in *The Habit of Being*, pp. 349–
    351.

Novelist John Hawkes and his family stopped to visit O'Connor, whose work Hawkes admired, in 1958, and soon O'Connor was writing to Hawkes, "I am very much taken with your books and their wonderful imaginative energy" (27 July 1958). Though Hawkes did not share O'Connor's religious convictions, the two writers seem to have sensed an affinity in their visions of a vio-lent modern world. As O'Connor wrote about Hawkes's The Lime Twig *(1961), "You suffer this like a dream. It seems to be something that is happening to you, that you want to escape from but can't. . . . Your other books I could leave when I wanted to, but this one I might have been dreaming myself" (9 October 1960).*

In this letter O'Connor explained the reli-gious beliefs that underlie Wise Blood *and her forthcoming novel* The Violent Bear It Away.

Your letter made me want you to read my novel now, so much so that I was tempted to send it to you (carbon) but I think this would be an in-fringement on your time and friendship, so I am sparing you. If FS&C have bound half-galleys I'll get them to send you a set. Sometimes publishers send these to me and they are very easy to read. Anyway, I would like to tell you something about this novel (much of which you have rightly antici-pated) and its kinship to *Wise Blood*.

I don't think you should write something as long as a novel around anything that is not of the gravest concern to you and everybody else and for me this is always the conflict between an attrac-tion for the Holy and the disbelief in it that we breathe in with the air of the times. It's hard to be-lieve always but more so in the world we live in now. There are some of us who have to pay for our faith every step of the way and who have to work out dramatically what it would be like with-out it and if being without it would be ultimately possible or not. I can't allow any of my charac-ters, in a novel anyway, to stop in some halfway position. This doubtless comes of a Catholic edu-cation and a Catholic sense of history — everything works toward its true end or away from it, every-thing is ultimately saved or lost. Haze is saved by virtue of having wise blood; it's too wise for him ultimately to deny Christ. Wise blood has to be these people's means of grace — they have no sacraments. The religion of the South is a do-it-yourself religion, something which I as a Catholic find painful and touching and grimly comic. It's full of unconscious pride that lands them in all sorts of ridiculous religious predicaments. They have nothing to correct their practical heresies and so they work them out dramatically. If this were merely comic to me, it would be no good, but I accept the same fundamental doctrines of sin and redemption and judgment that they do.

Now in the new book, all this is still there but it is a more ambitious undertaking. The great-uncle is not a puritan here, as you saw. He is a prophet. And the boy doesn't just get himself saved by the skin of his teeth, he in the end pre-pares to be a prophet himself and to accept what prophets can expect from their earthly lives (the worst). That was a shortened version of the first chapter. In the real first chapter it is brought out that the old man considers himself a prophet and that he has stolen the boy away from the school-teacher in order to raise him up to take his place as a prophet when he dies. As soon as the old man dies, the boy is left alone with the threat of the

He visited his daughter in town once a year and ~~didnotxwearxhis~~
~~oxoxxhix~~ wore the black suit that he expected to be buried in. He had got
up late ~~that~~ yesterday morning--not until seven o'clock--and had put on the suit and
~~the~~ his black felt hat and had gone down the stairs ~~and~~ that led into the cold kitchen
to ~~fixxhix~~ prepare his breakfast. ~~The~~ His boys were sleeping late too, but
his grandson, Serene Jr., was sitting at the bare table, drinking a cup
of cold ~~black~~ coffee. He had on the new light blue suit that they had
~~boughtxhimxyankee~~ ordered for him and a pale grey hat. The hat was too
big ~~Seemsbig~~ but they expected his head to grow. ~~The hat appeared to be~~ The brim was
~~balanced~~ and ~~the~~ ~~potately~~ ~~coming down~~ down ~~the oddxangle~~
over his ~~eyes~~ forehead ~~andxz~~ so that ~~they~~ disease could ~~hardly~~ not be seen. ~~withoutxlooking~~
The cook stove was already laid and the old man lit a match to it and
took the skillet off the nail. He was irked to see the boy ready to
go and did not speak to him. He went out on the back porch and returned
in a ~~xxxxxx~~ minute with a piece of fat back that he had got out of the refrigerator
~~they~~ kept on the porch. He threw ~~thix~~ it into the skillet and then
he came over to where they the ~~boy~~ child was hunched over his cup of coffee.
He put his big red fist beside the coffee ~~xxxx~~ cup and let it remain there
and drank the last swallow of coffee.
until the boy removed the cup to his mouth. "It ~~xixix~~ ain't nothing in
town," the old man said in a gravel voice, "that it ain't already out
here."

"I never said it was anything in that town," the boy said, putting the cup down. "I was born
in a city. I was born in a city, population 300,000." and lived there until I
~~was four years old.~~
"It ain't anything in a city either," the old man said.

The boy pushed his chair back and got up quickly. He was ~~xxx~~ eleven
~~years old~~ but very small for his age. His face was carefully expressionless.
They could not keep him in school except by beating him, or make him rise
from the third grade at all. He went out the back door, quickly, with
the hat (so far) pulled down that it cut off any view of his grandfather.
"Come back here and get your breakfast," the old man shouted. moving to the
door.
"I've ate," the boy called back and disappeared around the corner
house.
of the

First page from an early draft for The Violent Bear It Away *(The Flannery O'Connor Collection, Ina Dillard Russell Library, Georgia College)*

Lord's call. He heads for the schoolteacher and the burden of the book is taken up with the struggle for the boy's soul between the dead uncle and the schoolteacher.

The modern reader will identify himself with the schoolteacher, but it is the old man who speaks for me.

I hadn't thought about the cross-shaped face as meaning anything but that he was marked out for the Lord — or at least marked out as one who will have the struggle, who will know what the choice is. Haze knows what the choice is and the Misfit knows what the choice is — either throw away everything and follow Him or enjoy yourself by doing some meanness to somebody, and in the end there's no real pleasure in life, not even in meanness. I can fancy a character like the Misfit being redeemable, but a character like Mr. Shiftlet as being unredeemable. Mr. Head's redemption is all laid out inside the story.

This is too much about me and my works. I read *The Velvet Horn* [by Andrew Lytle] and I was entirely taken with it. I didn't follow all the intricacies of the symbolism but it had its effect without working it all out . . . I'll be waiting for *The Lime Twig* and will prepare the other two members of the Georgia Hawkes Appreciation Society. And I do appreciate your interest in this book of mine. It's not every book that gets itself understood before it has been read.

LETTER:
Flannery O'Connor to John Hawkes, 20 November 1959; in *The Habit of Being*, pp. 359–360.

In October 1959 O'Connor sent Hawkes a copy of the manuscript for The Violent Bear It Away. *This response to his comments clarifies O'Connor's belief in the literal existence of the devil; he is not just a metaphor or a "psychological tendency."*

I have been wanting to write and thank you for sending back the manuscript and for reading it and marking it and for all you did to help me. It was a great help . . .

I don't think I'll be able to keep out of the city and stick to what you call the pure whiskey and coffin and Bible land. The fact is that all the inhabitants of the coffin and Bible land have left it and are in the city. To write about Haze and Tarwater, that's where you have to go. I don't know that I am through writing about Tarwater. I've left him right at the beginning. I keep wondering about how the children of God will finish him off. The ones that will do it will be these country people in the city.

You set me to thinking if I had really intended three representations of the Devil. I had meant for Meeks and the pervert at the end to take on the form of Tarwater's Friend, and when I first set out I had in mind that Rayber would echo all his friend's sentiments in a form that the reader would identify himself with. With trial and error I found that making Rayber pure evil made him a caricature and took away from the role of the old prophet since it left him nothing worth trying to save. I have been reading about some cases of possession in the 19th century. It appears that we have a certain privacy from the Devil, who cannot read our thoughts directly but can only decide what we are thinking from our acts. Apparently the Devil possessing a man keeps his own name and personality and the possessed keeps his, and can keep his soul inviolate while being possessed. And the Devil is most tortured to have to call his own name. This has nothing to do with Rayber here, but I find it interesting. I want to be certain that the Devil gets identified as the Devil and not simply taken for this or that psychological tendency . . .

My best to you and Sophie.

BOOK REVIEW:
Granville Hicks, "Southern Gothic with a Vengeance," review of *The Violent Bear It Away, Saturday Review*, 43 (27 February 1960): 18.

The Violent Bear It Away was published on 8 February 1960 by Farrar, Straus & Cudahy, with whom O'Connor had signed a contract in April 1958, after her editor left Harcourt, Brace. O'Connor found the reviews for The Violent Bear It Away *"amusing." As she told Robert Giroux, who was once again her editor, "Even the ones who report favorably don't seem to have read the book" (6 March 1960). One of the most positive and most astute of the reviews was written by Granville Hicks.*

Flannery O'Connor is a Southerner and a Catholic, and both of these facts are important. Her material, up to a point at any rate, comes from her region, and is roughly of the sort described as Southern Gothic. Her attitude towards the material derives, as she has herself pointed out, from her religious convictions. But she is a particular kind of Southerner and, if she will forgive a heretic for saying so, a particular kind of Catholic. Her work is highly individual, and the better it becomes, the clearer its individuality is.

"The Violent Bear It Away" (Farrar, Straus & Cudahy, $3.75) is better than her first novel, "Wise Blood," and as good as the best of her short stories, which is to say that it is first-rate. She has been working on it for a long while (a chapter appeared in *New World Writing* in 1955) and it is a firm, strong, disciplined book. From now on there can be no doubt that Miss O'Connor is one of the important American writers.

The novel has a breathtaking first sentence:

> Francis Marion Tarwater's uncle had been dead for only half a day when the boy got too drunk to finish digging his grave and a Negro named Buford Munson, who had come to get a jug filled, had to finish it and drag the body from the breakfast table where it was still sitting and bury it in a decent Christian way, with the sign of its Saviour at the head of the grave and enough dirt on top to keep the dogs from digging it up.

This is Southern Gothic with a vengeance, and it gives a taste of the violence and horror to come. Like "Wise Blood," the book is one of grotesques, but this does not mean that the characters are fantastic or incredible. On the contrary, it becomes impossible not to believe in them.

Francis Marion Tarwater, who is fourteen, has been brought up by the uncle — great-uncle really — whom he fails to bury. The old man, a fanatic, in his own opinion a prophet, a moonshiner on the side, kidnaped the boy, taught him what he wanted him to know, trained him to become his successor. The boy's only other relative is a true uncle, a schoolteacher named Rayber, and it is to him that young Tarwater now turns.

The conflict between the boy and his uncle becomes the novel's central theme. Rayber himself, when he was seven, was exposed to the old man's fanaticism, but he escaped and, as he believes, achieved enlightenment. Now he wants to save his nephew, but Tarwater is recalcitrant. At the same time, however, Tarwater is by no means sure that he wants to adopt the prophetic role for which he has been prepared. In particular he hesitates before the task that, above all else, the old man imposed upon him: the baptizing of Rayber's feeble-minded son.

Both the boy and the man are divided within themselves. Tarwater has a tough, worldly streak, represented by an inner voice that gives him practical counsel, and from the beginning he struggles against his great-uncle's design for him, even though the compulsion to obey is strong. Rayber, for his part, has been more deeply influenced by the old man than he likes to admit, and he has to wage a hard fight against his fanatical tendencies. The rationalism he so glibly expounds is no more than skin deep.

Nevertheless, Rayber is diligent in his effort to lead Tarwater out of the darkness of superstition into the light of reason, and he tries one stratagem after another. He has, however, no chance of success, for the boy rejects out of hand the teacher's way of life. If he is not to become the prophet his great-uncle wanted him to be, then he will follow the bidding of his own dark impulses. His struggle reaches its climax in a scene with Rayber's half-witted child, but the climax is indecisive, for, against his will, he baptizes the child even as he drowns him. In the end, after Tarwater's further resistance, the triumph of the old man is complete.

In the essay she contributed to "The Living Novel" Miss O'Connor wrote:

> . . . when I look at stories I have written I find that they are, for the most part, about people who are poor, who are afflicted in both mind and body, who have little — or at best a distorted — sense of spiritual purpose. . . . Yet how is this? For I am no disbeliever in spiritual purpose and no vague believer. I see from the standpoint of Christian orthodoxy. This means that for me the meaning of life is centered in our Redemption by Christ and that what I see in the world I see in its relation to that . . . My own feeling is that writers who see by the light of their Christian faith will have, in these times, the sharpest eyes for the grotesque, for the perverse, and for the unacceptable . . . The novelist with Christian concerns will find in modern life distortions which are repugnant to him, and his problem will be to make these appear as distortions to an audience which is used to seeing them as natural.

The people in "The Violent Bear It Away," then, are not merely grotesques, and their grotesqueness is not portrayed for its own sake; they are distortions. The old man is warped by fanaticism; he is ugly, intemperate, unloving. Young Tarwater, before he too becomes a fanatic, has found no better alternative than cynicism and violent action. As for Rayber, his rationalism is superficial and preposterously inadequate. He is, indeed, as we realize after the drowning of the child, a dead soul.

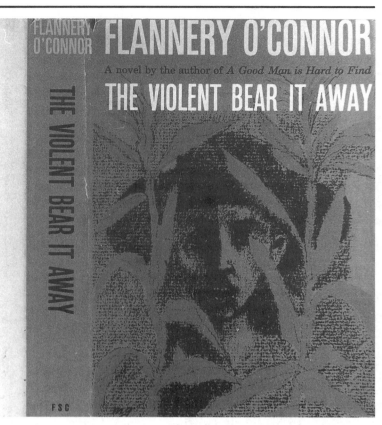

THE TALENT OF FLANNERY O'CONNOR, one of the most original among younger American writers, was recognized soon after the publication of her first short stories. . . . Miss O'Connor's work, however, has a characteristic which does not occur in the work of any of her contemporaries. Its presence in everything she writes, coupled with her extraordinary talent, makes her, I suspect, one of the most important writers of our age. . . . In Miss O'Connor's vision of modern man—a vision not limited to Southern rural humanity—all her characters are "displaced persons." They are "off center," out of place, because they are victims of a rejection of the Scheme of Redemption. They are lost in that abyss which opens for man when he sets up as God. This theological framework is never explicit in Miss O'Connor's fiction. It is so much a part of her direct gaze at human conduct that she seems herself to be scarcely aware of it. I believe that this accounts to a great extent for her power. It is a Blakean vision, not through symbol as such but through the actuality of human behavior; and it has Blake's explosive honesty.

CAROLINE GORDON

FARRAR, STRAUS AND CUDAHY
101 FIFTH AVENUE, NEW YORK 3

FSC

Dust jacket for the novel that O'Connor's friend Brainard Cheney called "the boldest most brilliant achievement of a young writer whose work includes already some of the most original and important American fiction of this century"

Yet Miss O'Connor exposes none of these characters to the contempt of the reader. She is not attacking error but portraying poor erring men. She writes about them with great compassion, and does justice to their virtues.

Miss O'Connor tells the story with stark power, making every detail carry its full weight. The conflicts she describes are wonderfully sustained and intensified, and the characters are even more fully revealed. What happens seems, when it has happened, to have been inevitable. Miss O'Connor is thoroughly in control of her world; she knows it and she knows where she stands in relation to it. Her prose is strong, supple, at times full of beauty, never pretentious. From any point of view, "The Violent Bear It Away" is a distinguished piece of work.

BOOK REVIEW:
Donald Davidson, "A Prophet Went Forth," review of *The Violent Bear It Away, New York Times Book Review*, 28 February 1960, p. 4.

Vanderbilt University English professor Donald Davidson, though generally sympathetic to O'Connor's religious position, appears to have been uncertain of how to interpret her fiction.

Flannery O'Connor's new novel, like her preceding works, is strong medicine, but now we know, as we did not earlier, that the medicine is for the soul, and is not just realistic Southern calomel and Epsom salts. The cryptic title comes from the twelfth verse of the eleventh chapter of Matthew and reads: "From the days of John the Baptist until now, the Kingdom of Heaven suffereth violence, and the violent bear it away."

The layman may stand thunderstruck before a Biblical text so difficult and disputable. The invitation to read the novel for a religious, even allegorical, meaning is no less definite. To declare that meaning is another matter, although on its face the narrative seems plain and simple and is written with consummate skill and power.

The 14-year-old Tarwater boy, orphan child of an unmarried mother, has been reared by his great-uncle — "a bull-like old man with a short head set directly into his shoulders and silver protruding eyes that looked like two fish straining to get out of a net of red threads." The old man is at feud with Tarwater's younger uncle, Rayber — who wanted to raise the boy up to a skeptical bookish education. Instead, the great-uncle kidnapped the infant, baptized him, and gave him a primitive religious education in his wilderness clearing at Powderhead, Tenn. When Rayber comes with a social-welfare woman to reclaim Tarwater, the old man blasts them off with a shotgun. From this time until the old man's sudden death, Tarwater feels sure he must be a prophet and must first of all go forth and baptize his cousin Bishop — the idiot child of Rayber and the welfare woman.

The action proper of the novel begins at the point where the young Tarwater leaves his great-uncle's corpse sitting upright at the breakfast table and starts to dig a grave. Later, he goes to a hidden still and drinks himself into unconsciousness. Awakening, he revolts against his mission and hitch-hikes to the city, where Rayber essays to convert him to modernism. Another revulsion seizes Tarwater. He drowns the idiot in a lake and starts back to his lonely clearing. A truck driver questions him:

"'How come your pants-legs are wet?' the driver persisted.

"'I drowned a boy,' Tarwater said.

"'Just one?' the driver asked.

"'Yes.' He reached over and caught hold of the sleeve of the man's shirt. His lips worked • • • Then all at once the sentence rushed out and was gone. 'I baptized him.'"

Home again, Tarwater finds that Buford, his Negro neighbor, has finished the grave. Looking around him, he sees in a vision the supernatural burning bush and the miracle of the loaves and fishes, and knows he must accept his mission.

The novel is superior in conception and execution to anything Miss O'Connor has previously published. If the meaning is muddled, or indecipherable, the fault is probably in the fact that the three main characters are so isolated from the general human context. In the end, we can found no firm generalization upon them, but tend to view them as irresponsible creatures belonging to some arbitrary world of fantasy.

LETTER:
Flannery O'Connor to John Hawkes, 14 April 1960; in *The Habit of Being,* pp. 389–390.

In this letter, written while reviews of The Violent Bear It Away *were still appearing in various periodicals, O'Connor explained her Roman Catholic perspectives on human manifestations of evil and divine grace, as they are exemplified in "A Good Man Is Hard to Find."*

Thanks for your letter of some time back. I have been busy keeping my blood pressure down while reading various reviews of my book. Some of the favorable ones are as bad as the unfavorable; most reviewers seem to have read the book in fifteen minutes and written the review in ten . . . I hope that when yours comes out you'll fare better.

It's interesting to me that your students naturally work their way to the idea that the Grandmother in "A Good Man" is not pure evil and may be a medium for Grace. If they were Southern students I would say this was because they all had grandmothers like her at home. These old ladies exactly reflect the banalities of the society and the effect is of the comical rather than the seriously evil. But Andrew [Lytle] insists that she is a witch, even down to the cat. These children, yr. students, know their grandmothers aren't witches.

Perhaps it is a difference in theology, or rather the difference that ingrained theology makes in the sensibility. Grace, to the Catholic way of thinking, can and does use as its medium the imperfect, purely human, and even hypocritical. Cutting yourself off from Grace is a very decided matter, requiring a real choice, act of will, and affecting the very ground of the soul. The Misfit is touched by the Grace that comes through the old lady when she recognizes him as her child, as she has been touched by the Grace that comes through him in his particular suffering. His shooting her is a recoil, a horror at her humanness, but after he has done it and cleaned his glasses, the Grace has worked in him and he pronounces his judgment: she would have been a good woman if *he* had been there every moment of her life. True enough. In the Protestant view, I think Grace and nature don't have much to do with each other. The old lady, because of her hypocrisy and humanness and banality couldn't be a medium for Grace. In the sense that I see things the other way, I'm a Catholic writer.

I hope you are writing and that *The Lime Twig* is on the way. Also that you all may be going to Florida this year and will stop for a longer visit with us.

INTERVIEW:

Robert Donner [Richard Gilman], "She Writes Powerful Fiction," *Sign*, 40 (March 1961): 46–48; in *Conversations with Flannery O'Connor*, pp. 44–50.

After the publication of The Violent Bear It Away, *several admirers of O'Connor's fiction traveled to Milledgeville to interview her. One of the most interesting interviews was conducted by Richard Gilman, who visited O'Connor in September 1960. (O'Connor began experiencing the symptoms of lupus in late 1950, not spring 1951, as reported here.)*

Milledgeville, Georgia, is a quiet town of some 10,000 inhabitants which lies about a hundred miles from Atlanta, whose predecessor as the state capital it was before the Civil War. Among its other distinctions, one might mention the fact that it was the birthplace of Oliver Hardy, of Laurel and Hardy fame, and that among its current residents is Mrs. Barbara Powers, the wife of the U-2 pilot who was shot down last spring over Russia and convicted of espionage.

When I was there last fall, Milledgeville was being visited by several reporters seeking interviews with Mrs. Powers, who had just returned from Moscow. My own purpose in coming, however, was quite different. I had come to see Flannery O'Connor, one of the most highly regarded of younger American writers.

Her short stories and novels have been receiving increasing praise from critics and readers both in this country and abroad. One English writer has called her the most impressive talent America has produced since the war, while an American critic, Granville Hicks, has said, "If there is a young writer who has given clearer evidence of originality and power than Flannery O'Connor, I cannot think who it is."

For commentators such as these, as well as for the small but dedicated public that admires her work (she is by no means a "popular" writer), what stands out in Miss O'Connor's writing is its moral quality, wedded to a high order of imagination. For the people she writes about — poor, rural Southern Protestants mostly — are caught up in situations of spiritual conflict that point to something much wider than themselves: they are universal dramas that we all participate in. Love and lovelessness, community and loneliness, faith and despair — these are the poles of her art, as they are the poles between which all of us lead our lives.

Yet there is nothing sermon-like about these stories. Miss O'Connor is concerned in her vocation as an artist to render life as she sees it, with exact truth, leaving the *explicit* moral and theological lessons to be drawn by those whose function it is. The way she approaches life is deeply shaped by her Catholic faith, however. As she says, "The Catholic writer, in so far as he has the mind of the Church, will feel life from the standpoint of the central Christian mystery: that it has for all its horror, been found by God to be worth dying for."

For various reasons — among them the fact that she lives far from any center of cultural activity, that her work differs in its underlying religious vision from that of most of her contemporaries, and that she has a painful illness that requires her to go about on crutches — a legend to the effect that she is a recluse, living in complete isolation, has grown up around Flannery O'Connor.

Even before I met her I learned that this picture was thoroughly distorted. Riding on the bus from Atlanta through the red-clay country of central Georgia, I fell into conversation with a young man who had noticed that I was reading *Wise Blood*, Miss O'Connor's first novel. He was a student at the University of Chicago, on his way home from the summer session, and he told me that he was well acquainted with the writer and that her home was the scene of frequent gatherings in which lively conversations on life and literature took place. "Oh, no," he said, as our bus pulled in, "she's certainly not a hermit, though she's not an extrovert either."

Miss O'Connor was waiting for me in a car driven by her mother. A brown-haired, slender woman in her thirties, she greeted me warmly, speaking in a soft voice with a medium-rich Southern accent. Before we went to their farm home, a few miles outside of Milledgeville, the O'Connors showed me the town — the old, pillared mansions along the wide residential streets, the red-stone buildings of the Georgia State College for Women, which Miss O'Connor had attended, the crumbling one-time governor's mansion now occupied by the president of the college, the little Church of the Sacred Heart where Milledgeville's Catholics worship. Then we drove the short and pleasant ride out to the farm.

I had read that Miss O'Connor raised peacocks as a hobby, and indeed there they were, strutting around the main house in lordly possession, although it wasn't the season for their splendid tails to be in bloom. "I like having them around," Miss O'Connor said, as we sat on the steps in the late afternoon sunshine and fed a hen and her five brown chicks from a can of dried corn kernels, chatting at random while Mrs. O'Connor prepared dinner.

Later we sat on rocking-chairs on the porch while night insects fluttered against the screens and the sound of some animal could be heard occasionally from the darkness outside. I asked Miss O'Connor for a brief autobiographical sketch, which she readily gave me, though I could see that her modesty and reticence made it something of a chore for her to talk about herself.

She was born March 25, 1925, in Savannah, where her father was in the real estate business ("there aren't any artists in my background"). Later he became an appraiser for the FHA and in 1938 the family moved to Milledgeville, which was Mrs. O'Connor's home town. Flannery (she was christened *Mary* Flannery, dropping the first name when she began to publish, though her friends and relatives still use it) attended Peabody High School and in 1942 entered Georgia State College for Women, earning her degree in three years under the accelerated wartime curriculum.

She had majored in the social sciences and had thought of becoming a teacher ("I'm rather glad things didn't work out that way"), but after her graduation she was granted a fellowship at the University of Iowa and began to write. Her first published story appeared in the literary magazine *Accent* in 1946 and from then on her career progressed steadily.

Her first novel *Wise Blood* (a bizarre, savagely funny, and deeply felt story about a young religious fanatic) was begun in 1948, the year she left Iowa, and published in 1951. Its final pages were composed under trying circumstances, for in the spring of 1951, while she was staying with friends in Connecticut, she suffered a severe attack of *lupus,* a disease of the rheumatic order, and had literally to sweat out every word as she put it on paper.

Since then she has been on cortisone, which keeps the malady in check, though there is no known cure. She returned to Milledgeville, where her mother had purchased a farm (her father had died in 1941), and has lived there ever since, writing and publishing regularly. From my own knowledge I filled in the rest of her biography.

Ten of her stories were published in 1955 under the title of *A Good Man is Hard to Find,* and her second novel, *The Violent Bear it Away,* a powerful story of a youth caught between the life of reason and that of prophecy, appeared early this year. Her stories have earned several important literary awards, including the O. Henry prize, and she has been the recipient of grants from both the National Academy of Arts and Letters and the Ford Foundation.

When she was describing her illness to me, her tone was remarkably matter-of-fact, without a trace of self-pity. And I discovered that, while the disease naturally limits her movements, it hasn't kept her rooted to one spot. She has participated in a number of writers' conferences and given readings at colleges as far north as Minnesota (where she recently read her work to the students at the College of St. Catherine in St. Paul). In 1957 she traveled to Lourdes on a pilgrimage with her mother and a party of townspeople.

When we began to talk about her work itself, she became much more animated, although she retained that note of half-humorous detachment I had observed before. "I don't have any theory of literature," she said. "I simply keep doing things the wrong way over and over until they suddenly come out right . . . That's one reason why I'm such a slow worker. *The Violent Bear it Away* took me seven years to write — of course I did other things from time to time — and I can't seem to turn out more than two stories a year. I have to have a "story" in mind — some incident or observation that excites me and in which I see fictional possibilities — before I can start a formal piece. But I do try to write at least three hours every morning, since discipline is so important."

She doesn't read many novels, she said, nor is she much of a reader in general. Among her favorite authors are Dostoievsky and Hawthorne, and she returns to them at regular intervals. Of the books she does read, many come to her from the Atlanta diocesan paper, for which she reviews frequently.

We discussed the reactions to her work among different kinds of readers. One that continually surprised her, she said, was the occasional charge that her stories lacked compassion for their characters. I suggested that this stemmed from the difficulty some people had in accepting a vision of humanity in its true behavior, with its passions, prejudices, conflicts, hungers, and secret dreams revealed to the eye, and with no explicit "uplifting" or consoling message to ease the shock. The humor in her writing was enough, it seemed to me, to demonstrate that her work was far from being deficient in sympathy and love.

More than that, a true Christian sense of existence is at the center of her work. What has made her a thorny writer for some readers is that her optimism is not on the surface. She had written once, "If the Catholic writer hopes to reveal mysteries, he will have to do it by describing truthfully what he sees from where he is. A purely affirmative vision cannot be demanded of him without limiting his freedom to observe what man has done with the things of God."

And I reflected on some of her stories: how behind the cruel, sardonic, often terrifying events that take place in them there is a hidden radiance, a light made up of hope and faith in ultimate salvation, and hope and faith in mankind, struggling, involved in evil, seeking to extricate itself, falling back and rising again.

But to be misunderstood is the frequent fate of writers. Miss O'Connor told me an amusing anecdote in illustration. One of her stories had been sold to television. When finally presented it had been turned upside down — a pointed, ironical tale of avarice, betrayal, and the birth of moral insight having become a piece of sentimental, easy-to-take escapism. The morning after the telecast, she was approached in town by an acquaintance who had never before indicated the slightest awareness of Miss O'Connor's stature as an artist. "Why, Mary Flannery," the woman said to her, "I do declare, I never dreamed you could do such nice work."

It was getting late. We rose and Miss O'Connor started checking the double locks on both the front and rear doors. When I asked her why all the precautions, she said, "Well, on one side of town there's the largest insane asylum in the world and on the other a home for delinquent boys. So we have to be careful about uninvited guests."

As I was going upstairs, she called after me, "Don't be alarmed if you hear something that sounds like 'Help!' It's only the peacocks." Nevertheless I was pretty badly shaken when I did hear it, just before I fell asleep.

After breakfast the next day, we took a tour of the farm. It's an impressive one, 1,700 acres stretching over hilly countryside and including pasture-land for a herd of a hundred cattle and the shetland ponies which are raised as a sideline, and an extensive stand of timber. As we rode across the fields to visit the ponies grazing among shrubs and small trees in a corner of the pasture, Flannery's mother explained that she had recently sold the timber rights to her trees to a lumber company, the buzzing of whose saws we could hear across the blue, hazy air.

The writer's mother, incidentally, struck me as an amazingly competent woman, of a pioneer-like stamina and courage. Though she employs a Polish refugee family and several Negro laborers to run the place, it was clear that the reins of the complex operation were in her hands.

Back in the house again, Miss O'Connor and I settled down to more conversation. I wanted to know about her family's roots in the area, and she told me that her great-grandfather had settled in Milledgeville around the time of the Civil War. It was her great-grandmother who had had the Catholic Church built: before that, Mass for the few local Catholics had been celebrated in her parlor by a visiting priest. Today there are about two hundred Catholic families and, Miss O'Connor commented, they get along amiably enough with their Protestant neighbors.

From this we passed to a discussion of the phenomenon of Southern writers, who occupy so large a position in American literature. "I think it's because the Southerner possesses a story-telling tradition" Miss O'Connor said. "When a Southerner wants to make a point, he tells a story; it's actually his way of reasoning and dealing with experience." The South, she added, while changing rapidly, was still largely rural and its people were therefore closer to the land and to the legends and myths which spring from it.

I reflected that the people in her stories possessed that earthiness and quality of permanence she was describing, and that her humility as a writer lay in her willingness to write about them and to find in their lives the material for her art, even though they were not on the surface what we think of as "representative" or typical.

A few days after my visit, I looked up the scattered writings of Flannery O'Connor that I hadn't yet read. In an essay called "The Church and the Fiction-Writer," which had appeared in *America*, I came upon a passage that perfectly expressed her credo as a creative writer. "What the fiction writer will discover," she had written, " . . . is that he cannot move or mold reality in the interests of abstract truth.

The writer learns, perhaps more quickly than the reader, to be humble in the face of what is."

PANEL DISCUSSION:

"Recent Southern Fiction: A Panel Discussion, Wesleyan College, 28 October 1960," *Bulletin of Wesleyan College* (Macon, Ga.), 41 (January 1961); in *Conversations with Flannery O'Connor*, pp. 61–78.

On 27 October 1960 O'Connor gave a talk titled "Some Thoughts on the Grotesque in Southern Fiction," at Wesleyan College in Macon, Georgia. The next day she participated with Caroline Gordon, Katherine Anne Porter, and Madison Jones in a panel discussion moderated by Louis D. Rubin, Jr., an English professor then teaching at Hollins College in Virginia.

Rubin: I suppose you know what a panel discussion is — for the first thirty minutes the moderator tries his best to get the panel members to say something and for the last thirty minutes he does his best to shut them up. I hope we can do that tonight. My own position here with these four distinguished Southern writers on my left is something like the junior member of that famous and often narrated legal firm — Levy, Ginsberg, Cohen, and Kelly. Kelly presses the suits. I thought the first thing we might talk about, if we may, would be writing habits. That is something everyone has one way or another. Mr. Jones, suppose I ask you, how do you write?

Jones: Well, you mean just physically speaking?

Rubin: Yes. What time of the day?

Jones: Well, I usually write from about 8:30 to 12 or 12:30 in the morning.

Gordon: Every day?

Jones: Well, every day except Sunday.

Gordon: You're a genius.

Rubin: How about you, Miss Porter?

Porter: Well, I have no hours at all, just such as I can snatch from all the other things I do. Once upon a time I tagged a husband around Europe in the Foreign Service for so many years and never lived for more than two years in one place and never knew where I was going to be and I just wrote when I could and I still do. Once in a while I take the time and run away to an inn and tell them to leave me alone. When I get hungry, I'll come out. And in those times I really get some work done. I wrote two short novels in fourteen days once [*Noon Wine* and *Old Mortality*] but that was twenty-five years ago.

Rubin: How about you, Miss Gordon?

Gordon: I made a horrible discovery this summer. I had a great deal of company and they all wanted to help me with the housework and I discovered I would have to stop writing if I let them do it because my writing and my housework all go together and if they washed the dishes then I didn't get any writing done. That's just my system that I have developed over the years — it works for me except it maddens my friends, because they like to help me wash the dishes.

Rubin: You mean your whole day is part of a very closely worked in regimen?

Gordon: I didn't discover it until this friend came and insisted she wanted to help me.

Rubin: How about you, Miss O'Connor. Do you do your writing along with the dishwashing?

O'Connor: Oh, no. I sit there before the typewriter for three hours every day and if anything comes I am there waiting to receive it. I think there should be a complete separation between literature and dishwashing.

Porter: I was once washing dishes in an old fashioned dishpan at 11 o'clock at night after a party and all of a sudden I just took my hands up like that and went to the typewriter and wrote the short story "Rope" between that time and two o'clock in the morning. I don't know what started me. I know I had it in mind for several years but the moment came suddenly.

Rubin: If that's what dishwashing does, then I'm going to buy a box of Duz in the morning. What I think you all seem to show is that there is no right way or wrong way, I suppose.

Porter: I think Grandma Moses is the most charming old soul. When they asked her how she painted — and they meant, I am sure, how she used the brush — she said, "Well, first I saw a masonite board to the size I want the picture to be." And I think that is what we do.

Rubin: It all sounds like alchemy to me.

Gordon: That is one question that people always ask a writer. How many hours he or she puts in a day. I've often wondered why that is and I just discovered fairly recently. I think they expect you to say you are writing all of the time. If you are mowing the grass you are still thinking about what you are going to write. It is all the time.

Rubin: I always remember reading something the late Bernard DeVoto remarked — that one of his hardest jobs was keeping his wife from thinking that if he looked up out of the window, then that meant he wasn't doing any work at the moment, so that she could ask him about some spending money or something of the sort.

Gordon: I used to have a dentist — an awfully good one — but I quit him because when he was going to hurt me he would say, "Now just relax and think about your novel." I couldn't take that.

Jones: I have always found that when something is going well, I can't think about it at all unless I am right over the paper. Unless I am at work, I can't even get my mind on it away from my environment.

Rubin: Let me change the subject. I'll let Miss Porter answer this one. Miss Porter, do you consider yourself a Southern writer?

Porter: I am a Southerner. I have been told that I wasn't a Southerner, that anyone born in Texas is a South-westerner. But I can't help it. Some of my people came from Virginia, some from Pennsylvania, but we are all from Tennessee, Georgia, the Carolinas, Kentucky, Louisiana. What does it take to be a Southerner? And being a Southerner, I happen to write so I suppose you combine the two and you have a Southern writer, haven't you? What do you think? I do feel an intense sense of location and of background and my tradition and my country exist to me, but I have never really stuck to it in my writing because I have lived too nomadic a life. You know my people started from Virginia and Pennsylvania toward the West in 1776 or 1777 and none of us really ever stopped since and that includes me. So why should I stick

to one place or write about one place since I have never lived just in one place?

Rubin: Miss O'Connor, how about you?

O'Connor: Well I admit to being one. My own sense of place is quite unadjustable. I have a friend from Michigan who went to Germany and Japan and who wrote stories about Germans who sounded like Germans and about Japanese who sounded like Japanese. I know if I tried to write stories about credible Japanese they would all sound like Herman Talmadge.

Rubin: Does the State Department know about *this?* How about you, Mr. Jones?

Jones: I feel more or less like Miss O'Connor. No matter where I was or how long I might live there — although my attitude might change — I still have the feeling that everything I would write would be laid in the country that I feel the most communion with, that is the central Tennessee area, or at least a part of it. My imagination just feels at home there. Other places I have been have never tempted me to write about them so I think I am a Southern writer.

Rubin: Miss Gordon, how about you?

Gordon: I agree with him. I wouldn't think about writing anything about anybody from Princeton. They just don't seem to be important. That's dreadful but that's the way I feel. Your own country — that's the first thing you knew — that's important. I did write one story once that was laid in France but it was fifteen years after I lived there. But I think the thing about the Southern writer — I believe there is such a thing — and I think he is very interesting because he knows something that not all other writers in America today know. I feel that very strongly.

Porter: He usually knows who he is and where he is and what he is doing. Some people never know that in a long lifetime. But you see, I write out of my own background about what I know but I can't stay in one place. I write about a country maybe ten years after I have been in it. But that is a part of my experience too, and in a way it is an egotistic thing to do because it is what happened to me. I am writing about my own experience, really, out of my own background and tradition.

O'Connor in 1961

Rubin: What do you mean by a sense of place? Do you mean simply your geographical knowledge?

O'Connor: Not so much the geography. I think it is the idiom. Like Mrs. Tate said, people in Princeton don't talk like we do. And these sounds build up a life of their own in your senses.

Gordon: And place is very important too I think.

Jones: And I think it is a check in a way, too, of the honesty in your writing. Somehow in writing you have a way to check yourself by the kind of intimacy you have with your community and home.

Rubin: I don't think myself there is any doubt that there is such a thing as a Southern Writer — capital S, capital W — and that when you pick up a book, a novel, a short story, it doesn't take you very long before you have the feeling that this is

by a Southerner. I suppose there are Southern writers that fool you. I mean that you don't think are Southerners. I think that you could pick up some Erskine Caldwell for instance, particularly his later work, and you would never think that this man is from 50 miles from where Flannery O'Connor lives but at the same time —

Gordon: But he says things which are not so. For instance, I forget in what story he has the best hound dogs in the neighborhood down in the well and all of the men are just sitting around talking. None of the men are getting the dogs out of the well. That just couldn't happen. Simply couldn't happen. You can't trust him on detail.

Rubin: I like some of the things in the early Caldwell work.

Gordon: Oh, at times he's very amusing.

Rubin: I was thinking about this the other day. Let's take writers such as Caldwell and Faulkner or Eudora Welty. You think of them as being poles apart. But when you compare either of these writers, with, let's say, Dos Passos, you notice that the Caldwell people and the Welty people are more or less responsible for their own actions. In the stuff Caldwell wrote about 1930 or so he was trying to show, for example, that what was wrong with Jeeter Lester was society and the share cropping system and things like that, but when he wrote about Jeeter Lester you couldn't help feeling that the main reason Jeeter Lester was what he was was because he was Jeeter Lester. Whereas in a book like *USA* I don't think you had this feeling — I think you do accept the author's version of experience that society is what causes it. I think that the individual character somehow being responsible for his own actions is very typical of the Southern writers, and I think this is why we have produced very few naturalists as such. Do you think there is something to that?

Gordon: Why I think we have produced wonderful naturalists.

Rubin: Well, I was using the word in the literary sense.

Gordon: I just don't think you can use it that way. Every good story has naturalistic elements. Look at the sheep, cows and pigs in Miss Porter's story, "Holiday."

Rubin: Well, I was using the word in the philosophical sense of the environment-trapped hero and such as that.

Porter: Don't you think that came out a great deal in the communist doctrine of the locomotive of history — you know, rounding the sharp bend and everybody who doesn't go with it falls off of it — that history makes men instead of men making history, and it takes away the moral responsibility. The same thing can be said of that cry during the war that nobody could be blamed because we are all guilty until we stopped realizing that one has been guiltier perhaps than the other. This whole effort for the past one hundred years has been to remove the moral responsibility from the individual and make him blame his own human wickedness on his society, but he helps to make his society, you see, and he will not take his responsibility for his part in it.

Rubin: Well that's very interesting. I think right there is the difference between Caldwell and Dos Passos. Caldwell was consciously writing out of just that propagandistic position. He wanted to show that these people were victims. Yet because he was a Southerner, because he was writing about these people, they wouldn't behave. They became people instead of symbols.

Gordon: I would like to say one other thing about the Southern writer. I think we have some awfully good Southern writers and I believe one reason they are so good is that we are a conquered people and we know some things that a person who is not a Southern writer cannot envisage as happening. For him they never have happened. We know something he does not know.

Rubin: You know that this isn't necessarily the greatest nation that ever was or ever will be.

Gordon: Well, we know that a nation can go down in defeat. A great many men committed suicide after the Civil War and anyone I have ever heard of left the same note. He said, "This is a great deal worse than I thought it was going to be." Some of them eighty years old. Edmund Ruffin, for example.

Rubin: Tell me this now. Do you think that this is as true of the young Southerner growing up today as it was for the generations of Southerners who wrote the books in the 1920's and 30's?

Gordon: I think the most terrible thing I have ever read about the South was written by my young friend here [Miss O'Connor] — worse than anything Faulkner ever wrote. That scene where that lady, I forgot her name, but her husband is dead and now she gets in a tight place and she goes into the back hall behind some portieres. I can just see them, too. Some of my aunts had portieres. And she sits down at a roll-top desk which is very dusty and has yellow pieces of paper and things, and communes with his spirit. And his spirit says to her, "One man's meat is another man's poison" or something like "The devil you know is better than the devil you don't know." I think that's the most terrible thing that's ever been written about the South. It haunts me.

Rubin: Do you really think that this is changing?

Gordon: Well, I would say here is a young writer who has this terrible vision and such a vision could only come out of great concern.

Rubin: I wondered though. Nowadays I go to my own home town of Charleston, South Carolina, and it still looks the same downtown but you go outside of the city and everything about it looks just like, well I won't say Newark, New Jersey — it's not that bad — but let's say Philadelphia, and I just wondered if the same environment that operated even on Miss O'Connor will still have the emotional impact that it has had on Southern writing, whether the sense of defeat that we were just mentioning is still going to prevail. I think the notion that the South alone of the American sections knew that it is possible to lose a war, that it is possible to do your very best and still lose, is something that has been very true of Southern life, but I wonder whether in the post-Depression prosperity this is still going to be so? I have a feeling that it isn't.

Gordon: I do too.

Porter: It is happening already. There are some extremely interesting young writers. Walter Clemons — I don't want to speak of Texas writers altogether — there is one named George Garrett and there are several others — William Humphrey, Peter Taylor, among them, and I think they are probably the last ones who are going to feel the way they do. And I think these young people are probably the last because I don't see anyone coming after them at all and even they have changed a great deal because they don't have the tragic feeling about the South that we had, you know.

Gordon: One of Peter's best stories and he says it is his best story is "Bad Time." Do you know that story? It's a beaut.

Porter: Yes. But I don't see anybody else coming after and these are greatly changed. You think of young Clemons and then think of ones just before and they are changed. More of them are city people; they are writing about town life. And a kind of life that didn't really interest us, even though we were brought up partly in town. It was the country life that formed us.

Gordon: Peter is kind of a missing link. But he writes about country people going to town.

Jones: I noticed that in the collection of new Southern writings more than half were set in urban areas.

Rubin: You mention William Humphrey and to me he is symptomatic of this change. That book [*Home From The Hill*] to me started off extremely well and then suddenly nose-dived, and it nose-dived precisely at the point where the protagonist could no longer do the Faulknerian sort of thing, the hunt and things like that, and was just an adolescent in the city, and it seemed to me we just couldn't take the person seriously enough. Humphrey was still trying to write like Faulkner in a sense — the wrong kind of milieu in the wrong kind of place — and to me the book failed, and this is symptomatic.

Porter: He is an extremely good short story writer. He preceded that book with a number of very good short stories, I think, but he did want to write a successful book if he possibly could, you know, and he got the idea of what is success mixed up with what would be good sales and so he spoiled his book by trying to make it popular.

Rubin: He succeeded in that.

Porter: He did and good luck to him. He was my student for years and I thought he was going to turn out better than that, I must say.

Rubin: I have a feeling about the Southern writing in the last ten years, and that includes Miss O'Connor by the way — and I certainly don't mean it as an insult, Miss O'Connor. There is a kind of distance to the life you describe, a kind of esthetic distance, as if the people are far away from the writer, and this sometimes produces an extremely fine emotional effect. Take for example the difference in Styron's *Lie Down in Darkness* and Faulkner's *The Sound and The Fury*, where in both cases you have someone walking around in a northern city holding a time piece getting ready to take his or her life. Somehow or other the protagonist in the Faulkner novel is still a Yoknapatawpha County citizen. Somehow the protagonist in the Styron novel is away from that, she has left it, she couldn't go back to it if she wanted to or anywhere like that, and to me this feeling runs through so much of the most recent Southern writing. The Southern community is moving farther and farther away. You write about it and do it beautifully, but the distance is farther. You can't take it as seriously.

Jones: But don't you think in *Lie Down in Darkness* that as long as he is at home, Styron makes you feel closer to the character? I mean, that last business about the girl seems to be pretty bad.

Rubin: What I think about that book is that the book takes place in a Southern city, Port Warwick — something like Newport News, but I don't feel that the family in the book are essentially what they are because of the community at all. I think that is what Mr. Styron wanted them to be. He wanted Peyton Loftis to suffer because of several generations, etc., but I don't think she does. I think it is purely because of these particular people involved. Their little private things are apart from the community, and I don't get the same sense of community even when they are writing about things in Port Warwick that you would have in a Faulkner novel.

Porter: I have a feeling about Styron, you know the way he develops piles of agonies and horrors and that sort of thing, and I think it masks a lack of feeling. I think he has all the vocabulary of feeling and rhythm of feeling and knows he ought to feel but he does not. I can't read him with any patience at all. I want to say, "Take off those whiskers, come out of the bushes and fight fair."

Rubin: I find him a very provocative writer myself.

Porter: Well, you remember the story about the man and the two people who come to play cards, I think this was in Rome. They are terrible card cheats and everybody gets frightfully drunk and he winds up perfectly senselessly without any clothes on, robbed and beaten, in a horribly filthy hotel and his wife has to come and get him and you say — now let me see, what was it about? What did it mean? It means absolutely nothing. One feels, well, the police just should have put this one in jail until he sobered up. And such a thing is not interesting for the simple reason that the man to whom it happened is of no interest. That is my quarrel with him, and it is a quarrel, too.

Rubin: If there is anything to this feeling of distance, I have the feeling that the Southern writer now isn't taking the things that go on in the community with the same kind of importance. He takes it with equal importance, but with a different kind of importance than, let's say, Faulkner did. Take someone like Sutpen in Faulkner, or Colonel Sartoris. What they did seemed to Faulkner to be very logical and important, even though it may be mad, but at the same time he wasn't writing about it in the sense that he thought he was handling a sort of primitive, or something like that.

Jones: Well, in that kind of community I guess that when someone jumps in the water you feel the ripple, but now it is hard to feel it.

Porter: I think Styron's trouble may be he really is alienated, you know, from that place and he can't get back home himself. Thomas Wolfe said, "You can't go home again," and I said "Nonsense, that is the only place you can go. You go there all the time."

Rubin: He certainly can't write about Southerners in the sense that they are importantly in the South acting on Southern concerns. His last one takes place in Italy.

Porter: It's curious. He may be able to do it. He has been living there for years. But I don't know what is happening to him.

Rubin: Miss O'Connor, I know this is a question that writers don't think of and only literary critics like myself think of and ask, but do you think that the Southern community you see, that your relationship to it, is different from the way that Eudora Welty or Faulkner looks at the Southern community?

O'Connor: Well, I don't know how either Eudora Welty or Faulkner looks at it. I only know how I look at it and I don't feel that I am writing about the community at all. I feel that I am taking things in the community that I can show the whole western world, the whole edition of the present generation of people, of what I can use of the Southern situation.

Rubin: I surely agree with that.

Porter: You made that pretty clear yesterday. You know that was one of the things you talked about. It was most interesting.

O'Connor: You know, people say that Southern life is not the way you picture it. Well, Lord help us, let's hope not.

Rubin: Well, I think that this is one of the tremendous appeals that Southern writing has had — the universality of its creative materials — but to me there has been some relation between this universality and the particularity with which it is done. You couldn't have one without the other. But I think the fact that you are all writing about the South in the sense that this is the way the people talk, etc., somehow does make possible a meaningful, broader reading that people give it.

Jones: It does give you something to check yourself against.

Rubin: I think that is a very good notion. It is the thorough grounding in actuality.

O'Connor: Well, the South is not the Bible Belt for nothing.

Porter: Someone said that the resemblance of the real Southerner to the Frenchman was that we have no organized, impersonal abstract murder. That is, a good Southerner doesn't kill anybody he doesn't know.

Rubin: I wonder if even that isn't changing. Speaking of the Bible belt, I think that it has more than one relevance to what we are dealing with. I think it also involves this question of language. I think that Southerners do and did read the Bible a great deal and somehow, more in the King James Bible, this rolling feeling for language comes through.

Gordon: They read a lot of Cicero, too.

O'Connor: More than the language it seems to me it is simply the concrete, the business of being a story teller. I have Boston cousins and when they come South they discuss problems, they don't tell stories. We tell stories.

Rubin: Well look now, how about our audience? I am sure that our panel will be glad to parry any questions you would like to throw at them. Doesn't someone have a question or two to ask?

Question: Would someone care to comment on the great number of old people and children in Southern writing?

Porter: Well, they are very much there.

Gordon: How many children in that family you were reading about last night?

Porter: Well, there were eight under the age of ten — counting one not yet born — belonging to two women. That isn't bad, is it? And I have known them to do better than that. And with the old people who always seem to live forever and everybody always lived in the same house, all the generations. It was one way of getting acquainted with the generations. We simply would have old people and we would have children in the house together, and they were important, both ends of the line. It was really the ones in mid-life who took the gaff, didn't they? Because they had the young on one side and the old on the other.

Rubin: They were too young to be tolerated and not old enough to be characters.

Porter: A friend of mine said the other day, "Now there are only three degrees of age — young, mature and remarkable."

Question: Miss O'Connor, you said yesterday that the South was Christ-haunted instead of Christ-centered. I don't quite understand this and how it effects [*sic*] our Southern literature. Would you please explain this?

O'Connor: I shouldn't have said that, should I? Well, as I said, the South didn't seem to me as a writer to be Christ-centered. I don't think anyone would object to that at all. I think all you would have to do is to read the newspapers to agree with me, but I said that we seemed to me to be Christ-haunted and that ghosts cast strange shadows, very fierce shadows, particularly in our literature. It is hard to explain a flat statement like that. I would hate to talk off the top of my head on a subject like that. I think it is a subject that a book could be written about but it would take me ten or twelve years to do it.

Gordon: When I was young, old gentlemen sat under the trees reading. That was all they did all of the time, and shall we call it the movement which is sometimes called The Death of God, that controversy that Hegel the Philosopher had with Heine the Poet. There was quite a lot of talk about the death of God, but God crossed the border, and I think that is what you are talking about. It's cast its shadow.

O'Connor: It's gone underneath and come out in distorted forms.

Question: I would like particularly Miss Porter to comment on religious symbolism in her work — if you think there is any and how you go about it in your work.

Porter: Symbolism happens of its own self and it comes out of something so deep in your own consciousness and your own experience that I don't think that most writers are at all conscious of their use of symbols. I never am until I see them. They come of themselves because they belong to me and have meaning to me, but they come of themselves. I have no way of explaining them but I have a great deal of religious symbolism in my stories because I have a very deep sense of religion and also I have a religious training. And I suppose you don't invent symbolism. You don't say, "I am going to have the flowering Judas tree stand for betrayal," but, of course, it does.

O'Connor: I would second everything Miss Porter says. I really didn't know what a symbol was until I started reading about them. It seemed I was going to have to know about them if I was going to be a respectable literary person. Now I have the notion that a symbol is sort of like the engine in a story and I usually discover as I write something in the story that is taking on more and more meaning so that as I go along, before long, that something is turning or working the story.

Rubin: Do you ever have to try to stop yourselves from thinking about your work in terms of symbols as you are working?
O'Connor: I wouldn't say so.

Porter: No. May I tell this very famous little story about Mary McCarthy and symbols. Well, she was in a college and she had a writers' class and there was a young person who wrote her a story and she said, "You have done a very nice piece of work. You are on the right road, now go on to something else." And the young person said, "But my teacher read this and said, 'Well all right, but now we have to go back and put in the symbols.' "

Rubin: How about you, Mr. Jones?

Jones: Am I a symbol man? Well, I don't think so. The story is the thing after all and I don't see how a writer can think about anything but the story. The story has got to carry him. I think it is bound to occur to you finally that something you have come across — maybe in the middle of coming across it it might occur to you — that this has certain symbolic value and maybe you would to a certain extent elaborate it in terms of this realization, but I don't think it is a plan of any kind where you say I am heading for a symbol and when I get there I am going to do so and so to it. It just comes out of the context. Of course, writing is full of symbols. Nearly everything is a symbol of some kind but some of them expand for you accidentally.

O'Connor: So many students approach a story as if it were a problem in algebra: find X and when they find X they can dismiss the rest of it.
Porter: Well and then another thing, everything can be used as a symbol. Take two of the most innocent and charming sounding, for example, just in western Christianity, let us say the dove and the rose. Well, the dove begins by being a symbol of sensuality, it is the bird of Venus, you know, and then it goes on through the whole range of every kind of thing until it becomes the Holy Ghost. It's the same way with the rose which begins as a female sexual symbol and ends as the rose of fire in

Highest Heaven. So you see the symbol would have the meaning of its context. I hope that makes sense.

Question: Is tradition an important part of contemporary Southern writing?

Rubin: What about you, Miss Gordon, do you have a tradition you go back to when you are writing? You told me today that you are writing an historical novel.

Gordon: All novels are historical. I don't think I told you I was writing an historical novel. I said it went back to 1532.

Rubin: Well, that sounds pretty historical.

Gordon: The word has become so debased. I wrote two novels, one in Civil War times and one in pioneer times, but people didn't know how to read them. I wouldn't like to be accused of writing what is known as an historical novel.

Rubin: Well, instead of saying tradition, do you think Southerners do things in certain ways because that is the way they have always been done rather than thinking about it at all, and if so, is this the way you see the Southerner in what you write?

Gordon: Well, I don't see it that way. I sit there or I walk around or I wash dishes until I see these people doing something and hear them and then I record it as best I can.

Rubin: It is very hard to get people to talk in terms of these abstractions because I don't think anyone uses tradition with a capital T. And yet there is a lot of tradition in what they do.

Question: I meant white columns, magnolias, worship of family — tradition in this sense.

Gordon: Well, after the Civil War there was a school of literature foisted on us by Northern publishers. They demanded moonlight and magnolias and a lot of people furnished it to them and that idea stuck in peoples' heads ever since. If a Southerner writes a novel now, whoever is reviewing for the *New York Times* will make a point of saying it isn't moonlight and magnolias. It's all nonsense. We are a conquered nation and abominably treated and we paid the greatest tribute perhaps ever paid by any conquered nation. Our history was miswritten and our children were taught lies and therefore the Northerners could not bear the image of us as we were and therefore the Northern publishers would publish only novels full of white columns and magnolias.

Porter: But this very place right this minute is absolutely filled to the chin with moonlight and magnolias. All you have to do is look outside.

Rubin: I think the position of that particular role of moonlight and magnolias tradition in Southern literature is very true. In the case of someone like George Washington Cable, for example. He tried to write one book without it and it was a flop. Nobody paid any attention to it so he went back and wrote the flowery sort of war romances. This was the only thing he could write. I must say that this ain't so no more, and I think it has been people like Miss Porter who ended all that. Many people read their books for what the books *say,* instead of what the people *thought* they should say. I think that the tremendous importance of Southern literature in our own time represents a breaking away from the stereotype. Writers who have done this, having published their first books in the 20's and 30's, have performed a great service for future generations of Southern writers. Not that that was what you were trying to do at the time, but I think the young ones are going to be eternally grateful for it.

O'Connor: Walker Percy wrote somewhere that his generation of Southerners had no more interest in the Civil War than in the Boer War. I think that is probably quite true.

Rubin: I think there is something to that and yet I heard many an argument in the Army during the last war. You get one or two Southerners in a barracks with a bunch of Northerners and maybe the Southerners were just kidding but let anyone say anything too outrageous and the fight was on.

Jones: That's true. They'll still fight but they don't know what they are talking about. They have no real information and so it is more a matter of just being a personal insult.

Question: Do you think that the South is being exploited now for its immediate fictional gains, let's say commercial gain, etc., is it too popular? Is it too much *Southern* writing?

O'Connor: I don't know any Southern writers who are making a big killing except Faulkner, you know. We are all just limping along.

Rubin: I think when you have a group of very fine writers who approach a group of people and subjects in a certain way it is then easier to imitate that than to do something on your own. And therefore a lot of second rate writers will come along and imitate it, and I know I see the publisher announcement sheets every fall. On one page of almost all announcement sheets from every publishing house there is announced a new Southern writer and most of them are never announced more than once. But I do feel very definitely there is a great deal of writing about the South, because these people here have shown how it can be done, and therefore someone is not going to do something on his or her own when this is the best lead to follow.

Question: I would like to know if your writing is strictly for a Southern reading audience or if you have in mind any reading audience.

O'Connor: The *London Times Literary Supplement* had an issue on Southern writing once and they said that Southerners only wrote books, they didn't read them.

Porter: Well, that's just the opposite from the old South because they only read them, they never wrote them. At least before The War Between the States writing was not really a gentleman's occupation except as privately. He wrote letters, memoirs, and maybe essays. But they all had libraries and collections of books.

Rubin: The South has long had the reputation for being the worst market for books in the U.S., per capita, among the publishers. I think any Southern writer who wrote primarily for Southerners would have to write a syndicated column for a newspaper or he would starve to death. I don't really think that these people think in terms of who is going to read what they are going to write, unless I am mistaken.

Jones: I was just going to say that I don't know who I write for but it seems to me that I have a person or two who is my audience rather than any group. But I think about one person and perhaps the standards that I absorbed from that person tends to be my audience rather than any group. I hope that a group will buy a book but I don't think I direct a book at any large group of people.

Rubin: John Bishop wrote that he wrote his books to be read by Edmund Wilson and Allen Tate.

Gordon: But you see he never wrote but one novel. Well, I know I have one reader, a Frenchman. He is the only person I know of who understands my work and I think that is why I think about him but I don't think I would under other circumstances. He knows a great deal about techniques of fiction and, perhaps this is a little off the subject, but people very much dislike any revolution in technique. If an author uses a technique that has never been used before, everybody will dislike it. And there is no record of any literary critic ever recognizing an innovation in technique. It has never happened. It is always recognized by another artist. So I have gotten to the point that I write for the person who will know what I am doing.

Question: Mr. Jones, you mentioned this afternoon that Southern writers have a stronger than usual sense of guilt and natural depravity. If this is so, what means of redemption do you see as possible?

Jones: You asked me a very complex question. I don't know whether I can answer the whole thing or not. You said that Southern writers have a sense of natural depravity. Do I think they do? Well, I do have the feeling that if it is not still, it certainly was the case with the first important Southern writers in that there was very little question about the sense of man's guilt. There was a consciousness of that and a perfect willingness to accept it and I think that is very notable in all the best Southern writers of the last generation. I don't know why that should particularly be the case with Southern writers except partly because, as I said, of Southern Fundamentalism which has kept that fact before them. And perhaps the Civil War had something to do with it. Not that I feel that the Southerners felt guilty about the Civil War but perhaps even though we felt we were right before the war, nevertheless we were defeated and didn't achieve all we thought we could even though we thought we were right and something must be wrong. I am sure there would be a great many other reasons that some-

one else could elaborate on. Man is of a less than perfect nature.

Porter: I am sure that we are all naturally depraved but we are all naturally redeemable, too. The idea, Calvin really put it into action, that God somehow rewarded spiritual virtue with material things, which is to say that if you were living right God would reward you with health and money, a good reputation, or the goods of this world is to me an appalling doctrine. I happen to have a faith that says the opposite, you see, that goods of this world have nothing to do with your spiritual good and your standing with God and I think that this attitude of the South, when you say they felt that if they had been right God would not have permitted them to lose that war is dreadful, you know. I think it is a terrible fallacy and a terrible mistaken way to feel because some very good people have had the worst times in this world and have lost all their wars, don't you know, have lost everything altogether. Defeat in this world is no disgrace and that is what they cannot understand. If you really fought well and fought for the right thing.

Rubin: That is a very good point. You know, I think it is about time we finished. I would like to question you a bit on that Calvin business if it weren't. I think we had better say one thing. We have been talking about a number of characteristics and we say, now *this* is Southern, and *this* Southern, and then somebody comes along and says, well don't you think that New England writers, or Western writers, have a notion about the natural depravity of man? Is this something that was invented in the South? I think the answer would be is that there are a number of qualities that people assign to Southern writing and say, "This is true of Southern writing." It isn't the uniqueness of the qualities, but I would say the combination of a certain number of qualities at one time, which has made this achievement possible and I think that whatever the achievement is, it has been a considerable thing; and I, myself, am not particularly pessimistic about it continuing, what with the people seated at the table with me tonight. We have hashed over the problems of writers and writing in the South for about an hour now and tried to answer some questions, and I think we'll quit. I would like to say on behalf of the panel what a wonderful time we have had and how grateful we are to Wesleyan College and to everybody for coming.

ARTICLE:

James F. Farnham, "The Grotesque in Flannery O'Connor," *America*, 105 (13 May 1961): 277, 280–281.

While many reviewers misinterpreted O'Connor's fiction because they lacked knowledge about her religious views, this article in a Roman Catholic periodical accurately explains the connection between her theology and her fiction, focusing on her use of the grotesque and her understanding of the doctrine of grace.

One cannot skip to the lovely dawn of Easter morning without first having passed through Good Friday; the Resurrection itself is meaningless except as the culmination of the Passion. Those are the ever present themes that run through Flannery O'Connor's writing.

Had William Esty been thinking of this when he spoke of Miss O'Connor in the *Commonweal* (March 7, 1958), he might have found less validity in his reference to the "Paul Bowles-Flannery O'Connor cult of the Gratuitous Grotesque." Mr. Esty said of Miss O'Connor's grotesque characters and situations that "these overingenious horrifics are presumably meant to speak to us of the Essential Nature of Our Time, but when the very real and cruel grotesquerie of our world is converted into clever gimmicks for *Partisan Review*, we may be forgiven for reacting with the self-same disgust as the little old lady from Dubuque." Mr. Esty presumes rightly that Miss O'Connor is speaking to us of the Essential Nature of Our Time. Let us look at what the young lady from Milledgeville, Georgia, has said on the subject and then into her works.

First of all, Miss O'Connor is an artist, and Catholicism is one of her "circumstances," just as her living in the South is. This does not mean that her religion is a mere circumstantial accident, but it does mean that her religion is not the cause of, nor the cause for, the externalization of her vision as a Christian artist. The ultimate reason for her use of the grotesque is simply that this is the aspect of reality which her artistic talent is best able to produce. In a letter to the author she once said:

> Essentially the reason my characters are grotesque is because it is the nature of my talent to make them so. To some extent, the writer can choose his subject; but he can never choose what he is able to make live. It is characters like The Misfit and the Bible salesman that I can make live.

Miss O'Connor writes, then, of the ugly simply because she can give life to the ugly. This is the ultimate explanation, for we are not called upon to concern ourselves with the ways and means by which talents are allotted.

Of course, given this talent for the grotesque, there is the question of what Miss O'Connor is to do with it, what meaning she gets out of it or puts into it. She does not like the sentimentalism of much contemporary Christian art; and, while never allowing her artistic talents merely to be turned to antisentimentalistic propaganda, she attempts to combat sentimentalism, her chief tool being the use of the grotesque. She sees modern man as an often grotesque figure, a caricature of his true self, and in showing what man is she is showing what he could be. It seems to be Miss O'Connor's intention never to let us think of man's salvation unless we are aware — painfully at times — of what the Passion was intended to redeem.

The central theme found in Flannery O'Connor's writing is the redemption of man; but, since her talent inclines her toward the portrayal of sin, she shows the effects of the redemption (i.e., grace) in a negative manner. She reflects the beauty of virtue by showing the ugliness of its absence. In her essay on "The Fiction Writer and His Country" she writes:

> My own feeling is that writers who see by the light of their Christian faith will have, in these times, the sharpest eyes for the grotesque, for the perverse and for the unacceptable. . . . Redemption is meaningless unless there is cause for it in the actual life we live.

If Miss O'Connor could believe that her audience is one which thinks within the basic Christian rationale, she would find it unnecessary to dwell upon the deformation of humanity. But, since she writes for an audience which she thinks is to a great extent blind to grace, she feels that she must show them how bad *they* are, not simply how good somebody else is. When you cannot assume, she says in "The Fiction Writer and His Country," that your audience is aware of grace, "you have to make your vision apparent by shock — to the hard of hearing you shout, and for the almost blind you draw large and startling figures." Flannery O'Connor does not shout of the ugliness of man deformed by sin because of any gratuitous pleasure involved in her writing process. Rather, she is a Christian writer acutely aware of grace, a writer whose talents impel her to the portrayal of a contemporary society deformed by its disavowal of grace.

This is her esthetic of the physically and spiritually ugly. She sees society very much aware of its abnegation of grace; indeed, it is their realization of loss which makes her characters so awful. They are not dumb creatures plodding ahead in stolid unknowing. For the most part, they are aware that there is some great void in their existences. The Misfit, for example, in "A Good Man Is Hard To Find," as he prepares to murder a family just starting on its vacation, says to the grandmother:

> Jesus thrown everything off balance. It was the same with Him as with me, except He hadn't committed any crime and they could prove I had committed one because they had the papers on me. He thrown everything off balance. If He did what He said, then it's nothing for you to do but throw away everything and follow Him, and if He didn't, then it's nothing for you to do but enjoy the few minutes you got left the best way you can — by killing somebody or burning down his house or doing some other meanness to him. No pleasure but meanness.

Certainly, Christ's Passion has influenced this man, but he has perverted the grace. Here is humanity in its suffering, but the suffering is without meaning. "I call myself The Misfit . . . because I can't make what all I done wrong fit what all I gone through in punishment." The redemption of man is perverted, and without grace man finds suffering and injustice maddeningly incomprehensible. Miss O'Connor's most evil characters are acutely aware of Christ, making their pain more intense by their blasphemy of Him.

Thus it is with the Bible salesman in "Good Country People." While all along the cynical young woman named Hulga (her real name was "Joy," but she relished the cacophony of "Hulga") thought that she was leading the Bible salesman to his seduction in the barn, he was in fact intent upon stealing her artificial leg. After he has revealed to her that his suitcase contains not only Bibles which he sells, but dirty playing cards, contraceptives and whisky as well, her complacent cynicism collapses. "Aren't you just good country people?" she murmurs. "Yeah," he sneers, "but it ain't held me back none." "You're a perfect Christian," she hisses. To which he replies in a lofty and indignant tone, "I hope you don't think . . . I believe in that crap! I been believing in nothing ever since I was born!"

Here, again, Miss O'Connor does not portray people who have never been touched by grace. They are painfully aware of grace, but their lives are focused upon its perversion. The salesman under the guise of spreading the Word of God is actually disbursing evil.

Tom T. Shiflet in "The Life You Save May Be Your Own" is constantly appalled by the evil men do. "Nothing is like it used to be," he says. "The world is almost rotten." After marrying the idiot daughter of the farm woman for whom he works so that he can get her old Ford, he leaves his bride asleep in a roadside restaurant. Later, a young hitchhiker, in response to Shiflet's sentimental reference to his sweet old mother, replies that "My old woman is a flea bag and yours is a stinking polecat!" Shiflet is horrified by the evil within the human heart and he races into Mobile full of righteous anger, invoking God to "Break forth and wash the slime from the earth." This character, like most in Miss O'Connor's grotesque gallery of humanity, has "a moral intelligence," so he says, but so perverted is it that grace has given way to evil. Miss O'Connor's characters are not gratuitously grotesque; they are grotesque because she sees reality without grace as grotesque.

If such people as The Misfit, the Bible salesman and Tom T. Shiflet are images of graceless humanity, Hazel Motes in Miss O'Connor's first novel, *Wise Blood*, is an almost metaphysical perversion of the Saviour. Haze envisions himself as a new redeemer:

> I preach the Church Without Christ. I'm member and preacher to that church where the blind don't see and the lame don't walk and what's dead stays that way. Ask me about that church and I'll tell you it's the church that the blood of Jesus don't foul with redemption. . . .
>
> I'm going to preach it to whoever'll listen at whatever place. I'm going to preach there was no fall because there was nothing to fall from, and no redemption because there was no fall, and no judgment because there wasn't the first two. Nothing matters but that Jesus was a liar.

Haze cannot ignore redemption and cannot escape it. His only salvation lies in a new dispensation of the utter perversion of grace. His grandfather used to tell him that "he had been redeemed and Jesus wasn't going to leave him ever. Jesus would never let him forget he was redeemed." Haze had never sought redemption, but redemption had always hounded him. Throughout his life he has been abnormally aware of original sin. As a boy, he had put small stones in his shoes, laced them up very tightly, and walked through the woods to expiate for his sense of inherited guilt. Near the end of his public life after he had blinded himself with lime to confess his nihilistic religion of the denial of Christ and of grace, his landlady discovered in his shoes gravel, broken glass and pieces of small stone. In explanation he merely answered: "To pay."

Out of context these descriptions of Hazel Motes might seem morbid; but in context they present a figure of almost heroically tragic proportions, a figure reminiscent of Milton's Satan, a Christ of Evil. Consumed by evil as he is, Haze like Satan cannot ignore nor even long be away from Christ. His suffering is the realization of loss, of man's fall. So darkened is his spirit by the chaos of his soul that grace cannot penetrate it, and he plunges deeper into darkness. This, then, is Flannery O'Connor's theme, the fall of man brought up to date.

As Hazel Motes is a graceless Christ, so Francis Marion Tarwater of her recent novel, *The Violent Bear It Away,* is a perverted prophet of Old Testament stature. "The boy was very proud that he had been born in a wreck. He had always felt that it set him apart . . . that the plan of God for him was special." His face "expressed the depth of human perversity, the deadly sin of rejecting defiantly one's obvious good." His first mission was to baptize his cousin, and this he did by drowning the idiot child. We leave him at the end of the book with his public career as prophet before him. "His singed eyes . . . seemed already to envision the fate that awaited him, but he moved steadily on, his face set toward the dark city, where the children of God lay sleeping."

It is ironic that in one of the very few instances ("The River") where one can see grace to be in any way efficacious, it is in a child: in Harry Ashfield who renamed himself "Bevel" after the country preacher who baptized him at a revival meeting. The preacher had said: "You'll be washed in the river of suffering, son, and you'll go by the deep river of life." Bevel accepted the words literally and arose one morning, before his hungover parents were up, and left home to re-enter the river. He found it difficult at first to enter under the water, but

the waiting current caught him like a long gentle hand and pulled him swiftly forward and down. For

an instant he was overcome with surprise; then since he was moving quickly and he knew that he was getting somewhere, all his fury and his fear left him.

Miss O'Connor allows this child, who took the words of redemption literally, to find salvation. Such characters as Hazel Motes, the Bible salesman, The Misfit, Tom T. Shiflet and Marion Tarwater are so warped by their disavowal of grace that she cannot conceive of their being saved. Only in the ironically and pathetically contradictory sense of a redemption in evil can they be said to find self-realization or salvation.

In "The Fiction Writer and His Country," Miss O'Connor quotes Cyril of Jerusalem to his catechumens: "The dragon sits by the side of the road, watching those who pass. Beware lest he devour you." She comments that "It is of this mysterious passage past him, or into his jaws, that stories of any depth will always be concerned to tell." Much of the world's literature is concerned with man's relation to sin and evil. This is Flannery O'Connor's concern. Her particular talent is externalized by giving life to the grotesquerie of evil, but hers is not the "cult of the Gratuitous Grotesque." One word can make a great difference. Grotesque she is, but certainly not gratuitously grotesque.

INTERVIEW:
Joel Wells, "Off the Cuff," *Critic,* 21 (August–September 1962): 4–5, 71–72; in *Conversations with Flannery O'Connor,* pp. 85–90.

Spring 1962 was a busy time for O'Connor, who visited several college campuses. In this interview conducted between two speaking engagements in May, she discussed reviewers' tendencies to be confused by her fiction.

Early this May, one of my favorite writers of fiction, Flannery O'Connor, came north from her home near Milledgeville, Georgia, for a three-day stay at Rosary College in Chicago's suburb of River Forest. In spite of being on crutches (for the past six years due to an affliction called disseminated lupus) she travels frequently and alone. She had already been to a conference at Converse and to North Carolina State University before taking up the invitation to Rosary where she presided at five classes, gave an hour's talk to the entire student body and was the featured attraction at a tea.

Though understandably a little done in, she agreed to talk to me while I drove her from Rosary to South Bend, where she was due to speak at Notre Dame on "The Catholic Writer in the Protestant South." I met her at one o'clock on an unseasonably warm day and, after making our farewells to a Rosary delegation obviously sorry to yield her up, we got underway. Speaking in a soft and, to Chicago-hardened ears, definitely drawling voice, she said that the Rosary students had amazed her with their close knowledge of her work, sometimes to the point of embarrassing her by citing things which roosted on the very edge of her own memory. Her only complaint was the temperature of the buildings, which struck her as having hovered just above freezing most of the time. She admitted that this was probably psychological on her part since she had once come to Chicago in the dead cold of winter and had never fully recovered from the experience. About her forthcoming talk at Notre Dame she expressed doubts as to having much of a crowd since she understood she was going on in direct and simultaneous competition with the Junior Prom.

I asked her if she had any qualms about driving with an unknown quantity of roadsmanship such as I must surely represent to her. She said with candor (Miss O'Connor is a candid person: to a question as to what she thought of Tennessee Williams she replied, "Not much"; and her opinion of *To Kill a Mockingbird* is that "it's a wonderful children's book") that she was willing to risk almost anything as opposed to lurching about on a train with her crutches or the strong possibility of having to fly the ninety miles to South Bend in a "small plane," a species of aircraft which she identified with more emotion than precision as any that had to be boarded "near the tail on rickety tin steps." In the same spirit, I told her that I had illogical but real misgivings about driving with her since so many terrible things seem always to happen to people in her stories while they are out driving. She assured me that such things happen only in the South.

In the middle lane of Chicago's teeming Congress Street Expressway, flanked and bracketed by enormous and odoriferous diesel trucks, Miss O'Connor may well have upgraded sharply her opinion of small planes, but she showed no visible signs of distress. Since I was not going to be able to hear her talk at Notre Dame (for which, as it turned out, a good crowd of non-dancers did appear), I asked her whether she felt that being a Catholic writer in the South made her task as a novelist more difficult.

Some Northerners, for instance, seem to have a hard time believing that characters such as those with which she peoples her stories could possibly exist — the whole burden of their creation must rest on her talents without any helpful assistance from real-life prototypes. Then there is the additional obstacle that Northerners in general, and Catholics in particular, don't seem to look at life and religion in the biblical light that colors so much of Southern fiction. Did this leave her in a predicament — somewhat documented by sales figures — of facing heavy odds against wide popular understanding?

This was quite a woolly question, but Miss O'Connor who is not only candid but graciously tolerant, took it at more than face value. The people she writes about, she said, are real. Not in the literal sense of being copies from life, but as types which still exist in the South, not evident to tourists perhaps, but there all the same. They are real, and if they are people who deal with life on more fundamental, even more violent terms than most of us, this doesn't make them mythical monsters.

As for the lack of biblical understanding, she said: "The fact that Catholics don't see religion through the Bible is a deficiency in Catholics. And I don't think the novelist can discard the instruments he has to plumb meaning just because Catholics aren't used to them. You don't write only for now. The biblical revival is going to mean a great deal to Catholic fiction in the future. Maybe in fifty years, or a hundred, Catholics will be reading the Bible the way they should have been reading it all along. I can wait that long to have my fiction understood. The Bible is what we share with all Christians, and the Old Testament we share with all Jews. This is sacred history and our mythic background. If we are going to discard this we had better quit writing at all. The fact that the South is the Bible Belt is in great measure responsible for its literary preeminence now. The Catholic novelist can learn a great deal from the Protestant South."

I cited one of her college talks in which she had said "for the modern reader, moral distinctions are usually blurred in hazes of compassion; there are not enough common beliefs to make this a fit age for allegory; and as for anagogical realities, they either don't exist at all for the general reader or are taken by him to be knowable by sensation." Did she think that this was the basic problem confronting the Christian novelist? Could this eventually be so limiting that such a

O'Connor in 1962

writer will have to be content with writing only for a few?

"One of the Christian novelist's basic problems is that he is trying to get the Christian vision across to an audience to whom it is meaningless," Miss O'Connor agreed. "Nevertheless, he can't write only for a select few. His work will have to have value on the dramatic level, the level of truth recognizable by anybody. The fact that many people can't see anything Christian about my novel doesn't interfere with many of them seeing it as a novel which does not falsify reality."

I wondered if she was generally pleased with the critical reception given her most recent novel — *The Violent Bear It Away* — not in a vain sense, but simply with regard to the measure of understanding she saw evidenced. I mentioned Orville Prescott's review for the New York *Times*

in which he had said that while her talent for fiction was "so great as to be almost overwhelming," he had been unable to see any evidence of the Christian relationships she intended to convey, according to her own intentions set down in an article he had read in a symposium called *The Living Novel*, edited by Granville Hicks.

Miss O'Connor felt that this was a good example of what we had just been talking about. "If Mr. Prescott hadn't read that article I wrote for Granville Hicks he wouldn't have been looking so hard for relationships and would have taken it just as a novel," she said. "There were enough Catholic reviews which shared my own interpretation of it for me to feel that I succeeded well enough in doing what I intended to do." She mentioned one review in particular which appeared in the 1962 issue of an annual called *Kansas Maga-*

zine. "It was written by a Jesuit Scholastic, Robert McCown, whom I had never met or corresponded with beforehand. But he seemed to understand everything I did about the book."

What about those reviews which seemed to imply that she had tried to fit too great a burden of meaning to her novel, been too allegorical, too much and too obviously the careful builder? There were a few who came close to saying that she had tried too hard — that in her short stories she was the pure artist at work but in her novels, a great artist still, but one more obviously on the moral make. Had she consciously set out to get a bigger message across in the novels?

"Message," said Miss O'Connor, still being candid, "is a bad word. It took me seven years to write *The Violent Bear It Away* and I hope there's more to it than a short story. As for its being too allegorical and all the rest, I can't agree. I wanted to get across the fact that the great Uncle (Old Tarwater) is the Christian — a sort of crypto-Catholic — and that the school teacher (Rayber) is the typical modern man. The boy (young Tarwater) has to choose which one, which way, he wants to follow. It's a matter of vocation."

I asked if she would amplify something she had said to the effect that there are ages when it is possible to woo the reader and others when something more drastic is necessary. Did she deliberately set out to be more drastic in her work?

"I don't consciously set out to be more drastic," she said, "but this happens automatically. If I write a novel in which the central action is a baptism, I know that for the larger percentage of my readers, baptism is a meaningless rite; therefore I have to imbue this action with an awe and terror which will suggest its awful mystery. I have to distort the look of the thing in order to represent as I see them both the mystery and the fact."

Since there is (to my mind) a great deal of very rich humor in almost everything Miss O'Connor has written (among her stories she names as favorite a wryly comic little masterpiece called "The Artificial Nigger"), and also an evident and deep concern with religious and prophetic values, I was interested in getting her reaction to something that Evelyn Waugh had once said. In an interview recorded in Harvey Breit's *The Writer Observed,* Mr. Waugh talked about people — Protestants in particular — who thought that a religious subject could never be treated with humor. He felt that most young contemporary writers had lost all their delight in the material, that they wrote believing they had some sort of mes-

sage to deliver from their souls. He stated his own belief that words should be an intense pleasure in themselves, just as leather is to a shoemaker. People who didn't take that pleasure from writing, Mr. Waugh suggested, should become philosophers instead. And in any case, writers had no right to be like Lawrence or Hemingway, thinking they were prophets.

"I agree with Mr. Waugh that words should be an intense pleasure," said Miss O'Connor, "but I don't see the connection between this and his rejection of a prophetic function for the writer. It seems to me that prophetic insight is a quality of the imagination and that Waugh is as prophetic in this sense as the next one. There is the prophetic sense of 'seeing through' reality and there is also the prophetic function of recalling people to known but ignored truths. Certainly none of this precludes comedy — or the pleasure taken in producing it."

I had already heard from Sister Mary Bryan, Miss O'Connor's sponsor at Rosary College, that she had responded to questions as to what she intended to do when she got home by saying, "An awful lot of porch-settin'." She has no new novel underway, much as she wished she had. A long short story, amounting almost to a novella, was the most recent thing she had done and it would appear in the Summer issue of *The Sewanee Review.* She feels that her short stories don't seem to get any better but she intends to keep on writing them until another novel takes shape in her mind. She thinks it takes time to write good fiction, and knows it takes her a long time. Besides the two novels (her first was *Wise Blood* which will be brought out in a new edition this fall by Farrar, Straus & Cudahy) she has produced a total of seventeen short stories, not counting a few she chooses to forget.

I wondered if she had ever considered writing a play, or letting someone adapt any of her work for the stage or movies. She didn't think she would ever write a play herself, mainly because she wouldn't know how to go about it. One man has repeatedly expressed interest in producing a movie of her story "The River" but seems just as repeatedly hamstrung by lack of money. The Schlitz Playhouse presented a television adaption of another story, "The Life You Save May Be Your Own," in which an itinerant no-good agreed to marry a widow's idiot daughter to gain title to her car. He does, but after driving a hundred miles or so, abandons the girl in a roadside diner.

"I didn't recognize the television version," said Miss O'Connor, "Gene Kelly played Mr. Shiftlet and for the idiot daughter they got some young actress who had just been voted one of the ten most beautiful women in the world, and they changed the ending just a bit by having Shiftlet suddenly get a conscience and come back for the girl."

It was at this point that we reached the toll road exit for South Bend and turned off to drive along the road which separates the Notre Dame campus from St. Mary's College, where Miss O'Connor would be returning at commencement time to receive an honorary Doctor of Letters degree.

All in all, she admitted, thanking me for the ride, traveling with me had turned out to be better than in a small plane — though she probably wouldn't have had to talk so much on the plane.

As Truman Capote said of her, "She has some fine moments, that girl!"

LECTURE:

Flannery O'Connor, "The Catholic Novelist in the Protestant South," in her *Mystery and Manners: Occasional Prose,* edited by Sally and Robert Fitzgerald (New York: Farrar, Straus & Giroux, 1969), pp. 191–192.

O'Connor's speech at Notre Dame in May 1962 was one version of "The Catholic Novelist in the Protestant South," a talk she had been delivering in various forms since April 1960. The version published in Mystery and Manners, *the editors' composite of several late drafts, is closest to the speech she delivered at Georgetown University in October 1963, describing it to a friend as "always the same old talk but I refurbish it a little like an apartment for rent."*

In the past several years I have gone to speak at a number of Catholic colleges, and I have been pleased to discover that fiction seems to be important to the Catholic student in a way it would not have been twenty, or even ten, years ago. In the past, Catholic imagination in this country has been devoted almost exclusively to practical affairs. Our energies have gone into what has been necessary to sustain existence, and now that our existence is no longer in doubt, we are beginning to realize that an impoverishment of the imagination means an impoverishment of the religious life as well.

I am concerned that future Catholics have a literature. I want them to have a literature that will be undeniably theirs, but which will also be understood and cherished by the rest of our countrymen. A literature for ourselves alone is a contradiction in terms. You may ask, why not simply call this literature Christian? Unfortunately, the word Christian is no longer reliable. It has come to mean anyone with a golden heart. And a golden heart would be a positive interference in the writing of fiction.

I am specifically concerned with fiction because that is what I write. There is a certain embarrassment about being a storyteller in these times when stories are considered not quite as satisfying as statements and statements not quite as satisfying as statistics; but in the long run, a people is known, not by its statements or its statistics, but by the stories it tells. Fiction is the most impure and the most modest and the most human of the arts. It is closest to man in his sin and his suffering and his hope, and it is often rejected by Catholics for the very reasons that make it what it is. It escapes any orthodoxy we might set up for it, because its dignity is an imitation of our own, based like our own on free will, a free will that operates even in the teeth of divine displeasure. I won't go far into the subject of whether such a thing as a Catholic novel is possible or not. I feel that this is a bone which has been picked bare without giving anybody any nourishment. I am simply going to assume that novelists who are deeply Catholic will write novels which you may call Catholic if the Catholic aspects of the novel are what interest you. Such a novel may be characterized in any number of other ways, and perhaps the more ways the better.

In American Catholic circles we are long on theories of what Catholic fiction should be, and short on the experience of having any of it. Once when I spoke on this subject at a Catholic university in the South, a gentleman arose and said that the concept *Catholic novel* was a limiting one and that the novelist, like Whitman, should be alien to nothing. All I could say to him was, "Well, I'm alien to a great deal." We are limited human beings, and the novel is a product of our best limitations. We write with the whole personality, and any attempt to circumvent it, whether this be an effort to rise above belief or above background, is going to result in a reduced approach to reality.

But I think that in spite of this spotty and suspect sophistication, which you find here and there among us, the American Catholic feels the same way he has always felt toward the novel: he trusts the fictional imagination about as little as he trusts anything. Before it is well on its feet, he is worrying about how to control it. The young Catholic writer, more than any other, is liable to be smothered at the outset by theory. The Catholic press is constantly broken out in a rash of articles on the failure of the Catholic novelist: the Catholic novelist is failing to reflect the virtue of hope, failing to show the Church's interest in social justice, failing to portray our beliefs in a light that will make them desirable to others. He occasionally writes well, but he always writes wrong.

We have recently gone through a period of self-criticism on the subject of Catholics and scholarship, which for the most part has taken place on a high level. Our scholarship, or lack of it, has been discussed in relation to what scholarship is in itself, and the discussion — when it has been most valuable — has been conducted by those who are scholars and who know from their own experience what the scholar is and does.

But when we talk about the Catholic failure to produce good fiction in this country, we seldom hear from anyone actively engaged in trying to produce it, and the discussion has not yielded any noticeable returns. We hear from editors, schoolteachers, moralists, and housewives; anyone living considers himself an authority on fiction. The novelist, on the other hand, is supposed to be like Mr. Jarrell's pig that didn't know what bacon was. I think, though, that it is occasionally desirable that we look at the novel — even the so-called Catholic novel — from some particular novelist's point of view.

Catholic discussions of novels by Catholics are frequently ridiculous because every given circumstance of the writer is ignored except his Faith. No one taking part in these discussions seems to remember that the eye sees what it has been given to see by concrete circumstances, and the imagination reproduces what, by some related gift, it is able to make live.

I collect articles from the Catholic press on the failures of the Catholic novelist, and recently in one of them I came upon this typical sentence: "Why not a positive novel based on the Church's fight for social justice, or the liturgical revival, or life in a seminary?"

I take it that if seminarians began to write novels about life in the seminary, there would soon be several less seminarians, but we are to assume that anybody who can write at all, and who

has the energy to do some research, can give us a novel on this or any needed subject — and can make it positive.

A lot of novels do get written in this way. It is, in fact, the traditional procedure of the hack, and by some accident of God, such a novel might turn out to be a work of art, but the possibility is unlikely.

In this same article, the writer asked this wistful question: "Would it not seem in order now for some of our younger men to explore the possibilities inherent in certain positive factors which make Catholic life and the Catholic position in this country increasingly challenging?"

This attitude, which proceeds from the standpoint of what it would be good to do or have to supply a general need, is totally opposite from the novelist's own approach. No serious novelist "explores possibilities inherent in factors." Conrad wrote that the artist "descends within himself, and in that region of stress and strife, if he be deserving and fortunate, he finds the terms of his appeal."

Where you find the terms of your appeal may have little or nothing to do with what is challenging in the life of the Church at the moment. And this is particularly apparent to the Southern Catholic writer, whose imagination has been molded by life in a region which is traditionally Protestant. The two circumstances that have given character to my own writing have been those of being Southern and being Catholic. This is considered by many to be an unlikely combination, but I have found it to be a most likely one. I think that the South provides the Catholic novelist with some benefits that he usually lacks, and lacks to a conspicuous degree. The Catholic novel can't be categorized by subject matter, but only by what it assumes about human and divine reality. It cannot see man as determined; it cannot see him as totally depraved. It will see him as incomplete in himself, as prone to evil, but as redeemable when his own efforts are assisted by grace. And it will see this grace as working through nature, but as entirely transcending it, so that a door is always open to possibility and the unexpected in the human soul. Its center of meaning will be Christ; its center of destruction will be the devil. No matter how this view of life may be fleshed out, these assumptions form its skeleton.

But you don't write fiction with assumptions. The things we see, hear, smell, and touch affect us long before we believe anything at all, and the South impresses its image on us from the moment we are able to distinguish one sound from another. By the time we are able to use our imaginations for fiction, we find that our senses have responded irrevocably to a certain reality. This discovery of being bound through the senses to a particular society and a particular history, to particular sounds and a particular idiom, is for the writer the beginning of a recognition that first puts his work into real human perspective for him. What the Southern Catholic writer is apt to find, when he descends within his imagination, is not Catholic life but the life of this region in which he is both native and alien. He discovers that the imagination is not free, but bound.

For many young writers, Catholic or other, this is not a pleasant discovery. They feel that the first thing they must do in order to write well is to shake off the clutch of the region. They would like to set their stories in a region whose way of life seems nearer the spirit of what they think they have to say, or better, they would like to eliminate the region altogether and approach the infinite directly. But this is not even a possibility.

The fiction writer finds in time, if not at once, that he cannot proceed at all if he cuts himself off from the sights and sounds that have developed a life of their own in his senses. The novelist is concerned with the mystery of personality, and you cannot say much that is significant about this mystery unless the characters you create exist with the marks of a believable society about them. The larger social context is simply left out of much current fiction, but it cannot be left out by the Southern writer. The image of the South, in all its complexity, is so powerful in us that it is a force which has to be encountered and engaged. The writer must wrestle with it, like Jacob with the angel, until he has extracted a blessing. The writing of any novel worth the effort is a kind of personal encounter, an encounter with the circumstances of the particular writer's imagination, with circumstances which are brought to order only in the actual writing.

The Catholic novel that fails is usually one in which this kind of engagement is absent. It is a novel which doesn't grapple with any particular culture. It may try to make a culture out of the Church, but this is always a mistake because the church is not a culture. The Catholic novel that fails is a novel in which there is no sense of place, and in which feeling is, by that much, diminished. Its action occurs in an abstracted setting that could be anywhere or nowhere. This reduces its dimensions drastically and cuts down on those tensions that keep fiction from being facile and slick.

The Southern writer's greatest tie with the South is through his ear, which is usually sharp but not too versatile outside his own idiom. With a few exceptions, such as Miss Katherine Anne Porter, he is not too often successfully cosmopolitan in fiction, but the fact is that he doesn't need to be. A distinctive idiom is a powerful instrument for keeping fiction social. When one Southern character speaks, regardless of his station in life, an echo of all Southern life is heard. This helps to keep Southern fiction from being a fiction of purely private experience.

Alienation was once a diagnosis, but in much of the fiction of our time it has become an ideal. The modern hero is the outsider. His experience is rootless. He can go anywhere. He belongs nowhere. Being alien to nothing, he ends up being alienated from any kind of community based on common tastes and interests. The borders of his country are the sides of his skull.

The South is traditionally hostile to outsiders, except on her own terms. She is traditionally against intruders, foreigners from Chicago or New Jersey, all those who come from afar with moral energy that increases in direct proportion to the distance from home. It is difficult to separate the virtues of this quality from the narrowness which accompanies and colors it for the outside world. It is more difficult still to reconcile the South's instinct to preserve her identity with her equal instinct to fall eager victim to every poisonous breath from Hollywood or Madison Avenue. But good and evil appear to be joined in every culture at the spine, and as far as the creation of a body of fiction is concerned, the social is superior to the purely personal. Somewhere is better than anywhere. And traditional manners, however unbalanced, are better than no manners at all.

The writer whose themes are religious particularly needs a region where these themes find a response in the life of the people. The American Catholic is short on places that reflect his particular religious life and his particular problems. This country isn't exactly cut in his image. Where he does have a place — such as the Midwestern parishes, which serve as J. F. Powers' region, or South Boston, which belongs to Edwin O'Connor — these places lack the significant features that result in a high degree of regional self-consciousness. They have no great geographical extent, they have no particularly significant history, certainly no history of defeat; they have no real peasant class, and no cultural unity of the kind you find in the South. So that no matter what the writer brings to them in the way of talents, they don't bring much to him in the way of exploitable benefits. Where Catholics do abound, they usually blend almost imperceptibly into the general materialistic background. If the Catholic faith were central to life in America, Catholic fiction would fare better, but the Church is not central to this society. The things that bind us together as Catholics are known only to ourselves. A secular society understands us less and less. It becomes more and more difficult in America to make belief believable, but in this the Southern writer has the greatest possible advantage. He lives in the Bible Belt.

It was about 1919 that Mencken called the South the Bible Belt and the Sahara of the Bozarts [Bozart]. Today Southern literature is known around the world, and the South is still the Bible Belt. Sam Jones' grandma read the Bible thirty-seven times on her knees. And the rural and small-town South, and even a certain level of the city South, is made up of the descendants of old ladies like her. You don't shake off their influence in even several generations.

To be great storytellers, we need something to measure ourselves against, and this is what we conspicuously lack in this age. Men judge themselves now by what they find themselves doing. The Catholic has the natural law and the teachings of the Church to guide him, but for the writing of fiction, something more is necessary.

For the purposes of fiction, these guides have to exist in a concrete form, known and held sacred by the whole community. They have to exist in the form of stories which affect our image and our judgment of ourselves. Abstractions, formulas, laws will not serve here. We have to have stories in our background. It takes a story to make a story. It takes a story of mythic dimensions, one which belongs to everybody, one in which everybody is able to recognize the hand of God and its descent. In the Protestant South, the Scriptures fill this role.

The Hebrew genius for making the absolute concrete has conditioned the Southerner's way of looking at things. That is one of the reasons why the South is a storytelling section. Our response to life is different if we have been taught only a definition of faith than if we have trembled with Abraham as he held the knife over Isaac. Both of these kinds of knowledge are necessary, but in the last four or five centuries, Catholics have over-emphasized the abstract and consequently im-

poverished their imaginations and their capacity for prophetic insight.

Nothing will insure the future of Catholic fiction so much as the biblical revival that we see signs of now in Catholic life. The Bible is held sacred in the Church, we hear it read at Mass, bits and pieces of it are exposed to us in the liturgy, but because we are not totally dependent on it, it has not penetrated very far into our consciousness nor conditioned our reactions to experience. Unfortunately, where you find Catholics reading the Bible, you find that it is usually a pursuit of the educated, but in the South the Bible is known by the ignorant as well, and it is always that *mythos* which the poor hold in common that is most valuable to the fiction writer. When the poor hold sacred history in common, they have ties to the universal and the holy, which allows the meaning of their every action to be heightened and seen under the aspect of eternity. The writer who views the world in this light will be very thankful if he has been fortunate enough to have the South for his background, because here belief can still be made believable, even if for the modern mind it cannot be made admirable.

Religious enthusiasm is accepted as one of the South's more grotesque features, and it is possible to build upon that acceptance, however little real understanding such acceptance may carry with it. When you write about backwoods prophets, it is very difficult to get across to the modern reader that you take these people seriously, that you are not making fun of them, but that their concerns are your own and, in your judgment, central to human life. It is almost inconceivable to this reader that such could be the case. It is hard enough for him to suspend his disbelief and accept an anagogical level of action at all, harder still for him to accept its action in an obviously grotesque character. He has the mistaken notion that a concern with grace is a concern with exalted human behavior, that it is a pretentious concern. It is, however, simply a concern with the human reaction to that which, instant by instant, gives life to the soul. It is a concern with a realization that breeds charity and with the charity that breeds action. Often the nature of grace can be made plain only be describing its absence.

The Catholic writer may be immersed in the Bible himself, but if his readers and his characters are not, he does not have the instrument to plumb meaning — and specifically Christian meaning — that he would have if the biblical background were known to all. It is what writer, character, and reader share that makes it possible to write fiction at all.

The circumstances of being a Southerner, of living in a non-Catholic but religious society, furnish the Catholic novelist with some very fine antidotes to his own worst tendencies. We too much enjoy indulging ourselves in the logic that kills, in making categories smaller and smaller, in prescribing attitudes and proscribing subjects. For the Catholic, one result of the Counter-Reformation was a practical overemphasis on the legal and logical and a consequent neglect of the Church's broader tradition. The need for this emphasis has now diminished, and the Church is busy encouraging those biblical and liturgical revivals which should restore Catholic life to its proper fullness. Nevertheless the scars of this legalistic approach are still upon us. Those who are long on logic, definitions, abstractions, and formulas are frequently short on a sense of the concrete, and when they find themselves in an environment where their own principles have only a partial application to society, they are forced, not to abandon the principles, but in applying them to a different situation, to come up with fresh reactions.

I often find among Catholics a certain impatience with Southern literature, sometimes a fascinated impatience, but usually a definite feeling that with all the violence and grotesqueries and religious enthusiasm reflected in its fiction, the South — that is, the rural, Protestant, Bible Belt South — is a little beyond the pale of Catholic respect, and that certainly it would be ridiculous to expect the emergence in such soil of anything like a literature inspired by Catholic belief. But for my part, I don't think that this is at all unlikely. There are certain conditions necessary for the emergence of Catholic literature which are found nowhere else in this country in such abundance as in the Protestant South; and I look forward with considerable relish to the day when we are going to have to enlarge our notions about the Catholic novel to include some pretty odd Southern specimens.

It seems to me that the Catholic Southerner's experience of living so intimately with the division of Christendom is an experience that can give much breadth and poignance to the novels he may produce. The Catholic novelist in the South is forced to follow the spirit into strange places and to recognize it in many forms not totally congenial to him. He may feel that the kind of religion that has influenced Southern life has run hand in hand with extreme individualism for so long that there is nothing left of it that he can recognize, but

when he penetrates to the human aspiration beneath it, he sees not only what has been lost to the life he observes, but more, the terrible loss to us in the Church of human faith and passion. I think he will feel a good deal more kinship with backwoods prophets and shouting fundamentalists than he will with those politer elements for whom the supernatural is an embarrassment and for whom religion has become a department of sociology or culture or personality development. His interest and sympathy may very well go — as I know my own does — directly to those aspects of Southern life where the religious feeling is most intense and where its outward forms are farthest from the Catholic, and most revealing of a need that only the Church can fill. This is not because, in the felt superiority of orthodoxy, he wishes to subtract one theology from another, but because, descending within himself to find his region, he discovers that it is with these aspects of Southern life that he has a feeling of kinship strong enough to spur him to write.

The result of these underground religious affinities will be a strange and, to many, perverse fiction, one which serves no felt need, which gives us no picture of Catholic life, or the religious experiences that are usual with us, but I believe that it will be Catholic fiction. These people in the invisible Church make discoveries that have meaning for us who are better protected from the vicissitudes of our own natures, and who are often too lazy and satisfied to make any discoveries at all. I believe that the Catholic fiction writer is free to find his subject in the invisible Church and that this will be the vocation of many of us brought up in the South. In a literature that tends naturally to extremes, as Southern literature does, we need something to protect us against the merely extreme, the merely personal, the merely grotesque, and here the Catholic, with his older tradition and his ability to resist the dissolution of belief, can make his contribution to Southern literature, but only if he realizes first that he has as much to learn from it as to give it. The Catholic novelist in the South will bolster the South's best traditions, for they are the same as his own. And the South will perhaps lead him to be less timid as a novelist, more respectful of the concrete, more trustful of the blind imagination.

The opportunities for the potential Catholic writer in the South are so great as to be intimidating. He lives in a region where there is a thriving literary tradition, and this is always an advantage to the writer, who is initially inspired less by life than by the work of his predecessors. He lives in a region which is struggling, in both good ways and bad, to preserve its identity, and this is an advantage, for his dramatic need is to know manners under stress. He lives in the Bible Belt, where belief can be made believable. He has also here a good view of the modern world. A half-hour's ride in this region will take him from places where the life has a distinctly Old Testament flavor to places where the life might be considered post-Christian. Yet all these varied situations can be seen in one glance and heard in one conversation.

I think that Catholic novelists in the future will be able to reinforce the vital strength of Southern literature, for they will know that what has given the South her identity are those beliefs and qualities which she has absorbed from the Scriptures and from her own history of defeat and violation: a distrust of the abstract, a sense of human dependence on the grace of God, and a knowledge that evil is not simply a problem to be solved, but a mystery to be endured.

If all that is missing in this scene is the practical influence of the visible Catholic Church, the writer will find that he has to supply the lack, as best he can, out of himself; and he will do this by the way he uses his eyes. If he uses them in the confidence of his Faith, and according to the needs of what he is making, there will be nothing in life too grotesque, or too "un-Catholic," to supply the materials of his work. Certainly in a secular world, he is in a particular position to appreciate and cherish the Protestant South, to remind us of what we have and what we must keep.

ARTICLE:
John Hawkes, "Flannery O'Connor's Devil," *Sewanee Review*, 70 (Summer 1962): 395–407.

Hawkes, who discussed the nature of the devil with O'Connor for years, takes a fresh, unorthodox approach to her fiction in this article. He acknowledges her Christian perspective, quoting from her letters to him, but he argues that the voice of the devil in O'Connor's fiction is often indistinguishable from O'Connor's satirical authorial voice, stressing "the devil I have been speaking of is only a metaphor, a way of referring to a temperament strong enough and sympathetic enough to sustain the work of piercing pretension." O'Connor responded to this article, which he sent to her before publication, by saying, "I

like the piece very very much. . . . This is not to say that you have convinced me at all that what you say is perverse is perverse. . . . I think what you do is to reduce the good and give what you take from it to the diabolical. . . . I think you call them perverse because you like them" (5 April 1962). As she explained to another friend, "Jack Hawkes' devil is not a theological one. His devil is an impeccable literary spirit whom he makes responsible for all good literature." O'Connor shared Hawkes's admiration for Nathanael West, whose Miss Lonelyhearts (1933) she recommended to the Fitzgeralds in 1949–1950.

Eventually students of literature may come to think of Flannery O'Connor not only in terms of coldness, detachment and "black" humor, but also in terms of an older or more familiar tradition. In a letter not long ago she said, "I think I would admit to writing what Hawthorne called 'romances'. . . . I feel more of a kinship with Hawthorne than with any other American writer. . . . " Surely such an expression of kinship is a sober one, coming as it does from a comic writer whose humor was described as "slam-bang" and whose style was called "as balefully direct as a death sentence" by *Time Magazine*. But of course this comic writer is a serious writer — say, in her moral preoccupations, her poetic turn of mind and incredible uses of paradox — and her remark about her affinity with Hawthorne deserves juxtaposition, it seems to me, with a statement such as this one from Edwin Honig's book on allegory: "Melville's problem, like Hawthorne's, was to find a method whereby a vigorous moral and aesthetic authority could be recreated in fiction. For him, as for his predecessors, the challenge was to map out the relation of the unknown country of allegory to the known countries and conditions of contemporary actuality."[1]

That this statement is more appropriate to Flannery O'Connor than to most other contemporary American writers; that the problem and challenge it describes are curiously hers; that the authority it describes is precisely what lies behind her "brutal" laughter; that "unknown country" and "actuality" are precisely what her fiction combines in a mercilessly pleasurable tension — all this is reason enough for making the juxtaposition above. And also reason enough for raising and perhaps evading the final question of the extent to which Flannery O'Connor's work should be considered allegorical. But here I must mention my faith in the occult nature of minor coincidence since it was Melville's granddaughter, a lady I was once privileged to know in Cambridge, Massachusetts, who first urged me to read the fiction of Flannery O'Connor, and — further — since this experience occurred just at the time I had discovered the short novels of Nathanael West.

At that time — about ten years ago — the sudden confluence of West and Flannery O'Connor to me suggested twin guffawing peals of thunder (the figure is borrowed from "The Life You Save May Be Your Own") above a dead landscape quite ready for new humor, new vision, new and more meaningful comic treatments of violence. Though he died in 1940, West is the one writer who, along with Flannery O'Connor, deserves singular attention as a rare American satirist. I would propose that West and Flannery O'Connor are very nearly alone today in their pure creation of "aesthetic authority," and would also propose, of course, that they are very nearly alone in their employment of the devil's voice as vehicle for their satire or for what we may call their true (or accurate) vision of our godless actuality. Their visions are different. And yet, as we might expect, these two comic writers are unique in sharing a kind of inverted attraction for the reality of our absurd condition.

We may think of satire as "centralizing a dominant ideal by means of irony and analogy,"[2] and also as a form which "demolishes man's image of himself as a rational creature."[3] It may be that most generally in West's satiric fictions the "dominant ideal," never more than implied, is merely the serenity of dissolution, or release from the pains of sexual struggle and from the dead-end of an impossible striving toward God, all of this brought to "pitch" (to use Faulkner's word) by the comedy of the sexual struggle itself. Though Flannery O'Connor's "dominant ideal" is likely to be as difficult to discover as West's, it is nonetheless an absolute of which she is perfectly aware. She writes: "I don't think you should write something as long as a novel around anything that is not of the gravest concern to you and everybody else and for me this is always the conflict between an attraction for the Holy and the disbelief in it that we breathe in with the air of the times." Obviously West would never have made such a statement, and the polarity of the religious positions of these two writers is borne out in their novels.

West's preoccupation with the "Christ business" begins as joke in *The Dream Life of Balso Snell,* reaches a partly confused and sentimental climax in *Miss Lonelyhearts,* and in *The Day of the Locust* finally dwindles to sporadic and surface satires on the freak Hollywood church as bad answer. Whereas Flannery O'Connor's first novel, *Wise Blood,* concerns a circuit preacher's grandson who is so violently opposed to Christ that in the end, after an immolation that involves self-blinding (among other things), he is last seen by his worldly landlady as "going backwards to Bethlehem"; and *The Violent Bear It Away,* her recent and more ambitious novel, describes the metamorphosis of a similar young Fundamentalist into a prophet who accepts his burden and turns "toward the dark city, where the children of God lay sleeping."

But if West wrote less effectively whenever he attempted to take into account the presence or absence of God, while Flannery O'Connor would not write at all without what she calls the "attraction for the Holy"; or if it appears that Flannery O'Connor is writing about the spirit (the absurdity of disbelief), while Nathanael West was writing about the dream (the painful absurdity of sexual desire), at least I would say that the "pitch" of their comic fictions is very nearly the same. Both writers are demolishing "man's image of himself as a rational creature" (Flannery O'Connor, for instance, in her wonderfully unsympathetic portrait of the ridiculous school teacher, Rayber, in *The Violent Bear It Away,* and West in his creation of total and hapless dementia in *The Day of the Locust*). And both writers are reversing their artistic sympathies, West committing himself to the creative pleasures of a destructive sexuality, Flannery O'Connor committing herself creatively to the antics of soulless characters who leer, or bicker, or stare at obscenities on walls, or maim each other on a brilliant but barren earth. And finally both writers — one a Roman Catholic, the other a man of no particular religious drive — are remarkably similar in their exploitation of the "demolishing" syntax of the devil. But then a good many readers would mistake Flannery O'Connor's belief in the Holy for its opposite, in the same way that many readers might be misled into thinking of Nathanael West as a Christian *manqué.* The point is that in the most vigorously moral of writers the actual creation of fiction seems often to depend on immoral impulse.

It is obvious that West's distortions (his incorrigible giving way to joke, or his use of cathected patterns of physical detail in the place of conventional plotting) are constructed for the sake of psychological truth as well as from the sheer necessity for liberation from a constraining realism. Furthermore, it is obvious that his distortions depend in no way on an outside "framed" body of orthodoxy for their "authority." Once imagined, his comic vision *is* in fact its own authority. However, it needs to be said that Flannery O'Connor's work is just as great a violation of probability and of anticipated, familiar "reality" as West's. In *Wise Blood* two policemen turn out to be sadistic versions of Tweedledum and Tweedledee; in *The Violent Bear It Away* the devil himself quite literally appears, wearing a cream-colored hat and lavender suit and carrying a whiskey bottle filled with blood in the glove compartment of his enormous car; or, in this same novel, there is the comic fanaticism of the old great-uncle who continues to sit for a whole morning bolt upright at the breakfast table where he "died before he got the first spoonful to his mouth." And it also needs to be said that such fictive distortions of Flannery O'Connor are just as independent as those of Nathanael West.

Surely if the elements of Flannery O'Connor's fiction could be referred point for point to the established principles of a known orthodoxy, then many of the imaginative beauties and tensions of her fiction would disappear. But this is not the case. The very revivalist or circuit-preacher Protestant world of her fiction, with its improbable combination of religious faith and eccentricity, accounts in large part for the way in which "unknown country" and "actuality" are held in severe balance in her work. And then there is the creative impulse itself, so unflagging and so unpredictable as to become, in a sense, "immoral." Hovering behind the fiction, this impulse has about it the energy and unassailable paradox of the grandfather in *Wise Blood,* who was "a waspish old man who had ridden over three counties with Jesus hidden in his head like a stinger." Within her almost luridly bright pastoral world — usually created as meaningless or indifferent or corrupted — the characters of Flannery O'Connor are *judged,* victimized, made to appear only as absurd entities of the flesh. Or, sometimes, they are allowed to experience their moments of mystery. But the mysterious baptismal drowning of an idiot child (to take one central example from *The Violent Bear It Away*) is in certain ways quite similar to the call — "full of melancholy and weariness, yet marvelously sweet" — of a trapped quail about to be cut apart with a pair of tin shears and fried in a skillet (*The Day of the Locust*). In other words, and thinking of artistic commitment in conflict with "dominant ideal," the improbable

yet fictionally true Hollywood landscape of West is very like the improbable yet fictionally true "Free Thinking" evangelistic landscape of Flannery O'Connor. There is no security, no answer, to be found in either of these horrifying and brightly imagined worlds.

I have spoken of the devil's voice as vehicle for satire, and of the devil's "demolishing" syntax; and have suggested that there is a relationship to be found between fictive "authority" and "immoral" author-impulse in the comic works of West and Flannery O'Connor. To me it is important to stress these generalities because both West and Flannery O'Connor write *about* the devil, or at least about diabolical figures (most obviously Shrike in *Miss Lonelyhearts* and Tarwater's Friend — who is a literal *heard* version of the devil — in *The Violent Bear It Away*), but seem also to reflect the verbal mannerisms and explosively reductive attitudes of such figures in their own "black" authorial stances. When I suggested to Flannery O'Connor some time ago that as writer she was on the devil's side she responded at once — and of course to disagree.

Despite the comparison made above between the baptismal drowning of the idiot child and the "marvelously sweet" call of the trapped quail, it is clear that there is, actually, a considerable difference between the experiences of mystery as created by West and by Flannery O'Connor. No matter his preoccupation with the darkness of life, West could never have taken seriously an idea of the devil (as he could not an idea of the Holy), while on the other hand Flannery O'Connor has phrased this aspect of her concern with typical and shocking clarity: "I want to be certain that the devil gets identified as the devil and not simply taken for this or that psychological tendency." A statement as matter-of-fact as this one, with its explicit acceptance of the devil's existence and explicit renunciation of all his works, does little to help my argument concerning her "true" fictional allegiance — the more so since Flannery O'Connor herself has pointed out the difference between her devil (Lucifer, a fallen angel) and the authorial-devil I have been speaking of (to her no more than a subjective creation and rather alien to her thinking). But there is an interesting distance between the directness of her statement and profundity of belief, and the shifting, even deceptive substance of what Flannery O'Connor, with disarming humor and understatement, has called her "one-cylinder syntax." My own feeling is that just as the creative process threatens the Holy throughout Flannery O'Connor's fiction by generating a paradoxical fusion of improbability and passion out of the Protestant "do-it-yourself" evangelism of the South, and thereby raises the pitch of apocalyptic experience when it finally appears; so too, throughout this fiction, the creative process transforms the writer's objective Catholic knowledge of the devil into an authorial attitude in itself in some measure diabolical. This is to say that in Flannery O'Connor's most familiar stories and novels the "disbelief . . . that we breathe in with the air of the times" emerges fully as two-sided or complex as "attraction for the Holy."

Two passages from *The Violent Bear It Away* will illustrate the shifting substance of Flannery O'Connor's language and authorial attitude. The action of this novel is centered about a legacy of two obligations left to the young protagonist, Tarwater, by the old man (and Prophet) who is his great-uncle and who is also the medium through which the course of Tarwater's life is determined. One obligation is to bury the old man when he dies (which Tarwater fails to do because of the persuasive voice of his new Friend, the devil), and another is to baptize little Bishop, the idiot child (which Tarwater does manage to do, but against his will, and then only by drowning the "dim-witted boy"). The first passage below appears early in the novel and concerns the argument between Tarwater and his Friend over the burial; the second appears toward the end of the novel and concerns the lake in which the baptism finally occurs (the dialogue in both passages occurs in Tarwater's head, hence the absence of quotation marks; italicizing is mine):

Oh I see, the stranger said. It ain't the Day of Judgment for him (the old Prophet) you're worried about. It's the Day of Judgment for you.

That's my bidnis, Tarwater said.

I ain't buttin into your bidnis, the stranger said. It don't mean a thing to me. *You're left by yourself in this empty place. Forever by yourself in this empty place with just as much light as that dwarf sun wants to let in. You don't mean a thing to a soul as far as I can see.*

The first sight that met his eyes when he (Tarwater) got out of the car at the Cherokee Lodge was the little lake. It lay there, glass-like, still, reflecting a crown of trees and an infinite overarching sky. *It looked so unused that it might only the moment before have been set down by four strapping angels for him to baptize the child in.* A weakness working itself up from his knees, reached his stomach and came upward and forced

a tremor in his jaw. *Steady, his friend said, everywhere you go you'll find water. It wasn't invented yesterday.*

The Violent Bear It Away actualizes the truth of the devil's sentiments — Tarwater does not, in fact, "mean a thing to a soul" and lives only in the stalwart nausea of his resistance to the Prophet's calling and in the ultimate grim pleasure of his acceptance of that call. By the end of the novel we know that Tarwater will be destroyed by "the children of God," or destroyed by our godless actuality.

But surely in giving voice to his dry country-cadenced nihilism and in laying out the pure deflated truth of mere existence ("Forever by yourself in this empty place"), the devil is speaking not only for himself but for the author. Of course the devil is attempting to persuade Tarwater that he is exactly like everybody else in "this empty place," and is attempting to persuade Tarwater to *be* himself and to *do* what he wants, since given the fact of mere existence there is nothing else to be or do. While of course the author is dramatizing the opposite, that Tarwater is *not* like everybody else and that he is destined to suffer the extremities of the pain involved in the conflict between the "mean" earth and symbolic waters. However, the devil takes obvious pleasure in going about his own "bidnis" and the author takes a similar obvious pleasure in going about hers. And there are numerous examples to indicate that the author's view of "everybody else" is exactly the same as her devil's view. (There is the young mother "whose face was as broad and innocent as a cabbage" in "A Good Man Is Hard to Find"; there is the old woman who "was about the size of a cedar fence post" in "The Life You Save May Be Your Own"; or the mother who has two little boys who stand with faces "like pans set on either side to catch the grins that overflowed from her" in *Wise Blood*.)

In these last examples the creation of flat personality — each instance is a kind of small muffled explosion — depends on the extreme absurdity of juxtaposing the human and the inanimate, and I think that the fact of the reductive or diabolical value judgment is clear, though to be sure there are degrees of judgment and degrees of sympathy too in the range of Flannery O'Connor's wonderfully merciless creations of the human type. But even more clear perhaps, or at least more important, is the basic principle or association that fills out the devil's nihilism and defines the diabolical attitude that lies behind the reversal of artistic sympathy — that is, the "meanness"-pleasure principle. When Tarwater discovers what he takes to be his freedom — for him it is the license to do whatever he wants, and it comes to him while he is trying to dig his great-uncle's grave — his first thought is simply, "Could kill off all those chickens if I had a mind to. . . . " And Flannery O'Connor appears to reveal her own understanding of earthly (and, I would say, artistic) pleasure when she writes that "Haze (the protagonist of *Wise Blood*) knows what the choice is and the Misfit (the extraordinary convict in 'A Good Man Is Hard to Find') knows what the choice is — either throw away everything and follow Him or enjoy yourself by doing some meanness to somebody, and in the end there's no real pleasure in life, not even in meanness." I suspect that for many readers today such a principle or such a cold paradox of stringent alternatives would prove merely accurate or baffling or offensive. Yet here, I think, is the core of traditional satiric impulse, or the core of what we may call contemporary "anti-realistic" impulse.

However, to return to the italicized portions of the two passages quoted above from *The Violent Bear It Away*, and noticing the similarity between the devil's country-cadences or constructions and the author's, we might well ask how a reader baffled by the purity of the devil's attitude and intention is to react to an author capable of tilting our expectations *negatively* toward the apocalyptic by confronting us suddenly with the incongruous vision of "four strapping angels." Certainly this second passage about the lake is lovely and shocking both. We admire it essentially for the extreme compression within which the writer modulates through three distinct "voices." That is, we are taken abruptly but skillfully from the direct and unbiased allusion to spirituality (the "*crown* of trees" and "infinite overarching sky") to the dispersive ambiguity of "unused" (the word has the disturbing connotations of "unused" in the earthly pragmatic sense — say, unused for boating — and hence extends this comically "realistic" view of life into the other world — "unused" for baptism) to the thoroughly double-purposed "angels" and Tarwater's sickness of recoil and anticipation, and finally to the ultimate reduction of the devil's own absurdly pragmatic (and at the same time pathetic) view of "invented" water. Here the shifting voices and attitudes alone produce considerable tension. And even the devil's comic relief — at once poised on the edge of

incredibility but also actualizing simultaneously the range of our possible "resistance" and the sheer fact of the impossibility of resistance (even the devil knows the implication of "everywhere you go you'll find water") — is in a sense an unwanted comic relief. However, the center of the tension for the reader, himself ensnared in the meanness-pleasure paradox, still lies in the metaphor of the "four strapping angels." If we consider what the passage might have been like had "four" and "strapping" been omitted ("It looked so unused that it might only the moment before have been set down by angels for him to baptize the child in") we become aware, first of the enormous loss that would have resulted from such omission, and second that the basis for the figure as it stands is a *literalness* which in its faithfulness to rationality is at once appropriate and absurd. Since literalness is also the basis of Fundamentalism, we may say that the figure returns us to the two components (improbability and "attraction for the Holy") originally seen as constituting the apocalyptic half of Flannery O'Connor's fiction. Or we may say that through her exploitation of satiric and sympathetic impulses she is attempting to maintain the balance of that conflict grounded in the fictional possibility of redemption. But my own feeling is that the comic humanizing of the giant "strapping" angels cannot be explained away in this fashion, and that it actually represents those creative impulses of the writer which point toward the other side of her imagination — the demonic.

I would not say that Flannery O'Connor's uses of image and symbol are inconsistent, but rather — to pursue the lines of this argument — that they are mildly perverse. If the writer commits herself at least creatively to the voice and attitude of her imagined devil, or if her imagined devil is at least a partial heightening of her own creative voice and attitude, then we have only to compare "that dwarf sun" with the "crown of trees" in order to interpret the very strength of her authority as being in a way perverse. In Flannery O'Connor's fiction personified nature is often minimized (the devil's view of the sun, or this corresponding author-description from "The Life You Save May Be Your Own": "A fat yellow moon appeared in the branches of the fig tree as if it were going to roost there with the chickens"). Or it is made to assume a baldly leering attitude toward the jocular evil antics of the men in its midst (the "guffawing peal of thunder" from the same story). And if Bishop, the little idiot child, is intended to establish an innocence that points toward the apocalyptic, old Singleton, an insane comic figure in "The Partridge Festival," is intended to be exactly the opposite — crazy and lecherous and pointing toward the demonic. The danger inherent in any oversimplified effort to discover consistent patterns or systems of traditional symbolic materials in this fiction is obvious (thinking of idiocy or insanity as traditionally sanctified conditions) when all at once the windshield wipers of an automobile make "a great clatter like two idiots clapping in church" (*Wise Blood*).

Certainly Flannery O'Connor reveals what can only be called brilliant creative perversity when she brings to life a denuded *actuality* and writes about a "cat-faced baby" or a confidence man with "an honest look that fitted into his face like a set of false teeth" or an automobile horn that makes "a sound like a goat's laugh cut off with a buzz saw." This much, I should think, is happily on the side of the devil.

Since I have mentioned that Flannery O'Connor does not agree with my notion of her central fictional allegiance, it is only right to say that our disagreement may not be so extensive after all, and that she has written that, "Those moments (involving awareness of the Holy) are prepared for — by me anyway — by the intensity of the evil circumstances." She also writes, "I suppose the devil teaches most of the lessons that lead to self-knowledge." And further that "her" devil is the one who goes about "piercing pretensions, not the devil who goes about seeking whom he may devour." If Flannery O'Connor were asked where she would locate the center of her creative impulse, she might reply, "in the indication of Grace." But then again she might not. And I suspect that she would not reply at all to such a question. It may be, too, that I have been giving undue stress to the darker side of her imaginative constructions, and that the devil I have been speaking of is only a metaphor, a way of referring to a temperament strong enough and sympathetic enough to sustain the work of piercing pretension. To think so, of course, takes much of the pleasure out of the piercing.

I shall continue to evade the final question of whether Flannery O'Connor is a writer of allegories, and whether she is to be associated with Hawthorne because he wrote "romances" or because he had his own indebtedness to evil principle. Very likely the principle and the form are inseparable. At any rate, and though the landscape

is not as dead or mirthless as it was ten years ago, Flannery O'Connor's writing stands out against all those immediate fictions which are precious or flatulent or tending to retreat into the security of a constraining realism. The voice of her devil speaks with a new and essential shrewdness about what Nathanael West called "the truly monstrous."

1. Edwin Honig, *Dark Conceit; The Making of Allegory* (1959), pp. 102–103.
2. Ibid., p. 158.
3. Ibid., p. 163.

ARTICLE:

Brainard Cheney, "Miss O'Connor Creates Unusual Humor Out of Ordinary Sin," *Sewanee Review*, 71 (Autumn 1963): 644–652; in *The Correspondence of Flannery O'Connor and the Brainard Cheneys*, pp. 204–211.

O'Connor's friend and fellow Roman Catholic responded to Hawkes's article.

Man has always claimed the rights of a free will, the while he was trying to evade the responsibilities. But the consequences have been catching up with him uncommonly of late, after a prolonged and immoderate time of free wheeling.

These rights have proliferated during their long detachment. We isolated not merely the historical categories of liberty, such as religious, moral, political, and social, but later on those better described as irreligious, immoral, pressure-political, other-directed social. Indeed, of more recent times our rights have been limited only by mental hygiene and available police protection.

But now we have come to talk about responsibilities. Talk deep. And not only about responsibilities, but the reason for responsibilities, the ontological reason. This has become a talking point and even a viewpoint. And this is the case, not only in homiletics and moral philosophy, but in the arts as well.

Humanism has been under accelerating attack since the end of the last World War. The search for religious faith has recently become a literary land run. And there have been a half dozen notable attempts among novelists to dramatize Christian conversion. In these efforts, writers have resorted to the strategies of satire, irony, symbolism, allegory, fable, and even anecdote. And, to be sure, humor, too. It has remained to Flannery O'Connor (insofar as I have been able to discover) to create a brand of humor based on the religious point of view.

In a world as secular as ours the phrase "the religious point of view" requires definition. In this country in particular, the Protestant movement has added uncertainty to such a viewpoint. To address this issue to a more specific context, there appeared in *The Sewanee Review* (Summer, 1962) an article on Flannery O'Connor's work by John Hawkes, who apparently does not understand the religious viewpoint and, hence, the diabolism he would attribute to Miss O'Connor.

Perhaps the first element in the religious perspective to consider here is that of man's free will. In some idiom or other, as we know, all of the world religions have recognized man's deficiencies, for life both in the here and the hereafter. They have offered personal salvation at a price. The religious man must choose the costly way. This has had especial emphasis in the Judeo-Christian tradition. In the religious mythology which underlies our Western culture and civilization, the one restraint that an omnipotent God places on Himself is the freedom allowed man in the matter of following God's will. But there is no freeloading. Responsibilities represented in the Ten Commandments, the Beatitudes, and, among the orthodox, in the communion of a Christian church come along with Christ's redemption of us. It is from this orthodox view that Miss O'Connor sees the humor of man's predicament. And more.

Without recalling all of the reforms since the Reformation by which the unorthodox have watered down their Christian responsibilities, we haven't forgotten that the pabulum eventually became fare for an infant agnosticism. And this infant under modern force-feeding methods has grown into a gargantuan adolescent secularism. And the force-fed secularist has outstripped his begetters only to find that bone and flesh and blood (he is unsound and suffers strange ills) suffer consequences. From the Christian viewpoint these are the ills of the will — the free will.

It has been roughly a century since modern man, even in his churches, has thought of himself as cursed with a fallen nature. He has thought increasingly well of himself, in his new scientific independence. When the consequences of his irresponsibility began to catch up with him, he blamed first the narrow-minded in his church. Then he blamed society and machinery and practically everything in sight, except himself. The top sentimentalists blamed God. They blamed Him at first for being mean. More recently they blame

Him for *not* being — in other words, for not being as they think He ought to be. In the literary world they are called Existentialists, and/or Beatniks.

The genius of Miss O'Connor's humor is that she nowhere appears the partisan of human fallibility. This is the initial requirement of the orthodox outlook: the Christian must realize that he is as liable to human weaknesses as any sinner or the unbeliever. She gives us an apt simile for this viewpoint in her story, "The River": where Mrs. Cronin stood, staring into the room, "with a skeleton's appearance of seeing everything." We have the feeling that the skeleton itself, with nowhere to hide anything, must be able to see through us with its own inner visibility. That sense of conscience, that nakedness before God, is the source of religious realism and the premise for Miss O'Connor's humor.

She has given this nakedness an even sharper irony in her story "A Temple of the Holy Ghost." Although, for the fourteen-year-old girl with whom the viewpoint lies, the thought of the circus hermaphrodite as temple for the Holy Ghost is mysterious and awful, she has no sentimental complaint against the ways of God. It is Miss O'Connor's position that irony is only a human emotion.

Apparently this quite escapes Mr. Hawkes in his *Review* piece titled "Flannery O'Connor's Devil." In a *tour de force* remarkable only for foolhardiness, in which he brackets her with Nathanael West, Mr. Hawkes speaks of her "inverted attraction for the reality of our absurd condition."

Miss O'Connor has a genius for the grotesque, and she makes effective dramatic use of misfortunes in a God-given world. This is her *metier*. But I would challenge Mr. Hawkes to support with evidence the view he attributes to her. Nowhere in any of her work with which I am acquainted has she as author viewed our condition as being *absurd*.

From religion to politics to science to manners, sentimentality has been rife in this land for a long time. It is, to be sure, the human complaint. When scientists, after Galileo, established their Archimedean Point from which to view the physical world, it was, I suppose, inevitable that man would discover a new Reality, confusing himself again with God.

Under this error the world has grown more awful to contemplate, the longer man has looked at it — for the viewpoint was still human and human only, wherever it might be located in space or time, or however many eyes were at the knot-hole. Whatever he did to refine or lengthen his measuring stick, man could only measure the human limitation called distance. So erring modern man for a long time has now been trying to deny the existence of Infinity.

This is *not* the religious point of view. The religious view is not man looking at himself in the presence of time and space, however great, and certainly not this humanly-conceived time and space looking at man. It is man looking at himself in the presence of Infinity — Infinity for Whom there is no unknown nor unknowable, from Whom there are no secrets. Yet there is something very essential to be added to establish the religious view, and I add it here: an Infinity of Love and Compassion, as well as Awfulness.

Perhaps Miss O'Connor has introduced God's charity nowhere more subtly, or more dramatically, than in her disarming story "A Good Man Is Hard to Find." Recall the "secular" picture of the vulgar couple and the barbarous children and the quaint grandmother on a boring excursion that she first presents. Her satire here seems secular and that is what she intends.

The reader may not suspect what is going on until the Misfit dispatches "Bailey Boy" and the two children. Perhaps even then he will but reluctantly and tardily perceive that God has made the misfit of a secular world His agent, too; and that the grandmother is engaged in a religious ordeal, that the issue is not her mortal life, nor the lives of the invincibly ignorant members of the family, but her immortal soul.

Indeed, though she has a growing suspicion, the grandmother herself doesn't know until her moment of truth that God, Who can "write straight with crooked lines," is revealing Himself to her, is offering her the charity of salvation that a responding charity can win for her. Despite all of her ignoble efforts to save her own skin at all costs, despite her denying Him, He compassionately gives her a last chance.

Recall the dramatic paradox in which the Misfit, responsive to the grandmother's inferential denial, "Maybe He didn't raise the dead" — says, " 'I wasn't there so I can't say He didn't. . . . I wisht I had of been there,' he said, hitting the ground with his fist. 'It ain't right I wasn't there because if I had of been there I would of known. Listen lady,' he said in a high voice, 'if I had of been there I would of known and I wouldn't be like I am now.' [In modern error, but under conviction.] His voice seemed about to crack and the

grandmother's head cleared for an instant. She saw the man's face twisted close to her own as if he were going to cry and she murmured [in charity], 'Why you're one of my babies. You're one of my own children!' "

Mr. Hawkes sets out to show that Miss O'Connor and the late Nathanael West, for all their obvious differences, are joined in a "remarkably similar" diabolism. This would make a very pretty paradox if it could be supported. Mr. Hawkes's effort, it seems to me, fails in the case of both parties to his parallel.

I am not well acquainted with the work of Nathanael West and perhaps come to it too late to read it with any deep sympathy. Mr. Hawkes says, "West's preoccupation with the 'Christ business' begins as joke in *The Dream Life of Balso Snell*, reaches a partly confused and sentimental climax in *Miss Lonelyhearts*, and in *The Day of the Locust* finally dwindles to sporadic and surface satires on the freak Hollywood church as bad answer."

I have not been able to lay hand on *The Dream Life of Balso Snell*, but my conclusion on reading *Miss Lonelyhearts* (on which he largely bases his case) is that the "Christ business" is no more than a joke in it, too. True, Miss Lonelyhearts was the son of a Baptist preacher and retains sentimentally some garbled pulpit language, but he is not committed to it, nor does he really believe in it. Even as he sees it, it is a sentimentally fraudulent incarnation, palmed off through an utterly fraudulent newspaper enterprise — and, I might add, on people in sentimentally fraudulent trouble. No religion operates in the story; there is no work for the devil to do, and the devil doesn't waste his time on anything so pointless. Mr. Hawkes' anointed devil, Shrike, for all his sacrilegiousness and profanity, does not function as a devil. As Mr. Hawkes' comment on *The Day of the Locust* might suggest, religion operates to a far less degree in that novel, which is to say not at all.

Mr. Hawkes declares his inability to recognize the devil early in his essay, when he says, "their [Miss O'Connor's and Mr. West's] employment of the devil's voice as vehicle for their . . . true (or accurate) vision of our godless actuality. . . . " Throughout, Mr. Hawkes seems to be unable or unwilling to distinguish between his own sense of values and that of Miss O'Connor, the only one of the three who believes in the devil.

The whole essay is shot through with this. I quote: "Surely if the elements of Flannery O'Connor's fiction could be referred point for point to the established principles of a known orthodoxy. . . . "! My response is that they very well can. If they were referred to this "known orthodoxy," he might conceivably see that "the characters of Flannery O'Connor are not *judged,* victimized, made to appear only as absurd entities of the flesh" — as he erroneously concludes.

In the face of Miss O'Connor's own declaration of her belief in "the devil" (Lucifer, a fallen angel), Mr. Hawkes still persists: "My own feeling is that just as the creative process threatens the Holy throughout Flannery O'Connor's fiction by generating a paradoxical fusion of improbability and passion out of the Protestant 'do-it-yourself' evangelism of the South, and thereby raises the pitch of apocalyptic experience when it finally appears; so too throughout this fiction, the creative process transforms the writer's objective Catholic knowledge of the devil into an authorial attitude in itself in some measure diabolical."

Mr. Hawkes could only make such a wrongheaded conclusion from his substantially accurate analysis (though not "the creative process" threatening "the Holy," but the human fallibility of her characters) because of his invincible ignorance (it seems) of the Christian view of things. He concludes: "This is to say that in Flannery O'Connor's most familiar stories and novels the 'disbelief . . . that we breathe in with the air of the times' [quoting her] emerges fully as two-sided or complex as 'attraction for the Holy.' " To be sure and why not? This *disbelief* is party to our central religious conflict of the day. And I might add that it constitutes a strategic circumstance of Miss O'Connor's drama and satire.

May we allow Mr. Hawkes to pinpoint further his contention about Miss O'Connor's viewpoint? He quotes two passages from *The Violent Bear It Away,* giving dialogue between young Tarwater and the devil, as illustrating "the shifting substance" of Miss O'Connor's "authorial attitude." About the first, he says: "*The Violent Bear It Away* actualizes the truth of the Devil's sentiments — Tarwater does not, in fact, 'mean a thing to a soul'. . . . " This would belie the whole action of the book, the obvious intention of the story, and amounts to blind perversity on Mr. Hawkes' part, if he does not, indeed, have tongue in cheek. For he continues in this vein, saying: "But surely in giving voice to his dry country-cadenced nihilism and in laying out the pure deflated truth of

mere existence . . . the devil is speaking not only for himself but for the author." This smacks of the thumb screws and rubber hose and prepared confession of burlesque police work! And Mr. Hawkes' pietistic squeamishness over adjusting to the realism of Miss O'Connor's descriptive phrase "four strapping angels" might have come straight out of *Miss Lonelyhearts.*

I decline to believe that Mr. Hawkes is really serious in his contention about Miss O'Connor's diabolism. It is at variance with his appreciative acknowledgment: " . . . this comic writer is a serious writer — say, in her moral provocative use of paradox and her most original use of humor."

This brings us to the final element in Miss O'Connor's humor growing out of a religious viewpoint. I have referred to her *strategic circumstance* in today's issue of religious faith, and, while she has brilliantly made it hers in the context of our times, it is also timeless. As counterpart of faith, disbelief is always a circumstance of religious perspective, always an element in religious drama. However, the pervasiveness of the secular viewpoint today and the depth to which it has corrupted our sense of values, even among those of us who call ourselves orthodox Christians, constitutes so unparalleled a circumstance that it has provided for Miss O'Connor's genius a situation of humor that is, so far as I know, without precedent in our literature. Her humor bears a kinship to *Don Quixote,* but only collaterally.

The situation of humor is presented in "A Good Man Is Hard to Find." It is characteristic dramatic strategy of her short stories and it abounds in her novels too. She begins with familiar surfaces, in an action that seems secular at the outset, and in a secular tone of satire or humor. Before you know it, the naturalistic situation has become metaphysical, and the action appropriate to it comes with a surprise, an unaccountability that is humorous, grimly humorous, however shocking. It is paradox, to be sure, but it rests on a theology and a Christian perception more penetrating than most people in this world are blessed with.

Let us take, for example, her story "The Artificial Nigger." We begin here with nothing more uncommon than a rustic old man taking his rustic grandson for his first trip to the city. While their backwoodness is a bit grotesque and the old man's vanity provides touching humor, metaphysical drama doesn't overturn secular seeming until the man publicly denies his relationship to the boy to escape retribution and to give the humor a new dimension. Those familiar with her fiction may already have suspected a Tiger Christ in the "nigger" image, but who expected her brilliant *tour de force* with its compassionate irony in her "artificial nigger" as crucifix?

Mr. Hawkes concludes: " . . . if Bishop, the little idiot child, is intended to establish an innocence that points toward the apocalyptic, old Singleton, an insane comic figure in 'The Partridge Festival,' is intended to be exactly the opposite — crazy and lecherous and pointing toward the demonic."

But all of this is in accord with the religious view of the world's dichotomy. It is the genius of Miss O'Connor's Christian realism that her characters who are touched with Holiness reveal their human frailties and foibles too. The old prophet Mason Tarwater was a moonshiner and given to drunkenness at times.

Tactically this has an obvious satiric aim. But there is in it a deeper justification than dramatic tactics to get her prophets and saints by the censor; that is, make them credible to a secular world. The Christian knows that to life's very end the forces of God and of the devil carry on an unremitting and uncertain struggle for the possession of man's soul. What Miss O'Connor's humor so upsets is the smug, comfortable self-satisfaction, and/or, equally, the sentimental self-pity of the get of our secular day, who, in their invincible ignorance, have no notion of man's corruption — and even less of God's mercy! — a mercy that Miss O'Connor, consistent with her religion, reflects in her own compassion for her villains along with her heroes.

In *The Violent Bear It Away*, Mason Tarwater left a note for Rayber on Francis Marion's crib when he "delivered" him from it: "The prophet I raise up out of this boy will burn your eyes clean." The Rev. Robert M. McCowan in the *Kansas Magazine* perceives in the author's final words about Rayber, who is the object of her sharpest satire, this meaning:

"In her treatment of Rayber Miss O'Connor shows both a strength and a compassion which are rarely found together in the same artist. As he hears the cry of his child and he realizes that the prophecy of old Tarwater at last has its fulfillment, he stares with horror for the first time into the empty depths of his own soul. From this scene on we hear no more of him, but the logic of events easily suggests the sequel. With Rayber's life emptied of its one unifying force, and this at the hands of the boy whose confusion he had goaded into

action, we are left to imagine for ourselves the remorse and hatred of self which, his eyes now 'burned clean,' will be the first step of a complete spiritual conversion, or, this grace rejected, the last step of his hell on earth."

If we wish to go beyond the covers of this book for evidence to support Father McCowan's surmise that Rayber's eyes may have been *burned clean* to his conversion, we may recall a similar extreme unction that came to Haze Moates [sic] in *Wise Blood*.

Romano Guardini has described the Beatitudes as " . . . no mere formulas of superior ethics, but tidings of sacred and supreme reality's entry into the world." I do not bring in Guardini for rhetorical effect; his words have actual relevance for us. But we should realize here that this entrance is always a revolution. Miss O'Connor's art is committed to religious revolution against a secular world. Perhaps one can only grasp the overtones of her humor finally by holding firmly to an unsentimentalized appreciation of the Sermon on the Mount.

ARTICLE:
Sister Rose Alice, S.S.J., "Flannery O'Connor: Poet to the Outcast," *Renascence*, 16 (Spring 1964): 126–132.

Like Brainard Cheney, this Roman Catholic critic stresses the theological basis of O'Connor's fiction, elucidating its sly attacks on "the determined and atheistic humanitarian" who is "wildly defeated in story after story."

In the works of Flannery O'Connor, there is a faint flavor of Graham Greene, for Miss O'Connor is a Roman Catholic whose Catholicism informs her writing. In this she resembles Greene, but his cosmopolitan inhabitants of jungles are an almost total reversal of her jungle-bred inhabitants of the cosmos. Her allegories are not "Catholic"; indeed, even the word Christian sometimes seems too limited to encompass her studies of human nature. That her works are highly moral and constructed within the Christian frame of reference, no one will deny but it requires a certain skill to see through the individual to the symbol, beyond the sensational to the spiritual.

Miss O'Connor peoples her stories not with burnt-out intellectuals but with feverish quasi-primates in whom religion becomes allied with sheer animal cunning. Indeed their shrewdness would seem to antedate even the Old Testament heroes she favors as prototypes. Over and over again we encounter the primordial struggle for survival; we totter on the brink of the sub-rational chasm between puerility and senility; we face evil existing side by side with sincere religion — and indeed often flourishing within those confines — these are recurring patterns in Flannery O'Connor's writing. We can trace the flaming tracks of Elias across her thinking, and feel the darkness of the whale's belly closing around us. But in the thick of it, the shrillness of truth still scrapes against our inner sensibilities, for the very dynamism and impact of her style commands our attention and respect. If her Christians are repulsive, it is with the repulsiveness of a Job or of a Lazarus, covered with sores, deformed, outcast. And it is the comforters and Dives whom Miss O'Connor shows us as the determined and atheistic humanitarian, wildly defeated in story after story. The fact that criminals, the ignorant, the misfits, the lame, the displaced almost always appear on the side of religion is disconcerting; but this deliberate choice of the bizarre for her protagonists is one of Miss O'Connor's most powerful tools. Indeed the bizarre becomes almost banal, as in her ten short stories, two novels and the newest novella ["The Lame Shall Enter First"] (*Sewanee Review,* Summer '62), we meet one wretched "hero" after another. Only the most careful scrutiny and that within that "Christian frame of reference" enables us to grasp the supernatural allegations which render the natural horrors bearable. Her style has been described as "percussive and stabbing," and the description is apt. The drubbing and the piercing to which she subjects her characters make for something less than pleasant reading for it might be called a literary masochism. But there is the subtle insistence on the tragedy of "un-Redemption," the warping evil of unaided human nature, the ineluctable paradox of grace working through and within the humanly repulsive. This comes across as her almost obsessive theme.

One critic has said, "Miss O'Connor's vision of modern man ... is a Blakean vision, not through symbol as such but through the actuality of human behavior; and it has Blake's explosive honesty." It appears, however, that once the explosion of style has subsided, the behavior *is* the symbol, the external sign of the black turbulence underlying all her characterizations. The physical deformity and the mental unbalance which form the raw material for her characterizations are clearly symbols of the human condition as Miss

O'Connor views it. We must believe the author when she says that her characters are real "not in the real sense of being copies from life but as types which still exist in the South. . . . They are real, and if they are people who deal with life on more fundamental, even more violent terms than most people, this doesn't make them mythical monsters."

Let us choose a few of her characters and attempt an analysis of their human and literary qualities. First, in her novels. In *Wise Blood* we meet Hazel Motes, a twenty-two year old malcontent, who is enthralled by a "blind" itinerant preacher. The supposedly self-blinded charlatan and his degenerate daughter so thoroughly disillusion the boy that he is led by novel's end to a hideous self-mutilation and to death. At the height (or depth) of his disenchantment, however, he has founded a Church-without-Christ; he has preached a new jesus, a grisly travesty. As Miss O'Connor's first novel, *Wise Blood* contains in germ the same theme on which she will build all the variations of her later works. Motes is the benighted searcher for truth and God, wrestling with evil without and his own bruised nature within. He is faced with the eternal problem of evil and because it is garbed in the somber dress of religion, he is drawn to it as by a sinister magnet; at the same time, he is repelled by the sweet odor of sin. We too, oddly enough, find ourselves fascinated and repelled by both forces; hence the book, for all its patent allegory and less skillful literary manipulation, is compelling and significant. The very understandable human qualities of Hazel Motes — his unabashed curiosity about the maimed, his shattered idealism, his senseless bravado — transform the atypical physical into the typical *inner* projection of personality. And as a literary creation, he rankles in our minds satisfactorily.

The ten short stories, published under the lead title, "A Good Man Is Hard to Find," are, for the average reader, hardly more pleasurable. In one after the other, we find the exiled Adam, here deformed, here witless, here mutilated. In each case, a "futile" soul faces a fatalistic nihilism, the soul futile because it has successfully sidestepped Redemption, the nihilism fatalistic because the forces of evil assume the quality of a juggernaut. There is no conventional happy ending for Flannery O'Connor. Nor does she write with humor, as some critics have asserted. Unless we apply to her the description she uses of a character — "her mind, clear and detached and ironic anyway, was regarding him from a great distance, with amusement but with pity" — it is difficult to detect humor in any of her work. Her "happy ending" would have to be stated as the correct appraisal of modern man's vacuum mentality. This, and the fact that her characters seem to be etched in acid on an opaque surface, make the reading of her works a valuable literary experience.

"A Good Man Is Hard to Find" is a typically understated title for a story of rare violence. The wrangling family group, which Miss O'Connor so often employs, in this case sets out on a trip. Because of the nagging insistence of the grandmother, a side excursion is attempted but the direction is lost, there is an accident and the party is accosted by three escaping murderers. The blind and ruthless evil we meet in these three makes the petty incompatibilities of the family pale into insignificance; we are faced with an irrational and hence an almost irresponsible agent. This does not lessen the horrendous effect as, one by one, the "innocent" are slaughtered. The Misfit, as the leader of the three rightly calls himself, remains the most pathetic character in the story, the one for whom our sympathies are most actively aroused.

In "The River" we meet one of Miss O'Connor's favorite symbolisms, the drowning of a human person not yet warped by evil. This symbol of Baptism we will encounter in her major work, *The Violent Bear It Away;* it will again involve a child, the marvelously portrayed idiot-Bishop. The "innocent" in "The River" is the child of negligent parents who is taken by a nursemaid to an immersion baptismal ceremony. The unconscious skepticism of the child is totally overcome by the preacher's words — "You *count* now" — and the impression is as fixed as grooves in wax: "I *count*." We are more or less fatalistically prepared then for the child's effort to regain his sense of significance by returning to the river, which greedily sucks him into itself.

A TV version of another story, "The Life You Save May Be Your Own," was adapted (not surprisingly) to provide the type of happy ending that snugness of living rooms and smugness of minds must have. The one-armed protagonist, appropriately named Shiftlet, surmises his landlady/benefactress' ravenous desire for a son-in-law; her pretty daughter is both half-wit and deaf-mute. His smile "like a weary snake waking up by a fire" warns us that the promise of a battered car and money for a "honeymoon" are overpowering any small pity this maimed spirit might have for

one so much more afflicted than himself. So he marries her and starts out with the hysterically-relieved mother calling blessings on them — only to leave the helpless creature at a roadside diner, disclaiming her as a hitchhiker. Almost immediately we see Shiftlet picking up a rider; when that undesirable character evokes from Shiftlet a high-flown tribute to motherhood which is promptly and brutally rebuffed, the shock which engulfs him lets us see the full extent of his irresponsibility. We are told that he felt "the rottenness of the world was about to engulf him." The story ends powerfully with "a guffawing peal of thunder," but TV audiences were warmed to see him go back after the defenseless deaf-mute and presumably to a life of rectitude.

The use of imagery to depict fear, the sound and look and smell of it, is one of Miss O'Connor's strongest literary devices. In "A Stroke of Good Fortune," we are smothered by the same fear which Ruby experiences, fear of sickness, of pregnancy, of old age and death. "A Temple of the Holy Ghost" fills us with the fear of a homely twelve-year old, a fear of the unknown, of the freakish, even of the spiritual side of herself. The helpless shrinking which paralyzes the "genteel" faced with barbarism and senseless vandalism is set forth with tremendous impact in "A Circle of Fire." Perhaps the two most impressive stories in the collection, though, (partly because of their length which permits much more depth of characterization) are "Good Country People" and "The Displaced Person." In the first, the rational excellence of the one-legged heroine is attested by her Ph.D. but her moral degradation is seen in her effort to seduce the young itinerant Bible salesman. We are led to believe that he is of that unimpeachable stock, the salt of the earth ("good country people") — and so are both shocked and unwillingly triumphant when he turns into a completely immoral common thief, who, in a touch of consummate irony, makes off with the wooden leg!

"The Displaced Person" shows us a farm laborer hailed by his employer with "That man is my salvation! He saves me money!" Mrs. McIntyre's other help, however, feels a sinister threat in the D.P.'s great energy, and the pall of it soon lessens her own enthusiasm. Her only grievance is his non-conformity, but this becomes a positive phobia. Lacking any motive for dismissing him, she is as surely trapped as his disgruntled co-workers. It is an "accident" with a carelessly parked tractor that snaps the life-thread of this "innocent"; the onlookers shared "one look that froze them in collusion together." The brief denouement merely states the moral and physical collapse of the entire group, all of whom feel mercifully — and determinedly — "free" from any apprehensions of guilt.

Miss O'Connor claims as her own favorite "The Artificial Nigger" and I would suggest that this preference is based on the more theocentric theme. The mercy of God stands out in sharp relief in this tale of mutual hatred between the very young and the very old. The frustration of the young and the betrayal by the old, and yet the inevitability of their agonized dependence on each other, leave the reader with a strong image of the heinousness of man's petty rebellions against God and the largesse of God's mercy in the face of our misery. The theme of this story does seem to be more obviously and beautifully stated than are the themes in her other stories. Perhaps it would be more accurate to say again that this appears to be one of the most beautiful of the variations on the theme.

The work on which her reputation was most firmly established, however, is undoubtedly her novel, *The Violent Bear It Away*. Besides being a milestone in contemporary American literary style, it is also an impressive contribution to the deposit of Christian allegory. We are confronted with the triadic symbolism which we met in *Wise Blood* and which we shall see so unmistakably in her latest work, the novella, "The Lame Shall Enter First." The protagonist here is Tarwater, a boy in the image and likeness of his fanatic grandfather, and destined to fulfill the prophetic career so abruptly terminated by the old man's grisly death. Tarwater's chief objective is the baptism of his small cousin, Bishop — a white-haired idiot child born to an atheist-scholar, Rayber. With his mother long dead, the child is the quintessence of innocence, torn apart by the grotesque love of his father and the religious fanaticism of Tarwater. The end is inevitable: the slaughter of the innocent. The symbolic slaughter, the baptismal drowning. Throughout the book we find the struggle between the scholarly humanitarian materialist in Rayber and the savage conviction of the spirit in Tarwater. Brooding over the entire work is the wild-eyed presence of the dead grandfather, a fascinating research subject to Rayber, a hated life-source to the boy. The allegorical implication, we must presume, is the Christian Church, brooding over the death-agony of innocence in the world of materialism, sorrowing at

the same time over the crudity of the human instruments of redemption. All of this is present to the mature and perceptive reader; to the student, the novel could stand on its literary prowess alone.

Miss O'Connor has commented on this situation herself: "One of the Christian novelist's basic problems is to get the Christian vision across to an audience to whom it is meaningless. . . . His work will have to have value on the dramatic level, the level of truth recognizable by anybody." Her work *is* unquestionably of great value on the dramatic level. No one who has read the last two works has been spared a ghastly glimpse of depravity and decadence. Stylistically, Miss O'Connor's descriptive and narrative powers place her among the outstanding American writers of the past decade. For example, in *The Violent Bear It Away*, the passage describing the drowning of the slobbering idiot child:

> The bellow rose and fell, then it blared out one last time rising out of its own momentum as if it were escaping finally, after centuries of waiting, into silence. The beady night noises closed in again.

And:

> He [Rayber] stood waiting for the raging pain, the intolerable hurt that was his *due*, to begin, so that he could ignore it, but he continued to feel nothing. He stood light-headed at the window and it was not until he realized there would be no pain that he collapsed.

This climactic but unsensational type of writing, coupled with the subtle building up of suspense pressures and inevitability, makes Flannery O'Connor's writing stunningly effective. If she is preoccupied with one locale (the South), one theme and actually, an atypical stereotype in character, she remains a master of allegory and of imagery.

Flannery O'Connor's novella, "The Lame Shall Enter First," deserves special mention. The resemblance to the *Violent* is unmistakable: Rayber becomes Sheppard; Tarwater becomes Rufus; Bishop becomes Norton. The dead mother serves in a sense as the deus ex machina, for it is about her state in the after life that the plot revolves. (Interestingly enough, Miss O'Connor chooses not to use women in her longer works. We can only envisage her portrayal of an important woman character and look ahead to it hopefully). But the new story appears to be a new burst of an old energy, a further refinement of the earlier theme. And yet

PARKER'S BACK

Parker's wife was eighteen years old and plain. The skin on her face was thin and drawn as tight as the skin on an onion and her eyes were grey and sharp like the points of an ice-pick. Parker could not get over the fact that he had married her. She was ~~always~~ always on the look-out for sin, ~~She~~ did not like *it that* his new employer ~~being~~ *was* a woman.

"It's no cause for you to be working for a woman," she x said, drawing up her mouth over the word woman. "It's no reason you can't work for a man." They were sitting on the front porch on a black leather sofa that had been there when Parker rented the house. Every few minutes a car shot past on the highway in front of them and his wife's eyes swerved after it and then came back slowly to rest on Parker. "It isn't any reason for it being a woman," she insisted.

If Parker had thought she was jealous, he would have been elated. He tried to imagine that she was. He had not told her that the woman he was working for was an old woman, fifty years old or more and too dried up to have an interest in him except for getting as much work out of him as she could. Not, he knew, that an old woman wouldn't sometimes have an eye out for a young man, particularly if he were good-looking like himself--Parker had bright red hair with sideburns and small eyes of an almost aquamarine hue--but this old woman looked at him the way she looked at her rotary hay-baler, as if she had to put up with it because she didn't have any better. The hay-baler had broken down the first hour Parker was on it and she had set him at once to cutting bushes, saying out the side of her mouth to the nigger, "Everything he

Opening pages from a working draft for "Parker's Back," the last story O'Connor completed before her death on 3 August 1964 (The Flannery O'Connor Collection, Ina Dillard Russell Library, Georgia College)

96

Parker had to put up with her   2

touches, he breaks." He ~~would not have taken~~ the ~~old woman's~~
because he
~~sass if he had not~~ had to have ~~x~~the job. He had bought his

wife a washing machine and a refrigerator and two loan ~~xxxxxx~~

companies were waiting impatiently for him to miss a payment
on the truck
so they could come and take his truck, ~~which~~ was indispensible
him
to ~~Parker.~~

                         seven
       He had been married ~~to her~~ ~~xxx~~ months and still loved ~~her.~~ */his wife*
~~inspite of the fact that she was pregnant.~~
H~~e~~ couldn't understand what was wrong with him that he loved

her or what was right with her. ᔕhe wouldn't have anything

to do with him until he had married her--and that was the one

thing he had always said he would not do for any woman, living

or dead. He had lived with a few women and had left them when

their dispositions began to sour. Any~~xx~~ woman that would stay

sweet, he would stay with her, but life was too short,(he would

tell the one he was about to leav~~e~~) to live with a sour woman.

He had observed that they soured usually between five and ei~~g~~ht

months, but the one he had finally married had been like vinegar

from the first.

                                      his mind on
       ᔕefore he married her, Parker settled ~~xxxxxxxxxx~~ the problem

of marriage. ~~X~~ If it didn't make any difference if you <u>didn't</u>

marry the woman you were living with, he reasoned, then it

didn't make any difference if you <u>did</u> mar~~ry~~,the one you were

fixing to ~~xxxxx~~ live with. ᔛou could leave one you were

married to as easy as one you weren't. The lucidity of this

~~xxx~~ satisfied him ~~enough~~ before he was married, but after he

was married, the problem began to gnaw at him again. He be-

came suspicious ~~ofxhisxownxreasoningxcaxzifc~~ that there was
                                                just
some hidden flaw in this reasoning and that he ~~would wake~~ up
one ~~with the sure knowledge that he was~~
~~xxxx morning a realize it and find himself trapped.~~ *was already*
trapped and didn't know it.

refinement is hardly the word, for the bludgeoning of this work is a numbing process.

The "hero," Rufus, a reform school parolee with a hideous club foot, is befriended by Sheppard, a social worker with a mania for redeeming. "I'm above simple pettiness. I'm going to save you," is his repeated reply to the boy's vicious ingratitude. The innocent is Norton, the repulsive son of Sheppard, who is stupidly gluttonous and avaricious. That these three qualities in his own child — his "stupidity" and his lack of interest in all but food and money — are symptomatic, does not occur to Sheppard until it is too late. Rufus, treacherous and despicable, nevertheless feels a compulsion to convert Norton to the Bible and to a belief in his mother's continued existence. And so the war is waged. Nothing excites Sheppard "so much as thinking what he could do for such a boy" while Rufus shouts maniacally, "Even if I didn't believe it [the Bible], it'd still be true," and to prove his convictions, tears a page from the Bible and eats it. Both are statements of philosophical significance to the story, yet neither entirely prepares the reader for the outcome. Rufus spitefully violates his parole by vandalism and is taken by the police. Sheppard, in despair, turns to the attic where he has set up a telescope in a frantic effort to "improve" Rufus' mind. Only now does he realize that he must concentrate his efforts on his own bereft child. In the attic he finds Norton, convinced that he has seen his mother through the telescope and longing to be with her again, hanging dead from the rafters. One almost cannot bear to read on from the moment when Rufus laughs triumphantly at the failure of Sheppard to mold him to his own image; the repulsive good defeats the urbane evil and there emerges the pattern whereby we realize that the sacrifice has not yet been fully consummated. Still the death of the innocent is shattering.

To a new reader, Flannery O'Connor will undoubtedly bring a shudder, though we must admit part of the shudder to be the excitement of discovery. The reader of all her works, familiar with her central theme, will greet her novella as the most powerful variation she has yet produced. True, the element of suspense is superseded by a certain grim morbidity; the semi-fiendish zealot will triumph over the humanistic materialist and the innocent dolt will be destroyed. That, of course, is a gross over-simplification, but it serves at least as an inadequate summary of the recurring theme. But actually, as only twelve tones comprise the thematic material of all music, so the few

themes of all great literature are used and re-used by each generation. The message does not become time-worn. The universal truths can be re-stated endlessly, yet always with profit to the reader. The struggle between the rational and the animal in every human being — and the mysterious workings of the spirit on the supernatural level — these are certainly worthy themes for any Christian author. Flannery O'Connor has proven herself uniquely qualified to re-introduce and promulgate them to the American reading public of this decade.

LETTER:
Flannery O'Connor to "A," 6 December 1963; in *The Habit of Being*, p. 552.

"The Lame Shall Enter First," discussed in the preceding article, is one of the stories collected in Everything That Rises Must Converge (1965). *"Revelation," another story in the volume, is discussed in this letter, which also gives O'Connor's reaction to the media coverage of the assassination and funeral of President John F. Kennedy.*

I'm much cheered that the story ["Revelation"] makes the right kind of noise in your head, though I am fearful other heads will be less reliable. If the story is taken to be one designed to make fun of Ruby, then it's worse than venal. The only other person I've sent it to is Catharine Carver and I haven't heard from her. She's a Yankee and a stoic, a woman whose only happiness seems to be in work and endurance, and that is not real happiness but just non-misery. What she makes of it will be a kind of acid test though I don't propose to pay too much attention if she makes nothing of it.

I wasn't thinking of Mary Grace as the Devil but then the whole story just sort of happened — though it took me about eight weeks to write it. It was one of those rare ones in which every gesture gave me great pleasure in the writing, from Claud pulling up his pants leg to show where the cow kicked him, right on through. The last time I went to the doctor here, Ruby and Claud were in there. It was just after Charlene and Walter announced their nuptials and that was the subject of conversation in the waiting room. I was just taken with the conversation — much better than anything I had in the story . . .

I didn't hear the two ambulance drivers interviewed but I heard everybody else and his brother. I think the funeral was a salutary tonic

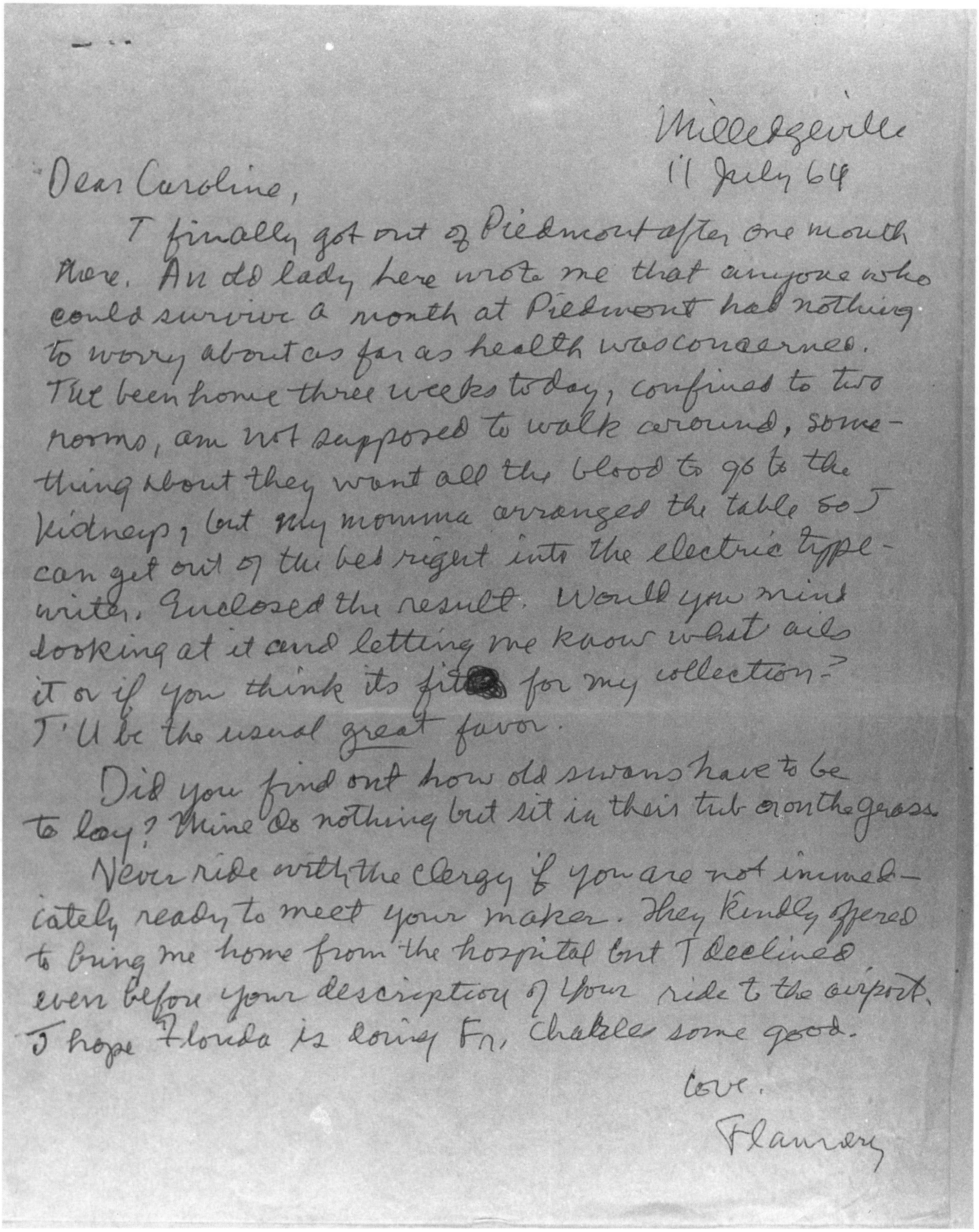

Milledgeville
11 July 64

Dear Caroline,

I finally got out of Piedmont after one month there. An old lady here wrote me that anyone who could survive a month at Piedmont had nothing to worry about as far as health was concerned. I've been home three weeks today, confined to two rooms, am not supposed to walk around, something about they want all the blood to go to the kidneys, but my momma arranged the table so I can get out of the bed right into the electric type-writer. Enclosed the result. Would you mind looking at it and letting me know what ails it or if you think its fit for my collection? I'll be the usual great favor.

Did you find out how old swans have to be to lay? Mine do nothing but sit in their tub on the grass.

Never ride with the clergy if you are not immed-iately ready to meet your maker. They kindly offered to bring me home from the hospital but I declined even before your description of your ride to the airport. I hope Florida is doing Fr. Charles some good.

love,

Flannery

Letter sent to Caroline Gordon with a draft of "Parker's Back" (Collection of Ashley Brown) for this back-slapping gum-chewing hiya-kid nation. Mrs. Kennedy has a sense of history and of what is owing to death.

I'm better. My trouble is anemia . . .

I have just read the galleys to Jack Hawkes' latest — *Second Skin* — and will give you same when you come. It's a little easier to follow than the others but when it's over you don't know any more what you've got. At least I don't. You probably will. He got a Ford Grant for next year, for which I'm glad.

LETTER:
Flannery O'Connor to Elizabeth McKee, 7 May 1964; in *The Habit of Being*, pp. 574–575.

The anemia mentioned in the preceding letter to "A" was caused by a benign fibroid tumor, which necessitated that O'Connor have surgery. The operation, performed in late February 1964, at first seemed to be a complete success, but complications developed, and O'Connor's lupus, which had been in remission, was reactivated. O'Connor went ahead with plans for a collection of her short stories, sending her agent, Elizabeth McKee, a tentative table of contents.

I have been thinking about this collection of my stories and what can be done to get it out with me sick. I am definitely out of commission for the summer and maybe longer with this lupus. I have to stay mostly in bed and am not supposed to get up and type except very short business letters. I was wondering if you have copies of the magazines the stories have been published in, if FS&G couldn't just print up the book from those? If I were well there is a lot of rewriting and polishing I could do, but in my present state of health I see no reason for me to spend my energies on old stories that are essentially all right as they are. Giroux seemed to want the book on their fall list and this is the only way I know to get it there. Will you call him up and discuss the matter with him and see what can be done? I think I'll be able to make any really necessary changes on the proofs.

If you don't have copies of all the magazines my mother may have the ones you don't. However she has her hands full right now as she has me in bed on one side of the house and my 81-year-old aunt, who has had a heart attack, on the other.

If we are going to make any money out of permissions, we'll have to get the book out.

The stories for inclusion are:
"Greenleaf" (*Kenyon*)

"A View of the Woods" (*PR?* or *Kenyon*)
"The Enduring Chill" (*Harper's Bazaar*)
"The Comforts of Home" (*Kenyon*)
"The Partridge Festival" (*The Critic*)
"The Lame Shall Enter First" (*Sewanee*)
"Everything That Rises Must Converge" (*NWW*)
"Revelation" (*Sewanee*)

This is not necessarily the order I want them in, but that can be worked out later with Giroux if he wants to go ahead and do it this way. Also which story I'll use for title.

LETTER:
Flannery O'Connor to Cecil Dawkins, 19 May 1964; in *The Habit of Being*, pp. 578–579.

In this letter to Cecil Dawkins, an English professor and writer from Alabama with whom she had been corresponding since 1957, O'Connor revealed the source for "Revelation" while exhibiting her determination to continue writing despite ill health.

I was cheered to hear from you and I'll be proud to get *Catch-22*. I got nothing better to do than give it a running start. That operation in February started up my disseminated lupus and I have been in the hospital again recently with that. I'm at home now but as the TV personality says "I ain't doing nuttin, just settin around." In fact for almost all of the time except when I go to the doctor once a week. Last week I had a blood transfusion and that made me feel considerable stronger. No pain, just extreme weakness with this lupus as the other symptoms can be controlled with the steroid drugs.

"Revelation" was my reward for setting in the doctor's office. Mrs. Turpin I found in there last fall. Mary Grace I found in my head, doubtless as a result of reading too much theology.

My aunt Mary had a heart attack in March and she is out here with us now, also a cousin from Kansas City who is helping my mama do some of the work . . .

Are you still working on the play? I guess I'll be using that "Enduring Chill" story in the collection. I suggested to Elizabeth [McKee] that maybe FS&G could print up the collection from the published stories. There's no use my wasting what little energy I can muster on busy-work. I do think some rewriting needs to be done on that particular story & I could do some on a couple of the others. However I haven't heard from her yet about it . . .

LETTER:
Flannery O'Connor to "A," 25 July 1964; in *The Habit of Being*, p. 594.

In her last letter to "A," written just ten days before her death, O'Connor explained one of Caroline Gordon's comments about "Parker's Back," O'Connor's last completed story. She also mentions having won a first prize in the O. Henry Awards for the story "Revelation."

No Caroline didn't mean the tattoos [in "Parker's Back"] were the heresy. Sarah Ruth was the heretic — the notion that you can worship in pure spirit. Caroline gave me a lot of advice about the story but most of it I'm ignoring. She thinks every story must be built according to the pattern of the Roman arch and she would enlarge the beginning and the end, but I'm letting it lay. I did well to write it at all. I had another transfusion Wednesday but it don't seem to have done much good.

We can worry about the interpitations of "Revelation" but not its fortunes. I had a letter from the O. Henry prize people & it got first.

OBITUARY:
"Flannery O'Connor Dead at 39; Novelist and Short-Story Writer Used Religion and the South as Themes in Her Work — Won O. Henry Awards," *New York Times*, 4 August 1964, p. 4.

O'Connor's death on 3 August 1964, from lupus or complications of the disease, was the subject of a respectful notice in The New York Times.

MILLEDGEVILLE, Ga., Aug. 3 (UPI) — Flannery O'Connor, one of the nation's most promising writers, died today. She was 39 years old.

Miss O'Connor had been ill for some years with a bone ailment that restricted her activity and forced her to use crutches.

She lived with her mother, Mrs. Regina O'Connor, on a 500-acre farm.

Work Highly Praised

In Miss O'Connor's writing were qualities that attract and annoy many critics: she was steeped in Southern tradition, she had an individual view of her Christian faith and her fiction was often peopled by introspective children.

But while other writers received critical scorn for turning these themes into clichés, Miss O'Connor's two novels and few dozen stories were highly praised.

In reviewing her second novel, "The Violent Bear It Away," for The New York Times in 1960, Orville Prescott described Miss O'Connor as a "literary white witch" whose "talent for fiction is so great as to be almost overwhelming."

"She writes with blazing skill about the most appalling horrors," he continued, "and sometimes makes them entirely real and perfectly natural."

In contrast Miss O'Connor saw herself as "a novelist with Christian concerns" who wrote her stories "in relation to the redemption of Christ." Many readers failed to see this relation, but they enjoyed her nevertheless.

Miss O'Connor was a Roman Catholic, but her main characters were Protestant Fundamentalists and fanatics. She suggested that the intensity of their faith was preferable to the tepid religion of a secularized churchman.

Miss O'Connor, who was born in Savannah, moved as a child to Milledgeville, a small town of mansions and farms. She lived in a two-story house set on a profitable farm. She did not take part in the business of the farm, except for raising the peafowl that strutted around the grounds, and, frequently, in her stories.

She wrote every day of the week when possible. "I write from 9 to 12," she once said, "and spend the rest of the day recuperating."

A self-portrait hanging in the family living room stressed Miss O'Connor's plain features. Sharing the painting is a peacock that, like Miss O'Connor, stares forward harshly.

In rating her among the most promising of the current generation of writers, critics frequently attempted to categorize her talent in terms of the South or her religious outlook. She did not object, but declared: "My characters are not sociological types. I write 'tales' in the sense Hawthorne wrote tales — though I hope with less reliance on allegory. I'm interested in the old Adam. He just talks Southern because I do."

Miss O'Connor was graduated from the Woman's College of Georgia, in Milledgeville, and in 1947 received a master's degree in Fine Arts from the University of Iowa. Her work at the Writer's Workshop there directed by Paul Engle resulted in publication. Stories appeared in such journals as the Sewanee Review, Harper's Bazaar, Partisan Review, and Kenyon Review, which last

happened to him. I'm glad Fr.
Charles is better. Cheers to you
& pray for me.
                    Love,
                        Flannery

Milledgeville
31 July 64

Dear Caroline,
    I do thank you for the re-
marks. I read both versions
and hope to do a little something about it all but I don't
know how much as the lid
has been put back on me. I
go to the hospital tomorrow for
another transfusion. The blood
count just won't hold. Anyway maybe I'll learn something
for the next set of stories. You
were good to take the time.
    One of the sisters at the Cancer
Home wrote me that the Rev. Fr.
(I presume she meant the Abbot)
had had a seige of being in the
hospital. She said he had
some torn ligaments in his
arm but didn't say what had

O'Connor's last letter to Caroline Gordon, thanking her for comments on "Parker's Back" (Collection of Ashley Brown)

year published a special collection of appreciation and criticism of Miss O'Connor.

Her first novel, "Wise Blood," published by Harcourt, Brace in 1952, was generally praised by the critics. Ten of her stories were published by Harcourt, Brace in 1955 under the title, "A Good Man is Hard to Find."

Her awards included O. Henry citations in 1955 and 1957, and a Ford Foundation grant in 1959.

Miss O'Connor's first-floor workroom was crammed with books and journals ranging from Faulkner to weekly Catholic newspapers. She read and reread the Bible, and made frequent allegorical comments in her stories. "The Violent Bear It Away," for example, is from Matthew, 11:12.

A collection of stories to be published next February by Farrar, Straus & Co. is entitled "Everything That Rises Must Converge." This is a line from the writings of the late Jesuit anthropologist and philosopher, Pierre Teilhard de Chardin.

Miss O'Connor's full name was Mary Flannery O'Connor, but she dropped the first name by choice many years ago.

BOOK REVIEW:
Richard Poirier, "If You Know Who You Are You Can Go Anywhere," review of *Everything That Rises Must Converge, New York Times Book Review*, 30 May 1965, pp. 6, 22.

Everything That Rises Must Converge, *a collection of nine stories written after the appearance of* A Good Man Is Hard to Find *in 1955, was published on 24 April 1965 with a biographical introduction by Robert Fitzgerald. Poirier's review, though not entirely positive, is a perceptive appreciation of the strengths and weaknesses of O'Connor's fiction.*

Short of any posthumous publication, these are the last stories we shall have from Flannery O'Connor. She died last summer at 38 [i.e., 39] in Milledgeville, Ga., a town where her family, old Georgian Catholic, has lived since before the Civil War. The introduction by her friend Robert Fitzgerald is thus understandably dedicatory, and yet it makes none of the excessive claims for her place in contemporary American literature that are always the anticipated embarrassment on such occasions. With respect to her work, the introduction observes what she herself would have considered a fitting humility. "To know oneself," she remarked in 1957, "is, above all, to know what one lacks. It

is to measure oneself against Truth, and not the other way around. The first product of self-knowledge is humility." "Measuring" of this kind is characteristic of her Catholicism, and of Mr. Fitzgerald's too, who tells us of their going daily to Mass during the months in 1949–50 when Miss O'Connor lived with the Fitzgeralds in Connecticut. His essay has clarity braced against exaggeration — which, as much as anything else, is evidence of his affectionate knowledge of the person and her work.

Humility in the claims made for oneself, for what one knows and values, is in fact the operative standard within the stories. Pride makes a fool at some time or other of nearly all of her characters. It gets expressed not grandly but within the grotesqueries of daily, mostly Southern life, and within simple people who are aware of no alternatives to that life, once pride is destroyed, except death or a strange God.

Everything that rises must indeed converge, joining the anonymity either of oblivion or the blessed. The pride of her characters may be for a new hat, a bit of money, a college degree or clean hogs; it is her particular genius to make us believe that there are Christian mysteries in things irreduceably banal. And in this too there is an aspect of Catholicism, most beautifully exemplified in the penultimate stanza of the "Paradiso," where Dante likens his poetic efforts in fashioning a vision of God to the work of a "good tailor."

Her characters seem damned precisely to the degree that they lack Miss O'Connor's own "measure" of their trivialities. They have no measure for them *but* pride, and they can therefore appeal for authority only to mundane standards that never threaten it, to platitudes and to prejudices, very often racial ones. Necessarily, she is a mordantly comic writer. She offers us the very sounds of platitude ("If you know who you are you can go anywhere," remarks the mother to her intellectualist son in the title story), or of prejudice (as in the imagined dialogue with God of the pretentious lady in "Revelation," who would have asked Him to make her anything but white trash: " 'All right make me a nigger, then — but that don't mean a trashy one.' And he would have made her a neat clean respectable Negro woman, herself but black.")

Except for sloth, pride is of all human failings the one that can be most difficult for a writer to translate into actions. Most often it expresses itself in a smugness of inaction, the hostilities it creates in others being the result merely of the

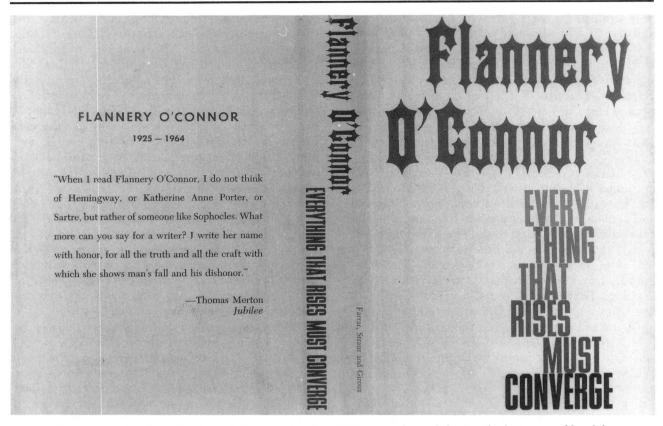

FLANNERY O'CONNOR

1925 — 1964

"When I read Flannery O'Connor, I do not think of Hemingway, or Katherine Anne Porter, or Sartre, but rather of someone like Sophocles. What more can you say for a writer? I write her name with honor, for all the truth and all the craft with which she shows man's fall and his dishonor."

—Thomas Merton
Jubilee

Dust jacket for the collection of short stories that O'Connor planned during the last year of her life

tones of voice, the gestures, the placidities which are its evidence. Miss O'Connor can produce as much violence from a quiet conversation as can other writers from the confrontations of gangsters or fanatics, though she can manage that, too.

The action in the best of these stories, "Revelation," is to a large extent dialogue, in which the veritable sounds of people talking gently in a doctor's office about everything from the heat to the ingratitude of children leads to a sudden but somehow expected flare-up of violence and disaster. With very little room for maneuver — most of her stories are about 20 pages long — she achieves transitions and even reversals of tone with remarkable speed, and she can show in people who have been almost preposterously flat a sudden visionary capacity. This absolute sureness of timing is, I think, what makes the reader assent to the religious direction which her stories take; from involvement in the most common stuff they move toward the Heaven and the Hell weirdly apprehended by her characters.

Miss O'Connor's major limitation is that the direction of her stories tends to be nearly always

the same. Caring almost nothing for secular destinies, which are altogether more various than religious ones, she propels her characters toward the cataclysms where alone they can have a tortured glimpse of the need and chance of redemption. The repetitiousness inherent in her vision of things is more bothersomely apparent in this collection than anyone would have guessed who read the various pieces over the interval of their periodical publication.

Story after story here and in her other fiction — "Wise Blood," "A Good Man is Hard to Find," "The Violent Bear It Away" — involves a conflict between parental figures and recalcitrant, precocious, generally snotty children aged anywhere from 8 to 36. The local result of this conflict is dialogue that comically mixes the parent's cant of "understanding" with muttering from children that has the velocity of a thrown knife. The ultimate result is usually the murder or suicide of one of the conflicting parties, often bringing with it some sort of distorted religious vision.

Of the nine stories in this present volume the casualty list is heavily parental. In "Everything

That Rises Must Converge," a mother dies in the arms of her remorseful son. In "Greenleaf," a mother is killed by a bull — not with the connivance but partly because of the irresponsibility of her bachelor sons.

In "A View of the Woods," a grandfather dies of a heart attack after physical combat with a 10-year-old granddaughter whom he can subdue only by strangulation. In "The Enduring Child," a son comes home to die but is kept alive, much to his distaste, by a mother who will probably kill him with her conversation.

In "Judgement Day," a father, staying with his daughter in New York, wants to die so that he can be taken back to Georgia — and achieves this ambition, partly by provoking a Negro into abusing him much as does the woman in "Everything That Rises." In "Revelation," an older lady is struck on the head by a book and then assaulted by a Wellesley girl, home from vacation, while she is telling the girl's mother that sometimes "I just feel like shouting, 'Thank you, Jesus, for making everything the way it is!' " In "The Comfort of Home," a mother is shot by her bachelor son who is aiming instead, maybe, at the convict girl whom she has introduced into the household. In "The Lame Shall Enter First," a son, wanting to find his dead mother in the heavens, hangs himself at the instigation of a convict boy to whom his father is proud of showing "kindness."

In one sense, Miss O'Connor's repetitiousness is an indication of how serious a writer she is. As against what might be called writers by occupation (who can of course always "pick" their subjects) she was obsessed by arrangements of life and language in which she saw some almost eschatological possibilities. And her religious commitment is the more powerful in determining the shape of her stories precisely because it is never made overt merely in rhetoric. It exists, as strong commitments often do, in a form unspoken, inseparable from the very processes of her sight and feeling. She may be the only writer of English or American fiction in this century whose style, down to the very placing of a comma, is derived from a religious feeling for the simplest actualities. Obviously, being a religious writer in this way is different from anything in, say, Graham Greene, who merely lugs theological rhetoric into stories that were by nature best left as mildly entertaining adventures.

I cannot describe her very rare distinctions in this vein more clearly than she did in an essay called "The Fiction Writer and His Country": "I

see," she wrote, "from the standpoint of Christian orthodoxy. This means that for me the meaning of life is centered in our Redemption by Christ and that what I see in the world I see in relation to that." To see the world from such a standpoint means caring about the possibilities of Redemption literally in what one sees, in the grossest things, and it is no wonder, therefore, that she has such a sharp eye for the grotesqueness and the pathos of the most ordinary vanities. But the test is in the reading and for that nothing better illustrates her intensely applied power than the story "Revelation." It belongs with the few masterpieces of the form in English.

BOOK REVIEW:
Guy Davenport, "The Top is a New Bottom" [excerpt], review of *Everything That Rises Must Converge, National Review,* 17 (27 July 1965): 658–659.

Southern writer Guy Davenport ranked O'Connor with William Faulkner and Eudora Welty.

[. . .] Flannery O'Connor, who died last August in her thirty-ninth year, had perfected an art of such integrity that she must be placed with Faulkner and Eudora Welty in the highest place among Southern writers. This is a futile evaluation in the world's eyes, for the literature of the South, honored for its imagination, its savagery of emotion, its bewildering and relentless critique of some disaster that it has been incapable of explaining for a century, is an unknown, unread, and almost wholly misunderstood literature. These nine stories, every sentence of which is written from a sense of moral outrage, reflect all over again that the Southern writer is moved by an anguish unknown to the rest of our literature.

Hawthorne and Twain, recoiling from man's lapse into bestiality, were drifting toward the Southerner's view of man in what seems to be a permanent retreat from civilization. For fifty years now the Southern writer has been saying that the South can arrive at nothing but the empty harvest of its own sterility. The South is outrageous. It is like nothing so much as the Old Testament, which, as Voltaire observed, must be true, as people do not tell that kind of lie about themselves. And like the Old Testament, the Southerner's account of the South proceeds, character after character, by insisting that the heights of human grandeur are far too low in the eyes of God. And, for the most part, far too low in the eyes of man.

The denouement of every Southern work of fiction is like Ahab's cry in his garden, when he met the accusing Elijah, *Alas, my enemy, hast thou found me?* For this is a literature without ideas, without politics, or theory. The South is not a place in the sense that France is a place; it is a disaster. What is so confusing is that its literature is not tragic. Tragedy can only appear in a people who have valid signs in their discourse — natural law, gods, norms of honesty, dignity, and so on. The South has none of these. Swift's Ireland, Goya's Spain of 1810, the Russia of Gorky's youth; these are comparable examples of moral emptiness.

Miss O'Connor's title, taken from Père Teilhard de Chardin, is ironic. All that rises does converge, but the risings she shows us are from such shallow and depressed beginnings that their convergences are merely pitiful. She deals with those tow-haired, razor-blade-eyed Southerners whose names are apt to be Whiflet (or Snops or Turbeyfield or Garnet), a people possessed by religion, whiskey, and self-hatred. In each story we find one of them ensnared and obliterated by the sheer littleness of his own being. It is wrong to place Miss O'Connor (or Faulkner or Eudora Welty) in the Gothic School, however freakish and shocking her themes. The astounding surface of her stories, as wildly grotesque as the best Gothic, is but the visual equivalent of the outrage she feels before a world stupid with selfishness. Not since the decade that gave us Carson McCuller's *Reflections in a Golden Eye* and Eudora Welty's *A Curtain of Green* has the Southern mind been so brilliantly examined. [. . .]

BOOK REVIEW:
Saul Maloff, "On Flannery O'Connor," review of *Mystery and Manners: Occasional Prose*, Commonweal, 90 (8 August 1969): 490–491.

The Fitzgeralds' edition of nonfiction writings by O'Connor, published on 12 May 1969, provides the basis for an understanding of her religious and aesthetic beliefs. Maloff recognized the connections between O'Connor's particular art and the broad concerns of all literary art.

Even if these "occasional" pieces — lectures, less formal talks, some critical essays and reviews, and miscellaneous articles — were not buttressed by the authority of the late Flannery O'Connor's fictions and thoroughly established reputation, they would be eminently worth collecting. Miss O'Connor could not have intended a collection; and her devoted friends and editors, the Fitzgeralds, tell us of their labors in cutting and pruning and splicing together fragments, in some instances, to make wholes of overlapping talks on the same or related subjects. Yet, remarkably, there is no oppressive sense of redundancy or padding; but rather a liberating one, of themes and variations, accretion and accumulation, a steady expansion of implication and statement to the point where the ideas essential to her life and art gathered toward the makings of something like a system.

Each piece — from those that seem little more than extended asides to those that clearly intend a summation of views — is singular, finely wrought and deeply felt; each bears the unmistakable imprint of her mind and play of her wit; and in each — how rare this is in expository prose — there is audible always the sound of her voice speaking; never the sound of a machine clattering. Except for the marvelous opening memoir of her life with the peacocks she raised, this volume records her lifelong preoccupation with the making of literature, the meaning and value of fiction.

Miss O'Connor wrote not as a theorist, nor even as a critic in any of the usual senses — nowhere in the volume does her attention come steadily to rest on a particular work or author. She wrote, as a writer of fiction reflecting on craft and art who in perfect confidence took herself and her work as sufficient instances of general problems about which universal assertions can be made; and when, in violation, almost, of her native temperament, she addressed herself to more theoretic questions — of regionalism, of being a Southern writer, of the "grotesque" in fiction, and especially of the vexed problem of religious belief, particularly Catholic belief and its relations to literature — she did so, one feels, as much because no one else could, or cared to, as because of the great pressures they exerted upon her as she practiced and sought to perfect her distinctive, recalcitrant art.

So to describe the book is to make it seem a writer's book aimed at other writers (which it is); but it is also to miss its special pleasure. "Special" because, though she provides it on every page, in every paragraph, it is not of the ingratiating kind. She does not court the reader; she doesn't seek to amuse or cajole or flatter so that she will be loved. Fiction was her life, its value transcendent. She is never consoling or reassuring. The defining quality of her mind was toughness, even harshness, impatience. She could be cranky, petulant, hectoring. She speaks with the wonderful arrogance of a writer who had come to know the exact dimensions of her powers — both scope and limitations; and who knew that though she had written relatively little, she was already among the American writers.

There was no doubt in her mind that she was born to write; that (in her terms) a gift had been given her; that it was her vocation, her calling; and that therefore to write at anything less or other than the intense pressure at which art is forged was sinful. From a writer less gifted, this would be intolerable pride; from her, we accept the terms in all their severity. The formidable claims are an altogether just estimate. Good fiction is hard to find; a good writer spares neither himself nor his readers. Not everyone can write; in fact few can: no one chose them though they may think they were called, though they may think that "anyone's unrestrained feelings are . . . worth listening to because they are unrestrained and because they are feelings." To "intrude upon the timeless" requires "the violence of a single-minded respect for the truth." Her truth, of course, was special and non-transferable; but shift the terms appropriately and it applies everywhere.

Exacting as all this sounds, Flannery O'Connor was never high-flown. She was pleased without the slightest condescension when a down-home country-woman remarked of some of her stories, "Well, them stories just gone and shown you how some folks *would* do"; she was pleased not only because the response was an honest one but because it is sound literary criticism, because, she remarks, it is "right": . . . "when you write stories, you have to be content to start exactly there — showing how some specific folks *will* do, *will* do in spite of everything."

But for the "little old lady in California" who informed her that when the tired reader comes home at night, he wishes to read something that "will lift up his heart" — for her, she has no time at all. And not because "it seems her heart had not been lifted up by anything of mine she had read," but because "if her heart had been in the right place, it would have been lifted up" — which can stand as an instance, at once, of her wit and critical self-knowledge, contempt for sentimentality, and her way of lifting up an extinct cliché bodily, standing it on its head and then on its feet again, fully alive.

God, alas, knows, the lady from California, whose name is Mrs. Legion, may have been Jew or Gentile, animist or Buddhist, or, serially, all; but one suspects she was Catholic, for the reason that Miss O'Connor reserved her finest wrath for those closest to her heart, her co-religionists (a term she would have hated), who like all other Americans with hearts in the wrong place wanted them lifted up. For her part, as a writer and a Catholic, as a Catholic writer, her aim in art was simply put: her "subject in fiction," she wrote, "is the action of grace in territory held largely by the devil." But she was a writer and not a theologian, and for a writer that is not sufficient knowledge. The "fiction writer," she wrote, and the statement, which recurs again and again with slight variation throughout the book, is virtually her motif, "presents mystery through manners, grace through nature, but when he finishes there always has to be left over that sense of Mystery which cannot be accounted for by any human formula." Of course there has to be no such thing. For "fiction writer" read "serious Catholic fiction writer"; but lower the case on Mystery and modify the final phrase, and it can stand as well as any other as a general statement about literary art, and, for herself, as credo. Only the most serious writer, of whatever kind, can venture to talk this way without disgracing herself and creating a scandal; and only a first-rate one can deliver the goods, which she did, again and again. She was simply describing not only the ideal she strove for but the end she actually achieved.

Now, this view of art has far more in common with the *serious* work of any real artist — of wavering, atrophied, vestigial, or no faith at all — than it does with the aggressive Philistinism of the canting letter-writers who reproach the writer for not lifting up their hearts; or (more to the point) the "pious trash" that passes for fiction among those who, hating art, batten on trash and do so in good conscience so long as trash breathes pieties and quotes Scripture. Miss O'Connor cites Cardinal Spellman's *The Foundling* — too obvious an example to be interesting; one trembles to think of others she had in mind when she spoke of pious trash — some, no doubt, masquerading as serious fiction.

The assault is devastating. What makes it of far more than parochial interest is its sweep of implication. Change the terms of immediate reference and the strictures apply exactly to all

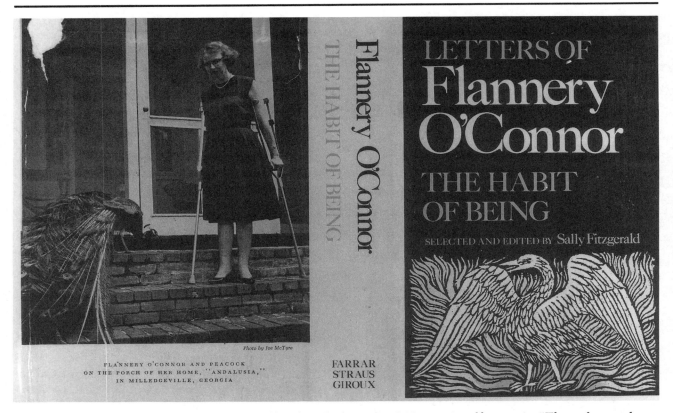

Photo by Joe McTyre

FLANNERY O'CONNOR AND PEACOCK
ON THE PORCH OF HER HOME, "ANDALUSIA,"
IN MILLEDGEVILLE, GEORGIA

FARRAR
STRAUS
GIROUX

Sally Fitzgerald described her 1979 edition of her friend's letters as O'Connor's self-portrait: "There she stands, to me, a phoenix risen from her own words: calm, slow, funny, courteous, both modest and very sure of herself, intense, sharply penetrating, devout but never pietistic, downright, occasionally fierce, and honest in a way that restores honor to the word."

bogus constructions, soft at the edges as at the center, which seek to uplift, edify, hearten, instruct, to "tidy up reality" — which seek all purposes that are not those of art, which has no purpose other than to be faithful to itself. Pious trash is not only trash; it is, to put a strict construction on it, also impious. Bad art, whatever its purity of intention, is bad politics, too; and bad morals; and bad theology. It is all these for the fairly simple reason that bad art necessarily lies; and good art, whatever its impurities, finally breaks through and transcends them to significant truths.

The range of Flannery O'Connor's occasional prose — which was not after all her métier — is necessarily limited, and many of her readers will take exception (as I do) to this or that formulation — on the South, on "pornography" and "obscenity," on some marginal matters; but at this distance from her death these no longer seem important. What is important is the luminosity and intensity of her best pages on the nature of fiction — the suppleness and radiance of her intelligence and the acerbity of her wit; and what is of

lasting importance is the body of work that underlies and amplifies them.

BOOK REVIEW:
Alfred Kazin, Review of *Flannery O'Connor: The Complete Stories, New York Times Book Review,* 28 November 1971, pp. 1, 22.

The Complete Stories, published on 8 November 1971, earned O'Connor a posthumous National Book Award. Kazin, who had met O'Connor at Yaddo in 1948, located the essence of her writing in her ability "to find people 'complete' in the smallest gesture, or in a moment's involuntary action that could decide a life forever."

The title sums up author, book and life: "Flannery O'Connor: The Complete Stories." She died in 1964 at the age of 39; she published 31 stories, of which 12 have been uncollected until now. Now they are all in one book, arranged in chronological order from the stories she wrote for her master's thesis at the University of Iowa to

"Judgment Day," a harrowing version of her brilliant early story about an elderly Southerner's exile in New York, "The Geranium." Since the stories here include the original openings and other chapters of her two novels "Wise Blood" and "The Violent Bear It Away" and since stories were more natural to her than novels, we do have almost all of Flannery O'Connor "complete" here. Especially when you reflect that the driving characteristic of her style, her mind, her particular faith, was to find people "complete" in the smallest gesture, or in a moment's involuntary action that could decide a life forever.

She could put everything about a character into a single look, everything she had and knew into a single story. She knew people with the finality with which she claimed to know the distance from hell to heaven. For her, people were complete in their radical weakness, their necessarily human incompleteness. Each story was complete, sentence by sentence. And each sentence was a hard, straight, altogether complete version of her subject: human deficiency, sin, error — ugliness taking a physical form.

I met her during the McCarthy period, under circumstances that persuaded me that she — or her friends — would have considered Jefferson Davis a Communist. I later visited her and her famous peacocks at her home in Milledgeville, Ga., in the company of her parish priest, who found her formidable in her fierce disapproval of his literary tastes. To tell the truth, what I liked most about her was her stories. She was not just the best "woman writer" of this time and place; she expressed something secret about America, called "the South," with that transcendent gift for expressing the real spirit of a culture that is conveyed by those writers (they are not necessarily the greatest, but neither do they ever die out of our minds) who become nothing but what they see.

Completeness is one word for it; relentlessness, unsparingness would be others. She was a genius. A mark of nongenius in story telling is to be distracted, to hint there are things to say that the author will get down to someday. Nongenius is nonconcentrating, and no matter how nasty it may be to people in the story, it is genial to itself. There is laxness in the air, self-conscious charm, a pensive mood of: What should come next?

O'Connor, as I must call her, was in story after story all there, occupying the mind and the whole life of a character who was as solidly on the page as if impaled on it. Her people were wholly

what they were, which wasn't much in "humane" terms. But they were all intact of themselves, in their stupidity, their meanness, their puzzlement, their Southern "ruralness." The South was her great metaphor, not for place but for the Fall of Man. Life for O'Connor was made up of absolutes; people were absolute, sharp, knives without handles. Hazel Motes all too believably blinds himself in "Wise Blood." Old Mr. Fortune, in "A View of the Woods," loves his granddaughter so deeply and identifies her with himself so wildly that of course he kills her without meaning to when she amazes him by balking his wishes. The young son of the dissolute city couple in "The River" is taken by his baby-sitter to see a country baptism, goes back by himself and drowns trying to find his new friend Jesus in the river.

The people were complete because the reader, not they, know all about them. They were nothing but their natures, and since there was nothing to life but people's natures, this made life moral. O'Connor's sentences, as ruthless as Stephen Crane's but less literary, always more objective than Hemingway's at his would-be toughest, measured like a rule, and came down flat. People in her stories are always at the end of their strength. They are at the synapse between what they are (unknown to themselves) and what they do. And these synapses, these flashes of connection, are so "complete," immediate, right, irreversible, that a particular feature of O'Connor's style is that a sentence is exact — not showily, as is the nature of rhetoric, but physically, the way different parts of a body fit each other. No one ever wrote narrative with more secret cunning, coming up with the minute differences that excite us in reading and cause us to respond. Yet no one ever wrote less "beautifully" in the contemplative, lyric Hemingway fashion. She was more devoted to the synonym than to the metaphor, for what she saw was the non-human that people always reminded her of: "He seemed mute and patient, like an old sheep waiting to be let out." "The rest of his face stuck out like a bare cliff to fall from . . . " "On the porch there were three little boys of different sizes with identical speckled faces and one tall girl who had her hair up in so many aluminum curlers that it glared like the roof." "When he finished, he was like something washed ashore on her, and she had made obscene comments about him, which he remembered gradually during the day."

Then there was the deadliness of observation without cruelty, funny because the different items "fit." "Mrs. Watts's grin was as curved and sharp as the blade of a sickle. It was plain that she was so well-adjusted that she didn't have to think any more." "He was chewing gum slowly, as if to music." "'He has a ulcer,' the woman said proudly. 'He ain't give me a minute's peace since he was born.'" Her sentences are more often disturbing in their laconic rightness than smart. She was not looking around her as she wrote. She was herself impaled on what her people were doing. There was nothing but that: one small circle.

Though she would have been only 46 by now, her stories already seem non-contemporary in their passion for the art of fiction. One realizes how diffuse and subjective the practice of fiction has become since O'Connor wrote the first stories in this book for her master's thesis at Iowa, which read as if she were going to be examined by Willa Cather and Stephen Crane. We live in such an age of commentary now. She had the dread circulatory disease of lupus from the time she began to write — her short career was a progress by dying — and I wonder if the sourness, the unsparingness, the breath-taking perspective on all human weakness in her work need as many translations into theology as they get in contemporary American criticism. As Josephine Hendin pointed out in "The World of Flannery O'Connor," there was an unreal and even comic gentility to her upbringing in Milledgeville that must have given O'Connor a wry sense of her aloneness as a woman, artist and Southerner who happened to be an Irish Catholic.

On the other hand, she was so locked up in her body that one can understand why life as well as her faith made her think of "this is my body, this is my blood." She touched the bone of truth that was sunk in her own flesh. Thus she lost herself in a story. And this was grace. Reading her, one is aware above all of a gift blessedly made objective, a giftedness reading the world. Words became true in her dramatic world, in action, gesture, death. That too was completeness of a kind, resting its weight perfectly in story after story. But fiction depended for her on an unyielding sense of our limits, and the limits could be raised only by death.

In "Greenleaf," the great story of a woman killed by the bull that her impossibly inefficient farmhand, Greenleaf, is always letting out, the woman stares at the "violent black streak bounding toward her as if she had no sense of distance, as if she could not decide at once what his intention was and the bull had buried his head in her lap, like a wild tormented lover, before her expression changed. . . . She had the look of a person whose sight has been suddenly restored but who finds the light unbearable."

BOOK REVIEW:
Guy Davenport, "Even as the Heathen Rage" [excerpt], review of *Flannery O'Connor: The Complete Stories, National Review,* 23 (31 December 1971): 1473–1474.

Davenport praised the universality of O'Connor's fiction, describing her as a devout Christian who nonetheless "knew the difference betweeen art and religion."

Flannery O'Connor (1925–1964) spent her last fourteen years on this earth at her family's farm outside Milledgeville, Ga. (the hometown of Oliver Hardy), a pleasant place that in the Confederate tradition had a name — Andalusia — and which was overrun with peacocks, the gaudiest and stupidest of God's creatures. What confined Miss O'Connor to Milledgeville was the dread disease *lupus erythematosus,* yet it is plausible that she would have lived there anyway, to be near the Scripture searchers and fireproof Baptists in whose Antinomian souls she saw the fingers of God kneading, kneading.

When Miss O'Connor first left her native Georgia to go to Iowa and study the art of fiction under the tutelage of Paul Engle, her dialect was so unintelligible to Western ears that she had to write on a pad to be understood. Indeed, all her life she liked to conduct literary conversations in demotic Milledgeville. When someone remarked on the wild imaginativeness of Southern writers, "Yep," she replied, "nobody likes to be on the tracks when the Dixie Special's comin' through." And of the grotesqueness of Southern literature she said simply, "We know a freak when we see one." She liked to point out that Southerners are still raised on the Bible, the grand rhythms and terse realism of which turn up in their prose as naturally as a shrug rises in a Frenchman's shoulders.

Miss O'Connor wrote two novels (*Wise Blood* and *The Violent Bear It Away*) and the 31 stories which are here gathered together for the first time by her editor Robert Giroux, who has provided an introduction and bibliographical notes. From Mr. Giroux we learn that Miss O'Connor was a writer of Flaubertian meticulousness. Nothing left her worktable over which she

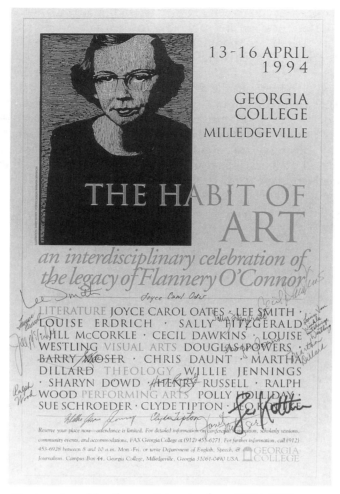

13-16 APRIL
1994

GEORGIA
COLLEGE
MILLEDGEVILLE

THE HABIT OF
ART

*an interdisciplinary celebration of
the legacy of Flannery O'Connor*

LITERATURE JOYCE CAROL OATES · LEE SMITH ·
LOUISE ERDRICH · SALLY FITZGERALD ·
JILL McCORKLE · CECIL DAWKINS · LOUISE
WESTLING VISUAL ARTS DOUGLAS POWERS ·
BARRY MOSER · CHRIS DAUNT · MARTHA
DILLARD THEOLOGY WILLIE JENNINGS
· SHARYN DOWD · HENRY RUSSELL · RALPH
WOOD PERFORMING ARTS POLLY HOLLIDAY ·
SUE SCHROEDER · CLYDE TIPTON ·

Reserve your place now—attendance is limited. For detailed information on conference registration, scholarly sessions, community events, and accommodations, FAX Georgia College at (912) 453-6271. For further information, call (912) 453-6928 between 8 and 10 a.m. Mon.-Fri. or write Department of English, Speech, & GEORGIA
Journalism, Campus Box 44, Georgia College, Milledgeville, Georgia 31061-0490 USA   COLLEGE

*Poster, signed by the participants, for a 1994 O'Connor
symposium (Collection of Barbara Brannon)*

had not agonized and rewritten draft after draft. It is a surprise to learn that in the age of Faulkner and Kafka she had such trouble with editors who wanted to soften her angular, outrageous stories into more conventional shapes. A German publisher claimed that German sensibilities would be shocked by some of Miss O'Connor's plots. One likes to think that when she heard of this delicacy of the Germans she had herself wheeled out to tell her peacocks about Dachau and Auschwitz. It would be like her.

But we are all Germans when we come to read Flannery O'Connor. She *is* shocking. For one thing, she was a Christian, and not a very civilized one, either. Her Christianity had that purity of the first centuries when to be civilized was the opposite of to be Christian. Miss O'Connor's Christians are the sort who end up in lion's mouths. The conventions of this world all fare terribly in

her hands. In our souls she sees the Gadarene swine grunting. Pride blinds our every look. The devil has us all, as we choose to be in his grasp, feel most comfortable with him, and know that we have his sympathy in all our affairs. He understands us.

Christ, however, is a diligent snatcher back of His own. It is this fierce love of God for His creatures that makes Flannery O'Connor's stories so disturbing and so powerful. Thomas Merton compared her art to Sophocles', whose protagonists are torn asunder by the claims of the gods and the world, but a more apt comparison might be with Tolstoy, who saw how uncomprehendingly men embody the will of God, and how trivial and transparent matter is, once we have learned to see the spirit inside it.

All of this sounds as if Miss O'Connor were a theologian constructing parables. Far from it.

Miss O'Connor knew the difference between art and religion, and never confused the two. She saw that her primary duty was to tell an engaging story. Her genius for the comic was superb, and her sense of the ridiculous was delicious. Only by being a writer of hair-raising insight could she deliver such a wallop to our moral complacency.

When Miss O'Connor writes about pride, for instance, she elicits all our sympathy. She makes her proud characters attractive, warm, interesting. We are all ready to welcome them as pleasant company when she begins to let the devil swish his tail. Conversely, she is fond of placing God's work in the hands of seeming idiots and bumpkins. God is without manners and can be most unseemly in His grabbing of souls, and no instrument is unworthy of His use.

These brilliant stories are some of the finest in modern literature. They have been read too long as grotesqueries from the midden of the late Confederacy. Their appeal is universal. Their integrity of design and moral perspicacity will insure their being around for a long time.

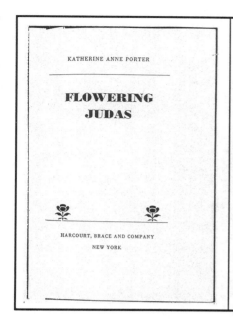

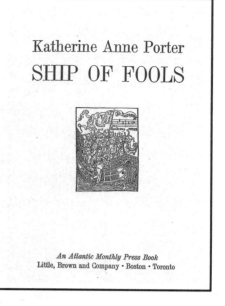

KATHERINE ANNE PORTER

(15 May 1890 – 18 September 1980)

See also the Porter entries in DLB 4: American Writers in Paris, 1920–1939; DLB 9: American Novelists, 1910–1945; DLB 102: American Short-Story Writers, 1910–1945, Second Series; and Yearbook: 1980.

MAJOR BOOKS:

My Chinese Marriage, as M.T.F. (New York: Duffield, 1921);

Outline of Mexican Popular Arts and Crafts (Los Angeles: Young & McCallister, 1922);

Flowering Judas (New York: Harcourt, Brace, 1930);

Hacienda (New York: Harrison of Paris, 1934);

Flowering Judas and Other Stories (New York: Harcourt, Brace, 1935; London: Cape, 1936);

Pale Horse, Pale Rider: Three Short Novels (New York: Harcourt, Brace, 1939; London: Cape, 1939);

The Leaning Tower and Other Stories (New York: Harcourt, Brace, 1944; London: Cape, 1945);

The Days Before (New York: Harcourt, Brace, 1952; London: Secker & Warburg, 1953);

The Old Order: Stories of the South from Flowering Judas, Pale Horse, Pale Rider, and The Leaning Tower (New York: Harcourt, Brace, 1955);

Ship of Fools (Boston & Toronto: Little, Brown, 1962; London: Secker & Warburg, 1962);

The Collected Stories of Katherine Anne Porter (London: Cape, 1964; expanded edition, New York: Harcourt, Brace & World, 1965);

The Collected Essays and Occasional Writings of Katherine Anne Porter (New York: Delacorte, 1970);

The Never-Ending Wrong (Boston: Little, Brown, 1977; London: Secker & Warburg, 1977);

This Strange, Cold World and Other Book Reviews, edited by Darlene Harbour Unrue (Athens: University of Georgia Press, 1991);

Uncollected Early Prose of Katherine Anne Porter, edited by Ruth M. Alvarez and Thomas F. Walsh (Austin: University of Texas Press, 1993).

BIOGRAPHY:

Joan Givner, *Katherine Anne Porter: A Life* (New York: Simon & Schuster, 1982).

BIBLIOGRAPHIES:

Robert F. Kiernan, *Katherine Anne Porter and Carson McCullers: A Reference Guide* (Boston: G. K. Hall, 1976);

Katherine Anne Porter—with her father, Harrison Boone Porter, in the photograph at left (circa 1916–1918)—was born on 15 May 1890 at her parents' farm in Indian Creek, Texas, and named Callie Russell Porter, after one of her mother's childhood friends. Her mother, Mary Alice Jones Porter (right, circa 1885) died in 1892. Callie Porter was the third of four surviving children.

After his wife's death Harrison Porter took his children to live in Kyle, Texas, with his widowed mother, Catherine Ann ("Cat") Skaggs Porter, photographed in 1891 (left) with eighteen-month-old Callie and her older sister Annie Gay (called Gay). Cat Porter died in October 1901, three years after the photograph of her granddaughter Callie (right) was taken.

On 20 June 1906 Porter married John Henry Koontz (left), a railway clerk. They were divorced in 1915. Having been raised as a Methodist, Porter (in 1912, at right) converted to Roman Catholicism, the religion of her husband's German-Swiss family.

Kathryn Hilt and Ruth M. Alvarez, *Katherine Anne Porter: An Annotated Bibliography* (New York & London: Garland, 1990).

LETTERS:
Letters of Katherine Anne Porter, edited by Isabel Bayley (New York: Atlantic Monthly Press, 1990).

INTERVIEWS:
Joan Givner, ed., *Katherine Anne Porter: Conversations* (Jackson: University Press of Mississippi, 1987).

LOCATION OF ARCHIVES:
The Papers of Katherine Anne Porter are in the McKeldin Library of the University of Maryland at College Park.

INTERVIEW:
Gordon K. Shearer, "What One Woman is Doing to Help Children," *Dallas Morning News,*

16 December 1916; in *Katherine Anne Porter: Conversations,* edited by Joan Givner (Jackson & London: University Press of Mississippi, 1987), pp. 3–5.

While she was married to Koontz, Porter began calling herself Katherine, legally assuming the name Katherine Anne Porter at the time of their divorce. After leaving Koontz in 1914, she worked as a movie extra in Chicago and a singer on the Lyceum Circuit in Louisiana. She contracted tuberculosis in 1915 and was hospitalized, first in Dallas and later at Carlsbad Sanatorium in San Angelo, Texas. Able to leave Carlsbad in 1916 but still weak, Porter went to Woodlawn Hospital in Dallas, where she was both a patient and an assistant who worked with the tubercular children at the hospital. Soon after arriving there, she started an informal, outdoor school to help these young patients keep up with their schoolwork — revealing an impulse toward social activism on behalf of ill or handicapped people that she exhibited throughout her life. This inter-

Porter and reporter Kitty Barry Crawford, whom she met at Carlsbad Sanatorium. Inspired by Crawford to become a journalist, Porter moved to Fort Worth in September 1915 and began writing theatrical reviews and society notes for the Fort Worth Critic, *a paper run by Crawford and her husband. In 1918, when Crawford went to Denver, Colorado, hoping to improve her health, Porter followed and took a job with the* Rocky Mountain News.

view also alludes to a short-lived school that Porter and her sister Gay ran in Victoria, Texas — not Corpus Christi, as mentioned below — in 1905, when they were attempting to support themselves and their father, who was never capable of providing for his family adequately.

"Academy Oaks" is a fitting title for Dallas County's first outdoor school. It has twelve pupils, and instruction is being given in all branches, from the primary department to fourth-grade lessons.

Back of the outdoor school is the heart of a free-air-loving girl. She is teaching this school under the trees she loves so well. Last summer, this girl,

Miss Katherine Anne Porter, was ill for several months. She chafed at the idleness of illness, at her inability to continue the outdoor life to which she had been accustomed since her childhood.

Then fate played her part. Miss Porter paid a visit to the Woodlawn Sanatorium, three miles north of Dallas. There she became interested in the tubercular children who were leading outdoor lives in a battle for health. They, too, were idle as she had been forced to be during her illness.

She saw the inviting meadow ground about the sanatorium, with its large shade trees and soft turf. She saw the children playing there, their screened galleries between the storm buildings where they sleep, and all the modern equipment which has been supplied to assist them to grow strong. Seeing all this, the question suggested itself: "What is being done for the growth of their minds?"

From that question sprang the Woodlawn Woodland School. The need of teaching for the children had been considered before, but teachers hesitated to risk health in such close association with the children. Miss Porter volunteered to become their teacher. She trusted to fresh air and a sunny disposition as her germicides. The teaching she knew she could master, for at one time she had been an instructor in elocution and folk-lore dancing in Corpus Christi.

It's a school without desks. The children gather under this tree or that, following the shade. The ground is the bench. A swing in one of the seats is an honor seat. Good pupils have it as a reward. Punishment? Of course. Discipline is required in this as in other schools. But it is not ordinary punishment. Whipping or a task to learn is not punishment therapeutically suited to a child whose temperature must not be raised. Miss Porter solved the punishment problem. If the pupil does not behave, the rest cure is applied. The pupil stays in bed instead of coming to school. Truancy is unknown.

Sunday was appointed by Miss Porter for a visit to her outdoor school. She could not have it interrupted weekdays by newspaper interviewers and cameramen. But the children gladly staged their outdoor school on Sunday, just as during the week, though some difficulties presented themselves.

"Jimmy" (that is not his real name, but all of the pupils are waiting to see their pictures and read this story, and he might be embarrassed if he were correctly named) hesitated to sit down as the pupils took their places on the soft turf under the afternoon oak.

"That's all right; sit right there on the ground!" said teacher.

Still he stood and said, "I can't."

"Yes, you can," replied Miss Porter. "Sit right down!"

"Naw, I can't," said Jimmy, grown desperate. "These are my other pants!"

He was assured that for once he might sit down in the dirt in his Sunday clothes, and school was called to order.

Remarkable aptitude is shown by these little outdoor scholars. Part of their progress is due to the personal attention the small class makes it possible for Miss Porter to give to each one, but she modestly attributes it to the fresh air and their natural brightness.

There's a touch of sadness, too. A tablet leaf is caught up by the breeze and goes sailing away with its unfinished "sum." A little girl starts after it, and you feel a tug at your heart, for she limps painfully.

Strangely precocious are some of these nature pupils. With the example of some of the grown-ups about them, they have strange, old-fashioned, hospitable ways.

"How have you been?" was the diagnostic greeting of a tiny curly-headed girl, not "Glad to see you!" or "Hello!"

If there's illness all about, Miss Porter counteracts it with cheerfulness and life. The children never are permitted to tire. At the slightest sign of fatigue or worry there is a turn to a new topic — maybe lessons are cast aside altogether and there is a folk-dance with easy steps requiring not too much exertion. Bright colors, too, are favored for their cheering effect.

To the casual visitor the apparent hardihood of these children who are under medical care comes as a surprise. On bright December days many of the boys go barefoot. On cold days, of course, there are wraps; but it's a severe day indeed that prevents the outdoor school.

Gary methods are used to a considerable extent. The books prescribed in other public schools are in use, and the course in other schools is followed. In this way it is hoped to keep the children apace with the boys and girls who go to ordinary school, so that when their cures are effected they may go on with pupils of their age.

CHILDREN'S STORY:
Katherine Anne Porter, "The Shattered Star," *Everyland*, 2 (January 1920): 422–423; in *Uncollected Early Prose of Katherine Anne*

Porter in 1919, soon after her arrival in New York

Porter, edited by Ruth M. Alvarez and Thomas F. Walsh (Austin: University of Texas Press, 1993), pp. 12–15.

In autumn 1918 Porter nearly died of influenza, an experience that "simply divided my life," she wrote later. "So that everything before that was just getting ready" for her career as a writer. The following autumn she moved to New York and rented an apartment in Greenwich Village. In January 1920 she published her first work of fiction, a children's story in a young people's magazine published by the Interchurch World Movement. "The Shattered Star" and the two subsequent stories Porter published in the February and March issues of the magazine are notable for their characters: the same sort of resourceful females and ineffectual males that appear in the fiction Porter later wrote for adults, including "María Conceptión," "The Cracked Looking-Glass," and "The Jilting of Granny Weatherall" — all written during the 1920s.

Some children of *Everyland,* we know, must have seen the Northern Lights, or Aurora Borealis, as the scientists call it — long, slender fingers of light wavering their faint blue or violet or white illumination from the northern horizon to the top of the sky. And of course everyone has asked the cause of this beautiful and mysterious radiance. When WE were small they told us it was the reflection of the sun shining on the ice of the Polar seas. Now they say it is the discharge of electricity through the atmosphere, influenced by the magnetic poles of the earth. Perhaps there are other theories. But we are sure that no explanation can be so delightful as this one of "The Shattered Star," which Miss Porter tells here to the children of *Everyland.* — The Editors.

In the days of long ago when fairies and demons were powerful, and everything in the world was a marvel, the Eskimo people lived on the side of the earth which is winter for nearly all the year, and they live there to this day. They loved their snow and icebergs, and long, still, frozen edges of the sea. They built their *igloos* (huts) of snow and burned their whale oil lamps with moss wicks, and made their garments of fur from the seals and the polar bears; and they treated their demons kindly, for fear of harm.

But in doing honor to the goddess of the ocean floor who loosed the fish to the Eskimo in the springtime, and in offering food to the visitors from the lower world who whistled in their ears on dark nights, they sometimes forgot the Moonman, a very powerful deity. In revenge he touched Nayagta, an Eskimo girl-child, when she was but a minute old, and claimed her for the people of the Moon.

Wrapped tightly in her swaddling clothes, Nayagta lay and watched the light from the oil bowl rippling in shadows on the walls of the ice hut until they shone with blue and green and silver light like stars shining in the sea. Sometimes they flowed like water tipped from side to side in a bowl. Nayagta loved this almost as much as she did the warmth of her mother's neck and shoulders as she lay cuddled into the furry *parka* (hood) that covered her mother's head. And she loved to hear her mother sing in a low voice, the same song always, that had only three notes in it.

But the demon who obeys the will of the Moon-man came and looked at the forehead of Nayagta. There was a mark, shaped like a seal, over her left eyebrow, which the finger of the Moon-man had drawn there. So the demon took the child, and stole from the igloo. The wolf dogs rose, bristling and shuddering, and howled as he passed.

Beyond the spaces of the Moon the demon carried Nayagta, and the spirits who inhabit that world received her, and made her their own. They taught her all they knew of magic, until at last she had more power than they, and they no longer had their will over her. And she wished to return to earth.

At this time, the demons were making their world anew, having tired of the old one. They had destroyed many things, but three treasures they could not give up. These were a star of surpassing brilliancy that glowed with all colors, a garden of warm pools and green trees and black shadows and scarlet birds, and a palace of white marble with ebony floors. They quarreled among themselves with bitterness, and wrought spells upon each other, and still they could not find places for the treasures.

So Nayagta leaped up from among them. She seized the garden and the star and the palace, and tucked them under her robe of white fur and cried, "I will give them all to my people!" So she returned to earth, through clouds and gray winds.

But she was changed beyond the knowledge of all those who saw her. Not even the oldest women of the great igloo remembered her. For time among the demons is not measured like our time, and Nayagta had been a thousand years growing up.

"See, I bring gifts!" said Nayagta, while they regarded her with wonder. And she drew forth the marble palace. They looked at it and shouted with joy, for they thought it was of snow. But when they went within and found it was made of strange substance, full of dark caves and many corridors, they were lost, and went about wailing.

Then Nayagta spread out the fair green garden, with its black shadows and scarlet birds, but the people languished and sickened beneath the green, lowering branches of the trees, and drooped with the fragrance of the thick-petalled flowers. Last, Nayagta drew forth the white-hot star, and it shone so radiantly that they were blinded, and wept with terror, hiding their faces and calling to her, "We do not know these things! They are evil!"

Nayagta wept also, when she saw how her people did not know her, and that her gifts were bringing them sadness. She gathered them up and went away again, earth-weary and troubled. This was strange, too, for she had not learned of these pains among the Moon-demons.

Merah, an Eskimo boy who loved Nayagta, came after her and plucked at the sleeve of her fur robe, saying, "Do not go away again to the Far Off places. Abide here in our igloo; my mother shall call you daughter, and I will call you wife. You shall harpoon whale and hunt the reindeer with me, and the *brix* (ledge) of our igloo shall be heaped with the fur of bear and the fur of seal."

But Nayagta answered, "You and your people have not wanted my star nor my garden nor my palace, nor any of the magic I brought you from the spaces of the moon. So I go again."

And Merah said, "Take with you your memory of us." And she answered, "No, I take only my magic and my star and my palace and my garden." But her heart grieved and she remembered.

She went, and she walked in grief and wrath, her feet left the earth, and with each step she rose higher. With her toe she kicked the stars in passing, and a shower of them went flying over the sea, scattering on the icebergs that lay along the edges of the world. As she went, she grieved, saying, "Since my people will not have my gifts, neither will I have them."

Then she cast the palace into the sea, where it turned to ice and stands forever with towers and minarets flashing in the sunlight. She cast the green garden another way, and it slipped over the sides of the earth into a place where no Eskimo has ever been. It is told in old tales that a strange race of folk dream and sing beneath its black shadows forever. She hurled the star into the heavens, where it shattered against the wall of the sky in fragments of fire, and there it blazes and dances and flames forever.

The Eskimos saw it and said, "Nayagta is remembering. Merah can also make magic!" Thereafter whenever a great gray cloud with black edges came whirling down in the time of deepest winter, howling with a great voice, the Eskimos said again, "Nayagta is remembering!" And they smiled as they smile now, for the Eskimo loves the blue ice, and the heavy sea, and the slow-moving bergs where the white bears climb and prowl. They sleep warmly in their huts of ice, and cook their food of fish and oil over the lamps with the moss wicks. They do not long for the vanished gifts of Nayagta.

But Nayagta, wrapped in a great whirling cloud of black and gray, comes up screaming her homesickness in the storm rack; or lies at peace on the edge of the sea watching her shattered star as it is mirrored deeply in the snow and frozen seas. It ripples like the light of the whale oil lamp on the walls of the igloo where Nayagta's mother used to sing three little notes as she swayed with Nayagta in her hood. And Nayagta remembers forever.

ARTICLE:

Katherine Anne Porter, "The New Man and The New Order," *Magazine of Mexico*, 1 (March 1921): 5–15; in *Uncollected Early Prose of Katherine Anne Porter*, pp. 51–61.

In Greenwich Village Porter became interested in Mexico through contact with a group of Mexican artists. One of them, Adolfo Best-Maugard, invited her to write the scenario for a Mexican ballet based on three Mexican dances. With music by Castro Padillo and sets by Best-Maugard, it was performed by Anna Pavlova several times over the next few years, most notably in Mexico City in 1923.

Having heard from Best-Maugard that the democratic election of President Alvaro Obregón was about to usher in a new and exciting era in Mexican history, Porter went to Mexico City in November 1920 and worked first as English-language editor of El Heraldo de Mexico *and later as editor of* The Magazine of Mexico, *published by American businessmen to encourage investment in Mexico. The magazine failed in April 1920, after publication of the second issue. "The New Man and The New Order," Porter's lead article in the first issue, reflects her initial optimism about the Mexican political situation, before some of the young, idealistic leftists she admired fell victim to political assassination.*

While in Mexico, Porter also completed an assignment she had accepted in New York, ghost-writing a novel based on the reminiscences of May Taim Franking, an American who had married a Chinese student and gone to lived with him in China. It was published in 1921 as My Chinese Marriage, *by M.T.F.*

It would be useless to deny that a man throws dice with death when he becomes president of Mexico. "He plays blind man's buff with La Muerte" says a Mexican writer. It is a high adventure, not to be undertaken lightly. Tremendous inner compulsion forces a man into the presidency of the Mexican Republic. In the past, this official has been infallibly one of these things — an egoist without horizons, an adventurer who loves danger, an idealist with a self sacrifice complex, a steel nerved dictator sure of his butchering strength. Once or twice it has been a fantastic combination of these qualities. But in all of them,

Cover for the first issue of the magazine Porter edited in Mexico

well acquainted with his country in its working dress; a man of straight literal mind, with a detached legal passion for setting disorder to rights. He became a soldier when the need for an honest fighting man became all too plain. He kept himself clear of the intricacies of professional diplomacy and politics through several years as general when Carranza was Chief of the Army. Later he became minister of War with this same Carranza as president, and somehow stood straight in this post too, not once fooled or circumvented by the devious methods of the President and his group of flattering shadows.

And now it is December 1st, 1920, and here is General Obregon about to become President of Mexico, after spectacular events, and a series of stupendous tragic blunders on the part of the fleeing Carranza. At twelve o'clock at night provisional President de la Huerta is to give over his office to General Alvaro Obregon. Preparations are all very festive, for everybody shares in a fiesta in Mexico. The city is strange with the voices of foreign people — we hear the shrill American voice, the tinkling Mexican voice, the gurgling Indian vocables, a scattering volley of French, truncated British speech, Spanish spoken in twenty different accents, for the South Americans are here in force. Here are the city Mexicans, rancheros grandiose in buckskin charros and great embroidered sombreros, Indians with sandaled feet and softly woven blankets luminous with color. They are all fearfully alive, fearfully bent on getting somewhere — the narrow sidewalks will not do, everybody takes to the street center, and disputes rancorously for place with the outraged drivers of cars.

Plainly, Obregon becoming President has a definite interest for all parts of the world, each part nursing its particular interest, its personal hope. Mexico is a mine unexploited, and all the riches to be had here shout from the gray earth, speaking all tongues, heard and understood of all men. Here are soils fit to grow anything human beings can use. Here are silver and gold, coal and oil — the air is redolent with the sound of these unctuous words. Men mouth them lovingly, and stare at vague and varied horizons.

Beauty is here too — color of mountain and sky and green things rooted in earth. Beauty of copper colored human things not yet wholly corrupted by civilization. Those things are well enough in their way, but business first. And our immediate business is getting this new President inaugurated, and finding out what he means to do with all the power vested in him.

the flair for personal magnificence, has made one-half of the formula. All things considered Mexico has borne with her presidents leniently, a divine patience has marked her dealings with her chance-appointed Chiefs. Some of them were aristocrats and all of them were opportunists. There was a dreamer once, hands raised in ineffectual blessings, dictators more than once, and the beautiful gold laced seekers of glory were the most numerous of all. But they shared ineluctably one glittering assortment of qualities — a baffling self sufficiency that blinded them to the importance of pacific international relations; a racial arrogance that made them not fusible with their neighbors; a personal pride that forbade them to learn the practical problems of their country; a startling ignorance of the conditions of labor and commerce and economics and industry that are the very life fluid of a nation.

It was high time Mexico had a simple working president with his feet firmly set in his native soil. After the scintillating procession of remote and inaccessible rulers, there came up from the land a farmer, Alvaro Obregon, prosperous and

Porter left Mexico in August 1921 and spent several months with the Crawfords in Fort Worth before returning to New York in early 1922. In April, invited by the Mexican government to work on a proposed American exhibition of Mexican folk art, she returned to Mexico and wrote Outline of Mexican Popular Arts and Crafts. *This catalogue was published in 1922 even though the U.S. government, which did not recognize the Obregón regime, refused to let the exhibition into the United States. This photograph, in which Porter is third from left, was taken in June 1922, on her return voyage to New York.*

Hours before the time of taking the oath the Camara is filled. The boxes of the ambassadors blaze with gold lace and glinting ceremonious swords and the jewels around the necks of the women. Next door are the governors' boxes, not quite so impressive, but gay with the gowns of the governors' ladies. Below, the diputados come in, leisurely, one at a time, each man uniformed in black dress suit, gleaming white shirt front, imperturbable dignity of demeanor. On the right hand side the aristocrats seat themselves. You notice a great many long Bourbon faces, with hair rolled back from thin brows. They are men with several centuries of power back of them, and they love the accepted order of things. What they think of this occasion no one knows. For Alvaro Obregon's face is not in the least Bourbon. He is Mexican, and a soldier, and a farmer, and a business man. On the left wing one notes a curious assortment of folk, evidently there by right, and vastly interested in the proceedings. One of them is Soto y Gama, thorn in the side of the old government, a man of wide education and culture, who rode his native mountains for seven years with a copy of Karl Marx, and another of the Bible in his pocket. Near him sits a wiry little nervous man, with an intrepid face, eyes tilted a bit at the corners. He is trim in his magpie uniform. His fingers drum the arm of his chair. He shifts about impatiently and crosses his legs repeatedly. He is Luis Leon, educated for an agricultural engineer, who could not work with the Carranza government for his conscience's sake, and therefore became a bull fighter — one of the best in Mexico. When Obregon came in, Leon came in also, and was elected diputado. So we see him sitting there, his plain black and white a long step from the silver embroidered splendor of his torero's cloak. And a longer step still, from the time he fought nine black bulls in a pen in Vera Cruz for the benefit of Zapatista revolutionists who mistook him for a spy. He did not have a torero cloak that day. He killed bulls, one at a time until there were no more bulls to be killed, and the revolutionists

mexico 1923

Porter during her third trip to Mexico, in summer 1923, as art editor for a special Mexican issue of Survey Graphic *(May 1924). By the time of this visit she had published "María Concepción," her first original work of adult fiction, in the December 1922 issue of* Century *and had begun other stories set in Mexico.*

are growing a trifle nervous. Two minutes until midnight. One minute. Half Minute. "My god," murmurs a man sitting next, "Something must have happened!" They are so accustomed to things happening at inaugurations in Mexico, they doubt if even so civilized and dignified a procedure as this can pass without exciting and untoward events.

A blare of trumpets sounds in the streets. Nearer. A great muffled shout, a sustained mellow roar soaks through the walls of the Camara. Another and milder roar inside, as the people rise to their feet. The clock hands point straight to twelve. The main portal swings back ponderously, and two men in plain dress suits, one wearing a white and green and scarlet ribbon across his chest, enter. The man wearing the ribbon has only one arm. The other has been left by the wayside between the farm and the President's chair.

The top gallery folk shout "Viva Obregon! Viva de la Huerta!" while the others applaud. President de la Huerta walks a step ahead of General Obregon. Presently, in not more than three minutes, they go again, and this time President Obregon walks a step ahead of citizen de la Huerta. But before this Mr. de la Huerta steps forward and embraces the new President. It has every evidence of heartiness and good will. And the incident is remarkable for being only the second of its kind recorded here. The old and the new have not been distinguished for amiable relations to one another.

Once again Mexico has a duly installed constitutional government. Splendor, pomp, militarism, democracy, and internationalism have combined in one grand pageant to do honor to the new regime. It has begun with a thick surface layer of good will and gayety, a hopeful way for a new government to begin. The jubilation and applause was an indication of harmony at the moment at least — a sincere, deep down desire for a better and more livable Mexico; an obliterating psychological moment when personal desires, ambitions and private interests sink into the common weal and an unbreathed hope that this nation will take its rightful place in the commonwealth of the world.

Being part and parcel of this grand spectacle, yet removed in sort of an impersonal observant way, one is compelled to pause and wonder. What will history say of this new man? What symbolism will designate the new order upon the destiny of the nation — this conglomerate and but little understood people?

were convinced of his vocation as he had declared it to them. They let him go, in order, as you see, that he might sit tonight with his wing collar chafing his chin, waiting for Obregon to come in and be made president. There is Felipe Carrillo, poet, friend of poets, champion of the Indians in Yucatan, who is also here on grave business.

There are others, on both sides of the house, who are worth watching. There is not an interest in all Mexico unrepresented by these seated men. They arrive in small groups, with the look of folk who have dined in peace and are now prepared carefully to consider the business of state. The diplomatic boxes and the governors' boxes are now rivaled by the society boxes, where ladies fling off great cloaks and sit bare shouldered in the chill spaces of the Camara. We in the Camara

Life is a substance they cannot get the feel of---

Goldfish or quicksilver here and yonder it slips;

Given their choice, which they aren't, they'd really rather

Go down to the boisterous sea, but not in ships.

So they go instead to live in the deep country,

Though it is not in their plan to follow a plow;

They love to eat what they neither sow nor gather,

They would live simply if some one showed them how.

They come back to town where everything's cut on the bias,
They point by turns with pride and view with alarm,

Call for reform which they find is too much bother,
                    they're against war
On principal ~~theyhatevnxnvaxd~~   and afraid to disarm.

They would do all sorts of brave things if they dared but they
dare not;

It would get them in trouble with living, breathing men:

So they stay in that soft land where the Wish is the father

To a loud cuckoo in a nest built by a wren.

                    Katherine Anne Porter

19 2 3 ?

Typescript for a poem Porter wrote in the 1920s (Papers of Katherine Anne Porter, Special Collections, University of Maryland at College Park Libraries). By this time Porter's early political idealism had been replaced by the attitude that politicians of all parties were self-serving people who wanted to manipulate the artist for their own purposes.

An unenviable position certainly is that of President Obregon. There are those who do envy, but surely from the point of personal ambition and aggrandizement and not from high minded service to country or as the solvent of the innumerable problems that hang over and wind about the presidential chair. He stands at the head of a nation that for a long time has been at utter discord with itself and its neighbors. Unharmonizing causes date back to the Spanish conquest and beyond. Republican form of government has never been successfully engrafted upon the Aztec and other primeval roots. There has been a steady oscillation between despotism and revolution. Constitutions have come and gone between volleys of musketry.

It has been well remarked that there never was a country for which God did more or man did less. Its very richness is its danger. Personal ambition and private self interest of those who constitute themselves the chosen few is rampant in Mexico today. It only exceeds the same virulent species of other nations in its tendency to subvert the ballot and the constitution by the rifle and the cannon, and by the richness of the prize sought. Neither does the exploitation by the arrogant few confine itself to Mexican citizenry. They are here from every point of the globe and the conflict for riches and prestige rage between race, color, and creed of every known angle and combination. There are plots for prestige, there are plots for political preference, there are plots for graft, great business interests are at stake, international problems of growing importance, an interweaving of selfish, private and governmental problems without end. Not hopeless to be true, unless the whole world is hopeless, for it may be truly said that for every problem of Mexico the rest of the world has a bigger one. Yet like the naughty boy in school, all eyes are on this turbulent one. For these great problems Destiny has handed the text book to President Obregon.

"Mexican Sovereignty must be kept inviolable." This is his answer to the first question of the first page. To this, every right thinking man of every nationality agrees. Only those who believe their own personal interest could be better served otherwise, can raise any objections to this and then only in whispered words in secret places. However the president has intimated by his public utterances that he does not consider sovereignty and provincialism as synonymous, that narrowness does not build a nation and that national rights as well as those of humans must work two ways, to the mutual best and equal division of interests and benefits — a sort of a national golden rule. If this policy is maintained as well as spoken, it will make the rest of the problems easy and many of them will disappear as corollary to the major premise.

Carrying for some years the title of General is the policy of the new man to be militaristic? Is the iron hand of Porfirio Diaz again to rule? The enormous mass of Mexican people, like all other nations, detest the tyranny of any army. The president's answer was given long ago. "I would rather teach the Mexican people the use of the tooth brush than to handle a rifle. I would rather see them in school than on battle fields. I prefer any day a good electrician, machinist, carpenter, or farmer to a soldier." A modern statement of "And their swords to plowshares beating, nations shall learn war no more." Yet this must not be taken for a high sounding platitude. President Obregon has his critics and severe ones but he is not accused of being unpractical and a dreamer of dreams for dreams' sake. He has method and is a disciplinarian — nerve if you please — as has been shown on many occasions. He hates and distrusts professional diplomacy and politics. He is a man of action primarily. He has a curious suddenness in action very disconcerting to the professional politician, accustomed to weaving situations deftly and slowly.

Granting he is right on the two great problems of sovereignty and citizenry the rest is comparatively easy. With a nation granting complete recognition of all rights legitimately acquired, it will soon be right with the other nations at issue whether to the North or more remote. With order, cleanliness, industry and labor established, Mexico with its riches would bound to the front. The capital of the world would come to its aid and capital is the one and only material need of this retarded, stunted and potential giant. With its great natural resources under development, debts would soon be paid, confidence restored, economic conditions adjusted, and bankruptcy turned to credit balances at the ports of the world. Being a farmer from the farm the land question should find easy solution at the president's hands.

To be right with his neighbors an individual must be right within himself. So it is with Nations. Possessed of brilliant mind, seasoned along the hard road of experience within his own land and broadened by travel without, President Obregon indicates by his words and actions that he has grasped the great principle of right dealing. At his first cabinet meeting he impressed most emphatically upon his collaborators the necessity of absolute morality in government. The English language employs the hard fibered word integrity, yet morality is broader and expresses the profundity of feeling of the new man for the desire to make the "Inner Chamber" of Mexico fit for the inspection of the world. Mr. Obregon knows, and the world will know, that he has enemies — many of them — strong and capable of deep hate, stopping at no thing to accomplish his downfall. Some will tell you he has done this or that discreditable thing in the past; others will say he will never stand to the end of his constitutional term. Yet strange to say none accuse him of stultifying official position to personal gain or placing personal ambition above his country's good. Close observation would lead one to the conclusion that he is the choice of a great majority of his people and that he is the strongest available man to fulfill their need and longing for peace. They want room for expansion of their business, freedom and opportunity to manage their own affairs in their own country, and in their own way. These rights they claim with a calmness of men standing on their own solid earth. The great majority, peace loving by nature, want that prosperity that comes from stable conditions and they see in their new president a man who sincerely and with only the personal interest of real service, desires that they have these rightful inheritances and their God given dominion. Others, only luke warm, wish him well for they too want peace and the other things that go with it. His antagonists, when asked to name a better man either admit it can not be done or by a national shrug of the shoulders refuse to nominate. Some go so far as to claim that with Mr. Obregon the last card has been played. If he can not bring about and maintain order in this troubled land, Mexico does not have a son capable of the task. This however, is only heard where zealous partisanship is strong or personal interest is involved. However two supremely important and terse questions arise and will not down wherever and whenever the possibility of failure from any source of Mr. Obregon's administration is discussed. These are the questions. Who? What?

Yet perhaps the new president's greatest distinction is in his knowledge that of his own self he can do nothing. He has frankly told his people this and given them the admonition that only by their co-operation could Mexico take its rightful place. He can guide, direct and counsel; give the most useful service, stamp out evil practices, and put down incipient revolutions, yet if the public con-

science is not attuned, General Alvaro Obregon must bow before defeat unavoidable though undeserved.

So in its last analysis the new order which is beginning with every evidence of permanence and stability rests with all the people of Mexico, from president to peon, each responsible according to his own degree and station in the scheme of destiny.

No better words can be found than those used by Waddy Thompson, Envoy Extraordinary and Minister Plenipotentiary to Mexico, in a book written in 1846, which were as follows: "God grant them success, both on their own account as well as for the great cause in which they have so long struggled, and under circumstances so discouraging."

Where President Obregon Stands
As Shown by Acts and Words of Recent Months.

Peace and rehabilitation.

Inviolability of Mexican Sovereignty.

Friendliness for the United States.

Honorable relations with all nations of the world.

Foreigners to enjoy absolute guarantees of personal safety.

An invitation to all bona fide investors to join in the rebuilding of Mexico and sharing in its opportunities.

Absolute integrity in governmental matters from the presidential chair down to the lowest official.

No question pending between Mexico and the United States but what can be settled in a satisfactory manner.

The border between Mexico and the United States to be as peaceful and relations as pleasant as that between the United States and Canada.

An open door to men of culture and morality; a barred portal to the exploiters of the poor and ignorant, the fomenters of discord and the preachers of anarchy.

A prompt, direct and decisive hand against lawlessness, banditry, vice, graft, political discrimination, favoritism, and the various insidious practices that have kept Mexico in ceaseless fomentation for the past decade.

INTERVIEW:
Kitty Barry Crawford, "Miss Porter Heads Clinic Campaign," *Fort Worth Record*, September 1921; in *Katherine Anne Porter: Conversations*, pp. 6–7.

Porter in Greenwich Village, circa 1923 (left). In 1925 she married Ernest Stock (right), an Englishman who had served in the Royal Flying Corps. They lived together for only a few months and were subsequently divorced.

During her 1921 stay in Fort Worth, Porter became publicity director for a project to raise money for a tuberculosis clinic. Kitty Barry Crawford, also involved in the campaign, interviewed her friend for a local paper.

"I can do everything a publicist does except write about myself."

That is what Miss Katherine Anne Porter, just the instant before I began to write this bit of copy, declared to me. And incidentally, that is why I am writing it at all.

Miss Porter is to have charge of a modest kind of campaign to create a fund for a clinic for the tuberculars in Fort Worth. She is to plan and direct efforts to obtain this fund along natural lines that will not interfere with the activities of other organizations already depending on public support. It is not to be a general drive, or solicitation from the public at large. More than one novel means of obtaining the money necessary to the equipment is being considered by Miss Porter and when the finance committee for the clinic has its full list of members, she will begin to put her plans into action.

Aside from a friendship of longstanding with me, Miss Porter has a special interest in the work she will undertake in Fort Worth. She was once a rest cure devotee herself, and spent several years in sanatoriums and resorts for the tuberculous. She believes that a well-conducted clinic for those whom it is not advisable to send away from home is a basic, necessary thing in every sizable city.

"There are hundreds here and in this vicinity, I am sure," said Miss Porter, "who cannot afford to pay the prices demanded by our best institutions, and who yet might bear the full expense of expert advice at home."

"A tuberculous patient is sent away from home always upon a chance. The doctor who advises a removal from familiar surroundings can never fully determine what effect this radical change will have upon the individuals moved. Altitude often affects people harmfully, causing insomnia and heart irregularity. Absence from home has a bad mental effect."

"In more than the majority of cases it would be better for the tubercular persons to stay at

Yudico came in tonight bringing his guitar, and spent the eve
singing for Mary. Mary

Mary sat in a deep chair at the end of the table, under the
light, a little preoccupied, infallibly and kindly attentive. She
is a modern secular nun. Her mind is chaste and wise, she knows a
great deal about life at twenty three, and is a virgin but faintly
interested in love. She wears a rigid little uniform of dark blue
cloth, with immaculate collars and cuffs of narrow handmade
lace made by hand. There is something dishonest, she thinks, in
lace contrived by machinery. She is very poor, but she pays a
handsome price for her good, honest lace, her one extravagance.

Being born Catholic and Irish, her romantic sense of adven
ture has guided her very surely to the lower strata of revolution
Backed by a course of economics at the Rand School, she keeps her
head cool in the midst of opera bouffe plots, the submerged
international intrigue of her melodramatic associates.

She had meant to organise the working women of Mexico into
labour unions. It would all have worked beautifult if there had
been any one else in the whole country as clear and straight minded ax
Mary. But there wasn't, and she has got a little new pucker of
trouble between her wide set grey eyes, wihtin four weeks of her
arrival. She doesn't in the least comrepehnd that revolution is
to the half dozen or so initiates who are managing it,
also a career, and finding herself subtly blocked and hundered
at every turn, she sets it down to her own lack of understanding
of the special problms of labour in Mexico.... She has been
bludgeoned into a certain watchful aquiescence by that phrase.
So that now she has the look of one expects shortly to find a
simple and honest solution of a very complicated problem. She
is never to find it....

1921

Notes on Mary Louis Doherty, one of the models for Laura in "Flowering Judas" (Papers of Katherine Anne Porter, Special Collections, University of Maryland at College Park Libraries). In Mexico in January 1921 Porter met Doherty, who had become a Communist fellow traveler and a sympathizer with the Mexican revolution while studying in New York at the Rand School. The revolutionary Yudico, also mentioned in these notes, was the model for Braggioni in "Flowering Judas."

home if they might have proper care and direction. Getting well is a long, tedious business, full of minute detail, and mistakes are always dangerous. Only the most expert attention will bring about the best results, and a clinic, with authoritative medical and nursing facilities, and modern equipment, will provide such attention."

"While I think that often it is best to send patients to other climates and environments, long experience has convinced me that hardly more than 10 per cent of those actually expatriated should have been removed from their familiar atmosphere."

Miss Porter will organize a finance committee immediately, and begin work on the creation of the fund.

BOOK REVIEW:
Louise Bogan, Review of *Flowering Judas, New Republic,* 64 (22 October 1930): 277–278.

After her return from Mexico in 1923 Porter spent the remainder of the decade living at various times in New York City, Connecticut, Massachusetts, and Bermuda. In addition to writing short fiction, essays, reviews, and even a few poems, she started work on a biography of Cotton Mather and a novel drawing on some of her Mexican experiences that she provisionally titled "Thieves' Market," "Many Redeemers," or "Historical Present." She never completed either of the book-length works, but parts of the novel became short stories, most notably "Flowering Judas."

By spring 1930 nine of Porter's stories had been published in magazines such as Century, New Masses, transition, *and* Hound & Horn *and in Alfred Kreymborg's prestigious anthology* The Second American Caravan *(1928). Porter had developed a reputation among other literary people, but it took a letter-writing campaign by friends such as Matthew Josephson, Edmund Wilson, Yvor Winters, Caroline Gordon and her husband Allen Tate to convince Harcourt, Brace to collect six of her nine previously published stories in a limited edition of six hundred copies. (In addition to the five stories Bogan mentions in this review,* Flowering Judas *also includes "The Jilting of Granny Weatherall.")*

Miss Porter's stories, here collected for the first time, have appeared during a period of some years in Transition, "The American Caravan" and in commercial magazines appreciative of distinguished writing. In each of the five stories in the present book, Miss Porter works with that dangerous stuff, unusual material. Two stories have a Mexican locale. Two contain passages which describe lapses into the subconscious and the dream. "Magic" briefly explores the survival of frayed but savage superstition. "Rope" follows the rise and fall of an hysterical mood, and "He" sets against simple human devotion an idiot's nonhuman power and suffering.

It is to Miss Porter's high credit that, having fixed upon the exceptional background and event, she has not yielded, in her treatment of them, to queerness and forced originality of form. With the exception of "Magic" (which I should prefer to think of as an experiment, since its effect is false, for reasons only too easily defined — the use of the fustian maid-to-mistress monologue, for one), the stories do not lean upon the doubtful prop of manner for its own sake. Miss Porter has a range of effects, but each comes through in its place, and only at the demand of her material. She rejects the exclamatory tricks that wind up style to a spurious intensity, and trusts, for the most part, to straightforward writing, to patience in detail and to a thorough imaginative grasp on cause and character. She has "knowledge about reality," and has chosen the most exacting means to carry her knowledge into form.

The fact, and the intuition or logic about the fact, are severe coördinates in fiction. In the short story they must cross with hair-line precision. However far the story may range, the fact and its essence must direct its course and stand as proof to the whole. The truth alone secures form and tone; other means distort the story to no good end and leave within the reader's mind an impression far worse than that produced by mere banality. Joyce's "Ivy Day in the Committee Room" depends wholly upon the truth of the fact; Chekhov's greatest stories, say "The Duel" and "Lights," have command of reasons in the first place, of emotion, taste and style secondarily. The firm and delicate writing in Miss Porter's "Flowering Judas," a story startling in its complexity, were it not based on recognizable fact, would be to no purpose. As it is, its excellence rises directly from the probity of the conception. It is as impossible to question the characters of the fanatical girl and the self-loving man — the "good revolutionist," who, softened to a state beyond principle, is fit only for a career — as it is to find a flaw or lapse it the style that runs clear and subtle, from the story's casual beginning to the specter of life and death at the end. "Rope," after "Flowering Judas," is perhaps the most remarkable story in the book. It makes no claim; its integration becomes apparent only when the reader tries to recount it to himself in any other form than its own. The mood is put together so accurately that its elements cannot be recombined.

"María Concepción" does not entirely come up to Miss Porter's standard. A slight flavor of details brought in for their own sake mars its intensity, and one does not entirely trust Maria's simplicity of motive. For the most part, however, the stories in "Flowering Judas" can claim kinship with the order of writing wherein nothing is fortuitous, where all details grow from the matter in hand simply and in order. Miss Porter should demand much work of her talent. There is nothing quite like it, and very little that approaches its strength in contemporary writing.

BOOK REVIEW:
Allen Tate, "A New Star," review of *Flowering Judas, Nation,* 131 (1 October 1930): 352–353.

Porter had known the Tates since the mid 1920s, learning from them to take pride in their shared Southern heritage. Through them she met Robert Penn Warren, one of Tate's compatriots among the Fugitive Poets at Vanderbilt University, and Andrew Lytle, who had been on the fringe of that group. Tate may have been the first critic to have recognized the aspect of Porter's talent that Eudora Welty summed up thirty-five years later when she commented, "Most good stories are about the interior of our lives, but Katherine Anne Porter's stories take place there; they show surface only at her choosing."

Miss Porter's stories have appeared in some of the more "literary" magazines whose circulation is not large, and her great distinction as a prose stylist has been known only to a few readers. This collection of six stories, which is her first book, is a limited edition of six hundred copies — evidence of the notoriously mysterious character of the publishing mind. It is doubtless better for the author to win six hundred readers of six stories in book form than to continue to be sampled by a thousand or ten thousand in the scattered and scattering medium of the magazines. But there is no reason why she should not win six or sixty thousand readers — unless indeed the formidable integrity of artistic purpose evinced in every one

of these stories is, according to superstition, necessarily detrimental to popularity.

This is not to say that Miss Porter is an author for the "few," or an experimenter writing for other craftsmen. I mean rather that she neither overworks a brilliant style capable of every virtuosity nor forces the background of her material into those sensational effects that are the besetting sin of American prose fiction. There is almost no American writer who escapes the one vice or the other. Of the former, the works of Hergesheimer and Cabell are conspicuously guilty types; types of the latter range all the way from the "social thesis" novels of writers like Miss Glasgow and Sinclair Lewis to the borings into Negro life of Mrs. Julia Peterkin and Du Bose Heyward.

The distinction to be drawn here concerning Miss Porter's work is this: while American fiction as a whole is chiefly occupied with the discovery and then the definition of its materials (witness Glenway Wescott's uneasy speculation on the Wisconsin background), Miss Porter already has a scene which is her instinctive, automatic, unconscious possession; a background that she does not need to think out, nor approach intellectually; a given medium which at once liberates the creative impulse from the painful necessity to acquire its material and sets it about the true presentation of it.

This is roughly the character of European fiction as opposed to the more uncertain, more speculative, and thinner American variety. To return to the two American vices — we have excellent precisians writing about nothing, or we have authors who never achieve a style because they lack that single, unitary mind which comes out of a fixed relation between the author and his material. The results, in the one case, are an excessive subjectivism or plain egomania, and, in the other, a continual blurring of the fictive characters in the constant rationalizing of their social condition. The character does not exist in his own complete and full-bodied right simply because his creator cannot distinguish him from the other rather similar examples of this or that social trend.

Miss Porter's mind is one of those highly civilized instruments of perception that seem to come out of old societies, where the "social trend" is fixed and assumed. The individual character as the product of such a background also has a certain constancy of behavior which permits the writer to ignore the now common practice of relating individual conduct to some abstract social

By the time Flowering Judas *was published Porter was in Mexico City attempting to complete "Thieves' Market." This 1930 photograph of Porter in her Mexican study was taken by Eugene Dove Pressly, whom Porter met soon after her arrival in Mexico and married three years later.*

or psychological law; the character is taken as a fixed and inviolable entity, predictable only in so far as familiarity may be said to make him so, and finally unique as the center of inexhaustible depths of feeling and action. In this manner Miss Porter approaches her characters, and it is this that probably underlies many of the very specific virtues of her writing.

For one thing, her style is beyond doubt the most economical and at the same time the richest in American fiction. Only in the first story, María Concepción, is there any uncertainty of purpose. In the five others there is not a word gone to waste — and there is no under-writing. There is none of that alternation of natural description and character exposition which is the hall-mark of formula-made fiction. There is much sensuous detail, but no decoration. For Miss Porter has a direct and powerful grasp of her material as a whole; this makes every sentence, whether of description, nar-ration, or dialogue, create not only an inevitable and beautiful local effect, but contribute directly to the final tone and climax of the story.

For another thing, Miss Porter's stories are never told in the same way. Each character, or set of characters, in the given scene requires a different approach; their own inherent quality, their inviolable isolation as human beings, determines the form; and no two of these six stories have anything like the same form. While the quality of the style is the same in all of them — there is the same freshness of imagery, the same rich personal idiom — the method is always different. And — this is her great distinction — the method is always completely objective. It would be difficult to "place" an art like this, unless we may timidly call on the word classical. For here is a combination of those sensuous qualities usually accredited to a dissociative romanticism, with a clear, objective, full-bodied outside world.

"Flowering Judas" is not a promising book; it promises nothing. It is a fully matured art. We may only hope to have more of it.

BOOK REVIEW:
Yvor Winters, Review of *Flowering Judas, Hound & Horn*, 4 (January–March 1931): 303–305.

Winters had published Porter's "Theft" in the November 1929 issue of Gyroscope, *a mimeographed quarterly he edited with Howard Baker, and he clearly regretted its omission from* Flowering Judas. *It was added to the expanded, 1935 edition.*

Miss Porter's book contains six stories, *María Concepción, Magic, Rope, He, The Jilting of Granny Weatherall,* and *Flowering Judas,* arranged in this order, which is the order of composition. Of these six tales, three deal with themes that are sharply limited. *Magic,* for example, tells of a prostitute who leaves a brothel because of brutal treatment from the proprietress and returns ostensibly as the result of a charm worked upon her in her absence, actually, one suspects, because of her physical exhaustion. What one has, however, is a static sketch of the brothel, the beating, the departure, the charm, the return. It is a good sketch, but it is nothing more. *Rope,* which is composed almost entirely in dialogue presented as indirect discourse, gives the rise and fall of a quarrel between a husband and wife, a quarrel that appears to be wholly the result of nervous fatigue. The timing is skillful; the details are admirable; but the quarrel remains a quarrel, presented in an almost crystalline fashion, indeed, but with no very wide implications. The next story, *He,* deals with a half-wit boy in a family benumbed by his presence; it is moving, but it is primarily a study in disease; one feels of this story as of the two preceding that it was intended to be an object of curiosity, a brilliantly executed fictive knick-knack, rather than a general symbol of experience.

Despite this objection, the three stories are written with such skill that they would suffice to give Miss Porter a very respectable place among contemporary fictionists; but they have probably been surpassed in some measure by one or two writers of lesser talents, notably by Mr. Morley Callaghan, who, at his best (*Last Spring They Came Over, A Cocky Young Man, A Girl with Ambition*), displays an irony in handling subjects roughly comparable to those of *Rope* and of *He* that is at once infinitely discreet and

cruelly devastating. Mr. Callaghan's irony exists in what one might call a pure state and can be applied to his limited subjects with extreme precision; Miss Porter's irony is inseparable from a very complex attitude, an attitude that is usually intensely tragic (in the most respectable sense of the word), that always, at any rate, involves much more than irony, and that requires a subject capable of carrying a considerable weight of feeling — when her irony is applied to such a subject as that of *Rope,* one feels, slightly, at least, that the irony is dragging a little too much else with it; and that the actual theme of the story is not quite an adequate embodiment of the tension one feels in the atmosphere. There is neither the ironic detachment of Mr. Callaghan nor the complete absorption of the author in the symbol that occurs in Miss Porter's more ambitious tales.

María Concepción, the earliest story included, is much richer than the three which follow it. It is the story of a Mexican girl who kills a rival for her husband's love. Such a story told by one of the contemporary objectivists, of whom Mr. Hemingway is the most popular and Mr. Callaghan the most distinguished representative, would probably have been given as nearly as possible from the point of view of the peasants themselves, perhaps in terms of their bare words and actions. Mr. Callaghan does this in *Soldier Harmon,* the story of a Sadistic pugilist. The norm toward which this sort of things tends, I suppose, is something like Little Black Sambo or the Sunbonnet Babies. Miss Porter follows the older tradition of treating her characters as important symbols, that is, from the point of view of the intelligent human; the story actually deals with her own feelings about the feelings of her people. This does not mean that she appears on the stage in person; her relationship to the story is felt in the quality of the perception. She has such precedent as the works of Hardy and Graham, to mention no others. Mr. Callaghan's only contribution, in his own name, to such stories, and it is a contribution he has made rather seldom, is, as I have said, his chemically pure irony.

María Concepción is technically straight narrative, marred a little by over-decoration. The last two stories in the book, *The Jilting of Granny Weatherall,* and *Flowering Judas,* employ a convention that makes for greater concentration, the convention of revery alternating with perceptions of the present. It is, however, a *convention,* rigidly controlled by the author, with no surrender on her

Eugene Pressly, photographed by Porter on 1 August 1932

part to a psychological flux, no weakening of her powers of selection and arrangement. The perceptions of the present, including a good deal of conversation, give the setting and the actual narrative progression that takes place between the first sentence and the last. The revery provides another dimension, the background and antecedent history. In this manner *The Jilting of Granny Weatherall* presents completely in some twenty-two pages the rich and tragic career of an old woman, along with a portrait of her household as they are gathered about her deathbed. There is no excess of simplification, no summary, no omission. The story is as complete and powerful as a fine poetic drama. *Flowering Judas,* with which most of the readers of this review will be familiar, covers as much ground, quite as successfully, though the actual length of time involved is considerably less. *Theft,* a story unfortunately omitted from this volume, but available in Mr. O'Brien's collection for 1930, raises to intense seriousness a device employed in *Rope,* that of using a simple occurrence as the ineluctable allegory of things much greater than itself, and yet of making that occurrence so real in itself that the obviousness of the allegory, far from being a weakness, is a source of tremen-

dous strength. I can think off-hand of no one who has succeeded in doing anything quite like it. *Theft,* again, employs a straight narrative method, but is much swifter and much more intense than *María Concepción. Theft* and the last two stories in the book seem to me to be major fiction. I can think of no living American who has written short stories at once so fine in detail, so powerful as units, and so mature and intelligent in outlook, except W. C. Williams; and one can make that exception for but one, I believe, of his compositions, *The Destruction of Tenochtitlan.* Even the Declamations of Mr. Kenneth Burke, if they are to be regarded as fiction, fall short of Miss Porter in firmness of detail and in organic progression.

LETTER:

Katherine Anne Porter to Caroline Gordon, 24 April 1931; in *Letters of Katherine Anne Porter,* edited by Isabel Bayley (New York: Atlantic Monthly Press, 1990), pp. 37–39.

In Mexico City a steady stream of visitors prevented Porter from completing her novel. As this letter to Gordon indicates, the most disruptive of her American guests was poet Hart Crane, who arrived at the house Porter was renting in the suburb of Mixcoac in April 1931 and decided to move in just as Porter learned that she had won a Guggenheim Fellowship and began making plans to travel to Europe with Pressly. "Gene, my best young man," mentioned in this letter, is Pressly, who was thirteen years younger than Porter. "The Ice House" is a story by Gordon that was about to appear in Hound & Horn. *Andrew is the Tates' friend Andrew Lytle, author of* Bedford Forrest and His Critter Company *(1931).*

One of the most important events during this stay in Mexico was Porter's visit to the Hacienda Tetlapayac, where Sergei Eisenstein was filming Qui Viva Mexico. *She spent several days there and used her observations for the long story* Hacienda *(1934), which she began writing in fall 1931. The story expresses her disillusionment with Mexico, about which she had once been so optimistic. Although she later made brief visits to Mexico, she never again lived there for extended periods of time.*

Dear Caroline:

News upon news, or so it seems from this vantage point. Edmund Wilson writes that he will be in Mexico in June. Janet Winters has a baby named Joanna, which of course you know. The news about that is Janet's calm way of disposing of the business in record time, a prize delivery, I call it, and her comment that it was hard to believe that she had really Joanna, "who is charming." And so home and no doubt back to the novel in ten days. This is the impression I received. Fancy writing letters with a five day old baby! Should not that woman be given a medal of some kind?

Peggy Cowley writes she is coming to Mexico in July. And others. But HART CRANE CAME! Did he! He bust in upon me one evening, screamed with joy over the garden, saw the big front room standing empty, declared he could live no where else in Mexico, and could he move out the next day? He was most lordly lit, and I thought it a drunken whim, and said, why naturally yes, and the next day he showed up cold sober with trunks and bags and in two days he was dug into that room with the victrola going, which has never stopped. He is wild with delight and enthusiasm. Gets out and waters the gardens and digs around the rose bushes, and suns himself on the tank ledge, and ramps up and down roaring fragments of Blake, Christopher Marlowe and Hart Crane. Goes to the market and comes back loaded down with grass mats and bandy legged tables. Gets up in the morning and feeds the turkeys and chickens First turning on the victrola. Goes four times a day for two litres of barrel beer wearing a red sweater and carrying a long blue glass pitcher. At the present moment he is pounding the piano, which I had not succeeded in moving out of the sala and now when I mention removing it he looks grieved. But its coming out just the same. Gene, my best young man, gets along with him up to a point. By supper time, Hart is usually nicely under the influence of beer — he seems to drink nothing else, and after two steins, Gene is apt to say, "Stop talking rot" when Hart gets explaining what all is wrong with my attitude towards Mexico. And so it goes. He wants to keep the house when We give it up, and that's a very good thing. This place is too lovely to let pass away entirely. And Its big enough, I presume, to hold us all until September.

All the Guggenheim Fellows for Mexico are here except Marsden Hartley. They must have taken the next boat. Such dispatch is not for me. But the novel gets on, I expect it to be gone by September 1. I've been remembering darkly all the things that happened in the country when YOU had Hart Crane in the same house, and I am still wondering how on earth this thing came about. The first night he got out and had a fight with a taxi driver and they went to the police station on a little matter of fare, another night he was raging about in the streets quite drunk, and a policeman came home with him, and we had — rather, Gene had — some pother to get the policeman out. He seemed to want sociability and a drink. Echoes of the riot ascended to my cloistered chamber, and the next day I lectured Hart in my most motherly Dutch Aunt style. He vowed that he had Made Resolutions — from this out I should see a changed man. So far, it holds. I would give a good deal to have again such ecstatic gayety and joy over Mexico as he has. He is happy in the sun as one of Blake's little skippling lambkins. We shall see!

I saw the announcement of "The Ice House" for the next number of H & H. God knows its time for them to have a good short story. The last, I think, was Kay Boyle's "Episode in the Life of An Ancestor." Have you read her novel? It is simply beautiful. At last I got hold of Faulkner's *The Sound and the Fury* and it curdled the marrow in my bones. I have never seen such a cold-blooded assault on the nerve-ends, so unrepentant a statement of horror as that book. And such good bold sound writing. That must be taken for granted, for only a very good writer indeed could do what he has done. It left me so shaken and unnerved I could hardly believe the face of the sun. Not, of course, that one doesn't read worse in the newspapers, every day. Not that I haven't myself seen a man burned at the stake. A few days ago a girl was taken into a beggar's flop-house here by two men dressed as policemen. They asked to leave her there because, they said, she was lying drunk in the street. When the keeper investigated the next morning she was dead, and a broken bottle had been forced into her womb. Not that things don't happen. But my *God!* There should be something in a work of art that gives you something to hang onto after the very worst has been told. Still, I want to read *As I Lay Dying*.

(See above. And the men were not policemen at all. They had taken off the uniforms in the alley-way as they left.)

It seems a long time since I heard from you. I do wish you had gone after the Fellowship business in time, and I hope you do next year. They seem to have a way of asking you to re-

Nordeutscher Loyd Bremen
An Bord des D. "Werra"

August 28, 1931

Caroline darling:

It simply was not possible to write until now.
And here we are six days out, already striking across
from the Caribbean Islands to the Canaries: fifteen days,
they tell me, from yesterday. Five days before, and probabl;
ten to fourteen more from the Canaries to Gijon, to
Southampton, to Bremen.. Then by train to Paris, and so
on down to Nice. We will have spent about five weeks on
this boat before we are finished.. A combination freighte;
and passenger ship, very steady, very broadbottomed and German in her
style, doing sixteen knots an hour and keeping a level keel.

I thought of all possible ways to get by to see you,
then go on and sail from New York and have it over, a week's
voyage, without simply spending the whole first quarter of
my allowance, and there was NO way. I wished to see my father
too, and had great plans to fly over to Brownsville. But
the money began to melt so alarmingly, I could do nothing but
ake the first boat and go on...

There is so much to say, but time to say it, too,
at last. My bad luck overtake me if ever again I go through the
hell of house wrecking which attends my every change of scene. I'm
going to live in rooms, or a room, in inns, pensions, hotels: I don't
know what, but never again shall I collect the odds and ends of a
household until I have a roof of my own to cover them.

The cats were found good homes, the dog was disposed
of to some one who wanted him, the baby turkeys and their mama went
to Teodora, and the sticks of furniture were peddled here and there
at five cents on the dollar, all this in the uproar of getting
necessary papers together, write a last minute review; Lord, why
tire you out with the list of things which make such a scramble at the
last second? You know all about getting off to Europe as we seem to
do it.

Katherine Anne Porter
c/o Caroline Gordon Tate

First page of the long letter to Caroline Gordon that was the genesis of Ship of Fools *(Princeton University Library)* new your application from one year to the next. You'd undoubtedly have it the next time. But its quite a lot of red tape to go over again. I am still sending doctor's certificates and receipts for material sent and so on. Its been going on since last November. But I hope you'll send your application again, and maybe we would see each other in Europe after all.

(Something has happened again to this spacer.)

I just have a letter from Andrew, telling about his eightyfive mile advance towards Mexico when he was recalled about Forrest . . . I wish he would come to Mexico. There's a man would talk sense about it.

Honey, do drop me a line when you have a minute. Which means of course, do take an hour and write me a long letter. I want to hear about you.

love,
Katherine Anne

From the uproar downstairs, I gather that Hart — it is now seven-thirty — has just broken a lamp and is howling in French at the Indian woman because she hasn't heated his shaving water. He is at the saturation point, I take it. Does he always behave like this? Something tells me the sala is shortly going to be vacant again.

LETTER:
Katherine Anne Porter to Caroline Gordon, 28 August 1931; in *Letters of Katherine Anne Porter,* pp. 46–60.

After seventeen unproductive months in Mexico, Porter embarked for Europe with Pressly on 22 August 1931, boarding the S.S. Werra *in Vera Cruz and sailing to Bremen. During the voyage Porter kept a log in the form of a long letter to Caroline Gordon. This letter and Porter's first-hand observations of Nazi Germany while she spent winter 1931–1932 in Berlin served as the basis for her novel* Ship of Fools *(1962), in which the characters Jenny Brown and David Scott are based in part on Porter and Pressly.*

Caroline darling:
It simply was not possible to write until now. And here we are six days out, already striking across from the Caribbean Islands to the Canaries: fifteen days, they tell me, from yesterday. Five

days before, and probably ten to fourteen more from the Canaries to Gijon, to Southampton, to Bremen . . . Then by train to Paris, and so on down to Nice. We will have spent about five weeks on this boat before we are finished . . . A combination freighter and passenger ship, very steady, very broadbottomed and German in her style, doing sixteen knots an hour and keeping a level keel.

I thought of all possible ways to get by to see you, then go on and sail from New York and have it over, a week's voyage, without simply spending the whole first quarter of my allowance, and there was NO way. I wished to see my father too, and had great plans to fly over to Brownsville. But the money began to melt so alarmingly, I could do nothing but take the first boat and go on . . .

There is so much to say, but time to say it, too, at last. May bad luck overtake me if ever again I go through the hell of house wrecking which attends my every change of scene. I'm going to live in rooms, or a room, in inns, pensions, hotels: I don't know what, but never again shall I collect the odds and ends of a household until I have a roof of my own to cover them.

The cats were found good homes, the dog was disposed of to some one who wanted him, the baby turkeys and their mama went to Teodora, and the sticks of furniture were peddled here and there at five cents on the dollar, all this in the uproar of getting necessary papers together, write a last minute review; Lord, why tire you out with the list of things which make such a scramble at the last second? You know all about getting off to Europe as we seem to do it.

Of course there was a farewellish kind of party, which kept us up until four, and at six we rose to take coffee and make the train. I had wanted to go by day for a last look at the famous mountains and the tremendous railway to Vera Cruz which winds through and over cliffs like something at Coney Island, magnified several hundred times . . . The *Werra* was stuck on a sandbank at Tampico, and expected to sail late from Vera Cruz . . . this was the first set-back. Then my letter of credit was sent by mistake in another name, and I didn't know whether I had any more money until two days before leaving . . . We set off, with hang-overs, after receiving notice that the boat would sail on time, after all. Then the fog shut out the valleys all the way, so it had been quite useless to tear myself out of bed at such an ungodly hour, and to sit miserably all day on an upright bench . . . At Vera Cruz a storm came up at three in the morning, with thunder like the crash of falling skyscrapers, and lightning struck the shaft of the elevator just twenty feet from my room. It burst in my face like a bomb, with an exasperated crack that almost deafened me. I lay with my blood congealed and bones shuddering, and thought bitterly that really, this was the last straw . . .

After three lovely smooth days we drew in at Habana, and there came on board 876 (exactly) third class passengers, all Spaniards from the Canaries and ports of Spain, who were being sent away from Cuba by public subscription because there is no work for them . . . This is a very small boat, small as any old Ward Line tub plying around the coasts . . . we have a cargo to the water line, and 1200 souls in space designed comfortably for five hundred . . . I had thought of going third class, since there is no second class, but when I saw the quarters I was glad I had not. Very miserable, hot, not clean, and rooms for only about a hundred persons . . . Well, they sleep on the deck in canvas chairs, very tired women surrounded by pale little children, very discouraged men who sit with their heads hanging; they get sick on the deck, and the sailors turn the hose on everything, and then they all pile back upon one another, in wet chairs, on wet decks, with damp clothing . . . They have no work waiting for them at the end, either. They are just going from a place they are not wanted to a place where they cannot be welcome. From misery through misery to more misery, and all of them decent looking people who cannot find work and bread.

As a young occulist from Texas, on his way to Vienna for a special clinic of some kind, commented: "It isn't as if they were dirty Bolsheviks." I was so startled by this remark, as a voice from the prehistoric times of the world, that I asked involuntarily, "Where are you from?" It seemed, Austin, Houston, and Corpus Christi, Texas. Still, so help me, they are talking that way in Texas. I got him located by swapping names with him for a while, and it isn't as if he were an ignorant hulk. He represents a great part of whatever enlightenment that place has to offer. "They don't deserve their hard luck," he said, "It isn't as if they were dirty Bolsheviks." His wife is with him, and a nice young electrical engineer from Kennedy, Texas, on his way to Berlin. My cabin mate is a hefty Swiss girl, whose father was for thirty years a mining engineer in Torreon, Mexico. A Spanish Zarzuela company — a kind of musical comedy troupe — is on its way back to Spain after the usual failure of hopes in Mexico City and Habana. The rest are Germans, Herr Doktors and Herr Professors and Herr Engineers and all that, with such typically German Frauen — vast, bulky, inert, with handsome heads and elephant legs, who drink beer all day long, swallowing a steinful in two drinks, smacking their lips and saying "Ja, Ja!" quite as the colored postcards had taught me to expect.

I am studying German attentively from the dinner lists, from stray signs and bathroom taps, and a grammar for beginners. But I really am reading up on French. And a short story is working around to be done on this long bee-line across the waters, which are getting very gradually a little more troubled. The ship's doctor says gloomily we are bound to run into weather. Pray that my sea-legs don't buckle under me. I have never been sea-sick except on one occasion when I went aboard sick already.

This is going to be a kind of log, Caroline; good bye until tomorrow.

Aug. 29. Last — it was Easter — a very gay festival — I found a blue Oaxaca pottery tea set for Nancy [Tate], a good one with pots and pitchers that really pour, and cups big enough for a girl like Nancy to take a mouthful from . . . Also a green glass water pitcher with three glasses of a sizeableness. Ever since then I have waited for some one to come by who could take it over the border and mail it to Nancy and nobody came. Thousands came, but no friend of mine. So I had a big tea set — coffee set, really — copied from it for myself, so Nancy and I should have dishes just alike, only different sizes, and they looked very fine, sitting side by side in their trays. I am carrying them with me in my suitcase, and maybe I shall see some one in Paris who will be coming back, and Nancy shall have her dishes yet. They are exactly for her and no one else. Give her my love and remembrance.

The attempts to make life on shipboard a little like life anywhere else is very sad. Life on shipboard should be something else. Night before last there was a dinner party for every one to get acquainted, and last night moving pictures . . . The people below deck were also recovered and in better spirits, and did the thing more successfully. They got out accordions and guitars, and sang and danced, making a tiny circle for the performers. The tired ones still slept through it all, and the full moon made their closed faces like silver masks. There was down there a huge fat man with a purple face and watermelon pink shirt, who got on at Vera Cruz. He had a voice like seven foghorns, and he roared and sprawled and guzzled beer and sang in a voice that drowned out the brass band and I think everybody looked forward with terror to so many weeks shut up with this noise. His wife and child came on at Habana, and he has been mute ever since, sitting around drooping like a grief-stricken elephant. Now and then you can see his wife lecturing him, coldly, calmly, patiently. He never says a word.

September 3. mid-Atlantic, and still going. There have been more moving pictures, and a dance. On gala nights we find at our plates little paper snappers, with toys inside, and a comic hat of paper with feather and ribbon. All of us put on our hats and grin vaguely at the others, who grin back, every body orders wine, the band strikes up "Wiener Blut" or some other Strauss waltz, and for the moment every one is acquainted with every one else. But nothing has changed, really half of us do not salute the other half on deck the next morning, and not from rancor but from indifference . . .

I think I have a very short short-story out of it: I mean to call it "Wiener Blut" and it is about a little fat man dancing a waltz . . . I have another in mind about selling out my house and leaving it, called ". . . And a Pleasant Journey" but the distressing thing is, nothing seems to come through. Everything forms vaguely and I catch it in random notes, and the ideas melt into one another. This has been a time of inner seethe — as when wasn't time just that? But I am done with worrying about it . . . or almost. Everything will get done, I feel sure of it.

Day before yesterday I saw three whales, enormous ones, swimming almost out of water, flashing white in the sun, spouting white fountains. There was nothing to do but scream "WHALES! WHALES!" climb up on the rail and almost fall overboard . . . They are a terrifying and gorgeous spectacle . . . Never before did I quite realize the immense lost depths of the sea . . . I used to swim about two miles out in the Gulf of Mexico near Corpus Christi, and whole schools of porpoises used to dive by, parting and sweeping around me and out to sea, and suddenly I would feel under me the awful waters and the unknowable life in them, and it seemed I would surely die of terror before I could get back to land . . . It was as dreadful as if you might be set down suddenly in the preglacial age in a wilderness of monsters . . . I

love the sea, but as an old-fashioned Christian loved God — with fear and trembling . . .

The heat is lessening gradually, the sunshine is paler, every evening heavy columns of cloud rear up and shine red over the waters, and then thunder and broad lightning, and more wind, but no storms, Gott sei dank! (I learned that from the stewardess, who is always being grateful to Divine Providence for one thing or another.) (It may not be spelt properly.) The people in the steerage seem to be getting on rather nicely. We have everything on board . . . A woman who may have a baby before we get to Bremen, a new-born one who came aboard when he was two weeks old, a little dying man who sits curled up on his pillows and coughs all day, a hunch-back, a woman who weighs nearly four hundred pounds; and a beautiful Spanish bride with her devoted bridegroom — married the day we sailed from Vera Cruz. She is a lovely creature, as romantic looking as the princess in a fairy tale, with the grace and silence and naturalness of a fine wild animal . . . She sits and walks all day with her long hand lying loosely in his, smiling and dazed. He is the most utterly happy looking person I ever saw, with an irregularly featured sensitive face . . . They are really something to see. They do not dance, nor wear paper hats, nor drink, nor play cards, nor grin. If ever I saw two persons walking in Eden, it is now.

The dinner bugle is blowing raucously. I must powder my face and fly. Always I am hungry. . . .

September 6, Sunday. Last night I stayed up until after midnight, a new thing for me, because half my life I am asleep. Gene and I walked round and round the deck, stopping around sailors who were washing down everything with hose. All evening the Asturianos on the deck below were singing. A drunken man was improvising verses on any theme, or single word, the people gave him. He would mutter to himself a few minutes, and then break into a long cry, sing his verse, and wind up with a slow, flatfooted dance step. The crowd would shriek with joy. At the other end of the ship boys were having wrestling matches, as usual. At midnight, they were settled down and asleep. Some lay in chairs, some on benches, others curled like snails into hammocks . . . all with their clothes on, no covering except now and again a sheet. Many had their faces covered with towels to keep out the deadly night air, and one man, in blue overalls, hung his great crooked bare feet out of his hammock, his head swathed like a

Porter married Pressly on 11 March 1933 in Paris. The guests who signed the marriage certificate (above) included British novelist Ford Madox Ford, American novelist Josephine Herbst (a close friend of Porter), and Sylvia Beach, owner of the Shakespeare and Company bookstore, a gathering place for American writers in Paris. Porter and Pressly separated in 1937 and were divorced the next year (Papers of Katherine Anne Porter, Special Collections, University of Maryland at College Park Libraries).

mummy. The most touching thing was the posture of nearly all of them . . . those shouting, singing, swearing Asturianos each lay in the pious attitude of a well-disposed corpse . . . on his back, hands clapped on his breast, feet crossed, and the occasional muffling white sheet gave the look of a cheerful morgue to the whole deck . . . At meal times they lift the canvas off the iron grating which gives light and air to the pit where they eat. And they sit down to mountains of fried potatoes, meat stew, piles of onions, bowls of cooked apples or apricots, huge pots of coffee. All those things are on the menu up stairs, only served in silver dishes and mounds of fresh napery, and in polite little specks, one at a time . . . Little by little I feel better about this voyage for them, because they are all looking better, and smoother, and happier, as does every face on board. The sea has been unbelievably friendly and beautiful, I am attached to this silly old ship. Fifteen days today.

If I were not keeping this kind of journal for you I could never believe it has been so long. This prelude is preparing me for life in an inn, a kind of community existence after my really anarchic freedom of Mixcoac. There, I was beginning to dread the appearance of a human face, any kind of face, the more clear space I had around me the more I needed, so that I managed quite habitually to keep two or three rooms between me and any one else, and I wanted the whole orchard to myself when I took a walk . . . Already I am accustomed to faces, all kinds, I sit here and write with the whole life of the ship revolving on the decks, and it is even comfortable to me.

There is a little hunchback man with downy dry hair and a shrivelled face who wears very gay neckties. On party nights he puts on his paper hat over one eyebrow and then sits on deck all evening with his head between his hands, eyes closed, listening to the music.

A Cuban woman about fifty years old, with short curled white hair and a waxy smooth face, follows various persons about, backs them into corners, and talks for two hours at a time, making strange desperate gestures, thumbs turned in flat to the palms. She leans forward and peers at the person she is talking to, as if she were communicating some dark important secret. She is very slender and was a tremendous beauty not so long ago. She tells every one the same: that her husband was killed fighting for the revolution in Cuba, that her sons are fugitives persecuted by the government. Her eyes are very dry and bright, she talks with a crying, complaining voice, eternally about her children who are lost, who have no place to rest, and how the government officials laughed at her when she went to them asking them not to persecute her children. Now they have exiled her to Teneriffe: it seems she is not married at all, nor ever was, but it is true that she has been very active helping the revolutionary students, and is being sent away, and her mind is unhinged. Cuba is her murdered husband, and the students are her children . . . There is a gang of university students on board, going to Gijon, but only because the university has been closed over their empty heads. Its all a great joke to them they must go somewhere else to finish learning the alphabet. All day they collect in knots and give college war-cries, then sing "Cucaracha": all about the unfortunate cockroach who can't run around any more because she lacks feet to run with: or has no marihuana to smoke: or no money in her purse: there are about forty verses in all, and they sing them through . . . Well, they have taken on La Loca, as they call her, have formed a Cucaracha club, elected her as president, made a verse in her honor, and escorted her around the deck, imitating her walk and smile at her back, prancing and grimacing, while she smiles at them, and makes a little speech: her hands dancing a ballet: "My sons were students who defied the government, and they were right. Youth must defy governments, even though it means persecution, exile, death. The young must not throw away their beautiful lives being stupid and living like half-dead things — leave that for an old woman!" She makes a very grand, old-fashioned bow. They shout and applaud, and wink at the other passengers. A stringy boy in Oxford bags like tucked up skirts lollops after her, at a safe distance and mimicks her frail complaining voice: "Youth, beautiful youth!" She walks on with them, her lace skirts flying, smiling blindly . . . Sometimes one of them will dance with her, and afterwards she stands talking, one hand under her breast, the other stroking her flank, a perfectly appalling expression on her face.

This morning the sky is pale and sunless, the water is grey for the first time. I woke up chilled under my single sheet, and put on a sweater. In an hour I had to take it off again, but we have crossed some line in the night, for it is early fall and not summer any more. Day after tomorrow morning we reach Teneriffe, but there is a rumor we shall not go ashore . . . just stop for a few hours. We pass Brest, le Havre, Boulogne, but do not stop there. The five passengers for Boulogne are going to be put off at Southampton to wangle themselves home as well as they may . . .

The ship's doctor is an old Heidelberg student with a grand hooked nose, a fine head, and two sabre scars across his cheek and forehead. He walks like an officer, and stands at attention apparently, for half an hour at a time, gazing at the water with the kindest, most serviceable pair of tan eyes you can imagine: they are almost maternally sweet and good. I went to him for help, having broken out with that dangerous tropical disease known as heat-rash. All over I was a welter. He gave me a lotion he had mixed for himself, being, he said, a martyr to heat rash. It worked like a charm. Was there anything else he could do for me? No, I was in perfect health otherwise. "You do not look to be a tough voman," he told me, "but it is possible you are very strong inside," and he tapped the front of his tunic. I said I thought I was fairly tough inside. He told me cheerful little anecdotes about his vife, like me a tough voman who did not seem so. She would insist on raising chickens, and they grew so tame they wandered all through the house, so that often she exhausted herself chasing them with a broom. He himself has a bad heart, and may drop dead at any time, but not, he hopes, until once more he can see that voman chasing herself with a broom after those chickens. . . .

Tuesday Night, September 8. Yesterday evening we sighted Palma, the first of the Canaries coming this way . . . It was a jagged rock-shaped, rock-colored mass rising abruptly from grey water . . . it is my idea of Spain — more Toledo than Seville. This morning I was waked by the engine giving three loud thumps, then stopping. There was Teneriffe — another long rock with peaked edges, with houses perched on levels hacked out with a chisel, apparently. Santa Cruz is lovely, and three things struck upon my eye: camels going loaded through the streets in company with burros, friars, fat and lean, of two orders, black and brown, slapping through the streets in their old-lady shoes and pork pie hats. And the milk-women in their short black dresses, bare legs, their heads swathed in a black shawl with a little round hat, secured in the back by an elastic under their knot of hair, carrying great flat trays loaded with battered milk cans. They have a charming walk, half-run, with rigid head and shoulders and wildly swaying hips . . .

We found a cafe called "El Quita Penas," (Forget Your Troubles) and sampled all the Canary wines from the great barrels along the wall. Malaga, Moscatel, Malavasia, Madeira, and the islands cognac, Tres Copas, and an orange liqueur something like Curacoa but not so good; with all this we ate a large Spanish lunch, and came away, just in the mood to hail a very small horse drawn veehickle something like a Victoria, but only half so large, and drive in great state to the very foot of the gangway, which was in the act of rising. We ascended just one jump ahead of the gangway itself, with shoals of hungry Syrians prowling below trying to sell us embroidered shawls . . .

It seems to me now I am having the loveliest time of my life — this is long after dinner, we are sober and the boat is rolling in heavy swooning swoops calculated to chill the pit of the stomach — so it isn't through a fog of Canary wine I write this . . . I was standing in a doorway surveying the sweet crooked streets with the soft, gay colored walls, feeling at home in the sound of Spanish all around me, when a brass plate across the walk suddenly announced that here was the Bank of British West Africa . . . A feeling that I was rather far from home came over me, just for a second. Tonight we are setting out off the coast of Africa; on Friday we will be at Vigo . . . news to me. This tramp freighter has changed her mind about where-all she's going about eleven times. We may even stop at Boulogne. The Boulogne passengers are invoking some old maritime law that says, when a ship takes on passengers for a certain port, she's bound to set them off there, and no where else, barring acts of God; so we're going to get a French visa at Vigo, and pop off at Boulogne if the Captain can be brought to see the light. When the steerage passengers swarmed up on deck with their bundles and laughed and wept at sight of their island, I envied them, and hope I might cry with joy to see some one place again . . .

When we left the harbor, the sea was so wild the pilot launch was almost swamped. The man at the wheel was drenched and had hard work to stay on board. The pilot came down the ladder like a spider dropping down his own web, swung into the launch, which almost capsized, took the wheel, and nosed her away; after a good sharp tussle, the engine went dead. The pilot just stood there, holding the wheel and looking up at the ship. I leaned out and waved my scarf at him. He took off his cap with a beautiful sweep and waved back.

The sailors have tied down the canvas storm curtains with hundreds of knots, the band is playing hoppety tunes, and those devil-possessed students are howling "Cucaracha" in the smoking salon. . . .

I haven't seen the map yesterday nor today, so to my shame I don't know whether we're just entering the Bay of Biscay or leaving it . . . Will let you know tomorrow, unless you're better at geography than I am, and know anyhow. . . .

More passengers are leaving . . . The ship is almost empty. About eighty first class, and the same number third. The Captain swears he will NOT stop at Boulogne. The Boulogne passengers must get off at Southampton: in little boats, with a keg of water and some biscuits, I suppose. We aren't going into the harbor even . . . But as you may have noticed, life on this ship is very uncertain, full of rumors, alarms, and excursions . . . One thing certain. We are on our way to Bremen, and will be set off there with due formality, armed with a ticket for Paris.

That reminds me. I read over your letters today, and have put in my note book the name of your little hotel, and we go there from the station . . .

(Hearing yelps outside, I put my head through the porthole to take a glimpse of Gijon. We are turning very slowly, and half a dozen launches are circling round filled with yelling friends of passengers, all waving, nearly all standing up in their bouncing walnut shells. A long row of Spanish ships are backed neatly into the dock like parked automobiles. Our gang plank is going down. Everything is grey and silent looking. My cabin mate looked out this morning while she was dressing, and said happily, "Oh, it looks like Europe already. Everything is so grey and misty!")

Which leads to the question about where I am going. It is really warmish near Nice, isn't it? Or Grasse? Kay Boyle wrote me that Ville Franche was a good place. I mean to stay only a little while in Paris. Not more than two weeks. I wouldn't think of trying to stay in Paris; it would be fool-hardy after all I've been told. . . .

Here ends this foolish note-book, made to amuse you a little and to remember my first Atlantic crossing by . . . It was a fairly good job, passing, as we did, Cuba, Africa, Portugal, Spain, with England, Germany a scrap of Belgium, and France to come . . . I feel like one of these tourists who rush through the world with eyes tightly closed, gaining momentum by the hour, counting on his fingers the lands he has travelled through . . . getting home with a souvenir spoon from each.

You cannot think how naively I should like to see the whole face of this world into which we are born strangers, and which we so often leave without ever acquainting ourselves with it . . . Then I think maybe one is always more at home in one place afterwards . . .

I love you very much, and never stop missing you. Love to Allen and Nancy. Tell Allen I have brought his extra copy of *Mr. Pope* all the way here with me, on the grounds that some day I shall mail it to him. I was re-reading some of the poems last night, and looked forward happily to the new book. These poems grow on me the more they are read . . . substance, and "tone" that mysterious and indispensable quality he attributes to the work of Ezra Pound also belong even more to his own . . .

Good bye for a short time

September 24. I don't expect you to be much astonished to hear that we are in Berlin. The French Consulate had not the faculty to grant visas to persons in transit . . . He told me this in French and I answered in Spanish, and we parted with mutual gestures of mystification . . . Then we did stop at Boulogne, after all! In the dead of night, with foghorns bellowing, the French pilot boat going twing-twing-twing under my porthole, the Spanish students disembarking drunk and roaring "Cucaracha." Then sharp quick nasal French voices on the deck above, and after a very short while, on we went, and I lay embittered, not knowing who to curse, that little worm of an agent in Mexico who assured me I could get a French Visa at any port, or the Captain, who assured me in Vera Cruz, while it was not too late, that he would not stop in Boulogne, or myself, who was fool enough not to prepare myself for any emergency . . . Still, it is done. So I decided to come on here, since I had always wished to, look about for a month, see if I could bear the cold if I had plenty of clothes and a warm house, and so

Photograph inscribed to Sylvia Beach (Princeton University Library)

come again in touch with the life-current of ideas and work, instead of just climate and a human vacuum . . .

The last of the voyage was very pleasant . . . When we passed the Isle of Wight, a great castle stood in a greensward, surrounded by little tender woods, and the grass shaven neatly to the lip of the sea . . . I thought as we passed along so near to the shores, that I was deceived again in my sense of smell, which brings me such strange whiffs on cross-currents of air. But it smelled of herbs and grass and grazing cows. I spoke of it to the Swiss girl. She said, "No, it is really true, I have passed here three times, and there is always that smell." At Southampton a little newsboy came aboard, and when I tried to buy a newspaper, I found that we could not understand each other at all . . . I do not know what dialect he spoke, but it was as foreign to me as German: broad, drawling, with vowel sounds I never heard anywhere else . . . In England and France, on this German boat, I felt as if I were passing through enemy territory . . . The English inspectors were saying something to our Captain, who replied in English: "Yes, this rule applies to German boats, I know. The Americans and the French can have everything." The Englishman sat silent with his eyebrows lifted . . . And the Germans said to me many times such things as: "We are not allowed to use the word champagne, but let me offer you some good German sparkling wine.". . . "We are not permitted to build airships of more than such-power". . . "Please don't say 'connoisseur' — we Germans no longer understand French." And so on. There is something real and undying in the hatred these two races have for each other. They hate in a way we cannot understand, I believe.

Well — at Bremen, some of the junior officers joined us after we left the boat, recommended a good cheap little hotel, and took us to the famous Rathskeller, where we drank beautiful Rhine wine and ate pig's knuckles with sauer kraut. I loved the enormous old wine tuns, each with names and a date — I remember 1580 something, painted, carved, decorated, with great bronze taps . . . but the whole place is a marvel of the most terrible German taste — great appalling blobs and festoons of carving, everything mixed up, writhen together with a horrid muscular energy without meaning or direction . . . I feel that this will bother me as I see more and more of it . . .

Went to sleep under a feather bed about 1 A.M. Got up at six thirty to catch the morning train for Berlin . . . took a third class compartment, astonished at its decency and comfort, with light and air and a little shelf table where we had coffee and bread and butter, and then hot broth and then fruit and more coffee, thus wearing away six mortal hours between sleep and nourishment . . . I was so tired by now I thoroughly wished to die . . .

Landed in Berlin, and checked our bags, got a map and a guide book, and simply roamed about the city until nearly evening. Then we picked a hotel from the guide book, came here, found a Mexican woman married to a German in charge of the place, who at once brought forth her Indian woman servant to wait on me . . . we have two stuffy rooms choked with feather pillows and plush table covers and knobby furniture and overstuffed divans, but praise God, the steam heat is on tonight; we get rooms, breakfast in bed, and maid service for twenty four dollars a month each, and that's as well as we can do in any pension we have yet visited — and they are not few . . . We have never eaten twice in any cafe, and have, by a simple hit or miss plan, sampled therefore about fifteen, with innumerable coffee shops and bars . . . No matter what the price, a platter of meat, potatoes, and vegetables is set before you fit to feed a starving family. The difference lies merely in the manner of getting it up. For 1 mark you get as much as for three marks . . . but it will be, meat, a gorgeous gosh-awful Gothic gob, potatoes, and vegetables cooked to goulash in meat broth . . . I foresee gout to the death, but I don't know yet what to do about it . . .

I know well there is a change coming over this German spirit: there are enough of these new houses with aluminum doors and window frames, thin firm concrete walls and lines of glass, orderly and bare as ships, their verandahs like decks . . . They are almost too bare and clean and pure, as if the builders were in an ecstasy of shearing away excrescences. In the shops I see beautifully designed furniture, clear colors, fine simple silver and dishes . . . There is a whole colony of new houses, built for the poor, for almost everybody is poor, where light, air, space, cleanliness, AND beauty have been the ends, with the greatest economy of means possible. I mean to see this: and some of the new films, and to hear some of the new music. Then I will be able to tell you something. In the meantime, I am bored with feather beds and figures of men and women who look like something by Albrecht Dürer . . .

But all of the persons I have spoken to, wherever, have soft voices and good manners. Their words of greeting and goodbye and thanks are very musical: it is all a great relief after the harshness, the nasty public manners, the shrillness and meanness of Mexico, where only the Indian gives any charm of being, and even that is the saddening courtesy and humbleness of a beaten creature who bows his way though life . . .

Write me once, anyhow, care the American Consulate General, Bellevuestrasse 8, Berlin, and by then I shall know where I am to be . . . I sent for my mail from Paris, and am trying to make up my mind to stick it through here, get my work done, and go south afterwards. It remains to be seen whether I can beat the cold . . . But a little time will show me.

Good bye and my love,
Katherine Anne

LETTER:
Katherine Anne Porter to Josephine Herbst, 3 August 1934; in *Letters of Katherine Anne Porter,* pp. 109–110.

Except for a brief visit home in spring 1936, Porter lived in Paris from spring 1932 until autumn

1936. During that time Katherine Anne Porter's French Song-Book *(1933),* her translations of seventeen French songs printed with the original French versions, and Hacienda *(1934) were published in limited editions by Harrison of Paris, a small publishing house run by Barbara Harrison and Monroe Wheeler with the assistance of novelist Glenway Wescott — all of whom Porter met soon after her arrival in Paris.*

As Porter mentions in this letter, she struggled with Hacienda, *continuing to revise it after publishing an early version in the* Virginia Quarterly Review *(October 1932). Porter was also at work on a novel, "Midway in This Mortal Life" (later called "Many Redeemers"), which she never completed. She published parts of the first section, "Legend and Memory," as the separate stories that she eventually grouped together as "The Old Order."*

At the beginning of this letter to Herbst, a close friend since the mid 1920s, Porter praises Herbst's story "Man of Steel," which she had just read in the January 1934 issue of the American Mercury *at Sylvia Beach's Shakespeare and Company bookstore. The story is based on Porter's brief marriage to Ernest Stock. In this letter Porter also comments extensively on her approach to writing fiction.*

Porter in Paris, 1933

Josie Darling:

As usual, Time does a grand sneak on me. I didn't realize how much of it has slid by until I happened on your story of the "Man of Steel" over at Sylvia's, in a *Mercury* dated, I think, just a year ago. It seems to me that almost your last letter was saying, "The story will appear next August . . ."

It is a very good story. Glenway Wescott once said, one was safe to write about any one, anything at all, because they either never recognize themselves as seen by others, or they pick out only the flattering things as applying to them, or they are so pleased to be taken for the subject of a story, they don't care what one says about them. As this is the first time I ever met myself in literature, I am still wondering which class I belong to . . . myself, I never used anybody I ever knew or any story about any one, complete. My device is to begin more or less with an episode from life, or with a certain character; but immediately the episode changes and the original character disappears. I cannot help it. I find it utterly impossible to make a report, as such. I like taking a certain kind of person, and inventing for him or her a set of experiences which I feel to be characteristic, which might well have happened to that person. But they never did happen, except in the story. Or if I take one episode as a starting point, it always leads to consequences which did not occur really. I believe that this is what fiction-writing means. Actually I think you have done much the same thing, because, while most of your episodes are perfectly recognizable, the *connections* and conclusions are very different from what happened, from my point of view . . . I mean to say, I know all the secret data of that unfortunate occurrence, what my own motives were, some things about the poor fool that explained some of the events, and so on. But you made a good and very logical story out of your materials, and I think it a good job . . . I have just finished a fiction version of "Hacienda," which will be published as a little book, and my struggles there taught me a great deal. For one thing, that I must not use *actual characters combined with their actual experience.* I must either write fiction, or report the facts. The combination

Porter in her Paris apartment, winter 1935–1936

for me is deadly. I cannot do it. I don't think my story is so bad, but I could have done better with it if I had not tried to stay within the frame of remembered events and actual personalities . . . That is merely the jumping off place for the imagination and that is where your story should begin, not end . . .

My novel started as autobiography, and after three pages I tore it up, named the whole first part "Legend and Memory" and began to write out of a fullness of *what I know in sum,* and not in detail or fact. And I have got by this not only more fact but more truth into what I am trying to tell; that is to say, it does no violence to the spirit of the life it is founded upon. That is all I can do.

BOOK REVIEW:
Eleanor Clark, "Cameos," review of *Flowering Judas and Other Stories, New Republic,* 85 (25 December 1935): 207.

In 1935 Harcourt, Brace published and expanded, trade edition of Flowering Judas, *adding "Theft," "That Tree," "The Cracked Looking-Glass," and* Hacienda *to the original collection.*

Miss Porter is not an easy author. Her scope is limited, and she counteracts this weakness by satire so pointed and compressed and such perfec-

tion of style that one is sometimes forced to concentrate more on word patterns than on the substance of a story. It is not absurd to speak of perfection in this context. One dares to use the word for miniatures.

These generalizations apply to Miss Porter's talent as a whole. They have to be qualified when one deals with the stories separately. Besides "Flowering Judas," two of the stories in this book, "María Concepción" and "The Cracked Looking Glass," would be almost perfect by any standard. In these two, and to a lesser extent in "He," the author has superimposed rhythm and melody on the confused feelings of an inarticulate person, not in such a way as to bring pattern into a life that lacks it, but rather to bring into the reader's senses, more often by sound than definition, the emphases inherent in a character's living. When Miss Porter is writing on this level one cannot be suspicious of restraint. The essentials are there, and we know them through an unfaltering series of trivialities. All the reticence, violence and power of María Concepción are in the carriage of her body when she takes her fowls to market.

In the title story a sensitive but inhibited girl is in love with a young Mexican revolutionary and in order to save him is forced to suffer the attentions of Braggioni, a labor organizer whose "gluttonous bulk has become a symbol of her many disillusions." Her lover kills himself in prison, she comes home and listens to Braggioni's singing. "He sighs and his leather belt creaks like a saddle girth." When he leaves her, sleep confuses her feeling with the symbolism of the Judas tree. It is impossible to imagine reverence of emotion conveyed with more precision than in this story, precision that gives a first impression of hardness as if its purpose were to clarify feeling into nonexistence, but that serves actually to lop off irrelevancies so that the impact of a mood is subtle and complete. The portrait of Braggioni is a triumph of deflation in few words, and this without comment from the author. The elements of his character are exposed, with rare cruelty, to each other, and automatically tear down his own image of himself.

The methods of this style — understatement, rigid selection and sympathetic music in words — are relatively unsuccessful in three of the new stories added to the original edition of "Flowering Judas." Particularly in "Hacienda," where the author is trying to describe a bustle of contradictory characters, the result is superficial and not pointed enough to give contour to any

Notes...

The uneasy morality, the exact code of manners, the women never daring to enjoy themselves or to be natural.. or the men, either The furtive trips of the men... where did they go? What did they do? Only to dri nk with other men, to swear a little, to be free of the piffling niceties of female society. To spit if they felt like it. To get for a moment into freer, looser air.

The young women like Amy. Full of curiosity, directness, honesty. But not allowed... Consequences of Amy's directness, too terrible. Brother, lovers or father or husband would most certainly feel obliged to shoot somebody. Amy's aWatteau shepherde s dress.
Amy's grave, with the poem. see note.

Amy and Gabriel. Fourth cousins. His race horse(remember his grand father disinherited him for race horses, see note). in le gend, finest horses, superlatively swift, champions, winning races, a brilliant gay life.... Amy's letter. The young stranger, the shooting (at) the scandal, the marriage, Amy's death. All told as seen and heard by
the incident of the Bourbonbottle in the carriage...
two romantic little girls..... then Uncle Gabriel in the life and Miss Honey.. Then Cousin Eva Parrington.

In Old Mortality —

Notes for "Old Mortality," first published in the Spring 1937 issue of The Southern Review (Papers of Katherine Anne Porter, Special Collections, University of Maryland at College Park Libraries). Memories of Amy, the central character of the first section of "Old Mortality," are woven through the remainder of the story.

Katherine Anne Porter   6/24/48

Old Mortality. Short Novel.

I have a feeling that these stories have been done and are
finished.

It is not an autobiographical story. But it is true some
one who represents the rememberer, the observer, is there. Just
the same the girl who is called Miranda is by no means intended
to represent myself. She is a single figure, the one who carries
the line, the thread of the argument.

It is a story of youth, childhood, growing up in society
full of legend, full of memory, of history. All ages are ages
of transition, but some a little more violent than others. The
time we live always seems the most difficult, the most unmanage-
able in all history. It is true that each man has more than he
can endure, no matter if he gives his life to thinking about it.
(or comprehend)

This is a story of youth being brought face to face with his
own time, which is not the time of his elders who brought him up.

My own experience was this: I was given the kind of education
and the kind of up-bringing that in no way whatever prepared me
for the world I was to face. When I was ready to step out in the
world supposedly grown up, I was as ignorant of the world as it
is possible to be.

You begin to question, you try to understand, and you try
to discover for yourself ways of meeting the world. And you
feel you cannot rely on anything that you were told or anything
you were taught because everything that you met in your experience
was simply, apparently another thing. And it takes years and years
in such a case to find out that they were indeed essentially well
prepared and well based and that you did have your weapons and
the essential knowledge, but they were so deeply concealed that
you couldn't find them in yourself, and that the change in the
world was a superficial change - you might say of fashion -
of speech.

This book is based on my own experience - true - by my own
experience that came to me from the family. The theme is not
about my problem.

The book is in three parts. First part - story of an aunt
of mine, my father's younger sister. She was dead nearly ten
years before I was born - and she was still as alive in the house as
if she had never left it.

*Porter's character Miranda appears in the stories collectively titled "The Old Order" (written in Paris),
as well as in "Old Mortality" and "Pale Horse, Pale Rider" (both completed in 1936–1937). More than a
decade later Porter made a series of notes (first page above) discussing the extent to which "Old Mortality"
is autobiographical (Papers of Katherine Anne Porter, Special Collections, University of Maryland at College
Park Libraries). Although these notes say that Porter is not Miranda, the character shares some of Porter's
experiences during youth and young adulthood. (In "The Old Order" and "Old Mortality" the character
Maria is based on Porter's older sister, Gay, while that of Paul is based on her brother, who was baptized
Harry Ray but later renamed Harrison Paul and always called Paul.)*

of the people involved. These few failures can be forgiven in a book that is primarily one of small patterns written with subdued and exceptional brilliance.

LETTER:

Katherine Anne Porter to Monroe Wheeler, 6 December 1936 [excerpts]; in *Letters of Katherine Anne Porter*, pp. 145–147.

After their return to the United States in 1936, Porter and Pressly separated, and Porter went to stay at an inn in Doylestown, Pennsylvania, where she wrote two of her best-known stories: "Noon Wine," which draws on the period after the death of her grandmother when Porter's father left her and her younger sister, Mary Alice, with the family of his cousin Ellen Skaggs Thompson on a farm near Buda, Texas, and "Old Mortality" (discussed in this letter to Wheeler), which draws on other events of her childhood and young adulthood.

. . . On my grandmother's farm, we used to have all the odds and ends that no one wanted in the other places, old secretaries, black walnut beds, mahogany chests, and sandwich glass. I remember the huge white hen with red comb which contained the breakfast boiled eggs. We thought it dowdy but practical. I could never afford to buy such a bird now. I don't really want one. I can look at one, and re-create a whole past, down to the least detail. I remember vividly things I had forgotten. I see windows stuffed with the things we sold en bloc to a second hand man for nothing. Short sighted, but I can't regret it. I shan't try to buy any of them back. [. . .]

As to work, I have had a let-down for the past two weeks; this happens, but it is not a mood I can tolerate, much less encourage. Good or bad ("hot or cold," remember the irreplaceable Bert Savoy?) they leave here on January first or a very few days after . . . The notion that *Harper's* might, by some persuasion, take a story of mine is very cheery-uppy. I'm money-mad, as you know, darling, and do think a twenty thousand word story is worth something more than I am apt to get for it from a smaller magazine. I have one, called "Old Mortality." It is in three parts, the first a story of romantic love and death, as patched together by a little girl listening to family reminiscence. In the second part, this little girl and her sister meet the hero of the romance, now grown old. Third part, one of the girls meets, when she is about

grown, a woman who had been an enemy of the heroine. That's really all. It is to be the first story in the collection. If *Harper's* publish it, they would have to get it in by the April number at the latest, as the book is scheduled for April. The March number would be even better. Shouldn't I send the copy to you? It would be splendid if it could be made to happen, but we will none of us be too badly upset if it doesn't. The story needs a clean copy. Otherwise it is ready. Let me know about this, I will send it where you think it should go.

The title comes from a pastiche I wrote on tombstone poetry in my part of the country. My version runs:

She lives again who suffered life
Then suffered death, and now set free
A singing angel, she forgets
The griefs of old mortality.

Don't you think that sounds like a tombstone poem of the 80's? I was interested also to find, when I visited an old cemetery last spring, that almost all the mottoes and quoted verses were secular, and classical . . . Interesting, I think. Not religious, and not sentimental poetry, except now and then, but fine tall quotations from Shakespeare and Dante and Milton. Well, my story exists and is ready to be published and I hope your good friend can help the editors to make up their minds to mewards. [. . .]

INTERVIEW:

Archer Winsten, "Presenting the Portrait of an Artist," *New York Post*, 6 May 1937, p. 17; in *Katherine Anne Porter: Conversations*, pp. 8–13.

In 1937 a Book-of-the-Month Club jury comprising Edna St. Vincent Millay, Pearl S. Buck, Christopher Morley, Heywood Broun, Hervey Allen, Dorothy Canfield, Ellen Glasgow, Sinclair Lewis, and other well-known writers of the day selected Porter as one of four authors of "outstanding merit" whose work had been insufficiently recognized by the general public. Chosen on the basis of books published between 1 May 1935 and 1 September 1936, each author was awarded $2,500.

This interview published on the occasion of the award includes several instances of Porter's tendency to embellish stories of her childhood and family background. For example, she was not a descendant of William Sydney Porter (O. Henry); she did not become a Roman Catholic until 1910, when she was nearly twenty; and she was never sent to a convent school in New Orleans. (When her fictional representative Miranda Gay elopes from a New Orleans convent in "Old Mortality," Porter is drawing the experiences of "Tante Ione," the wife of her father's younger brother Newell Porter.) Porter's first marriage lasted eight years, not three.

When the Book of the Month Club recently found itself with extra cash and a kindly impulse to give $2,500 to an author of outstanding merit whose work had not been appreciated by the great public, it chose Katherine Anne Porter for the award.

Her reputation, widespread among connoisseurs, was based on eleven short stories written and published during the past thirteen years and brought together in a volume called *Flowering Judas.*

In strong and simple prose they brought to the reader Mexico and Mexicans, the failure of a marriage, a quarrel, a few days in the making of a motion picture, the death of an old woman.

There were no tailor-made plots to gratify one's detective instinct with a tricky end. Something happened, something was said, some people live and, after the story was read, lived on. There was always the inescapable quality of the single observation, of the character portrayed, a capture of the truth.

She has been thought of as one who took a year to write three thousand words, a whole day to fit ten words into a sentence and half of another to weigh, polish, rearrange, and think about it. Editors, having read some of her stories, wrote in the editorial manner ". . . surely you have something on hand that we would like to see." But there was nothing, except maybe once a year. And editors considered her a most extraordinary writer. How strange not to have something on hand. And how much stranger not to sit right down and bat it out if the desk drawer happened to be depleted.

In such a case editors and others are apt to decide they are up against a stylist — that is, one to whom the manner of writing is so important that it is only by a major miracle that anything ever gets written. Ordinarily stylists can be identified by their thin volumes, rare publication, a small but appreciative public and an independent income.

Miss Porter had no independent income. Moreover, she has found it annoying to be called a stylist and what that implies.

In rebuttal she cites a recent twenty-one-day period in which she wrote 62,000 words, part of five short novels, which will soon appear under the Harcourt Brace imprint as *Pale Horse, Pale Rider.* There was also that autumn in 1927 when she sat down at 11 P.M. in her subleased apartment in West Fifty-second Street to write a story called "Rope."

She wrote it, dressed, went out to mail it to the first American Caravan, where it was published; returned home, and it was 2:10 A.M.

There are also the four complete novels and forty short stories she burned because she did not like them.

Do you understand? She is an artist.

She is now living in a first-floor apartment in a brownstone building on Perry Street in the Village. Her living room has a wall full of books, pale, unpainted furniture low to the floor, and a spinet.

The spinet, with its pearwood body, ebony and boxwood keys, a sounding board of 150-year-old fir, and its beech table and cover, is an exact copy of a French museum piece dated 1550. When she brought it from France last October, the steam heat and sea air warped the delicate instrument so that it has had to rest ever since.

She is a small woman with hair grayed almost to white and a young face. She has traveled far and done many things and remembers much because she has "an ungodly memory that won't let me forget anything except telephone numbers and the time of day."

When she was six years old she wrote, bound and hand-printed what she spelled "A Nobbel — The Hermit of Halifax Cave." There were no writers in the family — though she may have been very distantly related to O. Henry (Sidney [*sic*] Porter). No one encouraged her to become a writer. It was not done in those days in Texas, her native State.

She says, "My family felt that if one had talents they should be cultivated for the decoration of life, but never professionally."

From the beginning there was a determination to write. In school she learned proper things — dancing, elocution, penmanship. At home a grandmother born in 1827 — sixty-six years old when Katherine was born — took the place of her dead mother and insisted, "Children should be seen and not heard" or "Handsome is as handsome does."

So at the age of sixteen the convent girl ran away and was married, was divorced at the age of nineteen. A year later she left Texas.

She says "I had to leave the South because I didn't want to be regarded as a freak. That was how they regarded a woman who tried to write. I had to make a revolt, a rebellion, and I don't mean 'living your own life' either. When I left they were all certain I was going to live an immoral life. It was a confining society in those days."

In due time that society will find itself in the first part, "Legend and Memory," already completed, of a novel to be called *Many Redeemers*.

She went to Chicago and worked as an extra in the Essanay studios the very week that Gloria Swanson broke in as an extra. She was asked to go to the Coast with the company as a "guaranteed" extra when it moved. She refused, and she had a reason. Just as she had a reason for refusing to go to the Coast six years later when she was doing publicity work under Hunt Stromberg at the Selznick studios in New Jersey.

She says, "I knew. I just knew what it would do to me. I'm very luxury-loving. I have all the expensive tastes. I could fall into it like a cat into an empty pillow. I knew I was corruptible."

So she stayed in Chicago that time, was desperately poor, for she has always made her own way, and didn't get enough to eat all the time. Pretty soon she went back home with tuberculosis.

A few years later she was making good her recovery in Denver and working on the Rocky Mountain News as movie reviewer, drama critic and sob sister.

In 1920 she went to Mexico to study Mayan art, and found herself instead in the center of the Revolution. Being something of a rebel in her own quiet way, it was easy to plunge in on the side of Liberty, Equality and Fraternity. She taught dancing and physical culture in four of the new schools.

The experience provided her with a couple of stories and she stayed there off and on for eight years. In 1922 she brought the work of a couple of unknown Mexican artists to New York. They were Diego Rivera and Miguel Covarrubias.

One of the later stories she wrote with a Mexican setting was the one called "Hacienda," which told the events of a few days during Eisenstein's filming of "Thunder Over Mexico."

From the lips of one of the Russian characters she quoted the following: "Ah yes, I remember," he said on meeting some Southern women, "you are the ladies who are always being raped by those dreadful Negroes."

It is the kind of quotation that is unexpected in the writings of a woman trained in the Southern tradition, rebel though she was. But she has broken with the class from which she came, completely. She has come over and taken her stand, taken out her card in the Guild of Artists. She considers that her class, and she wants no other.

She feels that her life has had one pattern, the determination not to make writing a career — that is, not ever to allow her serious writing to be in any way influenced by demands of editors or public, as it would have to be if it were her livelihood.

"If I began to look upon it as a means to make money — I mean, for me it wouldn't do," she says.

Ghost writing, rewriting, editing, revising, all the different ways in which a writer works on other people's material — these she has done in order to keep going and to keep herself free.

She wrote steadily for years without ever an attempt at publication. Unlike the familiar tale of writers who collect basketfuls of rejection slips, she never had one. At the age of thirty she thought she had written a story worth printing and she sent it out and it was accepted. Since then she has had only one rejection. An editor asked her to send something to him. She sent the story she had just finished. It didn't please her and it didn't please him either.

There is a powerful element of self-confidence in her makeup. A story is written at fever heat, fast and without a break in the mood if she can help it. She goes over that copy with a pencil, marking out a few words and changing some. A clean copy is made, and that's the way it goes out. No one sees it but the editor to whom it is sent. She is the only one who knows what she is trying to accomplish, and therefore, logically, she is the best judge of whether or not she succeeds.

One of her greatest obstacles to increased production is libraries. Set her down in the midst of the dusty stacks of a big library and she is utterly content. In Basel, Switzerland, where she was able to go on a Guggenheim Fellowship in 1931, she found herself in the midst of the original documents of the Reformation. She wanted never to leave, never to stop her orgy of researching.

This side of her talent will be expressed in a book to be published after her next. It is "The Devil and Cotton Mather," the writing of which is almost finished. The next story of hers to appear, if you are interested, will be "Noon Wine," in *Story* magazine for June.

Besides writing, three things interest her: friends, revolution and cooking.

Friends — She likes them, can't resist; sees more of them than is good for work.

Revolution — She has been a so-called Fellow Traveler for many years, but whenever on the verge of joining up, some small thing prevented her, an incident, a statement, a person. It was always something that made her afraid for her mental freedom. A larger-scale example would be the Trotsky trials, which were profoundly disturbing to her. "Why," she asks, "should I have rebelled against my early training in Jesuit Catholicism only to take another yoke now?"

Cooking — "I'm a fanatical cook. I'm proud of the fact that I could hire out and be a good cook. I'm an imaginative cook. Some day, when I've finished all my books, I'm going to write a cookbook. I'm a perfectionist in cooking."

She thinks it would be wise for artists to be good cooks, since they seldom have enough money to eat in good restaurants and since their health and energy may depend on the food they eat.

An additional but purely personal interest is her husband, Eugene Pressly, whom she married in Paris in 1933 when he was in the United States Diplomatic Service.

This, quite by the way, is said by Miss Porter to be, with one exception, the only time she's ever been interviewed. Seeing the pencil and copy paper, she exclaimed, "It's going to be a real interview. You're going to take notes." And then, with marvelous restraint, she failed to add, "You'll have to let me see what you write before it's published."

The other interview occurred in Mexico City. Then, as now, she protested there was no reason to interview her. No one ever did. But the Mexican reporters and photographers insisted, taking a flock of pictures and jotting down terse statements about the beauties of Mexico and Mexico City. Finally they asked her to write her name on a piece of paper so it would be spelled correctly.

That done, they put their heads together. "Then you are not," they accused gravely, "Gene Stratton Porter?"

No, she was not.

This time, though, there has been no mistaken identity. A portrait of a sincere artist has been intended. It is a portrait of a woman who says about writing, "I don't think people really know what they do, and when they finish they don't know what they've done. We start out to do

a particular thing of course. But what you write is a sum of your experience and yourself."

LETTER:

Katherine Anne Porter to Glenway Wescott, 3 December 1937; in *Letters of Katherine Anne Porter*, pp. 153–155.

From autumn 1937 through spring 1938 Porter lived in New Orleans, completing "Pale Horse, Pale Rider" on time for publication in the Winter 1938 issue of The Southern Review, *whose editor, Robert Penn Warren, was an old friend. Warren's business manager/assistant editor was Albert Erskine, who would become Porter's fourth husband. After finishing "Pale Horse, Pale Rider," which draws on her nearly fatal bout with influenza in Denver in 1918, Porter returned to work on "Promised Land," which she had started nine months earlier. It eventually became* Ship of Fools, *published in 1962.*

Glenway my dear

Let me tell you what I have been doing and you will know better why I have not been writing to you when my delight is to send you letters such as they are. Just now, within this quarter hour, I have finished "Pale Horse, Pale Rider," and it would be quite useless to try to tell you what a thing it has been; this past month has been spent at it, quite literally, but it is done. The *Southern Review* editors have been snatching it page by page and having it set up, and here are the last dozen all ready to go tomorrow. Now I must begin at once on "Promised Land," which I hope to persuade *Harper's Bazaar* to take instead of the one I promised them, for it must be written next, no argument about that, and now is the time or never. I can't quite explain this steady energy, though I have had fits of it before, and it is the best thing in the world while it lasts . . .

Perhaps being on my own, with a real necessity to make money, and a real desire to have some sort of control of things that happen, are good enough as causes. Being here may have something to do with it. Here is an excellent place for me to be, apparently. But I want to be back in New York in the late spring, maybe yet in time for Julius Caesar and the Elizabethan farce, but at any rate in time to see all of you, for that is my real errand, before you begin scattering places as you may. That is my hope, to see you three at Stone Blossom and in 89th

Porter with Albert Erskine and Monroe Wheeler. Porter married Erskine, who was more than twenty years her junior, in New Orleans on 19 April 1938, ten days after her divorce from Pressly became final. Porter and Erskine separated two years later and were divorced in 1942.

street, and where ever else you may be. By that time my book will be out, and my hagridden conscience will be at ease momentarily, and maybe there will be more violets for me to transplant, or I can tamper a little with George's hawthorn hedge . . . Tell me, is that the pink-flowering thorn such as grew in the closerie at 70 bis rue Notre Dame des Champs? Did you ever see that little tree in full bloom? Promptly on the first of May it simply bloomed all over, and I thought it the pleasantest tree ever I saw, and some day I mean to have another just like it, I don't know where or how.

Nearly twenty thousand words, darling, laid neatly in rows on paper, at last . . . But most of them were written years ago, I almost know them by heart. I began this story in Mexico, went on with it in Berlin, Basel, Paris, New York, Doylestown, and now New Orleans . . . what a history. I need a method too. I hope you have found what you need, it is delicious news to hear your mood is better; I think you have simply emerged into another of your many phases, now you will do something else, whatever it is you have been preparing for. Bless you and bless you.

Maybe you will be glad to hear that in the rather dusty austerity of my attic, with no huswifly duties weighing me down, and a blithe disregard for my surroundings, I have developed my natural vanity again, and now go sleekly coiffed, curled, manicured, and spend three hours once a week in the hands of Julia, the Vieux Carré beautician who does the hair-dressing for the Petit Théâtre, also; she takes pride in me and turns me out smooth as a willow whistle. And I believe you will be glad to hear this.

I long to frequent you, too, my dear, and you are the only one I feel free to talk over the common predicament in which we find ourselves — literary predicament — One of the editors of the *Southern Review* wrote me today that the linotypers didn't like my story so far, because there were no bawdy spots in it. The editor told them there weren't going to be any, and one of them said, "I thought this woman was a proletarian sympathizer . . . but look at this story. Here's a couple dead in love and they don't sleep together."

And the editor added, "I think you may as well face the facts. You are not really a proletarian writer."....

With my love,
Katherine Anne

BOOK REVIEW:
Paul Rosenfeld, "An Artist in Fiction," review of *Pale Horse, Pale Rider, Saturday Review,* 19 (1 April 1939): 7.

The publication of Porter's 1939 book, which includes "Old Mortality," "Noon Wine," and "Pale Horse, Pale Rider," marked a high point in Porter's professional reputation. Rosenfeld was not the only reviewer to place her in the first rank of fiction writers. Lewis Gannett in the New York Herald Tribune *called her one of the great American writers; Clifton Fadiman in* The New Yorker *compared her to Hemingway, while Wescott, reviewing the book for* The Southern Review, *compared "Noon Wine" to John Milton's* Paradise Lost *(1667).*

Katherine Anne Porter moves in the illustrious company headed by Hawthorne, Flaubert, and Henry James. It is the company of storytellers whose fiction possesses distinct esthetic quality, whose feelings have attained harmonic expression in their work. Form, invention, and poetry to no uncertain degree were of the essence of the moving stories by this Texas woman collected a few years ago under the title "Flowering Judas." Even more definitely these properties distinguish the trio of tiny, affecting novels which comprise her present welcome volume. The book is that rare thing, the product of an accomplished artist in fiction.

Its artistic qualities do not draw attention to themselves. Beautifully modeled, petal-like sentences abound in the three novelettes. But unlike those of other conscious stylists, Kay Boyle for example, they never seem to stud the prose and pirouette in the direction of imaginary footlights. They move unobtrusively and precisely. So, too, do the narratives: without breaks and with inflexible steadiness and suppleness, easily, almost with sprightliness. Each of the narratives maintains its own tone — in the sense of effects of color and modulations and accents appropriate to the expression of its individual sentiment. And each of the poignant little dramas represented by them unfolds continuously and unpredictably, never betraying its ultimate turns, which arrive as shocks and surprises. Ideal beauty, a fugitive poetry, again and again flashes through the substance of the narratives. But the tone, too, invariably is unemphatic and quiet.

All these esthetic qualities are the expressive means of a singularly unified, rich feeling of life. This feeling, by and large, is a quick, subtle, sorrowful intuition of the eternal discord and harshness of things, their bittersweet, their baffling complexity. Wholly pessimistic this experience is not, since it recognizes — and with what keenness and delight — the smile of goodness, the shimmer of joy. Miss Porter's protagonists — simply drawn but solid and breathing — are gentle, naturally compassionate, but wrecked by fatal conflicts between character and circumstance, among them erotic fixations and maldevelopments. The first of them, the heroine of "Old Mortality" — who is seen through the wondering and half-comprehensive gaze of a child — is a brilliant, hysterical, anesthetic belle of the old days who flees from marriage into death. The second, the principal personage of "Noon Wine" — possibly the most touching and perfect of the triad of novelettes — is an easy-going Southern farmer who, deprived of self-confidence by the chronic invalidism of his wife, crazily commits a hideous crime in the effort to intercept a gratuitous act of inhumanity. And the half-starved little newspaper-woman of the story which lends its name to the volume finds a momentary lover in the boy who saves her from death, and then recovers to learn that he has died and left her in a void. Like the preceding tales, this last one with its magical recapture of the atmosphere of the war years leaves one at a peaceful distance from the world.

BOOK REVIEW:
"Novels of the Week: Away from Near-War Consciousness," review of *Pale Horse, Pale Rider, Times Literary Supplement,* 27 May 1939, p. 311.

The TLS *review for the British edition of* Pale Horse, Pale Rider *was respectful but less enthusiastic than the American responses.*

After war consciousness, post-war consciousness and crisis consciousness, there is something like white-war or near-war consciousness. It seems to be the worst of the lot and the most damaging to novelists and novels. No doubt imaginative talent has almost always chosen the wrong time to be born; no doubt, too, there is seldom a crop of masterpieces in the space of a few months. But it is plain that the going has of late become rougher and more difficult for the novelist, plain that by comparison with even a year ago the present standard of performance is appreciably lower. Good novelists turn out inferior stuff or none at all, while the competent commercial product is more visibly in the ascendant. On the whole, the most interesting novels this year have come from America, or at any rate from over the sea and far away, where a near-war consciousness has less than the whole field to itself or can be indulged with an air of greater detachment.

In reserving the week's nosegay for "Pale Horse, Pale Rider" something more is intended than making the best of a bad job. The book consists of three long short-stories — they are best described as short stories rather than *contes* or *novellas* or the "short novels" of the title-page — by an American writer with a previous collection of attractive quality to her credit. What gives distinction to Mrs. Porter's work is the strain of poetry in it. The poetry is consistently elegiac and therefore of a vulnerable kind in prose narrative; but it is nevertheless very welcome, and for a good reason. Ordinarily, if as story-teller you are going to get away from the burning topicalities and agitations of the immediate hour, two ways seem open. One is through the humdrum realism of eternal verities such as catching the 9.5, being unhappily married, finding a new love and watching the baby cut its first tooth. The other is through the doubtfully authentic thrill and glamour of the frozen North, the tropic sun or, say, Wellington's Peninsula campaign. Both fashions, it must be said, are a little too much with us at the moment. The thing that comes all too rarely in fiction nowadays, the thing that is most sorely missed and that reconciles so-called escapism with literature, is the poetic vision — the seeing eye, the invocatory and evocative power of words. Prose is not poetry; but good fiction never lacks a quality that must ultimately be called poetic. It is this that appears, perhaps rather more bravely than to discreet advantage, in each of the three stories in Mrs. Porter's volume.

In the first, "Old Mortality," two small girls learn the history of Aunt Amy, a Texan beauty of the nineties, who had been much loved, who had been unhappy and died young. The past is delicately conjured in family legend, in the flaunting airs and graces of the South, in dove-coloured velvet and eighteen-inch waists; the present materializes in the fat, shabby and lugubriously sentimen-

tal person of Uncle Gabriel, whose bride Amy had been for a few weeks. The effect is too deliberate, but all the same something of enchantment hangs over Amy and her capricious duel with death. "Noon Wine" is the story of a Swede who turned up one day at a small Texan dairy farm asking for work and stayed there for nine years. The man was blankly, oppressively silent, shut in on himself. It is the discovery that he had escaped from a madhouse that brings murder and self-destruction into a tale that had seemed to grow to idyllic shape. Again the effect is both suddenly piercing and slightly manufactured. The title-story, in which the child Miranda of "Old Mortality" has become a newspaper reporter, is an elegy-rhapsody of love in the last year of the War. It strikes tender and passionate notes, it captures vivid and arresting images, but it also cultivates beauty too assiduously.

That, indeed, is the failing of the book. The realistic and passionless transcript and the heroic romance are both being overdone just now, and it is a poetic sense such as Mrs. Porter tries to communicate in these stories that might best fortify the novelist not yet paralysed by war fever or enslaved by Miss Literature. But as for beauty, almost the last way of achieving it in a novel is by cultivating it.

LETTER:
Katherine Anne Porter to Cinina and Robert Penn Warren, 20 June 1940; in *Letters of Katherine Anne Porter*, pp. 181–183.

After separating from Erskine, with whom she had been living in Baton Rouge, Louisiana, Porter went to Yaddo, an artists' colony near Saratoga Springs, New York, where she was to remain for most of the next two years, moving into a house she bought nearby in autumn 1942. At Yaddo she hoped to complete her novel, which she had begun to call "No Safe Harbor," but the fall of France to the Germans reminded her of the time she had spent in Berlin in winter 1931–1932, and she wrote "The Leaning Tower," basing the characters on the other boarders in the pension where she had lived. In this letter to the Warrens she reflects on the war and the Nazis and mentions Hermann Göring, whom she had met while living in Berlin.

Dear Red and Cinina:
    From where I sit, I see the hills of Vermont shining very clearly this morning, and if I could

Dr. Charles W. Gerstenberg, president of the Society for the Libraries of New York University, presenting Porter the society's gold medal for Pale Horse, Pale Rider, *3 April 1940*

see a little beyond them, why there is Bennington, I am told. I arrived here on the third of June, and shall stay until time to go to Olivet. If we do not see each other before, we shall do so then. Albert sent me on your letter, what a letter it is. I suggested to Albert that he ask you to let him send it to *Time,* (or is it *Life?*) which publishes letters of experience from all sources. Naturally Passinetti's name would be reduced to an initial, a changed one, and you could sign with an initial too. But it is a valuable letter; it is hopeful, too, in a strange way. Perhaps of all the places we have been hoping for a peoples' revolt against Fascism, Italy may be the first, yet. But the wrongs done already cannot be undone by repentance.

I have been a little benumbed since the fall of Paris, its no good saying anything now. I am hoping, maybe all Americans are hoping, that we will just hold our own fort now, do a little housecleaning of Nazis and Fascist organizations; and South America might help by cleaning them out there, too. It seems to be a popular notion, too — Here at Yaddo where *all* is peace and sylvan beauty — wonderfully landscaped sylvan beauty, of course —

there was a Fascist cook who had a *crise* every time anybody said a word against her Party. And as everybody was always saying a word against it, there was riot. Finally the whole staff demanded that she be sent away, and she was. The present one is not so good a cook, but politically very satisfactory. She waves a butcher knife from time to time with threats against Hitler . . . The terrible thing is that this is a majestic sort of Nemesis overtaking a cowardly and divided world. If England had not backed Mussolini, in its fear of Russia, M . . . could never have kept his power. Having his power, if he had not supported Hitler at the crisis, Hitler could have been nipped. England, France and America combined in a race for trade in re-arming Germany, those three put the weapons in Germany's hand to destroy themselves. We are now selling to Japan all she needs to arm against us . . . I think we need not be surprised when the Furies come, having been so often and persistently invited.

I remember seeing a great Fascist parade in Boston, when I had got back from Europe after a good many years. Banners, slogans, Up Fascism, up Mussolini, with songs and marchings. I had got Europeanized in my point of view, I realized, as I stared with amazement. I wondered how far in the streets of Rome, Berlin, or Paris, a group of Americans, (even ten thousand of them, like these Boston Italians,) would have got with such a project. Can you see them, waving banners saying Up Roosevelt, American Democracy Shall Conquer the World, etc? Neither can I. They would never even have been permitted to gather, and rightly too. I remember my desolation at this sight, and the feeling that Democracy was bending backward, and would get a broken spine at that rate . . . There are Fascist and Nazi countries where Fascists and Nazis should live, and if they prefer the advantages of living in a republic, they should not be allowed to make the best of both worlds in any such way . . . In the last war I was all for tolerance. Now I should like to see boatloads of them simply deposited in the midst of those governments they are so loyal to. That is where they belong. I hope to see them there very soon. I am quite willing to help with the project. Goering once remarked that getting America would be an inside job. Its no good to be lackadaisical. We see what can happen, has happened to other countries.

Well, for twenty years the world has been piling up this monstrosity for itself, and now it is here, and its no good trying to shift blame or escape the consequences . . . The United States foreign policy has been of the criminal kind, and we shall all help pay for it.

The news this morning is that France does not accept the peace terms. That is good, that is right. Southerners who are after three generations still paying the oblique and heavy indemnity of total surrender, should be able to sympathize with the French point of view . . . I don't know at this distance what else we could have done, but France still has resources . . .

The Germans always coveted Paris so, and now they have it. I wonder how long it will take them to realize that they have not got Paris at all, but only another Berlin? Berlin is the best they can do, Paris will go with the French. That is something the Germans can never get through their strange heads: they still believe that if they can eat the heart of the brave enemy, they will have his qualities . . .

Good bye for the moment. Muy bien venida, and I hope you are rested by now, and comfortable.

With my love
Katherine Anne

MEMOIR:
Eudora Welty, "My Introduction to Katherine Anne Porter," *Georgia Review,* 44 (Spring/ Summer 1990): 13–27.

Eudora Welty was at Yaddo in summer 1941, when Porter was writing an introduction to A Curtain of Green *(1941), Welty's first collection of short stories, as well as working on the novel that became* Ship of Fools. *This memoir by Welty documents the beginning of their friendship and Porter's slow progress on her novel. In a letter to her nephew Paul Porter, Porter described Welty as "very imaginative and bold and complex, yet not in the least 'experimental' in the current sense of trying to break out of a tradition and start something new" (8 September 1941).*

When in 1937 Robert Penn Warren, Cleanth Brooks, and Albert Erskine, editors of *The Southern Review,* had decided to use two of my stories, the significance of that acceptance was not lost on me. They had thought my work good enough to take a chance on, to encourage. Still I had not been prepared for a letter out of the blue from Katherine Anne Porter after the stories appeared. She was not an editor, but a *writer,* a writer of short stories; she was out in the world, at Baton Rouge:

> 961 America Street
> Baton Rouge, Louisiana
> October 25, 1938

Dear Miss Welty:
Ford Madox Ford has been given control of the fiction department of the Dial Press, and asked me to help him look about for candidates for publication. I thought of you first, with your admirable short stories. It seems to me that if you have no other plans, and have a book length collection of stories, it would be an excellent idea to write to Ford, giving him some notion of your manuscript. He will then no doubt ask to see it.

Also, if you like, I would be glad to name you as candidate for a Guggenheim Fellowship for next year — rather, for application in the fall of 1939 and 1940 Fellowship. I have already named a candidate for this year. This is done by request of Secretary of the Foundation who looks constantly for likely candidates, and naturally is no sort of engagement or promise. But if you should care to apply, I should at once write a letter about you to Mr. Moe.

I take this liberty because of my admiration for your very fine work.

Katherine Anne Porter

I seized on the belief Miss Porter offered me; she was the writer of short stories I revered. Her letter was an act of faith, and I was able to recognize this. It also foretold something about her lifelong habit of mind: there was no mistaking the seriousness of her meaning; there never must be, with her, as all learned sooner or later about K.A.P. She spoke truth as she saw it about the written word, about the writing of the written word, the act itself.

She was to give encouragement to me from that time on in the ways that always applied to the serious meaning of a young writer's work — and life; as indeed she gave encouragement to many young writers.

Thus I'd sent along my stories to Ford Madox Ford, who turned out to think well enough of them to try to place them in England up until the time of his death not very long afterward. I'd applied for the Guggenheim in 1940 with Katherine Anne's blessing. It wasn't awarded on that first application. But it was the existence of Katherine Anne Porter's hopes for me themselves, successful and unsuccessful alike, that filled me with gratitude.

However I had been able to express this to her, she wrote back:

1050 Government Street
Baton Rouge, Louisiana
March 7, 1940

Dear Eudora:

Please remember that my recommendation of your work costs me nothing; that it gives pleasure, and is the best proof I can offer of my faith in your talent and hopes for the future. It is no doubt one of the marks of your seriousness of character and intention that you take obligation for any little help offered or received; in this case, let me assure you, a purely imaginary, self-assumed sense of obligation. Try not to remember it; I would much prefer your friendship, in the most unburdensome meaning of that word. And it would really disturb me if you felt in my debt for such a small thing as a word of praise from me.

I am still hoping that your luck will be good this year. Enough for the present, for if this year is good, the others can take care of themselves . . . [1]

Katherine Anne

And even if this year turns out *not* so good, that is no sign at all that the coming ones shall be unlucky!

In September 1940, as I was travelling to Vermont, she invited me to stop off at Yaddo, the artists' colony where she was spending a time working. She wrote to me afterwards:

Yaddo, Saratoga Springs
New York, September 18 1940

Dear Eudora:

It was simply lovely having you here even for such a little while, and I wish you could come back now, for I'm moved upstairs to a much pleasanter place and there are bedrooms all over the house, unoccupied . . .

Diarmuid Russell[2] wrote me, and I wrote him and he wrote me again and I just answered, so you see we are getting on splendidly. He gave me some advice which I followed and it worked; and he is a most secure admirer of you and your work, so it is delightful to know you are going to be looked after. He is really in earnest about it; says he finds himself mentally shaking his finger at editors about you. I feel serenely conscious that it is all going to end well. Yours will be a war of attrition, as mine was, Eudora. You just go the way you're going and the editors will fall in, in time. And you have all the time in the world, and all the gift you can handle; in fact, you've got a handful, perhaps more than you know.

I have out of a clear sky but not without premeditation, finished two short stories — whales, about eight thousand words each. One to S.R., one to Harper's Bazaar, as usual. I think I was working on the first when you were here. Well, there are two now. "Season of Fear" and "The Leaning Tower." That makes enough floating around for a collection, and I'm going to get out another book of short stories, willy-nilly; they can take it or leave it. We have *got* to beat down this conspiracy against collections of short stories . . . It's a long war, but we will win.

Katherine Anne

By 1941, Diarmuid Russell after two years' unremitting work had succeeded in placing all my stories in magazines, which had made them acceptable as a collection to a publisher who would risk a book of short stories. And now, John Woodburn of Doubleday, Doran in New York had by his long and patient work persuaded his house to publish it. The book was given a title, *A Curtain of Green*. To cap this, he had invited and persuaded Katherine Anne Porter to write an Introduction to it. She added to this wonderful news by writing to me:

Left to my own imagination, I should have decided that Faulkner
was the pen-name of a re-incarnation of the old Wild Green Man,
with vine-sprouts for hair and whiskers, bursting forth nine feet
tall from an unexpected corner of the Sacred Wood, waving a bottle
            life,   "(between swigs)
of the water of ~~~~~~ bawling "DOOM- DOOM,and serves us right!"
                    the Green Man
for at that point he turns, was we all know, into John the Baptist.

        His own Jean de lHomme, in fact, pronounced"Doom"so it isn't
my imagination at all, but Faulner's, who provided me with that
impression.
            harm to this image
        It does no good to hear from those who have seen him that
appenensn to all appearances he is an easy-mannered, spindling
gentleman, southern style, with a profound accent and a prepotent
quiet and harmless, they say, as a keg of gunpowder.
glint in his eye; this is just protective colring for the other man
that lives inside.

        He is in the great American tradition: all our best writing
men
men have cried Doom! in their various voices, even Whitman, whose
windy cheers and huzzas were the most desperate of all; in this land
founded, they say, on hope and renewal of faith, doom has been our
lot, if our poets know what they are talking about- and I believe the
mostly do.

Porter's notes on William Faulkner (Papers of Katherine Anne Porter, Special Collections, University of Maryland at College Park Libraries)

February 19, 1941–Olivet
[Olivet College, Michigan]

Dearest Eudora:

All the news about you is good news and makes me happy for you, and for myself, because nothing is better than to see you getting off so bravely.

I write with pencil because I am in bed with a crick in the neck which seems to be my way of having a cold, and all my paper, pens, etc., are on the other side of this blizzard-swept campus in my office. A splendid letter from Diarmuid full of rejoicing about you and the new baby.[3] Please tell him in your next I have his letter and will write when I am better able.

Meantime — Send the collection *with* "The Robber Bridegroom"[4] et al to Yaddo. I will do what I can to have it included — Above all, tell me *when, where* the preface should be sent; deadlines are my snare — But I will make it.

I know well already what I think of your work, but reading all the stories will give pointers.

No more for the moment. Albert Erskine will be delighted with this news. Meantime my love and good wishes, may all your good beginnings bring you to a happy end!

And soon after:

Yaddo, Saratoga Springs
New York, May 2, 1941

Dear Eudora:

Elizabeth Ames tells me you have been invited here for early June, and I hope you like the place and can stay a long time if you want . . . It will be lovely to see you. Mrs. Ames had said something about inviting you before the regular season, but I heard no more of it.

Your letter was useful and I am keeping it with my notes for the preface, just for the tone. We'll talk all that over when you get here . . .

Nothing more just now, I am at the last gasp of that novel, and must finish now before I do anything else. But after, I shall be free; and meantime I scribble down something else about your work as it comes to me, so the notes are piling up nicely against the day . . .

I got the deed to South Farm, today. So it is really mine, and the work is beginning on it almost at once . . . The end of the summer should see me in it. But believe me, this novel is the foundation of this whole thing, and it must go soon . . . I've written it so often, really, it is high time to let go, now!

Waiting to see you, with my love,
Katherine Anne

I showed your collection to Glenway Wescott, and he was pretty well bowled over. I said, "My money is on her nose for the next race," and he said, "Mine, too. She is marvelous." So your audience grows. He is a good friend to have — never will let his friends hear the last of you . . .

I arrived at Saratoga Springs as one in a dream.

Yaddo was in the old, rural, comfortably settled part of New York State west of Albany, near the town of Saratoga Springs. The estate was private and well guarded, though its gardens were, at that innocent time, open to the public. The Mansion faced you head-on as you approached it through forest trees; it was huge, elaborately constructed: it looked made by impulse for eternity, out of the rock on which it stood. The artists came for their summer at Yaddo solely by invitation. Elizabeth Ames gave her life to being its director — a woman of Quaker-like calm and decisiveness; she was beautiful and to some extent deaf. She stood ready for crises.

The artists — painters, composers, writers, sculptors — lived in the reaches of the Mansion, and beyond their rooms they were given studios to suit their particular needs; these stood hidden away among the old forest trees, at various calculated degrees of remoteness. Artists ate their lunch alone; it arrived in a tin box left silently outside their doors at noon.

Katherine Anne and I were enviably installed in the "farmhouse," a small frame building a distance away from the Mansion on its hill across the road. We shared the farmhouse with only two others, congenial both — a Canadian composer and an Armenian-American etcher, who *did* work all day in their respective studios.

Upstairs, across the hall from Katherine Anne's combined bedroom and studio, was my bedroom. My studio was downstairs in the farmhouse kitchen. On the outside of the studio door was a sign tacked up: "SILENCE. WRITER AT WORK WITHIN." My immediate work consisted of reading proofs of my forthcoming book, and that was over quickly. Already, though, my editor John Woodburn, in New York, had begun to write me little bulletins, instructing me to remind Katherine Anne about the Introduction: "And kid, you keep after her! She promised to write it *now*! Remind her we've got a deadline."

And I knew I couldn't do that.

In the early evening of each long summer's day, Katherine Anne — with her spring-heeled step, catching up her long skirts — and I set out in single file walking the woodland path up to the great stone Mansion for dinner. This was the only hour of the twenty-four when all the guests came out and showed themselves. They had supposedly been solitary all day behind their studio doors, working.

Within the Mansion, the atmosphere, even the hour, seemed changed; it was hushed, moody, and somehow public. The great room we entered spread out like a stage set for a grand opera on which the curtain might at any moment go up. An overture was in the making: an interior fountain close to us was murmuring, and offstage somewhere an organ began to growl; it was possible that one of the resident poets was still at work, thinking something through.

I began to feel apprehensive that we were all expected to *perform* here, that the assigned soloists and the combined chorus were *us.* The great hall was appointed with throne chairs, divans, velvet stools (one also noticed a sleigh), with candelabra, wine glasses, wine.

If I supposed our opera would be one about the arts, or artists, something like *La Bohème,* I wasn't on the right track. This was 1941. The company was in great part European. Elizabeth Ames had come to the aid of many artists who no longer had homes and were seeking refuge and a place to carry on their work. Our evening was indeed operatic, but it wasn't about the arts; it was about politics. Katherine Anne rose to the occasion — her clear voice would enter as if on cue with cries of *"Au contraire!"* One end of the great room gave onto the coming night; the window was a great tall frame holding the Yaddo moon, and I watched it climbing. Out there beyond and below the stone balustrade, the garden descended, with its statues of the Graces rising from the beds like another chorus. I could smell, without seeing it, the summer stock, the nicotiana. They made me think of home. That first night, I knew for certain only what the *garden* was doing.

From New York, John Woodburn, who was my champion, who had staked so much in bringing out this first book by an unknown, young, Southern, female, short-story writer, wrote to me nearly every day. "How far along is she? How's the Introduction coming?" "Keep after her, kid! Tell her one more time about the deadline!" "Get it out of her, baby."

Was she writing it indeed? If I heard from across the hall her little Olivetti typewriter start up, or still more, if I heard it stop, I felt like an eavesdropper. I let myself out of the house and walked down the road to Saratoga Springs.

It was lovely to arrive there, too, in the bright Northern summer morning. Lining either side of the main street, the great hotels stood facing each other under the meeting boughs of lofty elms, the United States Hotel and all its sisterhood: their red faces, their black iron columns across the front, twisted like Venetian barge poles, and the figures of black, turbaned, Oriental slaves mounted at the top of the steps with an arm crooked up to hold branching lamps with clusters of globes made for gaslight.

The length of the street was strung overhead with banners and flags bidding Welcome. Along the sidewalks I moved with a wonderful crowd of perambulators here for the waters, the races, the sights and parades: invalids, sporting people, sightseers, families stalled in circles on the sidewalk in a chorus of argument over what to do next. I visited the racetrack where the horses were working out, and the busy public halls where the waters were being dispensed.

By the time I walked home to Yaddo, I might be carrying onions, soup bones, maybe a fresh stalk of celery or bunch of carrots to Katherine Anne, who liked to keep the soup pot going on her little stove, as well as her windup gramophone going, and sometimes now her Olivetti going.

I knew it was to be a wonderfully happy and carefree summer for me — if only I didn't have Katherine Anne's awful deadline hanging over my head: the unmentionable.

Outside our farmhouse sat a brand new Studebaker car — it was Katherine Anne's. She had not quite learned to drive it yet. But I could drive it, and she said she had something to show me: we would take the day off from work!

It was a little distance off, in deep country: the house her letter had told me about securing the deed for. She confided that she was actually now in the very process of restoring it. She had christened it "South Hill." She would finish it, make it all her own, move into it, settle down and *write.* It became a part of nearly every day to jump into the Studebaker and drive out to South Hill.

She could count on a Mr. Somebody who came to see to everything. So a yellow-coned cement mixer churned away among the trees, and at times drowned out the birdsong, and the carpenters who stripped the upstairs walls now down to the laths found little feminine slippers that K.A.P. identified as being a hundred years old, and further came on — roused up — bees in the walls

AUTHOR'S APOLOGY

This novel was begun as a journal during my first voyage to Europe in August-September, 1931, from Vera Cruz to Bremerhaven on the North German Lloyd S. S. Werra. A small part of this journal was sent as a letter to a friend. I have always kept journals, without plan at first, then deliberately for use as source books and a help to recollection. From these notes a book began to take form almost at once, and I found myself writing in long scenes and situations which grew immediately out of present experience, so that all the main points of the story were written then and there, before the voyage ended. However, I distrust, for myself, snap judgments and instantaneous conclusions, preferring to view one experience in the light of others, earlier and later, so after the first general outline and the main events were written, I put it aside and worked on it only at long intervals ever since. In my case, "working" quite often means long stretches of almost subconscious brooding and making vast heaps of notes whose order and sequence and meaning are known only to myself.

There are a good many references, events and scenes which now appear almost suspiciously "timely" and the theme

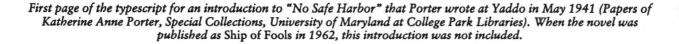

First page of the typescript for an introduction to "No Safe Harbor" that Porter wrote at Yaddo in May 1941 (Papers of Katherine Anne Porter, Special Collections, University of Maryland at College Park Libraries). When the novel was published as Ship of Fools *in 1962, this introduction was not included.*

too, which had been at work storing honey there for, she estimated, the same length of time. K.A.P. and I stretched out on the long sweet meadow grass in another part of the shade. At peace, we puffed on our cigarettes, and I listened to her tell the way she had discovered Joyce for herself: somehow a copy of *Ulysses* had been carried into this country and ended up on a secondhand book-stall in Galveston, Texas; Katherine Anne had walked by and just picked it up.

When the spirit moved us, we would jump into the Studebaker and ride all the way to Albany and there find six wonderful French antique dining-room chairs, or cinch a roll of ruby-red carpeting, perfect for the stairs when they were made ready to climb (at present we were crawling up a plank to reach the upstairs). All were now entrusted to storage. It was the clearest thing to K.A.P. that everything we engaged in all day long was South Hill in the making. There was supporting magic attached to finding treasures that would take their rightful place in it. There popped into my head the lovely little French virginal that Katherine Anne had showed to me, the very first thing, on the day when I'd come on her invitation to see her for the first time; it was in her new house in Baton Rouge. Where was the virginal now? I wondered, but did not ask. It must be in storage somewhere.

We sank into the luxury of talking books as easily as we sank into the long, sweet meadow grass; we had all day and a picnic lunch. We listened to the birdsong and the carpenters at work. Katherine Anne would often be laughing out loud.

But if it was hard for me, being there night and day with my very presence putting Katherine Anne on the spot, did I think of how hard it was for Katherine Anne? I am certain beyond a doubt that *I* could not have written the first line about anybody who was, at the time, staying in the house with me three steps away across the hall. And if that person knew about my purpose, and was waiting on me daily to set down the words on paper? And if at the same time that person had turned out to be a friend? I'm afraid the possibility never occurred to me that I *could* conclude my stay at Yaddo before my invitation was up.

Then the day came when she tapped at my door and came in holding out to me a whole sheaf of typewritten pages. "You may read this," she said, "if you would like." It was what she'd been working on, the first seventy-five pages of *No Safe Harbor* — her novel (which of course was to become, in the end, *Ship of Fools*). In allowing me to read it, and at its beginning, she had made me a

gift of her clear confidence in me. As far as I was concerned, the Introduction she was going to write for me had been conveyed to me by way of a blessing. If its significance was to relate to her literary trust in me, I had already received it.

The novel was years later on to appear in the finality of print, but what I had been living across the hall from was the immediacy, the presence, and something of the terror, of its pages coming into being one by one. I'd *heard* the living words coming through her fingers and out of her skin. I don't think I was ever again as stirred, and as captivated, to hold a fresh manuscript in my hands and realize what I held.

The summer was deepening, and with it the pleasures of Yaddo. By then, friendships had ripened among the set of artists, informality had caught up with formality, and picnics sneaked into the lazy noons. Katherine Anne made onion soup for her friends. That could take all day, and as we all agreed, it was worth every minute of it. There was music in the evening at the Mansion, but music was *always* to be heard at our farmhouse. The gramophone would be kept wound up and playing. K.A.P. kept stacks of French records, from Piaf back to Gluck, back to madrigals. In the performance of the opera *Orphée,* when the moment arrived that I listened for — Cerberus barking — a live little dog filled the role.

There was everything going on at once those days. Some way or another, the little Olivetti was seizing its chances, too. From across our hall, I heard it very well — its insistencies, its halts, and again its resuming, the long runs as if this runner could not now stop for breath. And we didn't leave out driving nearly every day to visit South Hill — what else was the Studebaker for?

At South Hill Katherine Anne and I sat in the meadow downhill from what was going on, and watched the building slowly come to pass before our eyes. For the plain, century-old house (looking something like an ark) that she was making her own, the elation, the intensity, the triumph, the impatience of her vision of it took hold of her afresh every day. It made me aware that the planner was profoundly a story writer.

As I look back now, I believe she was putting the house together like a story in her head, restoring to it its history — a story that had as much to do with her past as it had to do with her future. It was a work-in-progress she was highly conscious of, and scrupulously attentive to, a self-assignment she was meeting, an autobiographical deadline.

"How far along *is* the Introduction?" wrote John Woodburn to me. How hard this was on John too, and how well I knew it! He adored Katherine Anne. He had travelled up to Yaddo to ask her in person if she would write the Introduction; they'd celebrated the agreement in Saratoga Springs in the grandeur of the United States Hotel; and he was a sensitive man. *He* couldn't ask her a word about it now, either. But I could hear the groan in his words to me: "Get it out of her *now,* kid! Do you want our book *postponed?*"

It was postponed. The day the Introduction was due came and went, and at Yaddo I had never mentioned it to Katherine Anne. But I had *been* there. And I still was there — the live-in visitor from Porlock. I think now, in this long retrospect, that she made a daily brave attempt to forget about the interfering deadline for the moment at hand, and that what I was actually doing there was helping her forget it. At any rate, *this* was a success. And though I would not have known it at the time, this Introduction was undoubtedly only one of the things Katherine Anne was being pressed to do. She was constitutionally a besieged woman.

I'd begun to realize that the summer was of a kind not unexpected by Katherine Anne. Her whole writing life was one of interruptions, and interruptions of the interruptions. I was to learn that writers do generally live that way, and not entirely without their own collusion. No help ever comes, unless in the form of still another interruption.

The one thing that was uninterrupted in her life was her seriousness of intent. And when I look back, I seem to see her surrounded entirely by papers, by pages or galley sheets, by her work — "Old Mortality," "The Leaning Tower," and, on that blue typewriter paper, stretches of the novel. It seemed then that she was always writing. *Writing* — its conception — was ever-present to her. At Yaddo, at South Hill equally; writing was the future of her house, the *intention* of her house. And writing was — yes, even for her — very hard to do.

To me it came as no shock that writing itself, the act, might always be hard. The better the writer, the harder writing knew how to be. In fact, the harder Katherine Anne's work was for her, the more exhilarated, liberated my own spirits were accordingly. What I felt able to understand for myself was that writing well was for the writer worth whatever it took. The difficulty that accompanies you is less like the dark than like a trusted lantern to see your way by. I hoped proudly for myself that acknowledging and valuing the role of difficulty in writing well would re-

main always with me. Katherine Anne was helping me to recognize living with difficulty as a form of passion.

Certainly I was slower in learning to know Katherine Anne than I believed I was in the summer at Yaddo. Our friendship had shown me day after day the enchanting brightness she could shed around her, but it was later, through letters she wrote when we were no longer in the same place, laughing, that I became to any degree aware of the dark, its other side, which she lived with on its own terms in equally close commune. I wondered in retrospect if hers hadn't been the sort of exultation that can arise — must arise — out of some equally intense sadness, wondered if, as South Hill was taking shape before her eyes, there wasn't also something else in the course of being left behind. She was combatting unhappiness, even desolation, I now think, through that whole summer and for times longer than that, and bravely.

John Woodburn sent me the last of his bulletins in August, to Jackson where I'd returned: "Baby: Here is the Introduction, unproof-read, which I finally got out of Katherine Anne by distilling her. There was no other way. . . ."

In the end, of course, she had written her magnificent Introduction "very quickly," she told me. And all her generosity, her penetration, serenely informs it, doing everything in her power for the book and for its author, as she'd intended to do all the time.

It is time itself — there was never any use denying — that is forever the enemy. I learned in those early days that K.A.P. would always take on any enemy — and time in particular — with a deep measure of respect. The price of writing that Introduction had to have been the postponement of something else. As well we know, *Ship of Fools* suffered many another postponement to follow this, the one she assumed that summer for introducing *A Curtain of Green.*

Katherine Anne wrote to me:

Yaddo, Saratoga Springs, New York
August 27, 1941

Dear Eudora:

I go on missing you quite steadily, the whole place changed when you went, though the activities kept on. I got to Albany by bus, not too dull, and at good hours, but there was a grim air of business about the trips, no more pleasant escapade in the morning air, no unexpected finding of Hindu wool rugs, no fun, in a word. My eyes managed to give me the worst upset in my nerves of anything I have known in my life. I was almost reduced to a state of pure terror, night and day, for the better part of a week. My efforts to conceal my state made it worse; I wished to collapse, to tell my troubles, to call upon God for help. I cannot be blind, that is the one thing I would make no attempt to face . . .

. . . Far from being part of the pressure, your preface is gone, accepted, perhaps set up in galleys by now. I came home with my goggles on fine afternoons, sat down and batted out that opus in two evenings' very pleasant work, mailed it special delivery and received some very kind and pleasant words of rejoicing from John Broadside; so have that off your mind as it is off ours . . . Now of course I think of some other things I might have said to good effect, I wish I had gone a little more into certain stories, such as A Memory, Old Mr. Marblehall, and so on. But I can do it later when I write about your work again in another place. For certainly I expect to do so.

. . . I am being moved from North Farm to the Mansion for the month of September, since a new set are going to be settled here. This weekend must be spent packing, sending half my things to storage, taking mss. and music with me, and all. But I shall make quick work of it and work there as well as I can. South Hill is going faster, all at once, the plastering is begun, I should think that is a good sign. Every time I see it, I am pleased with it, it really is my house and just the one I wanted. And some day we will cook our supper on a charcoal grill in that terrace fireplace, maybe with snow outside, and the fire shining through the windows on it . . .

. . . To work, to work. It has always been later than I thought, but now it is later than ever . . . still I expect to make the deadline this time, the fourth for the novel . . . it just rolls along, I don't worry about it any more; there is this about all that space, it allows such a long line of continuity, and time for cumulative effect; and I always did know what I wanted to say in this book, my mind hasn't changed, and how could I write anything that didn't belong there? I trust myself, at last.

You trust yourself, too, darling. You are as good as there is in your time, and you have a long way to go and to grow, I can't see the end of it, thank God . . .

With my love,
K.A.

I missed her too, and a long life of correspondence started between us, easygoing and as the spirit moved us — about reading, recipes, anxieties and aspirations, garden seeds and gossip. She'd never let me thank her for the

Guggenheim, or Yaddo, or possibly even the Introduction, in any proper way. But *she* was a born thanker, for any miscellaneous trifle that might come in the mail from me, wanting to make her laugh:

Yaddo, Saratoga Springs, New York
October 7, 1941

Dear Eudora:
The sugar cane arrived in the most mysterious style, fascinating to think about: in one very short piece with the address tag on it, and a long stalk simply accompanying it, with not even a piece of string on it, unaddressed, un-everything, independent, unattached, there was nothing to stop it from going on to some destination it might have liked better, or turning in its tracks and bolting back to Mississippi again. But no, it stuck to its companion, and came in as it were under its own steam. And how good it tastes: I am still occasionally sitting down with a sharp knife and stripping off a section and gnawing away at it. My father told me once that when he was a little boy, strange and new to Texas, he and his slightly elder brother ran away to Louisiana because they were so homesick for the sight and taste of sugar cane. I put that in a story once. I know better now just how they felt, though . . .

Katherine Anne

Doubleday was giving a party for *A Curtain of Green* in November, in New York, and of course Katherine Anne's presence was called for. "I take for granted in some strange way that I am to be in New York for your party, it doesn't seem possible that I should miss it," Katherine Anne wrote from Yaddo on October 19. But on November 5, a telegram followed to tell me in New York, where I'd already arrived:

Dear Eudora, be happy and gay at your coming out party and remember me just enough to console me a little for not being there. All the good luck and reward in the world to you. You deserve everything. I hope to see you there or here before you go home. With my love, Katherine Anne.

She continued to work on restoring South Hill, and finally a letter arrived, dated August 28, 1942, on handsome letter paper only slightly different a shade of blue from her familiar typing paper, imprinted with SOUTH HILL, R.D. 3, Ballston Spa, New York. It reads in part:

Dear Eudora:
This is the very first letter on the very first page of the letter paper, and this is the first day I

have been here by myself. You can hardly imagine the confusion of household gear piled up here and there, but this nice south east room upstairs is in a bare and lovely order, with my table set up and the work-lamp ready, and when I look out I see the maples and the front meadow on my left and the corner of the sun room and part of the east meadow on the right.

. . . I must get settled in before the winter closes around us. Now you can think of me as here: Caroline Slade came this morning with a big, flat basket of vegetables from her garden, beautiful as a bouquet, every little carrot and tomato and celery head all washed and polished, and I put the parsley and some celery leaves in a bottle of sauterne vinegar at once, thinking you cannot begin too early with such things.

. . . Here all is weeds and unkemptedness, but the rosa regosa and white lilacs I planted in April are flourishing, it was a lucky rainy summer for I had to leave them to their fate almost at once. They didn't mind at all. They will be strong and fine for transplanting in the spring. They started as little dry sticks and are now green full little bushes. And so other things may go as well too . . .

For a few months her letters continued to be full of pleasure and happiness and invitations. But when winter arrived and closed her in, she grew too cold, and her old enemy pneumonia caught up with her and defeated her. South Hill, like some earlier dreams, but a dream completed this time, had to be put behind her.

By December 28, 1946, she was writing to me from Santa Monica, California. "I live within six blocks of the Pacific," she says. "Sometimes at midnight I hear that desperate creature beating its brains out on the beach, but musically. At last I have some of my books and music; this little place is like a birdcage, open and round, and I have sat here on the edge of my chair for a year, thinking any minute I may find a house of my own . . . I bought a little mountain top in the Mojave desert, after selling South Hill to the Willisons — did you read his *Saints and Strangers?* a fine piece of historical writing . . . I feel well. The novel is not finished, but I think now I have my road cleared a little, there is always so much to be done about other things, other people. But it does really seem that maybe I have reached the end of that, too."

1. The use of an ellipsis in K.A.P.'s letters, when the letters appear in their entirety, is her own. When I quote segments of her letters in passing, I have indicated by ellipsis that the quote is an excerpt.

2. My literary agent in New York in the newly formed firm of Russell & Volkening. Katherine Anne was considering his

offer to act as her agent. But she preferred in the end acting on her own.

3. His and Rose Russell's second child, William.

4. This short novel was later published separately by Doubleday.

BOOK REVIEW:
Howard Mumford Jones, "A Smooth Literary Texture," review of *The Leaning Tower and Other Stories, Saturday Review,* 27 (30 September 1944): 15.

Porter went to Washington, D.C., in January 1944 to fill out the ailing John Peale Bishop's term as fellow at the Library of Congress, where her old friend Allen Tate was serving as poetry consultant. She returned to Yaddo not long after the publication of The Leaning Tower and Other Stories *in September 1944. The reviews for the book, which sold twenty thousand copies within two weeks, were especially gratifying to Porter.*

Out of her work since 1934 Katherine Anne Porter has put together this slim volume of narratives and sketches in shorter form. The first seven concern one or another phase of the development of a Southern family, vaguely domiciled in Kentucky or Texas, and ruled, as is becoming customary in familial studies, by a grandmother who is much the best of the lot. The eighth is a tale of Irish life in New York, and the ninth and last, which gives the volume its title, is a study in the spiritual and economic decay of pre-Hitler life in Berlin. So far as any American can make clear the baffling obscurities of the German "soul," Miss Porter has done so in this sketch of student life in a Berlin *pension.*

The exquisite rightness of this author's art has been commented upon by many; and these sketches and tales reveal to that vague tribe, the discriminating reader, what fundamental brainwork goes into the creating of episodes that, on the surface, seem hastily thrown together. To be sure, this deftness is bought at a price; and the careful casualness of Miss Porter's approach sometimes reminds one of a cat stalking its prey with unnecessary caution. If some of these narratives were told in the straightforward narrative manner formerly characteristic of the short story, they might not lose in delicacy and might gain in dramatic power. But this is heterodox doctrine in an age which abhors the tightly built short story.

Perhaps nothing in American literary history is more amazing than the way the wheel has come full circle in this department of writing. When, after the Civil War, the monthly magazine began to be the most profitable vehicle for fictionists, the old-fashioned tale became outmoded, and with the rise of the local colorists, oddly enough, the short-story-with-a-plot came to supplant the sketch. At the opening of this century the short story was felt to be the American contribution *par excellence* to world literature, and writers as various as Sherwin Cody and Brander Matthews sought out its laws and defined its prerogatives. The climax of the tightly wrought tale was perhaps O. Henry, beyond whom neatness of plot could scarcely go; and as new influences came in, the short-story-with-a-plot seemed old-fashioned and the slice-of-life theory reigned in its stead. Now the slice-of-life theory also seems too simple, and in such a performance as "The Leaning Tower" we are really back with Washington Irving, just as, in the first seven of these narratives, we are in some sense back with John Pendleton Kennedy, learning about life at Swallow Barn.

Of course, it will be objected that we are not really back there, because Miss Porter's tales are more "sophisticated." But Washington Irving was sophisticated too; the smooth texture of his style was supposed to be the latest word in cosmopolitan ease, and the "Tales of a Traveler" was supposed to illuminate British life just as "The Leaning Tower" illuminates German life. Perhaps the vogue of Damon Runyon may mean that the short-story-with-a-plot may again return to favor in other places than the pulps.

All this has perhaps little to do with the volume under review. No change of fashion can antiquate the finesse of Miss Porter's pen, whose quiet manner and deceptively simple texture have something of the ease of Jane Austen. But it is at least an interesting query whether younger writers can afford to imitate her. Possibly another revolution in the approach to the short story and its artistic problems is not very far away.

BOOK REVIEW:
F. O. Matthiessen, Review of *The Leaning Tower and Other Stories*, Accent, 5 (Winter 1945): 121–123.

In addition to the title story, completed in 1940, Porter's 1944 book includes "A Day's Work," written in 1937, and "A Downward Path to Wisdom," written in 1939, as well as "The Old Order" stories, of which two — "The Witness" and "The Last Leaf" — were previously unpublished. The story called "The Old Order" in this

Marcella Comès Winslow, with whom Porter shared a house during most of her stay in Washington, D.C., painted this portrait of Porter at fifty-four.

book was retitled "The Journey" when Porter grouped the whole sequence under the collective title "The Old Order" in The Collected Stories of Katherine Anne Porter *(1965).*

Matthiessen attacks the "assumed superiority" of the novel to the short story, a prejudice that Porter — whose struggles to complete Ship of Fools *would seem to indicate that her natural talent was for the shorter form — faced throughout her career.*

Miss Porter's high reputation among nearly all schools of critics may now have reached the point where it is doing her a disservice. She is bracketed as "a writer's writer," which she certainly is, so far as that phrase implies that almost any other craftsman can learn important things from her about the handling of both language and structure. But the common reader has too frequently been led to believe that "style" is something esoteric, something to be relished apart from what it conveys, and that Miss Porter's relatively slim production must mean that she has not much to say. This misconception has also been nourished unwittingly by her admirers who like her quality so much that they want more and keep urging her to write a novel. But Miss Porter herself, when introducing the work of Eudora Welty, saw that for the master of the short story the novel may simply be the next trap ahead. The assumed superiority of the longer form is a product of our American supposition that bigger must be better, and has blown up many a lyric poet into an abortive epic bard, as well as the content adequate for a decent novel into a limp trilogy.

What we tend to forget is that in such a characteristically French form as the novelette, in the story of twenty to forty thousand words, we have also an American tradition. The kind of intensification that Melville gained in *Benito Cereno* and *Billy Budd,* and that James, working so differently, accomplished in *Pandora, The Coxon Fund, The Bench of Desolation* and a dozen others, would seem to have much to offer to our period whose syntheses are often so precarious that they may be lost through extension. Miss Porter has set her special signature on this form, as Hemingway has on the contemporary practice of the short story. Not that she hasn't worked brilliantly in short stories as well, but sometimes hers can seem too fragmentary, as, for instance, do the first half dozen pieces in this new volume in comparison with the more integrated structure of *Old Mortality,* which dealt with the same descendants of Kentucky against a Louisiana and Texas background.

Yet these very stories can demonstrate the searching originality of her content. She may seem to be dealing with the stock material of the local colorists, with older Southern manners and customs as they persisted down into this century. Yet you quickly realize, in "The Old Order" and "The Last Leaf," that the human relationships are being examined with a new depth and honesty, that the sentimental view of the devoted old slave living on serenely with her former mistress is punctured once for all by such a quiet observation as that Nannie thrived on "a species of kindness not so indulgent, maybe, as that given to the puppies."

Such discoveries of the living intricacy in any relationship are Miss Porter's most recurrent resource. A passage at the end of "The Grave," the last of this group, gives a very explicit clue as to how she comes into possession of her material. This passage records how Miranda, by a chance of seemingly irrelevant association, is suddenly struck with the full violence of an episode long buried in her childhood, by her first knowledge of the mystery of birth as it had come to her through seeing a pregnant rabbit that her brother had shot and was skinning. This passage, too long to quote here, reveals

Miss Porter's understanding of how much enters into any mature experience, of how deeply bathed in imaginative richness any event must be if it is to become a fluid and viable symbol.

The frequence with which violence lies at the heart of her discoveries helps to explain a main source of strength in her delicate prose. "The Circus," the best short story here, conveys the naked agony with which Miranda, too young to grasp the conventions, reacts to the dangers and brutalities of the show. What the others can take in the comic spirit presses upon her a first initiation into the pity and terror of life. Violence in modern fiction has been so often a substitute for understanding that Miss Porter's ability to use it to reveal ethical values is another of her particular distinctions, as she showed especially in *Noon Wine.* In "The Downward Path to Wisdom," one of the three longer stories in this collection, her control seems far less sure, since the brutalities which are poured down upon the helpless child by his elders are not sufficiently motivated to make a coherent pattern. Violence seems to have been manipulated almost for its own sake.

Still another of Miss Porter's distinctions has been her refutation of the local colorists and other narrow regionalists by her extraordinary ability to portray a whole series of different environments. It may only be our anticipation of so much variety from her that causes a story like "A Day's Work" to seem for the first time a repetition of material handled more freshly in "The Cracked Looking-Glass." In comparison with that earlier story, which was a sustained miracle of Irish feeling and rhythm, both the situation and characters here may seem slightly expected. But when we turn to the longest story, to the novelette which gives title to the volume, we have again the rare combination of virtuosity with moral penetration.

Here Miss Porter uses a controlling symbol in the way that James often did, since the leaning tower not only is a souvenir of the Berlin landlady's long past happiness in Italy, but also becomes a compelling image for the tottering balance of the German world in the year before Hitler's rise to power. Many best-selling accounts have now been written of that time, and yet it seems doubtful whether any of them will preserve its form and pressure longer than Miss Porter's presentation of it through the consciousness of a young American painter. The reason for her success may be suggested by a comment James once made when noting that Turgenieff's *Memoirs of a Sportsman,* dealing with the question of serfdom, had appeared in the very same year as *Uncle Tom's Cabin:* "No single episode pleads conclusively against the 'pecular institution' of Russia; the lesson is the cumulative testimony of a multitude of fine touches — in an after-scene of sadness that sets wise readers thinking . . . It offers a capital example of moral meaning giving a sense to form and form giving relief to moral meaning."

Some of Miss Porter's "fine touches" consist in her recurrent stress on the city's poverty, through Charles Upton's gradual realization of the difference from the depression he had left behind at home, where everybody took it for granted that things would improve, whereas in Berlin "the sufferers seemed to know that they had no cause for hope." No journalist or social historian analyzing the collapse of the republic has come closer to the central cause. And concerning the interpenetration of form and moral meaning, a comparison with Christopher Isherwood's *Good-Bye to Berlin* is instructive. Isherwood looked back to the same kind of student and boarding house life, and he dealt more explicitly with some of the manifestations of social decay. But his characters seem self-consciously worked up from a Freudian hand-book, or they exist to shock like the figures in a cinema thriller. They have none of the deep authenticity that springs from Miss Porter's humility and tenderness before life. She has been able to apprehend many kinds of Germans, ranging from the lumpish solemn mathematician who "loves study and quiet" to the young aristocrat whose new cheek-wound brings out in his expression a mixture of "amazing arrogance, pleasure, inexpressible vanity and self-satisfaction." Miss Porter does not slight the bestial brutalities in this hard city. No more, however, does she indulge in easy propaganda. When Charles Upton remarks lightly that Americans are sentimental and "like just everybody," the young mathematician stares at him earnestly and says: "I do not think you really like anybody, you Americans. You are indifferent to everybody and so it is easy for you to be gay, to be careless, to seem friendly. You are really cold-hearted indifferent people."

As a result of weaving back and forth through contradictions and incongruities, from one flickering center of human conviction to another, Miss Porter has done again what she did in *Pale Horse, Pale Rider*. She has created the atmosphere of a haunting moment of crisis. In that earlier novelette she gave us the end of the last war as it was felt in America through the crazy fever of the flu epidemic. Here, as she brings her group of students close together for a moment of New Year's Eve conviviality, what reverberates through their every speech and gesture is a premonition of disaster. In writing of Miss Welty, Miss Porter warned the artist against political beliefs, but here we can see that her remark was not the reactionary one that such a remark generally is. For she has penetrated into the economic and social sicknesses that brought on Fascism, but she has also held to her knowledge that the realm of the creator of fiction must be broader and more resilient than theories or opinions, that it can be nothing less than "that true and human world of which the artist is a living part."

BOOK REVIEW:

Diana Trilling, Review of *The Leaning Tower and Other Stories, Nation,* 159 (23 September 1944): 359–360.

Though many later readers prefer "The Old Order" sequence to "The Leaning Tower," the perceptive critic Diana Trilling — perhaps influenced by the times — was most impressed by the title story.

For all the virtues of the shorter pieces in Katherine Anne Porter's new collection of stories, "The Leaning Tower and Other Stories" (Harcourt, Brace, $2.50) — and I shall speak of them presently — it is the long title piece of the book which claims our enthusiasm and confirms Miss Porter's high literary reputation. Miss Porter's new novelette is not only the best thing she has ever written but by any measure one of the finest of modern stories. Perhaps, indeed, it was an error to combine in one volume this novelette, which is such a large achievement, with the rather fugitive sketches which precede it. The large work so overshadows the small that we tend to forget that even at its most fragmentary Miss Porter's writing is full of things to give pleasure.

The Leaning Tower is a remarkable literary-political document, not unrelated in method to Thomas Mann's story of the German inflation, Disorder and Early Sorrow. It is a story about Hitler which never mentions Hitler except as the unnamed subject of a photograph in a barber shop; it is an analysis of political forces without political analyses; it is a chapter of history which still manages, as literature, to stand outside and above history. Miss Porter is telling us about Germany in 1931, about the emotions that prepare national violence. Her narrative device is to follow an impressionable young Texan, who in the first freedom of maturity carries out the romantic resolution to visit the Berlin he had heard about from a childhood friend, as he becomes more and more frightened by the creeping awfulness of pre-Nazi German life. Nothing much happens to this Charles: he checks out of his hotel, he has his hair cut, he looks for lodgings, he becomes acquainted with the other tenants of his boardinghouse and celebrates New Year's Eve with them; but the eyes of Charles become the eyes of an ideal documentary camera. Miss Porter's story has neither action nor drama, in the usual sense, but slowly it borrows all the brooding drama of its time and place; in Miss Porter's Berlin of 1931 every house, every room, every piece of furniture or crockery, is a portent of a dreadful consummation. I think the underwritten climax of The Leaning Tower is its sole mistake in literary judgment: impression has mounted on fierce impression until the sense of a necessary explosion is almost unbearable; even as readers we require some of the ranting and roaring that climaxed this German story in actuality.

If space were available, a score of details could be dwelt on in praise of Miss Porter's novelette — the proportioning and pace of the story as a whole, its genius of visuality, the elegant use Miss Porter can make of colloquial language, the use to which she puts Charles's childhood attraction to the little German boy, the choice of a Pole as one of Charles's Berlin circle, the focus upon the Heidelberg scar of another of the lodgers, the endless avenue of horror which Miss Porter can open up by a dozen sentences of description of a hotel keeper and his wife, the instinct that led her to create the half-world cafe which is the scene of a Berlin New Year's party. In view of its achievements, it becomes unimportant that The Leaning Tower has one weakness in conception — the character of its protagonist. Much in the picture of Charles is beautifully handled, especially the litmus-paper quality which he has because he is a stranger in Germany, disconnected from the familiar even in language; but as an artist Charles is obscure and disconcerting. Granted that Charles is less an artist than he is young and American, the question is allowed to intrude upon us, whether he is a good artist or an artist as Hitler was once an artist. There seems to be a suggestion of the latter; but then, if she intends the parallel, Miss Porter would be introducing a chauvinism which, highly as she values the American spirit, is miraculously lacking from the rest of her story; for she would be saying, in effect, that the American temperament responds to frustration very differently from the German — a racial generalization whose truth is only devoutly to be wished.

As for the shorter pieces in "The Leaning Tower," although there is always the danger in writing as conscious as Miss Porter's, and particularly in very brief fiction, that carefulness will move over into preciousness, Miss Porter still manages to avoid this pitfall of the too wary; taste is her instrument rather than her nemesis. There is as much vigor as precision in her language, and this in itself distinguishes Miss Porter among present-day women writers, most of whom are so desperately given to breathy effects and soft figures of speech. In "The Source," for instance, Miss Porter writes the following sentence in description of cleaning-up day on a Southern farm: "Every mattress cover was emptied of its corn husks and boiled, every little Negro on the place was set to work picking a fresh supply of husks, every hut was thickly whitewashed, bins and cupboards were scrubbed, every chair and bedstead was varnished, every filthy quilt was brought to light, boiled in a great iron wash-pot, and stretched in the sun; and the uproar had all the special character of any annual occasion." Prose like this is not only in the best American tradition, from Mark Twain to Hemingway, but typical of Miss Porter's constant effort to keep her eye on the object.

Yet a faint perfume of sensibility does linger around Miss Porter's shorter stories, despite their vigorous objectivity, and I am puzzled to know whether this is because of their very abbreviated length or because of their subject matter. I have often written about the limitations of short fiction: it is an unsatisfactory medium, allowing not enough room for the play of the imaginative intellect and rather too much room for the display of personality; and even in Miss Porter the little gem of a piece reflects more of the light of its author than of the light of the world. But on the other hand this subtle self-extension may not be a result only of the small compass of Miss Porter's sketches; it may be a result of their common theme. With one exception all the shorter stories in "The Leaning Tower" are re-creations of what we can take to be Miss Porter's own childhood; and there seems to be a peculiar difficulty, these days, in writing about children or from the memory of childhood without making the author-child emerge, herself, too sensitive and cherished, too special a case. Perhaps even an attitude to fiction which is as sturdy and as educated as Miss Porter's is not proof against the prevailing attitude to childhood in our present culture.

BOOK REVIEW:
Robert Penn Warren, "Reality and Strength in These Tales," review of *The Leaning Tower and Other Stories, Chicago Daily Tribune, Books,* 15 October 1944, p. 17.

This review by an old friend was one of Porter's particular favorites.

The story goes like this: A nice, refined old lady who for 40 years had taught English in a state university said: "I like Katherine Anne Porter's stories so much because they are never sordid." When this remark was reported, perhaps with a touch of friendly malice, to the author she exclaimed: "What does she mean talking like that? I'll have her know I'm just as sordid as anybody!"

The anecdote has a moral. The old lady had been so lulled and bemused by the elegant rhythms and verbal felicities of Miss Porter's prose that she had, we presume, failed to attend to what a good many of the stories are about. Tho the "sordidness" of the stories is not exactly like what the old lady considered to be the sordidness of Hemingway's or Farrell's work, still it is worth remembering that the stories, for all their polish, fastidiousness, and calculated understatement, spring from issues of the real and frequently unpleasant business of living.

. . .

But with the present collection, "The Leaning Tower and Other Stories," it will be harder, even for the nice old lady, to forget this fact, for we have here in the title story — really a novelette — a quietly appalling picture of Berlin ripe for Nazism; in "The Downward Path to Wisdom," the first shock to a child of adult hatred and meanness; in "A Day's Work," the degradation of a family on relief.

Even the other items, which are of a gentler, more lyrical temper and look back to the childhood memories, never lose grasp on the issues in the world of fact or let complication dissolve in nostalgia. But in this book we simply have in a sometimes more obvious form what has always been present in Miss Porter's work, and it would be unnecessary to say so if it were not for the fact that there is a current tendency to praise the pres-

ent work at the expense of earlier for a "stronger grasp on reality."

It might be more accurate to praise these tales as enlarging, in a style perhaps more severe and taut, a body of stories already clearly defined — a body of stories distinguished for a remarkable combination of artistic poise and philosophical implication and narrative excitement.

BOOK REVIEW:
Edmund Wilson, Review of *The Leaning Tower and Other Stories, New Yorker,* 20 (30 September 1944): 72–74.

Porter liked this review, though with reservations. As she wrote to Monroe Wheeler after seeing an advance copy, "I think Edmund did me proud too, even if he seemed as he said a touch baffled. Our dear Edmund baffles easily where ladies-in-the-arts are concerned; I'm sure he has a feeling that dogs should not walk on their hind legs, however expertly, bless him."

Miss Katherine Anne Porter has published a new book of stories, her third: "The Leaning Tower and Other Stories" (Harcourt, Brace). To the reviewer, Miss Porter is baffling because one cannot take hold of her work in any of the obvious ways. She makes none of the melodramatic or ironic points that are the stock in trade of ordinary short stories; she falls into none of the usual patterns and she does not show anyone's influence. She does not exploit her personality either inside or outside her work, and her writing itself makes a surface so smooth that the critic has little opportunity to point out peculiarities of color or weave. If he is tempted to say that the effect is pale, he is prevented by the realization that Miss Porter writes English of a purity and precision almost unique in contemporary American fiction. If he tries to demur that some given piece fails to mount with the accelerating pace or arrive at the final intensity that he is in the habit of expecting in short stories, he is deterred by a nibbling suspicion that he may not have grasped its meaning and have it hit him with a sudden impact some moments after he has finished reading.

Not that this meaning is simple to formulate even after one has felt its emotional force. The limpidity of the sentence, the exactitude of the phrase, are deceptive in that the thing they convey continues to seem elusive even after it has been communicated. These stories are not illustrations of anything that is reducible to a moral law, or a political or social analysis, or even a principle of human behavior. What they show us are human relations in their constantly shifting phases and in the moments of which their existence is made. There is no place for general reflections; you are to live through the experience as the characters do. And yet the writer has managed to say something about the values involved in the experience. But what is it? I shall try to suggest, though I am afraid I shall land in ineptitude.

Miss Porter's short stories lend themselves to being sorted into three fairly distinct groups. There are the stories of family life in working-class or middle-class households (there are two of these in "The Leaning Tower"), which, in spite of the fact that the author is technically sympathetic with her people, tend to be bitter and bleak, and, remarkable though they are, seem to me less satisfactory than the best of her other stories. The impression we get from these pieces is that the qualities that are most amiable in human life are being gradually done to death in the milieux she is presenting, but Miss Porter does not really much like these people or feel comfortable in their dismal homes, and so we, in turn, don't really much care. Another section of her work, however, contains what may be called pictures of foreign parts, and here Miss Porter is much more successful. The story which gives its name to her new collection and which takes up two-fifths of the volume belongs to this category. It is a study of Germany between the two wars in terms of a travelling American and his landlady and fellow-lodgers in a Berlin rooming house. By its material and its point of view, it rather recalls Christopher Isherwood's "Goodbye to Berlin," but it is more poetic in treatment and more general in implication. The little plaster leaning tower of Pisa which has been cherished by the Viennese landlady but gets broken by her American tenant stands for something in the destruction of which not merely the Germans but also the Americans have somehow taken a criminal part (though the American is himself an artist, he finds that he can mean nothing to the Germans but the power of American money). So, in a fine earlier story, "Hacienda," a Mexican peon is somehow destroyed — with no direct responsibility on the part of any of the elements concerned — by a combination of Soviet Russians intent on making a Communist movie, the American business manager, and a family of Mexican landowners.

In both cases, we are left with the feeling that, caught in the meshes of a tangle of forces, some important human value has been crushed. These stories especially, one gathers, are exam-

ples of what Miss Porter means when she says in her foreword to "Flowering Judas" in the Modern Library edition, that most of her "energies of mind and spirit have been spent in the effort to grasp the meaning" of the threats of world catastrophe in her time, "to trace them to their sources and to understand the logic of this majestic and terrible failure of the life of man in the Western world."

But perhaps the most interesting section of Katherine Anne Porter's work is composed of her stories about women — particularly her heroine Miranda, who figures in two of the three novelettes that make up her previous volume, "Pale Horse, Pale Rider." The first six stories of "The Leaning Tower" deal with Miranda's childhood and her family background of Louisianians living in southern Texas. This is the setting in which Miss Porter is most at home, and one finds in it the origins of that spirit of which the starvation and violation elsewhere make the subjects of her other stories. One recognizes it in the firm little sketches that show the relations between Miranda's grandmother and her life-long colored companion, the relations between the members of the family, and the relations between the family and the Negro servants in general. Somewhere behind Miss Porter's stories there is a conception of a natural human spirit in terms of their bearing on which all the other forces of society are appraised. This spirit is never really idealized, it is not even sentimentalized; it can be generous and loving and charming, but it can also be indifferent and careless, inconsequent, irresponsible, and silly. If the meaning of these stories is elusive, it is because this essential spirit is so hard to isolate or pin down. It is peculiar to Louisianians in Texas, yet one misses it in a boarding house in Berlin. It is the special personality of a woman, yet it is involved with international issues. It evades all the most admirable moralities, it escapes through the social meshes, and it resists the tremendous oppressions of national bankruptcies and national wars. It is outlawed, driven underground, exiled; it becomes rather unsure of itself and may be able, as in "Pale Horse, Pale Rider," to assert itself only in the delirium that lights up at the edge of death to save Miranda from extinction by war flu. It suffers often from a guilty conscience, knowing too well its moral weakness; but it can also rally bravely if vaguely in vindication of some instinct of its being which seems to point toward justice and truth.

But I told you this review would be clumsy. I am spoiling Miss Porter's stories by attempting to find a formula for them when I ought simply to be telling you to read them (and not merely this last volume but also its two predecessors). She is absolutely a first-rate artist, and what she wants other people to know she imparts to them by creating an object, the self-developing organism of a work of prose. The only general opinion on anything which, in her books, she has put on record has been a statement about her craft of prose fiction, and I may quote it — from the foreword to which I have referred — as more to the purpose than anything that the present critic could say. Here is the manifesto of the builder of this solid little sanctuary, so beautifully proportioned and finished, for the queer uncontrollable spirit that it seems to her important to save:

"In the face of such shape and weight of present misfortune, the voice of the individual artist may seem perhaps of no more consequence than the whirring of a cricket in the grass, but the arts do live continuously, and they live literally by faith; their names and their shapes and their uses and their basic meanings survive unchanged in all that matters through times of interruption, diminishment, neglect; they outlive governments and creeds and the societies, even the very civilizations that produced them. They cannot be destroyed altogether because they represent the substance of faith and the only reality. They are what we find again when the ruins are cleared away. And even the smallest and most incomplete offering at this time can be a proud act in defense of that faith."

LETTER:
Katherine Anne Porter to Monroe Wheeler, 3 December 1945 [excerpt]; in *Letters to Katherine Anne Porter*, pp. 311–314.

Porter spent most of the late 1940s in California, working briefly and with little success as a screenwriter in 1945 and 1946 and teaching a course at Stanford University for the 1948–1949 school year. This letter to Wheeler, written from Paramount Studios after Porter had been in California for about ten months, expresses her distaste for the process of screenwriting.

Monroe darling:

Look where I'm, exclamation point. Rounding into my sixth week of a stretch of fourteen, and not even groggy yet. This is better, entirely. I am working with Charles Brackett — who did *Lost Weekend,* and a French professorial sort of person named Jaques Thery on an adaptation of *Madame Sans Gêne* for Betty Hutten [sic] — or have I told you this? In case I didn't, one evening at six o'clock they called me up and asked me to come to the studio all set to plunge in up to the eyebrows in the script. I asked why they couldn't wait until Monday, it then being Wednesday and they said, Golly, NO. Tomorrow at eleven a.m. you be here.

So I hastily broke my neck re-arranging my life for an indefinite period, showed up all eager on the hour, was greeted, kissed, handed around, lunched, patted on the head, shown my office, and about three o'clock Brackett said, Come on Darling, I'll drive you home . . . On the way he remarked casually that I needn't come back until I was sent for, they just wanted to be sure they had me, or words to that effect. So I sat out two weeks, drawing my wages with heavenly punctuality, then I was asked to drop in sometime if I felt like it. I felt like it the next day, and sat in a cribbage game with Billy Wilder, Thery and Brackett. They carry on a game every day about noon. (Do you play cribbage? I saw the prettiest little ivory board the other day and thought of you, I don't know why. Except that if you play cribbage you really need it.) They also got me into a discussion on the subject of abortion, with the Catholic censor, who was objecting to something in another picture of Brackett's. Then Mr. Thery remarked that when he was finished with me, I'd be able to write any scenario I wished with one hand . . . I sat around the office catching up on my correspondence and telephone calls, and went home about five. Not until last Monday, one week ago today, did I begin coming here every day, and four of them I have spent listening and watching Thery talk. I sit in a big arm chair and he gallops up and down the room before me, constructing a play. He really can construct one, but it has nothing to do with Sardou, or *Sans Gêne,* or fact or fiction or anything human . . . I keep interrupting, "yes but — " trying to tell him he is off the rails completely, but he never listens. If I do get the right of way, he stops and stares out the window and day dreams until I finish. Then he shakes his head as if he had water in his ears and starts galloping and talking once more . . . He has constructed and thrown away one play every session, and we are just where we were . . . This morning I came in at 11, and had a message from him he would be working with Billy Wilder today — he works with half a dozen writers and directors . . . So here I am darling, catching up on my correspondence some more . . .

But nobody else seems to be in the least worried, so I'm not either. I do know, there is evidence for it, that pictures do actually get made, somehow, and no doubt one I work on will finally emerge, too. It could be very interesting, a good comedy, but Thery is not funny. His way of working reminds me of a pack of cards somebody sent me once, called "Add-a-Plot." — No, Deal-A-Plot. You shuffled them and laid out five, and selected a hero, repeat for heroine, for theme, for treatment, and so down the line. Then you were supposed to go ahead and make a story out of what you had in hand . . . I feel that if they would let me alone I could get a decent play out of Sardou . . . but that is not the way it works, so I am just floating along. [. . .]

BOOK REVIEW:
Katherine Anne Porter, "They Lived With the Enemy in the House," review of *Apartment in Athens,* by Glenway Wescott, *New York Herald Tribune Weekly Book Review,* 4 March 1945, p.1.

In California, Porter returned to work on her novel, which she had decided to call Ship of Fools, *and by January 1946 she could write to Josephine Herbst that she had completed 240 pages. This review of a novel by her friend Glenway Wescott, written — like many works of the time — with the express purpose of helping the war effort, reveals the revulsion Porter felt at the photographs of Nazi atrocities published after the Allies began liberating German concentration camps in early 1945. The feelings Porter expressed in this review helped to shape the theme of* Ship of Fools. *As she wrote to Herbst on 23 January 1946, "My book is about the constant endless collusion between good and evil; I believe that human beings are capable of total evil, but no one has ever been totally good: and this gives the edge to good."*

Since this short history of what "happened" to a Greek family named "Helianos," is as current in its subject matter as a headline in this morning's newspaper, the important thing to know about "Apartment in Athens" is that it is first of all a work of honest, unembarrassed good literature. It is useful in the sense that no good work of art can ever be anything but useful, and timely because it can never come too early or too late. It is a story of the shapeless, immoderate miseries and confusions brought by the Germans upon this world for the third time within the memory of living men; it is even "propaganda" against this Germanic savagery, if you like, and if you would call Goya's "Disasters of War" by such a name. Mr. Wescott is said to have remarked that he wrote the book "to show how bad the Germans are" — but he has gone much further than that. Surely nobody need tell us at this time of day how bad the Germans are: they themselves first told us years ago; and then for years they have demonstrated their meaning precisely. Mr. Wescott has done something much more valuable than that: he has exposed and anatomized that streak of Germanism in the rest of us which made possible the Germany we know today. He does not indulge in any such generalization as this, but takes full advantage of the blessed craft of fiction, which calls for compression, limitation, severe choice of incident and a minute attention to those particular traits of character in the individual human being in a given locality and time. It is not his business to report corpses by the ton, destruction by the cityful, famine by thousands of square miles, losses on bombing missions by so much material. His scene is Greece; Athens; a poor four-room flat in a dingy street; his story the long painful education of Mr. and Mrs. Helianos in the true nature of evil, not only in their barbarous guest, but in themselves; and at last the true meaning of courage, a knowledge delayed so late it was almost useless, but not quite.

When the German captain chose their poor little flat for his quarters because it was convenient to his place of work, and began his highly instructed course of humiliation and terror in the household, Mr. and Mrs. Helianos were already experienced in defeat. Comfortable members of the upper middle class, the husband a mild-mannered middle-aged publisher with a civilized, poetic erudition, they had lost their first and best loved son at the battle of Mount Olympus; had been driven out of their house into a starveling neighborhood; had watched their small son and daughter dwindle with famine, the boy's brilliant mind gone savage and oblique, the girl stunned into half-wittedness by the sight of violence.

Mrs. Helianos has reason to believe that her brother has treasonable dealings with the Germans. She longs not to believe it, then wishes to believe it because by such means his life is saved; then tries to excuse him; then secretly hopes he is dead because by her logic the disgrace would be softened, she would be free to forget him. Mr.

Helianos comes of a bolder family, his male cousins are off in the mountains still fighting and doing underground work. He had always deplored in his rational, philosophic way, their reckless bravery while admiring their spirit. Still it seems to him at first that intelligent ruse, strategy, patience, a certain appearance of bending to the yoke while maintaining mental reservations, must in the long run overcome what he considers as mere raw blind force.

It is to be seen that even before the German captain came upon them they had set their feet in the longest and bitterest way. They become slaves in their own apartment to a pompous minor god with nasty personal habits and an epileptic instability of temper, the range of whose virtuosity in mean cruelties is endless. Helianos, still "trying to understand the Germans in general by this officer," and comparing notes with his Greek fellow sufferers, begins to grasp little by little that there was nothing unpremeditated in German behavior anywhere. They practised torture with "various tricks that were like surgery gone wrong, with little up-to-date mechanical contraptions."

Still, Helianos argues with himself and with his wife, whose feelings are deep, truly maternal and untinged with what, in spite of her loyal, impatient love, she considers her husband's male sophistries. He argues that they are better off than the people of Crete, where mere massacre had been carried out with the most acute disciplines and formalities. They are lucky in their officer — he belongs to the quarter-masters corps, not the ranks of killers and torturers. He did desk work and had intellectual interests. There is, he confesses weakly, even a certain charm about the fellow when he is not annoyed. Their chances for survival are more than fair.

It all comes to nothing in the deep places of their beings where they truly live and cannot avoid self-knowledge. They realize that "their having been able to bear it would be nothing to boast of. They thought of it as . . . a disease all through them, like vermin all over them. That would be their story and they would be ashamed to tell it."

Happily it is not their story. The captain, after a short sharp reign of terror, goes to Germany, has there an experience which shakes him, returns with the look of a haunted man, and becomes suddenly, frighteningly amiable to his prisoners. He draws Helianos into long strange conversations, in which he explains with the exaltation of mania his inhuman creed. He weeps and complains because the war has destroyed his wife and children, on the very soil of Germany the war has come and taken those sacred lives. Helianos listens, the divided, thoughtful, civilized man longing to be just even to his enemy, seeking the truth even from the very teeth of evil. But he cannot in the end, in spite of his own efforts, betray or degrade his spirit any longer. Without knowing, almost as if by a slip of the tongue, almost as if by mere childish credulity, he speaks the few words that open the trap that has been set there for him from the beginning, not purposely by the captain, but by the very nature of the situation.

From there the history of the Helianos family goes to its beautiful, reassuring end. It could be read now simply for what it has to tell us about the enemy, whom we helped to create. It might help us to recognize what it is in ourselves that has given him such power. As a work of literature it might do what no amount of newspaper print can accomplish in touching our hard hearts and stubborn minds. That could well be its purpose for now. But I cannot foresee a time when Helianos's letter to his wife, smuggled from prison, when he was dying under "questioning" and "did not always feel well" might not be read as poetry when happily, happily, its readers may no longer need the instruction it contains:

"I really know nothing about Americans. . . . Only I feel sure that they will be most important again when the war is over. Probably the Russians are ruthless, but the British have too much sense of honor and sentiment for the job that is to be done, and the Americans can influence the British . . .

"Tell Petros to warn them beyond the sea that it may happen to them, too, before the century is over. Nothing is too difficult for these great mystical, scientific, hard-working, self-denying Germans, possessed of the devil as they are, and despising every one else.

"I do not suppose that the Americans are indifferent to their fate and danger. I think that their worst mistake must lie in their hope of getting peace established for all time, as if it were a natural law needing no enforcement, so that they can relax and be frivolous and forget it. When they see that this is not possible then they lose hope altogether. They give it all up as a bad job and yield to their cynicism and fatalism. It is what happened after the other war. . . .

"What on earth do they mean when they speak of peace, forever? Naturally it can only be a little at a time, with good luck, and with an effort

173

Katherine Anne Porter   6/28/48

Abuse of vocabulary - and use of jargon of trades, sciences, psycho-analysis. Freudian - jargon of fashion.

Language changes every day. Difference of language between Chaucer's time to Shakespeare's, Fielding's to Hemingway's. It changes and it should. Sloppy use of badly misunderstood vocabulary of sciences, trades, professions.

I object to the use of Freudian case history transferred usually without change to fiction...The greater writer is the dedicated man who really means to practice his life for his lifetime in spite of the consequences, and who does it with a certain amount of selflessness.

You cannot learn anything useful to you, to practice literature from a medical book or a Freudian case history. Only thing you can learn - you get a kind of clue - if you have not already got them from reading of myths and legends, study of religions, and rather a little attention to the person sitting at your elbow who is the real source of your knowledge - only you mustn't look at him like that - that also is very bad.

If all this fails you, if you have not done it, do it now, and then after that you can take the very incomplete science which is called psycho-analysis and you can learn something there, too, for Freud has made a very good synthesis. But don't read people who write about Freud. Read Freud. Don't read commentators on the Bible. Read the Bible. Go to the source.

We have the most wonderful language of obscenity, and it will enrich itself, or it will be impoverished, according to our use of it.

We have a rather strange and I think charming use of the vocabulary of sports. We have a good rich slang. Some will survive and some will not and we can't tell which is which. I would not use an untried word. Use the strongest and best word for your meaning which is understood by the greatest number of people in the traditional sense. And I hope that doesn't sound too conservative. Because I have never been accused of that and I am getting ready to hear it any minute.

Certain vulgarity of words which we should chase out with steams and curses. We have almost lost the art of good old Elizabethan language.

drapes   contact
formal   dsinterested when it means uninterested

Porter's notes on the abuse of language and the Freudian case history in literature (Papers of Katherine Anne Porter, Special Collections, University of Maryland at College Park Libraries) and great vigilance and good management, day by day, year after year. Life is like that; everything on earth is like that; — have the Americans and the British forgotten? . . .

"When we are sick and we go to see a doctor, do we expect him to promise us immortality?" . . .

BOOK REVIEW:
Charles J. Rolo, "The artist as critic," in his "Reader's Choice," *Atlantic Monthly,* 190 (December 1952): 97–98.

In autumn 1949, when Porter returned to the East Coast and settled in New York City, much work remained to be done on Ship of Fools, *parts of which had been appearing in magazines since 1944 and continued to appear sporadically throughout the 1950s. During the four years she remained in New York, she accomplished little more than gathering together a collection of previously published critical essays and other nonfiction, published as* The Days Before *in late 1952. The book was generally well received, and although such collections rarely attract a great deal of attention, it helped to keep Porter's name before the public, as did the 1955 publication of* The Old Order: Stories from Flowering Judas; Pale Horse, Pale Rider; *and* The Leaning Tower, *which includes "The Jilting of Granny Weatherall," "He," "Magic," and "Old Mortality" in addition to six of the seven stories Porter later brought together under the collective title "The Old Order."*

In this review of The Days Before, *Rollo mentions an article on "Miss Stein's literary pretensions." When "The Wooden Umbrella" was first published (as "Gertrude Stein: A Self-Portrait") in 1947, it so upset Josephine Herbst that she published a response, virtually ending her longstanding friendship with Porter.*

The distance which separates André Gide from Katherine Anne Porter may seem prodigious, but Miss Porter's new book, *The Days Before* (Harcourt, Brace, $4.00) — a collection of her articles written during the past thirty years — reveals an artistic credo which, on certain points, has striking similarities to Gide's. In the Foreword, Miss Porter says she hopes the reader will find in these diversified articles the "connective tissue of a continuous central . . . preoccupation." This central preoccupation appears to be "the passion for individual expression without hypocrisy." The artist, she indicates, should reach for the inner

truth that is personal and particular to him — that is embedded in reality as he knows it. Her glowing tribute to her model artist, Virginia Woolf, concludes: "She was what the true believers have always called a heretic. . . . She lived in the naturalness of her vocation."

True art, Miss Porter remarks in her essay on Willa Cather, is "provincial" in the most literal sense in that it must have a province, a time and a place. And for that reason, she admires artists who have a strong sense of the importance of place; it keeps them closer to personal reality. "All the things I write of," she says, "I have known and they are real to me."

I have put last things first and have spoken of the "central preoccupation," because with this "connective tissue" one sees consistency and design in what might seem to be a potpourri, but actually comes close to being a self-portrait.

In the first section, there are twelve critical essays in which Miss Porter reveals herself obliquely in her evaluations. The article on Ezra Pound, while it brings out his aberrations, shows that to Miss Porter the crucial fact is his artistic perfectionism; she views him with sympathy because he was "a God-sent disturber of the peace in the arts, the one department of human life where peace is fatal." The first two books of Gertrude Stein elicit a favorable essay because they seem fresh, personal, and (to use Miss Stein's phrase) "everybody is a real one." Years later, Miss Porter writes a long, elegantly gossipy article, which says with infinite wit that Miss Stein, wishing to play the Genius, has deluded herself into monstrous self-indulgence. Without a trace of violence, it does to Miss Stein's literary pretensions what the executioner's crowbar did to the victim broken on the wheel. There are also pieces on Henry James, Eudora Welty, Katherine Mansfield, and others.

In the second section — "Personal and Particular" — Miss Porter speaks to us directly. This panel includes "Three Statements About Writing"; a "Portrait of the Old South" from which she hails, and other articles on places; and two discussions of the heaven and hell of marriage.

In the final section, "Mexican," Miss Porter writes about a people whose feeling for art she finds "cosanguine with my own," and whose struggles for freedom have stirred her.

It is common knowledge that Miss Porter is a beautiful writer, but in the intervals between her books, one is apt to forget what an extraordinarily fine artist she is. In these articles, there is an intelligence that races along; there is sanity, charm, and a love of the world. I have read much of the book twice, and I expect to reread much of it again.

LETTER:
Katherine Anne Porter to Eudora Welty, 20 February 1956; in *Letters of Katherine Anne Porter*, pp. 498–499.

Porter spent the 1953–1954 academic year as a visiting professor at the University of Michigan and went to Belgium for 1954–1955 as a Fulbright lecturer at the University of Liège. During these years she did little work on Ship of Fools, *but after her return to the United States in February 1955 she rented a house in Southbury, Connecticut, and resumed work on the novel in earnest.*

In this letter to Eudora Welty, Porter discusses another project, "Noon Wine: The Sources," which became one of her best-known pieces of nonfiction after Robert Penn Warren and Cleanth Brooks published it in their popular college text book Understanding Fiction. *The essay was also published in* The Yale Review *(September 1956). The "pieces about Circe" that Porter mentions in the last paragraph of this letter are Welty's short story "Circe" (first published as "Put Me In the Sky!" in* Accent, *Autumn 1949) and Porter's essay "A Defense of Circe" (first published in the June 1954 issue of* Mademoiselle*), the only piece of writing Porter completed while she was in Michigan.*

Eudora darling:

Your *Place in Fiction* brought me the pure pleasure I always have in reading anything you publish, and also something wonderfully timely to read, that is, something good and clear and true about your discoveries in the art of novel-writing, your considered point of view as to its practise: and all so vivid and *gay*, so beautifully illustrated — the little night-lamp, Eliza and the forty hounds of confusion — how you do clean up on *that* picture! the examples you give from other writers of what you mean, all all delights me, and doubly because it came just when I was in the middle of an attempt to explain, in a few well-chosen words, the sources in my life of "Noon Wine." I promised this to Robert Penn Warren for a collection of some sort he is getting together, and my God, I can compare the process only to tapping my own spinal fluid, so nearly does it come to the quick of memory, that is, numberless memories all fused together, sometimes no more tangible than dust-particles floating in a sunbeam; but the real diffi-

culty is explaining how, by the organic process of creation, the scattered and seemingly random events remembered through many years become fiction, that is — not a lie, really as I think you call it — but symbolic truth. I can only hope I am being a little less dull and more explicit in the piece I am writing. Place as a brimming frame: place as sense of form; as equilibrium — I am enchanted with the way your mind works it all out. I like your little side-blow at some of the new novels: confessions, rather than communications. I used to call them "case-histories" and there are now several little paper bound periodicals devoted entirely to this dreary school of couch-mutterers.

Bless you for writing it in the first place, and bless you for sending it. I hope sometime you will make a collection of these pieces: next to the *Odyssey*, perhaps it is about my favorite reading matter now — but there is so little of it, these lovely sparks flying off between the hammer and the anvil of a good writer's main work ... I hope you'll feel like doing a lot of them. ...

I think our pieces about Circe so near together a strange coincidence — after thinking about it for some 15 years I finally got to it in March 1954 in Ann Arbor.

With my love
Katherine Anne

INTERVIEW:
Winston Bode, "Miss Porter on Writers and Writing," *Texas Observer*, 31 October 1958; in *Katherine Anne Porter: Conversations*, pp. 30–38.

By 1958 Porter was able to report to friends that she had nearly completed a second draft of Ship of Fools. *Although there was still much work to be done on the novel, she accepted invitations to visit the University of Texas at Austin in autumn 1958 and spend the remainder of the semester as a visiting professor at the University of Virginia before going to Washington and Lee University in Lexington, Virginia, for the spring term.*

Bode interviewed Porter while she was in Austin and reported on a lecture that she based on "Noon Wine: The Sources," written at the request of Robert Penn Warren, not Allen Tate as reported here.

For many years Porter gave her birth date as 1894 — the date she gave Bode — rather than 1890, but when she reached seventy in 1960 she became proud of her age and started giving her correct birth date.

"Yes, I remember you," said the voice of Katherine Anne Porter. I had asked for an interview. "I've been answering the phone all morning with my mouth full of toothpaste. But I've finally got it out." She laughed a belly laugh. "It's the most amazing thing. Apparently" — the t's sharp — "the whole place is populated by old friends of mine. But they're all widows. Isn't that funny? All the uncles and brothers and fathers gone now."

We met in the dim tall-ceilinged lobby, she in her fur and rich hat, 64 and sporting lorgnette-type glasses ("I have others, but these are so much easier, don't you know"), looking at a letter we had opened on the way down, from the *Southwest Review.*

Her eyes are wide and a deep-lustered ageless grey green: "This is good. Write for the little magazines first . . . Some of the battles we won and you don't have to fight them again. When I was young there was a slick formula that was being used by the magazines and being practiced with great skill by a handful of craftsmen. But I wrote honest, and it was hard to get an honest story published. I think one man was responsible for the change. James Joyce with *Dubliners* broke the formula . . . Katherine Mansfield didn't write formula. Of course, I'd been writing my own kind of stories for years. But I was just a little girl from Texas in New York. My first story was published in *Old Century,* a respected magazine, like the *Atlantic Monthly.* That was "María Concepción," the first story I had finished. First finished, first published — in 1923. I had started many other stories, but I hadn't finished them. I was 29, and I had been writing since I was six or seven, and had been an apprentice for 15 years. But nobody ever saw a manuscript of mine except the editor I sent it to. There was an exception of a friend or two, whom I would show a manuscript to after it was all done and ready to be sent off.

"And then came the era of the little magazines. For 25 years I saved the stories for the poor dears because I wanted to keep them going. But now *Mademoiselle* will take the same stories and pay me $1,000, and you know, I'm going to take it. That's the battle we won for you. You don't have to starve in garrets and cellars as many of us did . . . The big magazines got the idea that people would read these stories and they started publishing them without changing a line. But they will not buy you if you are not known. You must send to the good small ones and then the big rich ones will buy your stories. They'll try to sidetrack you once they have you and make you write their

way, but if you're strong and hold out they'll buy the same stories the small magazines do . . . But it's a long haul. It takes about 40 years!" She laughed.

"In the early days people would say, 'I will go to Hollywood and save money and then write the way I want to.' But they never did. In the first place they didn't save money, and they ruined themselves. You can't hold yourself in contempt and do anything worthwhile.

"I would say to the young writers, you shouldn't side-step suffering if you have to go through it to get where you're going."

What did she mean by suffering?

"I mean whatever your human problem is. I mean facing it in life — not turning it into literature. Facing it, and not turning into a hobo like the beat generation, or a stuffed shirt . . . You'll have to write what you are. I wish I could remember who it was who said, 'If you don't want to give yourself away, don't write.' "

We discussed writers. I mentioned James Agee. She responded: "A first-rate artist, a wonderful example of the regional, the particular, used in such a way that the meaning is universal.

"He worked hard, and he played hard, and he used himself up all too soon. But he lived to the full, and perhaps that was the only way he could be. He just went over the dam chin first. I'm just awfully glad we had him while we did. But if someone could have stopped him and said, 'Look, save yourself. . . .' I regret him bitterly, as I do John Peale Bishop, who I think had so much promise and who had not reached his height.

"And I like Allen Tate." She smiled. "He has that sense of, of 'local habitation' . . . I don't like to quote Shakespeare, but sometimes we have to, don't we? . . ."

Her tone changed. "And then there are those like Jesse Stuart, who stay in one place — But I don't want to talk about other writers! After all, dog does not eat dog!

"I've come nearer getting exactly what I wanted than anyone I know. What is it? Not fame or notoriety, just having the people you want to read and like you. I have so little complaint. I haven't done as good work as I had hoped or expected to do. But that's why we don't quit. We're expecting the next one to be a masterpiece. You can't expect us to quit a way of life, to quit writing, any more than you can expect us to quit reading. I'll probably go on writing more and more. I've been so busy making a living, teaching and

Willa Cather: 1876-1947

Katherine Anne Porter

I never knew her at all, nor any one who did know her; do
not to this day. There exist large numbers of critical estimates
of her work, appreciations; perhaps even a memoir or two, giving
glimpse of her personal history — I have never read one. Her private
life never became public property, or her house a crossroads.
No romantic-erotic-scandalous
legends grew up around her name. She was not, in the popular
crutch-word to describe almost any kind of sensation, "exciting";
so far as I know, nobody, not even one of the Freudian school
of critics, ever sat up nights with a textbook in one hand and
her works in the other, reading between the lines to discover how
much sexual autobiography could be mined out of her stories.
I remember only one photograph— Steichen's— made in middle life,
showing a big plain smiling woman, her arms crossed easily over
a Girl-Scout sort of white blouse, with a ragged part in her hair.
She seemed, as the French say, "well seated" and not very outgoing. Even the earnestly amiable, finely shaped eyes, the left
one faintly askew, were in some mysterious way not expressive,
lacking as they did altogether that look of strangeness which a
strange vision is supposed to give to the eye of any real artist.
One doesn't have to be a genius absolutely to get this look, it
is often quite enough merely to believe one is a genius; and to
have had the wild vision only once is enough— the afterlight stays.

Well, Miss Cather looks awfully like somebody's big sister,
or maiden aunt, both of which she was. No genius ever looked
less like one, according to the romantic popular view, unless it
was her idol, Flaubert, whose photographs could pass
easily for the

*Page from the typescript and the corresponding proof sheet for an essay on Willa Cather that Porter wrote for
publication in the July 1952 issue of* Mademoiselle *(Papers of Katherine Anne Porter, Special Collections,
University of Maryland at College Park Libraries). Porter revised this essay before including it
in* The Days Before.

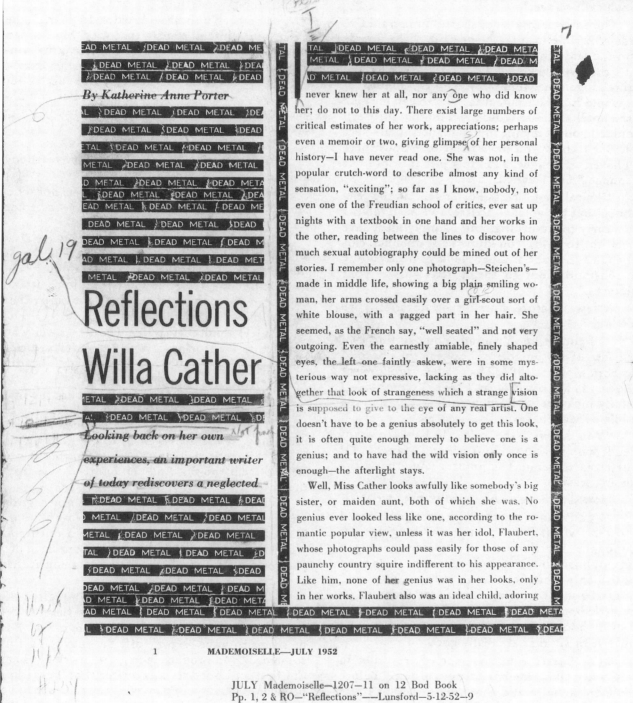

By Katherine Anne Porter

Reflections
Willa Cather

Looking back on her own experiences, an important writer of today rediscovers a neglected

never knew her at all, nor any one who did know her; do not to this day. There exist large numbers of critical estimates of her work, appreciations; perhaps even a memoir or two, giving glimpse of her personal history—I have never read one. She was not, in the popular crutch-word to describe almost any kind of sensation, "exciting"; so far as I know, nobody, not even one of the Freudian school of critics, ever sat up nights with a textbook in one hand and her works in the other, reading between the lines to discover how much sexual autobiography could be mined out of her stories. I remember only one photograph—Steichen's—made in middle life, showing a big plain smiling woman, her arms crossed easily over a girl-scout sort of white blouse, with a ragged part in her hair. She seemed, as the French say, "well seated" and not very outgoing. Even the earnestly amiable, finely shaped eyes, the left one faintly askew, were in some mysterious way not expressive, lacking as they did altogether that look of strangeness which a strange vision is supposed to give to the eye of any real artist. One doesn't have to be a genius absolutely to get this look, it is often quite enough merely to believe one is a genius; and to have had the wild vision only once is enough—the afterlight stays.

Well, Miss Cather looks awfully like somebody's big sister, or maiden aunt, both of which she was. No genius ever looked less like one, according to the romantic popular view, unless it was her idol, Flaubert, whose photographs could pass easily for those of any paunchy country squire indifferent to his appearance. Like him, none of her genius was in her looks, only in her works. Flaubert also was an ideal child, adoring

JULY Mademoiselle—1207—11 on 12 Bod Book
Pp. 1, 2 & RO—"Reflections"——Lunsford—5-12-52—9

genius

trouping the country, and I've had so many human calls on me."

Our interview was cut short. "I'm afraid I've made a terrible mistake," she said. "The people from the University are coming for me at 11:30 and I thought they said 12. You know on these lecture assignments, they put you on a treadmill. . . . But would it be convenient for you to call me here at the hotel at 2:30? Would you do that please? I could tell you all my life in ten minutes. I talk very fast. But I know you have those questions there you haven't asked me, and I talk just as fast on the telephone." She laughed.

"I'm relaxed," Miss Porter said on the telephone, "but my voice is hoarse. I've been talking since early this morning, and I simply must save myself for tonight. You know I got up much earlier than I thought and people have been calling me constantly. But go ahead, let's answer your questions."

A few "feature story" type questions, we said. Age?

"Of course I don't mind. You can find it in the backs of any number of books in the library. I was born May 15, 1894. That's a beautiful time of the year. I have a friend who says, You must feel awfully lucky being born right smack dab in the middle of May in Texas."

"You know," she said, "I have a lot of friends who were born in April and May. . . . Of course, as someone has pointed out, that's the lambing season!"

How did she feel about prolixity in writers?

"I don't have anything against prolixity. I hate that word! I don't have anything against abundance. But if you have a selectiveness, you don't publish so much. I've written bushels but I publish only what I choose to publish. Your output can be small, but you can be world famous on one little book of poems. After all, say you write 50 or 60 books. Out of that there are going to be only five or six that are really good."

Miss Porter said she started lecturing in 1936 when she came back from abroad. "Before that I did articles and that sort of thing. I was married part of the time. I did book reviews for the New York newspapers, and one way or another I made out. I wrote every day of my life and still do even on these little old trips. I write not to be taking notes, you understand, but because I like to get a thing down. Of course, it's a great change, to get out of the whirl and sit down and face that blank wall to write." Her musical voice

rang. "But nobody promised us the great things would all be wonderful."

"I've been a total widow for 16 years," she said, "and I intend to stay that way. My maiden name is Katherine Anne Porter, Porter is my family name. I never used my husbands' names except for social purposes. I'm not going to talk about my private life. It's not that I mind, but you understand there is nothing to tell. The only thing that counts is my work."

We asked where she was born.

"Why do you ask that? I thought everybody around here knew all that."

We discussed the fact that she was not written about too much in Texas. There was some joke about a revival.

"Yes I realize that! Well they know me elsewhere! I was born in Indian Creek, I think that is the name of a Community, in Brown County, and I was raised around Kyle . . . No, I didn't attend college, I went to girls' schools, convents, that type of thing."

"I feel about revival like whoever it was who heard that Henry James was being revived. He said, 'I hadn't heard he was dead.' I hadn't heard I was dead."

"Texas has no serious writers. I am the first serious writer Texas has produced. That is, up to now. There are two young writers who are very promising. William Humphrey has written a good book. 'Home is the sailor' . . . How does it go? 'Home from the sea And the hunter home from the hill.'

"Robert Louis Stevenson was not a good writer but that was a good poem. Now William Humphrey is really young — in his mid-thirties. If you start when you're 18 and work your head off, you're doing good to amount to something at that age."

"I thought William Goyen had a really brilliant and strange talent. When his first works came out I thought he had a first rate talent. But he seems to have — gone off. But maybe he will come back and produce more good work . . . I am the first and only serious writer that Texas has produced. These young people may turn out to be first rate. The woods are swarming with writers. In all this ferment, we're bound to get more good ones. But so far I am the only one. If you can show me others, I'll be glad to see them!"

In the hotel she had said, "What is more 'regional' than 'Noon Wine'? Than 'Old Mortality'?" I asked, "Are you a regional writer?" "Of course I'm not a regional writer. I think you

Recipients of honorary degrees at Smith College, 8 June 1958: Porter,
Janet Flanner, Barbara McClintock, Nadia Boulanger, and Mary Parsons

ought to write about what you know. But I don't know any first rate person who is a regional writer.

"I don't think we ought to have American lyric writers or French provincial writers or English country writers . . . I think we ought to drop two words: Americanism and regionalism. They are coins with the design rubbed off. They are cramping people with perfectly good instincts. Let the artist write what he can. I think we should be good writers."

The lecture hall was filled up, some sat in folding chairs in the aisles, and they piped the sound to two rooms upstairs. Miss Porter came out in a blue gown, stiffly and formally engaged the crowd, and bowed low. Her hair was dressed brilliantly. Her heart-shaped face looked sculptured, delicate and beautiful, and her lovely eyes were steady as they met the audience.

Dr. William Eckman of the English staff had introduced her as the first in the current series of lecturers in the University's Program in Criticism and as a woman who has "one of the solidest liter-

ary reputations in America." He said she would talk on "Noon Wine: The Sources."

"Noon Wine" had been bandied about in the papers all week as a story laid near Austin, around Buda.

Miss Porter fumbled in her purse and coughed a little and seemed apologetic and said, "You know, I've been meeting people all day and signing things and before I go a step further I want to say that" . . . more fumbling . . . "I got away with a perfectly good grey Parker pen!" She went into a deep laugh. More fumbling. "No, that's mine" . . . She lifted her chin. "I look upon this as a kind of beautiful family gathering. I shouldn't be surprised if there are some of you who know the place where I was born. It isn't on the map at all . . . I was taken away when I was 18 months old, and I haven't been back there for 45 years. I lived until I was ten years old with my grandmother, who died in the little farm town of Kyle . . . I think my first sight of the great world was when my grandmother brought me up here to be vaccinated . . .

My first look at a work of beauty was when she took me into the Capitol rotunda. We went all the way up to the top of the Capitol then. I understand they won't let you do that now."

"The people I knew accepted art . . . Van Cliburn doesn't seem a surprise to me. He's the sort of person I recognize. I can remember the school teacher who would catch the train once a week and come into Austin for piano lessons . . . They studied from the Germans, who came down on the piano from above . . . not like they do today all with the fingers . . . And the girls who taught school would go to Europe for the summer. Nobody thought much about it."

"People ask me what I write from, and I say, I write from experience, but I say experience is anything that happens to me . . . a flash of memory, a nightmare, a daydream . . . You can't start a work of art anywhere except where life starts. . . ."

". . . But many an experience that I use in a story happened to me so early I can hardly put it together . . . People ask me, 'Who was the person in real life who inspired you to write about the Swedish hired hand named Helton in "Noon Wine"? I say, 'Why his name was Helton and he was a Swedish hired hand.' He was someone I saw once propped up against the side of a shack playing tunes on a mouth organ. A lonely figure with thatched bleak hair between his eyebrows. And that's all I knew about him."

She prepared to read from her text and said perhaps the best way she could tell about the sources of "Noon Wine" would be to read what she had written Allen Tate about them.

She reached for her glasses and said: "You know I have wonderful eyes and can count the hairs of your eyebrows at 60 paces. I think it is perfect irony that I can see everything except print at 17 inches."

She looked up from the text. "I think everyone lives a story three times over . . . The first time is when the events occur . . . then when you remember them . . . and the third time is when you begin to put them into art . . . And there is a fourth time when people ask how it happened when they ask artists to explain themselves . . . Tracing the art through the labyrinth of experience . . . childhood memory . . . is really an impossible undertaking, a little like tapping one's own spinal fluid."

She read: "By the time I wrote "Noon Wine" it had become real to me almost in the sense that I felt not as if I had made that story out of my own memory of real events and imagined consequences, but as if I were quite simply reporting events I had heard or witnessed. This is not in the least true: the story is fiction; but it is made up of thousands of things that did happen to living human beings in a certain part of the country at a certain time of my life; things that are still remembered by others as single incidents; not as I remembered them, floating and moving with their separate life and reality, meeting and parting and mingling in my thoughts until they established their relationship and meaning to me. So I feel that this story is "true" in the way that a work of fiction should be true, created out of all the scattered particles of life I was able to absorb and combine and shape into new being . . ."

". . . The story wove itself in my mind for years before I intended to write it at all . . . When the moment came to write this story, I knew it; and I had to make quite a number of practical arrangements to get the free time for it, without fear of interruption. I wrote it as it stands except for a few pen corrections in just seven days of trance-like absorption in a small inn in rural Pennsylvania, from the early evening of November 7 to November 14, 1936. Yet I had written the central part, the scene between Mr. Hatch and Mr. Thompson, which leads up to the murder, in Basel, Switzerland, in the summer of 1932."

". . . I had been in Mexico, Bermuda, Spain, Germany, Switzerland and, best of all, in Paris for five years . . . And while I was there I was making notes of my own place . . . the south. (Looking at other countries) gave me back my past and my own home." She remembered "all the life of that soft black farming land . . . the rivers . . . the honey suckle . . . the heavy tomatoes, eaten ripe from the vine . . . the savory corn."

She told how she remembered her people, poor but not poverty-stricken, with origins in Kentucky and Tennessee, with a violence potential that broke through without warning . . . the feuds. She recalled their faces, with the prominent handsome noses with the diamond-shaped figure at the bridge, "I saw Pope Pius's picture in death the other day and I said, 'I know that nose. It looks like a Kentucky nose to me.' "

The incidents in "Noon Wine"? She didn't in the least remember the tobacco-chewing incident. But the men were always gathering in small knots, day after day, whittling and chewing and talking. She never had the courage to go close enough to hear what they were saying. She always wondered what could they find to talk about, day after day.

But all her childhood around Kyle there were sharp blades slicing tobacco. She remembered her father's knife was so sharp he could peel a pecan with four cuts through the hull, taking the meat out whole. There were blades everywhere — hoes, axes, knives, plow shares. But the children, for some reason, scarcely ever got hurt. She remembered her tall darkhaired booted relatives from West Texas, with guns in their shirts . . . You would go into a closet and there would be the long cold barrel of a shot gun or rifle, put there because the gun closet was full . . . She remembered shooting at targets and clay pigeons with her father . . . she could identify the sound of any kind of gun. And she remembered being on the patch of grass at the side of the house in a yard that was ever shrinking in size as her world became wider, and the town became smaller. She supposed she must have been small because of the way she remembered the way a table and people's legs looked to her . . . and she knew that there must have been others around her because there were always relatives around her. But all she remembered clearly was a shot gun shot breaking the stillness, followed by a wail of death.

She told of the bleary-eyed, slack, wild-talking man who came to her grandmother's one day after the shooting and the funeral. She could remember hearing him; "I swear it was in self-defense!"

"Lady, if you don't believe me, ask my wife. She won't lie."

The pitiable, shamed, bent figure sat and hoarsely said, "Yes, that's right. I saw it."

Was this the man who killed Pink Hodges? She didn't know. She remembered asking about the murder. But all she was sure of later was that it was in her ninth year.

"Suppose now," said Katherine Anne Porter, "I really saw all these persons in the flesh at one time or another? I saw what I have told you, a few mere flashes of a glimpse here and there, one time or another; but I do know why I remembered them, and why in my memory they slowly took on their separate lives in a story. It is because there radiated from each one of these glimpses of strangers some element, some quality that arrested my attention at a vital moment of my own growth, and caused me, a child, to stop short and look outward, away from myself; to look at another human being with that attention and wonder and speculation which ordinarily, and very naturally, I think, a child lavishes only on himself . . . This was a spiritual enlightenment, some tenderness, some first wakening of a charity in my self-centered heart. I am using here some very old-fashioned noble words in their prime sense. . . . I know well what they mean, and I need them here to describe as well as I am able what happens to a child when the bodily senses and the moral sense and that sense of charity are unfolding, and are touched once for all in that time when the soul is prepared for them; and I know that the all-important things in that way have all taken place long before we know the words for them."

INTERVIEW:

"Desegregation Ruling Criticized by Author," *Richmond News Leader,* 20 November 1958; in *Katherine Anne Porter: Conversations,* pp. 39–41.

As a native Southerner, Porter felt that the South had long endured unenlightened, hypocritical attacks on its segregationist heritage from other equally segregationist parts of the country. This belief informs the criticism leveled in this interview at the United States Supreme Court for striking down segregation in public schools. Despite her optimistic prediction in this November 1958 interview that Ship of Fools *would be published the following spring, she did not finish the book for nearly three more years.*

Katherine Anne Porter said here today the Supreme Court acted "recklessly and irresponsibly" in the school desegregation decision.

Her opinion on that issue popped up unexpectedly when deploring pressures to conform in the modern world, she said:

"I belong to the school of thought that believes the Supreme Court acted recklessly and irresponsibly in precipitating this crisis at the worst possible time when we already had enough crises on hand."

In the midst of saying it, the famous novelist paused to add, "I wonder what kind of trouble this may get me in, but I don't care."

("That's one of the pleasant things about growing old," she said. "As you perhaps have accomplished a little something, you feel more at home with yourself and the world and lose whatever fears you may have had.")

Miss Porter said she believed the justices "acted with moral irresponsibility because apparently they are ignorant of the true situation."

"That thing was taking care of itself very well," she added.

There is little conformity in Miss Porter.

She delivers fire-cracker opinions in soft, tentative tones, sometimes almost childlike, sometimes as if telling an engrossing fairy tale to a child.

She was dressed stylishly in black, a big silver filigree rose from Mexico on her lapel, a pizza-size gray felt hat from Paris over her soft white hair. She speaks with a wide-eyed verve and gaiety of a literary Tallulah Bankhead.

Asked what disappointed her most in contemporary America, she replied she didn't like "the way we have of taking on all the evils we were supposed to be fighting in Nazism, Fascism and Communism the oppression of the human spirit through the multiple making of petty, niggling laws."

("Although," she added, in an aside, "it's always been true that, in the strangest way, you tend to become like the thing you fight.")

What disturbs her, she said, is the tendency "to put the human spirit in a mould . . . to compress the individual into the lowest common denominator in human life."

Everything, she went on, is being organized into kinds of cartels, being done on a chain from education and government to motels and restaurants. In the attempt to make everything alike as possible, there is no room left for exploring and experimenting.

"The down-trodden minorities," she said, "are organized into tight little cabals to run the country so that we will become the down-trodden vast majority, if we don't look out."

The only things that make the world interesting, she said, "are the differences in nations and people. Why destroy that?"

Miss Porter, who likes to write of broad and subtle differences, says her favorite work always is her latest and the latest at the moment is "a great big smacking book. 200,000 words long" that will appear in late spring: *Ship of Fools.*

She got the idea when she won a Guggenheim Fellowship in 1931 and left Mexico, where she had been "attending and assisting a revolution," and traveled by ship to Europe "with the most unpleasant gang of people I ever knew."

Everything was "getting ready for the long fall," she recalls and all those aboard ship disliked each other for a variety of reasons.

"That's going to be my story," she said, "the time aboard ship from Vera Cruz to Bremerhaven, August 22 through Sept 17, 1931, an allegory of the ship of this world on a voyage to eternity."

It's going to depict the "inertia good people have toward the evils of this world, the things they allow to happen through indifference, laziness and confusion, too."

"Without knowing it," she said in another aside, "we are sometimes half in love with evil and don't stop it because it adds color and excitement to life."

She's "dead certain," she said, that the book is "the best thing I ever did," adding, laughing, "If I didn't think it was good, I wouldn't be doing it."

Her friends sometimes tease her, she said, because she is quite frank to agree when others praise something she owns and likes.

"If I didn't love it, I wouldn't have it around," she said. "And so it is with writing, I wouldn't waste my life on it if I didn't think it worthwhile. It's hard work and there are too many other wonderful things. I like too much just plain human living."

Sometimes plain living interferes. Her "lasting regret" is that she didn't have a better sense of management of life, time, and energy to finish her many projects.

"I'm leaving just bales," she said.

At times, she feels she has been wasteful, extravagant, and strewn herself around. But, she says, that has been her temperament from the restless activity of her childhood when, earlier than she can remember, she began writing, coloring, and sewing together little books.

"I was not a worldly person." she said, "but I was of this world in the sense that I wanted to touch, smell, see and be. I didn't figure it out. I just did it."

BOOK REVIEW:
Mark Schorer, "We're All on the Passenger List," review of *Ship of Fools, New York Times Book Review,* 1 April 1962, pp. 1, 5.

After spending spring 1959 at Washington and Lee, Porter, having received a generous Ford Foundation grant, decided to finish Ship of Fools *in Washington, D.C. Yet the many old friends there provided too much diversion. The only fiction she published in 1960 comprised two old stories that an assistant found when organizing her papers. "The Fig Tree," a story completed in 1929, was published in* Harper's, *and Porter was able to finish "Holiday," a story she had put aside in three versions in 1924; it won an O. Henry Award after its appearance in the December 1960 issue of* Atlantic Monthly. *Finally, under pressure from her publisher, Porter secluded herself in a quiet hotel on Cape Ann for most of spring and summer 1961, delivering the completed novel to her publisher in the fall, for publication on All Fools' Day 1962.*

The initial reviews for Ship of Fools *were generally favorable, with some reviewers, including Schorer, calling the novel a "masterpiece." The novel was a number one best-seller within a week of its publication, and before the month was out producer Stanley Kramer announced that he had bought screen rights for a guaranteed minimum of five hundred thousand dollars, with a contract providing for increased payments keyed to book sales.*

This novel has been famous for years. It has been awaited through an entire literary generation. Publishers and foundations, like many once hopeful readers, long ago gave it up. Now it is suddenly, superbly here. It would have been worth waiting for for another thirty years if one had had any hope of having them. It is our good fortune that it comes at last still in our time. It will endure, one hardly risks anything in saying, far beyond it, for many literary generations.

The novel is set in 1931. It opens on Aug. 22 in Veracruz, Mexico, when the Vera, "a mixed freight and passenger ship," is about to sail, and it ends on Sept. 17, when its passengers disembark in Bremerhaven. There are about fifty important characters, at least half of whom are major. Seventeen of the twenty-five major characters are Germans, returning to the homeland after a stay of one kind or another in Mexico. There are three Swiss, four Americans, a Swede, and a miscellany of Spaniards, Cubans and Mexicans.

Having for some years used "No Safe Harbor" as her working title, Katherine Anne Porter's final title acknowledges the organizing source of her conception in "Das Narrenschiff," Sebastian Brant's late fifteenth-century satire. Brant stayed only sporadically with his narrative conception of a shipload of fools sailing for the Land of Fools, digressing in all manner of didactic apostrophe, polemic, allusions and parallels, allegorical swellings. Miss Porter's voyage is a very real one, indeed, on her first passage to Europe.

If, like Brant's book, hers moves constantly from character to character, the dramatic point of view continually shifting, yet the controlling point of view, her perfectly poised ironical intelligence, is constant and in complete authority. If, now and then, her precise prose opens audibly into the overtones of allegory, these cannot be abstracted from the concrete details of the voyage. Yet all the time, as with any great work of art, something larger is in the air, and we know that we are on another ship as well, another voyage, sailing to another harbor.

Sebastian Brant did not exempt himself from the charge of folly but went so far as to make himself the captain of his ship of fools. Miss Porter says simply at the end of her little foreword, "I am a passenger on that ship." It will be a reader myopic to the point of blindness who does not find his name on her passenger list.

Probably many an eager graduate student is about to brush up on his German (Brant's dialect was Swabian) in order to read old Brant, and presently in certain periodicals we will be coming upon earnest analogical studies of the sort that followed upon the publication of Joyce's "Ulysses." Who knows what ingenious discoveries will be made? The Seven Deadly Sins will be marched out (and they are all unquestionably if most delicately here, but chiefly, and in every guise, "Accidia" — spiritual torpor, the paralysis of love), and someone may find in Miss Porter's two perfunctory priests not two perfunctory priests but modern instances of the corruption of the clergy in that late Middle Ages. Any such effort to get at the center of this novel would, of course, be nonsensical. "Ship of Fools," universal as its reverberating implications are, is a unique imaginative achievement.

If, as a conceptual convenience, Miss Porter has associated her novel with a medieval tradition of peculiarly harsh and not very witty satire, there is nothing (or almost nothing) harsh in her book. There is much that is comic, much even that is hilarious, and everything throughout is always flashing into brilliance through the illuminations of this great ironic style. At the same time, almost, everything that is comic is simultaneously pathetic; what is funny is also sad, moving to the point of pain, nearly of heartbreak.

No, all that is conceivably harsh in this novel is its magnificent lack of illusion about human nature and especially the human sexual relationship. Even that is not really harsh because all the sharp perception and unsparing wit of this total candor is exercised by an imaginative sympathy that is not withheld from even the greatest fool, not even from the Texan oaf, Denny, whom the gracious Mrs. Treadwell, suddenly outraged beyond endurance, beats into insensibility with the sharp heel of her lovely golden slipper.

There is no plot, not even, really, a story. Most of the major characters are presented in groups, chiefly family groups, each group with its own problem or project, and then there are a few solitary figures wandering the decks in isolation. And while the various groups become acquainted with one another and each reacts critically to the others and all interact, they are in fact all isolated. When they are not indifferent to one another, they are impelled by active hostility or chill malice. When they appear, within the groups, to be loving one another, they are usually destroying one another and themselves, if they have not already done so.

There are the Swiss Lutzes, with their stolid, unmarriageable daughter; the childless Huttens with their repulsive white bulldog, Bébé, who is nearly drowned, unfortunately not; the Baumgartners, he a hopeless alcoholic, and their frightened, defeated little boy; Jenny angel and David darling, Americans who are lovers but occupy separate cabins and who are hopelessly bound together in a symbiotic relationship based on hate and self-hate. There are an aged, miserly religious enthusiast, dying in a wheelchair, and his trapped young nephew; eight Spaniards who make up a zarzuela company — the women tarts, the men pimps — and their two demonic children called Ric and Rac. It is the Spaniards who organize the ship's party, which turns into a marvelous and absolutely disastrous Walpurgisnacht, in which every appearance of order is at last shattered and the real state of moral dishevelment is exposed in character after character, group after group of which I have named only a few.

Among the solitaries are the charming Mrs. Treadwell, a divorcée incapable of love; the attractive, gaudy Condesa, a political exile from Cuba put off on Tenerife, loved too late by the ship's doctor; the handsome Herr Freytag, returning to Germany to bring out before it is too late his beautiful Jewish wife, whom he is already beginning to resent. There are also Herr Lowenthal, the ship's pariah, a Jewish salesman of Catholic Church furnishings; a self-pitying hunchback; the Texas lout who pursues women like a sniffing dog and gets his highly satisfactory and entirely unexpected come-uppance.

Such catalogues as these cannot begin to suggest the brilliance and variety of characterization, nor the thematic unity (the fated and clumsy human quest for love and affection explicitly observed by Mrs. Treadwell) that binds all these to-

gether in the work of art even as separation is their condition in life. The Germans are particularly wonderful and horrifying creations, but even the best of the others do not escape the lash of irony or the relentless sharp prick of perception.

Set as the novel is in the years just before Hitler, and involved as it is with so many Germans and the impending German-Jewish crisis, one almost irresistibly compares it with another recent novel, Richard Hughes' "The Fox in the Attic." (The comparison is a little unfair, since the Hughes work is only the novel's first volume.) When Mr. Hughes moves from British manners to German politics, all becomes over-simplified, diagrammatic. Miss Porter, approaching the same historical situation, involves one more and more deeply in the sheer mess of human materials — these dreadful domestic relations, at once so funny and so unbearably sad.

If one is to make useful comparisons of "Ship of Fools" with other work, they should be with neither Sebastian Brant nor Richard Hughes, but with the greatest novels of the past hundred years. Call it, for convenience, the "Middlemarch" of a later day. And be grateful.

BOOK REVIEW:
Robert Drake, "A Modern Inferno," review of *Ship of Fools*, *National Review*, 12 (24 April 1962): 290–291.

Not all the reviews for Ship of Fools *were as laudatory as Shorer's, and Robert Drake was not the only critic to express the opinion that Porter's characters never learn from their experiences and that she was better at writing short stories than novels.*

Few distinguished reputations in contemporary American letters are based on slenderer evidence than that of Katherine Anne Porter — some twenty-odd short stories, with perhaps a novelette or two among them, and an assortment of critical essays. Indeed, there might be some who would insist that Miss Porter's reputation is based less on solid artistic achievement than on a self-created and perpetuated legend of it. Now I don't suppose there's a "literary person" in the United States who hasn't known for some time that Miss Porter was writing her first novel, though some seem to have been privileged to know it longer than others. (Writers, of course, no longer simply kiss and tell in diaries and letters; they do it at the round-table — and on tape too.) But after twenty years

December Atlantic ~~Page 1~~ *Main Text*

Katherine Anne Porter   3112 Q Street, N.W.
Washington, 7, D.C.

12 pages

31

(31)

HOLIDAY

By Katherine Anne Porter

1. line 30 (8)

At that time I was too young for some of the troubles I ~~keep~~ was having, and
I had not yet learned what to do with them. It no longer can matter what kind
of troubles they were, or what finally became of them. It seemed to me then
there was nothing to do but run away from them, though all my tradition, ~~background~~
background, and training had taught me unanswerably that no one except a coward ever runs away
from anything. What nonsense! They should have taught me the difference between
courage and foolhardiness, instead of leaving me to find it out for myself. I
learned finally that if I still had the sense I was born with, I would take
off like a deer at the first warning of certain dangers. But this story I
am about to tell you happened before this great truth impressed itself upon
me[,] that we do not run from the troubles and dangers that are truly ours, and
it is better to learn what they are earlier than later. *and if we don't run from the others, we fools.*

I confided to my friend Louise, a former schoolmate about my own age, not
my troubles, but my little problem: I wanted to go somewhere for a spring
holiday, by myself, to the country, and it should be very simple and nice and,
of course, not expensive, and she was not to tell any one where I had gone; but
if she liked, I would send her word now and then, if anything interesting was
~~happening~~. She said she loved getting letters, but hated answering them; and
she knew the very place for me, and she would not tell anybody anything. Louise
had then[,] she has it still[,] something near to genius for making improbable
persons, places, and situations sound attractive. She told amusing stories
that did not turn grim on you until a little while later, when by chance you
saw and heard for yourself. So with this story. Everything was just as Louise
had said, if you like, and everything was, at the same time, quite different.

" I know the very place," said Louise," a family of real old-fashioned
German peasants, in the deep blackland Texas farm country, a household in real
patriarchal style[,] the kind of thing you'd hate to live with, but is very
nice to visit. Old father, God Almighty himself, with whiskers and all; Old
Mother, matriarch in men's shoes; endless daughters and sons and ~~daughters~~
sons-in-law, and fat babies falling about the place; and fat puppies[,] my favorite
was a darling little black thing named Kuno[,] cows, calves, and sheep and lambs
and goats and turkeys and guineas roaming up and down the shallow green hills,
ducks and geese on the ponds. I was there in the summer when the peaches and

First page of the setting copy for "Holiday" in the December 1960 issue of Atlantic Monthly *(Papers of Katherine Anne Porter, Special Collections, University of Maryland at College Park Libraries). Porter based the story on a visit she and her sister Gay made to a German farming family in about 1913.*

a-borning, the novel, *Ship of Fools,* has now appeared; and it will doubtless be accorded all the respectful attention to which Miss Porter's reputation entitles it.

Ship of Fools is concerned with the voyage of the North German Lloyd *Vera* from Veracruz to Bremerhaven, August 22 to September 17, 1931, calling at Havana, Tenerife (Canary Islands), Spanish, French, and English ports. And Miss Porter has quite literally assembled all sorts and conditions of men on board "this simple almost universal image of the ship of this world on its voyage to eternity," as she calls it in a prefatory note. (Her source for this image is a fifteenth-century German moral allegory by Sebastian Brant, first published in Latin as *Stultifera Navis* in 1494.) And she has provided at the beginning a helpful *dramatis personae* (indeed, one is needed) — all the way from Captain Thiele, through assorted Germans returning to the Fatherland, a Swiss hotel-keeping family, an American divorcée, a chemical engineer, "Bohemian" artists, a Spanish dancing company, a Condesa being deported from Cuba (for political reasons), Mexican priests and a newly-wedded pair, and Cuban medical students going to study in France, on down to the "eight hundred and seventy-six souls" in steerage being deported from the Cuban sugar-fields back to the Canaries and various parts of Spain. What Miss Porter sets out to do, it seems, is to create a subtly woven tapestry depicting the Inferno in modern terms.

Anyone acquainted with her stories will know that her vision of reality is, in many ways, a theologically "orthodox" one, though she rarely dramatizes it in the "head-on," unblinking way of, say, a writer like Flannery O'Connor, whom some modern critical souls cannot accept because they say they cannot conscientiously "participate" in her vision. Significantly, they don't seem to have the same trouble with Dante: after all, that *was* a long time ago and we'll just hope it wasn't *really* true.

But an apprehension of Original Sin — call it selfishness, inclination to perversity and malice, the divided heart, or whatever you like — seems bred into every fiber of Miss Porter's sensibility, along with a profound soul-yearning, sometimes lyrically, sometimes starkly expressed, for that Other (God, Love, or whatever name you prefer) which will set free the "poor prisoner" from his isolated, sinful predicament as a human being.

In *Ship of Fools* Miss Porter has left not one human selfishness, folly, perversity, lust, or cruelty to escape from the searching glare of her inspection; the resulting diagnosis of the human condition is black enough to please Jonathan Edwards himself. There is William Denny, the chemical engineer, a walking embodiment of carnal lust of the most vulgar sort. (He has sex so much on the brain that there's hardly room for it anywhere else.) There are Ric and Rac, twin son and daughter of Lola of the Spanish dancing company (all either pimps or prostitutes), who seem the incarnation of malicious mischief in its most literal sense — juvenile Iagos. There are the "superior" Germans at the Captain's table, already, in 1931, mouthing Aryan racism, eugenics, euthanasia, and all the rest of it — drunk on ideas and abstractions (like Herr Professor Hutten), caressing (like the Captain) in their secret souls that dearest of all German words, *Verboten,* longing to impose *order* and *method* on a universe strangely reluctant to come to heel.

There is the American divorcée, Mary Treadwell, very much to the manner born, who has scorched her fingers in one attempt at love and can never, never run that risk again. There are the American "Bohemians," David Scott ("David darling") and Jenny Brown ("Jenny angel"), both trying desperately to emancipate themselves from their traditional "inhibiting" backgrounds and "express their personalities" in the world of painting and "free" living, yet irredeemably locked up inside their own petty egotism. There is the seemingly wise, compassionate Dr. Schumann, the ship's medical officer, who succumbs to the attractions of the Condesa and, in trying to sublimate his feelings, assists that unhappy, nearly mad lady down the road to drug addiction.

Through the closely wrought texture of this tapestry of total depravity weave, like the tail of a scorpion, the Cuban medical students in a seemingly endless conga-line, hysterically singing the obscener verses of "La Cucaracha." The catalogue is endless. At times, the voyagers simply take on the aspect of animals (indeed, they are often compared — in the other passengers' minds — to hyenas, monkeys, peahens, parrots, whatever animal seems appropriate); and Miss Porter seems to be the expert ringmaster putting her floating menagerie through their intricate paces. Back and forth, knot by knot across the Atlantic, Miss Porter weaves their sad stories in and out, letting in a little light, perhaps even suggesting the possibility of love and redemption, only to collapse such hopes with some new revelation of human folly or pride.

But to what end does all this lead? None, it would seem: the tapestry Miss Porter weaves with such care, and in such precise, really illuminating prose, has a good deal of the dynamic-static quality of Keats' *Grecian Urn;* the figures seem to move, yet do not move or change; they are exposed to life, yet do not seem to learn anything about it. And in the end they seem much as they were in the beginning. This mystery, like Keats' *Urn,* may tease us out of thought until we reflect that these sad souls are really in Hell — and a good orthodox, Dantesque Hell it is: they're there because they *want* to be there, indeed most of the time don't really *know* they're there. Deeper and deeper as we descend through the circles of this Inferno — and it would be hard to say just who takes pride of place in the lowest one — we realize that this is Miss Porter's grand design.

This is a wise book (one alternately marvels and shudders at Miss Porter's knowledge of the human heart); but how sad and unrelieved by any light: there is no *Purgatorio,* no *Paradiso* in Miss Porter's Divine Comedy. There seems no purgation by pity and terror, only an unqualified horror, and perhaps a weariness, at what she has come back from this shadowy world to tell us. Where are here the brooding lyricism of *Flowering Judas,* the moving tenderness of *Pale Horse, Pale Rider,* the alternating passion and serenity of *Maria Concepción?*

One wonders, finally, whether what Miss Porter has seen in her descent into the Inferno may not have been too much, even for her, and the book's structure and power suffered accordingly. Sin really *is* the dullest thing in the world, and there's the risk that all this piling up of "evidence" may be dull too. Here then is perhaps not so much a novel as a textbook on the pathology of sin. Furthermore, I'm afraid that for me, Miss Porter remains a short story writer: her "episodes" here are often brilliantly executed, but the whole structure of the book is more like a set of variations on a theme than a grand symphonic production. And sometimes, to borrow terminology from E. M. Forster, it's more *talk* than *song.* But Miss Porter has proposed a lofty end; and, if she does not always fulfill our expectations, we must nevertheless applaud a very distinguished effort — and one well worth waiting twenty years to read.

BOOK REVIEW:
Dorothy Parker, Review of *Ship of Fools, Esquire,* 58 (July 1962): 129.

Dorothy Parker reviewed Ship of Fools *with typical humor and hyperbole.*

Katherine Anne Porter's novel *Ship of Fools* took twenty years in the writing. There is never a slackening of its pace, never a lazily written passage, never a portrait roughed in. To those of us who, after filling a postcard, are obliged to lie down and have wet cloths applied to our brow, this is not a book. It's the Pyramid.

The first reviewers of the novel wrote of it to a man as allegorical, a word that always causes me to writhe with inferiority for I've had my difficulties in recognizing an allegory unless it, so to say, jumps up into my lap and licks my face. But Miss Porter made it, as she makes everything, beautifully clear in the brief explanation of her title which acts as preface. *Ship of Fools* is from a tale by Sebastian Brant published in 1494. "When I began thinking about my novel," she says, "I took for my own this simple, almost universal image of the ship of this world on its voyage to eternity. It is by no means new — it was very old and durable and dearly familiar when Brant used it; and it suits my purpose exactly. I am a passenger on that ship." She chose for the ship of her book the *Vera* out of Vera Cruz, bound for Bremerhaven. She peopled it as thickly as a battlefield. Indeed, the novel suggests a Meissonier battle scene in the perception with which each individual member of the hordes is rendered. The *Vera* is a German liner. The ship's officers are German, the year is 1931. Already there are hideous spurts of anti-Semitism — a man, impeccably Aryan, is banished from the captain's table because it had leaked out that the wife waiting at home is Jewish.

The passengers are in the thousands. In the steerage there are more than eight hundred Spaniards who had worked in the Cuban cane fields and were deported, when the sugar market collapsed, to whatever part of Spain they had come from, where no livelihood awaited them. Night and day they are jammed together on the deck, each one alone in his hopelessness, each one frantic in his bewilderment. The rest of the list are mostly Germans, and there are only four Americans — not one of whom should make us proud. There are some Cubans and Mexicans, a

Porter at the time she completed Ship of Fools

lone vehement Swede, and a gaggle of migratory Spanish dancers on the way back from being stranded in Mexico — four young women of many too many evenings and four of their slinky salesmen and, somehow attached to them, a pair of six-year-old twins, brats straight out of hell. The twins, knowing that the ladies and gentlemen of the group plan to steal pearls from an elderly Spanish noblewoman, fix their wagon by getting the pearls first and tossing them overboard. Crazed by the success of this caper they seize a poor old bulldog, a big bumbling creature not overbright and afflicted with seasickness from the moment the gangplank was up, but still the shining light in the life of two gentle souls, his owners. The twins throw the old dog overboard; a young man in the steerage sees, and jumps after him into the water. The dog is saved, but the man himself is drowned to live afterward in the indignant memory of the passengers as a fool.

There are very few glimpses of happy young love so far as I can see — these are of a Mexican honeymoon couple, and there is other young love in the persons of two American painters who, liv-

ing together without benefit of clergy, express their passions only by quarrels.

There is a fine portrait of a raffish old Spanish noblewoman — the one without her pearls — long resident in Cuba, now sent away into exile. She is attended by perhaps the most decent character in the book — a doctor who would like to help her and she, I suppose, would like to help him, but her help is always amatory. You cannot begin to go into the sadnesses of this pair, for she is going into exile and he is going back home to die of his long illness. There is . . . there is . . . there are . . . for heaven's sake who do I think I am trying to put twenty years of work into half a glossy page.

I never said it was a cheery book. I never said it was like those books that have so often been written about ship's companies — those bubbly bits of gaiety on the high seas. But I do say and I think I shall go on saying: My God, here is a book.

BOOK REVIEW:
"Clear Colours," review of *Collected Stories,*
    Times Literary Supplement, 9 January 1964,
    p. 21.

The disappointment Porter felt at the mixed reviews for Ship of Fools *and its failure to win any major book awards was eased when* The Collected Stories of Katherine Anne Porter *won a National Book Award and a Pulitzer Prize in 1966. The British edition, which includes fewer stories, was published first and was well received.*

"As for aesthetic bias, my one aim is to tell a straight story and to give true testimony," Katherine Anne Porter once wrote about herself. To see what she means by true testimony it is best to turn first to the three long short stories published here a quarter of a century ago under the title *Pale Horse, Pale Rider,* for these show her mature art at full stretch. The finest of them, "Old Mortality," tells the story of Amy, a Southern beauty who first jilts and then marries her second cousin Gabriel, and after six weeks of marriage dies through taking an overdose of drugs. But such a description is wretchedly inadequate, for the whole beauty of the story lies in the subtlety of its telling. This commonplace late-nineteenth-century tragedy is illuminated because it is seen through the eyes of Miranda, first as a child piecing together the mysterious bits and pieces told her about the dead and therefore distant Aunt Amy, then a year or two later when Miranda and her sister go to the races with their father and meet Uncle Gabriel, fat, drunken, and totally unimaginable as a romantic lover, and finally eight years later still when Miranda returns to the home from which she has become estranged through an elopement, for Uncle Gabriel's funeral. By these shifts of time and emphasis Miss Porter conveys different aspects of truth — Miranda's encounter in the last scene with a comic spinster of her childhood, an ardent advocate of votes for women, is a brilliant device in the new light it sheds on Aunt Amy and on relationships within the family. It is the shifts of time, too, that help her to show the shape, pattern and colour of life in the American South, and to suggest the immense gulf that opens between parents and children, between youth and age. At the end, returning home for the funeral, Miranda feels at last able to wrench herself free from the illusory past, "other people's memory of the past, at which she had spent her life peering like a child at a magic-lantern show." She asks herself, "Where are my own people and my own time?," and believes that she at least will not become caught in the mesh of legend.

This masterly story contains much of what Miss Porter has to say in other pieces about the South, for the past of which she seems to feel a wistful longing that makes one doubt her remark that she lacks "respect for caste of any kind, social, intellectual or whatever." A series of stories grouped together under the title "The Old Order," which deal with Miranda's family and the whole ambience of her early life, evoke with skill and unsentimental tenderness the world in which grandmother as a baby pointed to a pot-bellied Negro child and said, "I want that one to play with," and in which the pot-bellied child grew into Miranda's respected Nannie, an old woman linked in a curious relationship quite unlike that of slave and slave-owner with the grandmother who had wanted her as a plaything many years ago. Fine as they are, however, these stories and sketches lack the depth of "Old Mortality" and of some other pieces, in particular the other long story concerning Miranda, "Pale Horse, Pale Rider." This is an account of her love affair at the end of the First World War with a young soldier. From the beginning of the story Miranda has a premonition of death, and its whole atmosphere is one of a poetic unreality which reflects Miranda's feverish illness. She collapses, the young soldier nurses her, she is taken to hospital and then, when we are prepared for her death,

Miss Porter disconcerts us as she has done in other stories, with an ending in which Miranda recovers and the young soldier dies.

These two tales are the magnificent peaks of Miss Porter's achievement as a short-story writer, but there is much to admire in the earlier stories collected here as *Flowering Judas,* or in the later account of a young American's experiences in Berlin in the early 1930s, "The Leaning Tower." There is a passage in this story, vivid and savage as a George Grosz drawing, which describes fat Berliners staring into two shop windows, one filled with pig, "fresh, smoked, salted, baked, roasted, pickled, spiced, and jellied," the other with sugar pigs and chocolate sausages. These Berliners lead dogs which wear their winter clothes, wool sweaters, fur muffs, fleece-lined rubber boots. The unemployed, blind, mutilated, ill, beg on the pavements.

In spite of the social comment implied in such a scene and although she says that "politically my bent is to the left," Miss Porter is not in the least a political artist. She cannot be labeled in this way, any more than she can be called a Southern writer. Her work shows, indeed, few signs of social or literary influences, and the criticism that has compared her with Hemingway seems as maladroit as that comparing her with Katherine Mansfield. She is one of those original artists who half-deliberately develop their talents in isolation rather than by the exchange of ideas with friends, working through dozens of failures to the discovery of their talent's true nature. She has paid no attention to literary fashion and has not engaged in any kind of verbal experimentation, yet her temperament and sympathies make her entirely modern. Perhaps the most constant thing in her work is its continual fresh flow of feeling and sympathy. She seems both to be participating in the feelings of her characters and to be standing back so that she can make detached historical observations which contain no hint of moral comment. In her finest work this involves the use of a sensibility as delicately selective as that of any living writer. To tell a straight story and to give true testimony has been only the beginning of her art.

BOOK REVIEW:

V. S. Pritchett, "Stones and Stories," review of *The Lonely Voice,* by Frank O'Connor, and *The Collected Stories,* by Porter, *New Statesman,* 67 (10 January 1964): 47–48.

Himself a master of short fiction, V. S. Pritchett devoted most of his review of books by Porter and Frank O'Connor to praising Porter.

The novelist is concerned with many things; the short-story writer with one thing that implies many. Singularity and intensity are the essence of his art. This is obvious in the finest practitioners. They depend on a marked personal attitude. Where the novelist is immolated eventually in his subject, the story writer seems to depend on being perpetually visible: Frank O'Connor, who is entitled to talk on the subject, says that whereas in the novel there is always some character with whom the reader identifies himself, in the short story one is forced to identify oneself with the glance or, it may be, the vision of the writer, for so much is projected which is not actually put down. I doubt whether what Mr. O'Connor says about the novel is true, after adolescence. Since when did we, except in the most sophisticated sense, identify ourselves with Madame Bovary? A more interesting idea is that the short story flourishes in societies that are unformed, or are in a state of crisis, drift and fragmentation. This would certainly be true of the preeminence of Italian, Russian, American and Irish writers in the genre. Life has not turned their subjects into the novelists' solid pudding — they turn up like scattered ingredients. O'Connor is illuminating about aspects of Chekhov, and although hostile, very pointed about Kipling's oratorical manner. The notes on method are discerning.

Katherine Anne Porter's stories have rightly had the highest reputation in America since they first appeared in the early Thirties. Her scene changes often, a good sign. Her subjects bear out O'Connor's theory: Mexico, but in revolution; life in the decaying American South, in rootless New York, in hysterical post-1914 Berlin. Where she settles she writes from the inside. Her singularity is truthfulness: it comes out in the portrait of Laura, the virginal but reckless American schoolteacher in "Flowering Judas" who has ventured her political and personal chastity among the vanities and squalors of the Mexican revolution, perhaps as a religious exercise. She is a good old Calvinist-Catholic:

> But she cannot help feeling that she has been betrayed irresponsibly by the disunion between her way of living and her feeling of what life should be, and at times she is almost contented to rest in this sense of grievance as a private consolation. Sometimes she wishes to run away but she stays.

Laura wishes to live near enough to violent passion to be singed by it and is willing to pay for the experience in terrifying dreams. The Mexicans appeal to her because of their boundless vanity, their violence, their ability to forget and their indifference: Miss Porter austerely tests her characters against things that are elemental or ineluctable — a classical writer. There is a point at which life or circumstance does not give: when human beings come to this point she is ready for them. Braggoni, the Stalin-like Mexican revolutionary leader, is at this point: he is identified in a frightening, yet slightly fatuous and amicable way with the shady needs of revolution.

In the tale "Maria Concepcion" it is the respectable churchwoman, with her classical Christian sense of the rights of jealousy and vengeance, who murders and who is backed up by the villagers. Her husband will punish her: she accepts that. In "Noon Wine" we have an incompetent poor white farmer whose fortunes are saved by a Swedish hired hand down from Dakota. The hand speaks to no one, slaves night and day and consoles himself only by playing the harmonica. Years pass and then a blackmailer comes down from Dakota to reveal that the Swede is a murderous escaped lunatic. The farmer, faced with losing his saviour, kills the blackmailer. The Swede runs away, consoled by his harmonica. The poor farmer has nothing but a sense of social injustice. He kills himself out of self-pity.

Katherine Anne Porter does not find her tests only in these Verga-like subjects. The girl reporter and the soldier-boy in New York "dig in" in spiritual self-defense against the hysteria of the 1914 war. The choice is between reality and illusion and the reality is harder to bear. It is no reward. It is the same in the comic tale of the Depression: the domestic war between the out-of-work Irishman turned windbag and drunk and his avaricious and scornful wife who keeps him and ends by beating him up with a knotted towel. Violent: these classical heroes and heroines are always that. Again, in the comical sad history of the old Southern aunts and cousins one sees that Aunt Amy was wild, amusing, cruel and destructive because she knew she would soon die: she had inner knowledge of Fate. Killed, she could be a killer. Old Granny Weatherall fights to the last drop of consciousness on her death-bed because her pride will not really accept, even now, that she was once jilted as a girl. And that is not funny, it is terrifying. To every human being there eventually comes — Miss Porter seems to say — the shock of perception of something violent or rock-like in themselves, in others, or in circumstance. We awaken to primitive knowledge and become impersonal in our tragedies. There will arise a terrible moment of crisis, a kind of illness, when, for Laura, there will be *no* disunion between her way of living and her feeling for what life should be. She will discover what life is. It is something out of one's control, scarcely belonging to one, and that has to be borne as if one were a stone.

Miss Porter's singularity as a writer is in her truthful explorations of a complete consciousness of life. Her prose is severe and exact; her ironies are subtle but hard. If she is arbitrary it is because she identifies a conservative with a classical view of human nature. Laura listens to Braggoni with "pitiless courtesy" because she dare not smile at his bad performance on the guitar:

> He is so vain of his talents and so sensitive to slights that it would require a cruelty and vanity greater than his own to lay a finger on the vast careless world of his self-esteem.

Miss Porter has a fine power of nervous observation. Her picture of Berlin in the Isherwood period is eerie and searching. She sees everything that disturbs. She notices peculiar local things that one realises afterwards are true: how often, for example, the Berliners' eyes filled with tears when they were suddenly faced with small dilemmas. Hysteria is near to the surface. Yet the tears were a kind of mannerism. Her power to make a landscape, a room, a group of people, thinkingly alive is not the vague, brutal talent of the post-Hemingway reporter but belongs to the explicit Jamesian period and suggests the whole rather than the surface of a life. Her stories are thoroughly planted. It is true that she is chastely on the edge of her subjects, that one catches the wild look of the runaway in her eyes; but if her manner is astringent it is not precious. She is an important writer in the genre because she solves the essential problem: how to satisfy exhaustively in writing briefly.

BOOK REVIEW:
Granville Hicks, "A Tradition of Storytelling," review of *The Collected Stories, Saturday Review,* 48 (25 September 1965): 35–36.

Granville Hicks had found that Ship of Fools *"leaves the reader a little cold," but he considered "almost every story" in* The Collected Stories *"absolutely right." Though he got some of the facts wrong when he wrote this review, he was proba-*

bly right to conclude that Porter's reputation will rest on her short fiction. (His most obvious error is the statement that Porter began work on a study of Jonathan Edwards when, in fact, she started a biography of an earlier Puritan, Cotton Mather.)

In an interview that appeared in *Paris Review,* Katherine Anne Porter said, "We've always had great letter writers, readers, great storytellers in our family. I've listened all my life to articulate people. They were all great storytellers, and every story had shape and meaning and point." Flannery O'Connor often remarked that the habit of telling stories persisted in the South and was an important part of the inheritance of any Southern writer. Be that as it may — and not all of our good storytellers have come from the South, though several of them have — Miss Porter did somehow learn to write short stories of the highest order.

In *Collected Stories* (Harcourt, Brace & World, $5.95) we have all the stories that appeared in *Flowering Judas, Pale Horse, Pale Rider,* and *The Leaning Tower,* together with four stories not previously published in book form. Her first story written for publication, "María Concepción," is here, and it is one of the best, written with a firmness that she often equaled but never surpassed. She says that Carl Van Doren, who accepted the story for the *Century Magazine* in 1923, said to her, "I believe you are a writer!" She quickly proved that he was right.

She wrote several other stories about Mexico, including "Flowering Judas" and "Hacienda." She had gone to Mexico about 1920 to study the renascence of Mexican art, and not only the art but the whole life of the people had stirred her imagination. No doubt she would have become a writer if she had never crossed the Rio Grande, but Mexico did inspire her earliest and some of her best stories.

The collection called *Flowering Judas,* containing the Mexican stories and several others, appeared in 1930. Nine years later Miss Porter published *Pale Horse, Pale Rider,* which was made up of three short novels. (She objects, perhaps unreasonably, to both "novelette" and "novella.") In the first of these, "Old Mortality," she draws on family and personal material, setting forth the legend of Aunt Amy as reconstructed by a girl named Miranda, to be identified with the author. If Mexico was her first important theme, the strength of family ties was her second.

The title story, in which Miranda is the central character, has its climax in an extraordinarily vivid account of her nearly fatal illness during the flu epidemic of 1918. The third story, "Noon Wine," unlike its two companions, is a sternly objective study of farmers in Texas at the turn of the century. The volume showed that Miss Porter was as much a master of what Henry James called "the blessed *nouvelle*" as she was of the short story.

At this time, about 1940, it was announced that Miss Porter was working on a study of Jonathan Edwards and was also writing her first novel, tentatively called "No Safe Harbor." The biography was not finished, but the novel appeared in 1962 as *Ship of Fools*. Meanwhile a third collection of shorter fiction, *The Leaning Tower*, had been published in 1944. This included several excellent sketches of the life of her family in Texas, under the general name of "The Old Order." The title story, describing the experiences and impressions of a young American in Germany in 1931, was in some ways a new departure for the author and perhaps looked forward to *Ship of Fools*. A story that was not included in the original edition of *The Leaning Tower*, "Holiday," seems to me one of her best.

Discussing *The Leaning Tower*, Edmund Wilson wrote: "To the reviewer, Miss Porter is baffling because one cannot take hold of her work in any of the ordinary ways. She makes none of the melodramatic or ironic points that are the stock in trade of ordinary short story writers; she falls into none of the usual patterns and she does not show anyone's influence. She does not exploit her personality either inside or outside her work, and her writing itself makes a surface so smooth that the critic has little opportunity to point out peculiarities of color or weave. If he is tempted to say that the effect is pale, he is prevented by the realization that Miss Porter writes English of a purity and precision almost unique in contemporary fiction."

It is indeed difficult to define the exact quality of Miss Porter's stories and short novels. She has none of the wild inventiveness so startling in some of Faulkner's tales, nor does she build so surely to a climax as Hemingway did. She cannot create an atmosphere with Eudora Welty's richness and beauty, and one does not have the sense of experiencing an almost overwhelming revelation as one does with the best stories of Bernard Malamud and Flannery O'Connor. And yet one has the feeling, with almost every story, that it is absolutely right.

In her brief preface Miss Porter speaks of one of her stories: "'Holiday' represents one of my prolonged struggles, not with questions of form or style, but my own moral and emotional collision with a human situation I was too young to cope with at the time it occurred; yet the story haunted me for years and I made three separate versions, with a certain spot in all three where the thing went off track. So I put it away and it disappeared also, and I forgot it. It rose from one of my boxes of paper, after a quarter of a century, and I sat down in great excitement to read all three versions. I saw at once that the first was the right one, and as for the vexing question which had stopped me short long ago, it had in the course of living settled itself so slowly and deeply and secretly I wondered why I had ever been distressed by it. I changed one short paragraph and one line or two at the end and it was done."

She knew when the story wasn't right, although she didn't know why, and she knew when it was right. By and large, by her own account, she has not had problems of revision. "My stories," she said, "are written in one draft, and if short enough, at one sitting." She has also said, "I started 'Flowering Judas' at seven P.M. and at one-thirty I was standing on a snowy windy corner putting it in the mailbox." Obviously the story was right in her mind, or nearly right, before she sat down to put it on paper, and when she had written it out, it was close to perfection. With very few exceptions, the stories in this volume are first-rate, and I believe that it is on them, rather than on *Ship of Fools*, that her reputation will rest.

INTERVIEW:

Haskel Frankel, "The Author," *Saturday Review*, 48 (25 September 1965): 36.

After spending nearly a year, from autumn 1962 to autumn 1963, in Europe, Porter returned to the Washington area, where she lived for the rest of her life. This interview was conducted in the house in Spring Valley, Maryland, that she rented in 1964. Although she was still talking about publishing her biography of Cotton Mather, she never completed the book.

She is seventy-five years old and a truly beautiful woman. From her crown of white hair ("I've been on borrowed time since 1918, when I nearly died in the plague; that was when my hair turned white.") to her lovely legs Katherine Anne Porter is intensely alive.

We were seated at a six-foot circle of Vermont marble Miss Porter had had cut for her dining-room table in the twelve-room house she had leased just outside Washington, D.C., a year ago last June. "I think they describe this house as Jacobean," she said. "I call it 1905 American Stratford-on-Avon."

"I live like a hermit here. I'm not going anywhere, not traveling any more. I have an income now, thank God. I'm getting $1,000 on October 6 for yapping at the Library of Congress. This year I have refused $17,000 worth of speaking engagements — and I have lived on as little as $1,500 a year! It's just not worth it. I might die of it, and I have the utmost partiality for living."

She is a joy to listen to, a pleasure to watch, as she rattles on with a Southern softness to her speech, a touch of the Bankhead huskiness to her laughter. To underline an idea, she will slide her arm along the tabletop, lean toward you, and capture you in her eyes, which shade somewhere between amber and blue. She smiles, she laughs, she slurs a soft "honey" at you — she is all woman. And there are the little moments when, suddenly, her eyes are seeing something beyond the silver-gray silk walls of the dining room, a something that *was* that touches her face with a bygone sadness. And then, just as suddenly, she is back without telling you where she has been.

"I don't live in my art like a fish in water. I have an intensely private life. My relationships with family and friends are most important to me. I could have written fifty books during the time I've spent writing to family and friends. People have told me that they have sold letters of mine or willed them to universities. I'm farmed out all over the place. Those people who have sold me have forgotten that they also wrote to me. Well, I'm a magpie. I'm not going to let one of the letters I have out of my hands until I'm dead and gone."

Is she at work at the moment? "I have a medieval mystery in mind. And a book of occasional writings; I have twenty-five or thirty things to add to it. And there is my study of Cotton Mather and Salem witchcraft. I started it in 1928. I have added no fictions of my own. It's historical. Every bloody line — forgive me — is documented. I did eleven out of the twenty chapters in five months, working around the clock in Bermuda. Nobody knew me then. I wish it was that way now."

She arose to take me on a tour of her home. "I've lived for so long out of one suitcase. I decided that if I had to live under a roof, like others, I

Porter in 1965

I would not have anything that wasn't good. Well, everything here is original. It looks fine and expensive, and it is. The only folly is that." She pointed to a silver-based vase of glass etched with leaves and grapes. "It's nouveau art. I found it in Georgetown at the Child Jesus Thrift Shop. I couldn't resist that!"

In her home are the treasures that during the past forty years Katherine Anne Porter has discovered and loved: an eighteenth-century Waterford crystal chandelier in the dining room, an amber colored Lalique chandelier in the living room, a cupboard from Avila dating back to 1600, a bell jar containing a wire tree of hand-painted eggs presented for her on birthdays and holidays by a favorite nephew, a walnut trestle table that dates back to 1450 and belonged to a Fiesole monastery, Madame de Pompadour's dressing table, which she has in her bedroom. Katherine Anne Porter has created a showplace that is not for show.

"I am just the happiest person in the world," she said. "All the physical appetites have subsided a little, the mental and emotional have sharpened.

"I'm a tough person. If I weren't I wouldn't be here. I have no fear of death, no horror of it. I've been too near it. Twice in the past year I've been given the rites for the dying — once in Guadalajara, once in Dallas — but I've held on. I remember saying to the doctor in Dallas, 'Why didn't you let me go?' He looked at me slightly shocked. 'We can't do that sort of thing in hospitals,' he said. I told him, 'Well, the next time I'll stay at home!'"

ESSAY:
Eudora Welty, "Katherine Anne Porter: The Eye of the Story," in her *The Eye of the Story: Selected Essays and Reviews* (New York: Random House, 1977), pp. 30–40.

The December 1965 issue of The Yale Review *includes two perceptive essays about Porter's short fiction by two old friends, Eudora Welty and Robert Penn Warren. Welty's essay, revised for publication in her* The Eye of the Story: Selected Essays and Reviews *(1977), focuses on Porter's ability to portray the inner lives of her characters.*

In "Old Mortality" how stirring the horse race is! At the finish the crowd breaks into its long roar "like the falling walls of Jericho." This we hear, and it is almost like seeing, and we know Miss Lucy has won. But beyond a fleeting glimpse — the "mahogany streak" of Miss Lucy on the track — we never get much sight of the race with our eyes. What we see comes afterward. Then we have it up close: Miss Lucy bleeding at the nose. For Miranda has got to say "That's winning too." The race would never have got into the story except that Miranda's heart is being prepared to reject victory, to reject the glamour of the race and the cheering grandstand; to distrust from now on all evidence except what she, out of her own experience, can testify to. By the time we *see* Miss Lucy, she is a sight for Miranda's eyes alone: as much symbol as horse.

Most good stories are about the interior of our lives, but Katherine Anne Porter's stories take place there; they show surface only at her choosing. Her use of the physical world is enough to meet her needs and no more; she is not wasteful with anything. This artist, writing her stories with a power that stamps them to their last detail on the memory, does so to an extraordinary degree without sensory imagery.

I have the most common type of mind, the visual, and when first I began to read her stories it stood in the way of my trust in my own certainty of what was there that, for all my being bowled over by them, I couldn't see them happening. This was a very good thing for me. As her work has

done in many other respects, it has shown me a thing or two about the eye of fiction, about fiction's visibility and invisibility, about its clarity, its radiance.

Heaven knows she can see. Katherine Anne Porter has seen all her life, sees today, most intimately, most specifically, and down to the bones, and she could date the bones. There is, above all, "Noon Wine" to establish it forever that when she wants a story to be visible, it is. "Noon Wine" is visible all the way through, full of scenes charged with dramatic energy; everything is brought forth into movement, dialogue; the title itself is Mr. Helton's tune on the harmonica. "Noon Wine" is the most beautifully objective work she has done. And nothing has been sacrificed to its being so (or she wouldn't have done it); to the contrary. I find Mr. Hatch the scariest character she ever made, and he's just set down there in Texas like a chair. There he stands, part of the everyday furniture of living. He's opaque, and he's the devil. Walking in at Mr. Thompson's gate — the same gate by which his tracked-down victim walked in first — he is that much more horrifying, almost too solid to the eyes to be countenanced. (So much for the visual mind.)

Katherine Anne Porter has not in general chosen to cast her stories in scenes. Her sense of human encounter is profound, is fundamental to her work, I believe, but she has not often allowed it the dramatic character it takes in "Noon Wine." We may not see the significant moment happen within the story's present; we may not watch it occur between the two characters it joins. Instead, a silent blow falls while one character is alone — the most alone in his life, perhaps. (And this is the case in "Noon Wine" too.) Often the revelation that pierces a character's mind and heart and shows him his life or his death comes in a dream, in retrospect, in illness or in utter defeat, the moment of vanishing hope, the moment of dying. What Miss Porter makes us see are those subjective worlds of hallucination, obsession, fever, guilt. The presence of death hovering about Granny Weatherall she makes as real and brings as near as Granny's own familiar room that stands about her bed — realer, nearer, for we recognize not only death's presence but the character death has come in for Granny Weatherall.

The flash of revelation is revelation but is unshared. But how unsuspecting we are to imagine so for a moment — it *is* shared, and by ourselves, her readers, who must share it feeling the doubled anguish of knowing this fact, doubled still again when it is borne in upon us how close to life this is, to *our* lives.

It is to be remembered that the world of fiction is not of itself visible. A story may or may not be born in sensory images in a given writer's mind. Experience itself is stored in no telling how many ways in a writer's memory. (It was "the sound of the sea, and Beryl fanning her hair at the window" that years later and thousands of miles away brought Katherine Mansfield to writing "At the Bay.") But if the physical world *is* visible or audible in the story, it has to be made so. Its materialization is as much a created thing as are the story's characters and what they think or do or say.

Katherine Anne Porter shows us that we do not have to see a story happen to know what is taking place. For all we are to know, she is not looking at it happen herself when she writes it; for her eyes are always looking through the gauze of the passing scene, not distracted by the immediate and transitory; her vision is reflective.

Her imagery is as likely as not to belong to a time other than the story's present, and beyond that it always differs from it in nature; it is *memory* imagery, coming into the story from memory's remove. It is a distilled, a re-formed imagery, for it is part of a language made to speak directly of premonition, warning, surmise, anger, despair.

It was soon borne in upon me that Katherine Anne Porter's moral convictions have given her readers another way to see. Surely these convictions represent the fixed points about which her work has turned, and not only that, but they govern her stories down to the smallest detail. Her work has formed a constellation, with its own North Star.

Is the writer who does not give us the pictures and bring us the sounds of a story as it unfolds shutting out part of life? In Katherine Anne Porter's stories the effect has surely been never to diminish life but always to intensify life in the part significant to her story. It is a darkening of the house as the curtain goes up on this stage of her own.

Her stories of Mexico, Germany, Texas all happen there: where love and hate, trust and betrayal happen. And so their author's gaze is turned not outward but inward, and has confronted the mysterious dark from her work's beginning.

Since her subject is what lies beneath the surface, her way — quite direct — is to penetrate, brush the stuff away. It is the writer like Chekhov whose way of working is indirect. He moved indeed toward the same heart and core but by building up some corresponding illusion of life. Writers of Chekhov's side of the family are themselves illusionists and have necessarily a certain fondness for, lenience toward, the whole shimmering fabric as such. Here we have the professional scientist, the good doctor, working with illusion and the born romantic artist — is she not? — working without it. Perhaps it is always the lyrical spirit that takes on instantaneous color, shape, pattern of motion in work, while the meditative spirit must fly as quickly as possible out of the shell.

All the stories she has written are moral stories about love and the hate that is love's twin, love's impostor and enemy and death. Rejection, betrayal, desertion, theft roam the pages of her stories as they roam the world. The madam kicking the girl in "Magic" and the rest of the brutality in the characters' treatment of one another; the thieving that in one form or another infects their relationships; the protests they make, from the weakness of false dreams or of lying down with a cold cloth over the eyes, on up to towering rages — all this is a way of showing to the inward eye: Look at what you are doing to human love.

We hear in how many more stories than the one the litany of the little boy at the end of "The Downward Path to Wisdom," his "comfortable, sleeping song": "I hate Papa, I hate Mama, I hate Grandma, I hate Uncle David, I hate Old Janet, I hate Marjory, I hate Papa, I hate Mama . . . " It is like the long list of remembered losses in the story "Theft" made vocal, and we remember how that loser's decision to go on and let herself be robbed coincides with the rising "in her blood" of a "deep almost murderous anger."

"If one is afraid of looking into a face, one hits the face," remarked W. B. Yeats, and I think we must conclude that to Katherine Anne Porter's characters this face is the challenging face of love itself. And I think it is the faces — the inner, secret faces — of her characters, in their self-delusion, their venom and pain, that their author herself is contemplating. More than either looking at the face or hitting it, she has made a story out of her anger.

If outrage is the emotion she has most strongly expressed, she is using outrage as her cool instrument. She uses it with precision to show what monstrosities of feeling come about not from the lack of the existence of love but from love's repudiation, betrayal. From which there is no safety anywhere. Granny Weatherall, eighty, wise, affectionate and good, and now after a full life dying in her bed with the priest beside her, "knew hell when she saw it."

The anger that speaks everywhere in the stories would trouble the heart for their author whom we love except that her anger is pure, the reason for it evident and clear, and the effect exhilarating. She has made it the tool of her work; what we do is rejoice in it. We are aware of the compassion that guides it, as well. Only compassion could have looked where she looks, could have seen and probed what she sees. Real compassion is perhaps always in the end unsparing; it must make itself a part of knowing. Self-pity does not exist here; the stories come out trenchant, bold, defying; they are tough as sanity, unrelinquished sanity, is tough.

Despair is here, as well described as if it were Mexico. It is a despair, however, that is robust and sane, open to negotiation by the light of day. Life seen as a savage ordeal has been investigated by a straightforward courage, unshaken nerve, a rescuing wit, and above all, with the searching intelligence that is quite plainly not to be daunted. In the end the stories move us not to despair ourselves but to an emotion quite opposite because they are so seriously and clear-sightedly pointing out what they have been formed to show: that which is true under the skin, that which will remain a fact of the spirit.

Miranda, by the end of "Old Mortality" rebelling against the ties of the blood, resenting their very existence, planning to run away now from these and as soon as she can from her own escape into marriage, Miranda saying "I hate loving and being loved," is hating what destroys loving and what prevents being loved. She is, in her own particular and her own right, fighting back at the cheat she has discovered in all that's been handed down to her as gospel truth.

Seeing what is not there, putting trust in a false picture of life, has been one of the worst nightmares that assail her characters. "My dreams never renege on me, Mr. Richards. They're all I have to go by," says Rosaleen. (The Irish are no better than the Southerners in this respect.) Not only in the comic and touching Rosaleen, the lovely and sentient and tragic Miranda, but in many other characters throughout the stories we watch the romantic and the anti-romantic pulling each other to pieces. Is the romantic ever scotched? I believe not. Even if there rises a new refrain, even if the most ecstatic words ever spoken turn out to be "I hate

you," the battle is not over for good. That battle is in itself a romance.

Nothing is so naturally subject to false interpretation as the romantic, and in furnishing that interpretation the Old South can beat all the rest. Yet some romantic things happen also to be true. Miss Porter's stories are not so much a stand against the romantic as such, as a repudiation of the false. What alone can instruct the heart is the experience of living, experience which can be vile; but what can never do it any good, what harms it more than vileness, are those tales, those legends of more than any South, those universal false dreams, the hopes sentimental and ubiquitous, which are not on any account to be gone by.

For there comes a confrontation. It is then that Miss Porter's characters, behaving so entirely like ourselves, make the fatally wrong choice. Enter betrayal. Again and again, enter betrayal. We meet the betrayal that lies in rejection, in saying No to others or No to the self, or that lies with still more cunning in saying Yes when this time it should have been No.

And though we are all but sure what will happen, we are possessed by suspense.

It appears to me irrelevant whether or not the story is conceived and put down in sensory images, whether or not it is dramatic in construction, so long as its hold is a death-grip. In my own belief, the suspense — so acute and so real — in Katherine Anne Porter's work never did depend for its life on disclosure of the happenings of the narrative (nothing is going to turn out very well) but in the writing of the story, which becomes one single long sustained moment for the reader. Its suspense is one with its meaning. It must arise, then, from the mind, heart, spirit by which it moves and breathes.

It is a current like a strand of quicksilver through the serenity of her prose. In fiction of any substance, serenity can only be an achievement of the work itself, for any sentence that is alive with meaning is speaking out of passion. Serenity never belonged to the *now* of writing; it belongs to the later *now* offered its readers. In Katherine Anne Porter's work the forces of passion and self-possession seem equal, holding each other in balance from one moment to the next. The suspense born of the writing abides there in its own character, using the story for its realm, a quiet and well-commanded suspense, but a genie.

There was an instinct I had, trustworthy or not, that the matter of visibility in her stories had something to do with time. Time permeates them. It is a grave and formidable force.

Ask what time it is in her stories and you are certain to get the answer: the hour is fateful. It is not necessary to see the hands of the clock in her work. It is a time of racing urgency, and it is already too late. And then recall how many of her characters are surviving today only for the sake of tomorrow, are living on tomorrow's coming; think how we see them clearest in reference to tomorrow. Granny Weatherall, up to the last — when God gives her no sign acceptable to her and jilts her Himself — is thinking: "There was always so much to be done, let me see: tomorrow." Laura in "Flowering Judas" is "waiting for tomorrow with a bitter anxiety as if tomorrow may not come." Ordinary, self-respecting and — up to a certain August day — fairly well blessed Mr. Thompson, because he has been the one to kill the abominable Mr. Hatch, is self-tried, self-pleaded for, and self-condemned to no tomorrow; neither does he leave his sons much of a tomorrow, and certainly he leaves still less of one to poor, red-eyed Mrs. Thompson, who had "so wanted to believe that tomorrow, or at least the day after, life, such a battle at best, was going to be better." In "Old Mortality" time takes Miranda by the hand and leads her into promising herself "in her hope-fulness, her ignorance": "At least I can know the truth about what happens to me." In "Pale Horse, Pale Rider" the older Miranda asks Adam, out of her suffering, "Why can we not save each other?" and the straight answer is that there is no time. The story ends with the unforgettable words "Now there would be time for everything" because tomorrow has turned into oblivion, the ultimate betrayer is death itself.

But time, one of the main actors in her stories — teacher, fake healer, conspirator in betrayal, ally of death — is also, within the complete control of Miss Porter, with his inimical powers made use of, one of the movers of her writing, a friend to her work. It occurred to me that what is *seeing* the story is the dispassionate eye of time. Her passionate mind has asked itself, schooled itself, to use time's eye. Perhaps Time is the genie's name.

Laura is stuck in time, we are told in "Flowering Judas" — and told in the timeless present tense of dreaming, a brilliant working upon our very nerves to let us know precisely Laura's dilemma. There is in all Katherine Anne Porter's work the strongest sense of unity in all the parts; and if it is in any degree a sound guess that an im-

portant dramatic element in the story has another role, a working role, in the writing of the story, might this not be one source of a unity so deeply felt? Such a thing in the practice of an art is unsurprising. Who can separate a story from the story's writing?

And there is too, in all the stories, a sense of long, learning life, the life that is the story's own, beginning from very far back, extending somewhere into the future. As we read, the initial spark is not being struck before our eyes; the fire we see has already purified its nature and burns steadied by purpose, unwavering in meaning. It is no longer impulse, it is a signal, a beacon.

To me, it is the image of the eye of time that remains the longest in the mind at her story's end. There is a judgment to be passed. A moral judgment has to be, in all reason, what she has been getting at. But in a still further act of judiciousness, I feel, she lets Time pass that judgment.

Above all, I feel that what we are responding to in Katherine Anne Porter's work is the intensity of its life, which is more powerful and more profound than even its cry for justice.

They are excoriating stories. Does she have any hope for us at all? Well, do we not feel its implication everywhere — a desperate hope for the understanding that may come, if we use great effort, out of tomorrow, or if not then, maybe the day after? Clearly it has to become at some point an act of faith. It is toward this that her stories all point: here, it seems to me, is the North Star.

And how calm is the surface, the invisible surface of it all! In a style as invisible as the rhythm of a voice, and as much her own as her own voice, she tells her stories of horror and humiliation and in the doing fills her readers with a rising joy. The exemplary prose that is without waste or extravagance or self-indulgence or display, without any claim for its triumph, is full of pride. And her reader shares in that pride, as well he might: it is pride in the language, pride in using the language to search out human meanings, pride in the making of a good piece of work. A personal spell is about the stories, the something of her own that we refer to most often, perhaps, when we mention its beauty, and I think this comes from the *making* of the stories.

Readers have long been in the habit of praising (or could it be at times reproaching?) Katherine Anne Porter by calling her a perfectionist. I do not agree that this is the highest praise, and I would think the word misleading, suggesting as it does in the author a personal vanity in technique and a rigidity, even a deadness, in her prose. To me she is something more serious than a perfectionist. I celebrate her for being a blessed achiever. First she is an artist, of course, and as an artist she is an achiever.

That she hasn't wasted precious time repeating herself in her stories is sign enough, if it were needed, that she was never interested in doing the thing she knew already that she was able to bring off, that she hasn't been showing off for the sake of high marks (from whom?), but has patiently done what was to her her born necessity, quietly and in her own time, and each time the way she saw fit.

We are left with a sense of statement. Virginia Woolf set down in her diary, on the day when she felt she had seen that great brave difficult novel *The Waves* past a certain point in the writing: "But I think it possible that I have got my statues against the sky." It is the achieving of this crucial, this monumental moment in the work itself that we feel has mattered to Katherine Anne Porter. The reader who looks for the flawless result can find it, but looking for that alone he misses the true excitement, exhilaration, of reading, of rereading. It is the achieving — in a constant present tense — of the work that shines in the mind when we think of her name; and in that achieving lies, it seems to me, the radiance of the work and our recognition of it as unmistakably her own.

And unmistakable is its source. Katherine Anne Porter's deep sense of fairness and justice, her ardent conviction that we need to give and to receive in loving kindness all the human warmth we can make — here is where her stories come from. If they are made by the mind and address the mind, they draw their eloquence from a passionate heart. And for all their pain, they draw their wit, do they not, from a reserve of natural gaiety? I have wondered before now if it isn't those who were born gay who can devote themselves most wholeheartedly in their work to seriousness, who have seriousness to burn. The gay are the rich in feeling, and don't need to save any of it back.

Unmistakable, too, is what this artist has made. Order and form no more spring out of order and form than they come riding in to us upon seashells through the spray. In fiction they have to be made out of their very antithesis, life. The art of making is the thing that has meaning, and I think beauty is likely to be something that has for a time lain under good, patient hands.

Whether the finished work of art was easy or hard to make, whether it demanded a few hours or many years, concerns nobody but the maker, but the making itself has shaped that work for good and all. In Katherine Anne Porter's stories we feel their making as a bestowal of grace.

It is out of the response to her particular order and form that I believe I may have learned the simplest and surest reason for why I cannot see her stories in their every passing minute, and why it was never necessary or intended that a reader should. Katherine Anne Porter is writing stories of the spirit, and the time that fills those moments is eternity.

REVIEW ESSAY:
Robert Penn Warren, "Uncorrupted Consciousness: The Stories of Katherine Anne Porter," *Yale Review*, 55 (December 1965): 280–290.

Warren's essay argues for the essential modernity of Porter's seemingly traditional style.

In *The Collected Stories* of Katherine Anne Porter (Harcourt, Brace & World) we have all of the short stories, including four (one, "Holiday," a masterpiece) hitherto uncollected, along with five longer pieces — long stories and short novels. This is a large, solid book, and in its 500 packed pages we find the record of a life and the achievement of a rare, powerful, and subtle creative force. It is a beautiful and deeply satisfying book; and it promises to be a permanent and highly esteemed part of our literature.

Permanent: we may have some confidence in the permanence of this book because, from the beginning, forty-five years ago, the fiction of Katherine Anne Porter has been numinously present but never in fashion. It has had, very definitely, a public, and distinguished appreciation, but its appeal has always been intrinsic, and has never been derived from the accidents of context, social or literary, in which the work appeared. If we look back at the first collection, *Flowering Judas*, what do we find to remind us of the labels and textbook tags for the 'twenties? Or if we look back on the volume of long pieces, "Old Mortality," "Noon Wine," and "Pale Horse, Pale Rider," published in a volume that goes by the name of the last, what do we find that reminds us of the polemics and posturing or, in any obvious way, of the social passion of the 'thirties? Only one story in this collection, the title story of the collection called *The Leaning Tower*, has an air of topicality, and that is the only one which, by the rigorous standard proposed by the rest of the book, can be called a failure. Against the background of shifting fashions, this fiction has always seemed fixed. It seems to have been there always, a part of our spiritual landscape to which one may turn now and then, as to a tree, rock, or hill, for a moment of reorientation. Despite the great richness of detail and the subtlety of tonal variations, the final effect is one of a classic severity: the memory, as it were, of our own old, half-forgotten inner experiences, suddenly seen in a vital form.

There is, however, a paradox here. Though outside the flux of fashion and beyond the journalism of the chic, this fiction is profoundly, radically, modern. And that, of course, is why it sometimes seems, at first glance, to be outside of what, at a particular moment, may merely appear to be modern. Because of its radical modernism — its root modernism — this fiction often undercuts what is only the accident of a moment.

The most obvious example of this is in the short novel "Old Mortality." Here the legend of the Old South — appearing as a story of romantic family piety, with the beautiful and charming Aunt Amy, long dead, as the heroine — is subjected to a series of "unmaskings," is submitted to a series of tests by corrosives. The person who crucially confronts the legend of Amy, and for whom the unmaskings have a deep bearing on her own vision of life and on her own fate, is Miranda, a child when we first meet her, but at the end a grown girl.

As a child Miranda brings to the family stories merely the test of simple realism. If her romantic father can say, "Thank God, there never were any fat women in my family," the little girl remembers Aunt Keziah, up in Kentucky, "who, when seated, was one solid pyramidal monument from floor to neck." The corrosive of realism is succeeded by that of moral judgment, when Miranda discovers the disastrous effects of Aunt Amy's romantic story — this in the person of Cousin Gabriel, who, as a dashing young man, had married Amy but now is reduced to a whiskey-sodden, wheezing wreck of a man, a failing follower of the tracks, who tortures his present wife with the legend of Amy, a delusion from which he cannot disenthrall himself.

The next stages of the criticism of the legend occurs some years later when Miranda, on the train going back home to Gabriel's funeral, encounters Cousin Eva, who, like Gabriel, had been a victim of the romantic legend — poor, chinless Cousin Eva, who had failed as a belle and has spent her life teaching Latin in a female seminary or fighting gallantly for the cause of woman suffrage. Cousin Eva, out of the rancor of her old deprivation and defeat, offers Miranda two more kinds of unmasking for the legend. The gay parties of the legend had had a brutal economic undergirding; the parties and the love affairs were a "market." So here we have the very modern corrosive of Marx. But there is another very modern corrosive: "Cousin Eva wrung her hands. 'It was just sex,' she said in despair; 'their minds dwelt on nothing else. They didn't call it that, it was all smothered under pretty names, but that's all it was, sex. . . . None of them had, and they didn't need to have, anything else to think about, and they didn't really know anything about that, so they simply festered inside — they simply festered — ' " So the corrosive of Freud is added to that of Marx.

Cousin Eva, with Marx and Freud, speaks for modernism against the romanticism of which Miranda's father is the chief exponent, and thus far, in the various unmaskings of the Southern myth — i.e. the "past" in general — we find a fiction appropriate to its period, the 'thirties. But even as Cousin Eva speaks her piece about sex, "Miranda found herself deliberately watching a long procession of living corpses, festering women stepping gaily towards the charnel house, their corruption concealed under laces and flowers, their dead faces lifted smiling, and thought quite coldly, 'Of course it was not like that. This is no more true than what I was told before, it's every bit as romantic.' "

So Miranda retorts that her own mother had been "a perfectly natural woman who liked to cook" — and with the phrase "natural woman," she gropes out for some truth beyond all the formulations that have been offered her. She is now eighteen, she had eloped only a year before, she has run through her own "romance," and now she is seeking solid footing for her own life. She suddenly thinks she may find the "natural" truth upon returning home, with her father. But this is not to be. When she arrives she finds that there is a secret, unhealable breach between her and her father, and that it is Eva to whom he turns — Eva, who, with her modern unmaskings, had seemed the enemy of his romanticism.

It now appears that Eva and the father are merely the "poles," as it were, of the past, the terms of the dialectic of the past, and Miranda is left isolated to find her own "truth" without reference to that past. So we come to the end:

Ah but there is my own life to come yet, she thought, my own life and beyond. I don't want any promises, I won't have any false hopes, I won't be romantic about myself. I can't live in their world any longer, she told herself, listening to the voices back of her. Let them tell their stories to each other. Let them go on explaining how things happened. I don't care. At least I can know the truth about what happens to me, she assured herself silently, making a promise to herself, in her hopefulness, her ignorance.

The last five words of the story undercut, we may say, one set of assumptions in the story — the simplest being that the past can be "repudiated" in favor of absolute truth in the present. Truth, the last words would imply, is not an absolute, but inheres in the dialectic of the life-process. Each age must create its own truth, out of its own polarities, its own tensions, and this truth, however provisional, is what must constitute its vital commitment. Each age, each person in fact, lives only in the quality — the passion and profundity, and at the same time the critical awareness — of this existential commitment.

This story is, as we have said, the most explicit treatment of this theme, at least in historical and social terms. But it is implicit in "The Old Order." Here the character of Miranda again confronts, as in "Old Mortality," the past. Here is the struggle of the girl to find her own footing, but the struggle is not a simple objective one against the Old Order. She is involved in the values of that order, and the struggle is, finally, a subjective one, for she is fully aware of the virtues of the Old Order, and yearns for them. In "The Jilting of Granny Weatherall" we have a story which might well be in "The Old Order," and a character very close to the grandmother there. We find the toughness and self-reliance of Granny Weatherall (the name is significant), her loyalties and kindnesses, her well-earned pride in her triumph of life. On her deathbed she can think of "sitting up nights with sick horses and sick negroes and sick children and hardly losing one." The fusion of a will to life and a moral attitude, a clear notion of the rules of the game of life and of the stakes for which it is played — that was what the Old Order offered. The old-fashioned stout ones in these stories have what Faulkner in *Wild Palms* calls "the gift of living once and dying once instead of being diffused and scattered creatures drawn blindly from a grab bag and assembled."

The virtues of the Old Order appear, however, as in "Old Mortality," in the context of its limitations and defects. Since this fiction presents the Southern version of the Old Order, let us take, for example, the life of Nannie — the Black Mammy — as it winds in and out of the stories. There is the time when, as a pot-bellied child, scarcely more than a baby, she is sold at a slave-auction and the purchaser pokes her in the stomach, saying, "Regular crowbait." And the time when, a generation later, she is identified to the seller, now an old judge and respected citizen, who bawls out: "For God Almighty's sake! is that the strip of crowbait I sold to your father for twenty dollars?" Nannie finally airs the grievance to her mistress — whom, long after Emancipation, she had elected to stay with: " 'Looks lak a jedge might had better raisin',' she said gloomily, 'Looks lak he didn't keer how much he hurt a body's feelins.' " The episode, in its very mutedness, is more telling than a catalogue of atrocities. And how complex are the ironies in the fact that Nannie impugns the "raisin' " of the judge — a point on which the Old Order, at any social level, would have had most pride.

If Miranda can look back and yearn for the toughness, the sense of obligation, and the moral certitude of the Old Order, she knows that she cannot have them on the same terms. She must find her own terms, in the New Order; but this means that she may find herself, in the end, as much in conflict with its prevailing values as with any of the past. This is implicit in, for example, "Pale Horse, Pale Rider"; and the theme appears in "Flowering Judas" and is hinted at in the opening of "Holiday," and elsewhere. This is not to say that this theme is dominant, but it is often present, as a kind of under-theme, coloring and modifying whatever may be more dominant, providing another counterpoint or another irony.

The candor, the willingness to confront and explore inner tensions, the conviction that reality, the "truth," is never two-dimensional, is found in process not in stasis — all this gives the peculiar vibrance and the peculiar sense of a complex but severely balanced form to almost all of the other stories, even those not concerned with the generations or with an over-all society, but with more strictly personal issues. In a story like "Theft" the drama develops from the tension between "world-as-thief" and "self-as-thief," in a rigorous balance of argument subtly unfolding beneath the circumstantial surface of the narrative. In "He," as in

"Holiday," the drama develops from the tension between love and compassion, on the one hand, and the gross force of need and the life-will, on the other. In "Maria Concepcion" the drama lies in a contrast between the code of civilization and the logic of natural impulse. In "Noon Wine" it revolves about the nature of motive and of guilt. Did Mr. Thompson really see a knife in the hand of Mr. Hatch? Did he brain the monstrous Hatch to save Mr. Helton's life or to defend the prosperity which Helton had brought him? Or had some other, more mysterious force guided his hand? Poor Mr. Thompson — he can never know and therefore must put the shotgun muzzle under his chin.

The dark pit where motives twine and twist is a place well known, of course, to our modernity; it is the milieu of much modern fiction. It is the milieu deeply pondered and scrupulously reported by Katherine Anne Porter. Not only are "Noon Wine" and "Old Mortality" studies of the ambiguity of motive; such studies are also found in "Theft," "The Tree," and "He," to take only three examples. But it is important to see the difference in effect between her treatment of such ideas and that found in writers whom we think of as specifically modern. For one thing, Katherine Anne Porter never confounds the shadowy and flickering shapes of the psychological situation with vagueness of structure in the story itself, or permits the difficulty of making an ethical analysis to justify a confusion in form. The fallacy of expressive form is not found here. In fact, it may be plausibly argued that the most powerful tension in her work is between the emotional involvements (how great they can, at times, be!) and the detachment, the will to shape and assess experience; and the effect of this is sometimes to make a story look and feel strangely different, unanalyzably different, from the ordinary practice. But there is a deeper and more significant difference. A great deal of the current handling of the psychology of motive is a kind of clinical reportage. In two respects the work of Katherine Anne Porter is to be distinguished from this. First, she presumably believes that there is not merely pathology in the world, but evil — Evil with the capital E, if you will. Along with the pity and humor of her fiction there is the rigorous, almost puritanical, attempt to make an assessment of experience. Second, she presumably believes in the sanctity of what used to be called the individual soul. She may even go as far as Hawthorne does in "Ethan Brand," and elsewhere, in regarding the violation of this sanctity of the soul as the Unpardonable Sin. Not even those characters who are touched with evil

or fatuity are deprived of a vital rendering; the ethical judgment is not a judgment abstractly passed on a robot, and the difficulty of judging any human being is not blinked.

If neither the ethical bias in the fiction of Katherine Anne Porter nor the notion of the sanctity of the individual soul seems, at first glance, modern, let us recall that both are related to an issue which undercuts the clinical and reportorial concerns often passing for modernity. The issue is this: given the modern world of technology and the great power state, on what terms, if any, can the individual survive? The abstractions that eat up the sense of the individual — they call forth her most mordant ironies. Of Braggioni, the "professional lover of humanity" who cannot love a person, she says: "He has the malice, the cleverness, the wickedness, the sharpness of wit, the hardness of heart, stipulated for loving the world profitably." And oh, the beauty of that word *stipulated*!

The chic phrase is the "crisis of identity," and a consideration of that crisis lies at the heart of this fiction. It lies so near the informing heart, so deep in fact, that it can be missed; for Katherine Anne Porter sees the question in radical terms: ethical responsibility and the sanctity of the individual soul. Without that much, she might argue, what would "identity" mean? It is chic to discuss the crisis of identity, but it is not chic to explore it in terms that count — that, in fact, undercut the chic. One might conceivably state the issue here in theological terms. But there is no need to do so, and it might be irrelevant to the author's view. The logical terms are enough.

To take another approach to the whole question, there is a more personal aspect to the tensions underlying these stories. The story of Miranda is that of a child, then of a young woman, trying, in the face of the Old Order, and then of the New, to find her own values, to create her own identity. The exact ratio of fact and fiction in Miranda's story, and of autobiography and fiction in the portrait, is something which we cannot — and in one sense, the author herself cannot — know. It is not even important for us, or for the author, to know. Clearly there is a degree of overlap and projection, but, clearly again, there is one important difference between Miranda and her creator. The creator is an artist, and her own rebellions, rejections, and seekings, as shadowed forth however imperfectly and with whatever distortions, inevitably have some deep relation to this role in real life. No doubt the artist, in all periods, is stuck with some sense of difference, of even alienation, no matter how stoutly, or cynically, he may insist on identifying himself with his world; and in our period this alienation of the artist — even the "pathology of the artist" — is not only an element in his experience but often a theme of his work. It is, in one perspective, a theme of this book, in much the same sense that it is a theme of the work of Hawthorne, James, Kafka, or Mann. It is implicit, over and over, and in "Holiday" it finds something close to an explicit statement in this little lyric poem celebrating an artist's doom:

> I loved that silence which means freedom from the constant pressure of other minds and other opinions and other feelings, that freedom to fold up in quiet and go back to my own center, to find out again, for it is always a rediscovery, what kind of creature it is that rules me finally, makes all the decisions no matter who thinks they make them, even I; who little by little takes everything away except the one thing I cannot live without, and who will one day say, "Now I am all you have left — take me." I paused there a good while listening to this muted language which was silence with music in it; I could be moved and touched but not troubled by it, as by the crying of frogs or the wind in the trees.

The artist must find the right distance from life, put the right shape or frame on life, and at the same time must render, to a greater or lesser degree, its quality, its urgency. These paradoxical demands simply repeat the personal tensions of apartness and involvement. Such tension in this fiction has been peculiarly fruitful, because there is a willed candor in the author's assessment of her role. She knows the deep ambivalences in that role: the world — life — is a beloved enemy. If on one hand, life must be mastered in the dialectic of her form, on the other hand, life must be plunged into — or realized as though one had plunged into it and were totally immersed. The dialectic of her form is peculiarly severe, as I have tried to indicate in discussing "Old Mortality," and even in stories like "Flowering Judas" and "He," which seem at first glance more casually devised in their progression, will be found a deeply set logic. But in all the stories, even when the ordering is most rigorous, there is the same vividness of circumstantiality. The vividness of the details of the physical world is unwavering. The mouth of Braggioni, the fat revolutionist in "Flowering Judas," opens "round and yearns sideways, his balloon cheeks grow oily with the labor of song. . . . He sighs and his leather belt creaks like a saddle girth." When Granny Weatherall lighted the lamps, the "children huddled up to her and breathed like little calves waiting at the bars in the twilight." In "Virgin Violetta," in reference to Carlos: "His furry, golden eyebrows were knitted sternly, resembling a tangle of crochet wool." In "The Old Order," we have the annual arrival of the grandmother back at the farm: the "horses jogged in, their bellies jolting and churning, and Grandmother calling out greetings in her feast-day voice."

Here is a poetry of the rich texture of the world. It is a poetry that shows a deep emotional attachment to the world's body. But this is not a self-indulgent poetry, and its richness is derived from precision — precision of observation and precision of phrase. From, shall we say, the hard intellectuality that veins and hardens that love, that manifests itself elsewhere, and more fundamentally, in the dialectic of form.

As the love of the texture of the world is set against this intellectuality, so the world of feeling is set against the dialectic. It is a rich world of feeling. Gaiety, good humor, and humor abound here. The whole first section of "Old Mortality" spills over with it. In the second section we have the delicious humor of the little girls "immured" in the convent, and even in the last section, there are flashes of humor in the encounter with the formidable Cousin Eva.

Gaiety, good humor, and humor represent, however, only one segment of the spectrum of feeling found in this book. There is the heart-wrenching moment, for instance, at the end of "He," when all the tortured complexities of Mrs. Whipple's attitude toward her idiot son are absorbed into a sudden purity of focus. Or the moment in "The Old Order" when Nannie, after the words of the judge who had sold her years ago as "crowbait," bursts out to her mistress. Or in "Holiday," when the mute cripple, who works as a servant in the house of her own parents, shows the narrator the blurred photograph of a fat, smiling baby, and then turns it over to point to the name — her own name — written carefully on the back. Or in "Noon Wine," when after her husband has given her "a good pinch on her thin little rump," Mrs. Thompson says, "Why, Mr. Thompson, sometimes I think you're the evilest-minded man that ever lived," and then takes "a handful of hair on the crown of his head" and gives it "a good slow pull." Then: " 'That's to show you how it feels, pinching so hard when you're supposed to be playing,' she said, gently." Whether it is the bleak purity of emotion in "He," or this flash of unexpected warmth and tenderness in the life of the Thompsons, Katherine Anne Porter has the gift for touching the key of feeling. She never exploits this gift, never indulges in random emotionality; she knows that the gift must not be abused or it will vanish like fairy gold.

She knows, too, that shifts in feeling are essential if we are to sense the movement of life. A feeling suddenly explodes against the counterpoint of other feelings, other tones, as the pathos of the scene at the hotel in the second part of "Old Mortality" bursts against the humor associated with the little girls in the convent. And always, the feeling appears against the backdrop of the rigorously unfolding form of the story. Katherine Anne Porter has some austerity of imagination that gives her a secret access to the spot whence feeling springs. She can deny herself, and her own feelings, and patiently repudiate the temptation to exploit the feelings of the reader, and therefore can, when the moment comes, truly enter into the heart of a character; and in that self-denial may find, and affirm, herself. One hesitates to think what price may have been paid for this priceless gift.

I have been speaking of some of the tensions and themes in this book. They spring from the author's will to see "all" of a thing. She must explore, as it were, the inner resonances and paradoxes of her own sensibility. She is willing to undergo the painful discipline of trying to keep uncorrupted her own consciousness. One feels that for her the act of composition is an act of knowing, and that for her, knowledge is the end of life — and that for her, knowledge, imaginatively achieved, is, in the end, life. Without it, all the bright texture of the world and experience would be only illusion.

She knows, we are forced to believe, that if one is to try to see "all," one must be willing to see the dark side of the moon. She has a will, a ferocious will, to face, but face in its full context, what Herman Melville called the great "NO" of life. If stoicism is the underlying attitude in this fiction, it is a stoicism without grimness or arrogance, capable of gaiety, tenderness, and sympathy, and its ethical point of reference is found in those characters who, like Granny Weatherall, have the toughness to survive but who survive by a loving sense of obligation to others, this sense being, in the end, only a full affirmation of the life-sense, a joy in strength. On her deathbed, as we recall, Granny Weatherall, thinking of all the sick animals and people she had sat up with, night after night, can cry out in triumph to her long-

dead husband: "John, I hardly ever lost one of them!"

Like all strong art, this book is, paradoxically, both a question asked of life and a celebration of life; and the author of it knows in her bones that the more corrosive the question asked, the more powerful may be the celebration.

BOOK REVIEW:
Eudora Welty, "Post Mortem," review of *The Never-Ending Wrong, New York Times Book Review,* 21 August 1977, pp. 9, 29.

Porter's last two books were nonfiction: The Collected Essays amd Occasional Writings of Katherine Anne Porter *(1972) and* The Never-Ending Wrong *(1977). Her 1977 book is an account of her involvement in the 1927 protests against the executions of two anarchists, Nicola Sacco and Bartolomeo Vanzetti, for a 1920 armed robbery and murder in Boston. The Sacco-Vanzetti case was a cause célèbre for many artists and intellectuals, who believed that the two men were convicted and condemned to death on the basis of their political views rather than existing evidence. Porter made several attempts over the years to turn the notes she made in 1927 into an essay on her experiences and finally succeeded fifty years later. Some reviewers faulted* The Never-Ending Wrong *for being too much about Porter and not enough about the historical facts of the case, but Welty saw an important connection between the book and much of Porter's fiction: they warn of the way in which evil corrupts and victimizes the innocent and the not-so-innocent.*

As this is being written, the Governor of Massachusetts has issued a proclamation calling for a memorial day on Aug. 23, the anniversary of the electrocution of Sacco and Vanzetti in the Charlestown Prison for a holdup and murder, and his legal counsel has cited "the very real possibility that a grievous miscarriage of justice occurred with their deaths." It has taken the law exactly 50 years to acknowledge publicly that it might have made a mistake. But after that same 50 years, the renowned short-story writer and novelist Katherine Anne Porter has written a book, "The Never-Ending Wrong," also to be published on Aug. 23; and it seems to her that she still believes and feels today the same as she believed and felt at that time, on that scene.

This book of 63 pages, a "plain, full record of a crime that belongs to history" as she states in a foreword, was not intended to establish the guilt or innocence of Nicola Sacco and Bartolomeo Vanzetti, but rather to examine the guilt or innocence of those on the outside, all those gathered there, like herself, to see the final scene played out.

"I did not know then and I still do not know whether they were guilty . . . but I had my reasons for being there to protest the terrible penalty they were being condemned to suffer; these reasons were of the heart, which I believe appears in these pages with emphasis."

Her own participation was outwardly of little substance — a matter of typing letters Sacco and Vanzetti wrote to their friends on the outside, of showing up in the picket line and going through the motions of being arrested, jailed and bailed out. She knew herself to be largely in the dark about what was really going on. Questions rose out of personal feeling — deeply serious questions. She made some notes. This book, their eventual result, is a searching of a personal experience, whose troubling of the heart has never abated and whose meaning has kept on asking to be understood. The notes of that time have been added to, she says, "in the hope of a clearer statement," but the account is "unchanged in feeling and point of view."

The picket line in which she marched included the poets and novelists Edna St. Vincent Millay, John Dos Passos, Michael Gold, Grace Lumpkin, Lola Ridge. "I wouldn't have expected to see them on the same street, much less the same picket line and in the same jail."

By today's standards, the conduct of these exercises was almost demure. "I never saw a lady — or a gentleman — being rude to a policeman in that picket line, nor any act of rudeness from a single policeman. That sort of thing was to come later, from officers on different duty. The first time I was arrested, my policeman and I walked along stealing perplexed, questioning glances at each other; . . . neither of us wished to deny that the other was a human being; there was no natural hostility between us."

She made notes:

"*Second day:*

"He (taking my elbow and drawing me out of the line; I go like a lamb): 'Well, what have you been doing since yesterday?'

"I: 'Mostly copying Sacco and Vanzetti's letters. I wish you could read them. You'd believe in them if you could read the letters.'

"He: 'Well, I don't have much time for reading.' "

On the day they were all aware that the battle was lost, she said to him, "I expect this will be the last time you'll have to arrest me. You've been very kind and patient and I thank you." "Thank *you,*" he replied.

They were bailed out by the same kind soul every time they were put in jail. Edward James, Henry James's nephew, invariably appeared and put up the money for all of them, even those who did not wish to be bailed out, "getting us set free for the next round."

But, it appeared, Sacco and Vanzetti did not trust their would-be rescuers. "Many of the anxious friends from another class of society found [it] very hard to deal with, not to be met on their own bright, generous terms in this crisis of life and death; to be saying, in effect, we are all brothers and equal citizens; to receive, in effect, the reserved answer: No, not yet. It is clear now that the condemned men understood and realized their predicament much better than any individual working with any organization devoted to their rescue." They "knew well from the beginning that they had every reason to despair, they did not really trust these strangers from the upper world who furnished the judges and lawyers to the courts, the politicians to the offices, the faculties to the universities, who had all the money and the influence. . . . "

What they may not have known, says Miss Porter, was that "some of the groups apparently working for them, people of their own class in many cases, were using the occasion for Communist propaganda, and hoping only for their deaths as a political argument. I know this because I heard and I saw."

It was a certain Rosa Baron who made this clear through her own words to Katherine Anne Porter, who had expressed the hope that even yet the men might be saved. This "grim little person" headed Miss Porter's particular group during the Boston demonstrations, and what Miss Porter remembers most vividly through the 50 years of time are Rosa Baron's "little pinpoints of eyes glittering through her spectacles at me and her shrill, accusing voice: 'Saved? Who wants them saved? What earthly good would they do us alive?' "

"In the reckless phrase of the confirmed joiner in the fight for whatever relief oppressed humanity was fighting for, I had volunteered 'to be useful wherever and however I could best serve,' and was drafted into a Communist outfit all unknowing."

The account of her experience is clear and has the strength of an essence, not simply by virtue of its long distillation. It is clear through candor, as well. Miss Porter says of herself at this time:

"I was not an inexperienced girl, I was thirty-seven years old; I knew a good deal about the evils and abuses and cruelties of the world; I had known victims of injustice, of crime, I was not ignorant of history, nor of literature; I had witnessed a revolution in Mexico, had in a way taken part in it, and had seen it follow the classic trail of all revolutions. Besides all the moral force and irreproachable motives of so many, I knew the deviousness and wickedness of both sides, on all sides, and the mixed motives — plain love of making mischief, love of irresponsible power, unscrupulous ambition of many men who never stopped short of murder, if murder would advance their careers an inch. But this was something very different, unfamiliar."

"There were many such groups, for this demonstration had been agitated for and prepared for many years by the Communists. They had not originated the protest, I believe, but had joined in and tried to take over, as their policy was, and is. . . ."

Being used! The outrage she had found unbearable for the men on trial in court she realized was also the outrage being inflicted on those who had tried to help them, and on others more vulnerable than picketers in their line.

Through Miss Porter's eyes we see their wives, Rosa Sacco and Luigia Vanzetti, being marched through the streets at the head of a crowd massing at a rally, on the night before the scheduled execution.

" . . . and the two timid women faced the raging crowd, mostly Italians, who rose at them in savage sympathy, shouting, tears pouring down their faces, shaking their fists and calling . . . 'Never you mind. Rosina! You wait, Luigia! They'll pay, they'll pay!' It was the most awesome, the most bitter scene I had ever witnessed."

But the crowd assembled to await the execution itself was in contrast "a silent, intent assembly of citizens — of anxious people come to bear witness and to protest against the terrible wrong about to be committed, not only against the two men about to die, but against all of us, against our common humanity. . . . " The mounted police galloped about, bearing down on anybody who ventured beyond the edge of the crowd and rearing up over their heads.

"One tall, thin figure of a woman stepped out alone, a good distance into the empty square, and when the police came down at her and the horse's hoofs beat over her head, she did not move, but stood with her shoulders slightly bowed, entirely still. The charge was repeated again and again, but she was not to be driven away." Then she was recognized as Lola Ridge, and dragged to safety by one of her own; the strange, poignant, almost archetypical figure Miss Porter describes must remain indelible.

After that night was all over, the picketers themselves were given a trial; that is, "simply our representatives" (Edna St. Vincent Millay was one) "were tried in a group in about five minutes." The judge "portentously, as if pronouncing another death sentence, found us guilty of loitering and obstructing traffic, fined us five dollars each, and the tragic farce took its place in history."

The aftermath was numbness, silence; disbanding and going home. Miss Porter writes: "In all this I should speak only for myself, for never in my life have I felt so isolated as I did in that host of people, all presumably moved in the same impulse, with the same or at least sympathetic motive; when one might think hearts would have opened, minds would respond with kindness, we did not find it so, but precisely the contrary."

Katherine Anne Porter's fine, grave honesty has required of her, and she has given it to this account, a clarity of statement, a respect for proportion, an avoidance of exaggeration, a watchfulness against any self-indulgence, and a regard for uncompromising accuracy.

But the essence of the book's strength lies in its insight into human motivations, and the unique gifts she has brought to her fiction have been of value to her here as well — even in the specific matter of her subject. The theme of betrayal has always run in a strong current through her work. The worst villains of her stories are the liars, and those most evil are the users of others. Elements of guilt, the abandonment of responsibilities in human relationships, the betrayal of good faith and the taking away of trust and love are what her tragic stories are made of. Betrayal of justice is not very different from the betrayal of love.

And a nation is a living human organism. Like a person, a nation sometimes needs years to comprehend the full scope and seriousness of some wound that has happened to it or some act it has brought itself to perform. Though an experience in its history may have hurt it deeply, left a scar and caused it recurring discomfort and bad dreams, yet only slowly may its meaning grow clear to the sufferer.

"The never-ending wrong," says Miss Porter, "is the anguish that human beings inflict on each other," which she pronounces at the end "forever incurable." And she finds that "The evils prophesied by that crisis have all come true."

As no concerned citizen can argue, this book she has written out of her own life is of profound contemporary significance.

OBITUARY:
J. Y. Smith, "Prize-Winning Novelist Katherine Anne Porter Dies," *Washington Post*, 19 September 1980, B4.

In 1977 Porter suffered a series of strokes that affected her speech and left her unable to use her right arm. By late March 1980 her condition had deteriorated to the extent that she had to be placed in a Silver Spring, Maryland, nursing home, where she died on 18 September 1980.

Although Porter often told people, and may have believed herself, that her father, Harrison Boone Porter, was a descendant of Daniel Boone's brother and a cousin of writer William Sydney Porter (O. Henry), there is no evidence for either claim repeated in this obituary. It also misstates Porter's birth name, relying on information from Porter, who hated the name "Callie" and refused to acknowledge that her parents had named her simply Callie Russell Porter. Finally, Porter was married four times, not three (as stated here).

Katherine Anne Porter, 90, a writer who dazzled the literary world with the subtlety and power of her short stories and the author of one novel, "Ship of Fools," which added a fortune to her fame, died Thursday at the Carriage Hill Nursing home in Silver Spring. She had had a series of strokes.

Miss Porter's numerous honors included the Pulitzer Prize, awarded to her in 1966 for her short stories, the National Book Award for fiction in the same year, and the Gold Medal of the National Institute of Arts and Letters the following year.

Although her reputation is anchored most firmly in her short stories and novellas, of which she published five volumes, Miss Porter maintained that there was a coherence that ran through her shorter works and "Ship of Fools." Given

Miss Porter's reputation, it is not without irony, perhaps, that the appearance of the novel in 1963 was greeted more as a publishing than a literary event. But a publishing event it certainly was. The book went to the top of the best seller list and the film rights were sold for a reported $500,000. In fact, it met with less success with the critics than with the public.

Of this phenomenon Miss Porter said in an interview in 1970: "People don't read very attentively. Everything I've written, from 'Flowering Judas' to 'Pale Horse, Pale Rider' through 'Ship of Fools,' is one continuous line. But I suppose it's a horrible job to ask anyone to read five books just to find out what 'Ship of Fools' is about."

And Robert Penn Warren, himself a Pulitzer Prize-winning author and poet, said in a statement shortly before Miss Porter's death:

"She is certainly unsurpassed in our century or country — perhaps any time or country — as a writer [of] fiction in the short forms of story or novella. Her famous and only novel . . . though to a number of critics it has seemed little more than a collection of vignettes and episodes, with no significant unity, remains a memorable work.

"I myself am inclined to feel that, whatever sprawl can be found here is jerked into focus by sleight of hand, at the last moment, on the last page as it were — with the glimpse of the poor little German youth in the ship's band. But forgetting this book, her work remains a monument to a tremendous talent — even genius. It is permanent."

Virtually all critics wrote of Miss Porter's style, her control, the keenness with which she perceived and recorded emotion and character. And they spoke of her toughness. In the words of Warren, her toughness was "honed to a razor edge."

In addition to "Flowering Judas" published in 1930, and the celebrated "Pale Horse, Pale Rider," the title story of which is about a love affair involving a World War I soldier who dies of influenza, which appeared in 1938, Miss Porter's other story collections include "Hacienda: A Story of Mexico" (1934), "Noon Wine," (1937) and "The Leaning Tower and Other Stories" (1944). She also published several collections of her stories in addition to essays and other writings.

This relatively modest list by no means represents the total of her work, for Miss Porter made her living as a writer all of her life. She regarded much of what she did as hack work and

Porter on her eighty-fifth birthday

it took many forms, including magazine pieces and a time in Hollywood doing film scripts. She worked for a newspaper in Denver ("A newspaper is no place to learn to write," she remarked. "The truth is newspapers simply ruin writers"), was an actress in little theaters, took photographs, played the piano and collected old music, translated French ballads, 17 of which were published as "French Songbook" in 1933, studied ballet, rode horseback, and at all times was entirely her own person ("It is a disaster to have a man fall in love with me," she said. "They aren't content to take what I can give; they want everything from me.").

The stories about which she cared were another matter, and she spoke of this writing as "the single vital issue" of her life.

"I could not make a living writing because I would not write the kind of books editors wanted me to write because that was mine and I wouldn't tamper with it," she said on a television program in 1962.

The "one basic idea" of her work, she said, was that of "illusion, delusion and self-deception. People never know quite what they are, and they don't know how to treat other people. As a child, it struck me how little one person could under-

stand another. I've been told so often what I think and feel, and, of course, they've got it all wrong. I wish they'd keep out of my mind if they're going to muddle around like that."

In "Ship of Fools," these themes are presented as an allegory played out by 40 characters on a German ship, the Vera, sailing from Vera Cruz, Mexico, to Bremerhaven, Germany. Its theme is that good and evil exist in a symbiosis in which neither can exist without the other. Among the themes is the evil in German character and civilization that appears with the rise of Hitler.

Katherine Anne Maria Veronica Callista Russell Porter was born on May 15, 1890, at Indian Creek, a town near San Antonio, Tex. Her father was a farmer whose family contained some notable people. He was a direct descendant of Jonathan Boone, brother of the famous Daniel, and one of his second cousins was O. Henry (William Sidney Porter), the short story writer.

By Miss Porter's account, her family was literate, but not literary. "I was raised on a little farm in Texas, but I remember a first edition of Dr. Johnson's dictionary on the floor," she said.

Miss Porter was educated at girls' schools in Texas and Louisiana. In later life, she described herself as a "precocious, nervous, rebellious, unteachable child." Like many young women of her generation, she was taught to sing and loved it.

Her interest in literature was voracious and self-generating. It also was without formal guidance, a circumstance that has been cited in efforts to explain the force and originality of her work. She never went to college. But in the course of her long life she taught, read her work, or otherwise was formally in touch with students at more than 200 colleges and universities here and abroad. She began to write when she was a girl.

"I did not choose this vocation," Miss Porter said, "and if I had had any say in the matter, I would not have chosen it."

In 1918, during the great influenza epidemic, she nearly died of the disease. In the 1920s, she lived for several years in Mexico. In the 1930s, she lived in Paris and elsewhere in Europe, meeting, among others, Hitler and Goebbels, whom she described as "detestable and dangerous."

These experiences and her native Texas all provided settings for her stories. For more than 20 years, Miss Porter lived in Washington and its environs and maintained a residence in this area until her death.

On her 80th birthday, Miss Porter told an interviewer: "I have a good constitution and a heart like an ox. It scares me — I wonder how much it will take to kill me. I wouldn't want to live to be 97. But if I'd died 10 years ago, I would have missed some of the pleasantest experiences of my life. I'll hang on 'til 90 and see how it goes."

Against the day of her death, Miss Porter several years ago ordered a plain pine coffin with brass fittings from a firm in Arizona. She kept it in her house and planned to have it painted in the Mexican fashion.

Miss Porter was married and divorced three times. She leaves no immediate survivors.

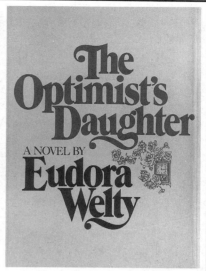

EUDORA WELTY

(13 April 1909–)

See also the Welty entries in DLB 2: American Novelists Since World War II; DLB Yearbook: 1987; DLB 102: American Short Story Writers, 1910–1945, Second Series; *and* DLB 143: American Novelists Since World War II, Third Series.

MAJOR BOOKS:

A Curtain of Green (Garden City, N.Y.: Doubleday, Doran, 1941; London: John Lane/ Bodley Head, 1943);

The Robber Bridegroom (Garden City, N.Y.: Doubleday, Doran, 1942; London: John Lane/Bodley Head, 1944);

The Wide Net and Other Stories (New York: Harcourt, Brace, 1943; London: John Lane/Bodley Head, 1945);

Delta Wedding (New York: Harcourt, Brace, 1946; London: Bodley Head, 1947);

The Golden Apples (New York: Harcourt, Brace, 1949; London: Bodley Head, 1950);

The Ponder Heart (New York: Harcourt, Brace, 1954; London: Hamilton, 1954);

Selected Stories of Eudora Welty (New York: Modern Library, 1954);

The Bride of the Innisfallen and Other Stories (New York: Harcourt, Brace, 1955; London: Hamilton, 1955);

Losing Battles (New York: Random House, 1970; London: Virago Press, 1982);

One Time, One Place: Mississippi in the Depression, A Snapshot Album (New York: Random House, 1971);

The Optimist's Daughter (New York: Random House, 1972; London: Deutsch, 1973);

The Eye of the Story: Selected Essays and Reviews (New York: Random House, 1978; London: Virago Press, 1987);

The Collected Stories of Eudora Welty (New York & London: Harcourt Brace Jovanovich, 1980; London & Boston: Boyars, 1981);

One Writer's Beginnings (Cambridge, Mass. & London: Harvard University Press, 1984; London & Boston: Faber & Faber, 1985);

Eudora Welty: Photographs, foreword by Reynolds Price (Jackson & London: University Press of Mississippi, 1989);

A Writer's Eye: Collected Book Reviews, edited by Pearl Amelia McHaney (Jackson: University Press of Mississippi, 1994).

Born in Jackson, Mississippi, Eudora Welty was the eldest surviving child and only daughter of Christian Webb Welty, an Ohio native who became a successful insurance-company executive (with his daughter, left), and Chestina Andrews Welty, a former schoolteacher from West Virginia (right).

BIBLIOGRAPHIES:
Victor H. Thompson, *Eudora Welty: A Reference Guide* (Boston: G. K. Hall, 1976);
Suzanne Marrs, *The Welty Collection: A Guide to the Eudora Welty Manuscripts amd Documents at the Mississippi Department of Archives and History* (Jackson & London: University Press of Mississippi, 1988);
Noel Polk, *Eudora Welty: A Bibliography of Her Work* (Jackson & London: University Press of Mississippi, 1994).

LETTERS:
Michael Kreyling, *Author and Agent: Eudora Welty and Diarmuid Russell* (New York: Farrar Straus Giroux, 1991).

INTERVIEWS:
Peggy Whitman Prenshaw, ed., *Conversations with Eudora Welty* (Jackson: University Press of Mississippi, 1984).

LOCATION OF ARCHIVES:
The major collection of Welty's papers is at the Mississippi Department of Archives and History in Jackson, Mississippi.

POEM:
Eudora Welty, "Once Upon a Time," *St. Nicholas,* 51 (November 1923): 108.

Welty's first publications appeared in the popular children's magazine St. Nicholas. *This poem —*

written when Welty was fourteen and a student at Central High School in Jackson, Mississippi — was entered in a competition marking the fiftieth anniversary of the magazine.

"Once upon a time" — that sounds
A great long distance back from now,
But that is when our dear ST. NICK
To our grandparents made its bow.

Oh, if those boys and girls of old
Could view this long, successful climb,
They'd wonder what ST. NICK will be
When *now* is "once upon a time!"

POEM:
Eudora Welty, "In the Twilight," *St. Nicholas,*
52 (January 1925): 328.

This poem, written when Welty was fifteen, won a Gold Badge in a St. Nicholas *readers' competition.*

The daylight in glory is dying away;
The last faded colors are fast growing gray;
The sun nears the beckoning portals of night,
And leaves to the skies his long, ling'ring light.

The sunbeams have hid 'neath a sad, misty veil,
And softened to shadows — dim, silvery, pale.
The Queen of the Night shyly peeps o'er the hill,
And reigns in her radiance — soft, cold, and still.
A lone cypress-tree, with its feathery grace,
Casts delicate shadows, like old Spanish lace,
On the cool, trembling waters that meet the
    gray sky,
And the moon rules supreme in her palace on
    high.

POEM:
Eudora Welty, "Burlesque Ballad," *The Spectator*
    (Mississippi State College for Women), 20
    (26 September 1925): 3.

When Welty graduated from Central High School in 1925, at age sixteen, her parents considered her too young to go away to an out-of-state college and sent her for two years to Mississippi State College for Women in Columbus, about 150 miles from Jackson. In 1927, encouraged by her parents, Welty transferred to the University of Wisconsin — Madison for her junior and senior years.
    This poetic parody of the fairy tale "Rapunzel" was Welty's first contribution to the

"A HEADING FOR AUGUST." BY EUDORA ALICE WELTY. AGE 10.
(SILVER BADGE)

Welty's first publication was this drawing, which won a Silver Badge in a St. Nicolas readers' competition and was published in the August 1920 issue of the popular children's magazine.

student newspaper at Mississippi State College for Women.

Up in a tall and silent tower
A maiden labored by the hour,
A nail file back and forth she drew
To saw the window bar in two.

She wept sad tears to show her grief,
And on the ground with dire relief
A pigeon caught them in his bill,
And quenched his thirst with right good will.

And then a knight came riding by
And heard the maiden sob and cry,
He sang a song to cheer her up.
She threw at him her drinking cup.

It struck the knight right in the nose
It knocked him down and soiled his clothes;
He looked above, she looked below.
And both were pierced by Cupid's bow.

The knight, he sighed in deep despair
How could he reach his lady fair?
No ivy hung upon the wall
And if there did, the knight would fall.

Up in the tower the lady fair
Unbound her coils of golden hair,
She let her locks fly out the casement,
They reached well nigh down to the basement.
Uprose the knight with right good will

213

PANDORA REGRETS HAVING OPENED THE BOX

Cartoon by Welty in the 12 February 1927 issue of The Spectator, *the student newspaper at Mississippi State College for Women*

And toward his love he climbed with skill;
He bent the bars and leaped inside
With outstretched arms he clasped his bride.

Then to a bar he bound her hair
And carefully lowered his lady fair;
He put a lock into his boot
And slid down like a chute-the-chute.

Alack! his spur did cut her head!
Alack! alas! it killed her dead!
The knight was grieved beyond repair
And strangled himself with her golden hair.

POEM:
Eudora Welty, "Desire," *The Spectator* (Mississippi State College for Women), 21 (16 October 1926): 3.

During her two years at Mississippi State College for Women, Welty contributed nine verse and prose pieces and one drawing to The Spectator. *This poem rises above its conventional theme with an allusion to John Keats's Grecian urn — and a hint of irony.*

I have found a purple flower in a far away place
And I wish that my hair were like swift night
clouds
So that I could wear the flower with the proper
grace —
    No use —
And I know a purple flower would surely come
to hate
My saintly silver vase —
So I crush my purple flower on the back door step,
    And bury all the leaves beneath the neat back
gate,
    And I tear the stem in stringy pieces all so nicely
brittle,
    And go inside and polish up my saintly silver
vase —

And laugh a little —
(Would you like to see the stain upon the back
   door step?)

SKETCH:
Eudora Welty, " 'I' for Iris — Irma, Imogene,"
   The Spectator (Mississippi State College for
   Women), 21 (27 November 1926): 6.

*This short prose sketch reveals some of Welty's
early thoughts about an artistic vocation and her
satirical bent.*

It was while I was sitting helplessly at the
table during one of those inevitable Ohio Sunday
dinners, wherein meat, bread, potatoes and kinfolks make a prim struggle for supremacy, that
one of the last named made the fatal suggestion.
Wouldn't it be nice if I should go to see the new
neighbor! She was an artist, they said significantly, and paused. It is generally believed among
my relatives that I have an artistic temperament,
although they go by only the first two syllables.
The artist had just bought the Laning Place and
was all by herself; wouldn't it be NICE if I should
go to see her.

Tuesday morning I decided I might as well
go on, and so I did not, meaning at all to build up
illusions on the way. But then the way had mar-
gins of apple trees, and the wind was good, and I
began to like the way her house looked, up the
road — just as though it had been cut out with
shiny scissors from very clean white paper and
pasted in pieces against the apple trees. The apple
trees themselves would have pleased Arthur Rack-
ham with their gray twistiness. I wondered if she
had come because of them. I rather hoped she had.

Her house had a card on the door — a large
square card with her name in very black letters —
"I. Smith." This was interesting: people who used
initials for their first names were always either very ashamed of them or were professional
enough to be nonchalant. And I reasoned that she
must be the latter kind, because if she were going
to be ashamed of her name, she would have ini-
tialed the Smith.

I knocked on the door, and a voice said
"Come in." As soon as I heard it, I knew she had
not come to draw the trees; her name was probably Iris and she painted sweet peas on china teacups. I was sorry about it, but I went in. Her studio was empty — the same voice told me to wait and
make myself at home — There weren't any teacups
lying about, but neither was anything else; she had

not finished moving things in yet, of course. Suddenly I saw a bottle of ink: suppose she were
named Irma and did banana plants; her voice
might be accounted for by describing it as ironic. I
was quite absorbed in giving her heavy pen
strokes and shell-rimmed glasses when the door
shut behind me. I. Smith had come in the room.

In ten minutes I knew all. She had two gold
teeth and a ready smile; she was just terribly sorry
she kept me waiting; she did the coat-suit page for
Peter's Latest Fashion's for Ladies and Young
Women — at Cincinnati, my dear — and her
name was Imogene Smith. Of course, I did not say
anything, but it really would not have mattered in
the least to me if she spelled it Smythe — and my
dear, wasn't this the deadest place in Ohio.

I think I might just as well claim my artistic
temperament.

INTRODUCTION:
Katherine Anne Porter, Introduction to *A Curtain
   of Green* (Garden City, N.Y.: Doubleday,
   Doran, 1941), pp. ix–xix.

*After completing her studies at Columbia Univer-
sity in 1931, the year her father died of leukemia,
Welty unsuccessfully sought work in New York
City before returning home to Jackson. At first
she worked part-time for a local radio station, and
later she did freelance newspaper writing. In 1935
she took a full-time job as "Junior Publicity
Agent" for the Works Progress Administration
(WPA) in Mississippi, traveling around the state
by car to write newspaper copy and take photographs. When her job ended in 1936, after Democratic defeats in state elections, she took a similar
job with the Mississippi Advertising Commission,
whose purpose was to attract industry and tour-
ism to the state. In 1936 and 1937 some of her
photographs of Mississippi black people were displayed in New York galleries. Some of these photographs have been published, most notably in
One Time, One Place (1971) and Eudora Welty:
Photographs (1989), but the Mississippi Department of Archives and History has negatives and
contact prints for many more that remain unpublished.*

*In March 1936 John Rood, editor of the
literary magazine Manuscript, had accepted for
publication two of Welty's short stories,
"Death of a Traveling Salesman" (May–June
1936) and "Magic" (September–October 1936).
By the end of the decade she had published eleven
more stories in magazines, including six in The*

Welty in 1929, the year she earned a B.A. in English from the University of Wisconsin. She studied advertising at the Columbia University School of Business in 1930–1931.

Southern Review, edited by Robert Penn Warren and Cleanth Brooks with the assistance of Albert Erskine, who recommended Welty's fiction to Katherine Anne Porter. In 1940 Welty won a fellowship to the Bread Loaf Writers' Conference in Middlebury, Vermont, where she renewed her acquaintance with Porter, who was continuing her efforts to interest book publishers in Welty's stories.

Since 1935 Welty had been trying to publish a collection of her stories, but even with help and encouragement from Porter and John Woodburn, an editor at Doubleday, Doran, she was turned down by several publishers before Doubleday, Doran reconsidered and agreed to publish A Curtain of Green. Porter, already an established author, agreed to write an introduction, helping to ensure the success of Welty's book.

Porter's introduction to the collection of seventeen stories, which was published on 7 November 1941, explains a dilemma that she and Welty faced throughout their careers: their natural inclinations were to write short fiction, but book publishers wanted novels.

Friends of us both first brought Eudora Welty to visit me three years ago in Louisiana. It was hot midsummer, they had driven over from Mississippi, her home state, and we spent a pleasant evening together talking in the cool old house with all the windows open. Miss Welty sat listening, as she must have done a great deal of listening on many such occasions. She was and is a quiet, tranquil-looking, modest girl, and unlike the young Englishman of the story, she has something to be modest about, as this collection of short stories proves.

She considers her personal history as hardly worth mentioning, a fact in itself surprising enough, since a vivid personal career of fabulous ups and downs, hardships and strokes of luck, travels in far countries, spiritual and intellectual exile, defensive flight, homesick return with a determined groping for native roots, and a confusion of contradictory jobs have long been the mere conventions of an American author's life. Miss Welty was born and brought up in Jackson, Mississippi, where her father, now dead, was president of a Southern insurance company. Family life was cheerful and thriving; she seems to have got on excellently with both her parents and her two brothers. Education, in the Southern manner with daughters, was continuous, indulgent, and precisely as serious as she chose to make it. She went from school in Mississippi to the University of Wisconsin, thence to Columbia, New York, and so home again where she lives with her mother, among her lifelong friends and acquaintances, quite simply and amiably. She tried a job or two because that seemed the next thing, and did some publicity and newspaper work; but as she had no real need of a job, she gave up the notion and settled down to writing.

She loves music, listens to a great deal of it, all kinds; grows flowers very successfully, and remarks that she is "underfoot locally," meaning that she has a normal amount of social life. Normal social life in a medium-sized Southern town can become a pretty absorbing occupation, and the only comment her friends make when a new story appears is, "Why, Eudora, when did you write that?" Not how, or even why, just when. They see her about so much, what time has she for writing? Yet she spends an immense amount of time at it. "I haven't a literary life at all," she wrote once, "not much of a confession, maybe. But I do feel that the people and things I love are of a true and human world, and there is no clutter about them. . . . I would not understand a literary life."

We can do no less than dismiss that topic as casually as she does. Being the child of her place and time, profiting perhaps without being aware of it by the cluttered experiences, foreign travels, and disorders of the generation immediately preceding her, she will never have to go away and live among the Eskimos, or Mexican Indians; she need not follow a war and smell death to feel herself alive: she knows about death already. She shall not need even to live in New York in order to feel that she is having the kind of experience, the sense of "life" proper to a serious author. She gets her right nourishment from the source natural to her — her experience so far has been quite enough for her and of precisely the right kind. She began writing spontaneously when she was a child, being a born writer; she continued without any plan for a profession, without any particular encouragement, and, as it proved, not needing any. For a good number of years she believed she was going to be a painter, and painted quite earnestly while she wrote without much effort.

Nearly all the Southern writers I know were early, omnivorous, insatiable readers, and Miss Welty runs reassuringly true to this pattern. She had at arm's reach the typical collection of books which existed as a matter of course in a certain kind of Southern family, so that she had read the ancient Greek and Roman poetry, history and fable, Shakespeare, Milton, Dante, the eighteenth-century English and the nineteenth-century French novelists, with a dash of Tolstoy and Dostoievsky, before she realized what she was reading. When she first discovered contemporary literature, she was just the right age to find first W. B. Yeats and Virginia Woolf in the air around her; but always, from the beginning until now, she loved folk tales, fairy tales, old legends, and she likes to listen to the songs and stories of people who live in old communities whose culture is recollected and bequeathed orally.

She has never studied the writing craft in any college. She has never belonged to a literary group, and until after her first collection was ready to be published she had never discussed with any colleague or older artist any problem of her craft. Nothing else that I know about her

could be more satisfactory to me than this; it seems to me immensely right, the very way a young artist should grow, with pride and independence and the courage really to face out the individual struggle; to make and correct mistakes and take the consequences of them, to stand firmly on his own feet in the end. I believe in the rightness of Miss Welty's instinctive knowledge that writing cannot be taught, but only learned, and learned by the individual in his own way, at his own pace and in his own time, for the process of mastering the medium is part of a cellular growth in a most complex organism; it is a way of life and a mode of being which cannot be divided from the kind of human creature you were the day you were born, and only in obeying the law of this singular being can the artist know his true directions and the right ends for him.

Miss Welty escaped, by miracle, the whole corrupting and destructive influence of the contemporary, organized tampering with young and promising talents by professional teachers who are rather monotonously divided into two major sorts: those theorists who are incapable of producing one passable specimen of the art they profess to teach; or good, sometimes first-rate, artists who are humanly unable to resist forming disciples and imitators among their students. It is all well enough to say that, of this second class, the able talent will throw off the master's influence and strike out for himself. Such influence has merely added new obstacles to an already difficult road. Miss Welty escaped also a militant social consciousness, in the current radical-intellectual sense, she never professed Communism, and she has not expressed, except implicitly, any attitude at all on the state of politics or the condition of society. But there is an ancient system of ethics, an unanswerable, indispensable moral law, on which she is grounded firmly, and this, it would seem to me, is ample domain enough; these laws have never been the peculiar property of any party or creed or nation, they relate to that true and human world of which the artist is a living part; and when he dissociates himself from it in favor of a set of political, which is to say, inhuman, rules, he cuts himself away from his proper society — living men.

There exist documents of political and social theory which belong, if not to poetry, certainly to the department of humane letters. They are reassuring statements of the great hopes and dearest faiths of mankind and they are acts of high imagination. But all working, practical po-

Welty's photograph of herself with friends Hubert Creekmore,
Margaret Harmon, and Nash K. Burger in Brown's Wells,
Mississippi, during the 1930s

litical systems, even those professing to originate in moral grandeur, are based upon and operate by contempt of human life and the individual fate; in accepting any one of them and shaping his mind and work to that mold, the artist dehumanizes himself, unfits himself for the practise of any art.

Not being in a hurry, Miss Welty was past twenty-six years when she offered her first story, "Death of a Traveling Salesman," to the editor of a little magazine unable to pay, for she could not believe that anyone would buy a story from her; the magazine was *Manuscript,* the editor John Rood, and he accepted it gladly. Rather surprised, Miss Welty next tried the *Southern Review,* where she met with a great welcome and the enduring partisanship of Albert Erskine, who regarded her as his personal discovery. The story was "A Piece of News" and it was followed by others published in the *Southern Review,* the *Atlantic Monthly,* and *Harper's Bazaar.*

She has, then, never been neglected, never unappreciated, and she feels simply lucky about it. She wrote to a friend: "When I think of Ford Madox Ford! You remember how you gave him

my name and how he tried his best to find a publisher for my book of stories all that last year of his life; and he wrote me so many charming notes, all of his time going to his little brood of promising writers, the kind of thing that could have gone on forever. Once I read in the *Saturday Review* an article of his on the species and the way they were neglected by publishers, and he used me as the example chosen at random. He ended his cry with 'What is to become of both branches of Anglo-Saxondom if this state of things continues?' Wasn't that wonderful, really, and typical? I may have been more impressed by that than would other readers who knew him. I did not know him, but I knew it was typical. And here I myself have turned out to be not at all the martyred promising writer, but have had all the good luck and all the good things Ford chided the world for withholding from me and my kind."

But there is a trap lying just ahead, and all short-story writers know what it is — The Novel. That novel which every publisher hopes to obtain from every short-story writer of any gifts at all, and who finally does obtain it, nine times out of ten. Already publishers have told her, "Give us first a novel, and then we will publish your short stories." It is a special sort of trap for poets, too, though quite often a good poet can and does write a good novel. Miss Welty has tried her hand at novels, laboriously, dutifully, youthfully thinking herself perhaps in the wrong to refuse, since so many authoritarians have told her that was the next step. It is by no means the next step. She can very well become a master of the short story, there are almost perfect stories in this book. It is quite possible she can never write a novel, and there is no reason why she should. The short story is a special and difficult medium, and contrary to a widely spread popular superstition it has no formula that can be taught by correspondence school. There is nothing to hinder her from writing novels if she wishes or believes she can. I only say that her good gift, just as it is now, alive and flourishing, should not be retarded by a perfectly artificial demand upon her to do the conventional thing. It is a fact that the public for short stories is smaller than the public for novels; this seems to me no good reason for depriving that minority. I remember a reader writing to an editor, complaining that he did not like collections of short stories because, just as he had got himself worked into one mood or frame of mind, he was called upon to change to another. If that is an important objection, we might also apply it to music. We might compare the novel to a symphony, and a collection of short stories to a good concert recital. In any case, this complainant is not our reader, yet our reader does exist, and there would be more of him if more and better short stories were offered.

These stories offer an extraordinary range of mood, pace, tone, and variety of material. The scene is limited to a town the author knows well; the farthest reaches of that scene never go beyond the boundaries of her own state, and many of the characters are of the sort that caused a Bostonian to remark that he would not care to meet them socially. Lily Daw is a half-witted girl in the grip of social forces represented by a group of earnest ladies bent on doing the best thing for her, no matter what the consequences. Keela, the Outcast Indian Maid, is a crippled little Negro who represents a type of man considered most unfortunate by W. B. Yeats: one whose experience was more important than he, and completely beyond his powers of absorption. But the really unfortunate man in this story is the ignorant young white boy, who had innocently assisted at a wrong done the little Negro, and for a most complex reason, finds that no reparation is possible, or even desirable to the victim. . . . The heroine of "Why I Live at the P.O." is a terrifying case of dementia praecox. In this first group — for the stories may be loosely classified on three separate levels — the spirit is satire and the key grim comedy. Of these, "Petrified Man" offers a fine clinical study of vulgarity — vulgarity absolute, chemically pure, exposed mercilessly to its final subhuman depths. Dullness, bitterness, rancor, self-pity, baseness of all kinds, can be most interesting material for a story provided these are not also the main elements in the mind of the author. There is nothing in the least vulgar or frustrated in Miss Welty's mind. She has simply an eye and an ear sharp, shrewd, and true as a tuning fork. She has given to this little story all her wit and observation, her blistering humor and her just cruelty; for she has none of that slack tolerance or sentimental tenderness toward symptomatic evils that amounts to criminal collusion between author and character. Her use of this material raises the quite awfully sordid little tale to a level above its natural habitat, and its realism seems almost to have the quality of caricature, as complete realism so often does. Yet, as painters of the grotesque make only detailed reports of actual living types observed more keenly than the average eye is capable of observing, so Miss Welty's little human monsters are not really caricatures at all, but individuals exactly and clearly presented: which is perhaps a case against realism, if we cared to go into it. She does better on another level — for the important reason that the themes are richer — in such beautiful stories as "Death of a Traveling Salesman," "A Memory," "A Worn Path." Let me admit a deeply personal preference for this particular kind of story, where external act and the internal voiceless life of the human imagination almost meet and mingle on the mysterious threshold between dream and waking, one reality refusing to admit or confirm the existence of the other, yet both conspiring toward the same end. This is not easy to accomplish, but it is always worth trying, and Miss Welty is so successful at it, it would seem her most familiar territory. There is no blurring at the edges, but evidences of an active and disciplined imagination working firmly in a strong line of continuity, the waking faculty of daylight reason recollecting and recording the crazy logic of the dream. There is in none of these stories any trace of autobiography in the prime sense, except as the author is omnipresent, and knows each character she writes about as only the artist knows the thing he has made, by first experiencing it in imagination.

Welty at the time of A Curtain of Green, *in the backyard of her family home in Jackson, Mississippi*

But perhaps in "A Memory," one of the best stories, there might be something of early personal history in the story of the child on the beach, alienated from the world of adult knowledge by her state of childhood, who hoped to learn the secrets of life by looking at everything, squaring her hands before her eyes to bring the observed thing into a frame — the gesture of one born to select, to arrange, to bring apparently disparate elements into harmony within deliberately fixed boundaries. But the author is freed already in her youth from self-love, self-pity, self-preoccupation, that triple damnation of too many of the young and gifted, and has reached an admirable objectivity. In such stories as "Old Mr. Marblehall," "Powerhouse," "The Hitch-Hikers," she combines an objective reporting with great perception of mental or emotional states, and in "Clytie" the very shape of madness takes place before your eyes in a straight account of actions and speech, the personal appearance and habits of dress of the main character and her family.

In all of these stories, varying as they do in excellence, I find nothing false or labored, no diffusion of interest, no wavering of mood — the approach is direct and simple in method, though the themes and moods are anything but simple, and there is even in the smallest story a sense of power in reserve which makes me believe firmly that, splendid beginning that this is, it is only the beginning.

"But now that so much is being changed, is it not time that we should change? Could we not try to develop ourselves a little, slowly and gradually take upon ourselves our share in the labor of love? We have been spared all its hardship . . . we have been spoiled by easy enjoyment. . . . But what if we despised our successes, what if we began from the beginning to learn the work of love which has always been done for us? What if we were to go and become neophytes, now that so much is changing?"*

*The Journal of My Other Self, by Rainer Maria Rilke. Translated by M. D. Herter Norton and John Linton. Published by W. W. Norton & Company, Inc.

BOOK REVIEW:
Marianne Hauser, Review of *A Curtain of Green, New York Times Book Review,* 16 November 1941, p. 6.

After Welty signed with literary agent Diarmuid Russell in May 1940, he was able to sell several of her stories to mass-market magazines, including Atlantic Monthly *and* Harper's Bazaar, *which paid better than the literary journals that had been publishing her short fiction and gave her more visibility. In early 1942 she won an O. Henry Award second prize for "A Worn Path," which had been published in the February 1941 issue of* Atlantic Monthly *before it was collected in* A Curtain of Green. *The sale of that book to Doubleday, Doran allowed Welty to devote full time to her writing, and she spent part of summer 1941 at Yaddo, an artists' colony near Saratoga Springs, New York, where Porter was working on the introduction for* A Curtain of Green. *Though reviews of the book were favorable, many appeared to have been cribbed from Porter's introduction.*

Few contemporary books have ever impressed me quite as deeply as this book of stories by Eudora Welty. It seems to me almost impossible to discuss her work detachedly. Reading it twice has not given me any critical distance, but has only drawn me closer into its rich and magic world. To explain just why these stories impress one so appears as difficult as to define why an ordinary face, encountered by chance in the street, might suddenly reveal miraculous beauty, through a smile perhaps, or through an unexpected expression of sadness.

Many of the stories are dark, weird and often unspeakably sad in mood, yet there is no trace of personal frustration in them, neither harshness nor sentimental resignation; but an alert, constant awareness of life as a whole, and that profound, intuitive understanding of life which enables the artist to accept it.

It is this simple, natural acceptance of everything, of beauty and ugliness, insanity, cruelty and gentle faith which helps the author create her characters with such clear sureness. Lily Daw, the feeble-minded girl who wanted to marry a xylophone player, the little clubfooted Negro, the two hitch-hikers or the traveling salesman are only a few of the many characters which the reader will not easily forget.

On each page one senses the author's fanatic love of people. With a few lines she draws the gesture of a deaf-mute, the windblown skirts of a Negro woman in the fields, the bewilderment of a child in the sickroom of an old people's asylum—

and she has told more than many an author might tell in a novel of six hundred pages.

How does she achieve this? Through the colorful flexibility of her style, the choice of her plot, the clever handling of her climax? Partly, but not essentially. Miss Welty's writing is not intellectual primarily, and what makes it so unique cannot be learned in short-story courses. As Katherine Anne Porter tells in her fine introduction, Miss Welty has never studied the writing craft at any college, or belonged to any literary group. She was born a writer, and could do nothing else but write. Her art is spontaneous, and of that poetic quality which values the necessity of form by instinct. Her stories escape any technical analysis. To point out that they are right in form seems to me quite as superfluous as to state that a tree is right in form.

Her descriptions of people and things never remain mere observations, but become, as it were, part of a deeper law and meaning, not through conscious symbolism or abstraction, but merely because they are so completely seen and felt. There is in some of her stories an almost surrealistic note, an intimate fusion of dream and reality, reminiscent at times of Kafka.

The background of most of the stories is a small town in Mississippi, the author's native State. However, there is nothing particularly regional about them. They could in a way happen anywhere, though certainly not to any one. For the mood and atmosphere of each story form a close unity with its specific characters.

There are no wars going on behind the scenes, no revolutions or headline-disasters. The tragedies which Miss Welty invokes occur in the backyards of life. She needs no outside stimulus to recreate the depths of human suffering.

If Miss Welty's writing is detached from immediate controversial subjects, it has nothing to do with "escapism." I would not think it necessary to make this point if the word had not become a standard expression for any type of literature that does not report or lecture. Escapism is not so bad a word, though if applied thoughtfully one might find that many a war story or newspaper report might come under its heading. But Miss Welty's stories never escape from anything, except from the danger of literary falsehood. She rather explores, follows up and remains within her story to the last to bear the responsibility of her deeper knowledge.

I feel certain that her stories will live for a long time. Her talent is of that rare kind which holds, even at its strongest moments, a hidden

John Woodburn, Eudora Welty, Doubleday chief associate editor Ken McCormick, Eugene Armfield of Publishers' Weekly, Carnegie Hall president Robert Simon, Welty's agent Diarmuid Russell (standing at right), and Russell's partner, Henry Volkening, at the Doubleday, Doran party to celebrate the publication of A Curtain of Green, *Murray Hill Hotel, New York, November 1941*

wealth of still greater strength, unexpressed as yet. This is why I believe that we can expect much from her in the future, and even more.

BOOK REVIEW:
Louise Bogan, "The Gothic South," review of *A Curtain of Green*, *Nation*, 153 (6 December 1941): 572.

Louise Bogan was one of several early reviewers who attempted to force Welty's fiction into a "Southern Gothic" mold instead of recognizing her originality.

The definite Gothic quality which characterizes so much of the work of writers from the American South has puzzled critics. Is it the atmosphere of the *roman noir*, so skillfully transferred to America by Poe? Or is it a true and indigenous atmosphere of decaying feudalism? Faulkner treats the horrifying and ambiguous situations thrown up by a background which has much in common with nineteenth-century Russia in a style darkened and convoluted by, it would seem, the very character of his material. Eudora Welty, who is a native and resident of Mississippi, in the stories of this volume has instinctively chosen another method which opens and widens the field and makes it more amenable to detached observation. She proceeds with the utmost simplicity and observes with the most delicate terseness. She does not try mystically to transform or anonymously to interpret. The parallel forced upon us, particularly by those of Miss Welty's stories which are based on an oblique humor, is her likeness to Gogol.

The tramp musicians, the inhabitants of a big house (either mad, drunk, or senile), the idiots and ageless peasant women, the eccentric families tyrannized over by an arch-eccentric, the pathetic and ridiculous livers of double lives, even the Negro band leader with his sadism and delusion of grandeur — all these could come out of some broken-down medieval scene, and all could be

2

had proved his recovery ~~established.~~ He had not even been sorry

to let the trained nurse go. He did not like illness. He distrusted

it, as he distrusted the road without signposts. It angered him.

He had given his nurse a really expensive bracelet because she

was ~~leaving, having neatly~~ packed up ~~illness in~~ her bag and ~~taken~~

~~it off again.~~

~~But~~ In ~~his~~ fourteen years on the road, ~~stocking small town general~~

~~stores with men's and women's low-priced shoes,~~ Bowman had never been

ill before, and never had an accident. He had gradually put up at

better hotels, ~~although some of them~~ were ~~always~~ stuffy in summer and

drafty in winter; ~~and he had known several, no, many fine women in~~

~~his territory. Sometimes on Christmas he went to his family, who~~

had moved to ~~Texas~~. . . He always wore rather wide-brimmed black

hats, and in the wavy hotel mirrors had looked something like a bull-

fighter, as he paused on the landing, walking downstairs to supper. . .

~~In this lonely road he was remembering himself as if he were another~~

~~person, and rather more fondly than he usually thought of himself.~~

He leaned out of the ~~window~~ again, ~~instead of wiping the dust off~~

~~the windshield. He seemed unable to keep his mind on what he was~~

~~doing, on what he ought to do. He was thinking of himself and how~~

~~he felt; perhaps that was how he had lost his way.~~

Bowman had wanted to reach Beula by dark, ~~as he could~~ go to bed

and sleep off his fatigue. That was fifty miles away, on a graveled

road. ~~And he was ready to admit now that this road went nowhere.~~ It

was only a cow-trail. How had he ever come to be in such a place?

He ~~took off his hat~~ and wiped the sweat from ~~the top of his head.~~

He had made the Beula trip ~~occasionally~~ before. But he had

never seen this hill or this petering-out path before, or that

cloud, he thought shyly, looking up and then down, blinded--any

more than he had seen this day before. ~~He was simply lost.~~ Like

Second page of a draft for "Death of a Traveling Salesman" (Eudora Welty Collection—Mississippi Department of Archives and History)

223

treated completely successfully — with humorous detachment, combined with moments of tenderness and roaring farce — by the author of "The Inspector General" and "Dead Souls." Like Gogol, Miss Welty opens the doors and describes the setting, almost inch by inch. She adds small detail to small detail: the fillings in people's teeth, the bright mail-order shirts of little boys, the bottles of Ne-Hi, the pictures of Nelson Eddy hung up like icons. We see what happens to representatives of an alien commercial world — here, traveling salesmen: how they become entangled against their will in this scene, which goes on under its own obscure decomposing laws; or dissolve back into it, symbolically enough, in delirium and death. Even the women in the beauty parlor have a basic place in the composition; they are not so much modernly vulgar as timelessly female — calculating, shrewd, and sharp. Miss Welty's method can get everything in; nothing need be scamped, because of romantic exigencies, or passed over, because of rules of taste. Temperamentally and by training she has become mistress of her material by her choice of one exactly suitable kind of treatment, and — a final test of a writer's power — as we read her, we are made to believe that she has hit upon the only possible kind. But it is a method, in Miss Welty's hands, only suitable for her Southern characters on their own ground. The one story dealing with the North, Flowers for Marjorie, goes completely askew.

Katherine Anne Porter, in her preface, surveys with much insight the nature and scope of and the dangers attendant upon the specialized talent of the writer of short stories. She warns against "the novel," a form held up to the short-story writer as a baited trap. She does not warn against the other trap, the commercial short story, and the other tempter, "the agent." It seems impossible that Miss Welty, equipped as she is, should fall into line and produce the bloated characters and smoothed-out situations demanded by "commercial" publications. But other finely equipped persons have given in. As for the novel, she needs only the slenderest unifying device, something analogous to "a smart *britchka,* a light spring-carriage of the sort affected by bachelors, retired lieutenant colonels, staff captains, landowners possessed of about a hundred souls," to produce one whenever she wishes.

BOOK REVIEW:
Alfred Kazin, "An Enchanted World in America," review of *The Robber Bridegroom, New*

York Herald Tribune Books, 25 October 1942, VIII: 19.

Doubleday, Doran published The Robber Bridegroom, *the short novel Woodburn had decided to omit from* A Curtain of Green, *as a separate book on 23 October 1942. It is one of a series of Natchez Trace stories that Welty set in different time periods along that historic five-hundred-mile trail running between Nashville, Tennessee, and Natchez, Mississippi. ("A Worn Path" in* A Curtain of Green *is also a Natchez Trace story.) Kazin admired the rich fantasy elements and the sense of history in* The Robber Bridegroom, *which Welty describes as a fantasy, "not a* historical historical *novel."*

The only trouble with our contemporary literature of native folklore and Americana is that it has so rarely been literature at all. It has inspired a staggering mass of legend and biography, of historical romance and doggerel and wistful bluster, that is the candid expression of our present sense of insecurity. It has driven us back, if only vicariously, upon the past we want, the past we transform so lovingly into myth, the past we need as transparently as the Russians need Alexander Nevsky, who was no Leninist, and the French St. Joan. But while it has given us a pride in the fondled memory of our frontier world, the ring of creation, of that depth of understanding and imaginative participation which comes from something more than access to grandfather's papers or the facile technicolor of the costume romance, has not been in it.

It is here that Miss Eudora Welty comes in. For Miss Welty is one of those young writers who are turning easily and naturally to our native materials, particularly in the South, where the sense of the past can be so much deeper, so much more insistent and sly than anywhere else in America, and she is also one of those who can never think of the forms in which they work as moulds into which library studies in Americans are to be poured. She begins with the imagination, with her own world apprehended, her particular object clearly and intensely seen. She begins with that perhaps indefinable sense of grace, so dear to our American craftsmen nurtured in the short story, which has always made for so vivid, if subterranean, a tradition of style in modern American writing. But most important, she begins with something not usually associated with our serious artists in fiction — a sense of joy. There is a lightheartedness in this book, an easy welling poetry of pleasure, that only a very young writer can know, a writer not too far from the myths of her childhood, but now in gleeful satiric command of them. Here, and not in the synthetic cuteness of the costume romance, is what so many have been trying to capture by dint of will and bibliography alone — the lost fabulous innocence of our departed frontier, the easy carelessness, the fond bragging and colossal buckskin strut. And Miss Welty can capture it only because she is not trying to produce historical chromos at all, only because she is writing out of a joy in the world she has restored, and with an eye toward the comedy and poetry embedded in it.

That joy is the great thing in "The Robber Bridegroom," and explains why it is cast as a fairy tale. We have moved here into a world where the image we all carry of the past has been restored to a pure frame of myth. Mike Fink blusters into it, and the long spinal river at New Orleans, and the bayous in whose region the story takes place; but the episodes are designed in fantasy, the characters are as representative of virtue and greed and vice as in any fairy tale, and the raven croaks the time. There is the favorite picaresque hero of fairy tale — the handsome outlaw, Jamie Lockhart, who swaggers in disguise with his band at night, but is a courtly and dashing gentleman by day. The heroine, Rosamond, has, of course, a wicked stepmother, Salome, who, in turn, employs the wicked or mutilated gamins of the wood to spy on poor Rosamond when she goes off with her Jamie. Nor, as in the archetypal fairy tale, do the lovers really know each other's identity until the end. Rosamond's father is incensed against the bandit with the mane of yellow hair who took his daughter off, but hires Jamie himself to find her — and Jamie already has her, and doesn't know it. And the stepmother sends off a character, "Goat," so-called because he can butt his way in and out of anything, to betray her. And there are Indians, and the living head of a decapitated criminal in a box crying "Let me out!" and panthers out of the poetry of William Blake, and always the woods at night.

Any summary of Miss Welty's tale is impotent and just a little silly. What composes the book is a series of fairy-tale incidents dense beyond retelling, the traditional comedy of errors perched crazily on wickedness and innocence. But the point is this: the simplicity of fairy tale has here become the echo of the legendary primitiv-

ism of the frontier — the very fact of its being legendary to us. We are in the black forest of Cinderella and magic boxes, of wicked stepmothers and elfs who are older than the rocks on which they sit; but this is the forest of Davy Crockett of Tennessee, and the river mud on which Mike Fink pushed his flatboat, and the poetry that is the unspoken poetry in Huck Finn. Miss Welty is a very conscious artist, so conscious that she has burnished the myth simply by restoring it on its most imaginative level, given it back by letting all the cardinal illusions of childhood stream free. And now she sits back and laughs a little, as we must laugh with her in her pleasure, for imaginatively childhood is free, and the images so many. How we can get here, in "fairy tale," what the solemnity of history can not give us! How we pierce here to the truth that is in the lovely lie of fairy tale, where there are so many tacit lies, or incomplete truths, in the truth of adulthood! Listen to Mike Fink:

"You doubt that I am Mike Fink? Nevertheless, it is true!" . . . He doubled up his fists and rippled the muscles on his arms up and down, as slow as molasses, and on his chest was the finest mermaid it was possible to have tattooed at any port. "I can pick up a grown man by the neck in each hand and hold him out at arm's length, and often do, too," yelled the flatboatman. "I eat a whole cow at one time, and follow her up with a live sheep if it's Sunday. Ho! Ho! If I get hungry on a voyage I jump off my raft and wade across and take whatever lies in my path on shore. When I come near the good folk take to their heels and run from their houses! I only laugh at the Indians, and I can carry a dozen oxen on my back at one time, and as for pigs, I tie them in a bunch and hang them to my belt!"

If this is an enchanted world, the black forest of childhood, it is also one into which the sadder, newer world is breaking. And the slow, long roll of disenchantment can be heard at the end, where the Indians capture all the characters and decide their fate, as the axe that broke the trees only led the way for the machine that would break the forest. Every myth we tell each other today, or try to restore, is only the symbol of our own longing, and turns upon itself. Not the smallest part of Miss Welty's rather exquisite achievement is the skill with which she reminds us that the enchanted forest is for us to recapture — and is forever dead.

BOOK REVIEW:
Diana Trilling, Review of *The Wide Net*, *Nation*, 157 (2 October 1943): 386–387.

Welty in 1942, the year she won a Guggenheim Fellowship. The fellowship was renewed for travel in France, Italy, England, and Ireland in 1949–1950.

Welty won O. Henry Award first prizes for "The Wide Net" (1942) and "Livvie" (1943), collected in The Wide Net and Other Stories. *The book was published on 23 September 1943 by Harcourt, Brace, where John Woodburn had gone to work the previous November. Trilling was not the only reviewer to prefer the stories in* A Curtain of Green *to those in* The Wide Net, *a collection of eight stories — seven set along the Natchez Trace — in which Welty combined motifs from mythology and folklore with essentially realistic subject matter.*

In her latest collection of short stories, "The Wide Net" (Harcourt, Brace, $2.50), Eudora Welty has developed her technical virtuosity to the point where it outweighs the uses to which it is put, and her vision of horror to the point of nightmare. Of course even in her earlier work Miss Welty had a strong tendency toward stylism and "fine" writing; she liked to move toward the mythical, and she had a heart for decay and an eye for the Gothic in detail. But she also had a reliable and healthy wit, her dialogue could be as normally reportorial of its world as the dialogue of Ring Lardner, and for the most part she knew how to keep performance subservient to communication; she told her story instead of dancing it, and when she saw horror, it could be the clear day-to-day horror of actual life, not only the horror of dreams. There was plenty of surrealist paraphernalia, if you will, in a story like The Petrified Man — the falling hair of the customer, and the presence of the three-year-old boy amid the bobbie-pins and sexual confidences of the beauty parlor, the twins in a bottle at the freak show, or even the petrified man himself. But compare to The Petrified Man the story Asphodel from Miss Welty's current volume, with its Doric columns and floating muslins, its pomegranate stains and blackberry cordial and its "old goats and young," and you will recognize the fancy road up which Miss Welty has turned her great talents.

The title story of Miss Welty's new volume is its best story but not typical. An account of a river-dragging party which starts out to recover the body of a supposed suicide but forgets its mission in the joys of the occasion, The Wide Net has its share of the elements of a tour de force, but it has more communicated meaning than the rest of the stories in the book, and it best fuses content and method. Of the six other stories Livvie is the only one which I like at all, and the only story, in addition to The Wide Net, which I feel I understood. Yet the volume as a whole has tremendous emotional impact, despite its obscurity. However, this seems to me to be beside the point, for the fear that a story or a picture engenders is likely to be in inverse proportion to its rational content: witness the drawings of children or psychotics, or most of surrealist art; and Miss Welty employs to good effect the whole manual of ghostliness — wind and storm, ruined buildings, cloaks, horses' hooves on a lonely highway, fire and moonlight and people who live and ride alone. But the evocation of the mood of horror or of a dreamlike atmosphere has become an end in itself, and if, for each story, there is a point of departure in narrative, so that I can report, for instance, that First Love is about a deaf-and-dumb boy who falls in love with Aaron Burr, or that Asphodel is about a tyrannical half-mad Southern gentlewoman, or that A Still Moment is a legend of Audubon, still the stories themselves stay with their narrative no more than a dance, say, stays with its argument. This, indeed, is the nature of "The Wide Net": it is a book of ballets, not of stories; even the title piece is a *pastorale macabre*.

Now I happen to think that to make a ballet out of words is a perversion of their best function, and I dislike — because it breeds exhibitionism and insincerity — the attitude toward narrative which allows an author to sacrifice the precise meaning of language to its rhythms and patterns. The word sincerity has lost caste in the criticism of serious writing, I know. But this seems to me unfortunate. We live in a very crafty literary period in which what aims to be art but is only artful is too often mistaken for the real thing. When an author says "Look at me" instead of "Look at it," there is insincerity, as I see it. The test of sincerity is wasted in the sphere of popular art, where criticism has sent it; most popular art is nothing if not sincere, and where it is not, it is usually because it is aping the manners of its betters. In these new stories Miss Welty's prose constantly calls attention to herself and away from her object. When she writes," . . . Jenny sat there . . . in the posture of a child who is appalled at the stillness and unsurrender of the still and unsurrendering world," or "He walked alone, slowly through the silence, with the sturdy and yet dreamlike walk of the orphan," she is not only being falsely poetic, she is being untrue. How does the walk of an orphan differ in its sturdiness and in its dream quality from the walk of a child with two parents? How would you even explain "unsurrender" to a child, and wouldn't a child be appalled precisely by the *surrender* of the world, if the concept could reach him? This is the sin of pride — this self-conscious contriving — endemic to a whole generation of writers since Katherine Mansfield and most especially to the women of that generation.

Somewhere between Chekhov and Katherine Mansfield the short story certainly went off its trolley. I think it is Miss Mansfield who must be held responsible for the extreme infusion of subjectivism and private sensibility into the short fiction of our day. In Miss Welty's case the subjectivism takes the form, as I say, of calling attention to herself by fine writing; in stories for a magazine like the *New Yorker,* which happily has no taste for fine writing, the form it takes is rather more subtle — the calling of attention to oneself for one's fine moral perceptions. This is a point I shall develop next week in discussing several other current collections of short stories, including those of Sylvia Townsend Warner.

I have spoken of the ballet quality of Miss Welty's stories: in this connection I am reminded of the painter Dali and — via Dali — of the relationship between the chic modern department store and much of modern fiction. (One day I should like, in fact, to trace what I see to be the direct line of descent from Miss Mansfield to Bonwit Teller.) Although the suspicion intrudes itself that Dali works with his tongue in his cheek, Miss Welty's dedication is of course unquestionable: this should be said at once. Still, the resemblance in performance and the subtle cultural kinship between the two is striking. Both Dali and Miss Welty are mythologists and creators of legend, both take their metaphor from dreams, and yet both are devoted naturalists; and each has a mother-country — Dali, Spain; Miss Welty, the Natchez country — whose atmosphere and superstition permeate his work and whose confines are determining beyond the power of travel or maturer experience to enlarge them. Rather more suggestive, however, than these similarities is their common service to what amounts to a myth of modern femininity.

For if it seemed a strange day for both art and commercialism when Bonwit Teller engaged Dali to do its windows, actually it was not so revolutionary as it looked. In the making of modern myths, the American department store has been at least abreast of the American artist. The chic department-store mannequin is surely one of the great metaphors of our time; the displays of merchandise one of the great abstractions, based upon naturalism, of our art. But more fundamental, we recall the slogan created a few years ago by Bonwit Teller, "Have you that cherished look?" and we realize that it was the department store which stated most unmistakably (so unmistakably, indeed, that the slogan was dropped) the modern woman's dream of herself. Here in all its economic nakedness is the narcissism which is so widely supported in current female writing, including Miss Welty's. This mythologizing of the feminine self, whether by means of clothes or prose, is as far from femininity as from feminism.

There is now running in the magazines an advertisement for a Schiaparelli product, "Shocking Radiance," the illustration painted by Dali. "Shocking Radiance," it appears, is four oils — for the body, the face, the eyelids, and the lips — and to promote its sale Dali has painted a Venus rising from her shell, attended by a trio of sprites, one of whom pours a libation on her breast, while another holds before her the mirror of her self-regard. Even at the risk of satirizing Miss Welty's stories, I suggest a study of this Schiaparelli-Dali advertisement to see the *reductio ad absurdum* of the elements in Miss Welty's latest work which

He could understand God's giving Separateness first and then giving Love to follow and heal in its wonder; but God had reversed this, and given Love first and then Separateness, as though it did not matter to Him which came first. — "A Still Moment."

Dust jacket for the volume that includes seven of Welty's Natchez Trace stories. Writing to Diarmuid Russell on 23 November 1940, Welty commented, "I believe that the Natchez Trace, like many another beautiful and time-worn place, casts a spell . . . ; and if I can show this spell, in a few of its dramatic or its modest aspects, that is what I hope to do."

have no place in such a serious and greatly endowed writer.

REVIEW ESSAY:

Robert Penn Warren, "The Love and the Separateness in Miss Welty," review of *The Wide Net and Other Stories, Kenyon Review*, 6 (Spring 1944): 246–259.

Warren responded to Diana Trilling's criticism of The Wide Net, *comparing Welty's method to that of much modern literature. His essay remains one of the most influential works of Welty criticism.*

If we put *The Wide Net,* Eudora Welty's present collection of stories, up against her first collection, *A Curtain of Green,* we can immediately observe a difference: the stories of *The Wide Net* represent a specializing, an intensifying, of one of the many strains which were present in *A Curtain of Green.* All of the stories in *A Curtain of Green* bear the impress of Miss Welty's individual talent, but there is a great variety among them in subject matter and method and, more particularly, mood. It is almost as if the author had gone at each story as a fresh start in the business of writing fiction, as if she had to take a new angle each time out of a joy in the pure novelty of the perspective. There is the vindictive farce of "The Petrified Man," the nightmarish "Clytie," the fantastic and witty "Old Mr. Marblehall," the ironic self-revelation of "Why I Live at the P.O.," the nearly straight realism of "The Hitch-Hikers," the macabre comedy and pathos of "Keela, the Outcast Indian Maid." The material of many of the stories was sad, or violent, or warped, and even the comedy and wit were not straight, but if read from one point of view, if read as a performance, the book was exhilarating, even gay, as though the author were innocently delighted not only with the variety of the world but with the variety of ways in which one could look at the world and the variety of things which stories could be and still be stories. Behind the innocent delight of the craftsman, and of the admirer of the world, there was also a seriousness, a philosophical cast of mind, which gave coherence to the book, but on the surface there was the variety, the succession of surprises. In *The Wide Net* we do not find the surprises. The stories are more nearly cut to one pattern.

We do not find the surprises. Instead, on the first page, with the first sentence, we enter a special world: "Whatever happened, it happened in extraordinary times, in a season of dreams . . ." And that is the world in which we are going to live until we reach the last sentence of the last story. "Whatever happened," the first sentence begins, as though the author cannot be quite sure what did happen, cannot quite undertake to resolve the meaning of the recorded event, cannot, in fact, be too sure of recording all of the event. This is coyness, of course; or a way of warning the reader that he cannot expect quite the ordinary direct lighting of the actual event. For it is "a season of dreams" — and the faces and gestures and events often have something of the grave retardation, the gnomic intensity, the portentous suggestiveness of dreams. The logic of things here is not quite the logic by which we live, or think we live, our ordinary daylight lives. In "The Wide Net," for example, the young husband, who thinks his wife has jumped into the river, goes out with a party of friends to dredge for the body, but the sad occasion turns into a saturnalian fish-fry which is interrupted when the great King of the Snakes raises his hoary head from the surface of the river. But usually, in the present stories, the wrenching of logic is not in terms of events themselves, though "The Purple Hat" is a fantasy, and "Asphodel" moves in the direction of fantasy. Usually the events as events might be given a perfectly realistic treatment (Dreiser could take the events of "The Landing" for a story). But in these cases where the events and their ordering are "natural" and not supernatural or fantastic, the stories themselves finally belong to the "season of dreams" because of the special tone and mood, the special perspective, the special sensibility with which they are rendered.

Some readers, in fact, who are quite aware of Miss Welty's gifts, have recently reported that they are disturbed by the recent development of her work. Diana Trilling, in her valuable and sobering comments on current fiction, which appear regularly in the *Nation,* says that the author "has developed her technical virtuosity to the point where it outweighs the uses to which it is put, and her vision of horror to the point of nightmare." There are two ideas in this indictment, and let us take the first one first and come to the second much later. The indictment of the technique is developed along these lines: Miss Welty has made her style too fancy — decorative, "falsely poetic" and "untrue," "insincere." ("When an author says 'look at me' instead of 'Look at it,' there is insincerity . . .") This insincerity springs from "the extreme infusion of subjectivism and private sensibility." But the subjectivism leads not only to insincerity and fine writing but to a betrayal of the story's obligation to narrative and rationality. Miss Welty's stories take off from a situation, but "the stories themselves stay with their narrative no more than a dance, say, stays with its argument." That is the summary of the argument.

The argument is, no doubt, well worth the close attention of Miss Welty's admirers. There is, in fact, a good deal of the falsely poetic in Miss Welty's present style, metaphors that simply pretend to an underlying logic, and metaphors (and descriptions) that, though good themselves, are irrelevant to the business in hand. And sometimes Miss Welty's refusal to play up the objective action — her attempt to define and refine the response rather than to present the stimulus — does result in a blurred effect. But the indictment does not treat primarily of such failures to fulfill the object the artist has set herself but of the nature of that object. The critic denies, in effect, that Miss Welty's present kind of fiction is fiction at all: "It is a book of ballets, not of stories."

Now is it possible that the critic is arguing from some abstract definition of "story," some formalistic conception which does not accommodate the present exhibit, and is not concerning herself with the question of whether or not the present exhibit is doing the special job which it proposes for itself, and, finally, the job which we demand of all literature? Perhaps we should look at a new work first in terms of its effect and not in terms of a definition of type, because every new work is in some degree, however modest, wrenching our definition, straining its seams, driving us back from the formalistic definition to the principles on which the definition was based. Can we say this, therefore, of our expectation concerning a piece of literature, new or old: that it should intensify our awareness of the world (and of ourselves in relation to the world) in terms of an idea, a "view." This leads us to what is perhaps the key statement by Diana Trilling concerning *The Wide Net*: she grants that the volume "has tremendous emotional impact, despite its obscurity." In other words, she says, unless I misinterpret her, that the book does intensify the reader's awareness — but *not* in terms of a presiding idea.

This has led me to reread Miss Welty's two volumes of stories in the attempt to discover the issues which are involved in the "season of dreams." To begin with, almost all of the stories deal with people who, in one way or another, are cut off, alienated, isolated from the world. There is the girl in "Why I Live at the P.O." — isolated from her family by her arrogance, meanness, and sense of persecution; the half-witted Lily Daw, who, despite the efforts of "good" ladies, wants to live like other people; the deaf-mutes of "The Key," and the deaf-mute of "First Love"; the people of "The Whistle" and "A Piece of News," who are physically isolated from the world and who make their pathetic efforts to reestablish something lost; the travelling-salesman and the hitch-hikers of "The Hitch-Hikers" who, for their different reasons, are alone, and the travelling-salesman of "Death of a Travelling Salesman" who, in the physically and socially isolated backwoods cabin, discovers that he is the one who is truly isolated; Clytie, isolated in family pride and madness and sexual frustration, and Jennie of "At the Landing," and Mrs. Larkin of "A Curtain of Green," the old women of "A Visit of Charity" and the old Negro woman of "A Worn Path"; the murderer of "Flowers for Marjorie" who is cut off by an economic situation and the pressure of that great city; Mr. Marbelhall in his secret life; Livvie, who, married to an old man and trapped in his respectable house, is cut off from the life appropriate to her years; Lorenzo, Murrell, and Audubon in "A Still Moment," each alone in his dream, his obsession; the old maids of "Asphodel," who tell the story of Miss Sabina and then are confronted by the naked man and pursued by the flock of goats. In some of the cases, the matter is more indirectly presented. For instance, in "Keela, the Outcast Indian Maid," we find, as in "The Ancient Mariner," the story of a man who, having committed a crime, must try to reestablish his connection with humanity; or in the title-story of *The Wide Net*, William Wallace, because he thinks his wife has drowned herself, is at the start of the story cut off from the world of natural joy in which he had lived. "The Petrified Man" and "A Memory" present even more indirect cases, cases which we shall come to a little farther in the discussion.

We can observe that the nature of the isolation may be different from case to case, but the fact of isolation, whatever its nature, provides the basic situation of Miss Welty's fiction. The drama which develops from this basic situation is of either of two kinds: first, the attempt of the isolated person to escape into the world; or second, the discovery by the isolated person, or by the reader, of the nature of the predicament. As an example of the first type, we can remember Clytie's obsessed inspection of faces ("Was it possible to comprehend the eyes and the mouth of other people, which concealed she knew not what, and secretly asked for still another unknown thing?") and her attempt to escape, and to solve the mystery, when she lays her finger on the face of the terrified barber who has come to the ruinous old house to shave her father. Or there is Jennie, of

"At the Landing," or Livvie, or the man of "Keela." As an example of the second type, there is the new awareness on the part of the salesman in "The Hitch-Hikers," or the new awareness on the part of the other salesman in the back-country cabin. Even in "A Still Moment" we have this pattern, though in triplicate. The evangelist Lorenzo, the outlaw Murrell, and the naturalist and artist Audubon stand for a still moment and watch a white heron feeding. Lorenzo having seen a beauty greater than he could account for (he had earlier "accounted for" the beauty by thinking, "Praise God, His love has come visible"), and with the sweat of rapture pouring down from his forehead, shouts into the marshes, "Tempter!" He has not been able to escape from his own obsession, or in other words, to make his definition of the world accommodate the white heron and the "natural" rapture which takes him. Murrell, looking at the bird, sees "only whiteness ensconced in darkness," and thinks that "if it would look at him a dream penetration would fill and gratify his heart" — the heart which Audubon has already defined as belonging to the flinty darkness of a cave. Neither Lorenzo nor Murrell can "love" the bird, and so escape from their own curse as did, again, the Ancient Mariner. But there remains the case of Audubon himself, who does "love" the bird, who can innocently accept nature. There is, however, an irony here. To paint the bird he must "know" the bird as well as "love" it, he must know it feather by feather, he must have it in his hand. And so he must kill it. But having killed the bird, he knows that the best he can make of it now in a painting would be a dead thing, "never the essence, only a sum of parts," and that "it would always meet with a stranger's sight, and never be one with the beauty in any other man's head in the world." Here, too, the fact of the isolation is realized: as artist and lover of nature he had aspired to a communication, a communion, with other men in terms of the bird, but now "he saw his long labor most revealingly at the point where it met its limit" and he is forced back upon himself.

"A Still Moment," however, may lead us beyond the discussion of the characteristic situation, drama, and realization in Miss Welty's stories. It may lead us to a theme which seems to underlie the stories. For convenience, though at the risk of incompleteness, or even distortion, we may call it "Innocence and Experience." Let us take the case of Audubon in relation to the heron. He loves the bird, and innocently, in its fullness of being. But he must subject this love to knowledge; he must kill the bird if he is to commemorate its beauty, if he is to establish his communion with other men in terms of the bird's beauty. There is in the situation an irony of limit and contamination.

Let us look at this theme in relation to other stories. "A Memory," in *A Curtain of Green*, gives a simple example. Here we have a young girl lying on a beach and looking out at the scene through a frame made by her fingers, for the girl can say of herself, "To watch everything about me I regarded grimly and possessively as a need." (As does Audubon, in "A Still Moment.") And further: "It did not matter to me what I looked at; from any observation I would conclude that a secret of life had been nearly revealed to me. . . . " Now the girl is cherishing a secret love, a love for a boy at school about whom she knows nothing, to whom she has never even spoken, but whose wrist her hand had once accidentally brushed. The secret love had made her watching of the world more austere, had sharpened her demand that the world conform to her own ideas and had created a sense of fear. This fear had seemed to be realized one day when, in the middle of a class, the boy had a fit of nose-bleed. But that is in the past. This morning she suddenly sees between the frame of her fingers a group of coarse, fat, stupid, and brutal people disporting themselves on the sand with a maniacal, aimless vigor which comes to climax when the fat woman, into the front of whose bathing suit the man had poured sand, bends over and pulls down the cloth so that the lumps of mashed and folded sand empty out. "I felt a peak of horror, as though her breasts themselves had turned to sand, as though they were of no importance at all and she did not care." Over against this defilement (a defilement which implies that the body, the breasts which turn to sand, had no meaning), there is the refuge of the dream, "the undefined austerity of my love."

"A Memory" presents the moment of the discovery of the two poles — the dream and the world, the idea and nature, innocence and experience, individuality, and the anonymous, devouring life-flux, meaning and force, love and knowledge. It presents the contrast in terms of horror (as do "The Petrified Man" and "Why I Live at the P.O." when taken in the context of Miss Welty's work), and with the issue left in suspension, but other stories present it with different emphases and tonalities. For instance, when William Wallace, in "The Wide Net," goes out to dredge the river, he is acting in terms of the meaning of the loss of his wife, but he is gradually drawn into the world of the river, the saturnalian revel, and prances about with a great cat-fish hung on his belt, like a river-god laughing and leaping. But he had also dived deep down into the water: "Had he suspected down there, like some secret, the real true trouble that Hazel had fallen into, about which word in a letter could not speak . . . how (who knew?) she had been filled to the brim with that elation that they all remembered, like their own secret, the elation that comes of great hopes and changes, sometimes simply of the harvest time, that comes with a little course of its own like a tune to run in the head, and there was nothing she could do about it, they knew — and so it had turned into this? It could be nothing but the old trouble that William Wallace was finding out, reaching and turning in the gloom of such depths." This passage comes clear when we recall that Hazel, the wife who is supposed to have committed suicide by drowning, is pregnant: she had sunk herself in the devouring life-flux, has lost her individuality there, just as the men hunting for the body have lost the meaning of their mission. For the river is simply force, which does not have its own definition; in it are the lost string of beads to wind around the little negro boy's head, the cat fish for the feast, the baby alligator that looks "like the oldest and worst lizard," and the great King of the Snakes. As Doc, the wise old man who owns the net, says: "The outside world is full of endurance." And he also says: "The excursion is the same when you go looking for your sorrow as when you go looking for your joy." Man has the definition, the dream, but when he plunges into the river he runs the risk of having it washed away. But it is important to notice that in this story, there is not horror at the basic contrast, but a kind of gay acceptance of the issue: when William Wallace gets home he finds that his wife had fooled him, and spanks her, and then she lies smiling in the crook of his arm. "It was the same as any other chase in the end."

As "The Wide Net," unlike "A Memory," does more than merely present the terms of contrast, so do such stories as "Livvie" and "At the Landing." Livvie, who lives in the house of wisdom (her infirm husband's name is Solomon) and respectability (the dream, the idea, which has withered) and Time (there is the gift of the silver watch), finally crosses into the other world, the world of the black buck, the field-hand, in his Easter clothes — another god, not a river god but a field god. Just after Solomon's death, the field-hand in his gorgeous Easter clothes takes Livvie in arms, and she drops the watch which Solomon had given her, while "outside the redbirds were flying and criss-crossing, the sun was in all the bottles on the prisoned trees, and the young peach was shining in the middle of them with the bursting light of spring."

If Livvie's crossing into the world of the field god is joyous, the escape of Jennie, in "At the Landing," is rendered in a different tonality. This story assimilates into a new pattern many of the elements found in "A Memory," "The Wide Net," "Livvie," and "Clytie." As in the case of Clytie, Jennie is caught in the house of pride, tradition, history, and as in the case of Livvie, in a house of death. The horror which appears in "A Memory," in "Clytie," re-appears here. The basic symbolisms of "Livvie" and especially of "The Wide Net" are again called into play. The river, as in "The Wide Net," is the symbol of that world from which Jennie is cut off. The grandfather's dream at the very beginning sets up the symbolism which is developed in the action:

> The river has come back. That Floyd came to tell me. The sun was shining full on the face of the church, and that Floyd came around it with his wrist hung with a great long catfish. . . . That Floyd's catfish has gone loose and free. . . . All of a sudden, my dears — my dears, it took its river life back, and shining so brightly swam through the belfry of the church, and downstream.

Floyd, the untamed creature of uncertain origin, is William Wallace dancing with the great catfish at his belt, the river god. But he is also, like the buck in "Livvie," a field god, riding the red horse in a pasture full of butterflies. He is free and beautiful, and Jennie is drawn after him, for "she knew that he lived apart in delight." But she also sees him scuffling playfully with the hideous old Mag: the god does not make nice distinctions. When the flood comes over the Landing (upsetting the ordered lives, leaving slime in the houses), Floyd takes her in his boat to a hill (significantly the cemetery hill where her people are buried), violates her, feeds her wild meat and fish (field and river), and when the flood is down, leaves her. She has not been able to talk to him, and when she does say, "I wish you and I could be far away. I wish for a little house," he only stares into the fire as though he hadn't heard a word. But after he has gone she cannot live longer in the Landing; she must set out to find him. Her quest leads her into the woods (which are like an underwater depth) and to the camp of the wild river people, where the men are throwing knives at a tree. She asks for Floyd, but he is not there. The men put her in a grounded houseboat and come in to her. "A rude laugh covered her cry, and somehow both the harsh human sounds could easily have been heard as rejoicing, going out over the river in the dark night." Jennie has crossed into the other world to find violence and contamination, but there is not merely the horror as in "Clytie" and "A Memory." Jennie has acted out a necessary rôle, she has moved from the house of death, like Livvie, and there is "gain" as well as "loss." We must not forget the old woman who looked into the dark houseboat, at the very end of the story, and understands when she is told that the strange girl is "waiting for Billy Floyd." The old woman nods, "and nodded out to the flowing river, with the firelight following her face and showing its dignity."

If this general line of interpretation is correct, we find that the stories represent variations on the same basic theme, on the contrasts already enumerated. It is not that there is a standard resolution for the contrasts which is repeated from story to story; rather, the contrasts being basic, are not susceptible to a single standard resolution, and there is an implicit irony in Miss Welty's work. But if we once realize this, we can recognize that the contrasts are understood not in mechanical but in vital terms: the contrasts provide the terms of human effort, for the dream must be carried to, submitted to, the world, innocence to experience, love to knowledge, knowledge to the fact, individuality to communion. What resolution is possible is, if I read the stories with understanding, in terms of the vital effort. The effort is a "mystery," because it is in terms of the effort, doomed to failure but essential, that the human manifests itself as human. Again and again, in different forms, we find what we find in Joel of "First Love": "Joel would never know now the true course, or the true outcome of any dream: this was all he felt. But he walked on, in the frozen path into the wilderness, on and on. He did not see how he could ever go back and still be the boot-boy at the Inn."

It is possible that, in my effort to define the basic issue and theme of Miss Welty's stories, I have made them appear too systematic, too mechanical. I do not mean to imply that her stories should be read as allegories, with a neat point-to-point equating of image and idea. It is true that a few of the stories, especially some of those in the present volume, such as "The Wide Net," do approach the limit of allegory, but even in such cases we find rather than the system of allegory a tissue of symbols which emerge from, and disappear into, a world of scene and action which, once we discount the author's special perspective, is recognizable in realistic terms. The method is similar to the method of much modern poetry, and to that of much modern fiction and drama (Proust, James, Kafka, Mann, Isak Dinesen, Katherine Anne Porter, Pirandello, Kaiser, Andreyev, O'Neill, for example); but at the same time it is a method as old as fable, myth, and parable. It is a method by which the items of fiction (scene, action, character, etc.) are presented not as document but as comment, not as a report but as a thing made, not as history but as idea. Even in the most realistic and reportorial fiction, the social picture, the psychological analysis, and the pattern of action do not rest at the level of mere report; they finally operate as expressive symbols as well.

Fiction may be said to have two poles, history and idea, and the emphasis may be shifted very far in either direction. In the present collection the emphasis has been shifted very far in the direction of idea, but at the same time there remains a sense of the vividness of the actual world: the picnic of "The Wide Net" is a real picnic as well as a "journey," Cash of "Livvie" is a real field-hand in his Easter clothes as well as a field god. In fact, it may be said that when the vividness of the actual world is best maintained, when we get the sense of one picture superimposed upon another, different and yet somehow the same, the stories are most successful. The stories which fail are stories like "The Purple Hat" and "Asphodel" in which the material seems to be manipulated in terms of an idea, in which the relation between the image and the vision has become mechanical, in which there is a strain for atmosphere, in which we do find the kind of hocus-pocus deplored by Diana Trilling.

And this brings us back to the criticism that the volume "has tremendous emotional impact, despite its obscurity," that the "fear" it engenders is "in inverse ratio to its rational content." Now it seems to me that this description does violence to my own experience of literature, that we do not get any considerable emotional impact unless we sense, at the same time, some principle of organization, some view, some meaning. This does not go to say that we have to give an abstract formulation to that principle or view or meaning before we can experience the impact of the work, but it does go to say that it is implicit in the work and is

having its effect upon us in immediate aesthetic terms. Furthermore, in regard to the particular work in question, I do not feel that it is obscure. If anything, the dream-like effect in many of the stories seems to result from the author's undertaking to squeeze meaning from the item which, in ordinary realistic fiction, would be passed over with a casual glance. Hence the portentousness, the retardation, the otherworldliness. For Miss Welty is like the girl in "A Memory":

> ... from any observation I would conclude that a secret of life had been nearly revealed to me, and from the smallest gesture of a stranger I would wrest what was to me a communication or a presentiment.

In many cases, as a matter of fact, Miss Welty has heavily editorialized her fiction. She wants us to get that smallest gesture, to participate in her vision of things as intensely meaningful. And so there is almost always a gloss to the fable.

One more word: It is quite possible that Miss Welty has pushed her method to its most extreme limit. It is also possible that the method, if pursued much farther, would lead to monotony and self-imitation and merely decorative elaboration. Certainly, the tendency to decorate elaboration is sometimes present. Perhaps we shall get a fuller drama when her vision is submitted more daringly to the fact, when the definition is plunged into the devouring river. But meanwhile *The Wide Net* gives us several stories of brilliance and intensity; and as for the future, Miss Welty is a writer of great resourcefulness, sensitivity, and intelligence, and can probably fend for herself.

BOOK REVIEW:
John Crowe Ransom, "Delta Fiction," review of *Delta Wedding, Kenyon Review,* 8 (Summer 1946): 503–507.

Published on 15 April 1946, Welty's first full-length novel, Delta Wedding, *was written during World War II, when both her brothers and many friends were serving in the military. The novel grew out of Welty's visits to the family of one of these friends, John Robinson, while he was overseas. After the Robinsons allowed her to read the diaries of a female ancestor, an early settler in the Mississippi Delta region. Welty was inspired to write a short story,* "The Delta Cousins," *which at Diarmuid Russell's urging she turned into the novel* Delta Wedding, *sending pieces of it as they*

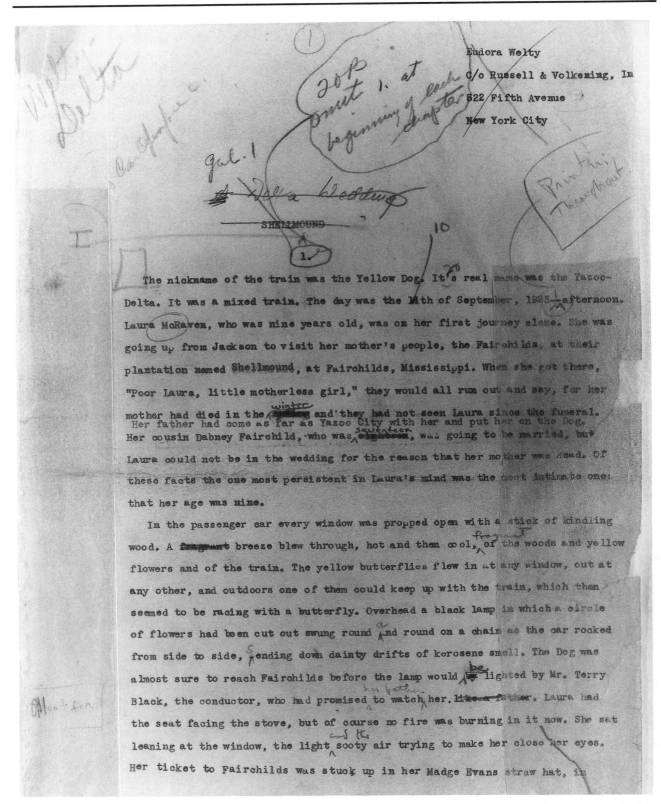

First page of the setting copy for Delta Wedding, *with revisions by Welty and editorial emendations and annotations (Eudora Welty Collection — Mississippi Department of Archives and History). "Shellmound" was the working title for the novel.*

were written to John Robinson in Italy to remind him of home.

Set on a Southern plantation in 1923, the novel was criticized by liberal Northern critics such as Isaac Rosenfeld and Diana Trilling, who accused Welty of lacking social consciousness. Trilling, who renewed some of the objections to Welty's style that she had voiced in her review of The Wide Net, *accused her of sentimentalizing a way of life that was fast disappearing. Even Welty's fellow Southerner John Crowe Ransom, who praised* Delta Wedding, *wondered if the novel were "one of the last novels in the tradition of the old South." Yet later critics have pointed out that Welty's underlying pattern of symbol and myth portrays the traditional culture of the plantation aristocracy as hollow and codified, with new vitality brought into the family by outsiders who refuse to be bound by it. The novel is now considered one of Welty's finest works, and in 1986 the Book-of-the-Month Club listed it as one of sixty American novels that should be included in "the well-stocked bookcase."*

Miss Welty's stature as an artist increases continually. We knew her last as the author of "The Wide Net" and its companion short stories, and very substantial these short stories were. She gave us rural characters who contrasted with the norms of their society by being earthy, and scandalous; they were pagans, descendants of the people in myths and folk-tales. Robert Penn Warren described their curious behaviors in this light. Their role was to retain the primitive attitudes to nature, and their vagaries were in the service of natural religion. Each was worth a good story. But not worth a novel; quaint characters become simply and painfully repetitious in a long narrative. And now, in her fourth book, we have from Miss Welty a full-length formal novel, with a content which is really capable of sustained presentation. She writes here according to some of the solidest canons of fiction.

The characters are so many as to confuse us at first, but soon they begin to compose with great clarity into what the English would call a county family. I should be prepared to suppose that a novel, ideally, is like an epic in that the individual actions are seen against the background of the cultus, the social establishment. Here a single family supplies that establishment, though the assumption would be that it is a representative family. The restriction greatly reduces the scope of the action as compared, let us say, with that of a novel

by Jane Austen — who liked to take a simple theme but to involve in it a whole cluster of families. The plot has to do only with a wedding in the family, and the preparations and brief aftermath last but a week. Nor are the Welty characters turned out as handsomely as those in Austen. Indeed they are not English, they are Southern; they are the Fairchilds of that Deep South which is the Delta country of Mississippi. I am glad that Miss Welty did not want them aristocratic and picturesque, as if to perpetuate some tradition of Southern novelists, or as if to produce a commodity in characters fit to sell to some movie firm. They have a cotton plantation, and from their economic status follows a certain social status. The time, however, is 1923, not eighty years earlier.

What a family sense they have! They look at each other with little starts of love and understanding. They stop to be glad for their own happiness, and then for their faults and failures if necessary, confident that everything is according to the mysterious requirements of the family, as well as knowing that an unvarying beatitude might dull the sense for happiness, which has to run perilously close to the tragic sense. It is needless to remark that this is a woman's book — I don't think the same inference was prompted by the short stories — and a modern one. Miss Welty in her present phase resembles Virginia Woolf more than does any other novelist of my acquaintance; the Fairchilds' wedding is the perfect analogue for Mrs. Dalloway's party. I am sure the resemblance is fortuitous. Miss Welty's prose, like her people, is her own; it is every bit as clean as Virginia Woolf's, and if it is not quite so flexible it does not need the literary range of a Bloomsbury style. Both writers confer an extreme self-consciousness upon their characters when these have recourse to their interior monologue. A scene or action is doubly beautiful when the observer stops to register it in that sense; or perhaps becomes then truly beautiful, and bears an unexpected testimony to Kant's idea that first we take a spontaneous pleasure in the object, and only presently find the object beautiful when we introvert our attention and discover the pleasure it gave us. Being an admirer of the beauties thus attested in Mrs. Woolf's books, I admire also the autochthonous beauties now achieved similarly by our own writer. Both like to take firm possession of what is beautiful, though it has to be caught on the wing; as if this were what their civilizations had trained them for, and invited them to. Their technique, if it makes us think of Kant, reminds us also of Wordsworth, who was always memorizing in his verse some specimen moment of happiness which might go, so to speak, into his winter album.

The Fairchilds are a gentle, spirited, and interesting family, perfectly realized. If there seems to be a preponderance of females, that is lucky for the special grade of communication that has to be made to the reader. They even do most of the reporting upon the males, though it is not of the management of the plantation or the ordering of business that they tell, much less of political discussions. They show the objective contribution of the males to the scene and theatre of the piece; they even read and translate for us the masculine sensibilities, these being remarkably acute though not so fine as their own.

Since I have slipped into a dramatic locution, I must say that Miss Welty's narrative method is not technically dramatic. She passes continually back and forth between the drama of dialogue and external action, on the one hand, and interior monologue on the other. But the figure of drama occurs to me at this point as useful in another way. The Fairchilds have so much self-consciousness along with their naturalness that it is as if they were actors, and their common life the drama they enacted daily. They are brought up to have this sense of themselves, and it affects them with a certain sophistication, and a public responsibility. The Fairchild servants share it. So they all enact a comedy of love together. Each actor must improvise his lines, since the development of the action is never wholly of his determination and cannot be foreseen. But he knows he must register in the right tone, and give generous leads to the other actors. The language which they address to each other is not specially remarkable in any literary sense, but there are other ways than language in which to register dramatic effect. The total effect is complex and rich.

But we come now to a kind of critical sequel which is not comedy. It is certain that Miss Welty's book is going to meet with many animadversions; probably we could categorize them, the several varieties of them, in advance. And though my own admiration is explicit, I am going to admit to fears and reservations which distress me a great deal.

Her objectors will stand on the authority of American life as they know it. Some will not be able to give credence to her exhibit of so exotic a minority culture in action down in the South. Others will project themselves into it faithfully, but even if they find it not too disagreeable they will have to disapprove it on principle.

Perhaps I had better disclose that I must have lived more than as long if not as deep in the South as has Miss Welty, and spent besides some fifteen years at one time or another looking at the South from points outside it, i.e., *ex partibus infidelium*. These points my be vantage points for the critic; who accordingly may devote himself to problems in Southern life which in theory are extremely pressing, but in fact are far from irrupting incessantly into the consciousness of Southerners at home.

How can Miss Welty's Fairchilds afford to live so casually on their sensibilities, seizing expertly upon the charming experiences that life brings them yet apparently heedless of the moral and material shortcomings of their establishment? I have been careful to intimate that in the background of the Fairchild behaviors, if rarely brought to explicit attention, there is the sense of a material culture, i.e., an objective economic and social establishment. The planter family is a microcosm of the collective society. To its members their establishment seems strong enough, with provisions that are adequate in some fashion from day to day; it has been going a long time. There is no particular worrying about it, nor idea of overhauling it. But this is not the same as saying that it is really too early for them to be worrying, and even re-ordering; nor as saying that when they do begin on the repairs there will only be a little tinkering needed. It has been a favorite conviction of mine that there can hardly be an art of living where there is not moral and material security, like a capital fund stored up by original thrift. I have no doubt that the Fairchilds have a high art, but I am inquiring about what looks like the obsolescence of their capital investment.

It would be political sense which would look after this sort of investment. Now Miss Welty's characters have copious vitality but they do not waste it on politics. The energy they have put into sensibility is not available when presently they might be projecting new models for society. I believe this has always been the way of the South. Political interest is occasional; it is intense when a polity has to be founded, but afterwards only as emergency requires; it makes a formal recovery periodically at election times, when it proceeds cheerfully to delegate the routine of departmental government. And so far as I am concerned this is not a bad political philosophy, relegating politics as it does a certain "place"; but only provided the political interest does not die of inanition over the interim periods, which is quite a proviso. In other words, I think politics is the means and not the end of life, like some other activities such as war, or even money-making, which it is barbarous to pursue beyond your need of them. This not the occasion to argue that position, but I want to assure Miss Welty of one reader's philosophical rapport with her.

I feel sure that the pattern of Southern life as Miss Welty has it is doomed. The Delta establishment will be disestablished, and at a time not far off. Like any artist, Miss Welty must be given to pondering her literary strategy in the light of the climate of public discussion. Where will she find the material of her further novels? The time of *Delta Wedding* was 1923, but that is already long ago. Her reader will probably identify it as the time of her childhood — if ignorant of the biographical data on Miss Welty as I am — and the child Laura, who is one of the precocious juvenile reporters in fiction, as herself; and he might even conclude that there was no strategic conception behind this novel other than that Miss Welty was nostalgic for a kind of life that already passed beyond recognition, and had to go back to it in imagination. But at any rate the mechanical cotton-picker had not been made and marketed then; nor had the mechanical cultivators broken into the cotton patch; they are among the instruments of revolution. Nor were relations between the black folk and the white folk strained as now, even in the Delta, they are coming to be. Both races accepted the Fairchild establishment; they had tolerances on both sides, and made mutual accommodations. But the distribution of the material benefits of this society was wholly arbitrary, even if strictly according to pattern, and the handsome sensibility of the Fairchilds was at the expense of the shabbiest kind of moral obtuseness. I expect the readjustment of racial relations in the South to be the more painful in the degree of its belatedness. But there will be many innovations, and all that cut deep into ancient habit will be painful.

In short, I am forced to wonder if *Delta Wedding* may not be one of the last novels in the tradition of the old South.

BOOK REVIEW:
Herschel Brickell, "Dragons in Mississippi," review of *The Golden Apples, Saturday Review*, 32 (27 August 1949): 9.

Published on 18 August 1949, The Golden Apples is a collection of seven stories about characters who live in or have ties to the fictional town of Morgana, Mississippi. The title comes from "The silver apples of the moon, / The golden apples of the sun," the concluding lines of William Butler Yeats's "The Song of the Wandering Aengus," a poem about a mythic hero's quest for a silver trout that transforms itself into an elusive "glimmering girl" when he catches it. The Golden Apples includes a similar wanderer, King MacLain.

The book earned Welty her best and most perceptive reviews to that date. Herschel Brickell praised the way in which mythological and literary allusions contribute to the unity of the stories, an aspect of the book much discussed by later critics.

This is the fifth book by a master-hand in the medium of short fiction, who has earned a secure place at the top of the list of living story-writers. As a poetical chronicle of an imaginary Mississippi town called Morgana, the name itself significant of Miss Welty's legendary approach to her subject, it comes close to being a novel in the completeness of its picture of a linked group of people, although its component parts range from the conventional short story length to the long short story, each a separate and complete work.

Indeed, a number of the stories have appeared separately in magazines, and one, at least, "The Whole World Knows," in an anthology, where it won recognition as one of Miss Welty's best efforts. It is a singularly moving tale of a man betrayed by his wife, whom he loved, and his pathetic efforts to cope with his tragedy. Another, "Music from Spain," has been published separately in a limited edition by the Levee Press.

As good as these separate parts proved to be, the full impact of a highly original piece of writing can only be had by reading the whole book, which has a definite pattern. In the first story, "Shower of Gold," which leaves no doubt that Miss Welty is writing at two levels, of things as they are, and of their relationship to classical and medieval mythology, the narrator is Mrs. Fate Rainey — Miss Katie — whereas the last story is concerned with Miss Katie's death and burial, rounding out a strange cycle of human conflicts, of many people in many situations.

The dominant figure is an earth-god called King McClain, who vanishes after begetting twins by Miss Snowdie Hudson, an albino, only to reappear at intervals, always eager and able to replenish the earth. King is marked for death as the book closes, but not until his imprint has been left on the reader's mind, as well as on the community.

From her earliest stories, Miss Welty's writing has had a high degree of individuality. Her memory for colloquial speech is unbelievably accurate, and her antic imagination, coupled with her profound compassion and understanding, gives us people much realer than real, stranger, yet more believable than the living.

Here is Mississippi observed and remembered, but it is a Mississippi where "they heard through falling rain the running of the horse and bear, the stroke of the leopard, the dragon's crusty slither, and the glimmer and the trumpet of the swan." Dragons in Mississippi? Yes, says Miss Welty, as everywhere else, and makes the reader believe it.

Anyone in search of writing of consistent beauty, of an individual outlook on life, of an impressive knowledge of Southern small towns, and of the play of a rare imagination, will find delight in more than one reading of "The Golden Apples," apples not to be squeezed of all their poetic juice in a single run. This is not a book for all readers, but followers of Miss Welty's work will find it one of her finest achievements to date, a work of literature that will richly reward the discriminating.

BOOK REVIEW:
Hamilton Basso, "Morgana, Mississippi," review of *The Golden Apples, New Yorker,* 25 (3 September 1949): 63–64.

Southerner Hamilton Basso also recognized Welty's accomplishment in The Golden Apples, *but his remarks reveal the tendency of critics near the middle of the twentieth century to measure young Southern writers against William Faulkner. More-recent critics would hesitate to state as categorically as Basso that Welty's work is derived from Faulkner's, and many would rank her with Faulkner.*

The town of Morgana, Mississippi, is not to be found on any map, but because of Eudora Welty's new novel, "The Golden Apples" (Harcourt, Brace), it is now just as real a place as another piece of Mississippi that has not yet come to the attention of Rand McNally — William Faulkner's Yoknapatawpha County. Like Faulkner, Miss Welty is a Mississippian in good standing; according to the vital statistics supplied by her publishers, she was born in Jackson, where she

still lives. It is my notion, though, that her real birthplace is Yoknapatawpha County. And it is obvious that she has been greatly swayed by this early environment; its mark is on her every page. In a lesser writer, this inheritance would tend to result in the worst kind of imitativeness. Miss Welty, however, is not a lesser writer. Although she derives from Faulkner and has been clearly influenced by him, she is not in the least imitative; hers is one of the most original talents in the business, and every line in this novel is absolutely hers. What she has done is take Faulkner's method, refine and sharpen it into a quite different instrument, and use it to accomplish her own purposes. This in itself is no meagre achievement. But I don't want to convey the impression that "The Golden Apples" is interesting solely as a technical exercise; Miss Welty's technical skill is only a most incidental part of it. Her book is best described as the chronicle of a small Southern town that can be taken to represent not only all small Southern towns but the whole Deep South. Again, though, I don't want anybody to be misled. This is in no sense a "regional" novel. Its people talk Southern, act Southern, and eat Southern, just as the people in Gogol's "Dead Souls" talk Russian, act Russian, and eat Russian, but they have a universal application. It is highly unlikely that their exact counterparts can be found in, say, Oxnard, California, or Sheffield, Massachusetts, where a different set of geographical and climatic influences is at work, but their problems and preoccupations, their joys and sorrows, are basic everywhere.

Yet I doubt that a better book about "the South" — one that more completely gets the feel of the particular texture of Southern life, and its special tone and pattern — has ever been written. (Faulkner has done the job up brown, of course, but his saga of Yoknapatawpha County now runs to ten volumes.) I am not sure that anyone not moderately familiar with the South can fully appreciate Miss Welty's accomplishment; it is not likely that those who have never seen a little girl holding a wide-open magnolia blossom can comprehend the absolute rightness of Miss Welty's saying of one of her characters that she "carried in the magnolia bloom like a hot tureen." A lack of familiarity with the South need not, however, stand in the way of enjoying the book; it is not necessary to have gone down the Mississippi on a raft to get lost in "Huckleberry Finn."

The chronicle of Morgana, as Miss Welty sets it forth, is told by a number of people at different times, and one event is sometimes seen from several points of view. The book begins with a certain Mrs. Fate Rainey, who tells in her own words the story of the two people who figure most prominently in it — King MacLain, an unpredictable, shiftless, far-wandering ne'er-do-well, and his wife, Snowdie. It ends, forty years later, with a description of Mrs. Rainey's funeral, at which King MacLain is one of the chief mourners. In between, the reader is introduced to various other inhabitants of Morgana: Virgie Rainey, who plays the piano at the picture show; Miss Eckhart, the town's music teacher; the MacLain twins; little Loch Morrison and his sister Cassie; their father, who owns the local newspaper; their mother; a whole gaggle of small girls; and, among others, Miss Perdita Mayo, who prides herself on being a woman "that's been clear around the world" in her rocking chair.

In the course of telling about these characters, Miss Welty gets to their hearts and the heart of Morgana; we come to know it all. Her book is so full of good things that one is tempted to go on about them endlessly. I shall mention only a few: a handling of children that is rather wonderful, an eye for significant detail, a nice sense of the comic and the bizarre, and, above everything else, a gift for language. All these excellences are not combined on every page, and Miss Welty's novel has its ups and downs, but I think that only once has she failed to bring things off. This is in a chapter devoted to a meeting in the woods between King MacLain and a young country-woman named Mattie Will Holifield. Mattie's husband is along, practicing with a .22, and before she and King can get together, he has to be disposed of. Miss Welty's way of getting rid of him is to have King fire a shot in his direction, which causes him to fall down and knock himself cold. Not only did I find this a bit contrived, but the episode, while done in the author's own manner, seemed almost a burlesque of Faulkner. But then I am so grateful for Miss Welty's novel that I am inclined to regard this defect (if I am correct in calling it a defect) as the one flaw that, according to an old Chinese theory of aesthetics, should appear in every work of art.

BOOK REVIEW:
V. S. Pritchett, "Bossy Edna Earle Had a Word for Everything," *New York Times Book Review,* 10 June 1954, p. 5.

Many reviewers saw Welty's short novel The Ponder Heart, *published on 7 January 1954, as a less significant work than the stories in* The Golden Apples. *They tended to agree with V. S. Pritchett's assessment of the novel as "one of Miss Welty's lighter works." Recent critics, however, have taken* The Ponder Heart *somewhat more seriously, pointing to its thematic connections to other works in the Welty canon.*

In some ways the novelists of the American South have the independent force of the writers of the Irish revival; in other ways, to an English critic, they recall the rich and ineradicable pockets of Scottish and Welsh regionalism; in their more decorative and ironical phases, the neo-peasant writers like T. F. Powys. In any case, they are all brilliant deviationists from a main tradition. They are a protest by old communities, enriched by wounds, against the success of mass, or polyglot, culture. They make a pawky local bid against the strong hand of the centralized society we live in.

This individuality has its dangers. Sometimes the regional writer becomes the professional topographer of local oddity. With one sophisticated foot outside his territory, he sets out to make his folk quaint or freakish (the abnormal becomes a matter of local pride), and he can be said to condescend to and even exploit them. He may even go so far as to suggest that people are not real until they are eccentric and decorative and then we have the disastrous impression that the author is philandering with his characters. (This was a great vice in James Barrie's comic Scots.) Of course isolated provincial societies *do* live a sort of family life, all rough and tumble but fundamentally close-knit, where mild lunatics, simples, notorious public nuisances, gossips and embarrassing relations have a great importance as personalities.

Indeed it is an awkward fact that there is more personality in the small worlds than in the big ones. All the critic can do is to warn against accepting the more endearing clichés of this expanded family reminiscence.

As Eudora Welty's new *nouvelle* shows, it all depends on depth and technical skill, and in Miss Welty's case on a sardonic comic brio. She has written some excellent short stories in the last ten years and an especially brilliant first volume, so that she comes to her subject with a good deal of experience. She has had the art to place her Uncle Dan in a complex position in the narrative. He is embedded in the mind of a bustling, hoydenish, bossy niece, a girl of fierce practical capacity,

Kay Bell

Eudora Welty

"One of America's distinguished prose stylists. . . . She is interested in people—their lives, their destinies, the irony attendant upon their comings and goings, and she writes of the unusual in terms of the usual."

—*N. Y. Herald Tribune Book Review*

Dust jacket for the short novel Welty published in 1954. Her first popular success, the book sold 10,883 copies in less than two months and was adapted for the Broadway stage by Joseph Fields and Jerome Chodorov, whose dramatic version ran for 149 performances in 1956.

snooty manners and possessive temperament, who will scornfully defend the old idiot partly because she passionately loves him, partly to keep her head up among the neighbors. She is the soul of small-town pugnacity and self-conceit and has an endless tongue.

It is part of the beauty of the telling that this young limb, Edna Earle, runs a small hotel (the setting is unmistakably Miss Welty's native Mississippi) and is forcing a traveling salesman to listen to her. She is really a more considerable character than Uncle Dan and it is her apparent normality which sets off his idiocy perfectly. The underlying suggestion that she may be as dotty as he is adds to the pleasure.

Uncle Dan is an amiable freak with a low I.Q. He has one dominant passion: he loves everybody with childish ingenuity. His love takes the delicate form of an irresistible desire to give everything away. He sheds property as a tree sheds leaves. He is a saint of the compulsion to distribute, and in the course of the tale even distributes himself twice in marriage. Edna Earle keeps a prim, head-tossing silence about what went on in

these marriages — one of them he described as a "trial"; certainly his wives left him in time, though without rancor. The bother about people who are not all there is that one can never be quite sure of the nature of what is there: it is likely to be unnerving. Once or twice it was thought that Uncle Dan ought to be put away, but uncle had a sort of somnambulistic instinct for last-minute success. When his father took him to the asylum, it was father, not the son, who found himself consigned.

Edna Earle's narrative is remarkable for its headlong garrulity and also for its preposterous silences and changes of subject at the crises of the tale. She is a respectable young scold with a long tradition in English sentimental comedy. If it was a shade tricky and arch of Miss Welty to make her tell the tale, she has the advantage of being able to bring a whole town to life in her throwaway lines and she has the scolds of Scott, Stevenson and Katherine Mansfield behind her in the world of feminine tongue rattling. Her breathless, backhanded, first person singular has been caught, word by awful word, in all its affectionate self-importance, by a writer with a wonderful ear. "The Ponder Heart" is one of Miss Welty's lighter works, but there is not a mistake in it.

BOOK REVIEW:
William Peden, "The Incomparable Welty," review of *The Bride of the Innisfallen and Other Stories*, *Saturday Review*, 38 (9 April 1955): 18.

The title story in The Bride of the Innisfallen and Other Stories, *published on 6 April 1955, was written in spring 1951 at Bowen's Court, the home of Anglo-Irish novelist Elizabeth Bowen in County Cork, Ireland, where Welty visited during travels in England and Ireland. (The two writers had met in 1949 and remained friends until the end of Bowen's life.) Reviews of Welty's earlier books had sometimes criticized her fiction for obscurity, but nowhere were such charges voiced as strongly as in the reviews for* The Bride of the Innisfallen and Other Stories, *with Orville Prescott calling two of the stories "wanly Bowenesque" and another "gruesomely Faulknerian" (New York Times, 8 April 1955). William Peden was less critical than Prescott, but the two reviewers shared the belief that Welty had somehow strayed from her true gift.*

Welty in 1955, the year she received the William Dean Howells Medal from the American Academy of Arts and Letters

In recent years the name of Eudora Welty has virtually become synonymous with artistry, integrity, and intelligence in American fiction; any full-length book by the "Mississippi Marvel" is a literary event of magnitude. Miss Welty's first stories began appearing in the good magazines in the late Thirties. First published in book form ("A Curtain of Green") in 1941 with a warmly appreciative introductory essay by Katherine Anne Porter, they were enthusiastically and justifiably praised. With subsequent books of fiction like "The Wide Net," "Delta Wedding," and most recently "The Ponder Heart" Miss Welty has more than lived up to the expectations of her earliest admirers. In an age of increasing literary sensationalism, exhibitionism, commercialism, and vulgarity her work has been something to cherish.

But "The Bride of the Innisfallen," her new collection of seven stories, short and not so short, is in some ways a disappointment, at least to this reviewer, who has to confess that he is often confused by certain aspects of Miss Welty's work. The title story is a richly allusive, lavishly embroidered account of a group of travelers, mostly Irish or Welsh but including an American young

woman, enroute from Paddington to Fishguard to catch the *Innisfallen,* the boat to Cork. The group includes a man from Connemara whose commentary consists largely of variations of the epithet "*Oh* my God," a middle-aged lady who sticks out her tongue at "everything just left behind," a little boy who whistles "Funiculi, Funicula," a pregnant young woman, and a schoolgirl avidly reading "Black Stallions of the Downs." There is much — and magnificent — talk about kidnaping, and Killarney, and a poisoned parrot among other things. Finally the travelers arrive at Fishguard, board the *Innisfallen,* and the American young woman reaches her destination, where at the close of the story she sends her husband a portentous wire and walks meaningfully into the "lovely room full of strangers" of an Irish pub.

Within this framework Miss Welty displays to the full her power of evoking a sense of place so real as to be almost magical. She is equally skillful in suggesting the essence of her numerous characters. But the story seems top-heavy, overburdened by a mass of detail and obscure or undecipherable symbol. Unnecessarily indirect and self-consciously elliptical, "The Bride of the Innisfallen" seems not so much a story as a highly specialized, highly *private* game. Only the initiated are invited to participate, the uninitiated can jolly well go about their own prosaic business. This excruciatingly perceptive story seems to be almost a parody of Miss Welty's effectively individualistic method; even after several readings I could neither accept it on a realistic level nor understand it on any other level.

It is difficult, however, to be objective about Miss Welty, whose devotees will probably hug "The Bride" to their bosoms. The collection as a whole certainly demonstrates that for sheer virtuosity and variety she is just about in a class by herself. This remarkable volume includes such diverse pieces as "Ladies in Spring" (Miss Welty is at her best in this portrayal of a small boy, and his dad and Miss Hattie the p. o. lady and the girl that dad has been playing around with) and "Going to Naples" (a robust mock-epic of the love life of Gabriella Serto, one of the screamingest, bawlingest, and plumpest heroines of recent years). What a writer!

INTERVIEW:
Bernard Kalb, "The Author," *Saturday Review,* 38 (9 April 1955): 18.

In a brief interview that accompanied William Peden's review of The Bride of the Innisfallen and Other Stories *Welty provided a brief overview of her career. Because of the illnesses of her mother and brothers, she was to write little for the next fifteen years. Her brother Walter died in 1959, and her mother and brother Edward died within days of one another in 1966.*

Three novels and four short-story collections ago — the mid-Thirties, to be exact — Eudora Welty, by then an ex-radio writer and ex-freelance newspaperwoman, tried to crash literature with a handful of candid photographs of rural-Negro life in Mississippi. "I tried to *sell* those pictures to fiction editors," she reminisced the other day in her hometown of Jackson, "thinking or hoping if they liked my pictures (which I thought were fine) they might be inclined to take my 'stories' (which I felt very dubious about, but I *wondered* about them — they being what I cared about), but they weren't decoyed. Once a year for three or four years I carried around the two bundles under arm on my two-weeks' trip to New York, and carried them home again — not much downcast, perhaps because I simply loved writing, and was going to do

it anyway." Finally, one sunny day in 1936, *Manuscript,* which had never seen a photograph of hers, accepted "Death of a Traveling Salesman," and that was that. *The Southern Review* and *Prairie Schooner,* among others, promptly jumped on the bandwagon; by 1941 she had enough stories to publish "A Curtain of Green," which had the critics foaming with admiration. All sorts of accolades have since piled up: O. Henry prizes, two Guggenheim Fellowships, election in 1952 to the National Institute of Arts and Letters, and an honorary LL.D. in 1954 from Wisconsin, where she got her B.A. a quarter of a century earlier. Jackson (pop. 98,271, capital of Miss.) is her great love. "I never felt that anywhere but Jackson was my home and base," she said, then switched to her new book. "I tried some stories laid in locations new and strange to me (result of a Guggenheim, that let me go to Europe), and tackled with some pleasure the problems the stories set me of writing from the outside, where my honest viewpoint had to look in from. The inside kind of story where the outside world is given, I'll always come back to, as I do in a number of stories in the new book; for the interior world is endlessly new, mysterious, and alluring."

BOOK REVIEW:
Granville Hicks, "A Belated Tribute to Short Stories by Eudora Welty and Flannery O'Connor," review of *The Bride of the Innisfallen and Other Stories* by Welty and *A Good Man Is Hard to Find and Other Stories* by O'Connor, *New Leader,* 38 (15 August 1955): 17.

In this brief review Granville Hicks avoids the pitfall of trying to force Welty and O'Connor into the same Southern mold and makes perceptive observations about the two writers' strengths.

This is a belated tribute to two collections of short stories, both by Southern women. They are Eudora Welty's *The Bride of Innisfallen* and Flannery O'Connor's *A Good Man is Hard to Find.* Harcourt, Brace published both of them last spring at $3.50 each.

Miss Welty is a Southern writer, not in the sense of belonging to a school or being a professional regionalist but simply in the sense of writing about an area of the South. As deeply rooted in her native state as her fellow-Mississippian, William Faulkner, she has succeeded, just as he has, in transcending her region.

Welty accepting a Brandeis University Creative Arts Award from university librarian Louis Kronenberger, 24 April 1966

This is not to say that the South hasn't given Miss Welty a great deal. In one of the stories in the present volume, "Kin," the narrator, after a long absence in the North, is visiting her aunt and cousin in the small Mississippi town in which she was born. "Aunt Ethel and Kate, and everybody I knew here," she reflects, "lived as if they had never heard of anywhere else, even Jackson." A degree of isolation, a degree of stability, the maintenance of family ties, the preservation of family and community and regional lore — all these provide a setting in which Miss Welty's talents operate with wonderful effectiveness.

Yet these talents can also operate without the setting, as three of these stories demonstrate. One of the three is a poetic retelling of the story of Circe and Ulysses, quite unlike anything the author has done before, though she has always had a fondness for legends. The other two seem almost calculated to prove her independence of the static qualities of Southern society, for they deal with situations that are in their nature ephemeral. "Going to Naples" describes an Atlantic crossing

on an Italian vessel, while the title story is devoted to the passengers in a compartment on the boat train from London to Fishguard. Yet in portraying the transient relationships that develop in such circumstances, Miss Welty manages, almost as well as in her best stories of the South, to suggest the depths of human personality.

Miss Welty has two great gifts. The first is her ability to create an atmosphere so real and so dense that the reader finds himself immersed in it. The second is her skill in searching out and in suggesting, usually by indirection, the subtler reaches of character. Her fondness for the oblique and the parabolic leads her at times into obscurity, and at times (as, for instance, in so essentially melodramatic a story as "The Burning") makes her seem awkward and prissy. But when subject and sensibility and method all match, as generally they do, she can provide as much pleasure as any writer now living.

Miss Welty's book gives me what I have learned to expect from her work, but Miss O'Connor's comes as a surprise: I hadn't realized she was so good. All ten of her stories are laid in Georgia, her native state, and her people are either poor or are fighting hard to maintain what advantages they have. But the book is not so much a description of a certain segment of the population as it is the expression of a mood.

Several of her characters are physically defective, with a hand missing or a leg, or they are feeble-minded; most of the others are morally or spiritually deformed. What typically happens is that characters are confronted with situations to which they are inadequate. In the title story, a painfully commonplace family stumbles into extermination. In "The Artificial Nigger," an old man cannot cope with the city and is led into a betrayal of his grandson. In "A Circle in the Fire," a woman of great self-reliance is challenged and beaten by a trio of young hoodlums. And in "The Displaced Person," another very competent woman is destroyed by being compelled to face the problems of her responsibilities to other persons.

It would be hard to exaggerate the competence with which Miss O'Connor goes about the telling of these stories. Each of them is hard and sharp and dramatic. And each of them leaves, as it is meant to do, a nasty taste in the reader's mouth. This nastiness, however, is not gratuitous on the author's part. On the contrary, it is clear that Miss O'Connor regards human life as mean and brutish and that she makes this judgment from an orthodox Christian point of view. But one does not have to believe in original sin to be affected by the stories. Miss O'Connor's vision of life is presented with such conviction and such intensity that, for the moment at any rate, it authenticates itself. If there is a young writer — Miss O'Connor is 30 — who has given clearer evidence of originality and power, I cannot think who it is.

BOOK REVIEW:
Louis D. Rubin, Jr., "Everything Brought Out In The Open: Eudora Welty's *Losing Battles,*" *Hollins Critic,* 7 (June 1970): 1–12.

During the long hiatus between The Bride of Innisfallen and Other Stories *in 1955 and the novel* Losing Battles *in 1970, Welty published three works of fiction in* The New Yorker. *Two were short stories sympathetic to the civil rights movement:* "Where Is the Voice Coming From?" *(9 July 1963) and* "The Demostrators" *(26 November 1966). The third was* The Optimist's Daughter *(15 March 1969), which was heavily revised before it was published as a book in 1972. After the deaths of her mother and brother Edward in*

1966, Welty went back to "a suitcase full of earlier drafts" and completed her longest and most popular novel, Losing Battles, *published on 13 April 1970.*

Miss Welty when last seen, in 1955, published *The Bride of the Innisfallen,* her third collection of short stories (fourth if you count *The Golden Apples*). Thereafter, and for fifteen years, silence, the only exceptions being a little privately-printed essay, *Place in Fiction,* and a few magazine pieces. So it has been a long time between books.

Now comes, in the year 1970, the 61st of the author's age, her longest novel, *Losing Battles,* an affair of some 436 pages all told, being the story of a family reunion in the northeastern Mississippi community of Banner. This particular place in fictional Mississippi is too small even to be a town, and most of what happens does so on a farm up a hillside several miles away from the post-office and the general store. The elapsed time is something more than 24 hours of a summer day and night in the 1930's. Most of what takes place is talk. The talk begins when Miss Beulah Renfro, grand-daughter of Elvira Jordan Vaughn, "Granny," puts in an appearance on the second page, after some 500 words of place-setting, shouting, "Granny! Up, dressed, and waiting for 'em! All by yourself! Why didn't you holler?" Thereafter everybody talks, all the time. It ends with a hymn, "Bringing in the Sheaves."

When Eudora Welty's people talk, it is a special kind of talk. They do not talk *to,* they talk *at.* Part of the reason that they talk is to communicate, but part of the reason is to dissemble, to mask, to hide. They converse obliquely, chattering away all the time but never entirely revealing themselves or saying what they think; and the barrier, the mystery that results, lies at the center of the high art of Eudora Welty.

I say high art, because the more I read and think about Miss Welty's fiction, the more I suspect that she is not merely a good writer, one of the very best of the half-a-dozen fine women writers that the South has produced in the past half-century, but a major author, one of the three or four most important writers to come out of twentieth-century America. Her best fiction — *The Golden Apples,* some of the stories, now *Losing Battles* — goes beyond story-telling, beyond people and places, to those truths of the human heart that only the greatest art can reveal. There is only one other Southern writer of her generation in her

103.

The baby ran behind the quilt ~~hanging there~~ *again* and Gloria caught
her ~~when she came out~~ on the other side. But she was already
sliding, slick as a fish, from her arms when she got her back
onto the porch, and running ahead of her mother again.

Aunt Nanny headed off Lady May, and breathing hard she crouched
and scooped up the baby in her arms. ~~"Didn't you know it?"~~ I've
come to steal you!" But Lady May squirmed free and ~~in her leaf
hat she~~ charged up and down a little path that kept opening between
their knees, over their patting feet.

~~"But where's she going, where's she going so soon?" Uncle Noah
Webster teased Gloria.~~

~~"That's for the future to say," she replied.~~

"Well, in case anybody forgets how long Jack Renfro's been gone,
feel the weight of _that_," said ~~Miss Lexie~~, and ~~stopping the baby~~
with her broom, she caught her and loaded her onto Granny Vaughn's
lap.

~~Granny waked then.~~ *Even* ~~Before~~ her eyes ~~even~~ opened, ~~she~~ *Granny* had put
both arms out. Lady May, the soles of her feet wrinkling like
the old lady's forehead, went to the weakest and most tenacious
embrace she knew. They hugged long enough to remind each other
that *perhaps* they were rivals.

"Yes sir! I've *already* started to wondering when she's going to talk
and what she's fixing to say," Miss Lexie said.

"And what's Jack know about his baby?" asked Aunt Cleo.

"Not a thing in this world. She's his surprise!" cried Aunt
Birdie. "What else would she be?"

"Makes it so nice she's a girl," Aunt Beck softly said.

~~From somewhere out of sight, a mocking bird was sending up
jets of song. "Go on, then," said Aunt Cleo.~~

Page from a draft for Losing Battles *(Eudora Welty Collection — Mississippi Department of Archives and History)* league: her fellow Mississippian William Faulkner, the greatest of them all.

Eudora Welty does it the hard way, and what is happening and what it means has to sink in, in retrospect, after reading the story. The writer she most resembles, I think, is Thomas Mann. That is to say, she is not technically experimental to any notable degree, and when you read her books you have to let the story pile up, until it is done. Then when you think over what you have read, you begin to perceive the ramifications, the events begin to link up, the people take on their meaning *sub specie aeternitatis* as it were, and the depth, the profundity of what you have seen happen in the story now begins to emerge. It isn't like the searing, tragic art of a Faulkner, for example, which holds you enthralled and breathless as a great elemental drama thunders toward climax and conclusion. The surface of her fiction is always deceptively mundane, matter-of-fact, usually funny. The difference between Miss Welty's fiction and that of less gifted authors is that her fiction doesn't lie on the surface, and the surface is anything but superficial yet, paradoxically, everything is contained right there in the surface.

This is the chief difficulty with *Losing Battles,* one that may prevent it from attaining the massive popularity of so many lesser novels by lesser but more flamboyant novelists, and that gets in the way of immediate recognition for its author. What must be overcome, if the wisdom of *Losing Battles* is to be savored in its fullness, is its density of surface. Every line must be read carefully. It cannot be skimmed. *Losing Battles* is not difficult in the way that many novels are difficult. It hasn't an opaque surface that hides the story and the meaning behind a texture of dense language and obscure reference. Everything is out on the surface, but the art *is* the surface, and every inch of the surface must be inspected. This means that you have to follow the conversations and note the narrative directions and take in every word, every phrase, holding it all in suspension, letting it accumulate. Many of us don't like to read that way; we haven't the patience to follow every footpath and byway in a novel that takes approximately the same amount of time to read as it does for the events themselves to happen. So we tend to go racing through, and we miss the detail and so the story; and we can, if we want, say that this constitutes a criticism, an adverse judgment, a limitation of the art. Fiction that demands more attention than one is willing to give, we can say, is to that extent unsuccessful art. To which Miss

Welty might reply (along with Lawrence Sterne, James Joyce, Thomas Mann and one or two other artists with the same shortcoming), "Oh, but you see, what I have to show you can't be shown in any other way than this, more's the pity, so that you'll have to choose whether *you* want to know what I have to tell you, in which case you'll have to let me show it to you the only way I know it, or whether *you don't* want to know it. For if I tried to show it any other way, *it* wouldn't *be*. You would instead be getting something else, something other. I'll do my best to divert and amuse and please you all along the way, but it must be along *this* way, for there isn't any other."

Of course Eudora Welty wouldn't say that. She would let her art, at whatever risk and at whatever cost, speak for itself, as she has always done. But she might point out, as she has in *Place in Fiction,* that

> . . . the business of writing, and the responsibility of the writer, [is] to disentangle the significant — in character, incident, setting, mood, everything, from the random and meaningless and irrelevant that in real life surround and beset it. It is a matter of his selecting and, by all that implies, of changing, "real" life as he goes. With each word he writes, he acts — as literally and methodically as if he hacked his way through a forest and blazed it for the word that follows. He makes choices at the explicit demand of this one present story; each choice implies, explains, limits the next, and illuminates the one before. No two stories ever go the same way, though in different hands one story might possibly go any one of a thousand ways; and though the woods may look the same from outside, it is a new and different labyrinth each time.

Losing Battles begins with the wait for the various grandchildren of Granny Vaughn and their families to arrive at the family residence, now the home of her granddaughter Beulah Beecham Renfro and her husband Ralph, and located way up at the end of a winding road north of the town of Banner. Among the most eager of those who are doing the waiting is a daughter-in-law Gloria Renfro, whose husband Jack has been away at the state penitentiary at Parchman since the day of their wedding. All are certain that Jack will get home for Granny's birthday reunion, however, not only to honor Granny and rejoin his wife but to see his little daughter, Lady May, for the first time. And soon Jack arrives, in good spirits, not at all resentful or embittered at his incarceration. He is overjoyed at seeing Gloria again, delighted with Lady May, and properly attentive to everyone present (though he does find time to get Gloria off by herself and renew relations properly). All the other relatives arrive, too, and everyone is in high spirits, remaining so for the entire occasion.

Unexpected guests at the reunion, and most reluctant to be there, are Judge Oscar Moody and his wife Maud Eva. It was Judge Moody who had sentenced Jack to his two years in prison, for fighting with Curly Stovall, the storekeeper at Banner, but nobody seems to mind that, Jack least of all. The Judge and his wife are present because their fancy Buick automobile has, hilariously and improbably, become lodged against a tree, far up on a hillside, after the Judge swerved off the road to avoid running over Lady May and Gloria. For the ensuing 24 hours the Buick remains there, teetering over the edge, its motor still running, with Aycock Comfort, a friend of Jack's, seated in it to keep it balanced. Not until the next morning, in just about as wild and as comic an episode as Miss Welty has ever created, is the Buick rescued, somewhat the worse for wear, and taken, tied between a school bus and a truck and with a pair of mules harnessed behind to do the braking, down the hill side and into the community of Banner.

At the reunion, people talk, sing, play, gossip. Among the numerous topics discussed are Granny's youth, the family's history, the obscure antecedents of Jack's wife Gloria, and the life, death, and influence upon the men and women of the Banner community of Miss Julia Mortimer, longtime teacher at the Banner school. Miss Julia has just died, at the nearby town of Alliance, but she is to be buried in the Banner cemetery. Gloria had been Miss Julia's protégé, and had married Jack against her wishes.

All the Vaughns and Renfros and Beechams and the related descendants and cousins and kin at the reunion, and all the other townsfolk of Banner community as well, have been Miss Julia Mortimer's pupils, and she has vexed them all. In the mingled rage, guilt and nostalgia with which they speak of her, whether oblique or direct, the nature of their vexation becomes apparent. For in what she was, what she wanted them to do, what she sought to force them to learn about the world and themselves, she was a threat to the entire Banner community. It was her objective to make the people of Banner, her pupils, realize and confront the ultimate consequences of their humanity.

What all these generations of men and women want to do — do, indeed, succeed in doing for the most part — is to go about their lives and their family and community doings innocently and unthinkingly, meeting birth, life, love and death as they arise, without the dread and the knowledge of anticipating or asking why. In so doing, they are not only helpless against time and change, but unable to deal with their circumstance. Miss Julia Mortimer had sought to force them to see who they were and what they were doing. As Gloria Renfro, who has come closest to being marked by Miss Julia's imprint, expresses the matter, in a rare moment of confrontation,

> Miss Julia Mortimer didn't want anybody left in the dark, not about anything. She wanted everything brought out in the wide open, to see and be known. She wanted people to spread out their minds and hearts to other people, so they could be read like books.

That statement, uttered by Gloria after the funeral, and as she sees that she may not be able to win her husband Jack away from the family and into a life of their own, amounts to a confession that Gloria has been marked by Miss Julia's determination, even though by marrying Jack she had done her best to escape the mantle placed upon her.

Gloria's statement, I suggest, comes very close to being a statement of Eudora Welty's artistic credo. For in *Place in Fiction*, we find her saying much the same thing. She is writing about the importance of place in grounding fiction in reality. "The good novel," she says, "should be steadily alight, revealing. Before it can hope to be that, it must of course be steadily visible from its outside, presenting a continuous, shapely, pleasing, and finished surface to the eye." For place

> has a good deal to do with making the characters real, that is, themselves, and keeping them so. The reason is simply that, as Tristram Shandy observed, "We are not made of glass, as characters on Mercury might be." Place *can* be transparent, or translucent: not people. In real life, we have to express the things plainest and closest to our minds by the clumsy word and the half-finished gesture; the chances are our most usual behavior makes sense only in a kind of daily way, because it has become familiar to our nearest and dearest, and still demands their constant indulgence and understanding. It is our describable outside that defines us, willy nilly, to others, that may save us, or destroy us, in the world; it may be our shield against chaos, our mask against exposure, but whatever it is, the move we make in the place we live has to signify our intent and meaning.

Thus the novelist, by selecting and defining people in a place — "the more narrowly we can examine a fictional character, the greater he is likely to loom up" — can through his focus provide awareness, discernment, order, clarity, insight — "they are like the attributes of love." The novelist seeks, hopes to write so that "the exactness and concreteness and solidity of the real world achieved in a story correspond to the intensity of feeling in the author's mind and to the very turn of his heart," since "making reality real is art's responsibility."

It is from just that kind of searching recognition that people seek diligently and determinedly to hide, and in Eudora Welty's fictional world, families and communities exist to enable their members to hide from reality. For as Gloria Renfro understands and tells her husband Jack, "people don't want to be read like books," whether by others or by themselves. In Miss Welty's work, we sometimes come upon people who realize this. We find characters who shrink from such knowledge, and also a precious few who, like Miss Julia Mortimer, do not thus shrink.

In Miss Welty's first novel, *Delta Wedding*, Laura McRaven travels to Shellmound, the family seat of the Fairchilds in the Delta country. For the Fairchilds (except for one of them, Shelley) everything that happens is gentled, humanized, incorporated into their ordered world. Violence, death, terror — a cyclone, a shooting, a train that runs over and kills a girl — are denied; the Fairchilds pretend that such things never exist, and that the protected, comfortable family world that is Shellmound can go on forever. The community existence, the constant coming and going in company with each other, protects the private loneliness of each participant by being carried on as if such secret knowledge did not exist. In the family, certain things are known, and so those who are in the family can deal with each other in terms of the known, thus avoiding inquiry into private matters. As Shelley Fairchild records in her diary, "we never wanted to be smart, one by one, but all together we have a wall, we are sulf-sufficient against people that come up knocking, we are solid to the outside. Does the world suspect? that we are all very private people? I think one by one we're all more lonely than private and more lonely than self-sufficient."

Shelley, who knows this but for the time being at least will take part in the pretense, and little cousin Laura McRaven, who is from Jackson and knows things about the outside world that will not fit into Shellmound's version of life, realize what is going on. "My papa has taken me on trips — I know about geography. . . . ," Laura insists. But she goes unheard: ". . . in the great confines of Shellmound, no one listened." Yet Shellmound is doomed, for change is inevitable, and the vague uneasiness that the peaceful, contained version of reality that Shellmound comprises will soon disintegrate is present throughout the book. Only Shelley, and Laura, will not be entirely helpless in its face; for only they, of all the Fairchilds, know that it is bound to happen.

The Golden Apples, published in 1949, is the masterpiece of all the books. In a set of seven closely-related narratives, together comprising forty years of human experience in the town of Morgana, Miss Welty sets forth a profound and hauntingly beautiful account of human beings in time, banded together to screen out the knowledge of their mortality. The inhabitants of Morgana — King MacLain, far-wanderer, Morgana's favorite fertility symbol; his twin sons Ran and Eugene, marked for life (and for death) by their father's heritage; the Morrison children, Loch, who can leave Morgana, and Cassie, who can stay; Miss Eckhart, the German music teacher who brought "*the* Beethoven" to Morgana and thus left her impress on those able to receive it (or unable to escape it); and, most of all, Virgie Rainey, who duelled with time, place, and Miss Eckhart all the way — these are unforgettable people; and so, to only a lesser degree, are a host of minor characters.

"Time goes like a dream no matter how hard you run, and all the time we heard things from out in the world that we listened to but that still didn't mean we believed them," declares Virgie's mother, Miss Kate Rainey, to a stranger at the outset (and *only* to a stranger, for like Prufrock and Guido, Miss Katie Rainey would not dare say what she did to anyone who might report it in Morgana). It was not that Morgana did not believe the news from the world outside, so much as that its citizens strove not to believe it. King MacLain left town for years — and left his wife Miss Snowdie to raise the twins — but he always came back, usually at key moments, and at the end he attends Miss Kate Rainey's funeral, knowing he will be the next to die. Yet King never "left" Morgana; though separate from the town, he was never separate from its ways. He played by its rules, and operating within them, took what he wanted. Those rules were: never remind us that time, death and art exist, and are not accountable by Morgana's ways of measurement. Do not, in other words, tell us that we do not control our fate.

Poor Miss Eckhart — Lottie Elisabeth Eckhart, who taught Virgie Rainey to play "Für Elise" and to master the Liszt concerto, and who said that "Virgie would be heard from in the world, playing that" — never learned those rules. She set a metronome in front of her piano pupils, let it tick away remorselessly, timelessly, in absolute disdain of Morgana clock-time; Virgie Rainey, outraged, demanded it be put away. When a terrible thing happened to her — attacked, raped — she would not leave town, and take from Morgana the knowledge that desperate things did happen, and that people survived as people even so. When the man she loved so timidly and inchoately was drowned, she nodded her head in helpless rhythm at the graveside, and then sought to throw herself into it — and Morgana could not countenance the evidence that there was grief that terrible or feeling that desperate.

At the end of her story — "June Recital," the heart of the book, Miss Welty's supreme creation — she comes back to Morgana from her place at the county poor farm, goes inside the old MacLain house where she had once lived and taught, and while her erstwhile pupil Virgie Rainey and a sailor boy cavort around and upon a mattress upstairs, sets her metronome to ticking and tries to set fire to the house. She fails at it, as with all she ever attempted; she is led away, back to the poor farm, and when Virgie Rainey, racing out of the still-smoking house, runs past her, they do not say a word or exchange a glance. For they were both, as Cassie Morrison divines, "human beings terribly at large, roaming on the face of the earth. And there were others of them — human beings, roaming, like lost beasts."

But Loch Morrison, too young to understand what was going on, retrieves the metronome, fetches it up to his room, waits to hear it begin ticking of its own volition: "All by itself, of its own accord, it might let fly its little door and start up."

"You'll go away like Loch," Cassie calls out to Virgie many years later, after Virgie's mother's funeral. "A life of your own, away — I'm so glad for people like you and Loch, I am really." Loch has long since departed, but not before, in the story entitled "Moon Lake," he has successfully given artificial respiration to a drowned orphan, tirelessly, rhythmically, with no heed to clocks, the steady in-out, in-out rhythm of elemental life-giving itself — and of generation, of sex, as the scandalized Morganans sense instinctively while they watch him at work. They must bring him down to their size; Jinny Love Stark, already a determined citizen though still a child, will "tell on him, in Morgana tomorrow. He's the most conceited Boy Scout in the whole troop; and's bow-legged." But Loch Morrison is one of those who

will leave, because he cannot pretend that Morgana is the world.

Yet it is Virgie Rainey — the gifted one, who battled Miss Eckhart all the way, sought to deny her own self, took a job playing "You've Got To See Mama Every Night" at the movie house rather than going on with "*the* Beethoven," went away briefly but came right back, sought fulfillment in a succession of lovers — who was most marked by Miss Eckhart. At the close, forty years old, unmarried, alone, ready at last to leave for good, she realizes that like the old music teacher, she too saw things in their time, in the rhythms of art and life and of ultimate human existence. Miss Eckhart had "offered, offered, offered — and when Virgie was young, in the strange wisdom of youth that is accepting of more than is given, she had accepted *the* Beethoven, as with the dragon's blood. That was the gift she had touched with her fingers that had drifted and left her."

So brief a summary, and of only the main plot-relationship at that, can do little justice to what is in *The Golden Apples*. It is, I think, an even more successful work than *Losing Battles,* but perhaps I say this for having known *The Golden Apples* for two decades, while *Losing Battles* is still to be lived with. But one recognizes at once, in the new novel, that Miss Julia Mortimer, with greater success, and Miss Lottie Eckhart, with lesser success, fought the same battle, representing for their fellow townsfolk the possibility, and the threat, of a greater and more ultimate discovery and self-revelation, and so were both feared and shunned. And similarly, Virgie Rainey and Gloria Renfro are of the same kind: both have been touched with the dragon's blood, and neither may put aside the legacy, struggle though they do. When the family accepts Gloria that day at the reunion, it is only with suspicion. They want her to become part of their common conspiracy, even down to the way she wears her clothes. As Aunt Beck says to Gloria, "you're just an old married woman, same as the rest of us now. So you won't have to answer to the outside any longer." But they ought not be so sure as that; "some day yet," Gloria tells her husband, "we'll move to ourselves." That is not what Miss Julia Mortimer had in mind for her; but neither is it what the Renfros and Beechams and Vaughns want, either.

Miss Julia Mortimer is dead when the family reunion that constitutes *Losing Battles* takes place, and she never appears as a character, but increasingly her presence comes to dominate the story. At the last, as the inhabitants of Banner watch the long funeral procession from Alliance and the burial in the Banner cemetery — there are hundreds of persons present, former students from distant states, a governor, a Catholic priest, a judge (for that was what Judge Moody was doing in the neighborhood), dignitaries and plain folk both — we realize that the spinster school-teacher has been a worthy adversary indeed to the family, and to all that makes human beings seek to flee from themselves and others. She has, in her time, made time run.

All of this is not told, or pointed out, as one goes along; it is realized as the reader begins putting together the experience of the bright, thick-textured surface of people, doings, and talk that constitutes this novel. *Losing Battles* is not, as it moves along its way, a somber book. It is alive in humor and merriment, and especially after we get into it well, filled with almost constant humor and diversion. But there are no shortcuts. It demands that the reader invest time and attention without stint, for as long as it takes to read it through. What it requires is sentence-by-sentence participation. What it provides, for those willing to take part, is delight ending in wisdom.

BOOK REVIEW:
Jonathan Yardley, "The Last Good One?," review of *Losing Battles, New Republic,* 162 (9 May 1970): 33–36.

Jonathan Yardley, a long-time admirer of Welty's writing, was not the only reviewer to prefer her short fiction to her novels.

Possibly the most foolish thing Eudora Welty ever did was write *The Ponder Heart.* Published sixteen years ago, that charming (*too* charming?) little tale won her fame, probably a modest fortune, a long run on Broadway when the adaptation appeared, a legion of women's-book-club admirers, and a severe case of misinterpretation. That the disease will be cured by *Losing Battles,* a milestone in her career if not her best book, is problematical; but it ought to be.

The trouble with Eudora Welty is that she is a Southerner, a woman, and she can twang your heartstrings like a Union Grove fiddler. The consequence is that she is dismissed or accepted, according to your point of view, as a regionalist whose view does not extend beyond the first hill, as a "woman's writer," and as a teller of simple, sentimental tales, some of them vaguely elusive but all of them quite within the mental reach of the Wednesday Lecture Club. Her very name conspires against her; like that of another equally misunderstood Southerner, Calder Willingham, "Eudora Welty" somehow has the ring of contrivance, or self-parody, of the Old South risen again.

The truth is of course a good deal more complicated, as is Eudora Welty. The South is certainly important to her work, but as is the case with any great regionalist, ultimately it is merely a convenient device for the exploration of themes which are anything but regional; she uses the Mississippi hills and delta as Bernard Malamud uses the New York ghetto stores and apartments. Her femininity only enriches her work, especially her marvellous portraits of men; and her spinsterhood adds yet another complicating dimension. The facade of simplicity with which most of her work is coated is a ruse, for underneath it are extraordinary depth, range and deliberate ambiguity. The sheer variety of her work is quite stunning. Unlike Faulkner, who usually mined one vein, she has explored a broad range of subjects and styles. She has roamed from the enchanting fantasy of *The Robber Bridegroom* to the harsh realism of "Powerhouse" (vastly overrated, I have always thought); from London and the decks of a transatlantic liner to the rich Mississippi lowlands of *Delta Wedding* and the hard Mississippi hills of *Losing Battles;* from the warm nostalgia of *The Ponder Heart* to the deftly bitter hometown social commentary of "Lily Daw and the Three Ladies." It is quite impossible to read such stories as "A Wide Net" and "Death of a Travelling Salesman" and dismiss her as a giddy regional sentimentalist. The stories are wonderfully light and gentle and touching, but there is nothing soft about them. Thematically they are complex — sometimes incredibly difficult — and varied; each is essentially about love, yet each is embroidered with other themes which achieve equal validity and meaning. Reading her best work, one peels off layer after layer of mood and meaning, each more subtle and more difficult to find than its predecessor. Miss Welty's use of simile may be unparalleled in contemporary American fiction, for its wry/sly humor and inventiveness and quiet grace, each simile a quick flash of the sharpest vision from *Losing Battles:* "An old Ford coupe, that looked for the moment like a black teakettle boiling over and being carried quick off the stove, crossed the yard"). Her symbols are at once obvious and subtle; you are made aware that they are there, you need no Annotated Version to find them, yet you are never pounded over the head with them. And there are moments when her prose is ethereal in its perfection, so that you tingle because every word is right. A moment in *Losing Battles,* when the young wife greets her ebullient husband home from the pen, is incomparable:

> They divided and there stood Gloria. Her hair came down in a big puff as far as her shoulders, where it broke into curls all of which would move when she did, smelling of Fairy soap. Across her forehead it hung in fine hooks, cinnamon-colored, like the stamen in a Dainty Bess rose. As though small bells had been hung without permission on her shoulders, hips, breasts, even elbows, tinkling only just out of ears' range, she stepped the length of the porch to meet him.

For a greeting such as that, so rich in magic and mystery, any man would gladly suffer Parchman Prison.

Losing Battles occupies an important but somewhat ambiguous place in the body of Miss Welty's work. It is by far her longest work, some 150 pages longer than *Delta Wedding,* and by that very fact assumes the air of Major Statement. Though it explores Miss Welty's customary themes with her customary skill, its motivating impulse seems to be not theme but nostalgia; in that respect, and others as well, it rather resembles *The Reivers,* though I hasten to deny any suggestion that it is derivative. Intriguingly, it is the other half of the coin of *Delta Wedding,* a novel to which it bears only passing resemblance yet with which it is symbiotic; for if *Delta Wedding* is the story of the wealthy downstate family into which Troy Flavin marries, *Losing Battles* is the story of the upstate hill country from which he comes. Add to those two novels *The Ponder Heart,* and we have a trilogy which could be called "Eudora Welty's Mississippi."

The framework of *Losing Battles* is the 90th birthday of Granny Vaughn, which becomes the occasion for a reunion of her huge and boisterous clan. The novel is rich in quick, hilarious incidents (Miss Welty proves that her humor can be rambunctious as well as wry/sly), in surprises, and in tall tales that would do honor to Sut Lovingood or William Faulkner; but its plot is negligible. It is basically a description of a ritual, a celebration of the idea and fact of family. (Interestingly the central characters are not the members of the family but those who are outside it trying to change it.) She manages subtly to establish the family as a symbolic microcosm of the whole human community, and yet to demonstrate its cruelties and narrowmindedness. In a country and a region which

have romanticized "family," and at a time when the institution is either changing or disintegrating, she simultaneously celebrates it and notes its decline. There is a scene in which the women of the family subject an orphan who may be an illegitimate relative to harmless but harrowing horrors: "A melony hand forced warm, seed-filled hunks into Gloria's sagging mouth. 'Why, you're just in the bosom of your family,' somebody's voice cried softly as if in condolence." She is no sentimentalist.

Thus, though the celebration of the dignity and strength of the family is earnest, it is also tinged with irony, as in the book's title.

Losing Battles is indeed about people doing precisely that: Miss Julia losing her battle to educate the people of Banner, Gloria losing her battle to escape the family's clutches, the family losing its battle against the eroding land, all varieties of little battles being lost along with the larger ones. Yet defeat is not at all what *Losing Battles* is about. It is rather a book about victory, about survival:

> The tree looked a veteran of all the old blows, a survivor. Old wounds on the main trunk had healed leaving scars as big as tubs or wagon wheels, and where the big lower branches had thrust out, layer under layer of living bark had split on the main trunk in a bloom of splinters, of a red nearly animal-like.
> "Too late to pull it up now," said Granny, looking from one face to another, all around the table.

The passage is quintessential Welty. Simple, gently humorous on its face, upon closer inspection it reveals unsuspected depths: the theme of pure survival, and its dignity, established; the rootedness of both the tree and the family — "too late" to pull up either — quietly emphasized; and the sense of family, the communion around the table, again heightened. Such subtlety and care are the work of genius.

There is an important difference, though I fear it will be widely ignored, between Miss Welty's concept of "survival" and Faulkner's of "endurance." Faulkner's was a stolid sort of thing, a stubborn plodding, noble in an elemental way but hardly as dramatic or as forceful as Faulkner imagined it to be. Miss Welty's is a battle against great odds, a battle in which there is exuberance to be found and which itself assumes a very clear dignity. "I haven't spent a lifetime fighting my battle to give up now," Miss Julia writes to Judge Moody. "I'm ready for all they send me.

There's a measure of enjoyment in it." It may well be that this good-humored acceptance of the struggle is a more meaningful affirmation than anything Faulkner gave us; it is hard to think of a thought more affirmative, more appreciative of the human condition, than this: a victory is gained if one engages himself fully in the battle, even if he "loses" the battle. A phrase recurs in Miss Welty's work: "coming through." It is the coming through that counts.

When we have sufficient perspective to make oracular judgments, we may well decide that *Losing Battles* occupies, paradoxically, a less important place in Eudora Welty's fiction than it does in Southern fiction. The novel is very good, but it is too long and a trifle out of focus. I would send the uninitiated to the short stories first because a handful are among the best in our literature; to *The Robber Bridegroom* second, because it is a very nearly perfect romance; and to *Delta Wedding* third, because it is her best long work. *Losing Battles* falls into the middle of the list — though one must remember how uncommonly distinguished the entire list is. But within the context of Southern fiction, *Losing Battles* is quite another matter. If I am correct in guessing that it is a work motivated in large measure by nostalgia, then it is a nostalgia not merely for a lost South but for a lost Southern literature. Undoubtedly someone will come along to prove me wrong, but I suspect that *Losing Battles* is the last "Southern novel" — or should I say the last good one. There is nothing self-consciously or affectedly Southern about it, yet in mood, setting and central concerns it is very much in the tradition that began when Faulkner sat down to write *Sartoris*. That tradition is now four decades old, and dying an early death. The reason is very simple: the essential ingredient of the tradition is reverence for and understanding of the past, but young Southerners no longer have a past that has anything *unique* to teach. Eudora Welty's generation is the last to know intimately the Southern land before the highways and quick-food joints took over, to know the Southern myth before it grew stale, to know the Southern family before it disintegrated. When Eudora Welty writes about yesterday's South she does so naturally and easily, because it is her South. Yet most of the young Southern writers are producing fiction that is pallid and imitative and contrived, more "Southern" than a truckload of hominy. The explanation, again, is simple: they are trying to create, or recreate, a world that *is not* theirs — a world they know only

through the writers they have read and now unconsciously ape. "The woods are full of regional writers," Flannery O'Connor wrote, "and it is the great horror of every serious Southern writer that he will become one of them." Now it is in style.

But if "the Southern tradition in literature" is falling into decline, what better way to kiss it off than with a big, funny, intricate and moving novel by Eudora Welty? By way of tribute to her and to this novel, nothing could be more fit than the words she wrote a year ago, for *Shenandoah*, to honor Jane Austen and her six novels:

> Great comic masterpieces that they are, their roots are nourished at the primary sources. Far from denying the emotions their power, she employs them to excellent advantage. Nothing of human feeling has been diminished; its intensity is all at her command. But the effect of the whole is still that of proportions kept, symmetry maintained, and the classical form honored — indeed celebrated. And we are still within the balustrades of comedy.

BOOK REVIEW:
Madison Jones, Review of *One Time, One Place,*
   New York Times Book Review, 21 November 1971, pp. 60, 62, 64.

One Time, One Place, a collection of some of the photographs Welty took while working for the WPA in the 1930s, was published on 6 October 1971. Southern novelist Madison Jones recognized the same artist's eye in her fiction and her photographs.

Few writers of fiction can match Eudora Welty's eye for the eloquent physical gesture or the compelling detail of posture or of dress. Much more than is common, her characters are revealed to us by a precision of physical rendering that evokes our perceptions like so many small starts of discovery. And this fictional distinction of Miss Welty's might have prepared us to expect at least something of what we find in her new book, which is not a work of fiction.

"One Time, One Place" is, except for the brief introductory essay, a collection of photographs taken by Miss Welty following her return from Columbia University to Mississippi in the 1930's. Those were the years of the Depression, and of the W.P.A. and as a publicity agent for the latter, Miss Welty found herself traveling about over all the 82 counties of the state. This gave her, as she tells us in her introduction, the chance to see, really for the first time, the nature of the place into which she had been born. Soon she was taking a camera with her. These photographs are the record of that first seeing.

There are 99 photographs, arranged, quite naturally, under the four classifications: "Workday," "Saturday," "Sunday" and "Portraits." A fairly small minority of the photographs have non-human subjects. There are country churches, a cane-syrup mill, houses and cabins in states of ruin or dilapidation, a grounded river boat converted into a dwelling. But most of the subjects are people, white and black ones, both single and in large or small groups, in city or small town or countryside. A majority of these, as Miss Welty remarks, were not aware, or were only peripherally aware of the camera, and are to be seen about their daily business or pleasure in the full naturalness of their lives. But even the portraits, in which the subjects are fully aware and look back at the camera, have something of the same unposed character, as though each one of these people knew, better than any camera could, exactly who and what he was.

As purely technical performances the pictures are of uneven value. In some of them, especially those taken indoors or in too stark a light, there is a blurring of feature or of background or both. But no apologies are in order, and Miss Welty offers none. The merit of the pictures, she says, lies in their subject matter. And necessarily they amount to "a record of a kind — a record of fact, putting together some of the elements of one time and one place."

The record has little about it to suggest the documentary. In some of the pictures there are, to be sure, evidences of material deprivation — ragged clothes, bleak and ramshackle dwellings. The modern eye is quick to perceive such evidences and, with characteristic bias, instinctively looks around for the more or less inevitable human consequences. But here, like one of those surprising issues in Miss Welty's fiction, such consequences do not follow. If there is sometimes sadness in these faces, there is also, and more often, joy and serenity and appetite for life. And just possibly some viewers of these pictures who are sternly given to the assumption of a necessary connection between poverty and dehumanization may be moved to re-think their position.

But it is pretty certain that Miss Welty had no such lesson in mind. She is interested in these people and places for the most human of reasons, that they are interesting, and she has recorded them in photographs that evoke with much subtlety varieties of character and experience.

One picture, captioned "Crossing the pavement," is of two elderly Negro women standing on a street corner of a country town, in preparation for crossing. Their backs are turned, but the face of one is visible in profile, thrust a little outward and glaring with anxiety down the apparently empty street. The effect is comic but also moving, for the picture has beautifully captured the image in the woman's mind of the bewildering and dangerous world of town.

Another, "Chopping in the field," shows the slight figure of a Negro girl with a hoe, her back to the camera, her upper torso vividly silhouetted against a flat, unbroken sky. The set of her legs and tilted head, and especially the arching of her back, convey the sense of her exertion. And yet, here, it is somehow like rest, too, or a kind of submission that cancels out the appearance of bodily strain.

As fiction writer Miss Welty has never been much afflicted by the demon of social concern; her steady engagement has been with the timeless things, leaving generalities to those with a taste for them. The same is true of her photography, at which she is no more like those makers of documentaries about the rural South than, as fiction writer, she is like the social realists. Some of the same physiognomies that appear in such documentaries appear also in Miss Welty's collection, but here they are barely recognizable. For Miss Welty does not show us masks — much less selected ones. She has had the patience — not to say the humanity and the art — to wait upon the unveiling of what the masks so often, especially from strangers, conceal.

Laboring under no compulsion to prove or support anyone's generality, she has been at liberty to be not only perceptive but also humane. In fact, an important difference between "One Time, One Place" and most of those documentaries is surely this: that Miss Welty's interest is the humanity of her subjects, and theirs, the absence of it.

If "One Time, One Place" should leave with the viewer any significant residue of sadness, it will likely be for the reason Miss Welty notes in her introduction. For the photographs, especially those of black people, surely do testify to the presence of an intimacy and a trust now almost entirely vanished. More than the span of years, this presence that dates these memorable pictures.

BOOK REVIEW:
James Boatwright, "The Continuity of Love," review of *The Optimist's Daughter, New Republic,* 166 (10 June 1972): 24–25.

Published on 23 March 1972, The Optimist's Daughter *was a critical and popular success and earned Welty a Pulitzer Prize for fiction. James Boatwright's review was one of many critical appreciations.*

Admirers of Eudora Welty's work have had a busy time of it since their *first* sight of *The Optimist's Daughter.* It was published in *The New Yorker* in the spring of 1969. At that time I was putting together an issue of *Shenandoah* as a tribute to Miss Welty, to which Reynolds Price contributed a detailed reading of the story, calling it her "strongest, richest work" — which was saying a lot but not, in my opinion, too much.

But that was before the publication, in April 1970, of the comic and epic *Losing Battles,* a long novel overflowing with both youthful energy and a serene, impartial wisdom. It was a book that a writing career and a body of work even as distinguished as Miss Welty's had hardly prepared us for. With the exception of *Delta Wedding,* her work had been essentially miniaturist: much in little, the perfectly controlled and executed novella and short story. As John Aldridge noted in his review [*Saturday Review,* 11 April 1970], *Losing Battles* challenged Faulkner on his home ground, in ambitiousness and scope.

Then Random House published last year Miss Welty's photograph album of her Mississippi neighbors in the 1930s, *One Time, One Place.* An object lesson in the proprieties of photographing other human beings, it showed us definitively that the documentary camera is not necessarily a savage or a sentimentally condescending eye but can have the complexity and truthfulness of vision of a gifted novelist. The preface, written over 30 years after the taking of the pictures, tells the reader as much about Miss Welty and her fiction — but indirectly, obliquely — as it does about the photographs.

Now, to further complicate our responses, to disarm our complacent notions about what the proper limits of energy and invention are, *The Optimist's Daughter* appears in book form, with the deceptively understated information that it "appeared originally in *The New Yorker* in a shorter and different form." To be specific, she has added 10,000 words to the original 30,000, has changed names, altered the order of some scenes, subtly modified some of the characters, added much to our knowledge of the protagonist's past and present. She has re-written and re-thought the book, so that it is both essentially the same and almost everywhere slightly different. To compare the two versions is another object lesson: we can observe the evolution, the accretion of a work of art as it is shaped by a master of narrative.

The story is stark and simple in its outline, a depiction of the trauma we suffer in witnessing the death of parents, in burying them. It's the order of nature: it occurs when most of us are middle-aged when we have learned, we think, what we are going to learn. An old dog learns new tricks. When before *have* we grown up? With our first job, with marriage, with the first child? Maybe, but they are not the same kind of event as this odd, painful liberation, which pulls the mind inward to a contemplation of our own lives as we witness the end of and make some final judgment on the lives of our parents, as we step free of them toward our own death.

The story told here, of course, is much more than its outline, as any story is. Laurel McKelva Hand flies hurriedly from Chicago to New Orleans, where her father is to undergo an operation. It is apparently successful, but Judge McKelva doesn't respond as he should and slowly drifts into death. Laurel and Fay, the Judge's young second wife, accompany the body back to the small Mississippi town where Laurel grew up and where her father still lived. The rest of the novel deals with the funeral, the gathering around of her friends and her father's friends, and Laurel's straightening out her affairs before she returns a few days later to her job in Chicago.

The abrasive conflict at the center of the novel is between Laurel and Fay. The usurping step-mother is younger than her step-daughter; she is not from the right sort of people, she's mean-spirited, totally self-absorbed. A blur of gold buttons and cheap costume jewelry, she bewails missing Mardi Gras; the judge is thoughtless enough to die on her birthday. But the real problem is not, I think, Fay's being unsuitable or unworthy; her entrance into Laurel's father's life is menacing in some as yet unspecified way, a deep wound, the desecration of holy ground, as Laurel makes explicit to Fay toward the end of the narrative. What is further involved here is a brooding on the nature of family and relationship itself.

It is only well into the story that we learn that Laurel is a widow, has been a widow for perhaps 20 or 25 years: her husband was lost at sea in World War II. She now presumably lives alone in Chicago, devoted wholly to her work as a fabric designer. It shouldn't surprise the reader then to learn that it was "still incredible to Laurel that her father, at nearly seventy, should have let anyone new, a beginner, walk in on his life, that he had even agreed to pardon such a thing." No beginner has walked into Laurel's life to replace her beloved Philip. Why? We aren't allowed much into Laurel's consciousness until the narrative begins to draw to a close, but we do learn that "her marriage had been of magical ease, of *ease* — of brevity and conclusion and all belonging to Chicago and not here," and that with Phil lost, "love was sealed away into its perfection and had remained there." *Ease, brevity, conclusion, perfection:* hardly the words to attach to the other relationships in the novel.

Instead, we are confronted with images of voracious need and hunger, love that is burdensome, endless, inconclusive, imperfect. At the hospital, Judge McKelva shares his room with crazy old Mr. Dalzell, who thinks the judge is his long lost son Archie Lee. Down the hall, the rest of the Dalzell clan, including the returned prodigal son, keeps its vigil. They are hilariously comic but something else too: steadfast, tenacious as snapping turtles. The Dalzells, gathered together in a lunatic confusion of loving gestures and burlesque pratfalls, are the first variation on the theme which builds throughout the narrative.

Fay has told Laurel that her family is dead, gone, every one of them: "Grandpa . . . that sweet old man, he died in my arms." But on the day of the funeral, a truckload of her family shows up: Fay's mother, a brother, a sister, a nephew — and finally Grandpa himself. In the midst of this long scene — which is, to my mind, brilliant beyond praise, a miraculous balancing of farce and the gravest pathos — Laurel recognizes what makes Fay's family seem familiar:

> They might have come out of that night in the hospital waiting room — out of all times of trouble, past or future — the great interrelated family of those who never know the meaning of what has happened to them.

Why don't they know? Because hunger, need and love are blind? (Literal eye trouble sends the judge to the hospital; Laurel's mother, Becky, had become blind and embittered in her long dying.) Toward the end of the book, as Laurel recalls her childhood vacations "up home" in West Virginia with her mother and grandmother, one particularly striking image stands out: the appearance of her grandmother's pigeons:

> . . . Laurel had kept the pigeons under eye in their pigeon house and had already seen a pair of them sticking their beaks down each other's throats, gagging each other, eating out of each other's craws, swallowing down all over again what had been swallowed before: they were taking turns. . . . They convinced her that they could not escape each other and could not themselves be escaped from. So when the pigeons flew down, she tried to position herself behind her grandmother's skirt . . . but her grandmother said again, "They're just hungry, like we are."

What the grandmother accepts, acquiesces in, Laurel hides from in terror. I think the implication is clear enough: Laurel has borne this image of relation, dependency, need through her life, and it has in part determined her vision, her demand for freedom, flight, escape — for clarity, for the knowledge of what has happened to you. She *did* marry, but the brevity, the unreal perfection of the marriage stand in contrast to what the nature of dependence actually is.

The strongest and most mysterious scene in the book is the account of Laurel's last night at home. When she enters the front door, a chimney-sweep loose in the house drives her into her parents' room, where she spends the night plunging into memory, following out affectionately but remorselessly what her parents' lives were: the high promises of their beginning, the eventual decline into sickness of Laurel's mother, the terrible failure of love to prevent pain and loss, love's betrayal. But Laurel's settling of accounts, seeing clearly the inescapable doom awaiting any hope of contingency, ends in a surprising way, a melting of resolve — "She lay there with all that was adamant in her yielding to this night, yielding at last. Now all she had found had found her." — ends with the resurrection of her dead husband.

> He looked at her out of eyes wild with the craving for his unlived life, with mouth open like a funnel's. . . . What would have been their end, then? Suppose their marriage had ended like her father and mother's? Or like her mother's father and mother's? Like —

She ran upstairs and on bare soft feet with the first's bedroom, and for an instant eight and shut the door

~~The same lady-like self-control with which Laurel had sent Major Bullock away and shut herself in with that bird rose in her to meet the intolerable.~~ *She closed the windows but the white* ~~She set up half the night waiting with her bedroom door locked, her south windows shut against the rain,~~ *And walked up and down the floor,* ~~listening, as unable to sleep as~~ *to the* ~~the blundering, frantic bird.~~ *the only horror* ~~Her pride and self-contempt both grew and grew as one. So far she had guarded Fay; but Fay would return.~~

She felt physically unable to sit at her table and write the letter a friend in Chicago was waiting for--a friend who ~~would~~ was not to be turned ~~away with~~ like another Major Bullock, a friend who with healthy Middlewestern impatience would <u>answer</u> her question, Must I keep my father's secret of how he was de-stroyed? ~~The answer she knew; she had accepted it at once that she must keep the secret. It was up to her now to understand what she had accepted.~~ Even if you have kept silent for the sake of the dead, you cannot rest in ~~the~~ *your* silence, as the dead rest *in theirs*. ~~Silently, Laurel struggled as if in alarm for her life.~~ She listened to the rain, the wind, the *blundering, frantic* ~~shuddering~~ bird, and wanted to cry out as the nurse cried out, "Abuse! Abuse!"

~~Sooner or later she would have to confront Fay alone. Fay's returning would be Laurel's departure, and at that moment how could Laurel not say, "I know what you did to Father, you destroyed him."~~

It was not punishment she wanted for Fay, she wanted acknowledg-ment out of her--admission that she knew what she ~~was doing~~ *had done.* Suddenly the question came to astound Laurel: does Fay know it herself? And

Page from "An Only Child," an early draft of The Optimist's Daughter *(Eudora Welty Collection — Mississippi Department of Archives and History)*

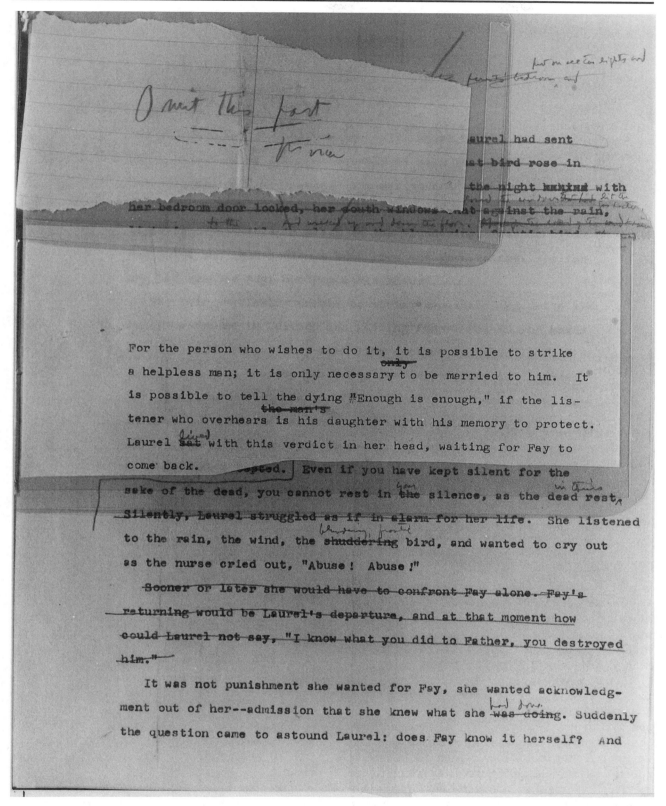

The same page with revision slips (Eudora Welty Collection — Mississippi Department of Archives and History). These paragraphs are an early version of a scene in the last section of the published book.

And it would have, wouldn't it? Their life would have ended in a blind blundering, the price paid for a lived life.

Fay's role in this painfully acquired knowledge of Laurel's is not a simple one, but I think it's something like this: Fay is Laurel's deepest fear, a figure of absolute isolation, totally incapable of love, in panicky flight from blood ties and the wounds of mortality, a grotesque parody of Laurel's own worst possibilities. In the showdown between Fay and Laurel in the novel's final scene, Fay is the instrument as Laurel affirms the shape of the lives of her parents, *lets go* of them, no longer tries to protect them — they don't need her protection, don't ask for it, they stand in memory in their complex and temporal imperfection, in their final dignity. Laurel returns to Chicago to what kind of life? No answer is given, but she has met a great fear and overcome it, "the deepest spring in her heart had uncovered itself, and it began to flow again." Or, as Laurel learns again, in her dream of Philip following his ghostly appearance to her — and what Fay does not know, cannot learn — life is meaningful and whole only in "the continuity of love."

ARTICLE:
Nona Balakian, "A Day of One's Own," *New York Times Book Review*, 27 May 1973, p. 23.

The state of Mississippi honored its best-known literary resident by declaring 2 May 1973 Eudora Welty Day. Nona Balakian covered the celebration for the New York Times Book Review.

A week before it was announced that she had won the Pulitzer Prize for her novel, "The Optimist's Daughter," Eudora Welty woke up one morning to find herself a local "celebrity," with her name on billboards and in neon lights. In a long career, never lacking in honors, it was a new kind of public/private tribute devised by proud fellow-Mississippians — and it went to everyone's heart, including the publicity-shy author's: for a full week (May 1–6) in her hometown of Jackson a whopping "Eudora Welty Celebration" was staged as part of the 10th annual Mississippi Arts Festival. An ingenious idea, which pooled the resources of some 1,000 enterprising committee members throughout the state and brought together a multitude of the writer's friends, it spotlighted the uniqueness of Miss Welty's career in American letters.

After a week of incessant rain, the sun beamed in recognition as Gov. William Waller, standing beside Miss Welty in the Old Capitol's House of Representatives (where Jefferson Davis once spoke), proclaimed May 2 "Eudora Welty Day" for the entire state. Some 500 fans of the novelist, among them school children and college students who had taken time from classes to attend the ceremonies, heard the Governor praise "the nation's foremost lady of letters . . . a woman of quiet dignity and charm. . . ."

Amid the clatter of radio and television equipment, photographers and such, Miss Welty in a pink dress sat quietly, obviously pleased, her blue eyes as unguarded as a young girl's. Later, in grateful response to the Governor's words and a standing ovation, she expressed wonder at the whole event: "If anything like this has ever been done to another author," she quipped, "then I think we can beat them." There were chuckles, and everyone relaxed — as everyone always does in Miss Welty's presence.

Before reading from her recent epiclike novel, "Losing Battles," she told her listeners: "Just think of it as voices." And, once past the lyrical beginning, she threw herself in the work, acting out all the parts with greatest relish. So complete was her identification with her characters that she might have been sitting in a room with them. The "voices" grew familiar: garrulous, lovable Eudora Welty characters in high comedy situations, enveloped by a deeply humane, poetic comprehension.

Though other local talent had its day in Jackson's grand Coliseum and surrounding fair grounds — with such outside stars as Renata Tebaldi, Edward Villella and Vikki Carr helping capture a record attendance of 150,000 — the first two days of the Festival were Miss Welty's own. On exhibit at the Department of Archives and History were her manuscripts, letters from editors, and a scrapbook with samplings of her reviews from over 30 years. A closed circuit television special featured dramatizations of her stories by local actors and an illuminating "conversation" with local critic Frank Hains. In a little church converted into a theater, a select audience saw the New Stage Theater's delightful adaptation of her comic extravaganza, "The Ponder Heart."

For the visitor from the East, the "celebration" had a fairy-tale quality. Writers in America are not supposed to be famous and happy at the same time: the "literary life" so often engenders tense, semi-tragic figures with glossy fronts that cover up a multitude of frustrations. Yet here was a writer perfectly attuned to her milieu, the lilt in her voice and simplicity of her manner giving her away as no words could. No gloss. No front. Only a sharp, intense responsiveness, a feeling of comradeship.

At a party in her family home (where she now lives alone, not too far from two adoring nieces and a sisterly sister-in-law) the rooms are aglow with the tremendous affection she inspires. "It's been like a funeral," she laughs, pointing to the flowers, the messages — the casseroles from solicitous neighbors. Her guests include distinguished literary agent Diarmuid Russell, her earliest editors Mary Louise Aswell and Lewis Simpson, her most gifted protégé the novelist Reynolds Price, a favorite author Ross Macdonald, and all the doting cosmopolite friends she has got to know from her annual visits to New York. As the talk shifts from old times to new happenings (not least the Watergate affair), not once does Miss Welty appear weary, or bored, or out of it.

Her equanimity and "positive feelings" have their source undoubtedly in a happy early childhood, but also in the fact, as she put it in a recent interview, that her work "has always landed safely and among friends." Indeed the letters on exhibit show that the first two stories she submitted found immediate publication in a little magazine in Ohio. Two years later, in 1938, Robert Penn Warren was seeking her out for the prestigious Southern Review and Ford Madox Ford's encouragement was firing the young writer with ambition. The one dissenting note came from a New York editor who complained there was no "market" for a volume of short stories and urged her to write novels instead. The novels were eventually produced, but not before her now classic volumes of stories, "A Curtain of Green" and "The Wide Net," won critical acclaim in the early 1940's.

Because the act of creating is a major joy in her life, Miss Welty feels no need to leave Jackson for long periods. The "experiences" are right there, waiting to be absorbed. Like Henry James's ideal writer, she is "blessed with the faculty which when you give an inch takes an ell . . . one of the people on whom nothing is lost."

"Place has the most delicate control over character," she has written, "location pertains to feeling." The "regionalism" attributed to her has given her work not only its rich texture but the contours of a separate world to hold up against the eternal one, that great mirror where qualities and flaws stand out in true proportion. But most of all, it has blessed her with her vivid Mississippians, with their immense sense of the singularity of people. "The living presence" of the individual which Eudora Welty's work all but sanctifies is in part a tribute to their human dimensions; in turn, by putting their very essence in her books, she has given them a surer sense of their own identity. But only a writer of stature could transform a city from a "crossroad of the South" to virtually a crossroad of the world.

INTERVIEW:

Charlotte Capers, "An Interview with Eudora Welty, 8 May 1973," Mississippi Department of Archives and History, Oral History Program (OHP 046), transcribed from tape TR 149, in *Conversations with Eudora Welty,* edited by Peggy Whitman Prenshaw (Jackson: University Press of Mississippi, 1984), pp. 115–130.

The day after the announcement that she had won a Pulitzer Prize for The Optimist's Daughter, *Welty was interviewed by her friend Charlotte Capers, a librarian at the Mississippi Department of Archives and History.*

Capers: This is Charlotte Capers, at my home, 4020 Berkley Drive, Jackson, on May 8, 1973, and I am about to interview Miss Eudora Welty, who yesterday, May 7, 1973, received the news that she had won the Pulitzer Prize for Fiction. Miss Welty has previously won many honors, and only last week was honored by the State of Mississippi, when Governor William L. Waller declared Wednesday, May 2, 1973, as Eudora Welty Day in Mississippi.

I'd like for Eudora to tell us something about the book for which she was awarded the prize, and her reactions on being informed that she had won.

Welty: Well, the book is a short novel, really a novella, I should say, which is not much different from a long story. I wrote it in 1969 and it was published in the *New Yorker* magazine. It was changed a little bit when I wrote it over for a book, but I suppose I changed every sentence with one word or two that no one would notice but the author. It was published in 1972. The title was *The Optimist's Daughter,* a title which I kept

"He's going to surprise us all. If we can make it stick, he's going to have a little vision he didn't think was coming to him! That's a *beautiful* eye."

"But *look* at him," said Fay. "When's he going to come to?"

"Oh, he's got plenty of time," said Dr. Courtland, on his way.

Judge McKelva's head was unpillowed, lengthening the elderly, exposed throat. Not only the great dark eyes but their heavy brows and their heavy under-shadows were hidden, too, by the opaque gauze. With so much of its dark and bright both taken from it, and with his sleeping mouth as colorless as his cheeks, his face looked quenched.

This was a double room, but Judge McKelva had it, for the time being, to himself. Fay had stretched out a while ago on the second bed. The first nurse had come on duty; she sat crocheting a baby's bootee, so automatically that she appeared to be doing it in her sleep. Laurel moved about, as if to make sure that the room was all in order, but there was nothing to do; not yet. This was like a nowhere. Even what could be seen from the high window might have been the rooftops of any city, colorless and tarpatched, with here and there other patches of rainwater. At first, she did not realize she could see the bridge—it stood out there dull in the distance, its function hardly evident, as if it were only another building. The river was not visible. She lowered the blind against the wide white sky that re-flected it. It seemed to her that the grayed-down, anony-mous room might be some reflection itself of Judge McKelva's "disturbance," his dislocated vision that had brought him here.

Then Judge McKelva began grinding and gnashing his teeth.

"Father?" Laurel moved near.

"That's only the way he wakes up," said Fay from her bed, without opening her eyes. "I get it every morning."

Laurel stood near him, waiting.

"What's the verdict?" her father presently asked, in a parched voice. "Eh, Polly?" He called Laurel by her childhood name. "What's your mother have to say about me?"

"Look-a-here!" exclaimed Fay. She jumped up and pattered toward his bed in her stockinged feet. "Who's *this*?" She pointed to the gold button over her breast-bone.

*Eudora—
this was
'small mirrors'
earlier? Letter?
later*

small mirrors

Segments of galley proofs for The Optimist's Daughter *(Eudora Welty Collection—Mississippi Department of Archives and History), with a query from Random House editor Albert Erskine and a response from Welty (above) and queries from Welty to Erskine (right)*

The last pigeonhole held letters her mother had saved from her own mother, from "up home."

She slipped them from their thin envelopes and read them now for herself. Widowed, her health failing, lonely and sometimes bedridden, Grandma wrote these letters to her young, venturesome, defiant, happily married daughter as to an exile, without ever allowing herself to put it into so many words. Laurel could hardly believe the bravery and serenity she had put into these short letters, in the quickened pencil to catch the pocket of one of "the boys" before he rode off again, dependent—Grandma then, as much as Laurel now—upon his remembering to mail them from "the court-house." She read on and met her own name on a page. "I will try to send Laurel a cup of sugar for her birth-day. Though if I can find a way to do it, I would ~~still~~ like to send her one of my pigeons. It would eat from her hand, if she would let it."

A flood of feeling descended on Laurel. She let the papers slide from her hand and the books from her knees, and put her head down on the open lid of the desk and wept in grief for love and for the dead. She lay there with all that was adamant in her yielding to this night, yielding at last. ~~All she had been learning had been coming too close, and~~ now all she had found had found her. The deepest spring in her heart had uncovered itself, and it began to flow again.

If Phil could have lived—

But Phil was lost. Nothing of their life together re-mained except in her own memory; love was sealed away into its perfection and had remained there.

If Phil had lived, ~~and I had lived on! If I had been afraid of nothing—nothing in the world. Afraid of nothing people might do and did do to each other in the name of loving each other—~~

She had gone on living with the old perfection un-disturbed and undisturbing. Now, by her own hands, the past had been raised up, and *he* looked at her, Phil himself—here waiting, all the time, Lazarus. He looked at her out of eyes wild with the craving for his unlived life, with mouth open like a funnel's.

What would have been their end, then? Suppose their marriage had ended like her father and mother's? Or like her mother's father and mother's? Like—

"Laurel! Laurel! Laurel!" Phil's voice cried.

She wept for what happened to life.

"I wanted it!" Phil cried. His voice rose with the wind in the night and went around the house and

Cap. N

Albert: do you feel this is better? E

Albert: I think well of deleting this too. By now, it must all be understood. Isn't it stronger and more of a shock to simply say again "If Phil had lived— E.

thinking I would change but never did. It's really an interior story of what went on in a young widow's mind in response to grief and loss and her adjustment to facing up to it, and acceptance of the meaning of the love in her life and affection. All this is shown in a family tangle of relationships.

Is this going into too much detail?

Capers: No.

Welty: It's all done by a series of confrontations, of only four or five people, plus a chorus of small townspeople who come to a funeral and come from here, there, and everywhere to speak as a chorus about love and death and so on.

Capers: I have heard it said and I have read it — that of all of your books, this was perhaps the most autobiographical. Is this correct?

Welty: Well, all my books are autobiographical in that I never have made up the feelings in them. I think that you have to experience emotion before you write about it, but usually I have the emotions acted out by a cast of characters and through situations that are better dramatic vehicles than my life happens to be, which is rather calm, but in the case of *The Optimist's Daughter,* I did draw on some of the childhood and early married experiences of my own mother. That's the only thing that is "factual"; and the character of Becky, the mother, is not the character of my mother, but it draws upon it. At any rate, there were letters and events and traumatic things in the life of my character, Becky, which came from my knowledge of my mother. This made it both meaningful and instructive — and hard for me to write.

Capers: I was going to say, I think it would be extremely hard . . . so close to you that it was painful.

Welty: I don't know. It was very painful; but also, it helped me to understand and so I don't know whether you'd call that autobiographical or not. The situation is made up, characters are made up.

Capers: Did it not help you to work through your own emotions after the death of your mother?

Welty: I think it did; although, I did not undertake it for any therapeutic reasons, because I don't believe in that kind of thing. I believe in really trying

to comprehend something. Comprehension is more important to me than healing; but, I suppose the by-product of that was being able to understand something better — my own feelings about it. It was helpful to me. But that's not important, really, because the important thing is if the novel itself was able to show these feelings I'm talking about, and what happens to people in such circumstances, and how they react on one another. It was just a story of relationships.

Capers: Well, it was, of course, beautifully done, and I think that the recognition it has been accorded proves that; but the thing that really rings so true to an old home-town girl is the chorus. I feel that I know a good many people in the chorus, but I think that these are almost typical people that do come to funerals, and that do stand by you and support you, and drive you mad and love you and worry you. The chorus you could pretty much spot, couldn't you, if you tried?

Welty: You mean, actually? No; you can spot that kind of person who goes on forever and ever.

Capers: Yes.

Welty: But the important thing again, to me, is that they are there, that they exist, and that they do come forward . . . I mean, the important thing to the story. It was an inevitable part of the story. Of course, it was the easiest to do.

Capers: Because there they are.

Welty: There they are, and you don't get on the inside of these people, they're self explanatory; so you're only on the inside of the figures through whom you're writing and you see these people through their eyes.

Capers: Well, do you feel that in *The Optimist's Daughter,* the place — the sense of place, which you have written a lot about and which I know you feel very strongly — is this very evident? Could these people have just as well been anywhere, or do you think these people, the principals and the chorus, are peculiarly Southern or peculiarly Mississippian?

Welty: I don't think, perhaps, they're peculiarly Mississippian. Well they may be, but I use place in this as I do in everything, but in a more complicated way; because the characters in it were not all of the location where the story happened. The character of Becky, the mother, has her deepest roots in another place, and that's the thing that most changed her life — a feeling of being out of place, in a place to which she has never really resigned herself; and the girl through whom the story is told, Laurel, has come from Chicago where she has attempted to change her life back into the past. She's coming from the opposite direction and must make her decisions in respect to the future, here, whereas the people who live in the little town have never changed. There's also the doctor who has left there and become another kind of being in a city. So I was using place in many ways — to define people, to explain them, and to be their lures and their despairs, etcetera, a little more complicated than having a story set in a place which never moves or changes.

Capers: Eudora, thank you very much for these very revealing remarks about your book. I would like to ask you now, since this is the book that has been recognized by the awarding of the Pulitzer Prize, if you know how the Pulitzer Prize is awarded, and by whom?

Welty: I got a telegram, which is all I know, saying that the trustees of Columbia University had awarded it, and it was signed by the president of Columbia. Those are the only facts about it that I know.

Capers: Would they have a committee?

Welty: I don't know. I asked some friend yesterday, and he said, "We've always understood that it's been very secret." Oh, this was someone I asked over the telephone. I believe it was Albert Erskine, somebody in New York.

Capers: Albert Erskine, who is your editor?

Welty: My editor at Random House. He telephoned me to tell me that he had heard the news, and I said, "I think it's wonderful," and he said, "Well, it won't do any harm."

Capers: (Laughter) Well, it won't!

Welty: So I asked him how it happened, and he said that it's all very secretive.

Capers: Does a cash award go with this?

Welty in 1972

Welty: That's what the paper said. I just read the paper and it said a thousand dollars went with each award.

Capers: Oh. Well, this is a marvelous thing for Mississippi, and as we have said previously, Mississippi has produced a few Pulitzer Prize winners before, but I don't think ever one for fiction. But you think William Faulkner, for fiction?

Welty: Well, it just seems natural that it would have been William Faulkner. I would love to get hold of some information about the whole thing. (Laughter).

Capers: (Laughter) I bet you would. Well, what do you do? Do you go somewhere to receive an accolade, or something?

Welty: I have no idea.

Capers: You don't know about ceremonies or —

Welty: The only thing said in the telegram was just what I told you. They didn't even say "letter follows," so I don't know if they'll ever tell me! (Both laugh).

Capers: Can you quote the telegram?

Welty: Yes, I think it said, "The Trustees of Columbia University have today awarded you the Pulitzer Prize for Fiction. Congratulations." Signed, the President, Mr. McGill, I think.

Capers: Dear old Mr. McGill!

Welty: That's all it was. It took ages to get here. By that time, I'd known it for about half an hour — or had been told it for about half an hour.

Capers: And you had been on television, and you had been interviewed.

Welty: And everything; and this was just people appearing at the door to tell me, and Frank Hains over the telephone.

Capers: And Frank Hains over the telephone was your first word?

Welty: He was my first word, so of course I was thrilled, but I was confused . . .

Capers: I'm sure.

Welty: And Winifred [Cheney] was visiting me at the time.

Capers: How happy that must have made her! Your winning the Pulitzer Prize has made Mississippians — your friends, and so many people in Mississippi — so happy. We have just had an occasion I'd like to talk to you about, which I think is unique, and that is the recognition of *you* by your fellow citizens of the State of Mississippi, and the great events associated with that recognition only last week. At that time, Governor William L. Waller, Governor of the State of Mississippi, proclaimed Wednesday, May 2nd, as Eudora Welty Day in Mississippi; and I do not know of another literary personality or another artist who has been so honored by any state; and this has made us all very happy. And I think the occasion itself was felicitous in the extreme. It was also historical, and if you don't mind, I'd like for you to tell me about your friends from Jackson and from out of the state who came to honor you. I believe the people started coming in on Sunday before Eudora Welty Day on Wednesday. Is that correct? Would you tell me about some of the people?

Welty: Yes, this was the most marvelous part of all, because it was really a gathering of my closest and oldest friends, throughout my whole life, both in Jackson and from away. I'd been hesitant to send them invitations. It seemed like such a long way to come for something; and then I thought, no, I'll just make my ideal list of who I'd most like to have, and ask them. I couldn't have lost by that, and it was marvelous how many people came. The ones that did come on Sunday were Diarmuid Russell, from New York, who is my agent, and has been since 1940, and his wife, Rosie. They stayed all week with me in Jackson. The first time they'd ever been to Mississippi. That was just wonderful!

Capers: I think they were delighted with Mississippi, and to be here. I'm interrupting you to say that for the benefit of the tape and transcription, this was all part of the Mississippi Arts Festival, Inc., for 1973. The Mississippi Arts Festival, Inc., sponsors a magnificent week of cultural events each spring, and the idea of Eudora Welty Day, I believe, was initiated by the Executive Committee of the Mississippi Arts Festival, Inc. Is that correct? This was part of the Arts Festival, and I wanted to make that reference for historical purposes, that the great feature of the Arts Festival, which each year brings celebrated people in all of the arts to Mississippi . . . that the special honoree this year was Miss Eudora Welty.

Welty: Yes, and really what made it so wonderful besides the fact of all the people gathering for me, was the really beautiful way it had been planned and carried out by these girls. I've never seen anything so lovingly planned, so thoughtful — just perfection was all you could call it. This was felt by all the guests.

Capers: Would you explain, amplify, about having friends meet friends at the airport?

Welty: Yes. Well part of their arrangements, which were complete, if there were ever complete arrangements, every guest was met at the airport; they were taken to their rooms in motels which had been set aside for them, and in the rooms were little bouquets of garden flowers, which I later heard many of them took back with them *when they left. The little roses would have opened, but they said that they were going to carry them back. They were taken to functions and taken home again. They were taken riding in cars and shown everything, taken to lunch in someone's home in little groups of six or eight. There was no end to the courtesy and to the pleasure that was given to them.

Capers: Well, it was a great pleasure for the people here who did it.

Welty: They showed that; and I think they all liked each other — that was the best thing. All my friends liked each other. That's something that happens in Paradise!

Capers: It really is.

Welty: For the time it lasted, it was just beautiful.

Capers: Well, I interrupted you when you were telling about Rosie and Diarmuid coming first. Rosie and Diarmuid Russell came and they stayed in your home, and they were the only out of town guests in your home. Then, other early arrivals were . . .

Welty: John and Catherine Prince, from Washington, who are young-old friends. I mean — they're old friends who are young. They live in Georgetown, and I've been to see them lots of times. I don't know what to tell you about them.

Capers: Well, that's enough — old friends.

Welty: Anyway, yes, old friends. Then, Reynolds Price, a young writer from Durham, North Carolina, who's been here many times, came, and gee, I can't go down this whole list.

Capers: Well, you can if you want to. Where's your list? Let's see. . . . What about . . . did Mr. Downs come?

Welty: Mr. Downs came.

Capers: I never met Mr. Downs.

Welty: Well, no wonder you never met him, because he never got my letter. Mr. Downs is from Denison University, and I've worked for him three or four times . . .

Capers: What is his job at Denison?

Welty: He's in the English Department there; and he said he thought the way to come would be by bus because that's the way I went to Columbus, Ohio, although I came to Columbus, Ohio, from Kentucky, which is a little easier. So he arrived by bus, and my letter didn't reach him so he didn't know he was invited to a party at my house for the out of town guests. All I knew was that he didn't come. He said he walked up and down in front of my house looking in and thought that must be my house.

Capers: He never got to your house?

Welty: He never got to my house . . . never got to my party! I saw him the next morning. That was the one sad story.

Capers: And his name is Mr. Linfield Downs?

Welty: Linfield Downs.

Capers: Lin Downs. Well, I'm sorry about Mr. Downs. Well, now, Mr. and Mrs. Lambert Davis got here.

Welty: They got here. He used to be my editor at Harcourt, Brace.

Capers: Say his name. I'm not sure I heard.

Welty: Lambert Davis. He retired from New York and publishing up there at an early age, because he couldn't stand New York any more; went down to Chapel Hill and became editor of the University of North Carolina Press, where he's lived happily ever after.

Capers: They're very nice.

Welty: They're *so* nice.

Capers: Now, the . . . Mr. and Mrs. William Meacham

Welty: They didn't get here . . . that's my relations. . . .

Capers: They were afraid of the flood.

Welty: They were afraid of the flood, and called up and said, "But it's flooded down there." I said, "No, it isn't." They said, "Well, you must not have been listening to the national news."

Capers: I heard that their travel agent warned them it was dangerous.

Welty: I don't know. She wrote to me after talking to me and said that they got phone calls and everything from people saying, "You don't dare go."

Capers: So they didn't come?

Welty: So they didn't come.

Capers: Well, that's real sad. Nona Balakian is an old friend?

Welty: She's an old friend on the *New York Times Book Review.*

Capers: Did you work with her?

Welty: I worked with her.

Capers: On the staff?

Welty: Yes, the time I worked there — one summer. And we're old friends. She had a lovely time, I think because she knew so many people.

Capers: She was real thrilled, though. She kept wanting to tell Nash Burger everything!

Welty: I know.

Capers: Michael Newton.

Welty: Michael Newton.

Capers: What is his official capacity? In the Arts?

Welty: Well, at present, I think he's vice president of the Associated Councils on the Arts. But I invited him here because he's an old friend from England whom I knew.

Capers: Oh! He's an Englishman?

Welty: Yes. I knew him when I was at Cambridge.

Capers: I didn't get to talk to him. I really didn't know much about him.

Welty: He's visited me in Jackson two or three times — so it has really nothing to do with the Asso-

ciated Councils on the Arts. But that's what he is, at present.

Capers: How about Joan and Olivia Kahn?

Welty: They're old friends of mine, and they're sisters, in New York. Joan is the mystery editor of Harper's Publishing House, and Olivia is a reader for several publishing houses and a fine painter.

Capers: Is E. J. Kahn their brother?

Welty: Their brother, yes.

Capers: Who writes short stories for *The New Yorker.*

Welty: Yes, and reports, too.

Capers: Well, of course, Mary Lou Aswell is one of your dearest friends.

Welty: One of my dearest friends, and, I guess, one of my oldest . . . since 1940. She was fiction editor of *Harper's Bazaar* when I first met her. She published my early stories.

Capers: Do you know the first story she published?

Welty: Oh, I can't think what it would be. I have such a poor chronological sense.

Capers: I knew she had published some of your earlier stories.

Welty: She published some of the stories in *The Golden Apples* — about three of them, I think — long stories which she had to get down on her knees to Mr. Hearst to save her space for.

Capers: Isn't that . . .

Welty: Wonderful!

Capers: Wonderful! doesn't she feel good today!

Welty: Oh! Yes! And so do I! (laughter)

Capers: Yes. Agnes Sims is a friend of Mary Lou Aswell's, and a friend of yours, of long standing. And a friend of mine, also.

Welty: And a friend of yours . . . and a painter.

Capers: Who lives in Santa Fe.

Welty: Yes, both she and Mary Lou come originally from Philadelphia.

Capers: Did they know each other in Philadelphia?

Welty: Yes, they knew each other long ago.

Capers: Well, now, we have known William Jay Smith in Jackson, Mississippi, before, but he appeared with Mrs. William Jay Smith this time.

Welty: Right.

Capers: And he is an old and close friend of yours.

Welty: That he is.

Capers: When did you first know Bill Smith?

Welty: I met him in Florence — Italy, not Mississippi. He had just gone over after being a Rhodes Scholar, and had been two years in England, then had moved on over to Italy. We've known each other in many parts of the world since, and he's now poetry consultant for the Library of Congress, and teaches at Hollins half the year, this summer at Columbia. We're old friends and he's a very fine poet.

Capers: Yes. I saw his thing on Venice in the *New York Times.*

Welty: Yes, beautiful!

Capers: Beautiful, very beautiful! Mr. and Mrs. Gwin F. Kolb, and I said, "No, that is not your name, it's not Kolb, it's Kolb." He's an old Jacksonian. Was he a friend of yours in Jackson?

Welty: No. I never did know him in Jackson. But he is at the University of Chicago, and when I went there to lecture, of course, he became my shepherd. We've been friends a long time. His wife, Ruth, is from here, too. Her name was Ruth Godbold, I think. They went to Millsaps, and met each other there.

Capers: I see. Mr. William McCollum — do I know him?

Welty: He came. He and Mr. Napier Wilt are both friends of the Kolbs.

Capers: I don't believe I met them.
Welty: Napier Wilt has retired now, but he was also on the English faculty at the University of Chicago.

Capers: I would like to ask you about Kenneth Millar, whose pseudonym is Ross Macdonald. He is a celebrated detective story writer, or writer, and is a friend of yours, and I'm interested in how you two met.

Welty: We met because he wrote me a letter after I had said, in an interview published in the *New York Times* with Walter Clemons, that I admired his work and had written him a fan letter, but had not risked sending it to him. So he wrote me a fan letter, which I answered, and we began to write letters over, oh, quite a while. Then I reviewed a book of his, *The Underground Man,* and we got to be friends again.

Capers: That was on the first page of the *New York Times Book Review.*

Welty: The *New York Times,* yes. I think so much of his work, and he's such a nice man. Then, in a typical Ross Macdonald fashion, we, unknown to each other, turned up at the same time in the same hotel in adjoining rooms in New York.

Capers: At the Algonquin?

Welty: At the Algonquin — and met then, and had some good conversations, and walked, and talked, and so on, and got to be good friends. So, I felt that he was almost like an old friend, especially after he dedicated his new book to me; so I invited him to come to this wonderful occasion for me, and he came, which I think was just wonderful — from Santa Barbara. I was sorry his wife couldn't come. She had planned to.

Capers: What's the title of his new book?

Welty: Sleeping Beauty.

Capers: I'm his fan, too. I can't wait to read it.

Welty: Oh! I know it! I'm going out today to try to buy some copies. Rosie wanted to take my inscribed copy home on the plane, but I wouldn't let her.

Capers: I don't blame you. Well, I thought he was a most attractive man, and I'm delighted that he came. Mr. and Mrs. Richard Ader were very nice people. They're from New York City, and I believe he's your lawyer. He's our lawyer.

Welty: He is. He is of the firm of Greenbaum, Wolfe and Ernst, and has been helping Charlotte and me over our literary matters. He had a wonderful time. He loved Mississippi — drove to Jackson by way of Columbus in a car, and then went on to Natchez. He telephoned me after they got back to New York that they had had such a wonderful time they only made the plane by seconds, and wanted to come back. I can't tell you how everybody was so sweet to them.

Capers: Who are the Brainard Cheneys? And the Lewis Simpsons? I didn't meet them.

Welty: Well, the Cheneys — I've known them a long time, too. They are from Smyrna, Tennessee, and their association is with the old Agrarian group. They're old friends of the . . .

Capers: The Vanderbilt people.

Welty: Yes. And I think she is the librarian at Vanderbilt, or was at one time, and writes book reviews. He's in politics somehow, in Tennessee, but he's also a novelist. They're old friends of Caroline Gordon's, and Robert Penn Warren's, Cleanth Brooks's and Allen Tate. At the time I made my list, they were all hoping to come, so I invited the Cheneys because I thought it would be good for them to see all of their old friends again.

Capers: I wanted to ask you about Robert Penn Warren.

Welty: Robert Penn Warren would have come, but he had a lecture date as close as Alabama on the night of this, and so, of course, he couldn't come.

Capers: And Allen Tate didn't get here.

Welty: Allen Tate had meant to come, but his health is frail, and he had spring flu just before. He had accepted . . . Caroline Gordon had accepted.

Capers: Yes. Where are they now? Caroline Gordon is in the East.

Welty: She's in Princeton. They're no longer married to each other.

Capers: No, I know. But is she writer-in-residence, or lecturer, at Princeton?

Welty: No. She's been writing up there, but she's just beginning a new sort of life out in Dallas, Texas, at the University of Dallas, where she's going to teach a course in Creative Grammar, which I think sounds wonderful.

Capers: Well, lots of grammar is very creative.

Welty: Yes, and there mostly isn't any grammar.

Capers: I know. Well, isn't she rather — isn't she of advanced years?

Welty: I think she's the oldest of that group, although I'm not quite certain how old she is. But she's of great vitality and vivacity.

Capers: Now, who is Mr. Shattuck?

Welty: Charles Shattuck is from the University of Illinois at Urbana, and my connection with him is that years ago, he and Kerker Quinn edited a well-known little magazine called *Accent.*

Capers: How do you spell "Kerker"?

Welty: K-e-r-k-e-r Q-u-i-n-n. He died, but Charles is still at the University of Illinois. But *Accent* had a long and honorable life, and they published a piece I wrote. Charlotte, you may know, on Ida M'Toy.

Capers: Oh, yes.

Welty: And we all got to be such friends over that. Then they invited me to come and lecture, and we've kept an acquaintance and friendship up, you know, over all these twenty-five years or so, and I was delighted he came; even though the Ozark Airline struck at the last minute and he had to go to Chicago and down. He's a delightful person, and he had a wonderful time.

Capers: Now, we did miss Mary Mehan.

Welty: Mary Mehan is an old friend also, in Santa Fe, who was struck down with a virus before she and her husband, Aristide — they would have loved to have come.

Capers: Well, it was a marvelous occasion. It was wonderful for us to be honored by the presence of these distinguished people. Most of all we enjoyed their demonstrated affection for you.

The day itself, I think, deserves some comment — Eudora Welty Day. And the reading in the House of Representatives of Mississippi's Historic Old Capitol, I don't think there's ever been such a crowd in the Old Capitol. It was a real tribute to you. I thought that it should also be noted that Governor Waller awarded you a "Distinguished Mississippian" plaque, which is well-deserved. Would you care to comment on the confusions of the day?

Welty: Well, the whole thing was so overwhelming to me. It also was beautifully run. I was the only one that didn't know quite what to do, and Charlotte is the one who should comment on this, but anyway . . . there in one room, semi-circular . . .

Capers: I'd like to know how you felt about it, because I will comment that I thought the arrangements were not good, there was a great deal of unnecessary confusion with the press and the television people. There should have been better planning, but as all these things did not work out — the main thing is how did you feel about it? It was your day!

Welty: I felt wonderful about it, and I was surprised by the lights and the TV and so on, but it just seemed like a dream in a way, in which various unexpected things turn up and it doesn't seem to bother you — you just go on. What really was present with me at every moment was the fact that in that one room were my oldest and best friends in Jackson and from around this country, all in one place for probably the only time in anyone's lives. How could they ever be in any one place again? Everything had converged that meant happiness and pleasure and joy for me, along with my family, and a beautiful day. And . . . well, I just thought it was beautiful.

Capers: Everyone thought you were beautiful, and your graciousness, under what must have been terribly straining circumstances, was remarkable. I felt that the arrangements for the press — well, apparently they hadn't been made at all, and it was bad to have all that interruption and confusion . . . but it did show one thing, and that is that you're the biggest "draw" we've ever had in Dixie! (Laughter). The night the lights went on in Mississippi! The day the lights went on in the Old Capitol! But, anyway, following the reading from *Losing Battles,* Eudora went to the Archives and History Building and received her fans, and was most gracious, and signed autographs for little children who'd come great distances to see her; and was joined, somewhat unexpectedly, by Mrs. Waller, who was very gracious and nice and is the wife of the governor, and who received with her. After this occasion, which was given by the Mississippi Arts Festival, Inc. (I think we should try to make this clear all along — the way that these things were planned by the Mississippi Arts Festival through its committees, some of which functioned a great deal better than others), then we moved on to the night, which was the climax of Eudora Welty Day. This was a big party, a lovely party given by the Mississippi Arts Festival, in the home of Mr. and Mrs. Arnold Turner, Jr., on Crane Boulevard, in Jackson, following a performance of *The Ponder Heart,* which was really a gift of love from New Stage Theatre to Eudora, because they gave her one whole night to ask her friends to be with her there. I enjoyed it more than the Old Capitol because I wasn't so tense about it. Would you like to say anything about the people that came to *The Ponder Heart?*

Welty: Well, it was all the same wonderful crowd that had been together all day. The Festival girls provided a bus. That was the only time we had any rain and it fell just as we were going to the theatre. They took everybody there dryly and securely in a chartered bus. The performance was wonderful, and I think everybody loved it . . . I'm sure they did.

Capers: And the whole house was yours for the night?

Welty: Well, except for the people that had their regular seats that night.

Capers: Did you have some regular ticket holders there?

Welty: Yes, no one was put out, but those who did not have season tickets for that night. Room was made for everybody, and it was just a beautiful performance.

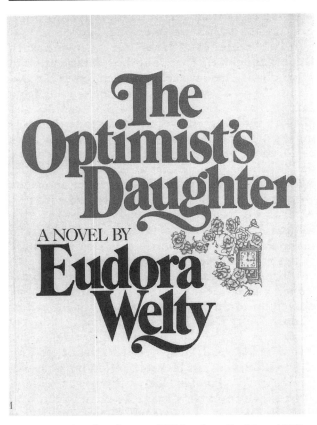

Dust jacket for the novel Welty described in a 1972 interview as "the first thing I've ever done that has direct autobiographical information in it"

Capers: And you had your old friends from high school and . . .

Welty: I had my old friends from high school — from Sunday School, Davis School, high school, everything. And they all came, and when someone who was an old friend couldn't come, then their family came in their place — like Lehman Engel. I asked his three girl cousins. I would have asked them anyway, but I mean, they all came because he couldn't, and they wanted to see me too, I know it. But it was all in the same spirit . . . I mean it was like some kind of reunion. I think we left out, Charlotte, back at the Old Capitol, about the exhibition . . . or do you want to go into that?

Capers: Yes, everything that you'd like to comment on.

Welty: Well, I thought that was beautiful!

Capers: I did too. I'm real delighted with it.

Welty: The Archives — as you know, having done this — has manuscripts and a lot of letters pertaining to things that happened in the course of my writing life, and these were all beautifully arranged by Patti Black, and they were heartwarming to me. When I saw those letters from John Woodburn . . . and also from a number of the people who were present — it was wonderful for them, they just kept going back and looking at it because it was strange — it was like looking into a prism or something. It gave you so many faces of things that everybody had had a part in . . . so really all of it belonged to everybody. It was really unique.

Capers: Well, the people at the Old Capitol really did work hard on that exhibition.

Welty: I know they did. It was obvious.

Capers: It was fine, I thought.

Welty: It was fine. They also had samples of the photographs they have, which was one more aspect of things. I don't see how anyone could have a more moving and meaningful tribute paid to them than my friends and fellow Mississippians did in this. I just can't conceive — I can't imagine people going into the detail and into the care and the study that brought all this about. It was really overwhelming.

Capers: It was really heartfelt, and I do not know of as many people anywhere who really wanted everything to be just right for you because they love you, and because they're proud of you. And so far as our collection goes, I think it's the greatest thing we have in the Department of Archives and History; and I'm really indebted — the State of Mississippi is really indebted to you, which I might as well say here, for the collection. I think you're about out of time, and I think we've hit the high spots of the day.

Welty: We'll have to . . .

Capers: We haven't gotten to the party but the party was great. I'd like to say that myself. It was a beautiful — what would you call it — it was an after-theatre black-tie supper.

Welty: It was an after-the-theatre, after-the-rain, after-everything, end-of-the-whole-beautiful-day party.

Capers: We had such a good time that we stayed till about two-thirty.

Welty: We stayed until about two-thirty. Every room in the house was filled with . . .

Capers: "The odor of roses and sweet girl graduates?"

Welty: Yes, and Becky Turner played the piano. It was in Jean and Arnold Turner's house, and given by her and Arnold, and Tay and Guy Gillespie (for the Arts Festival). They were the co-hosts and hostesses. It was a perfectly beautiful and perfect party. It was lovely. What else can you say about a party? It was also lively and animated. It was fun, it was beautiful!

Capers: Eudora, I thank you so much. I know you're in a great rush because you're just between all the excitement of receiving yet another distinguished award, and getting ready to go to New York Friday to attend — well, tell me where you're going.

Welty: I'm going to the annual ceremony of the National Institute of Arts and Letters in the Academy, and to a party being given for Diarmuid Russell in New York.

Capers: We'll take this up when you get back. Thank you ever so much for your time, and for being what you are.

INTERVIEW:
Alice Walker, "Eudora Welty: An Interview, Summer 1973," [excerpt] *Harvard Advocate,* 106 (Winter 1973): 68–72, in *Conversations with Eudora Welty,* pp. 131–144.

African-American novelist Alice Walker asked Welty about changing racial attitudes in Mississippi and how living in the South had influenced her writing.

AW: Did you think there was anything *wrong* with Mississippi [in terms of race] in those days, when you were young? Did you see a way in which things might change?

EW: Well, I could tell when things were wrong with *people,* and when things happened to individual people, people that we knew or knew of, they were very real to me. It was the same with my parents. I felt their sympathy, I guess it guided mine, when they responded to these things in the same way. And I think this is the way real sympathy *has* to start — from direct feeling for something present and known. People are first and last individuals, and I don't think of them in the mass when I feel for them most.

AW: How does living in Jackson affect your writing?

EW: It's where I live and look around me — it's my piece of the world — it teaches me. Also as a domestic scene it's completely familiar and self-explanatory. It's not everything, though — it's just a piece of everything, that happens to be my sample. It lets me alone to work as I like. It's full of old friends with whom I'm happy to be. And I'm not stuck, either, not compelled to stay here — I'm free to leave when I feel like it, which makes me love it more, I suppose.

AW: What do your friends think of your writing? Do they read it? Do any of them ever creep into your fiction?

EW: Oh yes. They do read it. But they don't creep in. I never write about people that I know. I don't want to, and couldn't if I did want to. I work entirely in terms of the imagination — using, of course, bits and pieces of the real world along with the rest.

AW: Do you write every day?

EW: No, I don't write every day — I write only when I'm in actual work on a particular story. I'm not a notebook keeper. Sustained time is what I fight for, would probably sell my soul for — it's so hard to manage that. I'd like to write a story from beginning to end right through without having to stop. Where I write is upstairs in my bedroom.

AW: In bed?

EW: Oh no, I write at a desk. I have a long room with six big windows in it, and a desk and typewriter at one end.

AW: What does it overlook? A garden? Trees?

EW: It overlooks the street. I like to be aware of the world going on while I'm working. I think I'd get claustrophobic sitting in front of a blank wall with life cut off from view.

AW: Do you have a "Philosophy of Life?" Some pithy saying that you quote to yourself when you seem inundated with troubles?

EW: No. I have work in place of it, I suppose. My "philosophy" is like the rest of my thinking — it comes out best in the translation of fiction. I put what I think about people and their acts in my stories. Of course back of it all there would have to be honesty.

AW: Many modern writers don't seem overly concerned with it.

EW: It's noticeable. Truth doesn't seem to be the thing they're getting at, a good deal of the time.

AW: In fact, much popular poetry, some of it black, engages in clever half-truths, designed to shock only. Or to entertain.

EW: Some of the black poets I've read I have not been able to understand. It hasn't so far as I know anything to do with race. I don't quite understand the virtue of the idiom they strain so over, the language — I don't see the good of it. I feel *tactics* are being used on me, the reader — not the easiest way to persuade *this* reader. It's hard to see the passion behind it.

AW: Oh. I understand the idiom and the language; I can see the passion behind it and admire the rage. My question is whether witty half-truths are good for us in the long run, after we've stopped laughing. And whether poetry shouldn't stick to more difficult if less funny ground, the truth.

EW: That's its real business. I don't believe any writing that has falsity in it can endure for very long. Its end will take care of itself.

AW: Let's hope. What are your thoughts on the Women's Movement?

EW: Well, equal pay for equal work, and so on, fine. But some of the other stuff is hilarious.

AW: Hilarious? Oh, you mean "the lunatic fringe," the flamboyant stances used to attract attention.

EW: Some of the effervescences. Of course, I haven't any bones to pick, myself. A writer never has the problem to face. Being a woman has never kept me from writing or from finding publication for my work.

AW: That's interesting. In the course I teach on black women writers I find that in critical studies black women writers are always given scant attention and sometimes none. They may have published with ease, as Zora Hurston did, but later they were forgotten. Until quite recently, of course. Of course, to many women your life would seem ideal. You have your work, which is substantial, both in what it gives you and what it gives others. You have a house of your own — a lovely one — and all the freedom you want. You are rare, a successful writer who is a woman!

EW: Well, I do have freedom. The successful part is not so much to the point. I think that any artist has it over other people.

AW: Well, some women artists feel that when they marry they must share too much of their time with their husbands and children. They feel they lose single-mindedness, energy they need to put into their own work.

EW: That of course I couldn't say — about husbands and children, I mean. But my tendency is to believe that all experience is an enrichment instead of an impoverishment. My own relationships with people are the things that mean the most to me. I couldn't say what marriage and childbearing would do, of course.

AW: But have you regretted not having been married and not having children?

EW: Oh, I would have been glad if it had come along. Yes I would have. Of course. It wasn't a matter of choosing one thing in place of the other. I think the more things the better.

AW: Over the years have you known any black women? Really known them.

EW: I think I have. Better in Jackson than anywhere, though only, as you'd expect, within the framework of the home. That's the only way I'd have had a chance, in the Jackson up until now. Which doesn't take away from the reality of the knowledge, or its depth of affection — on the contrary. A schoolteacher who helped me on week-ends to nurse my mother through a long illness — she was beyond a nurse, she was a friend and still is, we keep in regular touch. A very bright young woman, who's now in a very different field of work, began in her teens as a maid in our house. She was with us for ten years or more. Then she went on to better things — her story is a very fine one. She's a friend, and we are in regular touch too. Of course I've met black people professionally, in my experience along the fringes of teaching. Lecturing introduced us. The first college anywhere, by the way, that ever invited me to speak was Jackson State — years ago. I read them a story in chapel, as I re-member. Now I don't count meeting people at cock-tail parties in New York — black or any other kind — to answer the rest of your question. But I do know at least a few black people that mean a good deal to me, and I think they like me too.

AW: Have any of them ever crept into your fic-tion?

EW: No. As I said before, I never write about real people. You know, human beings are incapable of being made into characters, as is. They are so much more fluid, and so opaque in places where they need to be transparent and so transparent in places where they need to be opaque. But I think that what I put into a short story in the form of characters might be called certain *qualities* of people in certain situa-tions — no, pin it down more — some quality that makes them unique. I try to dramatize something like this in a way that can show it better than life shows it. Better picked out.

AW: Has it ever been assumed that because you were born and raised in Mississippi your black characters would necessarily suffer from a racist perspective?

EW: I hardly see how anyone could claim that. In-deed to my knowledge no one ever has. I see all my characters as individuals, not as colors, but as people, alive — unique.

BOOK REVIEW:
Louis D. Rubin, Jr., Review of *The Eye of the Story, New Republic,* 178 (22 April 1978): 32–34.

Welty, who has been publishing essays and book reviews since the 1940s and was on the staff of The New York Times Book Review *for six months*

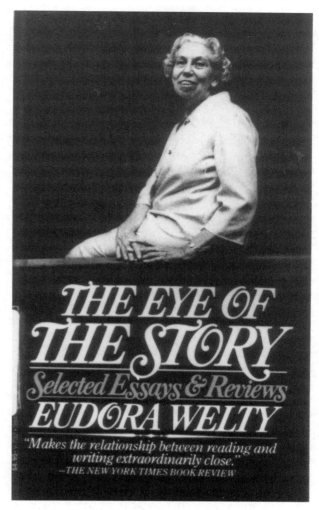

Cover for the first paperback edition of selections from Welty's selected literary criticism. The title comes from an essay on Katherine Anne Porter in which Welty explains how Porter's work "has shown me a thing or two about the eye of fiction, about fiction's visibility and invisibility, about its clarity, its radiance."

in 1944, collected some of her nonfiction writings on literature in The Eye of the Story, *published in April 1978. Louis D. Rubin looked at Welty's comments on other authors as clues for under-standing her own writing.*

When poets and novelists write literary criti-cism it's usually in order to make the world safe for their art. From this explanation I do not ex-clude Eudora Welty, provided it's understood that she isn't arguing for the merits of her own fiction, but for the integrity of fiction as a way of under-standing our lives. The truth is that she is always a little embarrassed when she is forced to discuss her own work: "I never saw, as reader or writer," she declares forthrightly, "that a finished story stood in need of any more from the author: for better or worse, there the story is." When she writes about writing fiction, therefore, she feels the responsibility to describe her own enjoyment of other writers' fiction and to make certain that the complexity of the literary imagination isn't short-changed.

The Eye of the Story is a splendid collection of non-fiction pieces written over the course of almost four decades. There are essays on individual writers — Jane Austen, Henry Green, Katherine Anne Porter, Willa Cather; essays on the arts of reading and writing; there is a fine batch of book reviews; and finally, a number of "personal and occasional pieces."

The most important items, I think, are those which are general in nature, and have to do with reading and writing, which Miss Welty believes is a very privileged kind of collaboration. The best of these is perhaps "Place in Fiction," written 20 years ago, a brilliant inquiry into the esthetic uses of locale in the fictional imagination. No one has a surer grasp of the importance of the imagination as a totality, a palpable and identifiable dimension in our experience of fiction, and no one has more respect for it. In this essay she explores ways in which place can interact, through technique and vision, with the writer's creative imagination to achieve by that process the ideal of fictional form.

Yet it is difficult to set even "Place in Fiction" over a gem of critical reading such as "Looking at Short Stories," first published almost 30 years ago. This piece takes up a group of short stories ranging from Crane's "The Bride Comes to Yellow Sky" to Faulkner's "The Bear," and offers some profound commentary on the short story as an esthetic entity, not experience but a shaped commentary on experience made available through style, design, plot, the significance given to events and characters. Of D. H. Lawrence she remarks that he is "writing of human relationships on earth in terms of his own heaven and hell, and on these terms plot and characters are alike sacrificed to something: that which Lawrence passionately believes to transcend both and which is known and found directly through the senses." This is not a comment on the author's psychology or his thematic concerns; it is a comment on the reader's relationship to the form of Lawrence's fiction.

Of Hemingway she notes that the man is, as writer, a moralist; his plots do not reveal, so much as they permit him to comment. "Action can be radiant, but in this writer who has action to burn, it is not. The stories are opaque by reason of his intention, which is to moralize. We are to be taught by Hemingway, who is instructive by method, that the world is dangerous and full of fear, and that there is a way we had better be." So that "as we now see Hemingway's story, not transparent, not radiant, but lit from without the story, from a moral source, we see the light's true nature: it is a spotlight."

There is formal insight and categorizing enough in this essay to furnish the structure for a full-fledged critical system — if, that is, Miss Welty herself were to work out the details. But in the hands of anyone less gifted than she at dealing with complex unities of the literary imagination, such a system probably wouldn't be any more useful than those we now possess, so we'd perhaps best leave her to her own fiction and be grateful for the essay as it now stands.

The obverse side of Miss Welty's impassioned belief in the splendid integrity of the fictional imagination is her notable distrust of those who would reduce it to a mere expression of personality. Thus her severe review of Arthur Mizener's biography of Ford Madox Ford. "The fact is," she says, "Mr. Mizener never makes the essential leap of mind to discover [Ford's *The Good Soldier*] as a complete entity, a world of itself and quite freed of its author." She wants a biographer to discuss a writer's discoveries of technique, not his psychological needs. She doesn't object to the writer's life as such; but she assumes that since what makes the particular person worth biographizing is the artistic achievement, then the artistic works ought not to be considered merely as psychological strategies for coping with life. Mizener, she says, "consistently treats the inventions of fiction as Ford's barefaced attempts to get away with something in his personal life by foisting these false versions upon the public." Sound cautionary doctrine, I think, and in this instance especially, very much to the point. But what Miss Welty may forget, I think, is that when you write a novel you place your imagination on public display, and if that imagination is compelling enough, there is no way to prevent readers from becoming intensely curious about the human being whose imagination they have been privileged to share.

The last section of this book is the most delightful, in part for just that reason. The author on the subject of Mississippi and Mississippians, including herself, is permitting us to see, with herself as guide, the time and place from which the art grew. Thus when, in downtown Jackson, we are invited to observe "the café with the fish-sign that says 'If They Don't Bite We Catch 'em Anyhow,'" we recognize very well just who it is that is showing that to us, and we can't very well be blamed, can we, for making the connections? Which is one way — but only one — to account for the pleasure we take in reading this fine collection.

BOOK REVIEW:
Carole Cook, "Critic, Friend, and Teacher," review of *The Eye of the Story: Selected Essays and Reviews, Saturday Review,* 61 (29 April 1978): 37, 78.

Carole Cook concurred with Rubin's assessment of The Eye of the Story, *praising Welty for turning "that dry art of criticism into a human, even moving practice."*

Without its storytellers, any nation would be reduced to the moral equivalent of a trading post, and after two generations of spinning the tales that have literally created the Delta country and the Natchez Trace (but not Yoknapatawpha County, which is another world also unto itself) for us outsiders — shy for one reason or another of Mississippi — it is sensible and honorable to regard Eudora Welty as a great national resource.

An ordinate amount of claptrap has been written about Eudora Welty. Critics and reviewers have picked over her work with a fussiness or, perhaps even worse, a glib glossiness. As for the burgeoning field of Welty scholars, her response has been to reiterate quietly that while she respects the difficulty of the work of the analyst, she cannot corroborate his schematic and symbolic interpretations of her stories — which are just that: stories.

But don't think for a minute that this is typical artistic disingenuousness on Welty's part. Nothing, let us hasten to say, is typical about Eudora Welty, even if she has sometimes found it convenient to make it seem that way. The introduction to her snapshot album of depression-era Mississippi, *One Time, One Place,* helps explain why her home state has been her locale. No professional photographer, no outsider, could ever have captured the naturalness of her subjects, but she was "part of it, born into it, taken for granted." From this unique vantage point, unseen

as the fly upon the wall, Welty has been able to write about all that is neither typical nor taken for granted in the life of the South. Originality of both subject and technique has been her one constant.

So we look to this collection of essays, reviews, and personal pieces — many of which, like Welty herself, have appeared in out-of-the-way places — to see what it reveals about her artistic creed and affinities. And lo, in addition to her canny insight into the work of her peers and masters and her great gift for pinpointing a writer's inspiration for coming to writing at all, many of these studies seem to be as much about Eudora Welty as about anything else.

For instance, all that she has to say about the noise and commotion in the novels of Jane Austen (whom Welty named once as her favorite author) — "the family scene! The dinner parties, the walking parties, the dances, picnics, concerts, excursions" — immediately conjures up the excitement of Dabney Fairchild's wedding, Granny Vaughn's ninetieth birthday party, Judge McKelva's funeral. And of whom exactly is she speaking when she asks how the future will treat this spinster who, confined to the world of her father's country parsonage, "could never have got to know very much about life" and then, thinking of Austen's intimate relations with the gentry, goes on to wonder, "Will they wish to call her a snob?"

Welty has said elsewhere of Chekhov, "He had the sense of fate overtaking a way of life, and his Russian humor seems to me kin to the humor of a Southerner. It's the kind that lies mostly in character," and it is through this prism of Welty's that we see Chekhov's reality. Aristocrats, kulaks, serfs, the Emancipation — all have a southern counterpart in the critic's mind.

When she illustrates an essay on Katherine Anne Porter (a longtime friend and an early supporter whose 1941 introduction to *Curtain of Green* is still one of the best essays around on the art of Eudora Welty) or on Willa Cather with a passage from one of their works that displays their insight into human character and their ability to crystallize transitory psychological states, we think to ourselves, Why, Welty herself could have written that! Her appreciation of Elizabeth Bowen's refined wit is an act of homage as well as of connoisseurship; her enthusiasm for the humor of S. J. Perelman makes one suspect that she may also have learned a trick or two here. While her high school peers, she confesses, "were studying 'How long, O Catiline, must we endure your orations?' I was taking in '"Gad, Lucy, You're Magnificent!" Breathed the Great Painter' . . . from a copy of *Judge* on my lap," and it is quite apparent from the bizarre, grotesque bits of humor that stud her stories, from her acute sense of the spoken language, and from her swift narrative pace that she had everything to gain by studying living American, rather than dead Latin, rhetoric.

Her respect for Faulkner goes without saying, but her awe of Virginia Woolf impresses us even more, because what Welty has gotten from her is so intangible. Yes, color and landscape from Faulkner, plot and irony from Austen, understatement from Chekhov, and so on down the seemingly endless list of Eudora Welty's accomplishments as a stylist. But it is Woolf who is her consummate artist, from whom she takes, I think, an entire attitude toward the act of writing. For Welty writes about Virginia Woolf as if she were an icon, a holy woman, a seeress of fiction.

If this were all there was to this volume — a series of touchstones for understanding Welty's stories — it would be quite enough. But as it happens, there is also a second dimension, another and more splendid gift from Welty to her readers. For in her studies of individual writers and in the more abstract section "On Writing" — which includes her defense of regional writing ("Place in Fiction") and of Faulkner, "the white Mississippian" ("Must the Novelist Crusade?") — she has made that dry art of criticism into a human, even moving practice. As critic, Welty is not lawgiver but friend and teacher. The words "feeling," "passion," "life," "communication," occur again and again in her attempts to lead her reader by the hand up to the books that have meant so much to her.

She explains at one point — referring most probably to the discovery of her own vocation — that "it's when reading begins to impress on us what degrees . . . of communication are possible between novelists and ourselves as readers that we surmise what it has meant, can mean, to write novels." *What it can mean to write novels.* This, it seems to me, is the real and very impassioned message behind all of Eudora Welty's criticism, and one that very few writers are in a position to transmit, because as she herself notes, story writing and critical analysis are entirely separate gifts, "like spelling and playing the flute."

The problem of criticism is that the meaning of writing is inseparable from the act of writing. There can never be a translation of a whole story into a commentary on its parts in which the story does not suffer. Welty's solution to this paradox is to treat the story as an intimate communication of feeling between just two persons — the writer and the reader, each bound to the other for the duration of the story by the moral responsibility the intimacy implies.

But whether she is writing fiction or criticism, Welty never forgets to be entertaining. She's as lively and engaging a critic as ever lived, and this is just another mark of her shrewdness. *The Eye of the Story,* which belies its occasional genesis, ought to be pressed posthaste into the hands of the young especially, for they are Eudora Welty's favorites, and also into the hands of serious readers and writers of all ages.

BOOK REVIEW:
Anne Tyler, "The Fine, Full World of Welty," review of *The Collected Stories of Eudora Welty, Washington Star,* 26 October 1980, D1, D7.

The publication of The Collected Stories of Eudora Welty *on 10 October 1980 provided an occasion for reassessing Welty's short fiction, and the reviews were far more favorable than those that had greeted Welty's volumes of short stories in the 1940s and 1950s. Novelist Anne Tyler, who has acknowledged Welty's influence on her own writing, offered a sensitive analysis of Welty's fictional world.*

In Eudora Welty's small, full world, events float past as unexpectedly as furniture in a flood. A lady with her neck in a noose sails out of a tree; a stabbed woman folds in upon herself in silence; a child pushed off a diving board drops upright, seeming first to pause in the air before descending; a car rolls down an embankment, rocks in a net of grapevines, and arrives on the forest floor.

All violent acts, come to think of it — but not at first glance. They are so closely observed, so meticulously described, that they appear eerily motionless, like a halted film. That child falling off the diving board, for instance: The lifeguard hangs his bugle "studiously" on a tree and retrieves her from the lake. He lays her on a picnic table, alongside a basket of tin cups and cutlery, and while he resuscitates her, another child with her poison ivy patches bandaged in dazzling white, fans her with a towel, and Mrs. Lizzie Stark, Camp Mother, arrives with a little black boy bearing two watermelons like twin babies. ("You can put those melons down," Mrs. Stark tells him. "Don't you see the table's got somebody on it?")

Or a young boy, spying on a vacant house, observes the following: While the watchman sleeps upstairs, his hat upon the bedpost, a sailor and his girlfriend lie on a mattress eating pickles, and an ancient lady strings the first-floor parlor with strips of paper. At next glance, the watchman's hat is seen to have turned on the bedpost "like a weathercock"; the sailor and his girlfriend are chasing each other in circles; the old woman holds a candle to the strips of paper, and two passing men, after breaking through a window, take a warmup jog around the dining room table, then charge on into the fire in the parlor.

Things happen, a girl in this story observes, like planets rising and setting, or like whole constellations spinning. And the town stays unsurprised; it simply watches people come and go, only hoping "to place them, in their hour or their street or the name of their mothers' people."

Placing, naming — isn't that why these stories work so well? Firmly pinned as butterflies, Eudora Welty's characters remain vivid after 30, 40 years, every dress fold and flash of eye caught perfectly: the deaf couple waiting in a railroad station, feeble-minded Lily Daw, old Phoenix Jackson traveling her eternal path through the pines. The running boards, rusty yard pumps, butter churns and powder-flash cameras have all but disappeared, but the people themselves remain so true that this volume, held in the hands, seems teeming with life. You can imagine that it's positively noisy, ringing as it does with voices laughing and scolding and gossiping, with the farmer calling out his buttermilk song and the Powerhouse band playing "Somebody Loves Me" and Virgie Rainey tinkling away on the Bijou picture-show piano.

The present collection contains all of Eudora Welty's published stories — four volumes' worth, along with two more recent stories not previously anthologized. *A Curtain of Green,* the first volume, was written in the 1930s. It contains some of her best-known pieces: "Why I Live at the P.O.," "Petrified Man" and "A Worn Path." *The Wide Net,* published in 1943, has for its motif the Natchez Trace, which runs alike through tales of the old-time outlaws who traveled it and the modern townspeople now living near it. The effect is a kind of river of time — or perhaps, more accurately, timelessness. Place (always central to Eudora Welty's writing) makes insignificant the mere passage of years.

In *The Golden Apples* (1949), place again provides the link. Morgana, Mississippi, is the setting for six of its seven stories, and even in the one exception, Morgana is a presence so haunting — at least to us, the readers — that San Francisco, where a Morgana citizen has moved, seems foreign and bizarre and jarring. What a relief, upon finishing that story, to turn the page and find ourselves back in Morgana! And how poignant and oddly satisfying to see Snowdie's pesky twin boys change to ordinary, not-very-happy men, to watch the little girls from that camp on Moon Lake grow settled and brisk and domestic, while King MacLain becomes a senile old gentleman!

The stories in *The Bride of the Innisfallen* (1955) move farther afield — to New Orleans, to Circe's island, to a boat train passing through Wales and a steamer bound for Naples. It's worrisome at first (will she still be Eudora Welty? the *real* Eudora Welty?), but not for long. Just look at the title story, where on a speeding train "two greyhounds in plaid blankets, like dangerously ecstatic old ladies hoping no one would see them, rushed into, out of, then past the corridor door. . . . " Yes, it's still Eudora Welty.

In the two stories not previously anthologized — "Where Is the Voice Coming From?" and "The Demonstrators" — the movement is less in place than in time. Both deal with the racial unrest of the '60s. Introducing them, Eudora Welty says that they "reflect the unease, the ambiguities, the sickness and desperation of those days in Mississippi." They do indeed; and they prove her to be the most faithful of mirrors. She writes about what *is*, not what ought to be. The "niggers" and "colored" of her '40s stories give way to the civil-rights leaders of the '60s. It's a whole little social history, offered without comment.

Now: Is she, in fact, a Southern writer? (Someone will be bound to ask.) Well, assuming there is such a thing, I believe she qualifies — not only through accident of birth and her characters' rhythms of speech but also because, in telling a story, she concerns herself less with what happens than with whom it happens *to,* and where. Everything must have its history, every element of the plot its leisurely, rocking-chair-paced (but never dull) examination.

Unlike Flannery O'Connor, she is kind, viewing her characters with genuine sympathy and affection. Or if unkind events occur, one senses that that's simply what happened; it's not a result of any willful twist from the author. She tells stories like a friend, someone you're fond of —

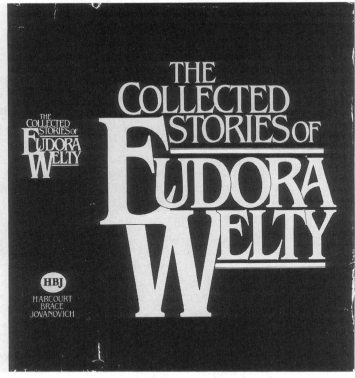

Dust jacket for the 1980 volume that includes all the short fiction from Welty's earlier books and two previously uncollected stories from the 1960s

sitting on her porch shelling peas, you imagine, and speaking in a genteel murmur, but then startling you with sudden flashes of humor and perception.

For me as a girl — a Northerner growing up in the South, longingly gazing over the fence at the rich, tangled lives of the Southern neighbors — Eudora Welty was a window upon the world. If I wondered what went on in the country churches and "Colored Only" cafes, her writing showed me, as clearly as if I'd been invited inside.

But what seems obvious only now, with the sum total of these collected stories, is that Eudora Welty herself must once have felt the need for such a window. The children in her stories are all eyes, soaking up other people's lives, feeling for the slightest crack that might allow them to slip into another person's existence. Over and over, they observe and conjecture and catalog, file away their mental notes, have moments when they believe they're in somebody else's skin. It's tempting to link these children directly to their creator. Such unblinking watchfulness could, years afterward, lead to some uncannily wise story-telling.

"Making the jump," she calls it in her preface. "What I do in writing of any character," she says, "is to try to enter into the mind, heart and skin of a human being who is not myself. . . . It is the act of a writer's imagination that I set most high."

A jump it may be, but she knows better than anyone that it's a jump made by very small increments, requiring supreme patience. Tirelessly, unhurriedly she assembles her details: the frazzled peacock feather dangling from a lightbulb, the lost ball on the roof, ladies' luncheons of colored cream-cheese flowers, electric fans walking across the floor, cake plates decorated with "rowdy babies," Mother's Helper paregoric bottles, Sweet Dreams mosquito repellent. And the piano recitals where "some untalented little Maloney" hands out programs, the photographer's backdrop of "unrolled, yanked-down moonlight," the name of a long-dead woman spelled out across the lawn in narcissus bulbs, the movie-theater sign requiring a deposit for coming in to talk, the saucepan of zinnias in an open mailbox with a note attached to the handle.

And if that's still not enough, she will find a way to *make* you see. She will spin a phrase a certain way so you have to stop dead, astonished, and then think it over and nod and agree — and thinking it over, haven't you conjured up the scene for yourself? A thorny old rose twines around a pavilion, "like the initial letter in a poetry book." On a spring day, the birds are "so busy you turned as you would at people as they plunged by." A woman passing a string of abandoned, boarded-up houses remarks that she is "walking in their sleep." A country man appears "home-made, as though his wife had self-consciously knitted or somehow contrived a husband when she sat alone at night." And a hat too big for the wearer "stood up and away from his head all around, and seemed only following him — on runners, perhaps, like those cartridges for change in Spight's store."

Then suddenness — an arresting incongruity — further convinces us that all this must be fact. (She couldn't just make these things up, you can hear a reader thinking.) In a crowded house where a death has occurred, a visiting relative pounces on a random child and tickles her violently — "speaking soberly over her screams, 'Now wait: You don't know who I am.'"

People are involved in strangely peripheral activities (tie-dyeing scarves, trying on lipstick) at crucial moments, or are caught by irrelevant sights, like the lavender soles of the lifeguard's feet or the black family's clothesline strung with cast-offs of the observer's relatives — his sister's golfing dress, wife's duster. More real than reality, these stories fairly breathe. We're taken in completely; we don't even raise an eyebrow, finally, when events as preposterous as miracles float by on the flood of her words.

The lighter stories are very, very funny — funny in their bones, as the best humor always is, so you'd have to read the entire story aloud from start to finish if someone asked why you were laughing. But how I'd love to be asked! Like a shot, I'd read "The Wide Net," with its motley collection of ne'er-do-wells joyfully assembling to drag the river. Yet on second thought, there's an undertone of sadness to that story, as there is to much of this collection. And some of the serious pieces can break your heart — the traveling salesman seeing, all at once, the vacancies in his life; or the little girl in "A Memory" constructing for herself, with infinite care, a small circle of protection against the ugly and pathetic outside world.

A few years ago, introducing a book of photographs she'd taken during the Depression, Eudora Welty remarked that her photos must have been attended by an angel of trust. Trust did seem to shine from those subject's faces — black and poor though most of them were. It was a mark of an innocent time, she suggested; but of course, it was more than that. People know, somehow, whom to open up to, and imaginary people know as surely as real ones. In Eudora Welty's stories, characters present themselves hopefully and confidingly, believing that she'll do right by them. Their faith is not misplaced. Eudora Welty is one of our purest, finest, gentlest voices, and this collection is something to be treasured.

BOOK REVIEW:
Reynolds Price, Review of *The Collected Stories of Eudora Welty, New Republic,* 183 (1 November 1980): 31–34.

Among the many celebratory reviews of The Collected Stories *was Reynolds Price's perceptive essay, which places Welty's fiction in the context of Western literary tradition. The review also attributes a growing resistance toward Southern fiction to a shift during the 1950s of "the center of critical power from the south to the northeast."*

American letters may still lack a novelist whose life work matches in weight the achievement of Dickens or Tolstoy, but our 20th-century masters of the short story bow to no one for stylistic elegance or emotional penetration. The past decade has brought in stout collections from three of the best — Flannery O'Connor, John Cheever, Paul Bowles — and of the certified living masters of the form, only Eudora Welty has resisted collection (though all but two of the stories were continuously available in separate volumes). A change of publisher stymied the project for several years, but finally here they are — 41 stories, the entire contents of her four individual collections plus two stories previously uncollected.

The best news is the availability, in a single package, of stories as good in themselves and as influential on the aspirations of other stories as any since Hemingway's. Second best — a quick check indicates that Welty has avoided the worst temptation of collectors, the revision of old work in hindsight. Thus some of the early stories are still clouded by a compulsively metaphoric prose (virtually everything is compared to, equated with, some other thing). And even an untypically hollow story like "The Purple Hat" or a misfire like "A Visit of Charity" has been perpetuated with the successes. Far better though to have them in the forms of their initial occurrence than obscured by a forged technical gloss or uselessly suppressed.

Only one sizable question may be asked. Would it have been better to break up the sequence of the original volumes and print the stories in order of composition (with an exception for *The Golden Apples,* whose stories are connected)? Such an arrangement would at least have made possible the inclusion of a few never-collected early stories as viable as two or three now canonized, and it would have clarified the reader's legitimate search for evolving themes and repetitions in a writer whose concerns have dived and surfaced in unusually patient cycles. But Welty presumably chose in favor of her first, chiefly musical placement; and she of all contemporary writers since Auden has spoken out most sternly against the bald historical-biographical curiosity of readers and critics. In any case, the original appearances of the components of the four volumes were closely grouped. Those in *A Curtain of Green* were published in magazines from 1936 to 1941, those in *The Wide Net* from 1941 to 1943, *The Golden Apples* from 1947 to 1949, *The Bride of the Innisfallen* from 1949 to 1954, and the two latest stories in 1963 and 1966. (Each of these volumes was followed by a novel — *The Robber Bridegroom* in 1942, *Delta Wedding* in 1946, *The Ponder Heart* in 1954, and the two late stories by *Losing Battles* in 1970 and *The Optimist's Daughter* in 1972.)

A long performance then and one which, though it has never lacked praise and devoted readers, has presented critics with the kind of fearless emotional intensity, the fixed attention to daily life, and the technical audacity that have mercilessly revealed the poverty of scholastic critical methods. In the 1940s the lucid early stories and *Delta Wedding* were automatically accused of gothicism and indifference to the plight of southern blacks. The connected stories of *The Golden Apples* set off a dismal and apparently endless hunt for mythological underpinning (a curse that the stories innocently brought on themselves). The internalized experiments of the long stories of the 1950s met with general bafflement. Though prizes descended and though a handful of stories were rushed into most anthologies while Welty fans round the land stood ready to burst into recitations from "Petrified Man" or "A Shower of Gold," it was only with Ruth Vande Kieft's discerning *Eudora Welty* in 1962 that the size of the achievement began to be acknowledged and mapped — the size and the peculiar pitfalls of the

stories as objects for contemplation, guides to action.

The difficulties are big, both of matter and of manner. As the center of critical power shifted in the 1950s from the south to the northeast, a vestigial resistance to southern fiction quickly enlarged and hardened. The south had had too long an inning as Literary Central; its writers were obsessed with the ruling classes of a society rotten with greed and racist inhumanity (as though Tolstoy, Flaubert, or Bellow had more exemplary subjects). Thus Welty's Christian white ladies and their ineffectual mates, her resigned fieldhands and maids, her garrulous white trash, were obstacles for a high proportion of trained readers. And no native, southern critics of distinction rose in succession to Ransom, Tate, and Warren to mediate such work to the nation. But even more daunting than the unabashed southern grounding of the work was the statement at its center, a quiet reiterated statement that declared two polar yet indissoluble things. Most disturbing of all, the statement proved itself by locating characters and actions of recognizable solidity and pursuing them with a gaze that occasionally seemed serpentine in its steadiness — or angelic (as in angel of judgment). On first acquaintance one might be tempted to link the Welty of the stories with an apparent progenitor and paraphrase the statement by quoting D. H. Lawrence's essay on Poe — "A ghastly disease love. Poe telling us of his disease: trying to make his disease fair and attractive. Even succeeding."

If we substitute *Homo sapiens* for Poe we do have a crucial beam for the scaffolding of any of Welty's stories. The fact was realized in other terms in Robert Penn Warren's important early essay, "The Love and the Separateness in Miss Welty." For the stories from first to last do say this clearly: "Human creatures are compelled to seek one another in the hope of forming permanent bonds of mutual service, not primarily from an instinct to continue the species" (children are only minor players in her cast), "but from a profound hunger, mysterious in cause, for individual gift and receipt of mutual care." ("Tenderness" is Welty's most sacred word.) "So intense is the hunger however that, more often than not, it achieves no more than its own frustration — the consumption and obliteration of one or both of the mates." (The words "bitter" and "shriek" occur as frequently, and weightily, as "tenderness.")

To that extent, Poe or even Strindberg is a truer ancestor to the stories than Virginia Woolf or E. M. Forster, who have often been mentioned. But such whimsical genealogies are of interest only to literary historians. They give little help to a reader whose aim is the enjoyment of and kinetic response to fiction that is so obviously the report of a particular pair of eyes on a particular place. For the dense matrix of observed life — mineral, bestial, human — which surrounds Welty's statement of the doomed circularity of love is the source of her originality, the flavor which quickly distinguishes a stretch of her prose from any other writer's.

> She knew that now at the river, where she had been before on moonlit nights in autumn, drunken and sleepless, mist lay on the water and filled the trees, and from the eyes to the moon would be a cone, a long silent horn, of white light. It was a connection visible as the hair is in air, between the self and the moon, to make the self feel the child, a daughter far, far back. Then the water, warmer than the night air or the self that might be suddenly cold, like any other arms, took the body under too, running without visibility into the mouth. As she would drift in the river, too alert, too insolent in her heart in those days, the mist might thin momentarily and brilliant jewel eyes would look out from the water-line and the bank. Sometimes in the weeds a lightning bug would lighten, on and off, on and off, for as long in the night as she was there to see.
>
> Out in the yard, in the coupe, in the frayed velour pocket next to the pistol was her cache of cigarettes. She climbed inside and shielding the matchlight, from habit, began to smoke cigarettes. All around her the dogs were barking. ["The Wanderers"]

Her monitoring senses record two main strands of data — the self-sufficient splendor of the natural world (in a number of American and European places) and the enciphered poetry of human thought and speech which rises, sometimes through fits of laughter, to moments of eloquently plain truth-telling. The first-written of the stories provides a pure example. In "Death of a Traveling Salesman," the lost itinerant shoe-salesman comes suddenly to understand the fertile union of a couple in whose home he has harbored after an automobile accident.

> Bowman could not speak. He was shocked with knowing what was really in this house. A marriage, a fruitful marriage. That simple thing. Anyone could have had that.

Somehow he felt unable to be indignant or protest, although some sort of joke had certainly been played upon him. There was nothing remote or mysterious here — only something private.

Such yearning for love is found in numerous other mouths in the stories, as character after character (male and female indifferently) reaches the boundary of illusion. But the second half of their repeated discovery is almost never spoken, by character or author. Only at the solitary ends of fated action do the characters perceive an inexorably closing circle. Having earned his vision, the salesman flees the scene of care and continuance and dies of heart failure, literally felled by his knowledge. Virgie Rainey at the end of "The Wanderers" is driven from her home and all she has known by the collapse of her dream of transcending love; and her first stopping place — perhaps her final destination — is a heightened awareness of the gorgeous nonhuman world that coils round our species (the only species, so far as we know, capable of contemplating that world). The casual pair who nearly connect in "No Place for You, My Love" are actually prevented by a watchful and judging world, the sunstruck land below New Orleans.

> At length he stopped the car again, and this time he put his arm under her shoulders and kissed her — not knowing ever whether gently or harshly. It was the loss of that distinction that told him this was now. Then their faces touched unkissing, unmoving, dark, for a length of time. The heat came inside the car and wrapped them still, and the mosquitoes had begun to coat their arms and even their eyelids.
>
> Later, crossing a large open distance, he saw at the same time two fires. He had the feeling that they had been riding for a long time across a face — great, wide, and upturned. In its eyes and open mouth were those fires they had had glimpses of, where the cattle had drawn together: a face, a head, far down here in the South — south of South, below it. A whole giant body sprawled downward then, on and on, always, constant as a constellation or an angel. Flaming and perhaps falling, he thought.

Similar ambush awaits the characters of her novels, though the greater length of a novel generally results in a more ambiguous, if not truer, statement. The stories preserve the naked cry — as sane, inevitable, and unanswerable as the evening call of a solitary beast from the edge of a wood.

No wonder that admirers of Welty's fiction have concentrated most of their scrutiny and affection on comic stories like "Why I Live at the P.O." or the numerous others that richly summon atmospheres of serene nature and the warm conglomerations of family life — weddings, funerals, reunions. The choice has been instinctive, a normal reflex of narrative hunger (which craves consolation, with small side-orders of fright or sadistic witness).

The favorites are certainly worthy. In previous American fiction, only Mark Twain displays as skillfully poised a comic gift, poised on the razor that divides compassion and savagery (Faulkner's comedy is oddly gentler). Welty's power over loving and tussling groups of kin gathered on magnetized family ground is matched only by the 19th-century Russians, as is her courage for the plain declaration of loyalty and duty. A story like "A Worn Path" is unimaginable in any hands but hers or Chekhov's (and it is only illustrative of my point that this uncomplicated tale of duty has evoked a blizzard of nutty mytho-symbolist explications). And her effortless entry into masculine minds as various as the traveling salesman, the younger salesman in "The Hitch-Hikers," the young husband of "The Wide Net," the black jazz-pianist of "Powerhouse," and the majestically thoughtless King McClain of *The Golden Apples* is a sustaining assurance (in the presently gory gender wars) that the sexes can occasionally comprehend and serve one another if they choose to.

But such selective attention — and the popular anthologies have been as monotonous as her admirers — has resulted in a partial, even distorted, sense of Welty as the mild, sonorous, "affirmative" kind of artist whom America loves to clasp to its bosom and crush with belated honors (Robert Frost endured a similar reputation, but he had handmade it assiduously). It is one of the qualities of genius to provide wares for almost any brand of shopper — it has taken ages to wrestle Jane Austen from the chaste grip of the Janeites or Dickens from the port-and-Stilton set — and Welty's stories have, without calculation, stocked most departments. But such an embarrassment of choice endangers understanding.

One can hope then that this first display of the whole supply in a single place will encourage readers not only to sample the random colors and harmonies of 20-odd masterpieces but to read all the stories in the roughly chronological order of their arrangement. I've already suggested the chief discovery or rediscovery to be made — a contemporary American genius of range as well as depth.

The breadth of Welty's offering is finally most visible not in the variety of types — farce, satire, horror, lyric, pastoral, mystery — but in the clarity and solidity and absolute honesty of a lifetime's vision. That it's a Janus-faced or Argus-eyed vision, I've also suggested — even at times a Gorgon stare. Yet its findings are not dealt out as one more of the decks of contradictory and generally appalling polaroids so prevalent in our fiction and verse. A slow perusal here — say a story a night for six weeks — will not fail to confirm a granite core in every tale: as complete and unassailable an image of human relations as any in our art, tragic of necessity but also comic (even the latest story, a chilling impersonation of the white assassin of a black civil rights leader, jokes to its end). As real a gift in our legacy as any broad river or all our lost battles.

INTERVIEW:
Anne Tyler, "A Visit With Eudora Welty," *New York Times Book Review*, 2 November 1980, pp. 33–34.

Welty expressed her feelings about rereading her short fiction while preparing The Collected Stories *for publication, described her practice of writing, and reminisced about her literary friendships to visitor Anne Tyler.*

She lives in one of those towns that seem to have outgrown themselves overnight, sprouting — on reclaimed swampland — a profusion of modern hospitals and real estate offices, travel agencies and a Drive-Thru Beer Barn. (She can remember, she says, when Jackson, Miss., was so small that you could go on foot anywhere you wanted. On summer evenings you'd pass the neighbors' lawns scented with petunias, hear their pianos through the open windows. Everybody's life was more accessible.) And when her father, a country boy from Ohio, built his family a house back in 1925, he chose a spot near Belhaven College so he'd be sure to keep a bit of green around them, but that college has added so many parking lots, and there are so many cars whizzing by nowadays.

Still, Eudora Welty's street is shaded by tall trees. Her driveway is a sheet of pine needles, and her house is dark and cool, with high ceilings, polished floors, comfortable furniture and a wonderfully stark old kitchen. She has lived here since she was in high school (and lived in Jackson all her

Welty receiving an honorary degree at Columbia University, 1982

life). Now she is alone, the last of a family of five. She loves the house, she says, but worries that she isn't able to keep it up properly. A porch she screened with $44 from the Southern Review, during the Depression, needs screening once again for a price so high that she has simply closed it off. One corner of the foundation has had to be rescued from sinking into the clay, which she describes as "shifting about like an elephant's hide."

But the house seems solid and well tended, and it's clear that she has the vitality to fill its spare rooms. Every flat surface is covered with tidy stacks of books and papers. A collection of widely varied paintings — each with its own special reason for being there — hangs on wires from the picture rails. One of them is a portrait of Eudora Welty as a young woman — blond-haired, with large and luminous eyes.

Her hair is white now, and she walks with some care and wears an Ace bandage around her wrist to ease a touch of arthritis. But the eyes are still as luminous as ever, radiating kindness and ... attention, you would have to call it, but attention of a special quality, with some gentle amusement accompanying it. When she laughs, you can see

how she must have looked as a girl — shy and delighted. She will often pause in the middle of a sentence to say, "Oh, I'm just enjoying this so much!" and she does seem to be that rare kind of person who takes an active joy in small, present moments. In particular, she is pleased by *words,* by ways of saying things, snatches of dialogue overheard, objects' names discovered and properly applied. (She likes to read technical manuals and diagrams with the parts labeled. Her whole face lights up when she describes how she heard a country woman confess to a "gnawing and a craving" for something. "Wasn't that a wonderful way of putting it?" she asks. "A gnawing and a craving.")

Even in conversation, the proper word matters deeply to her and is worth a brief pause while she hunts for it. She searches for a way to describe a recent heat wave: The heat, she says, was like something waiting for you, something out to *get* you; when you climbed the stairs at night, even the stair railing felt like, oh, like warm toast. She shares my fear of merging into freeway traffic because, she says, it's like entering a round of hot-pepper in a jump-rope game: " 'Oh, well,' you think, 'maybe the next time it comes by. . . . ' " (I always did know freeways reminded me of something; I just couldn't decide what it was.) And when she re-read her collected stories, some of which date back to the 1930's: "It was the strangest experience. It was like watching a negative develop, slowly coming clear before your eyes. It was like recovering a memory."

A couple of her stories, she says, she really had wished to drop from the collection, but was persuaded not to. Others, the very earliest, were written in the days before she learned to rewrite ("I didn't know you *could* rewrite"), and although she left them as they were, she has privately revised her own printed copies by hand. Still others continue to satisfy her — especially those in "The Golden Apples" — and she laughs at herself for saying how much she loves "June Recital" and "The Wanderers." But her pleasure in these stories is, I think, part and parcel of her whole attitude toward writing: She sees it as truly joyful work, as something she can hardly wait to get down to in the mornings.

Unlike most writers she imposes no schedule on herself. Instead she waits for things to "brood" — usually situations from her own life which, in time, are alchemized into something entirely different, with different characters and plots. From then on, it goes very quickly. She wakes early, has coffee and sets to work. She writes as long as she can keep at it, maybe pausing for a brief tomato sandwich at noon. (And she can tell you exactly who used to make the best tomato sandwiches in Jackson, back during her grade-school days when everybody swapped lunches. It was Frances MacWillie's grandmother, Mrs. Nannie MacWillie.)

What's written she types soon afterward; she feels that her handwriting is too intimate to re-read objectively. Then she scribbles revisions all over the manuscript, and cuts up parts of pages and pins them into different locations with dressmakers' pins — sometimes moving whole scenes, sometimes a single word. Her favorite working time is summer, when everything is quiet and it's "too hot to go forth" and she can sit next to an open window. (The danger is that any passing friend can interrupt her: "I saw you just sitting at your typewriter. . . . ")

Describing the process of writing, she is matter-of-fact. It's simply her life's work, which has occupied her for more than 40 years. She speaks with calm faith of her own instincts, and is pleased to have been blessed with a visual mind — "the best shorthand a writer can have." When she's asked who first set her on her path (this woman who has, whether she knows it or not, set so many later writers on *their* paths), she says that she doesn't believe she ever did get anything from other writers. "It's the experience of living," she says — leaving unanswered, as I suppose she must, the question of just how she, and not some next-door neighbor, mined the stuff of books from the ordinary experiences of growing up in Jackson, Miss., daughter of an insurance man and a schoolteacher; of begging her brothers to teach her golf; bicycling to the library in two petticoats so the librarian wouldn't say, "I can see straight through you," and send her home; and spending her honor roll prize — a free pass — to watch her favorite third baseman play ball.

And where (she wonders aloud) did she get the idea she was bound to succeed as a writer, sending off stories on her own as she did and promptly receiving them back? How long would she have gone on doing that?

Fortunately, she didn't have to find out. Diarmuid Russell — then just starting as a literary agent — offered to represent her. He was downright *fierce* about representing her, at one time remarking that if a certain story were rejected, the editor "ought to be horsewhipped." (It wasn't rejected.) And there were others who took a special interest in her — notably the editor John Woodburn, and Katherine Anne Porter. (Katherine Anne Porter invited her to visit. Eudora Welty was so overwhelmed that she only got there after a false start, turning back at Natchez when her courage failed.) A photo she keeps from around this period shows a party honoring the publication of her first book: a tableful of admiring editors, a heartbreakingly young Diarmuid Russell, and in their midst Eudora Welty, all dressed up and wearing a corsage and looking like a bashful, charming schoolgirl. She does not admit to belonging to a literary community, but what she means is that she was never part of a formal circle of writers. You sense, in fact, that she would be uncomfortable in a self-consciously literary environment. (Once she went to the writers' colony at Yaddo but didn't get a thing done, and spent her time attending the races and "running around with a bunch of Spaniards." She'd suspected all along, she says, that a place like that wouldn't work out for her.)

Certainly, though, she has had an abundance of literary friendships, which she has preserved and cherished over the years. She speaks warmly of Robert Penn Warren; and she likes to recall how Reynolds Price, while still a Duke student,

I

I.

LISTENING

In our house on North Congress Street, in Jackson, Mississippi, where I was born, the oldest of 3 children, 1909

We grew up to the striking of clocks. There was a mission-style oak grandfather clock standing in the hall, which sent its gong-like strokes up the sounding board of the stairs. Through the night, *it could* find its way into our ears. ~~however our bedroom pillows.~~ My parents' bedroom ~~Theirs~~ had a little clock that struck in bell-like notes, and though the kitchen clock did nothing but show the time, the dining room clock was a cuckoo-clock with ~~long~~ weights *on long chains* on one of which my baby brother, after climbing to the top of the china closet, once ~~~~ succeeded in hanging the cat for a moment, *not at all characteristic of him.* I don't know whether or not my father's *Ohio* family having been Swiss ~~~~ *back in* the 1700's *like him,* had anything to do with this; but we all of us have been, *at least* time-minded all our lives. This was good *at least* for a fiction writer, to have learned so penetratingly *and almost first of all,* about chronology.

~~Of course, if I did,~~ It was one of a good many things I learned, *about* without Knowing it; *a fund that* would be there when I needed it.

My father loved all instruments that would instruct and fascinate. His place to keep things was the drawer in the "library table" where lying on top of his folded maps ~~he kept~~ *was* a telescope with brass extensions, to find the moon and the Big Dipper after supper in our front yard, *and trips,* and to keep appointment with eclipses. *There was a folding Kodak that was brought out for Christmas, birthdays* ~~He also kept there~~ (a magnifying) *In the back of the drawer you could find* glass, a kaleidoscope, and a gyroscope in a black buckram box, which he would set dancing *for us* on a string pulled tight. He had also supplied himself with an assortment of puzzles of metal rings and intersecting links and keys chained together, impossible for the rest of us, however patiently shown, to take apart. *he had an almost childlike love of the ingenious.*

First page of a draft for One Writer's Beginnings *(Eudora Welty Collection — Mississippi Department of Archives and History)* met her train in a pure white suit at 3 A.M. when she came to lead a workshop. But some other friends are gone now. Elizabeth Bowen was especially dear to her. Katherine Anne Porter's long illness and death have left her deeply saddened. And Diarmuid Russell, she says, is someone she still thinks of every day of her life.

In a profession where one's resources seem likely to shrink with time (or so most writers fear), Eudora Welty is supremely indifferent to her age. She says, when asked, that it does bother her a little that there's a certain depletion of physical energy — that she can't make unlimited appearances at colleges nowadays, much as she enjoys doing that, and still have anything left for writing. (Colleges keep inviting her because, she claims, "I'm so well behaved, I'm always on time and I don't get drunk or hole up in a motel with my lover.") But it's plain that her *internal* energy is as powerful as ever. She credits the examples she's seen around her: Elizabeth Bowen, who continued full of curiosity and enthusiasm well into her 70's; and V. S. Pritchett, now 80, whose work she particularly admires. In fact, she says, the trouble with publishing her collected stories is the implication that there won't be any more — and there certainly will be, she says. She takes it as a challenge.

She does not, as it turns out, go to those ladies' luncheons with the tinted cream cheese flowers that she describes so well in her stories. (I'd always wondered.) Her life in Jackson revolves around a few long-time friends, with a quiet social evening now and then — somebody's birthday party, say. Her phone rings frequently just around noon, when it's assumed that she's finished her morning's work. And one friend, an excellent cook, might drop off a dish she's prepared.

Nor is she entirely bound to Jackson. She loves to travel, and she positively glows when describing her trips. "Oh, I would hate to be confined," she says. Her only regret is that now you have to take the plane. She remembers what it was like to approach the coast of Spain by ship — to see a narrow pink band on the horizon and then hear the tinkling of bells across the water.

When she talks like this, it's difficult to remember that I'm supposed to be taking notes.

Is there anything she especially wants known about herself — anything she'd like a chance to say? Yes, she says, and she doesn't even have to think about it: She wants to express her thankfulness for all those people who helped and encouraged her so long ago. "Reading my stories over," she says, "brings back their presence. I feel that I've been very lucky."

BOOK REVIEW:

C. Vann Woodward, "Southerner With Her Own Accent," review of *One Writer's Beginnings, New York Times Book Review,* 19 February 1984, p. 7.

Welty's memoir of her development as a writer, One Writer's Beginnings, *is a revised version of three lectures she delivered to inaugurate the William E. Massey lecture series at Harvard University in April 1983. In his review of the book the eminent Southern historian C. Vann Woodward discussed how Welty's nonsouthern roots set her apart from other Southern writers.*

In her introduction to Eudora Welty's first book, "A Curtain of Green" (1941), Katherine Anne Porter remarked of the young writer that "She considers her personal history as hardly worth mentioning." More than 20 years later, when pressed for biographical information again, she replied, "Except for what's personal, there is really so little to tell, and that little lacking in excitement and drama in the way of the world." In view of this reticence on the part of a major American writer, it is a good thing that Harvard University had the gumption to get Miss Welty to give a series of lectures on her life as a writer and the good sense to publish them in this small volume.

"One Writer's Beginnings" is not a misleading title. It takes two-thirds of the book to bring the author down to age 10, and yet this and the remaining part are all addressed to the origins of a writer and her art. She manages, in her informal and self-deprecatory way, to be quite informative about her real subject. "Children, like animals, use all their senses to discover the world," she writes. "Then artists come along and discover it the same way, all over again." An early interest in painting and in photography, a passion for words and for reading and a precocious gift and eagerness for listening are all relevant here. As a small child she would plant herself between adults and say, "Now, *talk.*" She listened for stories long before she wrote them. "Listening *for* them is something more acute than listening *to* them," she points out. Many of her stories, for example "Why I Live at the P. O.," are told wholly in monologue and many in dialogue. And as she rightly adds, "How much more gets told besides!"

in the telling. The telling is done in the authentic idiom of a time and space.

Of course, the place is almost always Mississippi — some particular part of it. She has lived in Jackson virtually all her life, and for all but her first six years in the same house. Since Mississippi, the poorest state, with the poorest schools, has produced a remarkable number of first-rate writers, some of whom have also clung to their native soil, Miss Welty regularly gets lumped with them as a member of the Mississippi School or the Southern School. Actually, there are no such schools, and if there were, Eudora Welty would have doubtful claim to membership, given the attributes usually put forth to define or characterize them.

One of the attributes most persuasively advanced is what Allen Tate called "the peculiarly historical consciousness of the Southern writers," which produced "a literature conscious of the past in the present." Tate had in mind a variety of things and examples too numerous to elaborate on here, but the past he meant was essentially a Southern past, and the writers' link with it was hereditary. And it was not just any part of the past but particularly the South of slavery, secession, Civil War, defeat, reconstruction, decline, Yankeefication and all that. As Denis Brogan once put it wryly — with reference to a certain Southern historian — "the *damnosa hereditas.*" Plenty of examples from Southern fiction will come to mind.

Those burdens are not to be found in the fiction of Miss Welty: Her first section, "Beginnings," provides some understanding of their absence. The hereditary link is missing. Her parents moved to Mississippi from "outside" — her father from rural Ohio and her mother from West Virginia — a few years before her birth in 1909. As a child, she got to know her Northern kin very well through summer visits — the talkative, musical, chaotic West Virginians as well as the more taciturn Ohioans, among whom "there wasn't much talking and no tales were told" and there was "all that country silence." Traces of those Yankee and border state relatives can be found in her fiction.

But Welty stories are almost entirely filled with Southerners, Mississippi Southerners, as authentically Southern as they come in their idiom, their gestures, their moods, their madnesses, everything to the finest detail. Black and white both, though mostly white. There are no Compsons or Sartorises, no hero with a tragic flaw, no doomed families with ancestral ghosts. With few exceptions — one thinks of "The Optimist's Daughter" — they are unsophisticated and very plain people.

Some are as objectionable as the Snopeses, but they are never types, only individuals. They never speak for the author, only for themselves or the community. Miss Welty writes with detachment and sympathy but without identification. She has no fictional spokesman, "I don't write out of anger," she says for "simply as a fiction writer, I am minus an adversary." It could be said that she is apolitical, nonideological, perhaps even ahistorical.

It is not that she is indifferent to history. The Natchez Trace runs right through her world. She even introduces historical figures — an imaginary encounter of Audubon, Lorenzo Dow, the evangelist, and John Murrell, the outlaw. In "A Still Moment," for example, Aaron Burr turns up in Natchez. But they appear from a legendary past, not as regional symbols or as "the past in the present." She passes over the Civil War with only one short story, and that as seen through the eyes of a totally uncomprehending slave girl. If the distinguishing "historical consciousness" were going to appear, it would be in "Delta Wedding," but it doesn't. Whole families pass in review, several generations of them, trailing no clouds of destiny, no hereditary curse, no brooding guilt or racial complications or torments of pride and honor. They are located in time and place but are never seen as the pawns of historical or social forces. That is not the Welty way. As much as she may admire that way in works of her contemporaries, she has left it to them.

She has her own way, and it would be a mistake to push her into any traditional category. Her fiction is often enigmatic, elusive, elliptical, difficult. Much is said between the lines or in the *way* it is said. Distinctions between love and hate, joy and sorrow, innocence and guilt, success and failure, victory and defeat are often left vague. So are the lines between dream and reality, fantasy and fact. One critic was brought up sharp by the suspicion that the whole story in "The Death of a Traveling Salesman" was hallucination on the part of the main character. The same sort of suspicion arises in that gem of a story "A Worn Path" or in "Powerhouse" or in "The Purple Hat." The author keeps her counsel. She records but never judges and often leaves enigmas enigmatic and mysteries mysterious.

The rich variety of her characters discourages generalization about them. Some are outsiders, loners, waifs, hitchhikers, rootless salesmen, the loveless and the unlovable. In one tour de force, two deaf mutes are made to communicate

Dust jacket for the memoir in which Welty concludes, "A sheltered life can be a daring life as well. For all serious daring starts from within."

elaborately, and in another two men with no common language spend a whole day together. The grotesque, the deranged, the deformed, the queer and the brutal all have parts to play, but they do not become a preoccupation. They are no more typical than judges, beauticians, housewives, ageless grannies, preadolescents, music teachers and hired hands.

Miss Welty seems at her best with sprawling families assembled for rituals, ceremonies or reunions. For example, the riotous romp and clatter of the Renfros and Beechams and the Banner community through "Losing Battles" or the familial convulsions and hilarities of "The Ponder Heart" and "Delta Wedding." In these novels, comedy, satire, tragedy, pathos, irony and farce are blended, often indistinguishably, by the disciplined spontaneity and exuberance of an artist who tells us, believably, that "the act of writing in itself brings me happiness."

In "One Writer's Beginnings," we find that in a turbulent period when authors commonly wrote in anger, protest and political involvement and many of them had reason to do so, one of

them led a sheltered, relatively uneventful life, never married and always made her home in a provincial community. The same could have been said of Jane Austen.

BOOK REVIEW:
Lee Smith, "Eudora Welty's Beginnings," review of *One Writer's Beginnings, Southern Literary Journal,* 17 (Spring 1985): 120–126.

Published on 20 February 1984, One Writer's Beginnings *spent forty-six weeks on* The New York Times *best-seller list. Southern novelist Lee Smith's review — which includes an anecdote about attending a party in honor of Welty, Eleanor Clark, and Robert Penn Warren — expands on Woodward's description of Welty as looking at the South as an "outsider," suggesting that any artist is an outsider by necessity. Smith also points out parallels and differences between* One Writer's Beginnings *and* The Optimist's Daughter.

One Writer's Beginnings is a crucial book for the serious Eudora Welty scholar; for the reader who has been charmed and beguiled and moved over the years by her wonderful stories and novels; and for the beginning or not-so-beginning writer who has any interest in where it all comes from, anyway: fiction, I mean, and what in the world it has to do with life. The book originated in a set of three lectures delivered at Harvard University in April, 1983, to inaugurate the William E. Massey lecture series, and it remains so organized. The individual essays are entitled "Listening," "Learning to See," and "Finding a Voice," with a generous selection of Miss Welty's family photographs sandwiched in. For an explicit discussion of fiction-writing techniques, readers must go elsewhere; these essays concern the development of a writers's *sensibility* rather than her craft — that inner ear, that special slant of vision, that heightened awareness of the world which distinguishes art from pedestrian fiction and which distinguishes Miss Welty's fiction particularly — her embrace of the gross world in all its lovely and awful specific detail. How did this come about?

First "Listening." Born in 1909 to life insurance executive Christian Webb Welty (1879–1931) and Chestina Andrews Welty (1883–1966), a passionate ex-schoolteacher from West Virginia, Miss Welty was "overprotected" (perhaps because of the first-born brother who died in infancy), greatly cherished, and greatly loved. The house at 741 North Congress Street in Jackson was full of books. "Neither of my parents had come from homes that could afford to buy many books, but though it must have been something of a strain on his salary, as the youngest officer in a young insurance company, my father was all the while carefully selecting and ordering away for what he and Mother thought we children should grow up with. They bought first for the future." Miss Welty "learned from the age of two or three that any room in our house, at any time of day, was there to read in, or be read to. My mother read to me . . . in the big bedroom in the mornings . . . in the diningroom on winter afternoons in front of the coal fire . . . in the kitchen while she sat churning, and the churning sobbed along with *any* story."

Mrs. Welty read "Dickens in the spirit in which she would have eloped with him." Consequently, Miss Welty tells us that ". . . there has never been a line read that I didn't *hear*. As my eyes followed the sentence, a voice was saying it silently to me. It isn't my mother's voice, or the voice of any person I can identify, certainly not my own. It is human, but inward, and it is in-wardly that I listen to it. It is to me the voice of the story or the poem itself." Along with the reading of stories went the "striking of clocks"; Mr. Welty, who "loved all instruments that would instruct and fascinate," came from an Ohio family of Swiss origins, and ". . . all of us have been time-minded all our lives." Thus the future writer learned "so penetratingly, and almost first of all, about chronology."

And Miss Welty grew up hearing stories — from the sewing lady, from her mother's friends. ("What I loved . . . was that everything happened in *scenes*.") The happy result was that "long before I wrote stories, I listened for stories. Listening for them is something more acute than listening *to* them." And she took note of the other sounds — the parents whistling an early morning duet, "The Merry Widow"; the hymns in Sunday School; the majestic cadence of the King James version of the Bible.

Miss Welty's brother Edward was born when she was three, her brother Walter three years later. Along with Edward came Miss Welty's sense of humor. "We both became comics, making each other laugh. We set each other off, as we did for life, from the minute we learned to talk."

The Weltys' summer trips to visit the two families in Ohio and West Virginia, undertaken in a five-passenger Oakland touring car, were essential to "learning to see." Mrs. Welty never quite got over having left the Andrews mountaintop home near Clay, West Virginia, in order to marry the young lumber company employee from Ohio; her five banjo-playing younger brothers never quite got over it, either — on the wedding day, Moses, the youngest, had gone out and "cried on the ground." Miss Welty's mother and her grandmother wrote letters back and forth every day of their lives. A different sort of life went on at Grandpa Welty's farm in southern Ohio. Compared to the boisterous Andrews clan, the Weltys were "scarce in the way of uncles and cousins and kin of an older generation." Nobody talked much. Grandma Welty — his second wife — had "each work day in the week set firmly aside for a single task." If "in the house it was solid stillness" (the organ was not played), in the huge, wonderful barn, "all you touched was warm." Although Mr. Welty had spent a sober childhood, by all indications, he was devoted to his father.

But it was the mountaintop — the wild, beautiful Andrews homestead — which would prove to be more important to the writer-to-be, for it gave Miss Welty her first sensation of "fierce independence." "Indeed it was my chief inheritance from my mother, who was braver. Yet, while she knew that independent spirit so well, it was what she so agonizingly tried to protect me from, in effect to warn me against. It was what we shared, it made the strongest bond between us and the strongest tension. To grow up is to fight for it, to grow old is to lose it after having possessed it. For her, too, it was mostly deeply connected to the mountains." And each summer trip "made its particular revelation," offering, finally, when the time came, *plot*: "When I did begin to write, the short story was a shape that had already formed itself and stood waiting in the back of my mind. Nor is it surprising to me that when I made my first attempt at a novel, I entered its world . . . as a child riding there on a train."

Now let me digress here a minute. Last spring, Miss Welty, Robert Penn Warren, and his wife, the writer Eleanor Clark, received honorary degrees from Wake Forest University, and I went to a party given in their honor, after the event. Miss Welty, looking tired but lovely, had been given a special seat on the veranda (there *was* a veranda) and a glass of special bourbon, which I'm sure she needed, as she was besieged by admiring fans and hangers-on — including me, completely mute the way I sometimes get in the presence of anybody I really respect. Everybody was asking questions about *One Writer's Beginnings*, which had just been published. One lady wanted to know whether or not Miss Welty considered herself a "real Southerner," since both her parents came from the North. At first Miss Welty seemed surprised by the question, and then she said *of course* she did, that she was *born* in Jackson, and she has lived there all her life. Miss Clark said *she* was reminded of a story often told by a friend of hers, a wonderful story involving a summer house and a cat who had had kittens in the oven. "But *nobody*," Miss Clark concluded, "considered them *biscuits*." The question-and-answer period resolved itself into general merriment.

Now I think there's some truth to be found here. And the third essay in *One Writer's Beginnings* is about this truth: how, in order to *write* what you see and what you hear, you have to be outside it, too. For the writer is ever the outsider, and the traveler. The writer is the girl in the summer dress at the window of the party — there but not there, seeing and hearing it all, in it but not of it, appreciating the *petits four* and the cut of a dinner jacket and the way the light comes shining in diamonds down from the chandelier, but know-

ing too the dark behind her, at the open window, feeling all the time the chill in the summer air. The first two essays also include this critical sense of being the observer.

In "Listening," Miss Welty tells an anecdote about a time when she was "taken out of school and put to bed for several months for an ailment the doctor described as 'fast-beating heart.' " Those nights, she was put to bed in a dark corner of her parents' room, the light carefully shaded with a piece of the daily paper, while they rocked in their rockers in a lighted part of the room and discussed their busy day. She can't remember what they talked about — it's not important, anyhow. "It was the murmur of their voices, the back-and-forth, the unnoticed stretching away of time between my bedtime and theirs, that made me bask there at my distance. What I felt was not that I was excluded from them but that I was included, in — and because of — what I could hear of their voices and what I could see of their faces in the cone of yellow light under the brown-scorched shade . . . I suppose I was exercising as early as then the turn of mind, the nature of temperament, of a privileged observer; and owing to the way I became so, it turned out that I became the loving kind." And in "Learning to See," those trips "were stories": because you've got to travel, you can't stay in the same place and see anything, or hear anything, you have to go and come back in order to notice what was there all along. As much as it is about anything, *One Writer's Beginnings* is about traveling.

At Mississippi State College for Women, we learn in "Finding a Voice," Miss Welty escaped the "life in a crowd" of the dormitory and walked to a fountain on campus to find some precious quiet in order to read a book of poems by William Alexander Percy which included a poem "written from New York City, entitled, 'Home.' "

> I have a need of silence and of stars.
> Too much is said too loudly. I am dazed.
> The silken sound of whirled infinity
> Is lost in voices shouting to be heard. . . .

She "said the poem" to herself, surrounded by Mississippi "silence and stars," but "This did not impinge upon my longing. In the beautiful spring night, I was dedicated to *wanting* a beautiful spring night. To be *transported* was what I wanted." Later, at the University of Wisconsin, she was "smote" by Yeats' "Song of the Wandering Aengus"; and it was there, too, that she learned the word for this — "The word is passion." To feel this, and then to bring it back to bear on whatever life we know; this is what writing is about. It's a scary, risky business.

In an earlier essay, "Place in Fiction" (from *The Eye of the Story: Selected Essays and Reviews*), Miss Welty wrote: "The truth is, fiction depends for its life on place. Location is the crossroads of circumstance, the proving ground of 'What happened? Who's here? Who's coming?' — and that is the heart's field." But, she goes on to say, place can*not* give theme. "It can present theme, show it to the last detail — but place is forever illustrative: it is a picture of what man has done and imagined, it is his visible past, result. Human life is fiction's only theme."

It is Miss Welty's characters who come, then, to mind — all round, all visible, all *talking,* from Edna Earle to Sister to old Mr. Marblehall to Fay — the whole host of them, peopling pages and pages. In "Finding a Voice," Miss Welty writes that characters "take on life sometimes by luck," but that she suspects it is "when you can write most entirely out of yourself, inside the skin, heart, mind, and soul of a person who is not yourself, that a character becomes in his own right another human being. . . ." Passion — the ability to be transported — is what enables you to write "entirely out of yourself."

She discusses the origin of Miss Eckhardt, the piano teacher in *The Golden Apples,* a character "miles away from that of anybody" she actually knew, including herself. And yet Miss Eckhardt "derived from what I already knew for myself, even felt I had always known. What I have put into her is passion for my own life work, my own art. Exposing yourself to risk is a truth Miss Eckhardt and I had in common." A character on the page, then, becomes a visible form of what is mute and inchoate in the personality. "Not in Miss Eckhardt as she stands solidly and almost opaquely in the surround of her story," Miss Welty writes, "but in the making of her character out of my most inward and most deeply feeling self, I would say I have found my voice in my fiction." Earlier, in "Place in Fiction," she wrote that "writing of what you know has nothing to do with security: what is more dangerous? How can you go out on a limb if you do not know your own tree? No art ever came out of not risking your neck. And risk — experiment — is a considerable part of the joy of doing, which is the lone, simple reason all writers of serious fiction are willing to work as hard as they do."

So passion makes the risk possible, and the risk is justified by the "joy of doing" — a view of writing which not all writers share with Miss Welty. For the self is the source of the art, as she makes clear; but many of us are fleeing into fiction, *away from* life — our memories are minefields.

It's instructive to read *The Optimist's Daughter* just before, or just after, you read *One Writer's Beginnings*. The parallels, the resemblances, the echoes are striking: the books in the house, the spunky mother from West Virginia whose death (reciting poetry in her blindness) so closely resembles Mrs. Welty's; the parents' courtship; the descriptions of "up home"; the "optimistic" father.

Here's the big difference: Fay. Laurel's father's second wife in *The Optimist's Daughter* ("without any powers of passion or imagination in herself") is one of "the great interrelated family of those who never know the meaning of what has happened to them." Fay is just awful. But Fay makes it fiction: she's the source of the conflict which is the theme of the novel — the past versus the future, change versus stasis — and the presence of conflict makes the difference between fiction and memoir. Fay is a blunderer, like the offensive handyman Mr. Cheek with his "familiar ways and blundering hammer"; like the grandmother's pigeons who "convinced (Laurel) that they could not escape each other and could not themselves be escaped from"; like, finally, the bird caught in the house after Laurel's father's funeral. Laurel cannot hide from the bird forever, although she hides from it for all of one night. At last she must catch it and set it free, as she must leave her mother's cherished breadboard for whatever uses the covetous Fay may find for it, realizing that "Memory lived . . . in the freed hands . . . and in the heart that can empty but fill again . . . in the patterns restored by dreams."

For the reader to go along pointing out what is *real* and *not real* in *The Optimist's Daughter* means nothing, then, finally — Fay and Laurel are equally real, and it's the heart's own truth which has made the novel. *The Optimist's Daughter* does, however, illustrate what Miss Welty says in "Finding a Voice": "Writing a story or a novel is one way of discovering *sequence* in experience, of stumbling upon cause and effect in the happenings of a writer's own life. This has been the case with me. Connections slowly emerge. Like distant landmarks you are approaching, cause and effect begin to align themselves, draw closer together. . . ."

*Dust jacket for the 1991, fiftieth-anniversary edition of
Welty's first book*

This is that "joy of doing" which Miss Welty alluded to in a different way in an earlier essay ("Katherine Anne Porter: The Eye of the Story") when she wrote about the "strong natural curiosity which readers feel to varying degree and which writers feel to the most compelling degree as to how any one story ever gets told. The only way a writer can satisfy his own curiosity is to write it . . . And how different this already makes it from telling it! Suspense, pleasure, curiosity, all are bound up in the making of the written story." We are always changing, too, Miss Welty reminds us towards the end of "Finding a Voice." "As we discover, we remember; remembering, we discover; and most intensely do we experience this when our separate journeys converge. Our living experience at those meeting points is one of the charged dramatic fields of fiction." For this is the point of *"confluence"* — that place where passion meets

life, and recognizes it, and the story is born, and born, over and over again.

BOOK REVIEW:
Stuart Wright, "Trying to Tell the Truth," review of *Eudora Welty: Photographs, Sewanee Review,* 98 (Summer 1990): lxxxiii–lxxxvi.

Drawn from the huge collection of her photographs at the Mississippi Department of Archives and History, Eudora Welty: Photographs, *published on 30 November 1989 with a foreword by Welty's friend Reynolds Price, provides a representative selection of Welty's photographic art. Reviewers once again noticed the relationship between her photography and her fiction.*

During what may well prove to be the most intensely creative and productive period in her long and distinguished literary career, the mid-1930s through the early 1950s, Eudora Welty's absorbing hobby was photography. She purchased her first camera in 1929, a Kodak with a bellows, and accidentally abandoned her third and last one on a bench in the Paris metro in 1950. Most of the pictures in *Photographs,* perhaps the most interesting ones photographically, were taken at the time she traveled through Mississippi (mostly by bus) as a publicist for the WPA, from about 1935 until 1941, the year *A Curtain of Green* was published. Miss Welty's job was that of journalist, or interviewer; so, she says, these pictures were made "not in conjunction with my job, but for my own gratification on the side."

Over the years Welty has spoken and written with characteristic modesty about her "snapshots" (her term), so I suppose one is compelled to view them together here as a sort of scrapbook, or family album, the work of an amateur, albeit a highly skilled amateur. This collection is superior to the earlier *One Time, One Place* (Random House, 1971) in two principal ways. First, the quality of reproduction is extremely fine, on coated paper, with images in sharp focus; second, the images are larger, more print-size (one can certainly forgive the overlap of a number of images because of the superior reproduction). Moreover there is noticeable variety in the Mississippi collection, which includes a number of genre shots omitted from the earlier volume, among them town- and cityscapes, and photographic mementos of Welty's European travels from the time of *The Golden Apples* and *Bride of the Innisfallen* stories (see especially the well-composed studies of Bowen's Court, County Cork, Ireland, home of Elizabeth Bowen). Most welcome, perhaps, among the additions are candid portraits, single and group, of friends, family, and literary acquaintances, including a marvellous study of Katherine Anne Porter and interesting snaps of Hubert Creekmore, Diarmuid Russell, John Woodburn, and Elizabeth Bowen.

From the beginning it appears that Miss Welty's desire to record "life as it was" was impulsive. Certainly she has been clear on one point: "I had no position that I was trying to justify, nothing I wanted to illustrate." And here is at least one major area of difference between her work and that of Farm Security Agency professionals such as Walker Evans and Dorothea Lange, who carefully composed (often contrived) their images to preserve with gleaming assurance and effect the timeless face of poverty and despair.

You have seen their faces. (I do not believe the honesty of their work is any more diminished for their methods than, say, Matthew Brady's depictions of the horrors of the Civil War, and he too was guilty of arranging his compositions for effect — recall, for instance, the dead Confederate sharpshooter in Devil's Den, at Gettysburg; there are a half-dozen different arrangements of the body and rifle, all inferior to the one frequently reproduced.) Margaret Bourke-White, who was working at the same time and in many of the same places as the FSA photographers, captures in softer focus and more sympathetic fashion many similar subjects; and Welty's work artistically resembles hers far more than that of either Evans or Lange. Nevertheless Bourke-White was working on a book in collaboration with Erskine Caldwell, whose message in unequivocal prose spoke of poverty and its attendant ills, effectively serving as a reminder that the poor will always be with us. But Eudora Welty insists that she "wasn't trying to exhort the public."

Perhaps Miss Welty's appropriate peers are other writers who have devoted themselves to photography and passionate amateurism. In the nineteenth century there were Oliver Wendell Holmes, Charles Kingsley, Samuel Butler, and most notably Lewis Carroll. In our own century, two writer-photographers stand out: Carl Van Vechten, who eventually gave himself over entirely to photography, and Wright Morris, a critically acknowledged professional who himself admits to a direct creative relationship between his photography and writing (unlike those of Welty, his views of structures and artifacts are largely unpeopled).

Of this group Lewis Carroll provides the most interesting parallel with Welty. Photography for both writers might in fact best be regarded as another aspect of the creative personality and as such is more important in the way it defines them as artists than in the actual comparative quality of their photographs. Both writers were skilled draftsmen and drew and painted from youth into adulthood. Miss Welty's first publications in fact were highly finished cartoons that appeared in *St. Nicholas Magazine* when she was in her early teens (she later contributed drawings and cartoons to her college literary magazine). Both Carroll and Welty maintained a high level of enthusiasm for photography for periods of just over two decades, and Carroll made literally hundreds of diary entries concerning his photographic activities. The years 1863–64 especially (*Alice's Adventures in Wonderland* was published in 1865) have been noted by scholars as significant for the great number and high quality of his images. Carroll, like Welty, invariably traveled with his camera, photographic plates, and chemicals, altogether a cumbersome affair. Both writers delighted in and wrote and spoke intelligently about the framing and composition of an image, a process for Welty resembling the construction of a short story. Both writers preferred to develop, trim, and mount their own photographs. That both of them excelled in portraiture, technological considerations notwithstanding (Carroll's beautiful young girls had to remain absolutely still for periods up to a minute-and-a-half, never less than forty-five seconds). However, it is noteworthy that neither Carroll nor Welty enjoyed being photographed, preferring instead to be on the other side of the camera.

When all is said and done, Eudora Welty hopes her photographs "will speak for themselves." "The same is true for my stories," she adds; "I didn't announce my view editorially . . . [but] tried to *show* it." And her pictures, like many of her stories, were "made in sympathy, not exploitation." (Welty is hard on Walker Evans, especially, on this point.) Her choice and treatment of subject were prompted by a desire "to tell the truth," not to "mock" the unfortunate or to intrude on their human privacy. Lewis Carroll's art sprang from his delight in the beautiful; but, again, both artists were concerned with the whole arrangement of the picture, the naturalness of it, the proper positioning of accessories (more in the case of Carroll), the framing of space around them.

That so many of Welty's photographs have immense charm and naturalness attests to the honesty behind her motives and passion. The best of them are simply composed yet clearly reveal a real depth of humanity in their subjects. We are grateful for and need the "stunned and frozen" faces Reynolds Price sees in Walker Evans, the naked "baffled pain" in much of Dorothea Lange's work. We are better too for the soft still moments, the occasional humor, the quiet inarticulateness of many of the faces Eudora Welty has shared with us from her family album; and we remain grateful for her enduring consummate artistic honesty.

Cumulative Index

Dictionary of Literary Biography, Volumes 1-148
Dictionary of Literary Biography Yearbook, 1980-1993
Dictionary of Literary Biography Documentary Series, Volumes 1-12

Cumulative Index

DLB before number: *Dictionary of Literary Biography*, Volumes 1-148
Y before number: *Dictionary of Literary Biography Yearbook*, 1980-1993
DS before number: *Dictionary of Literary Biography Documentary Series*, Volumes 1-12

B

Bersianik, Louky 1930- DLB-60

Bertolucci, Attilio 1911- DLB-128

Berton, Pierre 1920- DLB-68

Besant, Sir Walter 1836-1901 ...... DLB-135

Bessette, Gerard 1920- DLB-53

Bessie, Alvah 1904-1985 .... DLB-26

Bester, Alfred 1913- DLB-8

The Bestseller Lists: An Assessment Y-84

Betjeman, John 1906-1984 .... DLB-20; Y-84

Betocchi, Carlo 1899-1986 .... DLB-128

Bettarini, Mariella 1942- DLB-128

Betts, Doris 1932- Y-82

Beveridge, Albert J. 1862-1927 ...... DLB-17

Beverley, Robert
circa 1673-1722 .... DLB-24, 30

Beyle, Marie-Henri (see Stendhal)

Bibaud, Adèle 1854-1941 .... DLB-92

Bibaud, Michel 1782-1857 .... DLB-99

Bibliographical and Textual Scholarship
Since World War II Y-89

The Bicentennial of James Fenimore
Cooper: An International
Celebration Y-89

Bichsel, Peter 1935- DLB-75

Bickerstaff, Isaac John
1733-circa 1808 .... DLB-89

Biddle, Drexel [publishing house] ... DLB-49

Bidwell, Walter Hilliard
1798-1881 .... DLB-79

Bienek, Horst 1930- DLB-75

Bierbaum, Otto Julius 1865-1910 .... DLB-66

Bierce, Ambrose
1842-1914? DLB-11, 12, 23, 71, 74

Bigelow, William F. 1879-1966 ..... DLB-91

Biggle, Lloyd, Jr. 1923- DLB-8

Biglow, Hosea (see Lowell, James Russell)

Bigongiari, Piero 1914- DLB-128

Billinger, Richard 1890-1965 ...... DLB-124

Billings, John Shaw 1898-1975 ..... DLB-137

Billings, Josh (see Shaw, Henry Wheeler)

Binding, Rudolf G. 1867-1938 ...... DLB-66

Bingham, Caleb 1757-1817 .... DLB-42

Bingham, George Barry
1906-1988 .... DLB-127

Binyon, Laurence 1869-1943 .... DLB-19

Biographia Brittanica DLB-142

Biographical Documents I Y-84

Biographical Documents II Y-85

Bioren, John [publishing house] DLB-49

Bioy Casares, Adolfo 1914- DLB-113

Bird, William 1888-1963 .... DLB-4

Birney, Earle 1904- DLB-88

Birrell, Augustine 1850-1933 .... DLB-98

Bishop, Elizabeth 1911-1979 .... DLB-5

Bishop, John Peale 1892-1944 ...DLB-4, 9, 45

Bismarck, Otto von 1815-1898 ..... DLB-129

Bisset, Robert 1759-1805 .... DLB-142

Bissett, Bill 1939- DLB-53

Bitzius, Albert (see Gotthelf, Jeremias)

Black, David (D. M.) 1941- DLB-40

Black, Winifred 1863-1936 .... DLB-25

Black, Walter J.
[publishing house] DLB-46

The Black Aesthetic: Background DS-8

The Black Arts Movement, by
Larry Neal DLB-38

Black Theaters and Theater Organizations in
America, 1961-1982:
A Research List DLB-38

Black Theatre: A Forum
[excerpts] DLB-38

Blackamore, Arthur 1679-? DLB-24, 39

Blackburn, Alexander L. 1929- Y-85

Blackburn, Paul 1926-1971 ....DLB-16; Y-81

Blackburn, Thomas 1916-1977 ...... DLB-27

Blackmore, R. D. 1825-1900 .... DLB-18

Blackmore, Sir Richard
1654-1729 .... DLB-131

Blackmur, R. P. 1904-1965 .... DLB-63

Blackwell, Basil, Publisher DLB-106

Blackwood, Caroline 1931- DLB-14

Blackwood's Edinburgh Magazine
1817-1980 ....DLB-110

Blair, Eric Arthur (see Orwell, George)

Blair, Francis Preston 1791-1876 .... DLB-43

Blair, James circa 1655-1743 .... DLB-24

Blair, John Durburrow 1759-1823 ... DLB-37

Blais, Marie-Claire 1939- DLB-53

Blaise, Clark 1940- DLB-53

Blake, Nicholas 1904-1972 .... DLB-77
(see Day Lewis, C.)

Blake, William 1757-1827 .... DLB-93

The Blakiston Company DLB-49

Blanchot, Maurice 1907- DLB-72

Blanckenburg, Christian Friedrich von
1744-1796 ....DLB-94

Bledsoe, Albert Taylor
1809-1877 .... DLB-3, 79

Blelock and Company DLB-49

Blennerhassett, Margaret Agnew
1773-1842 ....DLB-99

Bles, Geoffrey
[publishing house] DLB-112

The Blickling Homilies
circa 971 ....DLB-146

Blish, James 1921-1975 ....DLB-8

Bliss, E., and E. White
[publishing house] DLB-49

Bliven, Bruce 1889-1977 ....DLB-137

Bloch, Robert 1917- DLB-44

Block, Rudolph (see Lessing, Bruno)

Blondal, Patricia 1926-1959 ....DLB-88

Bloom, Harold 1930- DLB-67

Bloomer, Amelia 1818-1894 ....DLB-79

Bloomfield, Robert 1766-1823 ......DLB-93

Bloomsbury Group DS-10

Blotner, Joseph 1923- DLB-111

Bloy, Léon 1846-1917 ....DLB-123

Blume, Judy 1938- DLB-52

Blunck, Hans Friedrich 1888-1961 ...DLB-66

Blunden, Edmund
1896-1974 .... DLB-20, 100

Blunt, Wilfrid Scawen 1840-1922 ....DLB-19

Bly, Nellie (see Cochrane, Elizabeth)

Bly, Robert 1926- DLB-5

Boaden, James 1762-1839 ....DLB-89

The Bobbs-Merrill Archive at the
Lilly Library, Indiana University ... Y-90

The Bobbs-Merrill Company DLB-46

Bobrowski, Johannes 1917-1965 .....DLB-75

Bodenheim, Maxwell 1892-1954 .. DLB-9, 45

Bodenstedt, Friedrich von
1819-1892 ....DLB-129

Bodini, Vittorio 1914-1970 ....DLB-128

Bodkin, M. McDonnell
1850-1933 ....DLB-70

Bodley Head DLB-112

Bodmer, Johann Jakob 1698-1783 ....DLB-97

Bodmershof, Imma von 1895-1982 ...DLB-85

Bodsworth, Fred 1918- DLB-68

Boehm, Sydney 1908- DLB-44

Boer, Charles 1939- DLB-5

C

E

Cumulative Index

M

T